151

Rolf E. Muuss
Harriet D. Porton

Goucher College

Adolescent Behavior and Society

A Book of Readings

fifth edition

McGraw-Hill College

Boston   Burr Ridge, IL   Dubuque, IA   Madison, WI   New York   San Francisco   St. Louis
Bangkok   Bogotá   Caracas   Lisbon   London   Madrid
Mexico City   Milan   New Delhi   Seoul   Singapore   Sydney   Taipei   Toronto

McGraw-Hill College

A Division of The McGraw·Hill Companies

ADOLESCENT BEHAVIOR AND SOCIETY: A BOOK OF READINGS,
FIFTH EDITION

This book is printed on acid-free paper.

3 4 5 6 7 8 9 0   FGR/FGR   0 5 4 3 2 1 0

ISBN 0–07–044422–6

Editorial director: *Jane E. Vaicunas*
Executive editor: *Mickey Cox*
Developmental editor: *Sarah C. Thomas*
Marketing manager: *James Rozsa*
Project manager: *Sheila M. Frank*
Production supervisor: *Deborah Donner*
Freelance design coordinator: *Mary L. Christianson*
Compositor: *Shepherd, Inc.*
Typeface: *10.5/12 Times Roman*
Printer: *Quebecor Printing Book Group/Fairfield, PA*

Freelance cover designer: *Elise Lansdon*
Cover image: © *PhotoDisc*

Library of Congress Cataloging-in-Publication Data

Adolescent behavior and society : A book of readings / [edited by]
   Rolf E. Muuss,   Harriet D. Porton. — 5th ed.
       p.   cm.
   Rev. ed. of: Adolescent behavior and society / editor, Rolf E.
Muuss. 4th ed. © 1990.
   Includes indexes.
   ISBN 0–07–044422–6
   1. Youth.   2. Adolescence.   I. Muuss, Rolf Eduard Helmut,   1924–
II.   Porton, Harriet.
HQ796.A3338   1999
305.235—dc21
                                  98–17908
                                    CIP

www.mhhe.com

This book is dedicated to the wife of the senior editor, Gertrude L. Muuss, who suffered serious health problems while the book was in production.

About the Editors

ROLF E. MUUSS received his teaching diploma from the Pädagogische Hochschule, Flensburg, Germany, his M. Ed. from Western Maryland College, and his Ph.D. from the University of Illinois. He was a research assistant professor in the Preventive Psychiatry Program at the Iowa Child Welfare Research Station, State University of Iowa. From 1959 until his retirement in 1995, he held the positions of professor, chairman of education, director of special education, and chairman of sociology and anthropology at Goucher College, where he was awarded the Elizabeth C. Todd Distinguished Professorship from 1980 to 1985. Professor Muuss also taught at the Johns Hopkins University, Pädagogische Hochschule Kiel, University of British Columbia, Towson State University, University of Delaware, University of Illinois, and Sheppard and Enoch Pratt Hospital Training Program for Psychiatrists. Listed in *Who's Who in the World,* he was elected Fellow in the American Psychological Society and two divisions of the American Psychological Association. Professor Muuss is a certified psychologist and served as a hearing officer for special education cases in the State of Maryland for 15 years. He has been a frequent speaker at both the International Congress of Pediatrics and the International Congress of Social-Pediatrics in Europe.

Professor Muuss is the author of six editions of *Theories of Adolescence* (1962, 1968, 1975, 1982, 1988, 1996), which has been translated into Dutch, Hebrew, German, Italian, Japanese, Portuguese, and Spanish. He is also the author of *First-Aid for Classroom Discipline Problems* (1962), Portuguese translation, and *Grundlagen der Adoleszentenpsychologie*

(1982). He has also published more than 100 research studies and articles in medical, psychological, and educational journals in the United States, Germany, England, Switzerland, and Sweden. In addition, he edited the four previous editions of *Adolescent Behavior and Society: A Book of Readings* (1971, 1975, 1980, 1990).

HARRIET D. PORTON earned her undergraduate degree at Towson State University and her M. Ed. in at-risk education at Goucher College. She has taught every level from first grade through graduate school but has spent the majority of her teaching career working with at-risk high school students. Currently Ms. Porton is an adjunct faculty member for Goucher College Graduate Programs in Education and serves as the Coordinator for Reconstitution-Eligible Schools for the Maryland State Department of Education. She has presented at numerous national conferences regarding at-risk youth, published several articles and a monograph, and served as a contributing writer and editor for the sixth edition of Rolf Muuss' *Theories of Adolescence* (1996).

Contents

Preface

It was the best of times, it was the worst of times.
It was the age of wisdom, it was the age of foolishness.
It was the season of light, it was the season of darkness.
It was the spring of hope, it was the winter of despair. . . .
—Charles Dickens in "A Tale of Two Cities"

The success of the previous editions, resulting in McGraw-Hill's request for a fifth edition of *Adolescent Behavior and Society*, has been inspiring to the editors. The first edition of this book was published almost 30 years ago by Random House; during this time the study of adolescence has changed dramatically. The increased scientific, political, and public attention given to this stage of development is an indication of the diverse and serious challenges posed by and for adolescence.

Adolescence, a poignant period of life, is often viewed as the "springtime of life," full of optimism, exuberance, almost endless energy, and challenging opportunities for the future. Adolescence is a wonderful time to explore self, others, and the world and to begin to make concrete preparations for adult life. The experiences of the first intense romantic feelings can be exciting, if not exhilarating. Emotional rejection—a common experience during adolescence—can be heart breaking. Obviously, the road to maturity is not all smooth sailing and can be characterized by occasional risk, temptations, obstacles, and numerous opportunities for derailment. Family and peers may serve as both stressors who aggravate the pain of growing up and as buffers who provide a shoulder to lean on and function as confidants and advisors when the adolescent must deal with adversity. Changing gender roles have helped to soften the lines that in the past have kept young women and men from reaching their potential. Young people must define and redefine themselves against many diverse and not always consistent messages about gender. Dickens's quote describing adolescence in France after the turmoil of the French Revolution applies equally today and captures the ideas of a rapidly changing world and the ambiguities inherent in adolescence.

Once a short, but socially recognized, transition period between the end of childhood and marriage, adolescence has been prolonged, in part as a result of societal demands for increasingly longer and more rigorous education. In addition, pubescence, the beginning of adolescence, occurs several years earlier than it did two centuries ago.

Even though this fifth edition includes many new selections, the purpose of *Adolescent Behavior and Society* remains basically unchanged.

1. To increase students' awareness of the needs and problems of adolescence and demonstrate some of the unique characteristics of this stage of life.
2. To familiarize students with current research and theory dealing with the psychological, sociological, anthropological, and educational status of contemporary adolescents.
3. To stimulate students to reflect upon the existential experience of their own adolescence and to become aware of the factors that influenced their development.
4. To expose students to the methods of scientific inquiry, to encourage critical thinking about developmental issues, and to reveal the complexities and limitations of developmental research.
5. To document the present, still quite incomplete, state of our knowledge about adolescence. Most of the authors presented in this anthology are nationally and even internationally recognized authorities in their fields; however, their methodologies and theoretical orientations differ, and some of their findings may have been challenged.
6. To provide students with a compilation of relevant and diverse material that adds to an understanding of adolescent development.

To allow flexibility for the use of the material and to avoid unnecessary duplication, some selections have been abridged, primarily in format (e.g., titles, subtitles, and footnotes). In some cases methodology, statistical procedures, and complex technical tables have been omitted to save space and enhance readability.

The text is organized into 13 parts and includes 40 specific articles, numbered consecutively. The editors have composed introductions for each of the parts. These introductions are not intended as formal abstracts; rather they provide an overview and a brief summary and offer glimpses into the main themes and findings of each reading. Frequently cross-references are used to related material in other parts of the book. Whenever any of the 40 selections are referred to in these introductions, they are identified by the article number in parentheses (1–40).

An anthology of this nature reflects the work of many contributors. We want to express our appreciation first and foremost to the authors whose articles, research reports, and papers have been reprinted. Without their generous support and willingness to grant permission to reprint their work, this edition never would have been possible. Much appreciation to the Mc-Graw-Hill reviewers who provided helpful evaluative feedback.

Several papers consist of unpublished material especially written for this book and thus constitute unique and much appreciated contributions. J. Loevinger's paper "Ego Development in Adolescence" (21) was written for the fourth edition; and is reprinted because of its theoretical significance. M. R. Stone and B. B. Brown's research report (15) dealing with high school crowds makes an important contribution to the literature dealing with peer groups. K. A. Schonert-Reichl and K. Beaudoin's paper (34) was presented at a Jean Piaget Society meeting but has not been previously published.

Finally, special thanks go to our colleagues Frona Brown and Barbara Gould who furnished support and astute editorial suggestions for two chapters (36 and 38) and to Marjorie Simon, our research librarian. We are grateful to all McGraw-Hill staff who participated in the production process. Special kudos to Beth Kaufman, who persuaded us to assemble a new edition, and to Sarah Thomas, who provided support in the completion process.

Rolf E. Muuss

Harriet D. Porton

PART ONE

ADOLESCENCE AS A SOCIAL TRANSITION

These are the best times of your life! You better enjoy them now,
before you know it, you will be weighted down with responsibility.
—JOHN S. DACEY

As a developmental stage, adolescence must be distinguished from childhood and adulthood and hence possess its own defining characteristics. It is a distinct phase in the human life cycle. Consequently, different cultures have utilized various markers, such as initiation or graduation ceremonies, new hair styles, and/or different clothing, to bring the new status of the initiated to the awareness of the community. Historically, adolescence seems to have been a relatively brief juncture between childhood and adulthood. However, by the second half of the nineteenth century Western societies experienced the impact of the industrial revolution and education for children became compulsory. As schooling became more widely available for adolescents, their roles in society, if not the very essence of the period, changed. As a result of earlier physical maturation, the challenging nature of today's job market, and the demands for prolonged and more technical education, adolescence has been expanded to include most of the second decade in life, and for those who pursue advanced educations, it often continues much longer.

Hamburg's insightful report (1) introduces both this section and the book to many of the critical issues in the lives of adolescents. Significant social changes influencing family life seem to have resulted in situations where teenagers need more help but actually have less access to support than ever before. For those adolescents whose cognitive time perspective and judgment are still limited, thinking through the long-range consequences of their behavior can be difficult. An adolescent's decision to become sexually active, experiment with drugs, and engage in antisocial behaviors may be a product of many factors, but the results of unwanted pregnancies, drug addiction, and crime are

1

often permanent. However, lacking necessary guidance, some adolescents make life-altering decisions by themselves. Hamburg reviews some of the more problematic adolescent behaviors and suggests effective interventions.

Is the current prolonged period of adolescence the function of an industrialized society? Or is it a social stage that is an outgrowth of reproductive cycles? Schlegel (2) supports the latter view through her analysis of a representative sample of nonindustrialized societies. Arguing against the theory that adolescence is simply a training period for future employment, Schlegel examines nonindustrialized cultures for cross-cultural patterns. She proposes a biosocial theory asserting that adolescence is a universal stage designed to prepare young people for their future role as parents. Although the duration of adolescence may differ between technologically advanced and nonindustrialized societies, even in those cultures where training already takes place during childhood, a period of social adolescence can be observed. Schlegel found that in these societies, after the work ends, boys generally do not participate in leisure time activities with men; instead they form age-sex peer groups that function on the periphery of adult male life. Girls, however, are encouraged to stay with the women, but they must defer to adult women and conform to their expectations. According to the biosocial theorists, in all cultures adolescents prepare for parenthood, but in industrialized nations they also prepare for their future occupations.

Theories describing adolescence are based on different assumptions and provide varied perspectives. Lerner's (3) theory, referred to as *developmental contextualism,* focuses on the multiplicity of interrelated influences that contribute to growing up. This theory provides a conceptual tool for understanding the reciprocal relationships between diverse contexts, and for explaining how an individual's behavior (cooperative vs. uncooperative) or appearance (attractive vs. unattractive) influences others' behavior toward him or her. Developmental contextualism has a natural affinity to contemporary concerns with diversity (Lerner, 30). Developmental contextualism is based on two key ideas: there are multiple levels of analysis, and these levels exist in reciprocal relationships. Any variable studied cannot be understood in isolation; rather it must be viewed in terms of its influence on other factors and other forces' influence on it. For example, observed ethnic or racial differences in academic achievement cannot be explained meaningfully by determining how Asian, African-American, or white students do on standardized tests. Academic performance is influenced by the peer group's endorsement of learning (Fordham & Ogbu, 18), parenting style (Steinberg et al., 19), family cohesiveness, and the way schools are organized (Blyth et al., 17), to mention just a few of the many interactive factors discussed in this book. When studying adolescents, therefore, neither internal variables (biological or psychological) nor external variables (peers, parents, or school) are seen as the primary forces for change;

rather growth is the result of the dynamics of relationships which affect each other. The idea of a multiplicity of interacting influences in all its complexity is depicted vividly in Figure 1 in the Lerner article.

Hamburg's theory examines the world of modern adolescents in a technological Western society; Schlegel's theory examines youth in nonindustrialized societies around the world; and Lerner's investigates the complex interactive relationships that shape adolescent development and how individuals influence others. As Thomas Jefferson once noted, ". . . theory is the most practical of men's instruments."

PREPARING FOR LIFE: THE CRITICAL TRANSITION OF ADOLESCENCE

DAVID A. HAMBURG
Carnegie Corporation of New York

From time to time, we read about the suicide or other self-destructive act of a young person at the very peak of success, recognition, and capability. How is it that such a person on the verge of great fulfillment can essentially snuff out his own life?

It may be useful to see this paradox in a historical and even an evolutionary perspective.

Adolescence in humans—and nonhuman primates—is a time when extensive changes occur in physiological and biochemical systems and behavior. The basic machinery of these neuroendocrine coordinations of puberty is of ancient origin and is essentially common to mammalian species. Its operation can be modified, however, by environmental influence and social context. Indeed, in humans, historically recent events have drastically changed the experience of adolescence, in some ways making it more difficult than ever before. Among these changes are:

- *The lengthening period of adolescence.* Biological changes in humans of the past two centuries induced by the control of infection and better nutrition, particularly in Western cultures, have lowered the average age of menarche. In the United States 150 years ago, the average age of menarche was 16 years; today it is $12^1/2$. The trend for boys is similar but

harder to document. At the same time, the social changes occurring during those centuries have postponed the end of adolescence—and of dependence—until much later. This phenomenon is a distinctly human evolutionary novelty. For a great many people the protracted period of adolescence introduces a high degree of uncertainty in their lives.

- *The disjunction between biological and social development.* While the human organism is reproductively mature in early adolescence, the brain does not reach a fully adult state of development until the end of the teenage years, and social maturity lags well behind. Young adolescents, age 10 to 15, are able to, and do, make many fateful decisions that affect the entire life course, even though they are immature in cognitive development, knowledge, and social experience.

- *Confusion in young minds about adult roles, and difficulty in foreseeing the years ahead.* In premodern times, preparation for adulthood typically extended over much of childhood. Children had abundant opportunity for directly observing their parents and other adults performing the adult roles that they would eventually adopt when the changes of puberty endowed them with an adult body and capabilities. The skills necessary for adult life were gradually acquired and fully available, or nearly so, by the end of puberty. In early ado-

Annual report of the Carnegie Corporation of New York, 1986, abridged.

lescence now, there is probably more ambiguity and complexity about what constitutes preparation for effective adulthood than was ever the case before. A great many young people are not even clear about what their parents do for a living. Moreover, the version of adult life that they see on television and to a lesser extent in other media creates only a shadow image of adult experience, a mix of reality and fantasy.

• *The erosion of family and social support networks.* Throughout most of human history, small societies provided durable networks, familiar human relationships, and cultural guidance for young people, offering support in time of stress and skills necessary for coping and adaptation. In contemporary societies, many trends reflect the erosion of such social support networks: extensive geographic mobility and migrations; the scattering of the extended family; and the rise of single-parent families, especially those involving very young, very poor, socially isolated mothers.

• *The easy access by adolescents to potentially life-threatening mechanisms, substances, and activities.* Adolescents are heavily exposed not only to sexuality but to alcohol and drugs, smoking (cigarettes and marijuana), vehicles, weapons, and a variety of other temptations to engage in health-damaging behaviors. While their use may appear to young people to be casual, recreational, and tension-relieving, their effects endanger themselves and others.

Despite the drastic biological, social, and technological changes surrounding adolescence that have taken place since the Industrial Revolution—and especially in this century—there appear to be fundamental human needs that are enduring and crucial to survival and healthy development, including most particularly—

• the need to find a place in a valued group that provides a sense of belonging;
• the need to identify tasks that are generally recognized in the group as having adaptive value and that thereby earn respect when skill is acquired for coping with the tasks;

• the need to feel a sense of worth as a person;
• the need for reliable and predictable relationships with other people, especially a few relatively close relationships—or at least one.

When these needs are met, the individual can say to himself something like, "I am a worthwhile human being. I have some useful skills. I can relate to other people. I have hope for the future." The longer and more complex the transition from childhood to adulthood, however, the more the adolescent experiences uncertainty and ambiguity in making such assertions. That is a basic dilemma of modern times.

There are a variety of major indicators showing that, in many contemporary societies, we are failing to provide avenues for the affirmation of fundamental needs to large numbers of adolescents. The historical recency of drastic social and cultural changes has outrun our understanding and institutional capacity to adapt. There is an urgent need to improve our capabilities for dealing with adolescent problems.

It may be necessary to think about creating a sea change in the preparation of young people for adult life, taking into account the drastic world transformation that has occurred and is still rapidly under way. In such a sea change, the crucial period of early adolescence must have an important role in our thinking. Is it possible to provide teenagers with the basis for making wise decisions about the use of their own bodies, about how to plan a constructive future? It is worth trying to think of ways of building capacity—social support networks—in every community for stimulating interest, hope, and skills among people in pursuing education and protecting their health.

THE BURDEN OF ILLNESS, IGNORANCE, AND WASTED POTENTIALITY

Early adolescence is a time of particular vulnerability even for those whose childhoods were not deprived. The combined physical, social, and emotional changes of that period intersect with the new intellectual tasks imposed upon youngsters in junior high school. A student's nascent sense of the future may be bleak, especially in areas of high joblessness and poverty. The pressures to experiment with sex, drugs—indeed many risk-taking behaviors—tend to be hard to withstand for some. Of course, most children weather the transition to adult life healthy and with opportunities for a fulfilling life. But a significant number of adolescents from many social groups drop out of school, commit violent or otherwise criminal acts, become pregnant, take up smoking, abuse drugs or alcohol, succumb to mental disorders, attempt suicide, or die or become disabled from injuries.

Nationally, one in four students does not graduate from high school. Dropouts limit their chances for success in the labor market and are more likely to require public assistance and engage in crime. For all social groups, the most frequent reason given for not completing high school is boredom!

One in ten girls becomes pregnant during adolescence. Although pregnancies among older teenagers have declined, pregnancies among those under age 15 have risen. In 1984, in the United States, girls 14 years old and under had 9,965 babies. The pregnancy rate for white American adolescents is more than twice that for teenagers in any other industrialized country. The rate for black girls is almost twice that for white girls. The Center for Population Options estimates that, in addition to the human toll, adolescent childbearing cost the nation $16.6 billion in 1985.

Similarly, illicit drug use in the United States is greater than that in any other nation in the developed world. In 1985, about 54 percent of high school seniors used marijuana at some time in their lives, and approximately 40 percent used some illicit drugs other than marijuana. The decline in marijuana use from 1979 to 1984 was reversed in 1985, which is disturbing enough, but the best single predictor of cocaine use is frequent use of marijuana during adolescence.

Cocaine today poses a significant threat to public health. In addition, more than 20 percent of American teenagers smoke cigarettes, and almost 6 percent are daily users of alcohol.

Alcohol use is an important contributor to motor vehicle accidents and assaultive behavior and the leading cause of death and injury among young people. Drinking patterns have changed remarkably among the young. Over the past two decades, alcohol use has become a more serious problem among 10- to 15-year-olds. A greater proportion of young adolescents drink alcoholic beverages than ever before. Teenagers have their first drinking experience earlier, drink larger quantities, and report more frequent intoxications. Although girls drink less than boys, the proportion of girls who drink and who report intoxication has risen more rapidly than that of boys.

Similar patterns have been observed among girls regarding cigarette smoking and probably the use of illegal drugs as well. A number of studies on smoking prevention have been carried out in the United States and Canada in junior-high school settings, focusing mainly on 12- and 13-year-olds. These studies show that the junior-high period is a critical time for the onset of smoking behavior. Very few students entering seventh grade smoke on a regular basis, but within a few years their smoking rate often more than triples. By the last year of high school, 30 percent of young people smoke to some extent, and $12^1/2$ percent smoke half a pack or more per day. In this group, girls now outnumber boys.

Suicides, although small in number, are increasing among teenagers and have recently drawn national attention through the media.

Add all these developmental casualties together, and we see that a substantial fraction of the age cohort is visibly damaged. Adolescent boys are at particular risk, having twice the death rate of adolescent girls. Indeed, until recently, teenagers were the only age group in the society for whom death rates were increasing.

Adolescence is characterized by exploratory behavior. Such experimentation is developmentally appropriate and socially adaptive for most people. But some of these behaviors carry high risks: the adverse effects may be near term and vivid; or they may be long term—a time bomb set in youth. Near-term damage includes sexually transmitted diseases or accidents related to alcohol use. Delayed consequences include cancer and cardiovascular disease in adult life, made more likely by high-calorie, high-fat dietary patterns, inadequate exercise, heavy smoking, or alcohol abuse. Long-term effects also entail a constriction of life options—for example, the school-age mother who drops out of high school, diminishing her lifetime employment prospects.

Although there have been recent encouraging declines or a levelling-off of some of these negative indicators and outcomes, the personal and social costs are still appalling. In financial terms alone, the costs reach into the billions of dollars per year. . . .

INTERVENTION: IS THERE ANYTHING USEFUL TO BE DONE?

When we face up to the serious problems and casualties of adolescence, it is easy to be overwhelmed and conclude that nothing can be done about them. Nonetheless, human ingenuity has been applied to the design of several innovations aimed at the prevention of developmental casualties, even in circumstances where other resources are sadly lacking. Lessons can be learned from such innovations and from concomitant research and experimentation in various parts of the world. If we care enough to make an intensive effort, we can devise ways to move forward through public and private policy to evaluate and replicate those interventions whose successes, though modest, are encouraging. . . .

One component of an adolescent's desire to smoke or drink or engage in other potentially harmful practices is to acquire credentials for entry into adulthood. Needless to say, these practices are not badges of authentic adult status; there are better standards of maturity and

adulthood. To convey positive concepts to young people, a variety of techniques have been used, including videotapes, group discussion, posters, and repeated role-playing with feedback from peer leaders.

One particularly promising intervention centers on peer-mediated approaches. For example, peer counseling can help in coping with the major transition from elementary to secondary school. Small groups of adolescents can come to understand essential features of human biology and behavior, how to communicate on vital but touchy subjects, and how to understand crucial evidence of the relationship between high-risk behavior and disease and disability. After modest but specific training, and with continuing supervision, adolescents may counsel other adolescents (usually slightly younger) who are in need of health and/or educational access. Such counseling tends to be helpful both to those who give it and to those who receive it.

There is abundant evidence that peer leaders who are highly respected and display valued characteristics tend to be influential in persuading young observers to adopt new patterns of behavior or modify old ones. High school peer leaders have proved to be capable of conducting prevention activities with junior-high school students, providing positive paradigms of mature adulthood. The peer leaders are trained by experienced personnel to guide junior-high school students in working out strategies for resisting destructive social pressure. The peer leaders chosen are individuals known to be liked and respected, able to communicate effectively, and committed to healthy life styles. Moreover, as demonstrably useful members of the community, they themselves enjoy opportunities for growth and often acquire a commitment to the concept of service. The long-term effects of peer counseling may be more important for the peer leaders than for the youngsters counseled. By being useful to others, adolescents can build a more durable basis for self-esteem than, say, by becoming experts on street pharmacology.

Though rigorous evaluation of peer programs is thus far limited, the outcome measures are sufficiently encouraging to justify an intensification of research to sort out the conditions under which peer programs are more effective and to understand better how these approaches work and for whom they work the most efficaciously. There is some evidence that a key element is the quality of supervision provided to the peer leaders.

Successes in changing unhealthy behavior have been reported by several different peer-based smoking prevention programs for adolescents. In addition to providing information about the near-term and long-term effects of smoking, such programs all employ peer-modeling and peer-counseling techniques to teach adolescents how to handle pressures that push them toward health-damaging behavior. The evidence from these programs is encouraging. Because the studies have not followed students long enough, we do not yet know whether the decision by a young person not to take up smoking is permanent or is simply delayed by two or three years. If the latter, even a delay in the adoption of any health-compromising behavior is significant because an older adolescent may then be intellectually and socially mature enough to make a more considered judgment. While most of these programs have been tried on white, middle-class populations, two large demonstrations in California are beginning to provide data on the effectiveness of these approaches with low-income, black, and Hispanic populations.

Experimental research at Stanford University is comparing a peer-group smoking program for seventh graders in a junior-high school with a comparison group in another, similar, school. The training sessions with a peer leader use a 45-minute classroom period roughly once a month over a nine-month interval. The sessions involve modeling, group discussion, skits, slogans, prizes—all oriented toward the understanding of peer influences and toward the acquisition and practice of ways to resist pressures to smoke. The findings indicate that such a cur-riculum of teaching resistance to social pressures may have a lasting effect. Follow-up after 33 months reveals the smoking rate for the control group to be about three times that of the experimental group.

Learning resistance to smoking inducement can be considered a kind of coping skill that may have wider utility. How to say no gracefully, how to resist pressures from valued persons, how to maintain grace and self-respect in adversity are involved in many life situations. More attention should be paid to the development of decision-making skills, of social skills, and of a realistic basis for self-esteem.

Research at Cornell University explicitly puts this line of inquiry into a broader context involving training for life skills. In this program, the preparation to resist social influences is treated as an important part of a variety of skills necessary for general competence. Because a sense of emerging competence in adolescence is so important for self-esteem, this view seems entirely appropriate. In practice, the program involves not only resistance training but also instruction on decision-making, assertiveness, ways of handling anxiety, and fundamental social skills. Moreover, the life-skills training is presented through various modes of leadership: 1) regular classroom teachers; 2) older peer leaders; and 3) outside helping professionals.

A research program at the University of Waterloo provides additional evidence of the effectiveness of smoking prevention by techniques of this sort. In this research, 22 matched schools were randomly assigned to an experimental group receiving intervention involving life-skills training and to a comparison group receiving no intervention. The intervention was begun in the sixth grade when the age of the students was typically 11 years, and booster sessions were given in the seventh and eighth grades—the junior-high school years. The groups included students who had begun smoking but were not yet addicted. The findings showed that the rate of smoking in the intervention group was less than half that of the comparison group. Longitudinal analysis was undertaken to find out what effect the intervention had on students at highest risk of adopting a regular smoking pattern. The result shows a typically strong impact on those who were at high risk because they were current, although not regular, weekly smokers when the intervention began. In other words, those who were actively experimenting with the behavior but who had not yet become addicted to it were effectively reached by this intervention.

Is alcohol consumption, where the situation is somewhat different, susceptible to the same intervention as is smoking, or does it require a different approach? What about cocaine, heroin, and other illicit drugs? Is it better to design programs that deal with a range of adolescent risk-taking behaviors and with underlying self-esteem and generalized coping skills? Are programs targeted narrowly to a specific problem such as pregnancy or drugs more effective? What interventions might be effective with populations at greatest risk in low-income, inner-city neighborhoods? The answers are not available now. Motivations other than those at work in middle-class populations might have to be tapped. Programs might have to start with younger children and deal with a wide range of problems in recognition of the earlier onset of serious difficulties. Community institutions including churches might be more effective bases than are schools, because of the low attachment to school and high dropout rates of the inner-city population. . . .

Research shows that problem behaviors manifested early tend to persist into later life. Exploration with alcohol and even problem drinking does not necessarily commit the young adolescent to a life course of this behavior, but it does alter the probabilities. Conversely, longitudinal studies have shown that early abstinence is a strong predictor of later healthful behavior. It makes sense, therefore, to orient the interventions toward early adolescence at a time when behavior patterns are not yet cast in concrete. Altogether, interventions focusing on the pre-

vention of any form of substance abuse at an early stage of adolescent development are most desirable. An important recurrent observation in the research on early interventions against smoking is that alcohol and other drug use tends to decrease along with decrease in smoking. This is an encouraging tendency that cries out for intensive follow-up.

With respect to health-sustaining behaviors, the evidence indicates that people with a strong sense of efficacy are more likely than others to adhere to preventive health practices. In seeking to build self-esteem, the adolescent must in effect ask himself, "What kind of a person do I wish to become? What capacities do I require to become that kind of person?" Much of adolescent behavior probably revolves around efforts to enhance a sense of efficacy with respect to valued dimensions of behavior and experience, and a good deal of adolescent behavior probably reflects an attempt to project that sense of efficacy when there is a deep underlying concern about it.

Young adolescents tend to believe that most of their peers engage in a particular kind of behavior, like smoking, whether or not this is the actual case. Indeed, there is a tendency across populations of adolescents to overestimate such behaviors by a factor of about six or eight. In one study, school children estimated that about two-thirds of their peers were smoking when the real figure was about one-tenth. Such erroneous appraisals are conducive to a kind of thinking that says, in effect, "Everybody does it, so I should, too."

Adolescents, moreover, tend to have a weak orientation to the future, especially in regard to the consequences of risk-taking behavior. College-bound adolescents tend to have a longer view of the future than those who do not pursue higher education, but in general, adolescents think, "It can't happen to me," or, "It's so far off that I can't think about it." They are focused on the here and now. Many youngsters, to the extent they think about it at all, have a dismal view of the future. They are doubtful about their own ability to influence events in ways that build toward a rewarding life. There is a crucial need to help adolescents acquire durable self-esteem, reliable and relatively close human relationships, a sense of belonging in a valued group, and a sense of usefulness in some way beyond the self. To shape these fundamental attributes in growth-promoting directions requires constructive models, mentors, and mediators. The challenge for preventive intervention is thus to help provide the building blocks of adolescent development and preparation for adult life.

One crucial task is to help adolescents learn about themselves. It may well be that a broader, more integrated, scientifically stronger approach would be intrinsically useful in education and applicable to a variety of adolescent problems. The life sciences offer a distinctive opportunity to stimulate early interest in science and to help youngsters learn how to deal more effectively with matters of deep human concern. Knowledge of human biology could be a particularly important factor in making decisions that relate to health—about the use of alcohol, cigarettes, or drugs; about diet and exercise; about sexuality; and about when and how to seek health care. Improvement of science education in human biology in junior-high school might further: 1) attract more young adolescents to the study of science and help continue that interest in high school and beyond, and 2) promote healthy behaviors among teenagers through the knowledge they gain about themselves and about what they can do to their own bodies and their own lives, both for better and worse. In the future, there may be considerable value in linking the science curriculum, preventive health care in the schools, and service by young people in the community.

Given the tragic burden of failure, illness, suffering, and cost to the nation embedded in the problems of adolescents, it is surprising that these issues are not higher on the national agenda. When there is a perceived crisis in certain problems, a significant amount of public effort can be directed toward eradication, as in the recent outcry over the illicit drug problem. However, such efforts on behalf of adolescents have rarely been equal in scale, quality, or approach to the magnitude of the challenge. They have mainly focused on the dramatic situation of the adolescent already in crisis rather than on early prevention and on the promotion of healthy adolescent development.

Moreover, ameliorative efforts have been plagued by professional divisions among health, education, and social service systems and by the lack of communication among people engaged in each of the individual problem domains. For example, although some promising changes are on the horizon, those conducting research on, or responsible for policies towards, delinquency do not commonly interact with those concerned with adolescent pregnancy. The latter in turn are isolated from those concerned with school dropout, drug abuse, or youth unemployment—even though in many cases they are dealing with the same young people. There is a similar gap between scholars and those who run programs for young people, with the result that scholars are deprived of the direct experience of practitioners, and innovative approaches go unevaluated, with their potential utility for other settings unknown. Meanwhile, many local organizations continue to pursue approaches that are plausible but lack evidence of effectiveness. Finally, there is a gap between all of these people and the general public, especially parents, who lack the kind of guidance in dealing with their adolescent offspring that is widely available to them concerning younger children. Although useful work is being done, there is no bright spotlight on adolescent development in the policy arena, no broadly integrative center for taking stock of existing approaches and stimulating new ones, no one institution where the different sectors of American society come together to pool their efforts in this field. . . .

A CROSS-CULTURAL APPROACH TO ADOLESCENCE

ALICE SCHLEGEL
University of Arizona

It is commonly assumed that adolescence is the creation of industrial society, with its need for occupational training that cannot well be accommodated during childhood. This assumption seems natural, since adolescence in industrial societies is generally viewed as the period of training for specialized manual and cognitive skills. Even Erik Erikson, who was aware of cross-cultural variation and wrote about childhood in American Indian societies, assumed that the psychological task of adolescents is to define themselves according to their adult occupations. He gave a new, psychological twist to the medieval concept of life as a series of steps, upward from the cradle to middle adulthood and from then on downward to the grave, by calling the fifth "stage of man," the one introduced by puberty, the stage of "identity versus role diffusion." Adolescents are uncertain as to who they are, and "it is primarily the inability to settle on an occupational identity which disturbs young people" (Erikson 1950:228).

Such a concept of adolescence, grounded in the view that production is the engine driving social organization, is not helpful in understanding adolescence in preindustrial societies. In places where productive tasks are learned during childhood or boys continue to work alongside their fathers even after they marry and bring wives into the home, boys should have no need for social adolescence. Even less should girls need such a stage, for by puberty almost everywhere most girls have mastered the skills they will require as wives and mothers. Nevertheless, anthropologists such as Mead (1928) and Elwin (1947) found adolescence in such places as Samoa or the hill country of central India.

The argument in this article is that adolescence as a social stage is a response to the growth of reproductive capacity. Where further training is required before the individual can assume adult social or occupational responsibilities, training can be accommodated during this period; but adolescence was not created to meet the needs of complex economic systems. The orientation here is away from the focus on cognitive and affective reorganization (common to psychologists) and the focus on role learning of sociologists (Bush and Simmons 1981) toward a biosocial theory.

It derives from the observation that the human life cycle includes a period between childhood and adulthood during which its participants behave and are treated differently than either their seniors or their juniors. A similar social stage has also been observed for sexually mature but unmated males among primates such as baboons and macaques (Walters 1987). During this stage,

Reproduced by permission of the American Anthropological Association from **Ethos** 23:1, March 1995. Not for further reproduction.

young males are extruded from the company of females and adult males and tend to be spatially and socially placed at the peripheries of these social groupings. In some cases, peer groups of adolescent males have been observed.

If a distinctive social stage is present across species, then adolescence is not a product of culture, although many of its features in humans are. The disjuncture between the physical readiness to engage in sexual activity and the social permission to reproduce implies that adolescence is a time of preparation for adult reproductive life. Social adolescents of all primate species, including humans, engage in sexual activity, but the birth of offspring is a rare occurrence. Older animals tend not to find the younger ones attractive: newly mature males and females tend to be selected as mates less than fully mature ones. A similar attraction pattern holds for humans, as only rarely is the accepted heterosexual partner for a social adolescent anyone other than another adolescent. Since human reproduction is embedded in kinship and marriage, and full social adulthood is almost everywhere associated with the married state, social adolescence across cultures can best be viewed as a time of preparation for marriage.

ADOLESCENCE AS A SOCIAL UNIVERSAL

The ubiquity of social adolescence was revealed in a cross-cultural study of tribal and traditional societies (Schlegel and Barry 1991) using data from 186 cases in the Standard Cross-Cultural Sample. For every society for which there is information (173), boys go through a social adolescence. Girls do as well, with one possible exception (175 societies).

In some instances, adolescence is socially marked and even institutionalized. The Navajo and the Melanesian Trobriand islanders, among others, have special terms for the person between puberty and marriage comparable to our term *adolescent*. The Mehinaku and other tribes of tropical Brazil, and some peoples elsewhere, seclude their postpubertal children for several years, seeing this as necessary for proper growth.

Boys' adolescence is generally longer than girls', as girls in many places are deemed ready for serious courtship or marriage proposals right after menarche. Boys, on the other hand, need more time, for reason that have more to do with social relationships than with occupational or role training.

In the eyes of those who have daughters to bestow, the boy just past puberty does not cut a very striking figure. The child may be the father of the man, but the older, adolescent boy is a better predictor of the man he will be. While it is true that bride-bestowers are interested in the kin of the future groom, they are also interested in acquiring the best son-in-law they can. They need time to look over candidates and to assess the value of any particular one. Adolescence gives them this needed period of assessment. The fact that age of marriage for boys is likely to be younger in matrilocal societies than in ones with other residence patterns may well be a consequence of this: it is easier to get rid of a disappointing son-in-law by sending him away than by bringing back a daughter. The extreme youth at marriage of heirs to thrones or high titles of nobility is made understandable by this explanation, for the social position of kings and high nobles supersedes their personal qualifications in the eyes of their in-laws.

When social adulthood is delayed beyond the late teens, there is generally a social stage that intervenes between adolescence and adulthood, a time when young people gain more privileges than adolescents without reaching those of adults. It is useful to distinguish this as a separate stage, youth, rather than to consider it a continuation of adolescence. The 18- to 20-year-old may not be socially mature, but he or she is very different from the 14- or 15-year-old. The line between adolescents and youths may be blurred, as when the unmarried young males between about 14 and the mid-20s constitute a single, often named, social category with specified duties to the community. Two examples are the *moran,* the warrior grade of the African Maasai (Llewelyn-Davies 1981), and the class of bachelors in preindustrial European villages and towns. Nevertheless, it is usually possible to distinguish differences in behavior, as juniors defer to seniors, and the older "boys" may be engaging in serious courtship, of which the younger ones are still only dreaming.

The discussion in the following pages will address some of the issues of adolescence that have caught the attention not only of scholars but also of those who deal with adolescents, that is to say, a broad spectrum of parents and concerned adults. The findings of cross-cultural research can be applied to topics of current interest such as gender differences and their origins, the management of adolescent sexuality, competitiveness and aggressiveness among adolescents, adolescent activities outside the home with peers and in the community, and the generation gap. Comparative research illuminates the breakdown of adult authority and the lowering of restraints on adolescent sexual activity and self-centered behavior, resulting in an explosion of teenage pregnancies and delinquency in many parts of the world.

THE SOCIAL SETTINGS OF GIRLS AND BOYS

Adolescents are not in school in the large majority of societies in the sample. Where schools exist, they are part-time (such as the Aztec Telpochcalli or the mosque schools of Turkish villages), or short-term (such as the African "bush schools"), or only for elite boys (such as the schools of early modern Europe). Boys and girls in these preindustrial societies spend most of their time with adults. Except for the boys in pastoral societies who herd animals away from the village, or forager boys who are not skilled enough to be taken on serious hunting expeditions, boys work alongside their fathers or other kin. Girls everywhere work with their mothers. While the cross-cultural study did not assess hours of leisure (Schlegel and Barry 1991), there

is considerable evidence that boys, like men, have more leisure time than girls and women.

There is a very widespread, possibly universal, pattern of social organization by age and sex. Girls and women aggregate, so that much of the association that girls have with other girls is when they are in a multi-age female assemblage. Boys associate with their fathers when they are working together, but when the tasks are done the boys do not join groups of men. They aggregate either at some distance from the adult men or at the periphery of the cluster of men. They are not incorporated physically or socially in the men's group, as girls are in the women's group. (There are similarities in human age-sex grouping to what primatologists call the "female assemblies," "male cohorts," and "bachelor bands" of terrestrial primates.)

With few exceptions, boys spend more time in the company of age-mates than girls do. Even when girls assemble away from women, their groups are smaller and less formally organized than are boys' groups. Girls together are likely to be engaged in conversation and unstructured play rather than in the goal-oriented activities with which boys' peer groups are frequently occupied.

The setting in which adolescent girls spend their days are hierarchical by age, girls deferring to women (see also Gilligan et al. 1988). Hierarchy inhibits competition for status, as there would be no point for girls to attempt to compete for leadership with adult women. It also promotes adherence to social norms, since the only way that junior participants will earn the respect and favorable attention of seniors is by conforming to their expectations. Consequently, girls learn an interactional style that emphasizes achieving their ends through such social skills as agreeableness and self-effacement.

Boys not only spend more time than girls do with age-mates, they also have more involvement with their peers. The peer group is egalitarian: even where the society is stratified or ranked (such as the Maori of Polynesia), leadership in boys' peer groups is achieved rather than ascribed. The egalitarian nature of a boy's peer group promotes competition among its members for leadership. Although boys almost everywhere show more competitive behavior than girls, their greater involvement in goal-oriented activities means that boys have to learn to cooperate at the same time that they are competing. Whereas competitiveness and cooperation are inversely related for girls, there is no correlation between these traits for boys.

The gender difference noted across cultures—that boys are more competitive, aggressive, and self-reliant than girls—may be partially due to the settings of adolescence. Boys learn a more aggressive style than girls, who attempt more to influence than to coerce. Girls are socialized for greater compliance than are boys, which is reflected in the much lower incidence of girls' than boys' antisocial behavior reported in the ethnographies. (This difference is unlikely to be an artifact of reportage, as it holds true regardless of the amount of information on adolescence.)

Sex separation characterizes most of the interactions of younger children as well as of adolescents (Whiting and Edwards 1988). It is my view that this separation begins in infancy and is due, in part, to the differential treatment of girl and boy infants by the mother. Mothers bind daughters to them more closely than sons and encourage sons to be more independent, a process that I call extrusion (see also Chodorow 1978). This is not rejection, but a subtle process in which infant and juvenile boys may cooperate by turning more than girls to the exploration of the surrounding environment. Extrusion can take a more direct form when the child is discouraged from remaining in the proximity of his mother and other women: "run along now" is more often said to little boys than to little girls. This kind of extrusion of small boys from multi-age assemblies of females is not unusual in human societies—I have witnessed it among Hopi Indian women—and a similar extrusion of juvenile males is common among troup-dwelling primates.

Sex separation becomes accentuated after young people enter social adolescence. This is true even in those societies in which adolescent boys and girls meet publicly for specified social occasions like dances or clandestinely for sexual encounters. In some places, boys' and girls' peer groups may cooperate in organizing activities, as they do in Transylvanian villages. Institutionalized nonsexual friendships between adolescent girls and boys, such as the *nwa ulo* relationship of the Afikpo Ibo of Nigeria (Ottenberg 1989), are very rare. It is only in the few places that have adolescent houses, where girls and boys relax and engage in sexual relations in the evenings, that there is much sustained interaction between the sexes.

THE CULTURAL MANAGEMENT OF ADOLESCENT SEXUALITY

Adolescent girls and boys are sexually active in the majority of societies in the sample. In spite of this, pregnancy out of marriage is rare. This has been widely attributed to adolescent subfecundity, in that females are rarely fully fertile for a year or two after menarche (see Whiting et al. 1986). When marriage occurs within a couple of years after menarche, by about age 16 or 17, the likelihood of premarital pregnancy is low.

Nevertheless, some societies, even those in which girls marry shortly after puberty, do prohibit sexual intercourse for adolescent girls. If girls are not permitted to engage in sexual relations, it is not expected that adolescent boys will either; in other words, there is only rarely a sexual double standard for adolescents. A double standard exists only where there are sexually available females: adolescent boys may be allowed to have heterosexual relations with prostitutes (although most will lack the goods to pay them); in some stratified societies, elite boys may not be severely sanctioned for seducing girls of lower classes or ranks. If there were a double standard in egalitarian societies without prostitutes, boys who could not approach girls sexually would turn to the wives of adult men—something these men are unlikely to encourage!

There are three factors that appear to underlie the attitude toward premarital sexual intercourse for girls (in other words, the value placed on virginity). The first is the length of adolescence, discussed above, as Whiting et al. (1986) have demonstrated.

The second factor is the economic or social value of children. Where children are an unqualified asset, they are likely to be welcome regardless of their legitimacy. Variations in the value of children as social or economic assets occur within as well as among societies. This can help to account for the high rates of bastardy in some periods and at some times in European history, in spite of the general Christian value on virginity.

The third factor underlying the value on virginity is the exchange of goods that accompany the marriage. Goody (1973) pointed out the association between dowry and virginity, but his explanation for this was inadequate: he said that the loss of virginity may "diminish a girls' honor and reduce her marriage chances" (1973:14). Such an explanation presupposes that virginity has some inherent value, which is improbable when more than half of the societies in the standard sample do not value it.

The results of a study of the value on virginity (Schlegel 1991) show that dowry-giving societies value virginity, but so do those practicing indirect dowry and gift exchange. Contrary to the belief of many that in bridewealth-giving societies men seek to "buy" virgins, in almost two-thirds of such cases in the standard sample, nobody cares whether the bride is a virgin or not.

The value on virginity in societies that give dowries or indirect dowries or exchange gifts can be understood as a mechanism for forestalling any paternity claims on a daughter's child. These claims are most likely to be made when property or a title accompanies the girl into her marriage. The upward mobility of a man through marriage is a possibility in rank or class societies; the seduction of a girl with property or from a high-ranking family is a temptation to the boy or man who would improve his position in life. Parental and fraternal surveillance of a girl's

behavior, and the socialization for guilt or shame at premarital sex, are widely effective methods for preventing a mésalliance through seduction. (For a fuller development of the argument, see Schlegel 1991.)

Although most ethnographers do not report on homosexual activities among adolescents, enough do to permit some tentative generalizations. Among those societies for which there was information (24 societies with information on both sexes, 13 with information only on boys), homosexual activity is more often permitted than prohibited, even when it is prohibited for adults. In a few societies in Melanesia, homosexual acts are institutionalized for all adolescent boys because the ingestion of semen is believed to be necessary for proper growth; there is no evidence that this practice leads to a preference for homosexual activity in adulthood or even that most men engage in it.

There is very little detailed information on girls' homosexual activity. One of the few reports available is by Gay (1986) on friendship relationships among older and younger Basotho girls of Lesotho, which sometimes include sexual stimulation. It is not improbable that casual sexual play is widespread among girls in societies that do not expressly prohibit it or that turn a blind eye to discrete erotic caresses.

In general, homosexual activity appears to be viewed as a substitute for relations with the opposite sex or just a natural feature of social immaturity that is set aside when adolescents become adults and can freely engage in sex with spouses and other opposite-sex partners. Homosexual play is reported even for societies that tolerate heterosexual adolescent relationships, such as the Nyakyusa of Tanzania (boys) and Basotho (girls). While opposite-sex partners may be available in theory, they are not always so in practice, or the shyness of young adolescents may inhibit them from approaching potential partners. In such cases, children may turn to others of their own sex.

The sexual activities of adolescents are tolerated or prohibited depending on the consequences of these activities for the adults who are responsible for them. But it is not only adults who monitor the sexual behavior of adolescents—peers also do it. Where young girls and boys are allowed a great deal of freedom, the group often pressures them to spread their favors. In the adolescent houses of the Muria, a hill tribe of India, the head girl and boy make sure that sleeping partners are rotated. Even where sexual play without penetration is permitted, such as the interfemoral intercourse practiced by the Kikuyu and other African peoples, participants are expected to change partners, and it would be selfish and unsociable to restrict one's attention to a special friend. The peer group protects itself against exclusive attachments to lovers, which would weaken the bonds of peers.

THE DEVELOPMENT OF THE SELF

When Erikson called adolescence the "stage of identity," he was echoing a widespread sentiment that adolescence is a time when young people set the patterns for their future lives. While the ethnographic literature does not lend itself to studying the process of personality development, it does give us a window onto the behavioral traits that adolescents exhibit and the kinds of relations they have with others.

It is clear that adolescence is a testing period for both sexes. Adolescents are newly arrived players, standing in the wings of the adult stage on which the dramas of kinship and marriage are played. They are on trial for the roles they will assume as spouses and affines. Memories are long in small communities, and one rarely has the opportunity to start over somewhere else. Present and future resources are finite in closed societies; adolescence must be a time of growing awareness of life's limitations.

Two behavioral traits that have long captured the attention of psychological anthropologists and social psychologists are competitiveness and physical aggressiveness. These traits, among others, were rated along an 11-point scale, separately for girls and boys, and the sample was divided

into societies above and below the means for testing (Schlegel and Barry 1991). Tests showed that their cross-cultural variation is associated with variations in the settings of adolescent life. These are the only two behavioral traits for which the means for girls and boys differed markedly.

This article has already discussed the differential setting of girls and boys and suggested that the hierarchical setting of the multiage female assemblage leads to a generally lower level of competitiveness among girls (boys' mean = 4.8, girls' mean = 3.2). In no society was the boys' score lower than the girls'. Aggressiveness shows a similar sex difference (boys' mean = 4.9, girls' mean = 3.4).

Both competitiveness and aggressiveness are related to what happens in the peer group and the household, the two social structures within which (unschooled) adolescents operate most of the time. Table 1 indicates that the size of the peer group is linked to competitiveness of boys. It also shows that the structure of the household is an associated factor, the stem-family household depressing competitiveness and the nuclear-family household stimulating it.

Table 2 shows that the amount of peer contact is related to aggressiveness for boys but not girls; as discussed above, much of the contact girls have with one another is in the multi-age female assemblage. Aggressiveness is associated with a higher degree of peer competitiveness for both sexes. The stem-family household reduces aggressiveness in boys, while the nuclear-family household raises it in girls.

The common factor in these various associations is the degree of involvement adolescents have with adults and with one another. While the peer-variable correlations are self-evident, the associations with household structure can be interpreted in light of the adult-to-child ratio.

The nuclear or two-generation family contains two core adults, the parents, although other adults such as widowed grandparents, unmarried aunts and uncles, servants, and boarders may also live in the household, usually as temporary members. Given four living children, the adult-to-child

TABLE 1
The Correlates of Competitiveness in Girls and Boys[a]

	Boys			Girls		
	N	r	p	N	r	p
Large peer group	52	.29	.039	28	.05	—
Stem-family household present	94	−.18	.088	57	−.19	(trend)
Nuclear-family household present	94	.21	.046	57	.24	.076 (trend)

[a]Competitiveness was rated on an 11-point scale separately for girls and boys.

TABLE 2
The Correlates of Aggressiveness in Girls and Boys[a]

	Boys			Girls		
	N	r	p	N	r	p
Stem-family household present	69	−.26	.031	46	−.11	—
Nuclear-family household present	69	.11	—	46	.35	.020
High peer competitiveness	44	.53	<.001	20	.62	.007
High peer contact	51	.30	.036	30	.04	—

[a]Aggressiveness was rated on an 11-point scale separately for girls and boys.

ratio is minimally 1:2. In the three-generation stem-family household, there are four adults, the senior couple (grandparents) and the junior couple (parents). Unmarried adult children of the senior couple (aunts and uncles) are also (often permanent) members of the household. Given four living children of the younger couple, the adult-to-child ratio is at a minimum 1:1. Competitiveness and aggressiveness show no significant associations with the extended-family household, comprising several married couples and their unmarried children. This category contains several forms, so that there is no clear adult-to-child ratio for the extended family as a structural type.

While adult-to-child ratio is only a proxy measure for the amount of contact and degree of involvement of adult and child family members, the two family forms do result in quite different household settings. Boys are responsive to both stem- and nuclear-family household structures, but girls' competitiveness and aggressiveness are associated only with the nuclear-family form. The nuclear-family household appears to be the form least conducive to an easy mother-daughter relationship. In the stem- or extended-family household, the daughter is in almost continual contact with her mother and the other adult women members of the family, each household forming a small female assemblage. In the nuclear-family household, the mother is the only permanent adult female member. Even when there are adult servants, they are subordinates, closer in status to daughters than to the mother. The nuclear-family household lacks a true female assemblage. In addition, when the mother is the only adult female in the household, or the one solely responsible for directing the female activities, she has less leisure time and is tempted to fob off much of the drudgery onto her adolescent daughter. This can lead to resentment on the daughter's part.

PARTICIPATION IN COMMUNITY LIFE

While younger children may be highly visible in the community as they play or run errands, they rarely contribute to community well-being. In a large number of societies, adolescents do. Peer groups of girls and boys may be expected to decorate neighborhoods at festival times, as they were in the traditional towns of Malaysia (Khadijah Muhamed, personal communication, 1982), or to organize dances and other festivities as in the preindustrial European village or town. They are also expected to do community labor, like the Micronesian teenagers of Palau. It is probably easier to mobilize the labor of adolescents when they are organized into formal age-sets; but even when they are not, they may do community work under the direction of adults or an appointed leader from their midst. The Muria adolescents mentioned above, who spend their nights relaxing in the adolescent houses, also work hard as peer groups for the public good, doing much of the drudgery connected with road repair or in preparation for weddings and funerals.

Adolescents may be called on to provide another kind of community service, the social "dirty work" that is beneath the dignity of adults. Under the tolerant eyes of their elders, adolescent boys in such far-flung places as the Ituri Forest of Zaire, the villages of early modern Europe, and contemporary American Chinatowns have been allowed to behave in ways that would be considered antisocial if they were not directed at social deviants or persons identified as community enemies. Their action is usually restricted to mockery, but it can go so far as the destruction of property or physical assault. Are the destructive youths of the modern world who burn crosses on the lawns of black householders in the United States, or destroy immigrant hostels in Germany, acting out the will of that segment of the community of which they are a part?

Whether or not adolescents take charge of specific activities for community welfare, almost everywhere they add to community life through the enjoyment they provide by their team sports and dances. While they display their strength and beauty to hoped-for boyfriends and girlfriends and try to impress important adults, they put on a show that entertains their audience of neighbors and kin.

RELATIONS BETWEEN GENERATIONS

The cross-cultural data do not indicate much sustained conflict between adolescents and older family members or other adults. There are several possible reasons for this apparent harmony.

One reason is that under circumstances in which conflict is likely to occur, there is some avoidance between adults and children. For example, there may be great potential for conflict in societies in which older men monopolize young women, marrying brides still in their physical adolescence and leaving adolescent boys with the knowledge that they will not find wives until they are well into their twenties. One would expect the older boys and youths to challenge their elders; one example of just this is the Australian Tiwi, whose young bachelors surreptitiously meet the young wives in the bush. When such affairs come to light, the senior male age cohort draws together and supports the aggrieved husband in his (mild) punishment of the offending junior. Youths and socially mature men among the Tiwi seem not to interact very much.

Even less do age cohorts of males interact in the age-graded societies of Africa, in which seniors also marry the girls of the juniors' generation. One stimulus to the formation of age-grades may be marriage across age cohorts, that is, when 12 to 15 years or more is the normal age difference between spouses. Age-sets serve to institutionalize the differences between age-cohorts in ways that promote social separation of them and to draw the lines that emphasize the power of the elders and the submission of the juniors. Females, on the other hand, are seldom organized into age grades. Even in those societies that recognize female age-grades, these are but pale reflections of the age-grades of boys and men. Girls, who marry young in almost all societies, do not have marital interests that compete with those of older women.

If one reason for a low level of conflict between adults and adolescents is institutionalized separation of boys and men, another is adolescents' understanding that they have no recourse to the authority of their families. Hopi girls, for example, may become so resentful of their mothers' authority that they run away, usually to the home of a paternal aunt. Nevertheless, they return when tempers have cooled, for they have no alternative (Schlegel 1973). In small and stable communities, where children are known to all adults, there is little that the child can do that will not be reported at home. The community reinforces the authority of the family.

While avoidance and suppression may account for some of the low level of overt conflict, it is probable that conflict simply does not arise much. It is not in the interest of children in most places to challenge the authority of their adult kin, for it is these kin who will give them the material and social support they need to move into adulthood. Deference and compliance attract the favorable attention of adults; rudeness or rebelliousness would get adolescents nowhere.

THE CHANGING PICTURE

The preindustrial world has practically disappeared, and with it have gone the earlier patterns of adolescent life. As nation-states expand their hegemony over formerly tribal peoples, they impose the changes that redirect the gender- and age-related behaviors of former times.

For adolescents, the most far-reaching change is the introduction of full-time schooling. For many adolescents in the advanced industrial nations, the teenage years have become a kind of "time out." Children are allowed this period of self-absorption, freed somewhat from parental surveillance and yet not given the responsibilities of adulthood. But misuse of this freedom extracts a heavy toll; Willis (1977) has shown how one variant of English working-class youth culture, which denigrates learning and rewards toughness in aggressive and sexual encounters, traps boys into a future of meaningless and ill-paid labor. Once they leave school and enter the workplace, the door snaps shut on these young men and their opportunities for more interesting and better-paid work have vanished. The adolescents who succeed in school are those who, like adolescents in preindustrial societies, have learned how to comply with the order imposed by adults.

Schooling for all will have different meanings to adolescents and their families in modernizing populations. Conditions are so variable that it is impossible to generalize: children whose grandparents were foragers, such as Inuit (Condon 1995) or Australian Aborigines (Burbank 1995), are likely to have very different perceptions from children who are the heirs of a long literate tradition, such as Moroccan town-dwellers (Davis 1995).

The one common factor is the shift in orientation from adults to peers. Schools put adolescents in a peer context for most of their days, reducing the amount of time they spend with adults and increasing the salience of their involvement with age-mates. What we learn about situated behavior from studies of unschooled societies raises questions about the effects, often unintended or unforeseen, of the transition to schooling.

CONCLUSION

This article has argued that the social function of adolescence across cultures is to prepare children for their adult reproductive careers; in this, the social adolescence of humans is similar to social adolescence among the higher primates. For humans, adolescence can also be a time of further preparation for adult occupational careers in those societies in which training beyond childhood is necessary.

As industrialization and the cognitive demands of a modern economy expand worldwide, the secondary function of adolescence takes on greater importance for boys and, increasingly, for girls as well. Adolescence for girls has been extended well beyond the age range found in most preindustrial societies. Societies that had no youth stage for boys now consider a period of further education, military service, or occupational testing a normal stage in the life cycle; in many cases, such a stage is coming to be considered normal or desirable for girls as well.

Erikson's (1950) concern with occupational identify as a feature of adolescent development is increasingly applicable to peoples who identify social status and style of life with the individual's occupation. It is a great historical misfortune that conception of the self should change in this direction at a time when there are too many adolescents worldwide to fill existing occupational niches. The result of population explosions is that poor and developing countries have more young people than can be accommodated by their economic systems. For many, perhaps most, young people in such countries, the cards are stacked against their reaching a satisfactory occupational identity, as they find themselves torn between the possibilities held before their eyes and the reality of few good jobs and poor preparation for those that do exist. Occupational identity cannot develop if there is no attainable occupation with which to identify.

Boys are unlikely to be recognized as adults in their reproductive lives, that is, to become socially recognized fathers responsible for the well-being of their children and accountable for them, unless they can help support children and their mothers. Girls, on the other hand, can claim reproductive adulthood by bearing and caring for children, regardless of where their support comes from. While it is impossible to determine exact chronological age of marriage when people do not keep account of dates, 15 to 17 seems to have been a common age in traditional societies outside of preindustrial Europe and Southeast Asia, where it was later. Thus, first pregnancy at age 17 to 19 is not unusual and may in fact be biologically desirable (Konner

and Shostak 1986). Teenage pregnancy is a worldwide norm, even though most such pregnancies have occurred within marriage. It is predictable that girls will begin their reproductive careers during their teen years when conditions permit. Such conditions include the toleration of sexual activity, the assurance of support for the child by the family or state welfare, and the absence of any well-defined occupational career plans that would be endangered by childbearing. (Burbank's study of Australian Aborigines 1995 illustrates such conditions.)

It is difficult to see any improvement in the prospects for adolescents in poor countries, or among the badly educated populations of the developed nations, without serious efforts to improve the education of girls and boys and at the same time make reproductive control available and attractive. Adolescents may be experiencing a "time out," but it is time that can easily be lost unless they have a clear sense of direction and the help of adults to clarify and achieve realistic goals. These are issues of great importance to all nations, as their future depends on the success of today's adolescents in successfully reaching adulthood.

REFERENCES CITED

Burbank, Victoria
    1995 Gender Hierarchy and Adolescent Sexuality: The Control of Female Reproduction in an Australian Aboriginal Community. *Ethos 23:* 33–46.
Bush, Diane M., and Roberta Simmons
    1981 Socialization Processes over the Life Course. In *Social Psychology: Sociological Perspectives.* M. Rosenberg and R. H. Turner, eds. Pp. 33–64. New York: Basic Books.
Chodorow, Nancy
    1978 *The Reproduction of Mothering: Psychoanalysis and the Sociology of Gender.* Berkeley: University of California Press.
Condon, Richard
    1995 The Rise of the Leisure Class: Adolescence and Recreational Acculturation in the Canadian Arctic. *Ethos 23:* 47–68.
Davis, Douglas
    1995 Modernizing the Sexes: Changing Gender Relations in a Moroccan Town. *Ethos 23:* 69–78.

Elwin, Verrier
    1947 *The Muria and Their Ghotul.* Bombay: Oxford University Press.
Erikson, Erik H.
    1950 *Childhood and Society.* New York: W. W. Norton.
Gay, Judith
    1986 "Mummies and Babies" and Friends and Lovers in Lesotho. In *Anthropology and Homosexual Behavior.* Evelyn Blackwood, ed. Pp. 97–116. New York: Haworth Press.
Gilligan, Carol, Janie V. Ward, Jill M. Taylor, and Betty Bardige, eds.
    1988 *Mapping the Moral Domain: A Contribution of Women's Thinking to Psychological Theory and Education.* Cambridge, MA: Harvard University Press.
Goody, Jack
    1973 Bridewealth and Dowry in Africa and Eurasia. In *Bridewealth and Dowry.* Jack Goody and S. J. Tambiah, eds. Pp. 1–58. *Cambridge Papers in Social Anthropology, 7.* Cambridge: Cambridge University Press.
Konner, Melvin, and Marjorie Shostak
    1986 Adolescent Pregnancy and Childbearing: An Anthropological Perspective. In *School-Age Pregnancy and Parenthood: Biosocial Dimensions.* Jane B. Lancaster and Beatrix B. Hamburg, eds. Pp. 325–346. New York: Aldine De Gruyter.
Llewelyn-Davies, Melissa
    1981 Women, Warriors, and Patriarchs. In *Sexual Meanings: The Cultural Construction of Gender and Sexuality.* Sherry B. Ortner and Harriet Whitehead, eds. Pp. 330–358. Cambridge: Cambridge University Press.
Mead, Margaret
    1928 Coming of Age in Samoa. Ann Arbor, MI: Morrow.

Ottenberg, Simon
    1989 *Boyhood Rituals in an African Society: An Interpretation.* Seattle: University of Washington Press.
Schlegel, Alice
    1973 The Adolescent Socialization of the Hopi Girl. *Ethnology 4:*449–462.
    1975 Situational Stress: A Hopi Example. In *Life Span Developmental Psychology: Normative Life Crises.* Nancy Datan and Leon H. Ginsberg, eds. Pp. 209–216. New York: Academic Press.
    1991 Status, Property, and the Value on Virginity. *American Ethnologist 18:*719–734.
Schlegel, Alice, and Herbert Barry III
    1991 *Adolescence: An Anthropologist Inquiry.* New York: Free Press.
Walters, Jeffrey R.
    1987 Transition to Adulthood. In *Primate Societies.* Barbara B. Smuts, Dorothy L. Cheney, Robert M. Seyfurth, Richard W. Wrangham, and Thomas T. Struhsaker, eds. Pp. 358–369. Chicago: University of Chicago Press.
Whiting, Beatrice B., and Carolyn P. Edwards
    1988 *Children of Different Worlds.* Cambridge, MA: Harvard University Press.
Whiting, John W. M., Victoria K. Burbank, and Mitchell S. Ratner
    1986 The Duration of Maidenhood across Cultures. In *School-Age Pregnancy and Parenthood: Biosocial Dimensions.* Jane B. Lancaster and Beatrix A. Hamburg, eds. Pp. 273–302. New York: Aldine De Gruyter.
Willis, Paul
    1977 *Learning to Labor.* Farnborough: Saxon House.

DEVELOPMENTAL CONTEXTUALISM, AND THE FURTHER ENHANCEMENT OF THEORY ABOUT PUBERTY AND PSYCHOSOCIAL DEVELOPMENT

Richard M. Lerner
Boston College

The changes that occur during puberty are the most visible developments of adolescence. Arguably, they also represent the features of adolescence about which the most has been written in the scientific literature. Such topics as normative and atypical hormonal changes; secular trends in menarche; the influence of pubertal transitions on family relations, on achievement, and on psychosocial adjustment; pubertal rites; menstrual beliefs; sexuality; adolescent pregnancy and childbearing; and the role of pubertally based changes and/or "drives" in ego and cognitive development are among those concerning scholars from disciplines such as medicine, biology, psychology, sociology, anthropology, history, and human development. Across this literature, puberty has been linked to developments at levels of analysis ranging from the biological, through the psychological, social, and cultural, to the historical.

Yet despite the prominence of conceptualizations about, and studies of, the role of puberty within and across these levels of organization, it is fair to argue—as do Adams, Day, Dyk, Frede, and Rogers (1992)—that theories of the explanatory role or functional significance of pu-

berty have not been articulated with the degree of precision or scope commensurate with the role attributed to puberty in the adolescent development literature. Indeed, as explained by Petersen and Taylor (1980), theories of the role of pubertal change in adolescent biopsychosocial development may be classified into two broad categories. "Direct effects" models stress that puberty has an unmediated influence on psychological functioning and social behavior. As epitomized by the psychoanalytic theories of A. Freud (1969) and Kestenberg (1967), these direct effect theories contend that biological change directly drives other changes of the person or that the biological processes (e.g., hereditary ones) that purportedly determine puberty are the same ones that shape personality and social functioning. The constitutional (somatic) theory of Sheldon (1940, 1942) is a case in point of this latter view.

"Mediated effects" models emphasize that the influence of pubertal change on the psychological and social behavior and development of the person occurs through an "interaction" with the environment—the context—within which the adolescent is embedded (e.g., Brooks-Gunn, 1987; Lerner & Lerner, 1989; Magnusson, 1988; Petersen & Taylor, 1980; Stattin & Magnusson, 1990). Although scholars following this general conception differ in regard to the meaning they attach to the term "interaction" and conceptualize, or model, the mediation of the context in

From Richard M. Lerner, *Journal of Early Adolescence,* Vol. 12 No. 4, pp. 366–368 and 377–388 (abridged). Copyright © 1992 by Sage Publications, Inc. Reprinted by permission of Sage Publications, Inc.

different ways, all agree that the role of puberty in psychosocial functioning will be different under distinct contextual conditions.

Because the quantity *and quality* of the research literature on adolescent development has burgeoned over the course of the past 2 decades, the need to adopt some sort of mediated effects model has become increasingly apparent (Petersen, 1988). In turn, contemporary scholarship finds little evidence for, or utility of, a direct effects conceptualization of the role of puberty in psychosocial functioning (e.g., see Adams, Montemayor, & Gullotta, 1989; Brooks-Gunn, 1987; Brooks-Gunn & Petersen, 1983; Lerner & Foch, 1987; Magnusson, 1988).

A representative instance of this view was provided by Stattin and Magnusson (1990):

> There are few reasons to believe that pubertal timing, except in some few obvious ways, has a unidirectional influence on behavior. There are even fewer reasons to assume that its influence generally should be interpreted in a causal way. As Brooks-Gunn and Petersen (1984) have pointed out, the mere fact that there exists a relationship between pubertal growth and social behavior does not imply a cause-effect relationship. What we witness might rather be the co-occurrence of different developmental factors. If so, the biological determinism model, which infers that observed changes in feelings, motivations, social relations, and so on are [causally] related to changes in the physical-bodily domain, has limited applicability. (p. 5)

Indeed, consistent with Stattin and Magnusson's view, there has been a compelling set of data generated indicating that puberty influences the adolescent's psychosocial behavior and development either in and/or through the context (e.g., the family, the peer group, or the school) within which the youth is embedded. However, due in part to the fact that the different scholars who have generated these data have done so through the use of different types of mediated effects models, there is considerably more information needed about the precise "parameters" of person and context that are involved in determining the conditions under which a particular instance of pubertal change interacts with the context to affect a specific instance of psychosocial functioning.

FEATURES OF DEVELOPMENTAL CONTEXTUALISM

Developmental contextualism rests on two key ideas. First, there are variables from multiple, *qualitatively distinct* levels of analysis, or levels of organization, involved in human life and development (e.g., biology, psychology, society, and history). Of course, this conception is one with which scientists adhering to virtually any theoretical viewpoint would agree. However, some scientists would pursue inquiries aimed at the investigation of variables from one level of organization, in isolation from other levels (i.e., they would adopt a "main effects" approach to science); in turn, others would adopt a reductionistic orientation, seeking to study, or at least interpret, variables from multiple levels in terms of one level—a level conceived of by these scientists as the core, constituent, or elemental level. Developmental contextualists would reject both of these approaches and, instead, would adopt a nonreductionistic, interlevel-synthetic orientation to the multiple levels involved in human life. This perspective would be followed because of the second key idea within developmental contextualism.

Variables from the several levels of organization comprising human life exist in reciprocal relation: The structure and function of variables from any one level influence, and are influenced by, the structure and function of variables from the other levels. This reciprocal influence among levels, this "fusion" (Tobach & Greenberg, 1984) of interlevel relations, is termed *dynamic interactionism* within developmental contextualism (Lerner, 1978, 1979). As a consequence of the ubiquitous existence of these dynamic interactions, the potential for change is a continuous property of the multiple, interrelated levels of organization comprising human life. In other words, because levels of organization exist in an integrated, or fused, system, relations between levels of organization and not an isolated level per se become the key focus of developmental analysis and changing relations among levels constitutes the basic process of human developmental change.

When applied to the level of the individual, developmental contextualism stresses that neither variables belonging to levels of analysis lying within the person (e.g., biological or psychological ones) nor variables belonging to levels lying outside the person (i.e., involving either interpersonal, such as peer group relations or extrapersonal—institutional or physical ecological—relations) are the primary basis—or cause—of the individual's functioning or development. Rather, the structure (or "form"; Pepper, 1942) of the system—the pattern of relations—at a given point in time (at a specific moment in history; Pepper, 1942) is the "event" causing the person's functioning; and changes in the form of these relations are the cause of developmental change. Simply, not only do "A" and "B" simultaneously influence one another, but any change in A or B is a function of the organization of variables within which they are embedded.

Optimism About the Potential for Change

Given this "configural," or formal (Pepper, 1942), but nonetheless change-oriented, view of causality, developmental contextualism is an optimistic view of the character of human development (Brim & Kagan, 1980). The system of person-context relations comprising human development means that at any point in the life span there is some probability that means exist for altering significantly an individual's structural and/or functional characteristics. Because these characteristics are conceptualized in relational terms, such alteration may be possible through interventions aimed at any of the multiple levels of organization within which the person is embedded. Of course, complete alteration of the person or, more precisely, of the person-context system is not possible: The structure and function of a level influences other levels both through affording some changes and through delimiting or constraining others (Lerner, 1984, 1992).

Humans have two coupled change-related characteristics: a capacity for change and powerful stabilizing processes protecting existing arrangements and capabilities. Actual change (as contrasted to the potential for change) results from the interaction of these two coupled characteristics. In other words, plasticity—systematic change in structure and/or function—is not absolute but only relative. Nevertheless, the relational character of human life and/or human change means that development is seen as more open to influence and change when considered from a developmental contextual perspective than from one associated with other organismically or mechanistically derived theoretical perspectives (Brim & Kagan, 1980).

The Nature-Nurture Issue

Finally, a key theoretical feature of developmental contextualism is that it represents a quite distinct position within the controversy that has been the core conceptual issue in developmental psychology (Lerner, 1976, 1986) and, arguably, within psychology as a whole (Anastasi, 1958): the nature-nurture issue. Within developmental contextualism, variables from levels of organization associated with a person's biological or organismic characteristics (e.g., genes, tissues, or organ systems) are held to dynamically interact with variables from contextual levels of organization (i.e., involving intrapersonal and extrapersonal variables), within which the biological or organismic characteristics are embedded.

Because of the presence of dynamic interactions, biological variables both influence and, reciprocally, are influenced by contextual ones. Accordingly, stances about nature-nurture relations, which stress either the core determination of human functioning and development by either context (e.g., cultural deterministic views) or biology (e.g., genetic or biological reductionistic, or deterministic views), are explicitly rejected by a developmental contextual perspective (Lerner, 1992). In developmental contextualism, biological and contextual factors provide facilitating and constraining conditions that "set the stage" and through different patterns of interaction may produce many different "plays" with a diversity of "plots." In other words, changes in the causal field of fused, interlevel relationships provide the basis of human developmental change; and interindividual differences in the content and timing of these relationships creates distinct developmental trajectories (i.e., multidirectionality in development across life).

The Application of Developmental Contextualism to the Study of the Role of Puberty in Psychosocial Behavior and Development

As discussed in several recent essays (e.g., Lerner, 1987; Lerner & Lerner, 1989; Lerner, Lerner, & Tubman, 1989; see also Stattin & Magnusson, 1990), ideas associated with developmental contextualism may be used, for both descriptive and explanatory purposes, to study the role of puberty in psychosocial development. For example, within the laboratory of Lerner and Lerner (1989; Lerner et al., 1989), the fused, interlevel associations depicted within developmental contextualism have been represented by a model such as that displayed in Figure 1. This model represents the fusions within the adolescent between biological (e.g., pubertal) characteristics and other physical, psychological, and behavioral attributes; in turn, fusions with the familial (e.g., parental), social network, community, societal, and cultural contexts are illustrated as well; finally, changes over time (history) in all these bidirectional, or reciprocal, relationships are represented in the model.

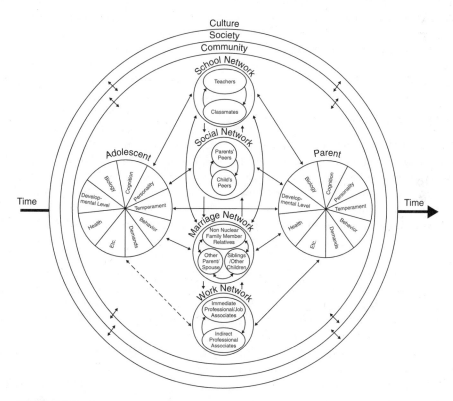

FIGURE 1
The Developmental Contextual Model of Development Used in the Research of Lerner and Lerner (e.g., Lerner & Lerner, 1989)

The descriptive use of the model, in regard to integrating extant data on puberty-psychosocial relations, may be illustrated by reference to the literature on menarche. This literature involves studies assessing the relationships, within the adolescent, of variation in timing of menarche (e.g., whether it occurs early, on time, or late) and other characteristics of individuality, for example, perceptions of self (Tobin-Richards, Boxer, & Petersen, 1983), cognition (Hamburg, 1974; Newcombe & Dubas, 1987; Petersen, 1983), or the experience of menstrual discomfort (Brooks-Gunn & Ruble, 1983). In turn, other studies assess how the occurrence of menarche is associated with a girl's relations with significant other people in her context (e.g., Anderson, Hetherington, & Clingempeel, 1989; Simmons, Blyth, & McKinney, 1983; Stattin & Magnusson, 1990; Steinberg, 1981; Steinberg & Hill, 1978). Such studies provide data illustrative of "adolescent effects" on the significant others in their social settings and constitute one component of the bidirectional effects (an adolescent → social context one) discussed in the literature on mediated effects models of puberty-context relations (Lerner & Foch, 1987; Magnusson, 1988; Petersen & Taylor, 1980; Stattin & Magnusson, 1990).

In contrast, other studies of menarche are "social context → adolescent" ones. These studies assess how adjustment to the transition of menarche is influenced by contextual features, such as parental demands regarding behavior desired in their adolescent children (e.g., Anthony, 1969; Windle et al., 1986), continuities or discontinuities in school structure (e.g., Crockett, Petersen, Graber, Schulenberg, & Ebata, 1989; Simmons & Blyth, 1987), or cultural beliefs regarding menstruation (e.g., Brooks-Gunn & Ruble, 1980; Ruble & Brooks-Gunn, 1979).

Additional studies in the adolescent literature assess how bidirectional relations between menarche and the social context (e.g., in regard to adolescents and their parents or peers) are associated with differences in developmental "outcomes" (e.g., the incidence of "adjusted" versus "problem" behaviors); these linkages are studied in relation to adolescents' embeddedness in more molar levels of the context, such as particular types of school or of physical activity settings (e.g., Brooks-Gunn, Attie, Burrow, Rosso, & Warren, 1989), different social classes (Hamburg, 1974; Simmons, Brown, Bush, & Blyth, 1978), different cultural or national settings (e.g., Lerner, Iwawaki, Chihara, & Sorell, 1980; Mussen & Bouterline-Young, 1964; Silbereisen, Petersen, Albrecht, & Kracke, 1989; Stattin, Gustafson, & Magnusson, 1989), or distinct historical eras (Elder, 1974; Nesselroade & Baltes, 1974).

To illustrate one instance of such findings, Stattin and Magnusson (1990) reported that in their study of 500 Swedish girls, minimal differences in social behavior (both problematic and well adjusted) in adolescence "will appear due to variations in maturational timing among females who do not engage with peers across the age border, who do not have peers outside the school environment, or who do not have stable opposite-sex relations" (p. 352). However, when girls do associate with these "nonconventional peers" Stattin and Magnusson found a greater role of puberty in social behavior.

Thus, at a descriptive level, the model shown in Figure 1 helps integrate extant portions of the puberty literature and, as such, also acts as a guide to studies of reciprocal puberty-context relations that need to be conducted. In turn, the relationships displayed in Figure 1 have been used as a basis for the formulation of theoretical models seeking to explain the nature of the outcomes derived from particular combinations of puberty and context.

Several instances of such theoretical formulations have been presented in the literature (e.g., Brooks-Gunn, 1987; Lerner & Lerner, 1989; Magnusson, 1988; Petersen, 1987; Stattin et al., 1989; Stattin & Magnusson, 1990). Despite the variation that exists in these instances of developmental contextual models, all involve (a) selection of a subset of the relationships displayed in Figure 1 and (b) specification of the conditions under which particular combinations of person and context are associated with specific developmental outcomes.

For example, in the Lerner and Lerner (1989) "goodness of fit" model, characteristics of physical individuality are predicted to be associated with healthy developmental outcomes when the characteristics meet the demands (or desires or expectations) of significant members of the adolescent's social context, for instance, peers, parents, or teachers; in turn, poor developmental outcomes are predicted when there is a poorness of fit (a mismatch, or incongruence) between the physical attributes the adolescent brings to a given social setting and the social demands of that context.

Several studies (e.g., Lerner, Delaney, Hess, Jovanovic, & von Eye, 1990; for reviews, see Lerner, 1987; Lerner & Jovanovic, 1990) have found that this developmental contextual, goodness of fit model is useful for understanding the role of physical (e.g., pubertal) variation in psychosocial behavior and development and adolescence. Moreover, the corresponding support in the literature for other developmental contextual models (e.g., Brooks-Gunn, 1987; Stattin & Magnusson, 1990) underscores the utility of such a family of theoretical approaches for advancing significantly knowledge of this key feature of adolescence.

REFERENCES

Adams, G., Day, T., Dyk, P., Frede, E., & Rogers, D. R. B. (1992). On the dialectics of pubescence and psychosocial development. *Journal of Early Adolescence, 12,* 348–365.

Adams, G. R., Montemayor, R., & Gullotta, T. (Eds.). (1989). *Advances in adolescent development,* Vol. 1. Beverly Hills, CA: Sage.

Anastasi, A. (1958). Heredity, environment, and the question "how?" *Psychological Review, 65,* 197–208.

Anderson, E. R., Hetherington, E. M., & Clingempeel, W. G. (1989). Transformations in family relations at puberty: Effects of family context. *Journal of Early Adolescence, 9,* 310–334.

Anthony, J. (1969). The reaction of adults to adolescents and their behavior. In G. Caplan & S. Lebovici (Eds.), *Adolescence: Psychological perspectives* (pp. 54–78). New York: Basic Books.

Brim, O. G., Jr., & Kagan, J. (1980). Constancy and change: A view of the issues. In O. G. Brim, Jr. & J. Kagan (Eds.), *Constancy and change in human development* (pp. 1–25). Cambridge, MA: Harvard University Press.

Brooks-Gunn, J. (1987). Pubertal processes and girls' psychological adaptation. In R. M. Lerner & T. T. Foch (Eds.), *Biological-psychosocial interactions in early adolescence* (pp. 123–153). Hillsdale, NJ: Lawrence Erlbaum.

Brooks-Gunn, J., Attie, I., Burrow, C., Rosso, J. T., & Warren, M. P. (1989). The impact of puberty on body and eating concerns in athletic and nonathletic contexts. *Journal of Early Adolescence, 9,* 269–290.

Brooks-Gunn, J., & Petersen, A. C. (Eds.). (1983). *Girls at puberty: Biological and psychosocial perspectives.* New York: Plenum.

Brooks-Gunn, J., & Petersen, A. C. (1984). Problems in studying and defining pubertal events. *Journal of Youth and Adolescence, 13,* 181–196.

Brooks-Gunn, J., & Ruble, D. N. (1980). Menarche: The interaction of physiology, cultural, and social factors. In A. J. Dan, E. A. Graham, & C. P. Beecher (Eds.), *The menstrual cycle: A synthesis of interdisciplinary research* (pp. 141–159). New York: Springer.

Brooks-Gunn, J., & Ruble, D. N. (1983). The experience of menarche from a developmental perspective. In J. Brooks-Gunn & A. C. Petersen (Eds.), *Girls at puberty: Biological and psychosocial perspectives* (pp. 155–177). New York: Plenum.

Crockett, L. J., Petersen, A. C., Graber, J. A., Schulenberg, J. E., & Ebata, A. (1989). School transitions and adjustment during early adolescence. *Journal of Early Adolescence, 9,* 181–210.

Elder, G. H., Jr. (1974). *Children of the Great Depression.* Chicago: University of Chicago Press.

Freud, A. (1969). Adolescence as a developmental disturbance. In G. Caplan & S. Lebovici (Eds.), *Adolescence* (pp. 5–10). New York: Basic Books.

Hamburg, B. (1974). Early adolescence: A specific and stressful stage of the life cycle. In G. Coelho, D. A. Hamburg, & J. E. Adams (Eds.), *Coping and adaptation* (pp. 101–125). New York: Basic Books.

Kestenberg, J. (1967). Phases of adolescence with suggestions for a correlation of psychic and hormonal organization: Part 1. Antecedents of adolescent organizations in childhood. *Journal of the American Academy of Child Psychiatry, 6,* 426–463.

Lerner, R. M. (1976). *Concepts and theories of human development.* Reading, MA: Addison-Wesley.

Lerner, R. M. (1978). Nature, nurture and dynamic interactionism. *Human Development, 21,* 1–20.

Lerner, R. M. (1979). A dynamic interactional concept of individual and social relationship development. In R. Burgess & T. Huston (Eds.), *Social exchange in developing relationships* (pp. 271–305). New York: Academic Press.

Lerner, R. M. (1984). *On the nature of human plasticity.* New York: Cambridge University Press.

Lerner, R. M. (1986). *Concepts and theories of human development* (2nd ed.). New York: Random House.

Lerner, R. M. (1987). A life-span perspective for early adolescence. In R. M. Lerner & T. T. Foch (Eds.), *Biological-psychosocial interactions in early adolescence* (pp. 1–6). Hillsdale, NJ: Lawrence Erlbaum.

Lerner, R. M. (1992). *Final solutions: Biology, prejudice, and genocide.* University Park: Pennsylvania State University Press.

Lerner, R. M., Delaney, M., Hess, L. E., Jovanovic, J., & von Eye, A. (1990). Early adolescent physical attractiveness and academic competence. *Journal of Early Adolescence, 10,* 4–20.

Lerner, R. M., & Foch, T. T. (Eds.). (1987). *Biological-psychosocial interactions in early adolescence.* Hillsdale, NJ: Lawrence Erlbaum.

Lerner, R. M., Iwawaki, S., Chihara, T., & Sorell, G. T. (1980). Self-concept, self-esteem, and body attitudes among Japanese male and female adolescents. *Child Development, 51,* 847–855.

Lerner, R. M., & Jovanovic, J. (1990). The role of body image in psychosocial development across the life span: A developmental contextual perspective. In T. F. Cash & T. Pruzinsky (Eds.), *Body images: Development, deviance, and change* (pp. 110–127). New York: Guilford.

Lerner, R. M., & Lerner, J. V. (1989). Organismic and social contextual bases of development: The sample case of adolescence. In W. Damon (Ed.), *Child developmental today and tomorrow* (pp. 69–85). San Francisco: Jossey-Bass.

Lerner, R. M., Lerner, J. V., & Tubman, J. (1989). Organismic and contextual bases of development in adolescence: A developmental contextual model. In G. R. Adams, T. Gullotta, & R. Montemayor (Eds), *Advances in adolescent development* (Vol. 1, pp. 11–37). Newbury Park, CA: Sage.

Magnusson, D. (1988). Individual development from an interactional perspective. In D. Magnusson (Ed.), *Paths through life* (Vol. 1, pp. 3–31). Hillsdale, NJ: Lawrence Erlbaum.

Mussen, P. H., & Bouterline-Young, H. (1964). Relationships between rate of physical maturing and personality among boys of Italian decent. *Vita Humana, 7,* 186–120.

Nesselroade, J. R., & Baltes, P. B. (1974). Adolescent personality development and historical change: 1970–1972. *Monographs of the Society for Research in Child Development,* No. 39.

Newcombe, N., & Dubas, J. S. (1987). Individual differences in cognitive ability: Are they related to timing of puberty? In R. M. Lerner & T. T. Foch (Eds.), *Biological-psychosocial interactions in early adolescence* (pp. 249–302). Hillsdale, NJ: Lawrence Erlbaum.

Pepper, S. C. (1942). *World hypotheses.* Berkeley: University of California Press.

Petersen, A. C. (1983). Pubertal change and cognition. In J. Brooks-Gunn & A. C. Petersen (Eds.), *Girls at puberty* (pp. 179–197). New York: Plenum.

Petersen, A. C. (1987). The nature of biological psychosocial interactions: The sample case of early adolescence. In R. M. Lerner & T. T. Foch (Eds.), *Biological-psychosocial interactions in early adolescence* (pp. 35–61). Hillsdale, NJ: Lawrence Erlbaum.

Petersen, A. C. (1988). Adolescent development. In M. R. Rosenzweig (Ed.), *Annual review of psychology* (Vol. 39, pp. 583–607). Palo Alto, CA: Annual Reviews, Inc.

Petersen, A. C., & Taylor, B. (1980). The biological approach to adolescence: Biological change and psychological adaptation. In J. Adelson (Ed.), *Handbook of adolescent psychology* (pp. 117–155). New York: Wiley.

Ruble, D. N., & Brooks-Gunn, J. (1979). Menstrual symptoms: A social cognition analysis. *Journal of Behavioral Medicine, 2,* 171–194.

Sheldon, W. H. (1940). *The varieties of human physique.* New York: Harper.

Sheldon, W. H. (1942). *The varieties of temperament.* New York: Harper.

Silbereisen, R. K., Petersen, A. C., Albrecht, H. T., & Kracke, B. (1989). Maturational timing and the development of problem behavior: Longitudinal studies in adolescence. *Journal of Early Adolescence, 9,* 247–268.

Simmons, R. G., & Blyth, D. A. (1987). *Moving into adolescence: The impact of pubertal change and school context.* Hawthorne, NJ: Aldine.

Simmons, R. G., Blyth, D. A., & McKinney, K. L. (1983). The social and psychological effects of puberty on white females. In J. Brooks-Gunn & A. C. Petersen (Eds.), *Girls at puberty* (pp. 229–272). New York: Plenum.

Simmons, R. G., Brown, L., Bush, D. M., & Blyth, D. A. (1978). Self-esteem and achievement of black and white early adolescents. *Social Problems, 26,* 86–96.

Stattin, H., Gustafson, S. B., & Magnusson, D. (1989). Peer influences on adolescent drinking: A social transition perspective. *Journal of Early Adolescence, 9,* 227–246.

Stattin, H., & Magnusson, D. (1990). *Pubertal maturation in female development.* Hillsdale, NJ: Lawrence Erlbaum.

Steinberg, L. D. (1981). Transformations in family relations at puberty. *Developmental Psychology, 17,* 833–840.

Steinberg, L. D., & Hill, J. P. (1978). Patterns of family interaction as a function of age, the onset of puberty, and formal thinking. *Developmental Psychology, 14,* 683–684.

Tobach, E., & Greenberg, G. (1984). The significance of T. C. Schneirla's contribution to the concept of integration. In G. Greenberg & E. Tobach (Eds.), *Behavioral evolution and integrative levels* (pp. 1–7). Hillsdale, NJ: Lawrence Erlbaum.

Tobin-Richards, M. H., Boxer, A. M., & Petersen, A. C. (1983). The psychological significance of puberty change: Sex differences in perceptions of self during early adolescence. In J. Brooks-Gunn & A. C. Petersen (Eds.), *Girls at puberty* (pp. 127–154). New York: Plenum.

Windle, M., Hooker, K., Lenerz, K., East, P. L., Lerner, J. V., & Lerner, R. M. (1986). Temperament, perceived competence, and depression in early- and late-adolescents. *Developmental Psychology, 22,* 384–392.

PART TWO

ADOLESCENCE AS A BIOLOGICAL TRANSITION

The hormonal changes of puberty are responsible for two extremely important biological metamorphoses: The body of the child becomes that of an adult, and the physical differences between the genders become pronounced.
—MODIFIED AND ADAPTED FROM M. A. LLOYD

Adolescence, the transitional period between childhood and adulthood, requires significant readjustments to physical, cognitive, and social changes and influences every aspect of an individual's life. While the debate continues about the extent to which biological development or social environmental forces determine the phenomenon of adolescence—and most evidence suggests that these factors really interact—there can be no doubt that fundamental physiological transformations occur during puberty. The physiological indicators that mark the onset of adolescence begin with an acceleration of physical growth patterns, the appearance of pubic hair for males and females, breast development and menstruation in females, and ejaculation and voice changes in males. The maturation of primary sex characteristics and the development of the secondary sex characteristics combined with body-image adjustments, feelings of sexual tension, physical attraction to others, uncertainties in social expectations, and major reorganization in cognitive structures (Piaget, 7) are hallmarks of this unique time in life.

For males, the dramatic increase in the production of testicular androgen during pubescence closely correlates with several behavioral and psychological manifestations characteristic of early adolescence, such as first ejaculation, beginning of masturbation, and early infatuations. Among females, menarche correlates with basic attitudinal and behavioral shifts from child's play to adult-like social recreational activities (social parties, dancing, dating, and interest in clothes and make-up) and an increasing awareness of body image. For both genders, sexual interest in others begins to emerge.

Tanner, a well-known British developmental physiologist, presents a precise and insightful account (4) of changes in primary and secondary sex characteristics associated with puberty. Researchers, scholars, pediatricians, and clinicians have utilized Tanner's criteria to assess progress through his widely accepted pubertal stages. However, rather than limiting his discussion to the strictly physiological aspect of growth, Tanner sees development in the context of its psychosocial implications. He emphasizes that "emotional attitudes are clearly related to physiological events." While the physiological growth of prepubertal boys is not basically different from that of young girls, the growth patterns of both sexes begin to diverge dramatically with the onset of puberty. Tanner refers to the process by which the bodies of males and females differentiate as *sex dimorphism*. The body differentiation extends beyond the maturation of the primary sex characteristics to include changes in height, patterns of fat deposit, weight, hips, breadth of shoulders, shape of pelvis, pitch of voice, and distribution of hair. The variation in the timing of these events fluctuates greatly not only among same age adolescents but also between the genders; generally speaking, these changes occur a year to a year and a half earlier for girls than for boys. However, when these differences become socially significant, such as breast development in girls, deviation from the peer group can cause anguish and pain, and alter the social and emotional adjustment of the individual. The extensive literature on early and late development to which Tanner refers attests to the profound connection between physiological development and its interrelationship with psychosocial adjustments. The long-range effects of physical maturation apparently reach into adulthood. Early maturing girls are likely to become sexually active at a younger age, to marry earlier, and to have a higher probability of divorce.

Eating disorders are indicators of problematic psychosocial adjustment. Cauffman and Steinberg (5) examine the relationship between menarchal status and dating on dieting and disordered eating behaviors among adolescent girls. Dieting seems to be more prevalent among girls who mature early because they are still adjusting to the weight gain typical of puberty and have not had sufficient time to adjust to their larger size. These girls tend to be more dissatisfied with their body image and try to regain their prepubertal physiques through dieting and disordered eating habits. This is especially true for those early maturing girls who have become involved in mixed-sex social activities; they seem more susceptible to social pressures to appear attractive, which they equate with being thin. This study along with other recent studies (36) considers the multiple, concurrent factors that influence dieting and pathological eating behaviors.

As extensively as menarche has been studied, its parallel among males, "semenarche" has received little research attention. The male experience of first ejaculation is reviewed by Stein and Reiser (6). Their descriptive study of adolescent camp counselors was designed to determine how boys remember the experience of semenarche and their experiences of their voices changing and the first appearance of pubic hair. It also considers how their education and interactions with family and peers affected their experience of these pubertal events. Despite sex education classes and some parental input, many of the participants remembered feelings of curiosity, surprise, and even confusion at the time of their first ejaculation. Although the event does not seem to cause a major trauma, participants' responses indicate that it is a very memorable, anxiety-arousing, highly charged event which could easily have provoked less anxiety if it were preceded by adequate education and understanding. Given the context of male peer relationships, the number of children being raised by single mothers, and the disproportionate number of female teachers, many boys are left to their own devices to interpret the experience of their first semenarche.

Adolescence is a time of multiple transformations. Each change interacts with others to create the need for even more adjustment. If young people have faulty information and inadequate emotional and cognitive preparation for puberty, their exposure to health risks is unnecessarily increased.

SEQUENCE, TEMPO, AND INDIVIDUAL VARIATION IN GROWTH AND DEVELOPMENT OF BOYS AND GIRLS AGED TWELVE TO SIXTEEN

J. M. TANNER
Institute of Child Health, London, England

For the majority of young persons, the years from twelve to sixteen are the most eventful ones of their lives so far as their growth and development is concerned. Admittedly during fetal life and the first year or two after birth developments occurred still faster, and a sympathetic environment was probably even more crucial, but the subject himself was not the fascinated, charmed, or horrified spectator that watches the developments, or lack of developments, of adolescence. Growth is a very regular and highly regulated process, and from birth onward the growth rate of most bodily tissues decreases steadily, the fall being swift at first and slower from about three years. Body shape changes gradually since the rate of growth of some parts, such as the arms and legs, is greater than the rate of growth of others, such as the trunk. But the change is a steady one, a smoothly continuous development rather than any passage through a series of separate stages.

Then at puberty, a very considerable alteration in growth rate occurs. There is a swift increase in body size, a change in the shape and body composition, and a rapid development of the gonads, the reproductive organs, and the characters sig-

naling sexual maturity. Some of these changes are common in both sexes, but most are sex-specific. Boys have a great increase in muscle size and strength, together with a series of physiological changes, making them more capable than girls of doing heavy physical work and running faster and longer. The changes specifically adapt the male to his primitive primate role of dominating, fighting, and foraging. Such adolescent changes occur generally in primates, but are more marked in some species than in others. Male, female, and prepubescent gibbons are hard to distinguish when they are together, let alone apart. No such problem arises with gorillas or Rhesus monkeys. Man lies at about the middle of the primate range, both in adolescent size increase and degree of sexual differentiation.

The adolescent changes are brought about by hormones, either secreted for the first time, or secreted in much higher amounts than previously. Each hormone acts on a set of targets or receptors, but these are often not concentrated in a single organ, nor in a single type of tissue. Testosterone, for example, acts on receptors in the cells of the penis, the skin of the face, the cartilages of the shoulder joints, and certain parts of the brain. Whether all these cells respond by virtue of having the same enzyme system, or whether different enzymes are involved at different sites is not yet clear. The systems have developed through natural selection, producing a functional re-

Reprinted by permission of *Daedalus,* Journal of the American Academy of Arts and Sciences, "Twelve to Sixteen: Early Adolescence," Fall 1971, vol. 100, no. 4, Cambridge, MA.

sponse of obvious biological usefulness in societies of hunter gatherers, but of less certain benefit in the culture of invoice clerk and shop assistant. Evolutionary adaptations of bodily structure usually carry with them an increased proclivity for using those structures in behavior, and there is no reason to suppose this principle suddenly stops short at twentieth-century man. There is no need to take sides in the current debate on the origins of aggression to realize that a major task of any culture is the channeling of this less specifically sexual adolescent energy into creative and playful activity.

The adolescent changes have not altered in the last fifteen years, or the last fifty, or probably the last five thousand. Girls still develop two years earlier than boys; some boys still have completed their whole bodily adolescent development before other boys of the same chronological age have begun theirs. These are perhaps the two major biological facts to be borne in mind when thinking of the adolescent's view of himself in relation to his society. The sequence of the biological events remains the same. But there has been one considerable change; the events occur now at an earlier age than formerly. Forty years ago the average British girl had her first menstrual period (menarche) at about her fifteenth birthday; nowadays it is shortly before her thirteenth. Fifty years ago in Britain social class differences played a considerable part in causing the variation of age of menarche in the population, the less well-off growing up more slowly. Nowadays, age at menarche is almost the same in different classes and most of the variation is due to genetical factors.

In this essay, I shall discuss (1) the growth of the body at adolescence and its changes in size, shape, and tissue composition, (2) sex dimorphism and the development of the reproductive system, (3) the concept of developmental age and the interaction of physical and behavioral advancement, (4) the interaction of genetic and environmental influences on the age of occurrence of puberty and the secular trend toward earlier maturation.

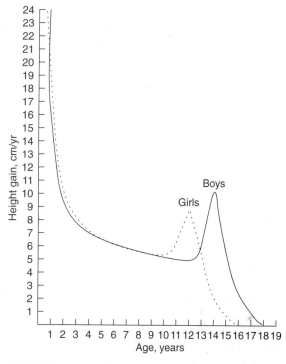

FIGURE 1   Typical Individual Velocity Curves for Supine Length or Height in Boys and Girls.
These curves represent the velocity of the typical boy and girl at any given instant. (*Source:* From J. M. Tanner, R. H. Whitehouse, and M. Takaishi, "Standards from Birth to Maturity for Height, Weight, Height Velocity and Weight Velocity; British Children, 1965," *Archives of the Diseases of Childhood,* 41 [1966], 455–471.)

GROWTH OF THE BODY AT ADOLESCENCE

The extent of the adolescent spurt in height is shown in Figure 1. For a year or more the velocity of growth approximately doubles; a boy is likely to be growing again at the rate he last experienced about age two. The peak velocity of height (PHV, a point much used in growth studies) averages about 10.5 centimeters a year (cm/yr) in boys and 9.0 cm/yr in girls (with a standard deviation of about 1.0 cm/yr) but this is the "instantaneous" peak given by a smooth curve drawn through the observations. The velocity over the whole year encompassing the six months before and after the peak is naturally somewhat less. During this year a boy usually grows between 7 and 12 cm and a girl between 6 and 11 cm. Children who have their peak early reach a somewhat higher peak than those who have it late.

The average age at which the peak is reached depends on the nature and circumstances of the group studied more, probably, than does the height of the peak. In moderately well-off British or North American children at present the peak occurs on average at about 14.0 years in boys and 12.0 years in girls. The standard deviations are about 0.9 years in each instance. Though the absolute average ages differ from series to series the two-year sex difference is invariant.

The adolescent spurt is at least partly under different hormonal control from growth in the period before. Probably as a consequence of this the amount of height added during the spurt is to a considerable degree independent of the amount attained prior to it. Most children who have grown steadily up, say, the 30th centile line on a height chart till adolescence end up at the 30th centile as adults, it is true; but a number end as high as the 50th or as low as the 10th, and a very few at the 55th or 5th. The correlation between adult height and height just before the spurt starts is about 0.8. This leaves some 30 per cent of the variability in adult height as due to differences in the magnitude of the adolescent spurt. So some adolescents get a nasty and unavoidable shock; though probably the effects of early and late maturing (see below) almost totally confuse the issue of final height during the years we are considering.

Practically all skeletal and muscular dimensions take part in the spurt, though not to an equal degree. Most of the spurt in height is due to acceleration of trunk length rather than length of legs. There is a fairly regular order in which the dimensions accelerate; leg length as a rule reaches its peak first, followed by the body breadths, with shoulder width last. Thus a boy stops growing out of his trousers (at least in length) a year before he stops growing out of his jackets. The earliest structures to reach their adult status are the head, hand, and feet. At adolescence, children, particularly girls, sometimes complain of having large hands and feet. They can be reassured that by the time they are fully grown their hands and feet will be a little smaller in proportion to their arms and legs, and considerably smaller in proportion to their trunk.

The spurt in muscle, both of limbs and heart, coincides with the spurt in skeletal growth, for both are caused by the same hormones. Boys' muscle widths reach a peak velocity of growth considerably greater than those reached by girls. But since girls have their spurt earlier, there is actually a period, from about twelve and a half to thirteen and a half, when girls on the average have larger muscles than boys of the same age.

Simultaneously with the spurt in muscle there is a loss of fat in boys, particularly on the limbs. Girls have a velocity curve of fat identical in shape to that of boys; that is to say, their fat accumulation (going on in both sexes from about age six) decelerates. But the decrease in velocity in girls is not sufficiently great to carry the average velocity below zero, that is to give an absolute loss. Most girls have to content themselves with a temporary go-slow in fat accumulation. As the adolescent growth spurt draws to an end, fat tends to accumulate again in both sexes.

The marked increase in muscle size in boys at adolescence leads to an increase in strength, illustrated in Figure 2. Before adolescence, boys and girls are similar in strength for a given body size and shape; after, boys are much stronger, probably due to developing more force per gram of muscle as well as absolutely larger muscles. They also develop larger hearts and lungs relative to their size, a higher systolic blood pressure, a lower resting heart rate, a greater capacity for carrying oxygen in the blood, and a greater power for neutralizing the chemical products of muscular exercise such as lactic acid.[1] In short, the male becomes at adolescence more adapted for the tasks of hunting, fighting, and manipulating all sorts of heavy objects, as is necessary in some forms of food-gathering.

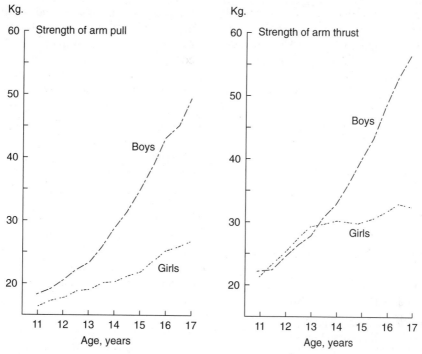

FIGURE 2   Strength of Arm Pull and Arm Thrust from Age Eleven to Seventeen.
Mixed longitudinal data, sixty-five to ninety-five boys and sixty-six to ninety-three girls in
each age group (From J. M. Tanner, *Growth at Adolescence*, 2d ed. [Oxford: Blackwell
Scientific Publications, 1962]; data from H. E. Jones, *Motor Performance and Growth*
[Berkeley: University of California Press, 1949].)

The increase in hemoglobin, associated with a parallel increase in the number of red blood cells, is illustrated in Figure 3.[2] The hemoglobin concentration is plotted in relation to the development of secondary sex characters instead of chronological age, to obviate the spread due to early and late maturing (see below). Girls lack the rise in red cells and hemoglobin, which is brought about by the action of testosterone.

It is as a direct result of these anatomical and physiological changes that athletic ability increases so much in boys at adolescence. The popular notion of a boy "outgrowing his strength" at this time has little scientific support. It is true that the peak velocity of strength is reached a year or so later than that of height, so that a short period may exist when the adolescent, having completed his skeletal and probably also muscular growth, still does not have the strength of a young adult of the same body size and shape. But this is a temporary phase; considered absolutely, power, athletic skill, and physical endurance all increase progressively and rapidly throughout adolescence. It is certainly not true that the changes accompanying adolescence enfeeble, even temporarily. If the adolescent becomes weak and easily exhausted it is for psychological reasons and not physiological ones.

SEX DIMORPHISM AND THE DEVELOPMENT OF THE REPRODUCTIVE SYSTEM

The adolescent spurt in skeletal and muscular dimensions is closely related to the rapid development of the reproductive system which takes

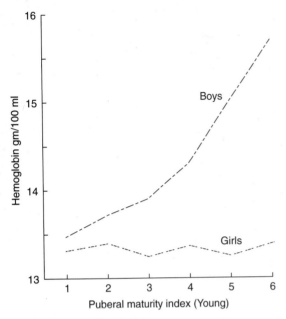

FIGURE 3   Blood Hemoglobin Level in Girls and Boys According to Stage of Puberty; Cross-Sectional Data.
(From H. B. Young, "Ageing and Adolescence," *Developmental Medicine and Child Neurology,* 5 (1963), 451–460, cited in J. M. Tanner, "Growth and Endocrinology of the Adolescent," in L. Gardner, ed., *Endocrine and Genetic Diseases of Childhood* [Philadelphia and London: Saunders, 1969].)

place at this time. The course of this development is outlined diagrammatically in Figure 4. The solid areas marked "breast" in the girls and "penis" and "testes" in the boys represent the period of accelerated growth of these organs and the horizontal lines and the rating numbers marked "pubic hair" stand for its advent and development.[3] The sequences and timings given represent in each case average values for British boys and girls; the North American average is within two or three months of this. To give an idea of the individual departures from the average, figures for the range of age at which the various events begin and end are inserted under the first and last point of the bars. The acceleration of penis growth, for example, begins on the average at about age twelve and a half, but

sometimes as early as ten and a half and sometimes as late as fourteen and a half. The completion of penis development usually occurs at about age fourteen and a half but in some boys is at twelve and a half and in others at sixteen and a half. There are a few boys, it will be noticed, who do not begin their spurts in height or penis development until the earliest maturers have entirely completed theirs. At age thirteen, fourteen, and fifteen there is an enormous variability among any group of boys, who range all the way from practically complete maturity to absolute preadolescence. The same is true of girls aged eleven, twelve, and thirteen.

In Figure 5 three boys are illustrated, all aged exactly 14.75 years and three girls all aged exactly 12.75. All are entirely normal and healthy, yet the first boy could be mistaken easily for a twelve-year-old and the third for a young man of seventeen or eighteen. Manifestly it is ridiculous to consider all three boys or all three girls as equally grown up either physically, or, since much behavior at this age is conditioned by physical status, in their social relations. The statement that a boy is fourteen is in most contexts hopelessly vague; all depends, morphologically, physiologically, and to a considerable extent sociologically too, on whether he is preadolescent, midadolescent, or postadolescent.

The psychological and social importance of this difference in the tempo of development, as it has been called, is very great, particularly in boys. Boys who are advanced in development are likely to dominate their contemporaries in athletic achievement and sexual interest alike. Conversely the late developer is the one who all too often loses out in the rough and tumble of the adolescent world; and he may begin to wonder whether he will ever develop his body properly or be as well endowed sexually as those others he has seen developing around him. A very important part of the educationist's and the doctor's task at this time is to provide information about growth and its variability to preadolescents and adolescents and to give sympathetic support and reassurance to those who need it.

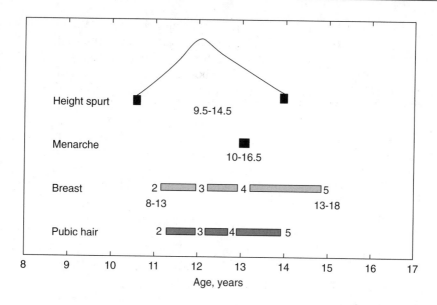

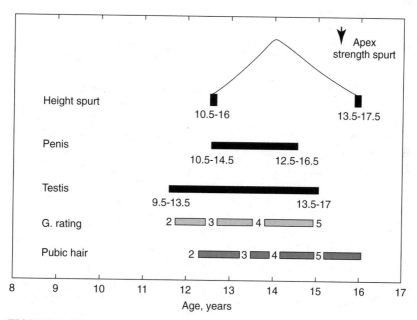

FIGURE 4   Diagram of Sequence of Events at Adolescence in Boys and Girls.

The average boy and girl are represented. The range of ages within which each event charted may begin and end is given by the figures placed directly below its start and finish. (From W. A. Marshall and J. M. Tanner, "Variations in the Pattern of Pubertal Changes in Boys," *Archives of the Diseases of Childhood*, 45 [1970], 13.)

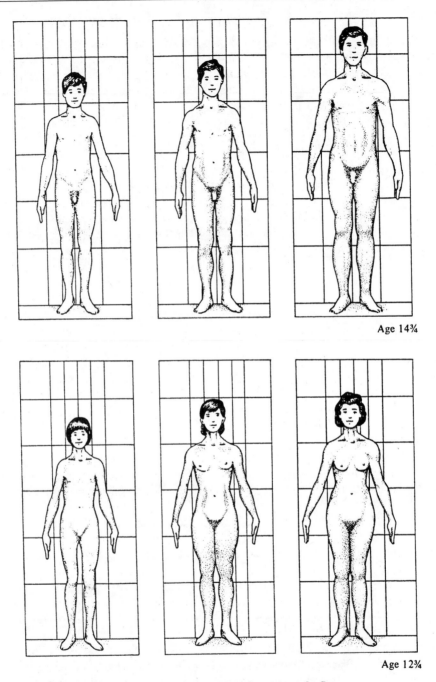

Age 14¾

Age 12¾

FIGURE 5   Differing Degrees of Pubertal Development at the Same Chronological Age.
Upper row three boys all aged 14.75 years. Lower row three girls all aged 12.75 years.
(From Tanner, "Growth and Endocrinology of the Adolescence.")

The *sequence* of events, though not exactly the same for each boy or girl, is much less variable than the age at which the events occur. The first sign of puberty in the boy is usually an acceleration of the growth of the testes and scrotum with reddening and wrinkling of the scrotal skin. Slight growth of public hair may begin about the same time, but is usually a trifle later. The spurts in height and penis growth begin on average about a year after the first testicular acceleration. Concomitantly with the growth of the penis, and under the same stimulus, the seminal vesicles and the prostate and bulbo-urethral glands enlarge and develop. The time of the first ejaculation of seminal fluid is to some extent culturally as well as biologically determined, but as a rule is during adolescence, and about a year after the beginning of accelerated penis growth.

Axillary hair appears on the average some two years after the beginning of pubic hair growth—that is, when pubic hair is reaching stage 4. However, there is enough variability and dissociation in these events that a very few children's axillary hair actually appears first. In boys, facial hair begins to grow at about the time the axillary hair appears. There is a definite order in which the hairs of moustache and beard appear; first at the corners of the upper lip, then over all the upper lip, then at the upper part of the cheeks in the mid-line below the lower lip, and finally along the sides and lower border of the chin. The remainder of the body hair appears from about the time of first axillary hair development until a considerable time after puberty. The ultimate amount of body hair an individual develops seems to depend largely on heredity, though whether because of the kinds and amounts of hormones secreted or because of the reactivity of the end-organs is not known.

Breaking of the voice occurs relatively late in adolescence; it is often a gradual process and so not suitable as a criterion of puberty. The change in pitch accompanies enlargement of the larynx and lengthening of the vocal cords, caused by the action of testosterone on the laryngeal cartilages. During the period of breaking, the pitch is variable, and the true adult pitch associated with full growth of the larynx may not be established until late adolescence. In addition to change in pitch, there is also a change in quality or timbre which distinguishes the voice (more particularly the vowel sounds) of both male and female adults from that of children. This is dependent on the enlargement of the resonating spaces above the larynx, due to the rapid growth of the mouth, nose, and maxilla which occurs during adolescence.

In the skin the sebaceous and apocrine sweat glands, particularly of the axillae and genital and anal regions, develop rapidly during puberty and give rise to a characteristic odor; the changes occur in both sexes but are more marked in the male. Enlargement of the pores at the root of the nose and the appearance of comedones and acne, though liable to occur in either sex, are considerably commoner in adolescent boys than girls, since the underlying skin changes are the result of androgenic activity. A roughening of the skin, particularly over the outer aspects of the thighs and upper arms, may be seen in both sexes during adolescence, but again is commoner in boys than girls.

During adolescence the male breast undergoes changes, some temporary and some permanent. The diameter of the areola, which is equal in both sexes before puberty, increases considerably, though less than it does in girls. Representative figures are 12.5 millimeters before puberty, 21.5 millimeters in mature men and 35.5 millimeters in mature women. In some boys (between a fifth and a third of most groups studied) there is a distinct enlargement of the breast (sometimes unilaterally) about midway through adolescence. This usually regresses again after about one year.

In girls the appearance of the "breast bud" is as a rule the first sign of puberty, though the appearance of pubic hair precedes it in about one in three. The uterus and vagina develop simultaneously with the breast. The labia and clitoris also enlarge. Menarche, the first menstrual period, is a late event in the sequence. It occurs almost invariably after the peak of the height spurt has been passed. Though it marks a definitive and probably mature stage of uterine development, it does not usually signify the attainment of full reproductive function. The early cycles may be more irregular than later ones and are in some girls, but by no means all, accompanied by dysmenorrhea. They are often anovulatory, that is unaccompanied by the shedding of an egg. Thus there is frequently a period of adolescent sterility lasting a year to eighteen months after menarche; but it cannot be relied on in the individual case. Similar considerations may apply to the male, but there is no reliable information about this. On the average, girls grow about 6 cm more after menarche, though gains of up to twice this amount may occur. The gain is practically independent of whether menarche occurs early or late.

NORMAL VARIATIONS IN PUBERTAL DEVELOPMENT

The diagram of Figure 4 must not be allowed to obscure the fact that children vary a great deal both in the rapidity with which they pass through the various stages of puberty and in the closeness with which the various events are linked together. At one extreme one may find a perfectly healthy girl who has not yet menstruated though she has reached adult breast and pubic hair ratings and is already two years past her peak height velocity; at the other a girl who has passed all the stages of puberty within the space of two years. Details of the limits of what may be considered normal can be found in the articles of Marshall and Tanner.[4]

In girls the interval from the first sign of puberty to complete maturity varies from one and a half to six years. From the moment when the breast bud first appears to menarche averages two and a half years but may be as little as six months or as much as five and a half years. The rapidity with which a child passes through puberty seems to be independent of whether puberty is occurring early or late. There is some

independence between breast and pubic hair developments, as one might expect on endocrinological grounds. A few girls reach pubic hair stage 3 (see Figure 4) before any breast development starts; conversely breast stage 3 may be reached before any pubic hair appears. At breast stage 5, however, pubic hair is always present in girls. Menarche usually occurs in breast stage 4 and pubic hair stage 4, but in about 10 per cent of girls occurs in stage 5 for both, and occasionally may occur in stage 2 or even 1 of pubic hair. Menarche invariably occurs after peak height velocity is passed, so the tall girl can be reassured about future growth if her periods have begun.

In boys a similar variability occurs. The genitalia may take any time between two and five years to pass from G2 to G5, and some boys complete the whole process while others have still not gone from G2 to G3. Pubic hair growth in the absence of genital development is very unusual in normal boys, but in a small percent of boys the genitalia develop as far as stage 4 before the pubic hair starts to grow.

The height spurt occurs relatively later in boys than in girls. Thus there is a difference between the average boy and girl of two years in age of peak height velocity, but of only one year in the first appearance of pubic hair. The PHV occurs in very few boys before genital stage 4, whereas 75 percent of girls reach PHV before breast stage 4. Indeed in some girls the acceleration in height is the first sign of puberty; this is never so in boys. A small boy whose genitalia are just beginning to develop can be unequivocally reassured that an acceleration in height is soon to take place, but a girl in the corresponding situation may already have had her height spurt.

The basis of some children having loose and some tight linkages between pubertal events is not known. Probably the linkage reflects the degree of integration of various processes in the hypothalamus and the pituitary gland, for breast growth is controlled by one group of hormones, pubic hair growth by another, and the height spurt probably by a third. In rare pathological instances the events may become widely divorced.

THE DEVELOPMENT
OF SEX DIMORPHISM

The differential effects on the growth of bone, muscle, and fat at puberty increase considerably the difference in body composition between the sexes. Boys have a greater increase not only in the length of bones but in the thickness of cortex, and girls have a smaller loss of fat. The most striking dimorphisms, however, are the man's greater stature and breadth of shoulders and the woman's wider hips. These are produced chiefly by the changes and timing of puberty but it is important to remember that sex dimorphisms do not arise only at that time. Many appear much earlier. Some, like the external genital difference itself, develop during fetal life. Others develop continuously throughout the whole growth period by a sustained differential growth rate. An example of this is the greater relative length and breadth of the forearm in the male when compared with whole arm length or whole body length.

Part of the sex difference in pelvic shape antedates puberty. Girls at birth already have a wider pelvic outlet. Thus the adaptation for child bearing is present from a very early age. The changes at puberty are concerned more with widening the pelvic inlet and broadening the much more noticeable hips. It seems likely that these changes are more important in attracting the male's attention than in dealing with its ultimate product.

These sex-differentiated morphological characters arising at puberty—to which we can add the corresponding physiological and perhaps psychological ones as well—are secondary sex characters in the straightforward sense that they are caused by sex hormone or sex-differential hormone secretion and serve reproductive activity. The penis is directly concerned in copulation, the mammary gland in lactation. The wide shoulders and muscular power of the male, together with the canine teeth and brow ridges in man's ancestors, developed probably for driving away other males and insuring peace, an adaptation which soon becomes social.

A number of traits persist, perhaps through another mechanism known to the ethologists as ritualization. In the course of evolution a morphological character or a piece of behavior may lose its original function and, becoming further elaborated, complicated, or simplified, may serve as a sign stimulus to other members of the same species, releasing behavior that is in some ways advantageous to the spread or survival of the species. It requires little insight into human erotics to suppose that the shoulders, the hips and buttocks, and the breasts (at least in a number of widespread cultures) serve as releasers of mating behavior. The pubic hair (about whose function the textbooks have always preserved a cautious silence) probably survives as a ritualized stimulus for sexual activity, developed by simplification from the hair remaining in the inguinal and axillary regions for the infant to cling to when still transported, as in present apes and monkeys, under the mother's body. Similar considerations may apply to axillary hair, which is associated with special apocrine glands which themselves only develop at puberty and are related histologically to scent glands in other mammals. The beard, on the other hand, may still be more frightening to other males than enticing to females. At least ritual use in past communities suggests this is the case; but perhaps there are two sorts of beards.

THE INITIATION OF PUBERTY

The manner in which puberty is initiated has a general importance for the clarification of developmental mechanisms. Certain children develop all the changes of puberty, up to and including spermatogenesis and ovulation, at a very early age, either as the result of a brain lesion or as an isolated developmental, sometimes genetic defect. The youngest mother on record was such a case, and gave birth to a full-term healthy infant by Caesarian section at the age of five years, eight months. The existence of precocious puberty and the results of accidental ingestion by small children of male or female sex hormones indicate that breasts, uterus, and penis will respond to hormonal stimulation long before puberty. Evidently an increased end-organ sensitivity plays at most a minor part in pubertal events.

The signal to start the sequence of events is given by the brain, not the pituitary. Just as the brain holds the information on sex, so it holds information on maturity. The pituitary of a newborn rat successfully grafted in place of an adult pituitary begins at once to function in an adult fashion, and does not have to wait till its normal age of maturation has been reached. It is the hypothalamus, not the pituitary, which has to mature before puberty begins.

Maturation, however, does not come out of the blue and at least in rats a little more is known about this mechanism. In these animals small amounts of sex hormones circulate from the time of birth and these appear to inhibit the prepubertal hypothalamus from producing gonadotrophin releasers. At puberty it is supposed that the hypothalamic cells become less sensitive to sex hormones. The small amount of sex hormones circulating then fails to inhibit the hypothalamus and gonadotrophins are released; these stimulate the production of testosterone by the testis or estrogen by the ovary. The level of the sex hormones rises until the same feedback circuit is reestablished, but now at a higher level of gonadotrophins and sex hormones. The sex hormones are now high enough to stimulate the growth of secondary sex characters and support mating behavior.

DEVELOPMENTAL AGE AND THE INTERACTION OF PHYSICAL AND BEHAVIORAL ADVANCEMENT

Children vary greatly in their tempo of growth. The effects are most dramatically seen at adolescence, as illustrated in Figure 5, but they are present at all ages from birth and even before. Girls, for example, do not suddenly become two years ahead of boys at adolescence; on the contrary

they are born with slightly more mature skeletons and nervous systems, and gradually increase their developmental lead (in absolute terms) throughout childhood.

Clearly, the concept of *developmental* age, as opposed to *chronological* age, is a very important one. To measure developmental age we need some way of determining the percentage of the child's growth process which has been attained at any time. In retrospective research studies, the per cent of final adult height may be very effectively used; but in the clinic we need something that is immediate in its application. The difficulty about using height, for example, is that different children end up at different heights, so that a tall-for-his-age twelve-year-old may either be a tall adult in the making with average maturational tempo, or an average adult in the making with an accelerated tempo. Precisely the same applies to the child who scores above average on most tests of mental ability.

To measure developmental age we need something which ends up the same for everyone and is applicable throughout the whole period of growth. Many physiological measures meet these criteria, in whole or in part. They range from the number of erupted teeth to the percentage of water in muscle cells. The various developmental "age" scales do not necessarily coincide, and each has its particular use. By far the most generally useful, however, is skeletal maturity or *bone* age. A less important one is dental maturity.

Skeletal maturity is usually measured by taking a radiograph of the hand and wrist (using the same radiation exposure that a child inevitably gets, and to more sensitive areas, by spending a week on vacation in the mountains). The appearances of the developing bones can be rated and formed into a scale; the scale is applicable to boys and girls of all genetic backgrounds, though girls on the average reach any given score at a younger age than boys, and blacks on the average, at least in the first few years after birth, reach a given score younger than do whites. Other areas of the body may be used if required. Skeletal maturity is closely related to age at which adolescence occurs, that is to maturity measured by secondary sex character development. Thus the range of *chronological* age within which menarche may normally fall is about ten to sixteen and a half, but the corresponding range of *skeletal* age for menarche is only twelve to fourteen and a half. Evidently the physiological processes controlling progression of skeletal development are in most instances closely linked with those which initiate the events of adolescence. Furthermore children tend to be consistently advanced or retarded during their whole growth period, or at any rate after about age three.

Dental maturity partly shares in this general skeletal and bodily maturation. At all ages from six to thirteen children who are advanced skeletally have on the average more erupted teeth than those who are skeletally retarded. Likewise those who have an early adolescence on the average erupt their teeth early. Girls usually have more erupted teeth than boys. But this relationship is not a very close one, and quantitatively speaking, it is the relative independence of teeth and general skeletal development which should be emphasized. There is some general factor of bodily maturity creating a tendency for a child to be advanced or retarded as a whole: in his skeletal ossification, in the percentage attained of his eventual size, in his permanent dentition, doubtless in his physiological reactions, and possibly in the results of his tests of ability. But not too much should be made of this general factor; and especially it should be noted how very limited is the loading, so to speak, of brain growth in it. There is little justification in the facts of physical growth and development for the concept of "organismic age" in which almost wholly disparate measures of developmental maturity are lumped together.

PHYSICAL MATURATION, MENTAL ABILITY, AND EMOTIONAL DEVELOPMENT

Clearly the occurrence of tempo differences in human growth has profound implications for educational theory and practice. This would espe-cially be so if advancement in physical growth were linked to any significant degree with advancement in intellectual ability and in emotional maturity.

There is good evidence that in the European and North American school systems children who are physically advanced toward maturity score on the average slightly higher in most tests of mental ability than children of the same age who are physically less mature. The difference is not great, but it is consistent and it occurs at all ages that have been studied—that is, back as far as six and a half years. Similarly the intelligence test score of postmenarcheal girls is higher than the score of premenarcheal girls of the same age.[5] Thus in age-linked examinations physically fast-maturing children have a significantly better chance than slow-maturing.

It is also true that physically large children score higher than small ones, at all ages from six onward. In a random sample of all Scottish eleven-year-old children, for example, comprising 6,440 pupils, the correlation between height and score in the Moray House group test was 0.25 ± 0.01 which leads to an average increase of one and a half points Terman-Merrill I.Q. per inch of stature. A similar correlation was found in London children. The effects can be very significant for individual children. In ten-year-old girls there was nine points difference in I.Q. between those whose height was above the 75th percentile and those whose height was below the 15th. This is two-thirds of the standard deviation of the test score.

It was usually thought that both the relationships between test score and height and between test score and early maturing would disappear in adulthood. If the correlations represented only the effects of coadvancement both of mental ability and physical growth this might be expected to happen. There is no difference in height between early and late maturing boys when both have finished growing. But it is now clear that, curiously, at least part of the height-I.Q. correlation persists in adults.[6] It is not clear in what proportion genetic and environmental factors are responsible for this.

There is little doubt that being an early or a late maturer may have repercussions on behavior, and that in some children these repercussions may be considerable. There is little enough solid information on the relation between emotional and physiological development, but what there is supports the common sense notion that emotional attitudes are clearly related to physiological events.

The boy's world is one where physical powers bring prestige as well as success, where the body is very much an instrument of the person. Boys who are advanced in development, not only at puberty, but before as well, are more likely than others to be leaders. Indeed, this is reinforced by the fact that muscular, powerful boys on the average mature earlier than others and have an early adolescent growth spurt. The athletically-built boy not only tends to dominate his fellows before puberty, but also by getting an early start he is in a good position to continue that domination. The unathletic, lanky boy, unable, perhaps, to hold his own in the preadolescent rough and tumble, gets still further pushed to the wall at adolescence, as he sees others shoot up while he remains nearly stationary in growth. Even boys several years younger now suddenly surpass him in size, athletic skill, and perhaps, too, in social graces.

At a much deeper level the late developer at adolescence may sometimes have doubts about whether he will ever develop his body properly and whether he will be as well endowed sexually as those others he has seen developing around him. The lack of events of adolescence may act as a trigger to reverberate fears accumulated deep in the mind during the early years of life.

It may seem as though the early maturers have things all their own way. It is indeed true that most studies of the later personalities of children whose growth history is known to show early maturers as more stable, more sociable, less neurotic, and more successful in society, at least in the United States.[7] But early maturers have their difficulties also, particularly the girls in some societies. Though some glory in their new possessions, others are embarrassed by them. The early maturer, too, has a longer period of frustration of sex drive and of drive toward independence and the establishment of vocational orientation.

Little can be done to reduce the individual differences in children's tempo of growth, for they are biologically rooted and not significantly reducible by any social steps we may take. It, therefore, behooves all teachers, psychologists, and pediatricians to be fully aware of the facts and alert to the individual problems they raise.

REFERENCES

1. J. M. Tanner, *Growth at Adolescence,* 2d ed. (Oxford: Blackwell Scientific Publications, 1962), p. 168.
2. H. B. Young, "Ageing and Adolescence," *Developmental Medicine and Child Neurology,* 5 (1963), 451–460.
3. Details of ratings are in Tanner, *Growth at Adolescence.*
4. W. A. Marshall and J. M. Tanner, "Variations in the Pattern of Pubertal Changes in Girls," *Archives of the Diseases of Childhood,* 44 (1969), 291, and "Variations in the Pattern of Pubertal Changes in Boys," *Archives of the Diseases of Childhood,* 45 (1970), 13.
5. See references in Tanner, *Growth at Adolescence,* and Tanner, "Galtonian Eugenics and the Study of Growth," *The Eugenics Review,* 58 (1966), 122–135.
6. Tanner, "Galtonian Eugenics."
7. P. H. Mussen and M. C. Jones, "Self-Concepting Motivations and Interpersonal Attitudes of Late- and Early-Maturing Boys," *Child Development,* 28 (1957), 243–256.

INTERACTIVE EFFECTS OF MENARCHEAL STATUS AND DATING ON DIETING AND DISORDERED EATING AMONG ADOLESCENT GIRLS

ELIZABETH CAUFFMAN AND LAURENCE STEINBERG
Stanford Center on Adolescence and Temple University

The prevalence of disordered eating among young U.S. women has increased markedly over the past several decades. At any one time, between one half and two thirds of all high school girls in the United States are on a diet, many of them unnecessarily (Rosen & Gross, 1987; Rosen, Tracey, & Howell, 1990). Stereotypical standards of beauty and social success transmitted through advertising and other mass media are often blamed for the prevalence of dieting and disordered eating among young U.S. women (Striegel-Moore, Silberstein, & Rodin, 1986). This account, however, does not explain why some young women develop eating disorders, whereas others, exposed to the same mass media, do not. The present study investigates the joint importance of two developmental factors believed to affect dieting and disordered eating in adolescence—pubertal maturation and socializing with members of the opposite sex—in a population of young adolescent girls.

According to Attie and Brooks-Gunn (1989), a developmental perspective considers eating problems during adolescence by placing them in the "context of challenges confronting individuals during this life phase" (p. 70). These challenges include pubertal development, the psy-chological and social changes that accompany it, and the process of moving into adulthood through increasing psychological autonomy from parents. A developmental framework may better explain why many eating problems generally arise during adolescence, because this is the phase of life in which so many physical and psychosocial challenges converge (Attie, Brooks-Gunn, & Petersen, 1990).

The present study begins from the premise that eating problems in young girls develop as a result of interactions between two distinct aspects of adolescent development: the specific challenges of puberty and the psychological and social challenges of early adolescence. Understanding the ways in which social factors and biological factors can interact in determining developmental outcomes is an issue of great importance to researchers and clinicians alike.

During puberty, girls undergo numerous physiological changes, predominant among them is a significant increase in body fat. This increase, which averages 24 lb (11kg; Young, Sipin, & Roe, 1968), leads many adolescent girls to become concerned about their body image, as they see it departing from what they perceive as ideal (Striegel-Moore et al., 1986). Consequently, girls become likely to diet in an attempt to return to a thinner, prepubertal physique (Brooks-Gunn, 1987; Dornbusch et al., 1984; Gralen, Levine, Smolak, & Murnen, 1990; Sim-

From *Developmental Psychology,* 1996, 32 (4), 631–635.

mons & Blyth, 1987). It is interesting that although psychosocial influences play a dominant role in the onset of eating disorders late in adolescence, physical variables are more predictive of eating problems during early adolescence (Attie & Brooks-Gunn, 1989). The timing of puberty is also an important consideration: Girls who mature early are at relatively greater risk of developing eating problems (Graber, Brooks-Gunn, Paikoff, & Warren, 1994), in part because their weight gain tends to be a larger fraction of their total body weight (Attie & Brooks-Gunn, 1989) and in part because they are heavier and more dissatisfied with their figures than are late maturers (Simmons & Blyth, 1987). In any case, however, one would hypothesize that dieting is more prevalent among girls who are still adjusting to the pubertal gain in body fat than among those who either are prepubertal or who have had sufficient time to adapt to the bodily changes of puberty.

Although pubertal maturation has been implicated in the onset of girls' eating problems, the relation between pubertal maturation and disordered eating may be due not to puberty per se but to other developmental changes that coincide with physical maturation. One such developmental change that generally accompanies puberty is the onset of heterosocial activity, including participation in mixed-sex social activities, the beginning of formal dating, and initial experimentation with sex. In the contemporary United States, girls typically begin to date between the ages of 12 and 13, which is also the average age of menarche in this country. Further evidence for the co-occurrence of dating and pubertal maturation is research indicating that the onset of dating occurs earlier among early versus late maturers (McCabe, 1984; Simmons & Blyth, 1987).

It is important to consider the effects of dating and other types of heterosocial activity on the eating behavior of early adolescent girls, for two reasons. First, there is a strong relation between girls' interest in opposite-sex popularity and their concern with appearance, body weight, and body shape (Simmons & Blyth, 1987). Con-

temporary U.S. society values thinness among women, and many adolescent girls view dieting as an important part of maintaining or enhancing their attractiveness to adolescent boys. Second, dating may increase young adolescents' vulnerability to depressed affect, which may in turn increase their risk for developing eating problems (Graber et al., 1994). Although one might assume that dating would increase girls' self-esteem, studies have found the reverse, at least among young adolescents: Junior high school girls who date have lower self-esteem than other girls (Simmons & Blyth, 1987). Barnett, Biener, and Baruch (1987) hypothesized that success in dating may actually signal movement from a focus on self and autonomy to a focus on pleasing others and, consequently, to a loss of autonomy and of one's sense of personal control.

Within a population of early adolescent girls who have begun socializing with boys, there is wide variability in the types and degree of heterosexual involvement observed, ranging from participating in mixed-sex group activities to having a "steady" boyfriend with whom one has a sexual relationship. The present study examines the effects on dieting of three different aspects of heterosexual activity. First, we consider social involvement in mixed-sex activities (e.g., going to parties where boys are present, going out in groups with boys). Second, we consider dating, as indexed by going out as a member of a couple. Finally, we consider physical involvement with boys (e.g., holding hands, kissing, petting). We predict that higher levels of involvement in all three respects will be associated with increased dieting behavior and, moreover, that these effects will be greater among girls in pubertal transition (i.e., those who have recently undergone menarche).

METHOD

Sample

The sample consisted of 7th- ($N = 58$, M age = 12.2 years, $SD = 0.5$) and 8th- ($N = 31$, M age = 13.1 years, $SD = 0.4$) grade girls. Fifty-seven (7th grade $N = 38$, 8th grade $N = 19$) attended a public junior high school in suburban New Jersey, and 32 (7th grade $N = 20$, 8th grade $N = 12$) attended a private school in a suburban area of California. The majority of the participants were White (85%), whereas the rest of our sample consisted of Asian Americans (8%), African Americans (1%), and adolescents from other ethnic groups (6%). On the basis of parent education level, the majority of our sample came from middle-class backgrounds (65% of fathers and 58% of mothers had obtained a college degree or better), whereas only a small portion were from lower-class families (6% of fathers and 2% of mothers had not completed high school). Of our sample, 76% came from two-parent, nondivorced families, whereas 24% were from divorced or separated families.

Procedure

The data for the present study come from questionnaires administered as part of a larger research program on adolescent attitudes and behaviors. A letter explaining the purpose and procedures of the study was mailed to the parents of all potential participants. Parents could withhold consent by returning a form enclosed with the letter to either the researchers or the school. Students were informed that their participation in the study was voluntary and that they could withdraw at any time. Of the potential participants, 5% were withdrawn from the study by their parents, and 7% were absent on the day of the study. The questionnaire was administered during regular class periods; two members of the research team were present to distribute questionnaires and ensure that all answers were voluntary and confidential.

Measures

The questionnaire contained a wide array of items concerning family background (including parent education, a proxy for socioeconomic status), psychosocial functioning, family and peer relations, and problem behavior. Of particular interest for the present analyses are our measures of menarcheal status, dieting, social involvement, dating, and physical involvement.

Menarcheal status. Participants were asked three questions specifically related to their menarcheal status. The first was a forced-choice question: "Have you had your period yet?" The next two questions concerned duration and regularity of menstruation, asking girls how long ago their first period occurred (less than 6 months ago, 6–12 months ago, or more than 12 months ago) and asking them to describe their monthly cycle (one period only, not every month, or every month). On the basis of their responses, participants were categorized as either (a) premenarcheal (have not yet had their first period), (b) menarcheal (had their first period less than a year ago), or (c) postmenarcheal (had their first period over a year ago). A number of researchers have verified that adolescent girls report their age at menarche accurately (Bean, Leeper, Wallace, Sherman, & Jagger, 1979; Brooks-Gunn, Warren, Rosso, & Gargiulo, 1987; Caspi, Lynam, Moffitt, & Silva, 1993; Petersen, 1983). For purposes of the analyses performed below, menarcheal status was dummy coded into two variables describing whether a subject is premenarcheal and whether a subject is menarcheal.

Dieting and disordered eating. Participants were asked if they were currently trying to lose weight (yes or no) and were categorized as either dieters or nondieters on the basis of their response to this question. The external validity of this question was established by Rosen and Gross (1987), who used parents, siblings, and friends to corroborate adolescents' dieting behaviors. Parents agreed with adolescents' self-report 82% of the time, and siblings and friends agreed 76% of the time.

The Eating Attitudes Test-26 (EAT-26), which is an abbreviated version of the 40-item EAT, was used to measure disordered eating (Garner & Garfinkel, 1979; Garner, Olmsted, Bohr, & Garfinkel, 1982). The format requires participants to respond on a 6-point scale (ranging from *always* to *never*) to how often they agree with a series of 26 statements. The most symptomatic response receives a score of 3, the second most symptomatic response receives a 2, the third a 1, and the rest are scored as zeroes. Although it is possible to use the EAT-26 scale to identify individuals who suffer from a clinical eating disorder, in a community sample of early adolescents, the prevalence of eating disorders that meet standard diagnostic criteria is quite low. In the present study, therefore, we use the EAT-26 scale simply as a continuous measure of disordered eating tendencies, with higher scores indicating more disturbed dieting behaviors.

The items of the EAT-26 cluster into three factor analytic subscales that assess a broad range of symptoms of anorexia nervosa and bulimia nervosa. The first factor, Diet, includes items indicative of dieting behavior and a drive for thinness (e.g., "I am on a diet much of the time" and "I am preoccupied with the desire to be thinner"). The second factor, Bulimia and Food Preoccupation, contains items related to bingeing and vomiting (e.g., "I have the impulse to throw up after meals" and "I have gone on eating binges where I feel that I may not be able to stop eating"). The third factor, Oral Control, reflects perceived social pressure to gain weight (e.g., "I feel that others pressure me to eat" and "I take longer than others to eat meals"). For the present analyses, total EAT-26 scores were used (in our sample, a = .88).

Heterosocial activity. Three aspects of heterosocial activity were assessed. A modified version of the Silverberg and Steinberg (1990) heterosocial scale was used to measure social involvement. Participants were asked how often during the past year they had engaged in various activities, including going out in groups to the mall or to the movies, going to school dances, and going to parties where boys and girls were present. Participants could respond to each item with four choices: 0 (*never*), 1 (*once or twice*), 2 (*three to seven times*), or 3 (*eight or more times*). Responses to six such items ($\alpha = .87$) were summed to create a scale of social involvement ranging from 0 (*not involved*) to 18 (*very involved*).

Dating was defined in the questionnaire as "going out with a boy either alone or with other couples." Participants were asked, "If you have ever had a date, how old were you on your first date?" Participants could respond that they have never had a date (these participants were classified as nondaters) or with the age at which they began dating (these participants were classified as daters).

In addition to the activities mentioned above, participants were asked how often they had a special boyfriend, held hands with a boyfriend, kissed a boyfriend, and "gone farther" than kissing with a boyfriend. Responses to these items ($\alpha = .93$) were used to index physical involvement. Adolescents were categorized into one of four physical involvement groups, defined as (a) nondaters (have never dated), (b) innocent daters (have dated, but not held hands, kissed, or gone farther than kissing), (c) experimenting daters (have dated, and held hands or kissed, but not gone farther than kissing), and (d) serious daters (have dated, held hands, kissed, and gone farther than kissing).

RESULTS

Plan of Analyses

Hierarchical logistic regression analyses were used to assess the effects of various factors on the dichotomous dieting variable, and standard hierarchical regression analyses were used to assess effects on the continuous EAT-26 variable. We controlled for the effects of chronological age by entering age as the first independent variable in each analysis. (This ensures that any observed differences among participants in different menarcheal or heterosocial categories are not simply a reflection of differences in age.) Analyses initially were performed for each school individually to check for school effects. In all cases, the results of individual school analyses were consistent with analyses of the entire sample. We therefore report only the results of analyses of the entire sample. For each of our three heterosocial activity variables (social involvement, dating, and physical involvement),

TABLE 1

Characteristics of the Study Sample

Variable	n	% dieting	EAT M	EAT SD
Dating				
Yes	40	60	13.22	9.90
No	48	29	7.85	6.93
Menarcheal status				
Premenarcheal	40	33	9.37	6.86
Menarcheal	19	63	12.37	9.80
Postmenarcheal	24	50	10.96	10.24

Note. EAT = Eating Attitudes Test.

analyses were performed using the following independent variables: (a) age, (b) menarcheal status (coded as a three-level categorical variable, premenarcheal, menarcheal, or postmenarcheal), (c) heterosocial activity, and, finally, (d) the menarche-heterosocial activity interaction. Table 1 provides general descriptive statistics for the sample.

Age alone showed no significant relation to current dieting behavior but showed a marginally significant relation to EAT-26 scores, $\beta = .214$, $t(1, 81) = 1.98$, $p < .06$, with older girls exhibiting higher scores. With age in the equation, menarcheal status was not a significant predictor of EAT-26 scores. There was a borderline relation between menarcheal status and dieting behavior, however: Menarcheal girls tended to be more likely to be dieting than their pre- or postmenarcheal peers ($b = .98$, $\chi^2 = 3.26$, $p = .071$).

Social Involvement, Dieting, and Disordered Eating

With age and menarcheal status already accounted for, logistic regression analyses revealed no significant effect of social involvement on current dieting behavior. Social involvement did, however, predict higher EAT-26 scores, with disordered eating more common among girls who are more socially involved than among those who are not active socially, $\beta = .274$, $t(4, 78) = 2.521$, $p < .05$. In addition, a significant interaction between social involvement

and menarcheal status (specifically, whether the participant is premenarcheal) was also observed, $\beta = -.863$, $t(6, 76) = -2.11$, $p < .05$, with the effect of social involvement on EAT-26 scores stronger among menarcheal and postmenarcheal girls than among premenarcheal girls.

Dating, Dieting, and Disordered Eating

Girls who date are significantly more likely to be dieting, even after taking into account the effects of age and pubertal status ($b = 1.37$, $\chi^2 = 7.39$, $p < .01$). An interaction between dating and menarche was also observed, with dating being most predictive of current dieting status among menarcheal girls ($b = 3.45$, $\chi^2 = 4.61$, $p < .05$). As expected, girls who were both dating and in the midst of menarche were the most likely to be dieting.

Regression analyses indicate that girls who date are more likely to exhibit disordered eating tendencies than girls who do not date, $\beta = .272$, $t(4, 78) = 2.41$, $p < .05$. A significant interaction between puberty and dating was also observed, $\beta = 1.25$, $t(6, 76) = 2.00$, $p > .05$, with the effect of dating on disordered eating being stronger among menarcheal girls than among premenarcheal or postmenarcheal girls.

Physical Involvement, Dieting, and Disordered Eating

Logistic regression analyses indicate that girls who are more physically involved with boyfriends are significantly more likely to be dieting, even after taking into account the effects of age and menarcheal status ($b = .570$, $\chi^2 = 5.82$, $p > .05$).

Physical involvement also predicted higher EAT-26 scores, indicating that disordered eating is more likely among girls who are physically involved with their boyfriends than among those who are not, $\beta = .435$, $t(4, 69) = 3.65$ $p < .001$. The interaction between physical involvement and menarcheal status in the prediction of dieting and EAT-26 scores was not significant, however, indicating that physical involvement and dieting behavior are similarly associated among girls at different stages of puberty.

DISCUSSION

Previous studies have suggested that girls who are in the midst of the pubertal changes accompanying menarche are more likely to engage in dieting behaviors than are premenarcheal or postmenarcheal girls (Attie & Brooks-Gunn, 1989; Gralen et al., 1990). The present study, however, indicates that although menarcheal status may, indeed, affect dieting and disordered eating, it does so mainly as a moderator of the dependence of dieting and disordered eating on girls' heterosocial activity. More specifically, dating is most strongly correlated with dieting and disordered eating tendencies among girls who have recently experienced menarche. These findings are consistent with those of Levine and Smolak (1992) and Smolak, Levine, and Gralen (1993), who reported that girls for whom puberty is synchronous with the onset of dating are at risk of developing abnormal eating behaviors.

Although previous studies also have identified links between dieting and dating, this study is the first to examine the particular role of physical involvement with a boyfriend as a predictor of dieting behavior. Our findings indicate that physical involvement with a boyfriend, in particular, increases the likelihood of dieting and disordered eating among adolescent girls. It is interesting that the association between physical involvement and dieting behavior is not moderated by menarcheal status. We suspect that girls who are sexually active with their boyfriends (even at these early stages of sexual activity and even among premenarcheal girls) are especially likely to be concerned about their physical appearance, particularly when such sexual activity is relatively new, as is likely among suburban 7th and 8th graders.

The fact that sexual activity (however innocent) is correlated with more symptoms of disordered eating is especially interesting, inasmuch as adults with eating disorders tend to be less sexually active (e.g., Brumberg, 1989; Johnson

& Pure, 1986; Strober, 1986). It thus appears that physical involvement in early adolescence leads to increased concern about appearance and attractiveness, but that when this concern becomes so great that it leads to disordered eating, the end result may be a diminution of the very activities that may have contributed to the disorder in the first place. The details of when and how this shift in emphasis from interest in sexual activity to feelings of sexual inadequacy occurs among women with clinical eating disorders remain to be determined, but establishing the point at which this shift occurs may be critical in understanding the developmental antecedents, course, and consequences of disturbed eating.

Involvement in mixed-sex social activities increases girls' likelihood of exhibiting disordered eating tendencies, and this effect is stronger among girls who have experienced menarche than among those who have not. The weight gains of puberty may make girls more susceptible to social pressures to appear attractive; alternatively, a more mature appearance itself may lead more mature girls to feel pressures to be "sexy" more strongly than those who are less physically mature.

Although this study breaks new ground by considering the effects of early, noncoital sexual involvement on adolescent dieting behavior, it is limited by its small sample size, predominantly White middle-class population, and cross-sectional design. We do not know if dieting or disordered eating precede, accompany, or follow girls' involvement in dating, although given the clinical literature on sexual activity among women with an eating disturbance, we think it more likely that social and physical involvement with boyfriends increase dieting, rather than the reverse. The use of menarcheal status as a measure of pubertal development, although certainly appropriate, nevertheless provides a somewhat incomplete account of participants' overall physical status. In addition, although self-report measures of menarche, dieting, and dating are generally accepted as valid and reliable, they are based on participants' interpretations of the questions asked; interpretations of the terms *dating* or *going steady,* in particular, may be different in different ethnic and cultural groups. Also, the narrow range of ages sampled in this study (typically, 12–13 years old) causes measures of menarcheal status and pubertal timing to be essentially equivalent (a postmenarcheal girl who is the same age as a premenarcheal girl is by definition an earlier maturer). To a certain extent, our premenarcheal participants are comparatively late maturers, whereas our postmenarcheal participants are comparatively early maturers. One might thus conclude that menarcheal timing, rather than menarcheal status, moderates the effect of social activity on EAT-26 scores, with late maturers being least affected. On the other hand, our finding that membership in the middle category of menarcheal status produces the strongest dating-dieting link suggests that this effect is not due simply to differences in timing, but is in fact a result of recent menarche. (Otherwise, one is led to the nonsensical conclusion that dating leads to dieting among girls with average pubertal timing, but not among those who are early or late maturers.) A longitudinal, multimethod study on the developmental course of dieting that included repeated, detailed measures of girls' heterosocial activities as well as their physical development, in a diverse population of young adolescents, would provide much-needed information about the processes through which weight-reducing behaviors are incorporated into some adolescents' behavioral repertoire.

Only recently have studies begun to consider the roles of multiple factors concurrently in the prediction of dieting and disordered eating. Through such studies, including the present one, it has become increasingly apparent that factors such as dating and menarcheal status are not simply additive in their effects on dieting behaviors, but that the importance of one factor is moderated by the other. Although dating increases the likelihood that girls will diet and show signs of disordered eating, dieting is related to dating most strongly among girls who have recently experienced menarche; at the same time, menarche is a strong predictor of dieting among girls who are socially active or dating, but not among those who have not begun mixed-sex social activities. Although the presence of an interaction does not, itself, answer the question of which variable is moderating which, it is our contention that dieting and disordered eating tendencies are determined primarily by social pressures, such as social activity, dating, and physical involvement with boyfriends, whereas pubertal development moderates the effects of these pressures by affecting an individual's susceptibility to them. The fact that our results are largely consistent with such a picture (in which social factors are moderated by physical ones) demonstrates the value of considering multiple convergent factors as predictors of dieting and disordered eating in early adolescence.

REFERENCES

Attie, I., & Brooks-Gunn, J. (1989). Development of eating problems in adolescent girls: A longitudinal study. *Developmental Psychology, 25,* 70–79.

Attie, I., Brooks-Gunn, J., & Petersen, A. C. (1990). A developmental perspective on eating disorders and eating problems. In M. Lewis & S. Miller (Eds.), *Handbook of developmental psychopathology* (pp. 409–420). New York: Plenum Press.

Barnett, R. C., Biener, L., & Baruch, G. K. (1987). *Gender and stress.* New York: Free Press.

Bean, J. A., Leeper, J. D., Wallace, R. B., Sherman, B. M., & Jagger, H. J. (1979). Variations in the reporting of menstrual histories. *American Journal of Epidemiology, 109,* 181–185.

Brooks-Gunn, J. (1987). Pubertal processes and girls' psychological adaptation. In R. M. Lerner & T. T. Foch (Eds.), *Biological-psychosocial interactions in early adolescence* (pp. 123–153). Hillsdale, NJ: Erlbaum.

Brooks-Gunn, J., Warren, M. P., Rosso, J., & Gargiulo, J. (1987). Validity of self-report measures of girls' pubertal status. *Child Development, 58,* 829–841.

Brumberg, J. J. (1989). *Fasting girls: The history of anorexia nervosa.* Cambridge, MA: Harvard University Press.

Caspi, A., Lynam, D., Moffitt, T. E., & Silva, P. A. (1993). Unraveling girls' delinquency: Biological, dispositional, and contextual contributions to adolescent misbehavior. *Developmental Psychology, 29,* 19–30.

Dornbusch, S. M., Carlsmith, J. M., Duncan, P. D., Gross, R. T., Martin, J. A., Ritter, P. L., & Siegel-Gorelick, B. (1984). Sexual maturation, social class, and the desire to be thin among adolescent females. *Developmental and Behavioral Pediatrics, 5,* 308–314.

Garner, D., & Garfinkel, P. (1979). The Eating Attitudes Test: An index of the symptoms of anorexia nervosa. *Psychological Medicine, 9,* 1–7.

Garner, D., Olmsted, M., Bohr, Y., & Garfinkel, P. (1982). The Eating Attitudes Test: Psychometric features and clinical correlates. *Psychological Medicine, 12,* 871–878.

Graber, J., Brooks-Gunn, J., Paikoff, R., & Warren, M. (1994). Prediction of eating problems: An 8-year study of adolescent girls. *Developmental Psychology, 30,* 823–834.

Gralen, S. J., Levine, M. P., Smolak, L., & Murnen, S. K. (1990). Dieting and disordered eating during early and middle adolescence: Do the influences remain the same? *International Journal of Eating Disorders, 9,* 501–512.

Johnson, C., & Pure, D. L. (1986). Assessment of bulimia: A multidimensional model. In K. D. Brownell & J. P. Foreyt (Eds.), *Handbook of eating disorders* (pp. 405–449). New York: Basic Books.

Levine, M. P., & Smolak, S. (1992). Toward a model of the developmental psychopathology of eating disorders: The example of early adolescence. In J. H. Crowther, D. L. Tennenbaum, S. E. Hobfoll, & M. A. P. Stephens (Eds.), *The etiology of bulimia nervosa: The individual and familial context* (pp. 59–80). Washington, DC: Hemisphere.

McCabe, M. P. (1984). Toward a theory of adolescent dating. *Adolescence, 19,* 159–170.

Petersen, A. C. (1983). Menarche: Meaning of measures and measuring meaning. In S. Golub (Ed.), *Menarche: The transition from girl to woman.* Lexington, MA: D. C. Heath.

Rosen, J. C., & Gross, J. (1987). Prevalence of weight reducing and weight gaining in adolescent girls and boys. *Health Psychology, 6,* 131–147.

Rosen, J. C., Tracey, B., & Howell, D. (1990). Life stress, psychological symptoms and weight reducing behavior in adolescent girls: A prospective analysis. *International Journal of Eating Disorders, 9,* 17–26.

Silverberg, S., & Steinberg, L. (1990). Psychological well-being of parents at midlife: The impact of early adolescent children. *Developmental Psychology, 26,* 658–666.

Simmons, R. G., & Blyth, D. A. (1987). *Moving into adolescence: The impact of pubertal change and school context.* Hawthorne, NJ: Aldine.

Smolak, L., Levine, M. P., & Gralen, S. (1993). The impact of puberty and dating on eating problems among middle school girls. *Journal of Youth and Adolescence, 22,* 355–368.

Striegel-Moore, R. H., Silberstein, L. R., & Rodin, J. (1986). Toward an understanding of risk factors for bulimia. *American Psychologist, 41,* 246–263.

Strober, M. (1986). Anorexia nervosa: History and psychological concepts. In K. D. Brownell & J. P. Foreyt (Eds.), *Handbook of eating disorders* (pp. 231–246). New York: Basic Books.

Young, C., Sipin, S., & Roe, D. (1968). Density and skinfold measurements: Body composition of pre-adolescent girls. *Journal of American Dietetic Association, 53,* 25–31.

A STUDY OF WHITE MIDDLE-CLASS ADOLESCENT BOYS' RESPONSES TO "SEMENARCHE" (THE FIRST EJACULATION)

JAMES H. STEIN AND LYNN WHISNANT REISER

University of Wisconsin Medical School and Yale University Medical School

The male experience of the first ejaculation has received little research attention. This invisibility is reflected in the lack of a generally accepted term in the English language for the event. "Semenarche"—a word meaning the beginning of semen—is a logical term for the first ejaculation (Sarrel, personal communication, 1987). This paper uses this designation and suggests the common adoption of this term as a name for the first ejaculation.

Research interest in male puberty and the significance of the first ejaculation has focused on biology (Kinsey, 1948; Tanner, 1971; Richardson and Short, 1978; Hirsch, 1988)—the psychological and social components of this phenomena have not been adequately addressed. This deficiency is found both in standard textbooks of psychiatry (Kaplan and Saddock, 1989) and pediatrics (Behrman, 1992) and in the psychoanalytic literature. Yet there are indications that semenarche is an important event.

Kinsey *et al.* (1948) concluded from his retrospective study of 4590 men that the first ejaculation was "the most significant of all adolescent developments" and stated that "the newly adolescent boy's capacity to ejaculate, [and] his newly acquired physical characteris-

tics of other sorts, do something to him which brings child play to an end and leaves him awkward about making further socio-sexual contacts." A questionnaire study of 146 male college students (Shipman, 1968) suggested that semenarche was an important and frightening experience because sex education for boys was inadequate. In contrast, Gaddis and Brooks-Gunn (1985) concluded from a small interview study of 13 adolescent boys that the first ejaculation was not as traumatic as previously reported.

This paper presents a descriptive and hypothesis-generating study of adolescent male camp counselors to determine how they remembered the experience of semenarche and other changes of puberty, and how their education and interaction with family and peers contributed to their understanding pubertal changes.

METHOD

Thirty-six white, middle-class, Jewish male camp counselors ranging in age from 15.7 to 21.5 years (average age of 18.4 years) enrolled in this study. This corresponds to 98% participation by the male counseling staff at this private camp. A written questionnaire was followed by a 45 minute audiotaped semistructured interview (with JS). The questionnaire served as an introduction to the topics that were more explicitly discussed

From *Journal of Youth and Adolescence,* Vol. 23, No. 3, 373–384, 1994. Copyright © 1994 by Plenum Publishing Corporation. Reprinted with permission.

in the interview. Using both research tools provided a measure of intrasubject reliability—questions in the questionnaire and interview were parallel and responses were consistent when compared (except for one exception described below). The research tools included questions regarding physical changes that accompanied puberty, education and sources of information about puberty, and psychological and social responses to these changes. Fearing that parents might consider this an explicit introduction of sexual topics, camp officials excluded campers aged 10–14 years from the study. Subjects were informed about the study by the camp director who presented it as a survey study of how boys experience the changes of puberty. They were interviewed individually in a private setting by a researcher who had been a former camper and counselor at the camp. Each discussant signed a release assuring confidentiality.

RESULTS

Age at Semenarche

When asked how old they were when they had their first ejaculation, most subjects initially claimed not to remember (responded "don't know" on the questionnaire, or answered "I don't know" in the interview). Five subjects left the question blank on the questionnaire. When restated in the interview as "What grade were you in?" and when more specific questions about context were asked, *all* remembered the circumstances of this event (although 2 still did not remember their age). The average age was 12.9 ± 1.5 years.

Context of Semenarche

Semenarche occurs in a number of different contexts—such as during sleep (nocturnal emission), masturbation, or in sexual activity with another person. In interview data, a wet dream was the most common context for semenarche (20 boys) and masturbation was the next (13 boys). In contrast to the agreement on other questions, there was a discrepancy between 4

subjects' answers to this in the interview and on the questionnaire. These subjects reported on the questionnaire that semenarche occurred during masturbation, but in the interview as a nocturnal emission. These subjects' discomfort during the interview was rated high by self-report and by the interviewer, and these subjects provided few descriptive details. This suggests that masturbation may be a more common context for semenarche than is reflected in the interview data. Three subjects experienced semenarche during heterosexual activity—2 having intercourse, one engaging in petting. No subjects reported that their first ejaculation occurred during homosexual activity.

Subjects were asked to rate the extent to which they experienced 22 feelings at semenarche (Table I). A 4-point scale (*not at all, a little, somewhat, a lot*) was adapted from Gaddis and Brooks-Gunn (1985). The final two categories (*somewhat* and *a lot*) were reported as "a lot" to facilitate comparison with Gaddis and Brooks-Gunn, who did the same. In the interview, subjects were encouraged to elaborate on any strong feelings that they may have had. Representative and interesting anecdotes are presented below. Many reported having had strong feelings (rarely negative) at their first ejaculation. The qualitative aspect of their response and conflict was more evident in the interviews:

> *My wet dream was kind of an experience that I didn't experience.* It had nothing to do with my mental attitude. I was sound asleep, I woke up the next morning and my sheets were pasty—I slept through it—After you wake up your mind is kind of happy and then you realize 'oh my god, this is my wet dream.' (Emphasis added)

Seventy-five percent of the subjects reported feeling surprised that they were so young when their first ejaculation took place and at the physical intensity of the first ejaculation. The extent to which a subject felt "surprised" was strongly correlated with feeling confused (Pearson $r > 0.60, p < .001$), embarrassed ($r > 0.52, p < 0.001$), scared ($r > 0.61, p < 0.001$), and out of control ($r > 0.68, p < 0.001$). Many of those who felt "surprised" also felt unprepared ($r > 0.52, p$

TABLE I.
Experience of Positive and Negative Feelings at Semenarche (Interview Data)[a]

Feeling		Percentage		
	Mean	Not at all	A little	A lot
Positive feeling				
Positive	2.4	28	14	58
Prepared	2.6	17	25	58
Pleasurable	2.4	36	8	56
Grown up	2.2	39	17	45
Excited	2.1	33	31	36
Glad	2.0	39	28	34
Relieved	1.9	42	25	34
Happy	1.8	44	33	22
Proud	1.5	61	28	11
Negative feeling				
Surprised	3.0	14	11	75
Confused	2.4	33	14	52
Embarrassed	2.0	47	25	27
Out of control	1.7	64	14	22
Upset	1.4	75	11	14
Dirty	1.4	81	6	14
Scared	1.5	64	25	12
Disgusted	1.5	67	22	12
Unhappy	1.3	78	17	6
Painful	1.1	92	6	3
Angry	1.1	94	6	0
Ripped off	1.0	97	3	0
Neutral feeling				
Curious	2.9	8	25	67

[a]$N = 36$. A 4-point scale was used, including (1) *not at all,* (2) *a little,* (3) *somewhat,* and (4) *a lot.* The percentage of subjects who responded "somewhat" are included above in "a lot."

< 0.001). "Surprised" did not correlate with "pleasure" or "happiness."

Subjects whose semenarche was a wet dream were more likely to initially confuse semen with urine. Eleven subjects (31%) reported that their first ejaculation reminded them of "urinating" or "wetting the bed."

> It took kind of awhile to click in—later in the day I finally figured out what the hell was going on. I thought I had pissed in my pants at first!

> It reminded me of peeing in my pants—that was my first reaction even though I'd never done it.

Subjects whose first ejaculation was during masturbation remembered more pleasure (two-tailed $t = 3.71$, $df = 31$, $p < 0.05$) and happiness (two-tailed $t = 2.08$, $df = 31$, $p < 0.05$) than did subjects whose first ejaculation was during a nocturnal emission. The latter, however, did not express more negative feelings. The data suggest that the source of difference was the conscious experience of an orgasm that accompanied masturbation.

Boys who experienced their first ejaculation while masturbating commented:

> My parents had these videotapes. I knew they were X-rated and I really wanted to see them. My parents were out of town. I knew they were hidden in their closet. I threw them in. I thought 'this is very interesting' and the next thing I knew— Bam!—I honestly didn't know what I was doing.

I think I was trying to masturbate—I didn't really—it was—the actual ejaculation came as a surprise—I knew what I was doing but didn't know what would happen—I—I remember—I remember—realizing what had happened but not really knowing exactly until later.

The only common negative feeling was confused (50%):

I was in my bed—I really didn't know what I was doing—just touching myself. I was at the point where I knew it would happen but I was confused—I really didn't know what was going on and was embarrassed because of it.

A boy who woke up after a nocturnal emission remembered:

I didn't know what it was so I blew it off, since the rest of the mornings I woke up normal. I thought I was just nervous or something.

Sixty-seven percent of the subjects remembered feeling curious, wondering how they could make the ejaculation happen again, when it would happen again, and if it would be different with a girl. This boy expresses that sense of wonder:

I was curious to see—I wasn't expecting to have sex or anything. It was just generally—I didn't know exactly how—would it happen again? It had never happened before.

In interviews, the strongest negative responses were related to embarrassment and feeling out of control, especially to less prepared subjects.

I was alone but I was very embarrassed because I was *out of control.* That was my major feeling—I was worried it would happen again. I put it together about a week later when I did it again. Then I figured it out. (Emphasis added)

The association with urination may also contribute to the sense of being out of control—some boys had expected ejaculation, like urination, to be under voluntary sphincter control. "I thought it was just like peeing."

I thought it would happen when I wanted it to, that I'd have control over it. I was scared about the *loss of control.* (Emphasis added)

The most stressful experience of semenarche, and the only one that was described as "painful," was that of a boy whose first ejaculation (at age 17) was with a woman. He was embarrassed about not having control over his body in the presence of another person.

It was a lot painful. It hurt. I don't know why. That's what I remember. It was enjoyable to have it done, not physically. I was just glad I got it over. The pain was indescribable.

In contrast to that subject's experience, many of the subjects described the experience as pleasurable:

Well at first I felt really—like it was weird cuz I had never felt that way before. But after a little bit it was—pleasurable. It was good—It felt good—You just have to feel it for yourself.

Some subjects, however, reported feeling uncomfortable with the unexpected intensity of the pleasure that they felt at the first ejaculation.

Education

Classes at school were the most common source of information about puberty in general. Nearly all of the subjects completed "health education" courses in fifth or sixth grade, and continued their education about physical development and human sexuality well into high school. In spite of having an extensive health and sex education curriculum, more than one-quarter of the boys recalled that classes failed to explain ejaculation. In the classes that did discuss ejaculation, the topic was postponed until the eighth grade, after many boys had already experienced their first ejaculation. The boys remembered that teachers put emphasis on informing students that pubertal changes were "normal" and "healthy." The subjects' responses reflected this focus, as many subjects described their first pubertal changes as a signal that they were "normal."

One boy whose semenarche was during masturbation at age 12 expressed these complicated feelings:

It didn't make me feel proud. It made me feel guilty, like I'd done something wrong. Those kind of feelings—The class didn't say anything. I still think it's something I shouldn't do—My only relief was that I was *normal*. (emphasis added)

Another boy whose semenarche was a nocturnal emission described a predominant sense of relief at being normal:

I woke up the next morning and noticed the wetness. I felt relieved. I expected it. I mean, people talked about it and the classes—sex ed—told about what happens and it happened. *It's a normal thing*—I didn't have much emotion attached to it. I felt prepared for it, but I never expected it—I didn't want anyone to know—I was glad that it happened. (emphasis added)

The only late-maturer in the study expressed this sentiment (relief at being normal) most strongly.

Forty-two percent of the subjects felt unprepared for semenarche. "Prepared" subjects reported feeling more "proud" and "positive" (two-tailed t = 3.02, df = 34, $p < 0.005$); "Unprepared" subjects, stronger negative feelings—more "confused" (3.87, 34, $p < .001$), "upset" (4.87, 34, $p < 0.001$), "scared" (3.18, 34, $p < 0.005$), "disgusted" (3.43, 34, $p < 0.002$), "out of control" (2.70, 34, $p < 0.02$).

For example, one boy stated:

I'm almost positive that it was a wet dream. The problem was that I didn't know what it was. It was just so—I never knew what it was. I was surprised I wet my bed—what did I do? I only found out a year later what it was.

Only one-third of the boys considered parents important sources of information about ejaculation. For those, this topic was usually discussed by a father alone or both parents together—in one case information about ejaculation was provided by a mother alone. Conversations about semenarche *after* it happened were rare. Only 2 subjects told their mother or father that their first ejaculation had occurred. Most boys were very secretive:

For the first time I knew something that they [parents] didn't—it was a private thing that nobody else knew.

Boys often hid the evidence of a nocturnal emission by changing the sheets themselves (some even performed midnight laundering). Others assumed their parents knew but did not mention it directly:

My mom, she knew I had them. It was all over my sheets, and bedspread and stuff, but she didn't say anything, didn't tease me and stuff. I was kind of glad. She never asked if I wanted to talk about it—I'm glad. I never could have said anything to my mom.

I don't remember when it happened or how old I was, but I didn't tell anyone. My friends, we didn't talk about it, but if it came up, you know we always played these games—'So have you done this, so have you done this, so have you done this'—I would say I had. But I didn't say 'By the way mom, my bed is wet.' I mean, I knew what an ejaculation was, and I knew that I hadn't wet my bed.

When a boy did tell someone, it was usually a friend. The boys' descriptions reveal more about the fragmentary quality of this kind of discussion with friends:

Before it I remember being in the boy's locker room at school and my friend telling me about having a wet dream and he said 'Oh, everyone has it' and I remember thinking and I remember lying and I remember experimenting with masturbation after that.

While it was going on no one wanted to say anything about it. We all kind of left it alone—After it happened and we knew what was going on, we laughed about it with friends. Laughed at guys' penises, you know.

I had no idea what—I had no idea what was happening—It just hurt and I said 'I gotta go,' so I found my friend and said 'I gotta talk to you' and it just went from there. He made me feel better—I was embarrassed about telling my friend—it just really hit me. I just told him. I didn't hold back cuz I wanted to know what was happening. I said 'I wanna know what happened.' He said 'Oh yeah, you came,' and I felt happy after that, glad it happened.

Pubertal Events

Seventy-eight percent of the subjects stated that the appearance of pubic hair was a memorable signal that puberty had started. However, as a group they felt that neither this biological change nor any other was in itself a symbol for their change in status and self-perception. A few boys like this one did assert the importance of the first ejaculation:

> The next morning I felt really gross—I knew what it was. I don't think it was pleasurable—I was embarrassed. I don't know, I just remember being in my bed and feeling that I had just—I knew I didn't wet my bed. I mean, I felt weird that this change had just happened—*it was pretty major. (Emphasis added)*

Less than 40% felt that the first ejaculation was important. More often they asserted, like this boy, that

> The things that I really remember are the things that I did sexually.

The events (Table II) that were most meaningful for this group were social—"making out" was very meaningful for 89%, "dating" for 83%, and "Bar Mitzvah" for 72%.

Only 10 subjects (28%) felt it was noteworthy that after the first ejaculation they were physically able to "get a girl pregnant." Most reported that they rarely considered the possibility that they could father a child. Their confusion is evident in their words:

> I never thought about getting a girl pregnant. I knew biologically that I could father a child.

DISCUSSION

The subjects comprised a homogeneous sample of boys with similar religious, educational, and

TABLE II.
The Significance of Social and Physical Events (Interview Data)[a]

Feeling		Percentage		
	Mean	Not at all	A little	A lot
Physical event				
Develop pubic hair	2.9	8	14	78
Growth spurt	2.8	8	31	61
Growth of penis	2.5	11	28	61
Develop facial hair	2.5	19	25	56
Develop acne	2.3	33	22	45
Voice change	2.3	25	33	42
First ejaculation	*2.3*	*19*	*42*	*39*
Develop axillary hair	2.1	22	44	34
Growth of testes	1.9	31	44	25
Social event				
Making out	3.3	8	3	89
Dating	3.2	6	11	83
Bar Mitzvah	3.0	14	14	72
Shaving	2.7	17	17	66
Using cologne	2.2	25	39	36
Change nudity practice	2.1	31	36	33
Showering	1.9	44	28	28
Using deodorant	1.9	39	36	25
Wearing jockstrap	1.8	50	28	22

[a]$N = 36$. A 4-point scale was used, such that (1) *not at all,* (2) *a little,* (3) *somewhat,* and (4) *a lot.* The percentage of subjects who responded "somewhat" are included above in "a lot."

socioeconomic backgrounds. They were socially well adjusted enough to be chosen as camp counselors. Because participation was high, this well-defined population can be *compared* to others, but cannot be used to generalize about other demographic groups. As in all retrospective studies, experiences subsequent to target events may have influenced memories of the event in an unquantifiable manner (recall bias). The average time since semenarche for our subjects was 5.5 ± 0.9 years, so it relied more on memory than the study of young adolescent boys conducted by Gaddis and Brooks-Gunn (1985). Although both of these study samples were small, the higher participation rate (90%) and larger sample size (36) suggest that this study had less selection bias than the study by Gaddis and Brooks-Gunn (1985, 62% participation, 13 subjects). Given these limitations, the study is meant to be descriptive and hypothesis generating.

The results were consistent with the descriptions of the events that signaled pubertal onset in the populations studied by Kinsey *et al.* (1948) and Tanner (1971). The average age of semenarche in Kinsey's study was about a year older, 13.88 years. Adolescent boys experience strong, but rarely negative feelings at semenarche, including surprise, confusion, curiosity, and pleasure. The conscious experience of orgasm allows those who experience their first ejaculation by masturbation to feel more "pleasure" and "happiness." Although boys whose first ejaculation is during a wet dream do not report more negative feelings, they more often confuse semen with urine, at least initially. Boys rarely discuss their first ejaculation and usually hide the evidence. Semenarche is not a socially recognized event and adolescent boys deny attaching much significance to it, especially in light of later sexual experiences.

The first ejaculation, biologically significant in sexual and reproductive functioning, is socially invisible. Thus, semenarche is not comparable to menarche as a significant symbolic developmental milestone. The lack of a name for the first ejaculation contributes to making this an invisible event and parallels the failure to label adequately the female external genitalia (especially sexual structures) in the education of girls (Lerner, 1976). The connection of the first ejaculation with sexuality makes it a charged event.

Despite sex education and hygiene classes at school and some parental input, many of the boys in this group felt unprepared for their first ejaculation, which occurred earlier than they expected. Education, including a specific discussion about ejaculation before semenarche occurs, can positively influence how boys experience pubertal transformation. Those who were prepared coped better, in contrast to the subjects interviewed by Gaddis and Brooks-Gunn (1985) and in agreement with Shipman's study (1968).

In view of the current crisis in the prevention of AIDS and unwanted pregnancies, the data from this study raise many questions about how best to educate boys about puberty and when to provide information. Education regarding semenarche frequently occurred *after* the boys had already experienced the event, so earlier sex education is clearly needed. In addition, emphasis should be placed on the fact that many boys are fertile at or before semenarche (Richardson and Short, 1978; Hirsch, 1988).

The difficulties in sexual education for preadolescents are many:

> Frequently, newly provided sexual information seems to be promptly forgotten. At times this rather amazing phenomenon may be due to a feigned ignorance in the service of secrecy, out of uneasiness with the subject matter or compliance with the cultural double standard. Frequently, though, it represents a genuine, unconscious denial of anxiety-producing knowledge. ("Normal Adolescence," 1968, p. 792).

In addition, a boy's ability to understand the physical changes of puberty is limited by his cognitive ability, which is usually still at the concrete or early formal operations stage (Piaget, 1972) when he experiences his first ejaculation. Sigmund Freud (1895/1959a, 1895/1959b) pointed out how persistently adults, particularly parents, avoided acknowledging childhood (and adolescent) sexuality. This observation is still accurate and is reflected in the boys' reports and in the paucity of empirical studies of childhood sexuality.

One boy suggested an approach to this problem in terms of a favorite series of childhood picture books:

> I would describe it [puberty] as 'Curious George.' *Because you really don't know what's going on unless you really get it explained by somebody who doesn't have a bias on it.* I always really liked Curious George—he always wants to find out more about things he shouldn't, and that's what puberty is. (Emphasis added)

This empirical survey study of a well-defined population of normal adolescent boys suggests that although the first ejaculation is not traumatic for the majority of boys, it is a memorable, highly charged event that is less anxiety producing if there has been prior education. There is a need for both prospective and retrospective studies documenting the experience of semenarche in other ethnic and socioeconomic groups in order to delineate the impact of this event upon subsequent psychosocial development and to clarify how best to respond to boys' curiosity in preparing them for puberty.

REFERENCES

Behrman, R. E. (1992). *Nelson's Textbook of Pediatrics* (14th ed.). W. B. Saunders, Philadelphia, PA.

Freud, S. (1959a). The Sexual Enlightenment of Children—an Open Letter to Dr. M. Furst, 1907. In *Standard Edition* (Vol. 9). London: Hogarth Press. (Originally published 1895.)

Freud, S. (1959b). On the Sexual Theories of Children, 1908. In *Standard Edition* (Vol. 9). London: Hogarth Press. (Originally published 1895.)

Gaddis, A., and Brooks-Gunn, J. (1985). The male experience of pubertal change. *J. Youth Adolesc.* 14: 61–69.

Hirsch, M., Lunenfeld, B., Modan, M., Ovadia, J., and Shemesh, J. (1988). Spermarche—The age of onset of sperm emission. *Sex. Active Teen.* 2: 34–38.

Kaplan, H., and Saddock, B. J. (1989). *Comprehensive Textbook of Psychiatry* (5th ed.). Williams & Wilkins, Baltimore, MD.

Kinsey, A. C., Pomeroy, W. B., and Martin, C. E. (1948). *Sexual Behavior in the Human Male.* W. B. Saunders, Philadelphia, PA.

Lerner, H. (1976). Parental mislabeling of female genitals as a determinant of penis envy and learning inhibitions in women. In *Female Psychology— Contemporary Psychoanalytic View,* ed. H. Blum. International Universities Press, New York.

Normal adolescence: Its dynamics and impact. (1968). In Group for the Advancement of Psychiatry (Volume VI, Report No. 68).

Piaget, P. (1972). *The Child's Conception of the World.* Littlefield Adams, Totowa, NJ.

Richardson, D. W., and Short, R. V. (1978). Time of onset of sperm production in boys. *J. Biosocial Sci. Suppl.* 5, 15–25.

Sarrel, P. M. (1987). Personal communication.

Shipman, G. (1968). The psychodynamics of sex education. *Family Coord.* 7, 3–12.

Tanner, J. M. (1971). Sequence, tempo, and individual variation in growth and development of boys and girls aged twelve to sixteen. *Daedalus* 100, 907–930.

PART THREE

ADOLESCENCE AS A COGNITIVE TRANSITION

The important thing is not to stop questioning.
—ALBERT EINSTEIN

At the turn of the twentieth century, Binet's testing of children in Paris inspired the systematic measurement of mental abilities and thus operationalized our understanding of intelligence. At the dawn of the twenty-first century, cognitive science, especially under the influence of Piaget's *Genetic Epistemology*, has supplanted earlier definitions and created new levels of appreciation for the processes involved in acquiring knowledge. Cognition is more than answering questions correctly or knowing specific information: it encompasses the reasoning by which children solve problems, and it refers to all processes involved in knowing, reasoning, thinking, problem solving, creativity, and—Piaget would agree with Einstein—even questioning. Cognition, no longer viewed in the context of learning alone has been applied to rather diverse fields, such as social cognition, identity formation, and moral and ego development.

For most of his life, Piaget (7) investigated the changes that take place in the process of children acquiring and modifying their knowledge. Later he expanded his theory to those cognitive advances that begin to emerge during puberty. At that transition, concrete problem-solving operations expand into abstract, formal, and logical operations. Formal cognitive structures allow young people to understand the properties of logic, to think in terms of probability, to develop hypotheses, and to think about thinking. These new abilities enable the adolescent to solve problems in a way that approaches the scientific method. According to Piaget, cognitive development, which depends, in part, on maturation, can be understood only in interaction of observations and experiences from which the individual constructs knowledge. Optimal growth in cognition is best achieved when the young person is in an intellectual environment that is stimulating and the learner is continuously exposed to moderately discrepant stimulation. According to Piaget, a teacher should never do for a child what the child can do for him/herself.

Piaget's influence on developmental psychology cannot be overemphasized since his theory has inspired the work of many who followed in his footsteps. Elkind's (8) postmodern appraisal of Piaget's work is an excellent case in point. Elkind recognizes Piaget's ground-breaking contributions "to our factual and theoretical understanding of adolescence." However, Elkind reminds us that all social scientists are bound by "the social-historical paradigms and discourses in which they live and work." One telling piece of evidence is that up until recently, females were rarely studied by scientists. This obviously limited view of differences between the genders does not necessarily reflect intentional neglect but rather the cultural norms of time and place. Although Piaget's work is open to that criticism, replication studies of his cognitive tasks have revealed few gender differences.

Banks (9) discusses ethnicity, social class, cognitive and learning styles, and the implications of these variables for teaching and learning. He goes on to examine their often poorly understood relationship. Beginning with the "cultural deprivation" hypothesis of the 1960s, claiming that poor children were culturally impoverished, Banks provides a historical perspective on the frequently observed low academic achievement of some ethnic minorities. His intent is to emphasize the need for understanding variations within and between ethnic groups thus to reveal how educators can reach all learners. Although social class differences have been studied for a century, the commonly observed differences in learning have been used to explain racial differences. However, by treating social class as synonymous with ethnicity, valuable insights have been overlooked since the lower performance of black children was explained on the basis of their social class. Differences in learning style, motivation, and attitude toward competition were neglected. Even the limited knowledge that was available was slow to be implemented by educators. For example, the goals of winning in competition, of becoming independent and self-reliant may hold true for many white male learners, but these goals are shared less frequently by females, blacks and American Indians. Therefore, Banks (9), as well as Fordham and Ogbu (18), caution educators not to apply their information-rich curriculum to all children without awareness of the forces that shape their diversity. Multicultural approaches and differentiated instructional materials must be provided, and equal emphasis must be given to relational, cooperative, and diverse cognitive styles.

Elkind (10) traces the idea of "egocentrism in thinking" through Piaget's stages. However, Elkind also includes emotional-social development and interpersonal awareness (or the lack thereof). His *egocentrism* provides insight into the limited social awareness of adolescents who, because of their egocentric cognitive ability, ascribe more social perceptiveness to the thoughts of others than is warranted. The egocentric adolescent assumes that everyone is aware of him/her and is focused upon his/her shortcomings. Actually most other adolescents appear equally preoccupied with being observed. All of them are reacting to an "imaginary audience" that is the creation of their still limited egocentric thought. An example of the irony implied in this type of thinking is a young man and woman preparing for their date. Both are trying to look their very best; however, when they actually meet, each is so preoccupied with his/her own appearance neither compliments the other. Many youth believe that their feelings and sufferings are so unique that nobody else can fully comprehend them, much less have the same experiences. This is what Elkind refers to as the "personal fable." Another component of adolescent egocentrism is the belief in one's own indestructibility—a "mishaps won't happen to me" attitude—which may lead to behavior that is loaded with danger.

INTELLECTUAL EVOLUTION FROM ADOLESCENCE TO ADULTHOOD

JEAN PIAGET

We are relatively well informed about the important changes that take place in cognitive function and structure at adolescence. Such changes show how much this essential phase in ontogenic development concerns all aspects of mental and psychophysiological evolution and not only the more 'instinctive', emotional or social aspects to which one often limits one's consideration. In contrast, however, we know as yet very little about the period which separates adolescence from adulthood and we feel that the decision of the Institution FONEME to draw the attention of various research workers to this essential problem is extremely well founded.

In this paper we would first like to recall the principal characteristics of the intellectual changes that occur during the period from 12–15 years of age. These characteristics are too frequently forgotten as one tends to reduce the psychology of adolescence to the psychology of puberty. We shall then refer to the chief problems that arise in connection with the next period (15–20 years); firstly, the diversification of aptitudes, and secondly, the degree of generality of cognitive structures acquired between 12 and 15 years and their further development.

From *Human Development*, 1972, *15*, 1–12. Reprinted by permission of S. Karger AG, Basel.

THE STRUCTURES OF FORMAL THOUGHT

Intellectual structures between birth and the period of 12–15 years grow slowly, but according to stages in development. The order of succession of these stages has been shown to be extremely regular and comparable to the stages of an embryogenesis. The speed of development, however, can vary from one individual to another and also from one social environment to another; consequently, we may find some children who advance quickly or others who are backward, but this does not change the order of succession of the stages through which they pass. Thus, long before the appearance of language, all normal children pass through a number of stages in the formation of sensorimotor intelligence which can be characterized by certain 'instrumental' behavior patterns; such patterns bear witness to the existence of a logic which is inherent to the coordination of the actions themselves.

With the acquisition of language and the formation of symbolic play, mental imagery, etc., that is, the formation of the symbolic function (or, in a general sense, the semiotic function), actions are interiorized and become representations; this supposes a reconstruction and a reorganization on the new plane of representative thought. However, the logic of this period remains incomplete until the child is 7 or 8 years old. The internal actions are still 'preoperatory' if we take 'operations' to mean actions that are entirely reversible (as adding and subtracting, or judging that the distance between A and B is the same as the distance between B and A, etc.). Due to the lack of reversibility, the child lacks comprehension of the idea of transitivity ($A \leq C$, if $A \leq B$ and $B \leq C$) and of conservation (for a preoperatory child, if the shape of an object changes, the quantity of matter and the weight of the object change also).

Between 7–8 and 11–12 years a logic of reversible actions is constituted, characterized by the formation of a certain number of stable and coherent structures, such as a classification system, an ordering system, the construction of natural numbers, the concept of measurement of lines and surfaces, projective relations (perspectives), certain general types of causality (transmission of movement through intermediaries), etc.

Several very general characteristics distinguish this logic from the one that will be constituted during the pre-adolescent period (between 12 and 15 years). Firstly these operations are 'concrete,' that is to say, in using them the child still reasons in terms of objects (classes, relations, numbers, etc.) and not in terms of hypotheses that can be thought out before knowing whether they are true or false. Secondly, these operations, which involve sorting and establishing relations between or enumerating objects, always proceed by relating an element to its neighboring element—they cannot yet link any term whatsoever to any other term, as would be the case in a combinatorial system: thus, when carrying out a classification, a child capable of concrete reasoning associates one term with the term it most resembles and there is no 'natural' class that relates two very different objects. Thirdly, these operations have two types of reversibility that are not yet linked together (in the sense that one can be joined with the other); the first type of reversibility is by inversion or negation, the result of this operation is an annulment, for example, $+ A - A = 0$ or $+ n - n = 0$; the second type of reversibility is by reciprocity and

this characterizes operations of relations, for example, if $A = B$, then $B = A$, or if A is to the left of B, then B is to the right of A, etc.

On the contrary, from 11–12 years to 14–15 years a whole series of novelties highlights the arrival of a more complete logic that will attain a state of equilibrium once the child reaches adolescence at about 14–15 years. We must, therefore, analyze this new logic in order to understand what might happen between adolescence and full adulthood.

The principal novelty of this period is the capacity to reason in terms of verbally stated hypotheses and no longer merely in terms of concrete objects and their manipulation. This is a decisive turning point, because to reason hypothetically and to deduce the consequences that the hypotheses necessarily imply (independent of the intrinsic truth or falseness of the premises) is a formal reasoning process. Consequently the child can attribute a decisive value to the logical form of the deductions that was not the case in the previous stages. From 7–8 years, the child is capable to certain logical reasoning processes but only to the extent of applying particular operations to concrete objects or events in the immediate present: in other words, the operatory form of the reasoning process, at this level, is still subordinated to the concrete content that makes up the real world. In contrast, hypothetical reasoning implies the subordination of the real to the realm of the possible, and consequently the linking of all possibilities to one another by necessary implications that encompass the real, but at the same time go beyond it.

From the social point of view, there is also an important conquest. Firstly, hypothetical reasoning changes the nature of discussion: a fruitful and constructive discussion means that by using hypotheses we can adopt the point of view of the adversary (although not necessarily believing it) and draw the logical consequences it implies. In this way, we can judge its value after having verified the consequences. Secondly, the individual who becomes capable of hypothetical reasoning, by this very fact will interest himself in problems that go beyond his immediate field of experience. Hence, the adolescent's capacity to understand and even construct theories and to participate in society and the ideologies of adults; this is often, of course, accompanied by a desire to change society and even, if necessary, destroy it (in his imagination) in order to elaborate a better one.

In the field of physics and particularly in the induction of certain elementary laws (many experiments have been carried out under the direction of B. Inhelder on this particular topic), the difference in attitude between children of 12–15 years, already capable of formal reasoning, and children of 7–10 years, still at the concrete level, is very noticeable. The 7- to 10-year-old children when placed in an experimental situation (such as what laws concern the swing of a pendulum, factors involved in the flexibility of certain materials, problems of increasing acceleration on an inclined plane) act directly upon the material placed in front of them by trial and error, without dissociating the factors involved. They simply try to classify or order what happened by looking at the results of the co-variations. The formal level children, after a few similar trials stop experimenting with the material and begin to list all the possible hypotheses. It is only after having done this that they start to test them, trying progressively to dissociate the factors involved and study the effects of each one in turn—'all other factors remaining constant.'

This type of experimental behavior, directed by hypotheses which are based on more or less refined causal models, implies the elaboration of two new structures that we find constantly in formal reasoning.

The first of these structures is a combinatorial system, an example of which is clearly seen in 'the set of all subsets,' ($2n^2$ or the simplex structure). We have, in fact, previously mentioned that the reasoning process of the child at the concrete level (7–10 years old) progresses by linking an element with a neighboring one, and cannot relate any element whatsoever to any other. On the contrary, this generalized combinatorial ability (1 to 1, 2 to 2, 3 to 3, etc.) becomes effec-

tive when the subject can reason in a hypothetical manner. In fact, psychological research shows that between 12 and 15 years the pre-adolescent and adolescent start to carry out operations involving combinatorial analysis, permutation systems, etc. (independent of all school training). They cannot, of course, figure out mathematical formulas, but they can discover experimentally exhaustive methods that work for them. When a child is placed in an experimental situation where it is necessary to use combinatorial methods (for example, given 5 bottles of colorless, odorless liquid, 3 of which combine to make a colored liquid, the fourth is a reducing agent and the fifth is water), the child easily discovers the law after having worked out all the possible ways of combining the liquids in this particular case.

This combinatorial system constitutes an essential structure from the logical point of view. The elementary systems of classification and order observed between 7 and 10 years, do not yet constitute a combinatorial system. Propositional logic, however, for two propositions 'p' and 'q' and their negation, implies that we not only consider the 4-base associations (p and q, p and not q, not p and q, not p and not q) but also the 16 combinations that can be obtained by linking these base associations 1 to 1, 2 to 2, 3 to 3 (with the addition of all 4-base associations and the empty set). In this way it can be seen that implication, inclusive disjunction and incompatibility are fundamental propositional operations that result from the combination of 3 of these base associations.

At the level of formal operations it is extremely interesting to see that this combinatorial system of thinking is not only available and effective in all experimental fields, but that the subject also becomes capable of combining propositions: therefore, propositional logic appears to be one of the essential conquests of formal thought. When, in fact, the reasoning processes of children between 11–12 and 14–15 years are analyzed in detail it is easy to find the 16 operations or binary functions of a bivalent logic of propositions.

However, there is still more to formal thought: when we examine the way in which subjects use these 16 operations we can recognize numerous cases of the 4-group which are isomorphic to the Klein group and which reveal themselves in the following manner. Let us take, for example, the implication p > q, if this stays unchanged we can say it characterized the identity transformation I. If this proposition is changed into its negation N (reversibility by negation or inversion) we obtain N = p and not q. The subject can change this same proposition into its reciprocal (reversibility by reciprocity) that is R = q > p; and it is also possible to change the statement into its correlative (or dual), namely C = not p and q. Thus, we obtain a commutative 4-group such that CR = N, CN = R, RN = C and CRN = I. This group allows the subject to combine in one operation the negation and the reciprocal which was not possible at the level of concrete operations. An example of these transformations that occurs frequently is the comprehension of the relationship between action (I and N) and reaction (R and C) in physics experiments; or, again, the understanding of the relationship between two reference systems, for example: a moving object can go forwards or backwards (I and N) on a board which itself can go forwards or backwards (R and C) in relation to an exterior reference system. Generally speaking the group structure intervenes when the subject understands the difference between the canceling or undoing of an effect (N in relation to I) and the compensation of this effect by another variable (R and its negation C) which does not eliminate but neutralizes the effect.

In concluding this first part we can see that the adolescent's logic is a complex but coherent system that is relatively different from the logic of the child, and constitutes the essence of the logic of cultured adults and even provides the basis for elementary forms of scientific thought.

THE PROBLEMS OF THE PASSAGE FROM ADOLESCENT TO ADULT THOUGHT

The experiments on which the above-mentioned results are based were carried out with secondary school children, 11–15 years, taken from the better schools in Geneva. However, recent research has shown that subjects from other types of schools or different social environments sometimes give results differing more or less from the norms indicated; for the same experiments it is as though these subjects had stayed at the concrete operatory level of thinking.

Other information gathered about adults in Nancy, France, and adolescents of different levels in New York has also shown that we cannot generalize in all subjects the conclusion of our research which was, perhaps, based on a somewhat privileged population. This does not mean that our observations have not been confirmed in many cases: they seem to be true for certain populations, but the main problem is to understand why there are exceptions and also whether these are real or apparent.

A first problem is the speed of development, that is to say, the differences that can be observed in the rapidity of the temporal succession of the stages. We have distinguished 4 periods in the development of cognitive functions: the sensorimotor period before the appearance of language; the preoperatory period which, in Geneva, seems on the average to extend from about $1^1/2$–2 to 6–7 years; the period of concrete operations from 7–8 to 11–12 years (according to research with children in Geneva and Paris) and the formal operations period from 11–12 to 14–15 years as observed in the schools studied in Geneva. However, if the order of succession has shown itself to be constant—each stage is necessary to the construction of the following one—the average age at which children go through each stage can vary considerably from one social environment to another, or from one country or even region within a country to another. In this way Canadian psychologists in Martinique have observed a systematic slowness in development; in Iran notable differences were found between children of the city of Teheran and young illiterate children of the villages. In Italy, N. Peluffo has shown that there is a significant gap between children from regions of southern Italy and those from the north; he has carried out some particularly interesting studies indicating how, in children from southern families migrating north, these differences progressively disappear. Similar comparative research is at present taking place in Indian reservations in North America, etc.

In general, a first possibility is to envisage a difference in speed of development without any modification of the order of succession of the stages. These different speeds would be due to the quality and frequency of intellectual stimulation received from adults or obtained from the possibilities available to children for spontaneous activity in their environment. In the case of poor stimulation and activity, it goes without saying that the development of the first 3 of the 4 periods mentioned above will be slowed down. When it comes to formal thought, we could propose that there will be an even greater retardation in its formation (for example, between 15 and 20 years and not 11 and 15 years); or that perhaps in extremely disadvantageous conditions, such a type of thought will never really take shape or will only develop in those individuals who change their environment while development is still possible.

This does not mean that formal structures are exclusively the result of a process of social transmission. We still have to consider the spontaneous and endogenous factors of construction proper to each normal subject. However, the formation and completion of cognitive structures imply a whole series of exchanges and a stimulating environment; the formation of operations always requires a favorable environment for 'co-operation,' that is to say, operations carried out in common (e.g., the role of discussion, mutual criticism or support, problems raised as the result of exchanges of information, heightened curiosity due to the cultural influence of a social group, etc.). Briefly, our first interpretation would mean that in principle all normal individuals are capable of reaching the level of formal structures on the condition that the social environment and acquired experience provide the subject with the cognitive

nourishment and intellectual stimulation necessary for such a construction.

However, a second interpretation is possible which would take into account the diversification of aptitudes with age, but this would mean excluding certain categories of normal individuals, even in favorable environments, from the possibility of attaining a formal level of thinking. It is a well-known fact that the aptitudes of individuals differentiate progressively with age. Such a model of intellectual growth would be comparable to a fully expanded hand fan, the concentric layers of which would represent the successive stages in development whereas the sectors, opening wider towards the periphery, correspond to the growing differences in aptitude.

We would go so far as to say that certain behavior patterns characteristically form stages with very general properties: this occurs until a certain level in development is reached; from this point onwards, however, individual aptitudes become more important than these general characteristics and create greater and greater differences between subjects. A good example of this type of development is the evolution of drawing. Until the stage at which the child can represent perspectives graphically, we observe a very general progress to the extent that the 'draw a man' test, to cite a particular case as an example, can be used as a general test of mental development. However, surprisingly large individual differences are observed in the drawings of 13- to 14-year-old children, and even greater differences with 19–20 year olds (e.g., army recruits): the quality of the drawing no longer has anything to do with the level of intelligence. In this instance we have a good example of a behavior pattern which is, at first, subordinate to a general evolution in stages [cf. those described by Luquet and other authors for children from 2–3 until about 8–9 years] and which, afterwards, gradually becomes diversified according to criteria of individual aptitudes rather than the general development common to all individuals.

This same type of pattern occurs in several fields including those which appear to be more cognitive in nature. One example is provided by the representation of space which first depends on operatory factors with the usual 4 intellectual stages—sensorimotor (cf. the practical group of displacements), preoperatory, concrete operations (measure, perspectives, etc.) and formal operations. However, the construction of space also depends on figurative factors (perception and mental imagery) which are partially subordinated to operatory factors and which then become more and more differentiated as symbolical and representative mechanisms. The final result is that for space in general, as for drawing, we can distinguish a primary evolution characterized by the stages in the ordinary sense of the term, and then a growing diversification with age due to gradually differentiating aptitudes with regard to imaged representation and figurative instruments. We know, for example, that there exist big differences between mathematicians in the way in which they define 'geometrical intuition': Poincaré distinguishes two types of mathematicians, the 'geometricians,' who think more concretely and the 'algebrists,' or 'analysts,' who think more abstractly.

There are many other fields in which we could also think along similar lines. It becomes possible at a certain moment, for example, to distinguish between adolescents who, on the one hand, are more talented for physics or problems dealing with causality than for logic or mathematics and those who, on the other hand, show the opposite aptitude. We can see the same tendencies in questions concerning linguistics, literature, etc.

We could, therefore, formulate the following hypothesis: if the formal structures described in part 1 do not appear in all children of 14–15 years and demonstrate a less general distribution than the concrete structures of children from 7–10 years old, this could be due to the diversification of aptitudes with age. According to this interpretation, however, we would have to admit that only individuals talented from the point of view of logic, mathematics and physics would manage to construct such formal structures

whereas literary, artistic and practical individuals would be incapable of doing so. In this case it would not be a problem of under-development compared to normal development but more simply a growing diversification in individuals, the span of aptitudes being greater at the level of 12–15 years, and above all between 15 and 20 years, than at 7–10 years. In other words, our fourth period can no longer be characterized as a proper stage, but would already seem to be a structural advancement in the direction of specialization.

But there is the possibility of a third hypothesis and, in the present state of knowledge, this last interpretation seems the most probable. It allows us to reconcile the concept of stages with the idea of progressively differentiating aptitudes. In brief, our third hypothesis would state that all normal subjects attain the stage of formal operations or structuring if not between 11–12 to 14–15 years, in any case between 15 and 20 years. However, they reach this stage in different areas according to their aptitudes and their professional specializations (advanced studies or different types of apprenticeship for the various trades): the way in which these formal structures are used, however, is not necessarily the same in all cases.

In our investigation of formal structures we used rather specific types of experimental situations which were of a physical and logical-mathematical nature because these seemed to be understood by the school children we sampled. However, it is possible to question whether these situations are, fundamentally, very general and therefore applicable to any school or professional environment. Let us consider the example of apprentices to carpenters, locksmiths, or mechanics who have shown sufficient aptitudes for successful training in the trades they have chosen but whose general education is limited. It is highly likely that they will know how to reason in a hypothetical manner in their specialty, that is to say, dissociating the variables involved, relating terms in a combinatorial manner and reasoning with propositions involving negations and reciprocities. They would, therefore, be capable of thinking formally in their particular field, whereas faced with our experimental situations, their lack of knowledge or the fact they have forgotten certain ideas that are particularly familiar to children still in school or college, would hinder them from reasoning in a formal way, and they would give the appearance of being at the concrete level. Let us also consider the example of young people studying law—in the field of juridical concepts and verbal discourse their logic would be far superior to any form of logic they might use when faced with certain problems in the field of physics that involve notions they certainly once knew but have long since forgotten.

It is quite true that one of the essential characteristics of formal thought appears to us to be the independence of its form from its reality content. At the concrete operatory level a structure cannot be generalized to different heterogeneous contents but remains attached to a system of objects or to the properties of these objects (thus the concept of weight only becomes logically structured after the development of the concept of matter, and the concept of physical volume after weight): a formal structure seems, in contrast, generalizable as it deals with hypotheses. However, it is one thing to dissociate the form from the content in a field which is of interest to the subject and within which he can apply his curiosity and initiative, and it is another to be able to generalize this same spontaneity of research and comprehension to a field foreign to the subject's career and interests. To ask a future lawyer to reason on the theory of relativity or to ask a student in physics to reason on the code of civil rights is quite different from asking a child to generalize what he has discovered in the conservation of matter to a problem on the conservation of weight. In the latter instance it is the passage from one content to a different but comparable content, whereas in the former it is to go out of the subject's field of vital activities and enter a totally new field, completely foreign to his interests and projects. Briefly, we can retain

the idea that formal operations are free from their concrete content, but we must add that this is true only on the condition that for the subjects the situations involve equal aptitudes or comparable vital interests.

CONCLUSION

If we wish to draw a general conclusion from these reflections we must first say that, from a cognitive point of view, the passage from adolescence to adulthood raises a number of unresolved questions that need to be studied in greater detail.

The period from 15 to 20 years marks the beginning of professional specialization and consequently also the construction of a life program corresponding to the aptitudes of the individual. We now ask the following critical question: Can one demonstrate, at this level of development as at previous levels, cognitive structures common to all individuals which will, however, be applied or used differently by each person according to his particular activities?

The reply will probably be positive but this must be established by the experimental methods used in psychology and sociology. Beyond that, the next essential step is to analyze the probable processes of differentiation: that is to say, whether the same structures are sufficient for the organization of many varying fields of activity but with differences in the way they are applied, or whether there will appear new and special structures that still remain to be discovered and studied.

It is to the credit of the FONEME Institution to have realized the existence of these problems and to have understood their importance and complexity, particularly as, generally speaking, developmental psychology believed that its work was completed with the study of adolescence. Fortunately, today, certain research workers are conscious of these facts and we can hope to know more about this subject in the near future.

Unfortunately the study of young adults is much more difficult than the study of the young child as they are less creative, and already part of an organized society that not only limits them and slows them down but sometimes even rouses them to revolt. We know, however, that the study of the child and the adolescent can help us understand the further development of the individual as an adult and that, in turn, the new research on young adults will retroactively throw light on what we already think we know about earlier stages.

INHELDER AND PIAGET ON ADOLESCENCE AND ADULTHOOD: A POSTMODERN APPRAISAL

DAVID ELKIND
Tufts University

Social scientists can never entirely remove themselves from the social-historical paradigms and discourses in which they live and work. Jean Piaget was no exception. Piaget reached maturity during the late modern period, when the social sciences were just emerging and struggling to establish their independence from philosophy and from one another. The reigning scientific philosophy of the era was positivism, the commitment to avoiding prejudice and preconceived ideas and to making experience the final arbiter in decisions regarding the nature of reality. It was, moreover, a period in which social scientists believed that the knowledge they gathered could be applied to human problems for the benefit of humankind. In his endeavors to create a unique discipline, genetic epistemology (Piaget,

1970a); in his belief that education should teach children to be critical and to test out ideas before accepting them (Piaget, 1964); and in his argument that child psychology should be the science of education (Piaget, 1970b), Piaget mirrored the guiding tenets of his time.

I start with these remarks because in this article I want to illustrate some of the ways in which Bärbel Inhelder and Piaget's (1955/1958) work on adolescence, as well as their limited forays into adulthood, were also a reflection, in part at least, of the prevailing social science attitudes toward adolescence and adulthood. I therefore do not enter here into the controversy over the adequacy or appropriateness of Inhelder and Piaget's formal operational model. Rather, my aim is to show how their highly original discussion of adolescent thinking and affectivity was nonetheless combined with many conventional modern ideas regarding adolescence and adulthood. My hope is that by looking at Inhelder and

From *Psychological Science,* 7, 216–220 (1996). Copyright © 1996 American Psychological Society. Reprinted with the permission of Cambridge University Press.

Piaget's work in this broader perspective, we can attain not only a fuller appreciation of the originality of their contribution but also a better grasp of the extent to which even the most original work is limited, in part at least, by the social-historical context in which it was done.

Accordingly, in this article I look at those facets of Inhelder and Piaget's work on adolescence that reflect the social science of their times rather than their own original thinking. To do this, I briefly review the basic, unquestioned, assumptions of modernity and then illustrate how these were mirrored in some facets of Inhelder and Piaget's work on adolescence.

THE DISCOURSE OF MODERNITY

Modern science was founded on what were taken as the self-evident truths of progress, universality, and regularity. Science grew by the progressive accumulation of knowledge that benefited the whole of humankind. Likewise, the aim of modern science was to discover the laws of nature that were universal and that transcended time and space. Newton's law of gravitation was the prototype of universal scientific laws such as the principles of electromagnetism and the conservation of energy. Finally, scientific laws were believed to be regular and to admit of no exceptions. "God," as Einstein said, "does not play dice with the universe." Surface irregularities such as phenotypes must be explained by underlying genotypic regularities.

The late-appearing social sciences took the principles of progress, universality, and regularity as necessary givens. Both Karl Marx and Max Weber were concerned with describing the evolution or progress of society. Both were concerned with the rise of capitalism, but they arrived at different explanations. Marx contended that all facets of society were determined by economic dynamics and that religion, for example, was a rationalization for capitalism. Weber, in contrast, believed that economics and capitalism grew out of religious values and that Protestants were more industrious than Catholics for reli-

gious reasons. Anthropologists such as Bronislaw Malinowski argued that their discipline had to do with documenting the progress of culture from primitive to modern society. Sigmund Freud, in turn, described the progress of the sexual instinct from the oral to the anal to the genital zones. Within behavioristic psychology, socialization came to be seen as the progressive acquisition of habits.

Equally prominent in the social sciences was the commitment to the belief in universality. Psychologists, sociologists, and anthropologists looked for the universal laws that governed the behavior of individuals, societies, and cultures. There was no question that such laws existed; the only question was how to find them and to demonstrate their validity. Georg Hegel regarded his dialectic as determining the evolution of all societies. Emile Durkheim believed that social phenomena such as suicide could be explained by universal societal experiences of alienation and anomie. Freud proposed that all dreams could be explained by the principles of primary-process thinking: condensation, substitution, and identification.

Finally, social scientists were also committed to the principle of regularity. Irregular behavior at the individual, social, or cultural level always had an explanation, usually by some principle or rule at another level of analysis. Freud explained irregular slips of the tongue and pen as the product of unconscious wishes and desires. Alfred Adler interpreted inordinate competition as reflecting an underlying inferiority complex. B. F. Skinner, in his description of operant behavior, presumed that all such behavior was in response to some stimulus (i.e., was lawful), even though the stimulus itself was unknown.

The unquestioned adoption by the social sciences of the tenets of physical science has become a focal point of the critical movement that has been labeled *postmodernism*. Michele Foucault (1974), for example, argued that as social scientists, we never study a universal "human nature" but only individuals. Inasmuch as Inhelder and Piaget's work embodies the belief in progress, universals, and regularity, it is open to postmodern analysis and critique. I attempt this with particular attention to some aspects of Inhelder and Piaget's work on adolescence and their meager references to adulthood.

PROGRESS

Piaget addressed the issue of progress in many different works and in many different contexts. As in the case of Marx and Weber, for Piaget the idea of progress itself was never in question. Rather, what Piaget challenged was the prevailing conception of the dynamics of progress. In *Behavior and Evolution,* for example, Piaget (1978) contended that behavior is the primary mechanism of evolutionary progress:

> The organism is an open system, a necessary precondition of whose functioning is behavior and . . . it is the essence of behavior that it is forever attempting to transcend itself and it thus supplies evolution with its principle motor. (p. 139)

For Piaget, in the beginning there was the act, and it was through action that the individual progressed both biologically and psychologically. Likewise, in his discussion of the stages of development, Piaget did not question the fact of progress, but argued for a nonconventional description of intellectual development:

> To revert to our earlier image, the pyramid of knowledge no longer rests on foundations but hangs by its vertex, an ideal point near reached and, more curious, constantly rising. In short, rather than envisaging human knowledge as a pyramid or building of some sort, we should think of it as a spiral, the radius of whose turns increases as the spiral rises. (Piaget, 1970a, p. 34)

At each stage of development, the child reconstructs the conceptions built at the earlier stage but now at a higher, more abstract level. On the one hand, to the extent that Piaget was discussing stages in the biological sense, it would be hard to challenge their progressive nature. The evidence is just too overwhelming that children think differently at different age levels and that these differences are loosely linked to biological maturation. On the other hand, when Inhelder and Piaget wrote about adolescent progress toward socialization, they fell back on the social science conventions of their day, and this is where their work can be challenged most successfully.

For example, in many different places, Piaget argued that socialization moves forward to the extent that the child is able to overcome his or her egocentrism by taking the other person's perspective:

> We might therefore describe the facts of mutual respect as follows: 1: A gives a command to B. 2: B accepts this command because he respects A. 3: But A puts himself mentally in B's place (this would be the new fact marking a departure from the egocentrism of the initial stages). 4: A therefore feels bound himself by the command he has given B. (Piaget, 1932/1948, p. 388)

For Piaget, then, it is the child's ability to take the other person's point of view that gives rise to cooperation, mutual respect, and a subjective notion of justice.

In Piaget's later writings, he was concerned with the child's construction of aspects of the physical world, such as concepts of space, time, and number, and the issue of socialization was given less attention. Piaget sought to demonstrate how intellectual operations are derived from the child's own actions upon the physical environment and that such mental activities are not a product solely of maturation or of learning. But in the book on adolescence, Inhelder and Piaget returned to the issue of socialization and once again evoked social perspective taking as a critical mechanism in overcoming (progress out of) adolescent egocentrism:

> From the standpoint of social relationships, the tendency of adolescents to congregate in peer groups has been well documented—discussion or action groups, political action groups, youth movements, summer camps, etc. . . . . Certainly this type of social life is not merely the effect of pressures towards conformity but also a source of intellectual decentering. It is most often in discussions between friends, when the promoter of a theory has to test it

against the theories of the others, that he discovers its fragility. (Inhelder & Piaget, 1955/1958, p. 346)

For Inhelder and Piaget, at each stage of development after the sensorimotor period, the child constructs egocentric structures which, when unconfirmed by peers, force the young person to take the other individual's point of view and to gain a more objective, socialized view of reality. This perspective-taking theory of socialization has been widely accepted and has been thoughtfully elaborated by Robert Selman (1980). The importance of perspective taking in socialization must, however, be questioned. This proposition derives from the assumption that progress in socialization necessarily parallels the progress in cognitive development.

Yet this contention does not hold up under examination. For one thing, it is very difficult even for us adults to take another person's point of view when it is different from our own. For example, the work of Carol Gilligan and her colleagues (e.g., Gilligan, Ward, & Taylor, 1988) has demonstrated how much of psychology is male oriented and fails to take the female perspective into account. Likewise, the very process of psychotherapy shows how difficult it is for men and women to put themselves in another person's position when it is different from their own. How can such an extraordinarily difficult and complex process be the everyday means of socialization of children?

To show where the error lies, it is useful to break perspective taking into several steps. The first step is the construction of an egocentric conception regarding oneself or the world, such as the early adolescent's construction of an imaginary audience (Elkind & Bowen, 1979). A second step occurs when this egocentric conception leads to experiential expectations (say the adolescent expects all of his or her peers to admire a new outfit worn to school). And a third step occurs when that expectation is disconfirmed (when peers fail to notice or comment on the outfit). In this sequence, the first thing the young person discovers is that other people do

not share his or her perspective. This realization leads to the next step, which is the alteration of the egocentric conception or expectation. Now the adolescent has to recognize that no matter how attractive he or she believes the outfit to be, other people did not see it that way. The adolescent may even decide that the outfit is not so attractive after all.

In this illustration, the adolescent discovers that other people do not share his or her perspective and modifies the egocentric conception without necessarily putting himself or herself in the other person's position. To use an example a little closer to home, suppose we write an article that we believe makes an important contribution, but the response to the article, no reprint requests, indicates that other people do not share our high opinion of the piece. We may continue to regard our work highly, while acknowledging that others—because of their obtuseness—are unable to see its value. In short, we can overcome our egocentrism without necessarily taking another person's perspective. The disconfirmation of our egocentric expectations is all that is required.

There is no question that social interaction is critical to socialization; it is only the nature of that interaction that is in question here. Inhelder and Piaget (1955/1958) suggested that when a young person's egocentric conceptions are challenged by peers, he or she is forced to take their point of view and to alter the egocentric conceptions accordingly. But as I have just suggested, social interaction can bring us to alter our egocentric conceptions without the necessity of our sharing the other person's perspective. Put somewhat differently, it is the social disconfirmation of our egocentric conceptions, rather than taking the other person's point of view, that is the critical dynamic of decentration.

The focus on perspective taking as the prime mechanism of socialization has, I believe, distracted developmentalists from looking at socialization more broadly. Elsewhere (Elkind, 1987), I have suggested that socialization comes about, in part at least, by the acquisition of what Erving

Goffman (1974) called frames—the rules, expectations, and understandings that govern repetitive social situations such as waiting in line. A good deal of socialization comes about by the learning of frames. Although such learning does have a developmental dimension, it is also determined by personality, temperament, family, society, and culture. These determinants are simply too variable in their effects for frames to develop in any regular, age-related progression.

UNIVERSALITY

The belief in universality presents special problems for psychology. Controversies over whether there are psychological universals range from situation versus trait theories of personality to issues regarding the possibility of "transfer of training." With respect to Piaget, the most obvious question regarding his work is whether the stages in the development of intelligence that he outlined are indeed universal.

It is important to distinguish between biological and psychological universals. Foucault (1978), for example, did not argue against the existence of biological universals such as human sexuality. He did, however, deny that there are universal psychological discourses regarding sexuality (such as that of repression). To the extent that the Piagetian stages are linked to our biological humanness, they have the same claim to universality as the rest of our biological heritage. This linkage is, however, less clear for the formal operations of adolescence than it is for the earlier operations of intelligence.

Although preoperations and concrete operations are acquired largely through the child's actions upon things, formal operations are acquired through activities not on objects themselves, but on symbols. A symbol system, or a discourse, is a cultural product and will vary from society to society and even from group to group within the society. Inhelder and Piaget were, therefore, quite postmodern in describing the attainment of formal operations as nonuniversal and dependent on the level of symbolic elaboration and the educational system of particular societies. Yet there is an assumption of universality that Inhelder and Piaget borrowed from sociology and never questioned in the way they critically examined the origins of formal operations themselves. This assumption is that young people move into adulthood by assuming adult roles:

> Thus to say that adolescence is the age at which adolescents take their place in adult society is by definition to maintain that it is the formation of the personality, for the adoption of adult roles is, from another and necessarily complementary standpoint, the construction of personality. (Inhelder & Piaget, 1955/1958, p. 350)

Inhelder and Piaget thus started from a very modern view of society wherein there was a clear dividing line between adolescence and adulthood and adult roles were clearly defined. Children and adolescents, for example, dressed differently than did adults, and wearing long pants and using makeup were rites of passage. Such role differentiation is much less evident in postmodern society, in which children and adolescents are hurried to grow up fast and developmental stages and limitations are increasingly denied (Elkind, 1981/1988, 1984, 1994).

One way to clarify this point is to use a distinction that Margaret Mead (1970) made regarding the effect of the rate of technological change on culture. She distinguished between three different types of cultures. In *postfigurative* cultures, wherein social change is very slow, all knowledge, values, and skills are acquired from the society's elders. Such societies are rich in tradition and ritual, and youths are inculcated with a respect for age and authority. In such societies, becoming an adult does indeed entail taking on adult roles. As I explain in the next section, this is the kind of culture in which Piaget spent his adolescence and that he and Inhelder apparently assumed was still in play—as it may still be to some extent in Switzerland.

But Mead described other cultures that were *cofigurative*. In such societies, the pace of technological change has speeded up, and young people often become more skilled than their parents and other adults. American society, she argued, was cofigurative until about midcentury. Over the past few decades, however, our society has become *prefigurative*. In America today, technological change is so rapid that the young must devote most of their time to learning the newly emerging knowledge, skills, and values. To such young people, the knowledge, skills, and values of the older adult society appear dated and of little practical utility. As a result, the young have little respect and veneration for parents in particular and society in general. In our contemporary society, becoming an adult often means creating or reinventing adulthood, because the social roles modeled by adults of the previous generation are no longer adaptive.

REGULARITY

Within Piaget's work in general, the assumption of regularity is perhaps most evident in the stage conception of intellectual development. The stages are said to evolve in a necessary sequence that is related to age. Although young people may attain these stages at different times and, depending on circumstances, the formal operations may not be attained at all, the sequence is nonetheless invariant. To the extent that the appearance of these stages is linked to biological maturation, the depiction of them as regular certainly seems warranted and is supported by a great deal of cross-cultural data.

In their book on adolescence, however, Inhelder and Piaget made some assumptions about regularities in adolescence that seem to arise more from the social science of their time, and perhaps from Piaget's own history, than from research. It is these regularities that I question here. In the following quotation, the authors suggested, as they did at other places in the book, that all adolescents construct some sort of life plan, or program:

The adolescent not only builds new theories or rehabilitates old ones, he also feels he has to

work out a conception of life which gives him an opportunity to assess himself and to create something new (thus the close relationship between his system and the life program). Secondly, he wants a guarantee that he will be more successful than his predecessors (thus the need for change in which altruistic concern and youthful ambitions are inseparably blended). (Inhelder & Piaget, 1955/1958, p. 342)

What is missing from Piaget's description is the social context in which young men in Switzerland were being educated. In an extraordinary account of *Piaget Before Piaget,* Fernando Vidal (1994) revealed how much the educational environment contributed to the intellectual pretensions of young Swiss adolescents just before the first world war:

One of the most distinctive aspects of Piaget's youth was his membership beyond school obligations, in the institutions that contributed to Neuchatel's reputation as an educational center. . . . Prominent among Neuchatel's educational institutions were various private learned societies and amateur clubs aimed at fostering knowledge through mutual instruction and independent research. Individuals, ideas, information and values circulated freely among all levels of the public and private systems. It is within such an institutional network—a small community where everybody knew everybody, and where learning was openly shared, that the young Piaget was educated. (p. 16)

There were a number of different clubs for young people that would meet individual interests. One of these was the Jura Club:

The Jura Club was the natural-historical counterpart of the historical society. Its founders, "professors and friends of youth" wished to acquaint young people aged nine to eighteen, with the study of natural sciences, with a focus on the fauna and flora of the Jura. Their goal was to occupy youth with "healthy, elevated things, necessary during the often dangerous moment of transition when, having finished school the adolescent has not yet taken his place in society, and is lured by frivolous pleasures and material enjoyments. (Vidal, 1994, pp. 18–19)

Although Piaget published in the Jura Club's magazine, he himself belonged to a club called The Friends of Nature.

> In early twentieth-century Switzerland, the "friend of nature" was still a familiar character who matched the well known prototype depicted by the Genevan educator, author, and pioneer cartoonist, Rodophe Toepffer (1799–1846). The "friend of nature" was a "fifteen-year-old philosopher" capable of spending entire days looking for specimens, classifying and perfecting his collections. Toepffer (1858, 65–66) together with many other naturalists and pedagogues, was convinced that natural history was accessible to adolescents because it required practically no specialized background and suited their supposedly typical energy, curiosity and individualism. (Vidal, 1994, p. 20)
>
> Apart from regular sessions, the Friends organized botanical, paleontological or zoological excursions. During the sessions, papers were presented, generally containing observations on animals, plants, or natural phenomena; readings were periodically held. (Vidal, 1994, p. 21)

There were many other youth clubs in Geneva, and teachers, professors, and intelligentsia from the community were all involved with young people. As Vidal (1994) concluded, "The intertwining of institutions, people and ideas in Piaget's youth produced a social network in which he continued to function for years to come" (p. 22).

All this is to say that when Inhelder and Piaget wrote their concluding chapter, Piaget in particular was probably reflecting upon his own adolescence. It is likely that all young people in Neuchatel, regardless of social class, were influenced by the intellectual ferment and the commitment of adults to education and avocations of youth. In such an environment, it is likely that most young men (there is no mention of young women constructing life plans) did construct a life plan inasmuch as this was more or less expected of them (for Piaget's life plan, see Piaget, 1918). In emphasizing the importance of the life plan in moving toward adulthood, Piaget was probably reflecting the social consensus (and male bias) of his time.

It is questionable, however, whether youths growing up in postmodern America, bombarded by television, by news of the declining work opportunities, world overpopulation, environmental degradation, and so on, are either as optimistic or as idealistic as Inhelder and Piaget portrayed them as being. Nor, in the absence of the social context of a Neuchatel, are many young people likely to create life plans.

Here again it is fascinating to see how Piaget and Inhelder, who were otherwise so careful to support their interpretations with data, extrapolated from personal experience. Perhaps it was the less familiar domain of socialization that led them to assume that what was the rule for Piaget and his cohorts growing up in Neuchatel would be the rule for adolescents in general. It is an open question whether Inhelder and Piaget believed that young women wrote life plans and whether such plans played a comparable role in their development.

CONCLUSION

I have tried to show how Inhelder and Piaget, despite their originality, reflected the scientific and societal givens within which they worked and wrote. The belief in progress may have led them to overestimate the role of perspective taking in the attainment of socialization. Likewise, their beliefs in universality may have led them to assume that the heady intellectual atmosphere of postfigurative, turn-of-the-century Neuchatel was characteristic of all societies. Finally, their belief in regularity encouraged them to overgeneralize the role of life plans in the lives of young men and to seemingly ignore the role of such life plans in the lives of young women.

In arguing that Inhelder and Piaget's work on adolescence in some ways mirrored the culture of their times, I do not mean to minimize the enormity of their contribution to our factual and theoretical understanding of adolescence. Indeed, their original achievement is even more remarkable considering the force of the social zeitgeist. My main point is that even the giants in our discipline can never entirely transcend the social, cultural, and historical context in which they live and work. It is a cautionary lesson for us all.

REFERENCES

Elkind, D. (1984). *All grown up and no place to go.* Reading, MA: Addison-Wesley.

Elkind, D. (1987). *Miseducation.* New York: Knopf.

Elkind, D. (1988). *The hurried child* (rev. ed.). Reading, MA: Addison-Wesley. (Original work published 1981)

Elkind, D. (1994). *Ties that stress.* Cambridge, MA: Harvard University Press.

Elkind, D., & Bowen, R. (1979). Imaginary audience behavior in children and adolescents. *Developmental Psychology, 15,* 38–44.

Foucault, M. (1974). Human nature: Justice vs. power. In F. Elder (Ed.), *Reflective water: The basic concerns of mankind* (p. 171). London: Souvenir Press.

Foucault, M. (1978). *The history of sexuality: Vol. I. An introduction.* New York: Random House.

Gilligan, C., Ward, J. V., & Taylor, J. M. (1988). *Mapping the moral domain.* Cambridge, MA: Harvard University Press.

Goffman, E. (1974). *Frame analysis.* New York: Harper.

Inhelder, B., & Piaget, J. (1958). *The growth of logical thinking from childhood to adolescence* (A. Parsons & S. Milgram, Trans.). New York: Basic Books. (Original work published 1955)

Mead, M. (1970). *Culture and commitment.* New York: Natural History Press.

Piaget, J. (1918). *Reserche.* Lausanne, Switzerland: Concorde.

Piaget, J. (1948). *The moral judgment of the child* (H. Gabain, Trans.). Glencoe, IL: Free Press. (Original work published 1932)

Piaget, J. (1964). The aims of education. In R. Ripple & V. Rockcastle (Eds.), *Piaget rediscovered* (pp. 17–19). Ithaca, NY: Cornell University School of Education.

Piaget, J. (1970a). *Genetic epistemology* (E. Duckworth, Trans.). New York: Columbia University Press.

Piaget, J. (1970b). *Science of education and psychology of the child* (D. Coltman, Trans.). New York: Oxford University Press.

Piaget, J. (1978). *Behavior and evolution* (D. Nicholson-Smith, Trans.). New York: Random House.

Selman, R. (1980). *The growth of interpersonal understanding.* New York: Academic Press.

Toepffer, R. (1858). *Nouveau voyages en zigzag.* Paris: Garnier.

Vidal, F. (1994). *Piaget Before Piaget.* Cambridge, MA: Harvard University Press.

ETHNICITY, CLASS, COGNITIVE, AND MOTIVATIONAL STYLES

JAMES A. BANKS
University of Washington at Seattle

ETHNIC MINORITIES AND ACADEMIC ACHIEVEMENT

The low academic achievement of some ethnic minority youths, such as Afro-Americans, Mexican Americans, and Puerto Rican Americans, is a major national problem that warrants urgent action at the local, state, and national levels. The problem is complex and difficult to diagnose because there is substantial disagreement among educational researchers, practitioners, and the lay community about what causes the wide discrepancies in the academic achievement of groups such as Blacks and mainstream White youths, and between Mexican American and Japanese American students. The writer has reviewed and discussed elsewhere the conflicting explanations and paradigms that have emerged since the civil rights movement of the 1960s to explain the low academic achievement of ethnic youths.[1]

The Cultural Deprivation and Cultural Difference Hypotheses

When national attention focused on the under-achievement of poor and ethnic minority youths in the 1960s, cultural deprivation emerged as the dominant paradigm to explain their educational problems.[2] Cultural deprivation theorists stated that lower-income and minority students were not achieving well in school because of the culture of poverty in which they were socialized. The cultural deprivation paradigm was harshly attacked in the late 1960s and during the 1970s.[3] Its critics argued that it promoted assimilationism and violated the cultural integrity of students from diverse income and cultural groups.

Researchers who rejected the cultural deprivation paradigm created a conception of the cultures and educational problems of lower-income and minority youths based on a different set of assumptions. They argued that these students, far from being culturally deprived, have rich and elaborate cultures. Their rich cultural characteristics are evident in their languages and communication styles, behavioral styles, and

From *Journal of Negro Education,* 57 (1988), 452–466.
Copyright © 1988 by Howard University. All rights reserved.
[1]J. A. Banks, "Multicultural Education: Developments, Paradigms, and Goals," in J. A. Banks and J. Lynch, eds., *Multicultural Education in Western Societies* (New York: Praeger, 1986), pp. 2–28.

[2]F. Reissman, *The Culturally Deprived Child* (New York: Harper, 1962); B. S. Bloom, A. Davis, and R. Hess, *Compensatory Education for Cultural Deprivation* (New York: Holt, 1965).

[3]C. A. Valentine, *Culture and Poverty: Critique and Counter-Proposals* (Chicago: University of Chicago Press, 1968); S. S. Baratz and J. C. Baratz, "Early Childhood Intervention: The Social Science Base of Institutional Racism," *Harvard Educational Review,* 40 (Winter 1970), 29–50.

values.[4] These theorists also contended that the cognitive, learning, and motivational styles of ethnic minorities such as Afro-Americans and Mexican Americans are different from those fostered in the schools.[5] These students, therefore, achieve less well in school because the school culture favors the culture of White mainstream students and places students from other backgrounds and cultures at a serious disadvantage. The school environment consequently needs to be reformed substantially so that it will be sensitive to diverse learning, cognitive, and motivational styles.

The Social Class Hypothesis

While the cultural difference paradigm has provided rich insights with implications for practice, it has devoted little attention to variation within ethnic groups. Learning and other social science theories should accurately reflect the tremendous diversity within ethnic groups such as Afro-Americans and Mexican Americans. While these cultures share a number of overarching beliefs, values, and behavioral styles, there are enormous within-group differences caused by factors such as region, gender, and social class. Diversity within ethnic groups has received insufficient attention within the social science literature and in the popular imagination.

While variables such as region, religion, gender, and social class create intragroup variation within ethnic groups, social class is presumably one of the most important of these variables.

Wilson's important and controversial book—in which he argues that the importance of race in the United States has declined and that class has created important divisions among Blacks—evoked a stimulating and acid debate about race and class in the United States.[6] Wilson believes that class is a major factor that stratifies the Afro-American community. Gordon also hypothesizes that class has a strong influence on ethnic behavior.[7] He writes, "With regard to cultural behavior, differences of social class are more important and decisive than differences of ethnic group. This means that people of the same social class tend to act alike and to have the same values even if they have different ethnic backgrounds."[8]

My aim in this article is to examine the social class hypothesis and to determine the extent to which ethnicity is class sensitive. I will do this by reviewing studies on cognitive styles, learning styles, and motivational styles which include social class as a variable. If social class is as powerful a variable as Wilson and Gordon state, then middle-class Black and White students should not differ significantly in their cognitive, learning, and motivational styles. However, middle-class and lower-class Blacks should differ significantly on these variables. Another, and perhaps more likely possibility, is that social class and ethnicity interact in complex ways to influence learning, motivation, and cognitive styles.

PROBLEMS IN STUDYING CLASS AND ETHNICITY

Several intractable problems confront the scholar who tries to determine the relationship between social class, ethnicity, and cognitive and motiva-

[4]G. Smitherman, *Talking and Testifying: The Language of Black America* (Boston: Houghton Mifflin, 1977); J. Hale, "Black Children: Their Roots, Culture and Learning Styles," *Young Children,* 36 (January 1981), 37–50; J. L. White, *The Psychology of Blacks* (Englewood Cliffs, N.J.: Prentice-Hall, 1984).
[5]M. Ramírez and A. Castañeda, *Cultural Democracy, Biocognitive Development and Education* (New York: Academic Press, 1974); B. J. Shade, "Afro-American Cognitive Style: A Variable in School Success?" *Review of Educational Research,* 52 (Summer 1982), 219–244; J. Hale-Benson, *Black Children: Their Roots, Culture, and Learning Styles,* rev. ed. (Baltimore: The John Hopkins University Press, 1986).

[6]W. J. Wilson, *The Declining Significance of Race: Blacks and Changing American Institutions* (Chicago: University of Chicago Press, 1978); A. Pinkney, *The Myth of Black Progress* (New York: Cambridge University Press, 1984).
[7]M. Gordon, *Assimilation in American Life* (New York: Oxford University Press, 1964).
[8]Ibid., p. 52.

tional styles. Most of the literature that describes the cognitive and motivational styles of ethnic students includes little or no discussion of social class or other factors that might cause within-group variations, such as gender, age, or situational aspects. Social class is often conceptualized and measured differently in studies that include class as a variable; this makes it difficult to compare results from different studies. Researchers frequently use different scales and instruments to measure variables related to cognitive, learning, and motivational styles. To operationally define social class, especially across different ethnic and cultural groups, is one of the most difficult tasks facing social scientists today.

The nature of social class is changing in the United States. Behavior associated with the lower-class fifteen years ago—such as single-parent families—is now common among the middle class. Social class is a dynamic and changing concept. This makes it difficult to study social class over time and across different cultural and ethnic groups. Many of the studies reviewed in this article used Warner's Index of Status Characteristics which was published almost forty years ago.[9]

Cognition and Learning Studies

Lesser, Fifer, and Clark studied the patterns of mental abilities in six- and seven-year-old children from different social-class and ethnic backgrounds.[10] They studied verbal ability, reasoning, number facility, and space conceptualization among Chinese, Jewish, Black, and Puerto Rican students in New York City. They found that the four ethnic groups were markedly different in both the level of each mental ability and the pattern among these abilities. In a replication study, Lesser, Fifer, and Clark studied middle- and lower-class Chinese, Black, and Irish Catholic first-grade students in Boston.[11] The replication data for Chinese and Black students were similar to the data on these groups from their earlier study. However, the data for the Irish Catholic students showed neither a distinctive ethnic-group pattern nor similarity of patterns for the two social classes.

Burnes studied the pattern of WISC (Wechsler Intelligence Scale for Children) scores of Black and White students who were upper-middle and lower class.[12] She found significant social-class differences in the scores of the students but no significant racial differences. No interaction effects were found for social class and race. The scores on the subtests for Blacks and Whites did not show a pattern by race or cultural group.

Backman studied six mental ability factors among 2,925 twelfth-grade students who had participated in Project TALENT.[13] She examined how the six mental abilities were related to ethnicity, social class, and sex. Sex accounted for a much larger proportion of the variance than did either ethnicity or social class. Sex was related significantly to both the shape and the level of the patterns of mental ability. It accounted for 69 percent of the total variance in the shape of the patterns. Ethnicity was the only other variable that showed a significant effect on the patterns. It accounted for 13 percent of the total variance: 9 percent associated with shape and 4 percent with level. The patterns of mental abilities of the social-class groups differed significantly in both shape and level. However, these

[9]W. L. Warner, *Social Class in America* (Chicago: Science Research Associates, 1949).

[10]G. S. Lesser, G. Fifer, and D. H. Clark, "Mental Abilities of Children from Different Social-Class and Cultural Groups," *Monographs of the Society for Research in Child Development,* 30, No. 4 (1965).

[11]Cited in S. S. Stodolsky and G. Lesser, "Learning Patterns in the Disadvantaged," *Harvard Educational Review,* 37 (Fall 1967), 546–593; reprinted Series No. 5, *Harvard Educational Review,* 1975, pp. 22–69.

[12]K. Burnes, "Patterns of WISC Scores for Children of Two Socioeconomic Classes and Races," *Child Development,* 41 (1970), 493–499.

[13]M. E. Backman, "Patterns of Mental Abilities: Ethnic, Socioeconomic, and Sex Differences," *American Educational Research Journal,* 9 (Winter 1972), 1–12.

differences accounted for only 2 percent of the variance and were considered by the investigator too small to be important.

A number of researchers have examined a variety of learning variables and cognitive functions related to ethnicity and social class. However, it is difficult to derive clear-cut generalizations from these studies. Siegel, Anderson, and Shapiro examined the categorization behavior of lower- and middle-class Black preschool children.[14] The children were presented with sorting objects, colored pictures, and black-and-white pictures. Lower-class and middle-class children differed in their ability to group only on the pictures. They used different types of categories. Lower-class children preferred to form groups based on use and interdependence of items. Middle-class children preferred to group items on the basis of common physical attributes.

Orasanu, Lee, and Scribner investigated the extent to which category clustering in recall is dependent on preferred organization of the to-be-recalled items and whether preferred organization or recall are related to ethnic or economic group membership.[15] Social-class status was related to the number of high-associate pairs the subjects produced in sorting. Middle-income children produced significantly more pairs than low-income children. Ethnicity was related to the number of taxonomic categories; White children sorted taxonomically more often than did Black children, who showed a preference for functional sorting. Ethnicity and social-class status were unrelated to amount recalled on the pairs-list tasks or to the amount of clustering. Although Black and White children showed differences in organizational preferences, there were no differences in recall.

Rychlak investigated the role of social class, race, and intelligence on the affective learning styles of 160 lower- and middle-income seventh-grade children who were equally divided by sex and race (White and Black).[16] The researchers hypothesized and found that, for all subjects, moving from positive to negative reinforcement value across lists resulted in less nonspecific transfer than does moving from negative to positive reinforcement across successive lists. They hypothesized that this general pattern would be more apparent for Blacks than for Whites and for lower-class than for middle-class subjects. Their hypotheses were confirmed. The White subjects reflected positive non-specific transfer across the lists regardless of whether they were moving from positive to negative or negative to positive levels of reinforcement value. However, Black subjects reflected a negative transfer when moving from positive to negative and a positive transfer when moving from negative to positive lists.

Family Socialization

Some evidence indicates that the socialization and intellectual environment of the homes of different racial groups vary even when they are members of the same social class as determined by an index such as Warner's Index of Status Characteristics.[17] Trotman compared the home environment ratings of fifty Black and fifty White middle-class families of ninth-grade girls to the girls' Otis-Lennon Mental Ability Test results, Metropolitan Achievement Test scores, and grade point averages.[18] She found that the home environments of middle-class White fami-

[14]I. Siegel, L. M. Anderson, and H. Shapiro, "Categorization Behavior in Lower- and Middle-Class Preschool Children: Differences in Dealing with Representation of Familiar Objects," *Journal of Negro Education,* 35 (1966), 218–229.

[15]J. Orasanu, C. Lee, and S. Scribner, "The Development of Category Organization and Free Recall: Ethnic and Economic Group Comparisons," *Child Development,* 50 (1979), 1100–1109.

[16]J. F. Rychlak, "Affective Assessment, Intelligence, Social Class, and Racial Learning Style," *Journal of Personality and Social Psychology,* 32 (1975), 989–995.

[17]Warner, *Social Class in America.*

[18]F. K. Trotman, "Race, IQ, and the Middle Class," *Journal of Educational Psychology,* 69 (1977), 266–273.

lies showed a significantly higher level of intellectuality than did those of middle-class Black families. There was an overall positive relationship between the family's home environment and the child's score on the Otis-Lennon Mental Ability Test. This relationship was stronger for Black than for White families. Trotman believes that there is a cultural difference in the home experience and parent-child interactions in Black and White families of the same social class, and that this difference may help to explain the variation in intelligence test performance by members of the two cultural groups.

Research by Moore supports the hypothesis that family socialization practices related to intelligence test performance is different within Black and White families of the same social class.[19] She compared the intelligence test performances of a sample of Black children adopted by Black and by White middle-class parents. She hypothesized that Black children adopted by Black families would achieve significantly lower WISC scores than Black children adopted by White families. Her hypothesis was confirmed. The children adopted by the White families scored significantly higher on the WISC than did those adopted by Black families. The 13.5-point difference in performance between the two groups is the level usually observed between Black and White children.

The studies by Trotman and by Moore support the hypothesis that the socialization practices of Black and White middle-class parents, at least as they relate to intelligence test performance, differ significantly. However, it cannot be inferred from these findings that family socialization practices do not vary within different social classes in the Black community. A study by Kamii and Radin indicates that the socialization practices of lower-lower and middle-class Black mothers differ in

significant ways.[20] These researchers directly observed how the mothers interacted with their preschool children and conducted interviews with the mothers in their homes. While they found that lower-lower and middle-class mothers differed significantly in some socialization practices, "not all mothers demonstrated the characteristics of their strata. Social class is thus not a determinant of behavior but a statement of probability that a type of behavior is likely to occur."[21]

Cognitive Styles

Theorists and researchers who support the cultural difference hypothesis, such as Ramírez and Castañeda, Hilliard, White, and Hale-Benson,[22] have been heavily influenced by the "cognitive style" concept pioneered by Witkin.[23] Witkin hypothesizes that the learning styles of individuals vary; some are field independent in their learning styles, while others are field dependent. Learners who are field independent easily perceive a hidden figure on the Embedded Figures Test, while field-dependent learners find it difficult to perceive because of the obscuring design.[24]

Ramírez and Castañeda used Witkin's concept in their work with Mexican American students. They substituted "field sensitive" for "field dependent," which they believe has nega-

[19]E. G. J. Moore, "Ethnicity as a Variable in Child Development," in *The Social and Affective Development of Black Children,* ed. M. G. Spencer, G. K. Brookins, and W. R. Allen (Hillsdale, N.J.: Lawrence Erlbaum Associates, 1985), pp. 101–115.

[20]C. K. Kamii and N. J. Radin, "Class Differences in Socialization Practices of Negro Mothers," *Journal of Marriage and the Family,* 29 (1967), 302–310; reprinted in *The Black Family: Essays and Studies,* ed. R. Staples (Belmont, Calif.: Wadsworth Publishing Co., 1971), pp. 235–247.

[21]Ibid., p. 244.

[22]Ramírez and Castañeda, *Cultural Democracy;* A. Hilliard, "Alternatives to IQ Testing: An Approach to the Identification of Gifted Minority Children" (Final report to the California State Department of Education, 1976); White, *The Psychology of Blacks;* and Hale-Benson, *Black Children.*

[23]H. A. Witkin, *Psychological Differentiation* (New York: Wiley, 1962); H. A. Witkin and D. R. Goodenough, *Cognitive Styles: Essence and Origins* (New York: International Universities Press, Inc., 1981).

[24]H. A. Witkin, "Individual Differences in Ease of Perception of Embedded Figures," *Journal of Personality,* 19 (1950), 1–15.

tive connotations.[25] Field-independent and field-sensitive students differ in some significant ways in their learning styles and behaviors. Field-independent learners prefer to work independently, while field-sensitive learners like to work with others to achieve a common goal. Field-independent learners tend to be task-oriented and inattentive to their social environment when working. Field-sensitive learners tend to be sensitive to the feelings and opinions of others.[26] Ramírez and Castañeda found that Mexican American children tend to be field sensitive in their learning styles, while teachers usually prefer field-independent students and assign them higher grades. The teaching styles of most teachers and the school curriculum also tend to reflect the characteristics of field-independent students. Mainstream Anglo students tend to be more field independent than ethnic minorities such as Mexican American and Black students. Although field-independent students tend to get higher grades than do field-dependent students, researchers have found that cognitive style is not related to measured intelligence or IQ.

Cohen,[27] who has influenced the works of Hale-Benson and Hilliard, has conceptualized learning styles similar to those formulated by Witkin. She identifies two conceptual styles, analytic and relational. The analytic style is related to Witkin's field-independent concept. The relational is similar to his field-dependent concept. Cohen found that these styles of thinking are produced by the kinds of families and groups into which students are socialized. Family and friendship groups in which functions are periodically performed or widely shared by all members of the group, which she calls "shared function" groups, tend to socialize students who are relational in their learning styles. Formal styles of group organization are associated with analytic styles of learning.

Several researchers have tested the hypothesis that ethnic minority students tend to be more field-dependent or relational in their learning styles than mainstream students, even when social-class status is held constant. Ramírez and Price-Williams studied 180 fourth-grade children to determine whether Mexican American and Black students were more field dependent than Anglo students.[28] Both the Black and the Mexican American students scored in a significantly more field-dependent direction than did the Anglo children. The social-class effect was not significant. Ramírez found that most teachers are significantly more field independent than are Mexican American students. However, their level of field independence does not differ significantly from that of Anglo students.[29]

Perney studied field dependence-independence among suburban Black and White sixth-grade students.[30] No information is given about the social-class status of the community. She found that the Black students were significantly more field dependent than were the White students. However, it was the scores of the Black females that accounted for most of the difference between the races. Black females were the most field-dependent subjects in the study. The females in the study, as a group, were significantly more field dependent than the males. Perney's study reveals that there are significant field-dependence differences between Black and White students and between males and females. However, it does not help us determine the extent to which field dependence is related or sensitive to social-class status.

---

[25]Ramírez and Castañeda, *Cultural Democracy.*
[26]Ibid.
[27]R. A. Cohen, "Conceptual Styles, Cultural Conflict, and Nonverbal Tests of Intelligence," *American Anthropologist,* 71 (1969), 828–856.

[28]M. Ramírez and D. R. Price-Williams, "Cognitive Styles of Children of Three Ethnic Groups in the United States," *Journal of Cross-Cultural Psychology,* 5 (1974), 212–219.
[29]M. Ramírez, "Cognitive Styles and Cultural Democracy in Education of Mexican Americans," *Social Science Quarterly,* 53 (1973), 895–904.
[30]V. H. Perney, "Effects of Race and Sex on Field Dependence-Independence in Children," *Perceptual and Motor Skills,* 42 (1976), 975–980.

Locus of Control and Motivation

Researchers have devoted considerable attention to locus of control and its influence on learning and motivation.[31] This psychological construct is related to how individuals perceive the relationship between their action and its consequences. Individuals who believe that consequences are a direct result of their actions are said to have internal locus of control or internality. Persons who believe that there is little or no relationship between their behavior and its consequences are said to have an external locus of control.

Researchers have found that internality is positively related to academic achievement.[32] Students who believe that their behavior can determine consequences tend to achieve at higher levels than students who believe that their behavior is determined by external forces such as luck, fate, or other individuals. Researchers have found that internality is related to social class and to socialization practices.[33] Higher-socioeconomic-status students tend to be more internal in their orientations than are lower-socioeconomic-status students.

Some researchers interested in minority education have devoted considerable attention to locus of control because of the percentage of ethnic minority students who are lower-class and consequently tend to be external in their psychological orientations.[34] Research rather consistently indicates a relationship between social-class status, internality, and academic achievement. A study by Garner and Cole indicates that while both field dependence and locus of control are related to academic achievement, field dependence is the more important factor; the achievers in their study were more field inde-

pendent.[35] However, when locus of control and field dependence were combined, locus of control dominated. The achievement of the groups ranged from high to low as follows: internal and field independent, internal and field dependent, external and field independent, and external and field dependent. A study by Battle and Rotter supports the well-established principle that locus of control is related primarily to social class rather than to race or ethnicity.[36]

THE PERSISTENCE OF ETHNICITY

As the above review of research indicates, our knowledge of the effect of social-class status on cognitive and motivational styles among ethnic minorities is thin and fragmentary. My review of such studies is representative but not exhaustive. This research does not give a clear and unmixed message about how sensitive ethnicity is to social-class status. Some researchers, such as Lesser, Fifer, and Clark, Trotman, and Moore, have found that ethnicity has a powerful effect on behavior related to learning and intellectual performance when social class is varied or controlled. Other researchers, such as Orasanu, Lee, and Scribner and Burnes, have derived findings that reveal the effects of social class on learning behavior or the effects of both class and ethnicity.

Collectively, the studies reviewed in this article provide more support for the cultural difference than for the social-class hypothesis. They indicate that ethnicity continues to have a significant influence on the learning behavior and styles of Afro-American and Mexican American students, even when these students are middle class. *In other words, the research reviewed in this article indicates that while ethnicity is to some extent*

[31]H. M. Leftcourt, *Locus of Control: Current Trends in Theory and Research,* 2nd ed. (Hillsdale, N.J.: Lawrence Erlbaum Associates, 1982).
[32]Ibid.
[33]Ibid.
[34]J. A. Vasquez, "Bilingual Education's Needed Third Dimension," *Educational Leadership,* 37 (November 1979), 166–168.

[35]C. W. Garner and E. G. Cole, "The Achievement of Students in Low-SES Settings: An Investigation of the Relationship Between Locus of Control and Field Dependence," *Urban Education,* 21 (July 1986), 189–206.
[36]E. S. Battle and J. B. Rotter, "Children's Feelings of Personal Control as Related to Social Class and Ethnic Group," *Journal of Personality,* 31 (1963), 482–490.

class sensitive, its effects persist across social-class segments within an ethnic group. However, the research also indicates that social class causes within-ethnic-group variation in behavior. Middle-class Afro-Americans and middle-class Whites differ in some significant ways, as do middle-class and lower-class Afro-Americans.

While the research reviewed herein indicates that cognitive and learning styles are influenced by ethnicity across social classes within ethnic groups, it suggests that locus of control is primarily a class variable. Whether students believe that they can exert control over their environment appears to be related more to their socioeconomic status than to their ethnic socialization or culture.

Why Does Ethnicity Persist Across Social Classes?

In his important and influential publication, Gordon hypothesizes that social-class differences are more important and decisive than ethnic-group differences.[37] He also states that people of the same social class will share behavioral similarities. Gordon emphasizes the importance of social class in shaping behavior. His "ethclass" hypotheses need to be revised and made more consistent with the research and thinking that have taken place during the last two decades.[38]

Gordon's hypotheses are not consistent with many of the studies reviewed in this paper. His ethclass hypotheses predict that social class has a stronger effect on behavior than ethnicity has on behavior. However, this does not seem to be the case for behavior related to the learning and cognitive styles of Afro-Americans and Mexican Americans. We need to examine why there is an inconsistency between Gordon's hypotheses and the research reviewed in this article.

I believe that this inconsistency results primarily from a major problem in social science

research in the United States related to the conceptualization and study of social classes within non-White populations such as Afro-Americans and Mexican Americans. The tendency in social science is to use standard indices such as occupation, income, and educational level to identify lower-class and middle-class populations within these groups and to compare them with White populations with similar occupational, income, and educational characteristics. The assumption is made that social-class groups within the non-White populations and those within the White population are equivalent.

The comparative study of social classes across ethnic groups in the United States creates problems in both theory construction and in the formulation of valid generalizations because significant differences often exist between Blacks and Whites with similar income, educational, and occupational characteristics. The study of the Black middle class is a case in point. Most middle-class White families live in a middle-class community, have middle-class relatives and friends, and send their children to middle-class schools. This may or may not be true of a middle-class Black family. Approximately 55 percent of Blacks in the United States are members of the lower class.[39] Many Black middle-class families have relatives who are working class or lower class. Black middle-class families often live in mixed-class neighborhoods, participate in community organizations and institutions that have participants from all social-class groups, and often visit relatives who live in the inner city.[40]

Many Blacks are also members of an extended family, which often includes lower- and working-class relatives. Lower-class relatives often play an important role in the socialization of their children. These relatives may serve as babysitters

[37]Gordon, *Assimilation in American Life.*
[38]H. P. McAdoo and J. L. McAdoo, eds., *Black Children: Social, Educational, and Parental Environments* (Beverly Hills: Sage Publications, 1985).

[39]J. E. Blackwell, *The Black Community: Unity and Diversity,* 2nd ed. (New York: Harper and Row, 1985).
[40]J. A. Banks, "An Exploratory Study of Assimilation, Pluralism, and Marginality: Black Families in Predominantly White Suburbs," document resume in *Resources in Education.* ERIC document 257-175.

for short and long periods for the middle-class family. There is a strong expectation within the Black extended family that the individual who becomes middle class will not forsake his or her family and should help it financially when necessary.[41] Unlike many middle-class White families, which tend to function highly independently within a largely middle-class world, the middle-class Black family is often a first-generation middle-class family that exists within an extended family and a community network that have definite group expectations for it and strongly influence its behaviors and options. Many of the generalizations made here about Black families are also true for Mexican American and Puerto Rican American middle-class families.[42]

THE PERSISTENCE OF ETHNICITY: THEORY AND RESEARCH IMPLICATIONS

To reformulate Gordon's ethclass hypotheses to make them more consistent with research that has taken place in the last two decades, we need to recognize the persistence of ethnicity when social-class mobility takes place. This is especially the case when an ethnic group is non-White and is a part of a group that has a disproportionately large working-class or lower-class population. Significant differences exist for the individual who is middle class but functions within a community that is primarily working class or lower class, and for the individual who is middle class but who functions within a predominantly middle-class community. Taking these factors into account, we may reformulate one of Gordon's hypotheses to read: With regard to cultural behavior, ethnicity continues to influence the behavior of members of ethnic groups with certain characteristics when social mobility

occurs. This means that while people of the same social class from different ethnic groups will exhibit some similar behaviors, they will have some significant behavioral differences caused by the persistence of ethnicity.

When studying race, class, and ethnicity, social scientists need to examine *generational middle-class status* as a variable. There are often important behavioral and attitudinal differences between a Black individual who grew up poor and became middle class within his or her adulthood and a Black who is fourth-generation middle class. Many of the middle-class Afro-Americans and Mexican Americans described in existing research studies are probably first-generation middle class. Such individuals are sometimes compared with Whites who have been middle class for several generations. Generational social-class status needs to be varied systematically in research studies so that we can learn more about the tenacity of ethnicity across generations.

Other Research Implications

We need more replications of studies related to race, class, and cognitive styles. One of the major problems with the research is that various researchers formulate different questions, study subjects of different ages who attend different kinds of schools, use different statistical analysis techniques, and use different instruments to measure the same variables. Important lines of inquiry on problems related to ethnic groups and cognitive styles are begun but not pursued until valid generalizations and theories have been formulated. Lesser, Fifer, and Clark published a pathbreaking study that described the patterns of mental abilities of ethnic minorities in 1967. However, we know little more about patterns of mental abilities in ethnic groups today than we knew in 1967. Neither the original researchers nor other students have pursued this line of inquiry in any systematic way. As a result, the research on learning patterns among ethnic minorities remains thin and fragmented, and provides few insights that can guide practice.

---

[41]E. P. Martin and J. M. Martin, *The Black Extended Family* (Chicago: The University of Chicago Press, 1978).
[42]J. W. Moore and H. Pachon, *Mexican Americans,* 2nd ed. (Englewood Cliffs, N.J.: Prentice-Hall, 1976).

THE PERSISTENCE OF ETHNICITY: IMPLICATIONS FOR PRACTICE

Teachers and other practitioners reading the review of research in this article are likely to be disappointed by the fragmentary nature of the research that exists on ethnicity, social class, and cognitive styles. It is difficult to find such studies. Nevertheless, we can glean some guidelines for practice from the research.

The research suggests that students will come to the classroom with many kinds of differences, some of which may be related to their ethnic group, their social-class status, or social class and ethnicity combined. Research suggests that Afro-American and Mexican American students tend to be more field sensitive in their learning styles than are mainstream Anglo-American students. This means that Mexican American and Afro-American students are more likely to be motivated by curriculum content that is presented in a humanized or story format than are mainstream Anglo students. The research also suggests that middle-class students tend to be more internal than are lower-class students. This suggests that teachers will need to work with many lower-class students to help them to see the relationship between their effort and their academic performance.

It is important for teachers to understand that the characteristics of ethnic groups and socioeconomic classes can help us to understand groups but not individual students. All types of learning and motivational styles are found within *all* ethnic groups and social classes. Many Afro-American students are field independent and analytic; many White students are field dependent and relational. The teacher cannot assume that every Mexican American student is field dependent and that every Anglo student is field independent. These kinds of assumptions result in new stereotypes and problems. There is a delicate and difficult balance between using generalizations about groups to better understand and interpret the behavior of groups, and using that knowledge to interpret the behavior of a particular student. Cox and Ramírez have described some of the difficulties that resulted when practitioners applied their research on cognitive styles:

The dissemination of research information on cognitive styles has also had a negative effect in some cases, arising primarily from common problems associated with looking at mean differences; that is, by using averages to describe differences between groups, the dangers of stereotyping are more likely. The great diversity within any culture is ignored, and a construct which should be used as a tool for individualization becomes yet another label for categorizing and evaluating.[43]

Teachers should recognize that students bring a variety of learning, cognitive, and motivational styles to the classroom, and that while certain characteristics are associated with specific ethnic and social-class groups, these characteristics are distributed throughout the total student population. This means that the teacher should use a variety of teaching styles and content that will appeal to diverse students. Concepts should be taught when possible with different strategies so that students who are relational in their learning styles as well as those who are analytic will have an equal opportunity to learn. Researchers such as Slavin and Cohen have documented that cooperative learning strategies appeal to ethnic-group students and foster positive intergroup attitudes and feelings.[44]

Teachers should also select content from diverse ethnic groups so that students from various cultures will see their images in the curriculum.[45] Educational equity will exist for all students when teachers become sensitive to the cultural diversity in their classrooms, vary their teaching styles so as to appeal to a diverse student population, and modify their curricula to include ethnic content. This is a tall but essential order in an ethnically and racially diverse nation that is wasting so much of its human potential.

---

[43]B. G. Cox and M. Ramírez, "Cognitive Styles: Implications for Multiethnic Education," in *Education in the 80s: Multiethnic Education,* ed. J. A. Banks (Washington, D.C.: National Education Association, 1981), pp. 61–71.

[44]R. E. Slavin, *Cooperative Learning* (New York: Longman, 1983); E. G. Cohen, *Designing Groupwork: Strategies for the Heterogeneous Classroom* (New York: Teachers College Press, 1986).

[45]J. A. Banks, *Teaching Strategies for Ethnic Studies,* 4th ed. (Boston: Allyn and Bacon, 1987).

EGOCENTRISM IN ADOLESCENCE

DAVID ELKIND
Tufts University

Within the Piagetian theory of intellectual growth, the concept of egocentrism generally refers to a lack of differentiation in some area of subject-object interaction (Piaget, 1962). At each stage of mental development, this lack of differentiation takes a unique form and is manifested in a unique set of behaviors. The transition from one form of egocentrism to another takes place in a dialectic fashion such that the mental structures which free the child from a lower form of egocentrism are the same structures which ensnare him in a higher form of egocentrism. From the developmental point of view, therefore, egocentrism can be regarded as a negative by-product of any emergent mental system in the sense that it corresponds to the fresh cognitive problems engendered by that system.

Although in recent years Piaget has focused his attention more on the positive than on the negative products of mental structures, egocentrism continues to be of interest because of its relation to the affective aspects of child thought and behavior. Indeed, it is possible that the study of egocentrism may provide a bridge between the study of cognitive structure, on the one hand,

and the exploration of personality dynamics, on the other (Cowan, 1966; Gourevitch & Feffer, 1962). The purpose of the present paper is to describe, in greater detail than Inhelder and Piaget (1958), what seems to me to be the nature of egocentrism in adolescence and some of its behavioral and experiential correlates. Before doing that, however, it might be well to set the stage for the discussion with a brief review of the forms of egocentrism which precede this mode of thought in adolescence.

FORMS OF EGOCENTRISM
IN INFANCY AND CHILDHOOD

In presenting the childhood forms of egocentrism, it is useful to treat each of Piaget's major stages as if it were primarily concerned with resolving one major cognitive task. The egocentrism of a particular stage can then be described with reference to this special problem of cognition. It must be stressed, however, that while the cognitive task characteristic of a particular stage seems to attract the major share of the child's mental energies, it is not the only cognitive problem with which the child is attempting to cope. In mental development there are major battles and minor skirmishes, and if I here ignore the lesser engagements it is for purposes of economy of presentation rather than because I assume that such engagements are insignificant.

From *Child Development*, 1967, *38,* 1025–1034. © 1967 by The Society for Research in Child Development, Inc. Reprinted by permission of the author and The Society for Research in Child Development.

Sensori-Motor Egocentrism (0–2 Years)

The major cognitive task of infancy might be regarded as the *conquest of the object.* In the early months of life, the infant deals with objects as if their existence were dependent upon their being present in immediate perception (Charlesworth, 1966; Piaget, 1954). The egocentrism of this stage corresponds, therefore, to a lack of differentiation between the object and the sense impressions occasioned by it. Toward the end of the first year, however, the infant begins to seek the object even when it is hidden, and thus shows that he can now differentiate between the object and the "experience of the object." This breakdown of egocentrism with respect to objects is brought about by mental representation of the absent object.* An internal representation of the absent object is the earliest manifestation of the symbolic function which develops gradually during the second year of life and whose activities dominate the next stage of mental growth.

Pre-Operational Egocentrism (2–6 Years)

During the preschool period, the child's major cognitive task can be regarded as *the conquest of the symbol.* It is during the preschool period that the symbolic function becomes fully active, as evidenced by the rapid growth in the acquisition and utilization of language, by the appearance of symbolic play, and by the first reports of dreams. Yet this new capacity for representation, which loosed the infant from his egocentrism with respect to objects, now ensnares the preschool children in a new egocentrism with regard to symbols. At the beginning of this period, the child fails to differentiate between words and their referents (Piaget 1952b) and between his self-created play and dream symbols and reality (Kohlberg, 1966; Piaget, 1951). Children at this stage believe that the name inheres in the thing and that an object cannot have more than one name (Elkind, 1961a, 1962, 1963).

The egocentrism of this period is particularly evident in children's linguistic behavior. When explaining a piece of apparatus to another child, for example, the youngster at this stage uses many indefinite terms and leaves out important information (Piaget, 1952b). Although this observation is sometimes explained by saying that the child fails to take the other person's point of view, it can also be explained by saying that the child assumes words carry much more information than they actually do. This results from his belief that even the indefinite "thing" somehow conveys the properties of the object which it is used to represent. In short, the egocentrism of this period consists in a lack of clear differentiation between symbols and their referents.

Toward the end of the pre-operational period, the differentiation between symbols and their referents is gradually brought about by the emergence of concrete operations (internalized actions which are roughly comparable in their activity to the elementary operations of arithmetic). One consequence of concrete operational thought is that it enables the child to deal with two elements, properties, or relations at the same time. A child with concrete operations can, for example, take account of both the height and width of a glass of colored liquid and recognize that, when the liquid is poured into a differently shaped container, the changes in height and width of the liquid compensate one another so that the total quantity of liquid is conserved (Elkind, 1961b; Piaget, 1952a). This ability, to hold two dimensions in mind at the same time, also enables the child to hold both symbol and referent in mind simultaneously, and thus distinguish between them. Concrete operations are, therefore, instrumental in overcoming the egocentrism of the pre-operational stage.

Concrete Operational Egocentrism (7–11 Years)

With the emergence of concrete operations, the major cognitive task of the school-age child becomes that of *mastering classes, relations, and quantities.* While the preschool child forms

---

*It is characteristic of the dialectic of mental growth that the capacity to represent internally the absent object also enables the infant to cognize the object as externally existent.

global notions of classes, relations, and quantities, such notions are imprecise and cannot be combined one with the other. The child with concrete operations, on the other hand, can nest classes, seriate relations, and conserve quantities. In addition, concrete operations enable the school-age child to perform elementary syllogistic reasoning and to formulate hypotheses and explanations about concrete matters. This system of concrete operations, however, which lifts the school-age child to new heights of thought, nonetheless lowers him to new depths of egocentrism.

Operations are essentially mental tools whose products, series, class hierarchies, conservations, etc., are not directly derived from experience. At this stage, however, the child nonetheless regards these mental products as being on a par with perceptual phenomena. It is the inability to differentiate clearly between mental constructions and perceptual givens which constitutes the egocentrism of the school-age child. An example may help to clarify the form which egocentrism takes during the concrete operational stage.

In a study reported by Peel (1960), children and adolescents were read a passage about Stonehenge and then asked questions about it. One of the questions had to do with whether Stonehenge was a place for religious worship or a fort. The children (ages 7–10) answered the question with flat statements, as if they were stating a fact. When they were given evidence that contradicted their statements, they rationalized the evidence to make it conform with their initial position. Adolescents, on the other hand, phrased their replies in probabilistic terms and supported their judgments with material gleaned from the passage. Similar differences between children and adolescents have been found by Elkind (1966) and Weir (1964).

What these studies show is that, when a child constructs a hypothesis or formulates a strategy, he assumes that this product is imposed by the data rather than derived from his own mental activity. When his position is challenged, he does not change his stance but, on the contrary, reinterprets the data to fit with his assumption. This

observation, however, raises a puzzling question. Why, if the child regards both his thought products and the givens of perception as coming from the environment, does he nonetheless give preference to his own mental constructions? The answer probably lies in the fact that the child's mental constructions are the product of reasoning, and hence are experienced as imbued with a (logical) necessity. This "felt" necessity is absent when the child experiences the products of perception. It is not surprising, then, that the child should give priority to what seems permanent and necessary in perception (the products of his own thought, such as conservation) rather than to what seems transitory and arbitrary in perception (products of environmental stimulation). Only in adolescence do young people differentiate between their own mental constructions and the givens of perception. For the child, there are no problems of epistemology.

Toward the end of childhood, the emergence of formal operational thought (which is analogous to propositional logic) gradually frees the child from his egocentrism with respect to his own mental constructions. As Inhelder and Piaget (1958) have shown, formal operational thought enables the young person to deal with all of the possible combinations and permutations of elements within a given set. Provided with four differently colored pieces of plastic, for example, the adolescent can work out all the possible combinations of colors by taking the pieces one, two, three and four, and none, at a time. Children, on the other hand, cannot formulate these combinations in any systematic way. The ability to conceptualize all of the possible combinations in a system allows the adolescent to construct contrary-to-fact hypotheses and to reason about such propositions "as if" they were true. The adolescent, for example, can accept the statement, "Let's suppose coal is white," whereas the child will reply, "But coal is black." This ability to formulate contrary-to-fact hypotheses is crucial to the overcoming of the egocentrism of the concrete operational period. Through the formulation of such contrary-to-fact hypotheses, the young person discovers the arbitrariness of his own mental constructions and learns to differentiate them from perceptual reality.

ADOLESCENT EGOCENTRISM

From the strictly cognitive point of view (as opposed to the psychoanalytic point of view as represented by Blos [1962] and A. Freud [1946] or the ego psychological point of view as represented by Erikson [1959]), the major task of early adolescence can be regarded as having to do with *the conquest of thought.* Formal operations not only permit the young person to construct all the possibilities in a system and construct contrary-to-fact propositions (Inhelder & Piaget [1958]); they also enable him to conceptualize his own thought, to take his mental constructions as objects and reason about them. Only at about the ages of 11–12, for example, do children spontaneously introduce concepts of belief, intelligence, and faith into their definitions of their religious denomination (Elkind, 1961a; 1962; 1963). Once more, however, this new mental system which frees the young person from the egocentrism of childhood entangles him in a new form of egocentrism characteristic of adolescence.

Formal operational thought not only enables the adolescent to conceptualize his thought, it also permits him to conceptualize the thought of other people. It is this capacity to take account of other people's thought, however, which is the crux of adolescent egocentrism. This egocentrism emerges because, while the adolescent can now cognize the thoughts of others, he fails to differentiate between the objects toward which the thoughts of others are directed and those which are the focus of his own concern. Now, it is well known that the young adolescent, because of the physiological metamorphosis he is undergoing, is primarily concerned with himself. Accordingly, since he fails to differentiate between what others are thinking about and his own mental preoccupations, he assumes that other people are as obsessed with his behavior and appearance as he is himself. *It is this belief that others are preoccupied with his appearance and behavior that constitutes the egocentrism of the adolescent.*

One consequence of adolescent egocentrism is that, in actual or impending social situations, the young person anticipates the reactions of other people to himself. These anticipations, however, are based on the premise that others are as admiring or as critical of him as he is of himself. In a sense, then, the adolescent is continually constructing, or reacting to, *an imaginary audience.* It is an audience because the adolescent believes that he will be the focus of attention; and it is imaginary because, in actual social situations, this is not usually the case (unless he contrives to make it so). The construction of imaginary audiences would seem to account, in part at least, for a wide variety of typical adolescent behaviors and experiences.

The imaginary audience, for example, probably plays a role in the self-consciousness which is so characteristic of early adolescence. When the young person is feeling critical of himself, he anticipates that the audience—of which he is necessarily a part—will be critical too. And, since the audience is his own construction and privy to his own knowledge of himself, it knows just what to look for in the way of cosmetic and behavioral sensitivities. The adolescent's wish for privacy and his reluctance to reveal himself may, to some extent, be a reaction to the feeling of being under the constant critical scrutiny of other people. The notion of an imaginary audience also helps to explain the observation that the affect which most concerns adolescents is not guilt but, rather, shame, that is, the reaction to an audience (Lynd, 1961).

While the adolescent is often self-critical, he is frequently self-admiring too. At such times, the audience takes on the same affective coloration. A good deal of adolescent boorishness, loudness, and faddish dress is probably provoked, partially in any case, by a failure to differentiate between what the young person believes to be attractive and what others admire. It is for this reason that the young person frequently fails to understand why adults disapprove of the way he dresses and behaves. The same sort of egocentrism is often seen in behavior directed toward the opposite sex. The boy who stands in front of the mirror for 2 hours combing his hair is probably imagining the swooning reactions he will produce in the girls. Likewise, the girl applying her makeup is more likely than not imagining the admiring glances that will come her way. When these young people actually meet, each is more concerned with being the observed than with being the observer. Gatherings of young adolescents are unique in the sense that each young person is simultaneously an actor to himself and an audience to others.

One of the most common admiring audience constructions, in the adolescent, is the anticipation of how others will react to his own demise. A certain bittersweet pleasure is derived from anticipating the belated recognition by others of his positive qualities. As often happens with such universal fantasies, the imaginary anticipation of one's own demise has been realized in fiction. Below, for example, is the passage in *Tom Sawyer* where Tom sneaks back to his home, after having run away with Joe and Huck, to discover that he and his friends are thought to have been drowned:

> But this memory was too much for the old lady, and she broke entirely down. Tom was snuffling, now, himself—and more in pity of himself than anybody else. He could hear Mary crying and putting in a kindly word for him from time to time. He began to have a nobler opinion of himself than ever before. Still, he was sufficiently touched by his aunt's grief to long to rush out from under the bed and overwhelm her with joy—and the theatrical gorgeousness of the thing appealed strongly to his nature too—but he resisted and lay still.

Corresponding to the imaginary audience is another mental construction which is its complement. While the adolescent fails to differentiate the concerns of his own thought from those of others, he at the same time overdifferentiates his feelings. Perhaps because he believes he is of importance to so many people, the imaginary au-

dience, he comes to regard himself, and particularly his feelings, as something special and unique. Only he can suffer with such agonized intensity, or experience such exquisite rapture. How many parents have been confronted with the typically adolescent phrase, "But you don't know how it feels. . . ." The emotional torments undergone by Goethe's young Werther and by Salinger's Holden Caulfield exemplify the adolescent's belief in the uniqueness of his own emotional experience. At a somewhat different level, this belief in personal uniqueness becomes a conviction that he will not die, that death will happen to others but not to him. This complex of beliefs in the uniqueness of his feelings and of his immortality might be called *a personal fable,* a story which he tells himself and which is not true.

Evidence of the personal fable is particularly prominent in adolescent diaries. Such diaries are often written for posterity in the conviction that the young person's experiences, crushes, and frustrations are of universal significance and importance. Another kind of evidence for the personal fable during this period is the tendency to confide in a personal God. The search for privacy and the belief in personal uniqueness leads to the establishment of an I-Thou relationship with God as a personal confidant to whom one no longer looks for gifts but rather for guidance and support (Long, Elkind, & Spilka, 1967).

The concepts of an imaginary audience and a personal fable have proved useful, at least to the writer, in the understanding and treatment of troubled adolescents. The imaginary audience, for example, seems often to play a role in middle-class delinquency (Elkind, 1967). As a case in point, one young man took $1,000 from a golf tournament purse, hid the money, and then promptly revealed himself. It turned out that much of the motivation for this act was derived from the anticipated response of "the audience" to the guttiness of his action. In a similar vein, many young girls become pregnant because, in part at least, their personal fable convinces them that pregnancy will happen to others but never to them and so they need not take precautions. Such examples could be multiplied but will perhaps suffice to illustrate how adolescent egocentrism, as manifested in the imaginary audience and in the personal fable, can help provide a rationale for some adolescent behavior. These concepts can, moreover, be utilized in the treatment of adolescent offenders. It is often helpful to these young people if they can learn to differentiate between the real and the imaginary audience, which often boils down to a discrimination between the real and the imaginary parents.

THE PASSING OF ADOLESCENT EGOCENTRISM

After the appearance of formal operational thought, no new mental systems develop and the mental structures of adolescence must serve for the rest of the life span. The egocentrism of early adolescence nonetheless tends to diminish by the age of 15 or 16, the age at which formal operations become firmly established. What appears to happen is that the imaginary audience, which is primarily an anticipatory audience, is progressively modified in the direction of the reactions of the real audience. In a way, the imaginary audience can be regarded as hypothesis—or better, as a series of hypotheses—which the young person tests against reality. As a consequence of this testing, he gradually comes to recognize the difference between his own preoccupations and the interests and concerns of others.

The personal fable, on the other hand, is probably overcome (although probably never in its entirety) by the gradual establishment of what Erikson (1959) has called "intimacy." Once the young person sees himself in a more realistic light as a function of having adjusted his imaginary audience to the real one, he can establish true rather than self-interested interpersonal relations. Once relations of mutuality are established and confidences are shared, the young person discovers that others have feelings similar to his own and have suffered and been enraptured in the same way.

Adolescent egocentrism is thus overcome by a two-fold transformation. On the cognitive plane, it is overcome by the gradual differentiation between his own preoccupations and the thoughts of others; while on the plane of affectivity, it is overcome by a gradual integration of the feelings of others with his own emotions.

SUMMARY AND CONCLUSIONS

In this paper I have tried to describe the forms which egocentrism takes and the mechanisms by which it is overcome, in the course of mental development. In infancy, egocentrism corresponds to the impression that objects are identical with the perception of them, and this form of egocentrism is overcome with the appearance of representation. During the preschool period, egocentrism appears in the guise of a belief that symbols contain the same information as is provided by the objects which they represent. With the emergence of concrete operations, the child is able to discriminate between symbol and referent, and so overcome this type of egocentrism. The egocentrism of the school-age period can be characterized as the belief that one's own mental constructions correspond to a superior form of perceptual reality. With the advent of formal operations and the ability to construct contrary-to-fact hypotheses, this kind of egocentrism is dissolved because the young person can now recognize the arbitrariness of his own mental constructions. Finally, during early adolescence, egocentrism appears as the belief that the thoughts of others are directed toward the self. This variety of egocentrism is overcome as a consequence of the conflict between the reactions which the young person anticipates and those which actually occur.

Although egocentrism corresponds to a negative product of mental growth, its usefulness would seem to lie in the light which it throws upon the affective reactions characteristic of any particular stage of mental development. In this paper I have dealt primarily with the affective reactions associated with the egocentrism of adolescence. Much of the material, particularly the discussion of the *imaginary audience* and the *personal fable* is speculative in the sense that it is based as much upon my clinical experience with young people as it is upon research data. These constructs are offered, not as the final word on adolescent egocentrism, but rather to illustrate how the cognitive structures peculiar to a particular level of development can be related to the affective experience and behavior characteristic of that stage. Although I have here only considered the correspondence between mental structure and affect in adolescence, it is possible that similar correspondences can be found at the earlier levels of development as well. A consideration of egocentrism, then, would seem to be a useful starting point for any attempt to reconcile cognitive structure and the dynamics of personality.

REFERENCES

Blos, P. *On adolescence.* New York: Free Press, 1962.

Charlesworth, W. R. Development of the object concept in infancy: Methodological study. *American Psychologist,* 1966, 21, 623. (Abstract)

Cowan, P. A. Cognitive egocentrism and social interaction in children. *American Psychologist,* 1966, 21, 623. (Abstract)

Elkind, D. The child's conception of his religious denomination, I: The Jewish child. *Journal of Genetic Psychology,* 1961, 99, 209–225. (a)

_____. The development of quantitative thinking. *Journal of Genetic Psychology,* 1961, 98, 37–46. (b)

_____. The child's conception of his religious denomination, II: The Catholic child. *Journal of Genetic Psychology,* 1962, 101, 185–193.

_____. The child's conception of his religious denomination, III: The Protestant child. *Journal of Genetic Psychology,* 1963, 103, 291–304.

_____. Conceptual orientation shifts in children and adolescents. *Child Development,* 1966, 37, 493–498.

_____. Middle-class delinquency. *Mental Hygiene,* 1967, 51, 80–84.

Erikson, E. H. Identity and the life cycle. *Psychological issues.* Vol. I, No. I, New York: International Universities Press, 1959.

Freud, A. *The ego and the mechanisms of defense.* New York: International Universities Press, 1946.

Gourevitch, V., & Feffer, M. H. A study of motivational development. *Journal of Genetic Psychology,* 1962, 100, 361–375.

Inhelder, B., & Piaget, J. *The growth of logical thinking from childhood to adolescence.* New York: Basic Books, 1958.

Kohlberg, L. Cognitive stages and preschool education. *Human Development,* 1966, 9, 5–17.

Long, D., Elkind, D., & Spilka, B. The child's conception of prayer. *Journal for the Scientific Study of Religion,* 1967, 6, 101–109.

Lynd, H. M. *On shame and the search for identity.* New York: Science Editions, 1961.

Peel, E. A. *The pupil's thinking.* London: Oldhourne, 1960.

Piaget, J. *The child's conception of the world.* London: Routledge & Kegan Paul, 1951.

_____. *The child's conception of number.* New York: Humanities Press, 1952. (a)

_____. *The language and thought of the child.* London: Routledge & Kegan Paul, 1952. (b)

_____. *The construction of reality in the child.* New York: Basic Books, 1954.

_____. *Comments on Vygotsky's critical remarks concerning "The language and thought of the child" and "Judgment and reasoning in the child."* Cambridge, Mass.: M.I.T. Press, 1962.

Weir, M. W. Development changes in problem solving strategies. *Psychological Review,* 1964, 71, 473–490.

PART FOUR

THE FAMILY

When I was seven, my father knew everything, when I was fourteen,
my father knew nothing, but when I was twenty-one, I was amazed at
how much the old man had learned in those seven years.
—MARK TWAIN

As children enter adolescence and begin to develop their own "philosophy of life," they frequently begin to question the rules, values, and belief systems of their parents. Many want more recognition and expect a different treatment from their family. Seeking a more egalitarian role in their family, adolescents, sometimes gracefully but sometimes aggressively, put pressure on the adults in their lives to make room "at the top." Theorists have described this intergenerational conflict as a crisis: Hall (storm and stress), Freud (detachment from parents), Erikson (identity crises), Blos (individuation process), and Sullivan (increasing interpersonal complexity) all depicted adolescence as a time of inevitable turmoil. Mark Twain's quote captures the spirit of these ideas. More recently, family-systems theory has contributed to this view by underscoring the stress that accompanies the change from a hierarchical parent-child relationship to a more egalitarian parent adolescent system.

Nevertheless, not all researchers agree that adolescence is synonymous with family discord. Data suggests that parent-adolescent relationships, except for a few exceptions, are neither more stressful nor more fraught with conflict than family relationships in any other stage of development.

Montemayor's (11) review of research brings some broad perspective to this controversy. The debate deals with whether a conflict between parents and adolescents is an inescapable developmental phenomenon or whether the inevitability of such conflict has been distorted by psychoanalytic theory and by the media's relentless focus on difficulties, thus giving the impression that troublesome youth have become the norm.

Montemayor reviews three components of the problem: (1) Are there age changes in conflict, such as before, during, and after adolescence? Data suggest, as does Mark Twain's observation, an inverted U-shape with lower levels of conflict existing before and after but increasing during pubescence. (2) What are the issues that cause conflicts? An analysis covering 50 years of research shows that the issues over which parent-adolescent conflicts arise have changed surprisingly little: they continue to include schoolwork, chores, social life, clothing, disobedience, and personal hygiene. (3) Is there a relationship between parent-adolescent conflicts and adolescent behavior? Like other theorists, especially Erikson, Montemayor maintains that some disagreement may be a normal, healthy, growth-producing component of autonomy development. In contrast, more serious and sustained family conflicts, such as emotional, physical, and sexual abuse or frequent, painful, demeaning confrontations, may contribute to more severe problems: running away, pregnancy, eating disorders, delinquency, school failure, even suicide.

In their ground-breaking longitudinal studies, Glueck and Glueck, as a lifetime endeavor, compared carefully matched groups of 500 delinquent and 500 nondelinquent boys from impoverished homes. They identified factors (physique, personality traits, recreational preferences, and family characteristics) which distinguished these two groups and resulted in a highly accurate scale for predicting delinquency. The following are some of the most powerful family characteristic predictors: (1) discipline of the boy by his father; (2) supervision of the boy by his mother; (3) affection of the father for the boy; (4) affection of the mother for the boy; and (5) family cohesiveness. Sampson and Laub (12) reanalyzed Glueck and Glueck's data and proposed the hypothesis that "family poverty inhibits family processes of informal social control, in turn increasing the likelihood of juvenile delinquency." In addition, children who have difficulty in managing their temperaments and who live in poverty seem to self-select antisocial behavior. The disciplinary practices, supervision, parental controls, and bonds of attachment (Glueck and Glueck's family factors) constitute contextual variables that influence the development of either delinquency or socially well-adjusted behavior.

Since juvenile crime has increased, studies that examine the relationship between parent-adolescent intimacy and problem behaviors are of practical importance. Field, Lang, Yando, and Bendell (13) investigated the relationship between the following variables: family intimacy, demographics, social and school factors, and problem behaviors such as drug use. Subjects who had higher self-esteem experienced less depression, expressed no suicidal ideation, and felt closer to their parents. Surprisingly, none of the variables was related to peer intimacy. When adolescents maintained positive connections with their families, they exhibited socially desirable behaviors and goals. Family interactions change as a function of development; however, those young people who reported continued family attachment also reported a greater sense of well-being than those who didn't. A nourishing family relationship appeared to serve as a significant insulator against self-destructive behavior. Resnick et al. (35) arrived at similar conclusions.

During adolescence the efforts to find a balance between dependence and independence, connection and autonomy are most pronounced and almost inevitable. Personal exploration is a part of identity formation. Actually, parent-adolescent conflict is not an either-or proposition but should be viewed as a continuum. For some, family relationships remain stable and harmonious and reveal no significant increase in conflict. For others, moderate, temporary, but not insignificant conflicts do erupt but do not lead to permanent disharmony. At the other end of the continuum, relationships are conflicted and there is little evidence of mutual trust and supportive family functioning. Kipke et al. (37) described the more extreme cases of family dysfunction, in which children become street youth.

Certainly the emergence of adolescent desires to have a voice, to disagree and to question can create stress, disharmony, and disengagement. There are theorists who believe adolescence inevitably creates family discord. However, others believe that this is a myth and that harmonious interactions are quite possible. Nevertheless, no one questions that the metamorphosis from child to adult requires some readjustment for everyone involved.

PARENTS AND ADOLESCENTS IN CONFLICT

RAYMOND MONTEMAYOR
Ohio State University

According to some, the young and the old are paired-off and engaged in a continual and oftentimes heated generational conflict that pits energy and idealism against wisdom and realism. Although the phrase "generation gap" was invented during the decade of the 1960s, the idea itself is not new. Indeed, as Goethals (1975) pointed out, the theme of generational conflict is a basic motif in the portrayal of the relations between generations and its origins are ancient, appearing in one of its most widely known forms in the myth of Daedalus and Icarus. Daedalus the wise and skilled craftsman constructs wings of wax and feathers by which both he and his son can escape from their tower prison. The father carefully instructs Icarus on the proper use of the wings and tearfully kisses him before they both set out on their flight to freedom, a flight that ends fatally for Icarus who impetuously disobeys his father and flies too close to the sun, melting the wax and plunging the boy into the ocean. If one side of the moral of this story is that to disobey one's parents may have disastrous, even fatal consequences, the other side is that the young must discover this for themselves. Thus the conflict—life must be experienced and the knowledge of

the old may serve as only a partial guide for the young, to the continual dismay of parents.

Does this charming story with its ancient warning accurately capture the essence of parent-adolescent relations, or does it merely highlight and bring to the fore one aspect of those relations? The interactions between parents and their adolescent sons and daughters are sometimes, perhaps even oftentimes, disagreeable and stressful. But are those interactions characterized by turmoil to the degree that it is both normal and normative for parents and their adolescent children to be in conflict?

THEORIES OF PARENT-ADOLESCENT CONFLICT

Virtually all adolescent theorists agree that the stage of adolescence is inherently stressful and that parent-adolescent relations are likely to be more conflictual than parent-child relations, but there is disagreement about what produces the stress. Explanations of parent-adolescent stress can be divided into two broad classes, those that emphasize individual characteristics and those that focus on family relations.

Traditionally, parent-adolescent stress has been viewed as the result of changes in adolescents brought about by puberty. A variety of adolescent factors have been proposed to account for

From Raymond Montemayor, *Journal of Early Adolescence*, 1983, *3*, 83–103. Copyright 1983 by Sage Publications. Reprinted by permission of the author and Sage Publications, Inc.

stress with parents, such as biological changes in levels of aggression (Hall, 1904), the appearance of adult sexuality (Blos, 1962; Freud, 1905/1953), the need for independence (Ausubel, Montemayor, & Svajian, 1977), and the search for an identity (Erikson, 1968). More recently, the cause of this stress has been laid on the parent's doorstep, and it has been suggested that many parents of adolescents experience a midlife disillusionment with their career and marriage which could lead to increases in parenting stress (Hill, 1980; Prosen, Towes, & Martin, 1981). Also, mothers have been regarded as at least partly responsible for some mother-adolescent difficulties. Specifically, it has been claimed that many mothers are reluctant to relinquish control of their adolescents, and that much mother-adolescent interaction revolves around her effort to keep her adolescent within the family circle, while the adolescent attempts to break free (Turner, 1970).

More recent attempts to explain parent-adolescent stress have not focused on the individual characteristics of adolescents or parents but have emphasized transformations of family patterns of interaction. The parent-child social system is pictured as relatively stable and predictable. Presumably, family members have spent years developing patterns of interaction which are known and acceptable to all. The physical, psychological, and social changes that occur during the adolescent period are thought to disrupt this smoothly functioning system and, it is argued, a readjustment of the parent-child system must occur in order to achieve a new homeostasis (Morton, Alexander, & Altman, 1976). The hierarchical parent-child system must be replaced by an egalitarian peer-peer system in which parents and adolescents occupy a more nearly equal status. During the replacement process family members must learn new behaviors based on their new statuses. This relearning is regarded as stressful for the participants and, until new relationships are established, conflicts due to poor communication and unmet expectations are supposed to be common (Boszormenyi-Nagy, 1973).

The above theorists postulate different mechanisms to account for conflict, but their theories all share three common features. First, adolescence is regarded as a major transitional period during which important qualitative changes occur in development. Adolescence is seen as a time when individuals enter adulthood and acquire mature forms of thought, emotion, and behavior. Second, the transition from childhood to adulthood is regarded as inherently stressful. It is widely held that adolescents experience the biological, psychological, and social changes that occur during puberty as disorienting and perturbing. Third, adolescents are thought to lack mature skills to cope with these changes and, therefore, experience a high degree of what has been referred to as "transitional stress."

The idea that parent-adolescent relations are stressful is widely accepted not only by adolescent theorists and many practicing clinicians, but also by many parents of adolescents and the adolescents themselves. For example, in one study of the difficulty of parenting children of various ages mothers reported more problems with their adolescents than with any other age group, especially in regard to the adolescent's moodiness, independence and discipline (Ballenski & Cook, 1982). In another study, a multidimensional scaling technique was used to examine late adolescents' perceptions of interpersonal relations. These college students described the typical parent-teenager relationship as most similar to the relationships of mother-in-law and son-in-law, and guard and prisoner (Wish, Deutsch, & Kaplan, 1976).

Given these perceptions, it is no wonder that clinicians, parents of adolescents, and adolescents have an interest in information on parent-adolescent conflict. Most self-help books written for parents of adolescents (e.g. Ginott, 1969; Schowalter & Anyan, 1979) and some written for the adolescents themselves (Gnagey, 1975) contain chapters on adolescent management skills and conflict resolution strategies. Apparently many parents have some temporary problems in these areas and some have serious difficulties with adolescent conflict. Within the past few years a number of treatment programs have been developed which are designed to help family members control parent-adolescent conflict. These approaches are based on social learning theory (Gant, Barnard, Kuehn, Jones, & Christophersen, 1981), behavioral contracting (Stuart, 1971), systems theory (Alexander & Barton, 1976), and communication skills training (Robin, 1981).

RESEARCH ON PARENT-ADOLESCENT CONFLICT

Although many clinicians, parents, and adolescents believe that conflict between parents and adolescents is widespread, this idea lacks credibility among professional social scientists. Recent articles on parent-adolescent relations often begin with a statement that these relations have not been found to be stressful (Coleman, 1978), and many adolescent textbook writers also attempt to persuade their readers of this view (e.g., Santrock, 1981). Few ideas in adolescent psychology are as accepted by researchers with such unanimity as the notion that parent-adolescent relations basically are not stressful. One gets the strong impression that most adolescent psychologists regard theories of parent-adolescent conflict as explanations in search of a problem. Yet one must wonder why in the presumed face of what is regarded as overwhelming evidence to the contrary the idea of parent-adolescent stress remains alive in the minds of many parents of adolescents and therapists.

Some have argued that the persistent belief in the notion of stressful parent-adolescent relations is the result of a variety of distortions. For example, as early as 1937, Reuter (1937) writes: "The assumption of a period of 'flaming youth' appears in large measure to be the creator of such 'flaming youth' behavior as the younger generation manifests. The assumption creates the reality" (p. 416). More recently, Bandura (1964) argued that the view that parents and adolescents are in turmoil is the result of such biases as mass media

sensationalism, an over interpretation of superficial signs of nonconformity, and inappropriate generalizations from samples of deviant adolescents. Without denying the fact that these biases do indeed exist, one wonders if they account for the complete story. Recent evidence indicates that many of today's adolescents have serious problems with drugs, alcohol, sex, and crime, and that these problems are at least partly the result of stressful parent-adolescent relations. Also, many adolescents who are not involved in these kinds of serious problems still report that they have some difficulty relating to their parents. Are clinicians, parents, and adolescents attempting to tell researchers something that they should be listening to? Just how fictional is the view of the stressed parent-adolescent relationship?

Evidence for the view that the parent-adolescent relationship is essentially calm and pleasant is not as convincing as many believe. Some writers conclude that parent-adolescent relations are unstressful without reporting any data whatsoever (Elkin & Westley, 1955; Westley & Elkin, 1957), while the results of the few classic empirical studies of this question are not clear-cut (e.g. Bandura & Walters, 1959; Douvan & Adelson, 1966; Offer, 1969; Offer & Offer, 1975). A thorough review of the literature in this area does not exist. Before we discard the idea that parent-adolescent relations are stressful, I would like to give it a fair hearing in order to examine what is known, point out the deficiencies of the literature which does exist, and suggest directions for future research.

One common way that parent-adolescent stress has been investigated is by examining generational differences in beliefs, attitudes, and values—the "generation gap." I have chosen to ignore these studies in this review and to focus on those investigations in which parents or adolescents were questioned about *actual* conflicts or disagreements, or measures of conflict *behavior* between parents and adolescents were obtained. The reason for this focus is that the overt expression of conflict poses a greater threat to a relationship than does the mere existence of attitudinal differences, which may or may not lead to arguments. Conflict has been shown to be a key element in the maintenance and dissolution of other types of relationships, particularly marriages (Gottman, 1979). The frequency and intensity of disagreements are better predictors of marital satisfaction and spouse involvement than are differences in attitudes or values. What is true for marriage probably is true for the parent-adolescent relationship as well, and studies of generational differences in attitudes reveal little that is important in our attempt to understand the quality of the relationship that parents and adolescents have with each other. An understanding of attitudinal similarities and differences between the generations is important for other reasons, however, and excellent reviews of this literature exist elsewhere (Bengtson & Starr, 1975; Bengtson & Troll, 1978; Braungart, 1975; Tolor, 1976).

In reviewing the literature on parent-adolescent conflict one curious fact quickly becomes evident—there is virtually no connection between the theories and the research in this area. For example, if an adolescent's desire for independence is thought to be partly responsible for parent-adolescent conflict then one would expect to find studies in which the relationship between different levels of this trait in adolescents were related to different levels of conflict. Studies which use adolescent or parent characteristics, or types of family organization to predict different levels of parent-adolescent conflict do not exist. Indeed, most studies in this area are not based on any formal theory of individual development, parent-child relations, or family life-cycle change. The research has been notably atheoretical. Strong hypotheses formally derived from theory have not been tested (see Edwards and Brauberger (1973), who examined several hypotheses derived from exchange theory, for a notable exception). If theory plays any part at all in the investigation of parent-adolescent stress it is as an a posteriori explanation of conflict, usually in terms of adolescents' need for autonomy. Therefore, different explanations about the causes of parent-adolescent conflict cannot be

evaluated, and the literature cannot be organized around tests of different theoretical models.

One way to organize the literature in this area is in terms of the two different research designs that investigators have employed to study this question. These designs correspond to two different interpretations of the parent-adolescent conflict issue. A number of researchers only studied a sample of adolescents or their parents and did not include a comparative sample of children or their parents. What hypothesis can be tested with this design? Without a comparison group only statements about adolescents are possible. It appears that researchers using this design are examining a notion about conflict such as the following: by an absolute standard parents and adolescents are miserable when they are together and their relationship is characterized by constant turmoil. How much conflict would have to be found between parents and adolescents before this hypothesis would be supported? Presumably, confirmation would require finding that over 50% of adolescents or parents of adolescents reported that their relationships were typically characterized by conflict and argument, or that parents and adolescents argue with each other over 50 percent of the time that they are together. This is a very strong interpretation of the conflict hypothesis, but it is the only version that could be tested without a comparison group. The second design used by researchers is to compare parent-child with parent-adolescent relations. With this design differences in relations can be investigated and a weaker, but equally interesting, version of the conflict hypothesis can be examined, which is that relations between parents and adolescents deteriorate during adolescence. Here the claim is not that parent-adolescent relations are bad, but that they are worse than parent-child relations. Confirmation of this hypothesis would not require that conflict be high during adolescence, merely higher than in childhood.

These two different research designs are used in this review to organize the literature on parent-adolescent conflict. First is an examination of whether conflict changes in frequency between childhood and adolescence and then again between adolescence and youth. Second, the literature on the extent of conflict with parents during adolescence is reviewed. Third, the relationship between parent-adolescent conflict and other adolescent behaviors is examined.

Conflict with Parents, before, during and after Adolescence

A number of investigators have examined the question of whether conflict with parents increases around the time adolescents enter puberty. Data gathered through interviews or self-reports of conflict are inconsistent on this issue. Block (1937) and Offer (1969) found that conflict was more common in grades seven and eight than at later grades. In other studies, however, quarreling was reported to be less frequent before age 15 than after (Johnstone, 1975; Liccione, 1955; National Center for Health Statistics, 1974; Powell, 1955). A variety of methodologies were employed in these studies which included administering questionnaires to parents or adolescents, interviewing adolescents, and obtaining projective measures of conflict from adolescents. These differences make strict comparisons among studies impossible and may explain some of the discrepancy among the findings. Another problem with these investigations is that children under 12 years of age generally were not examined. The absence of younger aged children makes it hard to establish the true rate of prepubescent conflict since some 12-year-olds would be prepubescent and others postpubescent.

Consistent results were reported in three behavioral observational studies of the relationship between conflict with parents and the pubertal status of children. Jacob (1974) observed the verbal interactions between parents and their sons who were either 11- or 16-years-old. The majority of males in these two age groups very probably were pre- and postpubescent. No important age differences were found for such process measures of family interaction as conversation interruptions and talk time. Age differences were reported for the two outcome measures, however. Eleven-year-olds initially disagreed with their parents more than did 16-year-olds, but the latter group had more influence over their parents which came at the expense of their mothers. In two other studies of 11- to 14-year-old boys conflict with mothers was reported to be greater during the early rather than the later part of the pubertal cycle (Steinberg, 1981; Steinberg & Hill, 1978). During audiotaped discussions, adolescents who were in an early pubescent stage were interrupted by their mothers more frequently but deferred to them less often than did more physically advanced boys. Taken together, the results of these three behavioral studies indicate that family relations undergo a transformation during early adolescence such that sons acquire more family power and influence at the expense of their mothers. This alteration of the mother-son relationship leads to heightened conflict. By middle adolescence mothers and sons have developed new forms of interaction based upon the sons' adult physical status and conflict subsides.

In a few studies possible age differences in conflict with parens were examined among adolescents who were between the ages of 13 and 17 years, and none were found (Block, 1937; Douvan & Adelson, 1966; Liccione, 1955; Moore & Holtzman, 1965; National Center for Health Statistics, 1974; Powell, 1955). For example, interviewers from the Department of Health, Education, and Welfare collected health surveys from a random sample of 6768 mothers with adolescents between the ages of 12 and 17 years (National Center for Health Statistics, 1974). As part of the survey mothers were asked how difficult their adolescents were to bring up. The percentages who answered "some" or "a lot" ranged between 9.8 percent for mothers of 12-year-olds and 15.5 percent for mothers of 15-year-olds, and the average was 13.0 percent.

Little is known about possible changes in conflict with parents as adolescents enter young adulthood, typically considered to begin between 18 and 21 years of age, but the evidence that is available is very consistent—conflict with parents decreases after about age 18 (Connor, Johannis, & Walters, 1954; National Center for Health Statistics, 1974; Powell, 1955; Sullivan & Sullivan, 1980). It isn't clear why this change occurs but at least two explanations are possible. One is that conflict declines when an individual acquires full adult status and becomes a peer of his parents. The other is that the lessened conflict is the result of a decrease in interaction time which follows the move away from home that often takes place around the age of 18. At present the latter explanation seems more likely, based upon a study by Sullivan and Sullivan (1980) of two groups of boys attending college, some of whom lived at home while others lived away. No changes were found in relations with parents before and after entry into college for those boys who remained at home, while among the boys who moved away there were increases in parental affection, quality of communication, and relationship satisfaction. Apparently absence does make the heart grow fonder.

Taken together, the results obtained from studies of conflict with parents at the start, during, and after adolescence indicate that conflict and age are related in an inverted U-shaped function; conflict increases during early adolescence, is reasonably stable during middle adolescence, and declines when the adolescent moves away from home. This conclusion is further strengthened by the converging findings from other types of investigations. For example, in studies of the family life-cycle it has been shown that satisfaction with parenting is at a low point when children are in their teenage years (Burr, 1970; Hoffman & Manis, 1978). Further, investigators of the "empty nest syndrome" have shown that the departure of adolescents from the home brings both an increase in marital satisfaction for women and an increased sense of well-being (Rubin, 1980). In general, mothers indicate that parental satisfaction is higher with a preteenage child or an older child who has moved away from the home than with a teenager.

On the basis of the research reviewed here it appears that some worsening of the parent-child relationship occurs during early adolescence. This deterioration has two components, an increase in parent-adolescent conflict and mothers' loss of power and influence over their adolescent. Let me suggest a few directions for future research based upon these findings.

First, we need to know why quarrels are associated with alterations in the mother-child relationship. It is probably not the case that the loss of mothers' power is the result of fatigue due to an increase in the total number of aversive interactions that they have with their adolescents. In fact, the number of intrusive interruptions undoubtedly declines greatly between childhood and adolescence. For example, Fawl (1963) conducted in-home observations of the interactions of middle-class mothers and their non-problem preschool children and reported that these mothers averaged 3.4 disturbances per hour. This rate is considerably higher than the infrequent arguments that mothers and adolescents have, as will be discussed shortly. It may be that a change in the nature of the arguments has a greater impact on a mother's declining influence than does an increasing reluctance to argue with her adolescent. A promising direction for research on possible differences in the types of arguments that mothers have with their children and their adolescents comes from Turiel's work on the development of reasoning about conventional or social issues (Turiel, 1975, 1977). Turiel has reported that adolescents around the age of 12 or 13 consider social conventions to be arbitrary, even when they are governed by formal rules. Adolescents at this stage may defer to a conventional rule for pragmatic reasons but reject the legitimacy of the rule. Thus, a child may agree that a parent has a right to establish a rule, even though he might argue about its execution (e.g., "Why do I have to be home at 8:00 P.M. instead of 9 P.M.?"), while an adolescent may question the very justification for the rule and, ultimately, the legitimacy of maternal authority itself (e.g. "Its no business of yours when I come in."). This type of an attack may be considerably more damaging to traditional maternal authority than the more frequent, but in the long run, less challenging irritations caused by children.

A second important area for investigation concerns family variation in transitional stress. It is time that we moved beyond the old tired debate of whether the transition between childhood and adolescence is stressful or not to a more important and interesting question—why is it that this transition is stressful for some families but not so for others? Burr and his colleagues have argued that the degree of difficulty that individuals experience as they undergo a transition from one role to another is highly related to their anticipatory socialization into that role (Burr, Leigh, Day, & Constantine, 1979). Individuals who are desirous of making a change and who know how to correctly act in their new role will have an easier transition than those who are reluctant to change or don't know the proper way to behave in their new role.

Recognition of the importance of role preparation may have important implications for the education and training of parents. It is interesting to note that most parent training programs focus on teaching soon to be or recent parents effective skills for managing infants and small children (Fine, 1980). These programs usually neglect the adolescent period, however, and do not emphasize enough the new abilities and problems that appear during adolescence and the crucial need to adjust parenting styles to these changes. The skills that are required to be a successful parent of a child may not be the same as those necessary during the adolescent years, and some parent-adolescent conflict may be the result of a parental deficit in adolescent management skills.

Parent-Adolescent Conflict

In this section those studies which included only a sample of adolescents, usually defined as indi-

viduals between the ages of 12 and 18 years of age, are reviewed. The earliest data on parent-adolescent conflict are reported in the Lynds' study of life in Middletown during the late 1920s (Lynd & Lynd, 1929). The Lynds administered a 12-item checklist to 730 students in grades 10 through 12 who were asked to check those issues "about which you and your parents disagree." Most adolescents checked between three and four issues. Those most often picked were "the hours you get in at night," and "the number of times you go out on school nights during the week." Over 43 percent of adolescents checked these problems as sources of disagreement between themselves and their parents. Issues which fewer than 14 percent of adolescents checked were "Sunday (or Sabbath) observance," and "clubs or societies you belong to."

Recently, the Middletown study was replicated and the same "Source of Disagreement" checklist was used to examine parent-adolescent conflict (Caplow, Bahr, Chadwick, Hill, & Williamson, 1982). Remarkably, the issues that were picked by the Middletown adolescents in the 1980s as most and least likely to lead to arguments with parents were virtually identical to those selected by adolescents living in the 1920s. Over 42 percent of contemporary adolescents checked "the hours you get in at night," and "home duties" as sources of disagreement. Again, "Sunday (or Sabbath) observance," and "clubs or societies you belong to" were reported to be the issues which led to the least amount of disagreement.

In most studies it has been shown that the majority of arguments between parents and their adolescents are about normal, everyday, mundane family matters such as school work, social life, and friends, home chores, disobedience, disagreements with siblings, and personal hygiene (Bath & Lewis, 1962; Caplow, Bahr, Chadwick, Hill, & Williamson, 1982; Douvan & Adelson, 1966; Hicks & Hayes, 1938; Landis, 1954; Lynd & Lynd, 1929; Montemayor, 1982; Offer, 1969; Remmers, 1957; Rosenthal, Note 1; Schaneveldt, 1973). Some researchers have concluded that these types of arguments are indicative of adolescents' growing desire for autonomy and independence from parents. This interpretation is certainly plausible, but one should not lose sight of the fact that normal socialization continues throughout adolescence. Based on the content of most parent-adolescent arguments, one might plausibly conclude that this conflict is the result of nothing more, nor less, than parents' continuing efforts to teach their children to delay gratification and to conform to a set of social and family rules. This task inescapably produces a certain amount of tension between socializer and the one socialized, a tension that is present throughout development. At this point it is simply not clear whether parent-adolescent conflict has a "deeper meaning" than this.

There are two especially notable features about the content of the arguments that adolescents have with their parents. The first is that parents and adolescents apparently rarely argue about such "hot" topics as sex, drugs, religion, or politics. The absence of overt conflict about these issues is all the more remarkable given the great differences that exist in the attitudes of adults and youth about these topics (Bengtson & Starr, 1975). The reason why these generational differences do not lead to much intrafamily conflict might be because the positions held by parents and adolescents do not directly affect day-to-day relations among family members. Parents and adolescents may feel that what is not relevant to daily family life need not be discussed, an attitude which would reduce conflict. For example, there is abundant evidence that the young are more sexually active today than were their parents (Hopkins, 1977). But this difference rarely brings adolescents into conflict with their parents since they simply do not discuss sexuality (Thornburg, 1981). Apparently most families cope with potentially explosive generational differences by silently ignoring them.

A second interesting aspect about parent-adolescent conflict is that over the years very little has changed in what parents and adolescents argue about. An examination of the 17 studies contained in Table 1 reveals that between 1929

and 1982 the same problems about daily family functioning appear in study after study. This conclusion also is true for the three studies done during the socially and politically turbulent years between 1966 and 1973 (Douvan & Adelson, 1966; Offer, 1969; Schaneveldt, 1973). Arguments about the crucial issues of the 1960s, such as civil rights, the Vietnam war, and college protest, never were mentioned by students as significant sources of disagreements between themselves and their parents. Adolescents today apparently have the same kinds of disagreements with their parents that their parents had when they, themselves, were adolescents. Modern family life undoubtedly is quite different in many important respects than it was 50 years ago, but one area that has not changed is what parents and adolescents argue about. The issues remain the same, but when adolescents become parents their perspectives on the issues are altered. So when adolescents complain that their parents don't "understand" them they must not be using the first definition of that word, "to grasp the meaning of," but the second, "to show a sympathetic or tolerant attitude toward."

When adolescents are given a list of possible sources of disagreements between themselves and their parents they pick three or four as typical of their relationship (Caplow, Bahr, Chadwick, Hill, & Williamson, 1982; Dinkel, 1943; Kinloch, 1970; Lynd & Lynd, 1929). In most families parents and adolescents argue about a small number of issues, while many aspects of their relationship apparently are peaceful and free of stress. This is a potentially important clinical finding and one that deserves further investigation. It may be that this pattern of conflict is characteristic of normal relations between parents and adolescents, while an abnormal pattern is one in which conflict pervades virtually every area of the relationship. Parents and adolescents in a distressed relationship do report more conflict than those in a non-distressed relationship (Prinz, Foster, Kent, & O'Leary, 1979), but the importance of how pervasive conflict is has not been examined.

TABLE 1

**Three Most Common Causes of Arguments with Parents According to Adolescents
(1929–1982)**

Study	Sample	Causes of Arguments
Lynd & Lynd, 1929	348 males, 382 females Grades 10–12	Males and females 1. The time I get in at night 2. Number of times I go out during school nights 3. Grades at school
Block, 1937	528 males and females Grades 7–12	Males 1. Won't let me use car 2. School marks aren't high enough 3. Insists that I eat foods I dislike Females 1. Objects to car riding at night with boys 2. School marks aren't high enough 3. Insists that I eat foods I dislike
Hicks & Hayes, 1938	57 males, 66 females Ages 11–16 yrs.	Males and females 1. Coming home late 2. Quarreling with siblings 3. Teasing siblings
Stott, 1940	1878 males and females	Males and females 1. Getting home late from a date 2. Disobedience 3. Being impudent, sassy
Punke, 1943	989 males, 1721 females High school students	Males and females 1. Social life and friends 2. Work and spending money 3. Clothes
Connor, *et al.,* 1954	119 females Ages 17–26 yrs.	Females 1. Dating and mate selection 2. Standard and values in activities with the world outside the family 3. Standards and values of personal appearance, conduct, and health
Landis, 1954	1900 male, 2410 females High school seniors	Males and females 1. My share of the work around the house 2. My spending money 3. My attitude towards my parents
Remmers, 1957	15,000 males and females High school students	Males and females 1. Afraid to tell parents when I've done wrong 2. Too strict about my going out at night 3. Too strict about family car

(continued on next page)

TABLE 1
Three Most Common Causes of Arguments with Parents According to Adolescents (1929–1982) *(continued)*

Study	Sample	Causes of Arguments
Bath & Lewis, 1962	103 females Ages 19–30	Females 1. Discipline 2. Responsibilities 3. Family rules and regulations
Douvan & Adelson, 1966	1925 females Grades 6–12	Females 1. Clothing 2. Friends 3. Driving
Offer, 1969	73 males High school freshmen	Males 1. Orderliness 2. Completion of tasks 3. Cleanliness
Kinloch, 1970	100 males and females College freshmen	Males 1. Eating dinner with family 2. Getting to use the car 3. Arguing Females 1. Arguing 2. Going around with certain boys or girls 3. Being home enough
Schvaneveldt, 1973	85 males, 145 females Ages 12–15 yrs.	Males and females 1. Performing home chores 2. Use of time 3. Attitudes towards studies
Johnstone, 1975	1261 males and females Ages 13–20 yrs.	Males and females 1. Studying 2. Spare time use 3. School
Cromer, 1978	80 males and females Ages 15–21 yrs.	Males and females 1. Who I go out with 2. The places I go 3. Physical appearance
Rosenthal, 1982	630 males and females Ages 13–16 yrs.	Males and females 1. Drinking and/or smoking 2. Time and frequency of going out 3. Doing jobs around the house
Caplow, *et al.,* 1982	442 males, 488 females Grades 10–12	Males 1. The time I get in at night 2. Home duties 3. My spending money Females 1. Home duties 2. The time I get in at night 3. The number of times I go out on school nights.

Some researchers have attempted to assess the overall frequency of conflict in non-clinic families with adolescents. In a number of older studies it was reported that a majority (Punke, 1943) or a substantial minority of adolescents (Douvan & Adelson, 1966) never quarreled with their parents or had little or no conflict with them (Bath & Lewis, 1962). In two studies in which the overall quality of family relationships was investigated, it was found that adolescents expressed a high degree of satisfaction with relations with their parents and reported little conflict with them (Moore & Holtzman, 1965; Offer, 1969). In an excellent epidemiological study, Rutter, Graham, Chadwick, and Yule (1976) examined adolescent turmoil among 200 14- and 15-year-olds living on the Isle of Wight. Mothers were asked if they had "any arguments with their adolescent children concerning when and where they went out, or about other activities," and a similar question was asked of the adolescents. Approximately 18 percent of mothers responded that they did, while about 36 percent of adolescents reported that they had these kinds of conflicts with their mothers. This response difference may reflect mothers' unwillingness to report a high degree of conflict, but it may also indicate that adolescents perceive more conflict with their mothers than their mothers perceive with them. For example, one could imagine a mother telling her adolescent to pick up his clothes. An adolescent's silent compliance might mask an underlying resentment, and he would consider the interaction a conflictual one while the mother would not. In general, when self-report measures of overall relationship conflict or satisfaction are obtained from adolescents or parents, both groups report that conflict is low and satisfaction high, although mothers may have a somewhat more positive view of the quality of the relationship with their adolescents than do adolescents.

Rather than obtain reports of overall conflict, a number of investigators have had adolescents report on amount of conflict with parents for a specified period of time. This methodological improvement results in a somewhat different picture of the parent-adolescent relationship. In one study, about 17 percent of adolescents reported that they had a quarrel or serious disagreement with their parents "yesterday" (Proper, 1972), a figure that indicates a fairly substantial amount of quarreling over a long period of time. In regard to frequency of parental discipline, in two older studies it was found that about 30% of adolescents indicated that they had been punished by their parents during the previous week (Stott, 1940) or were frequently scolded by them (Meissner, 1965).

Finally, in one recent study daily accounts of conflicts with parents were obtained from 64 high school sophomores (Montemayor, 1982). Interviewers telephoned each adolescent at home on three randomly selected evenings during a three week period. The adolescents were asked to recount the events of the previous day, including any conflicts that they had with their parents. Conflict was defined for the adolescents as follows: "Either you teased your parent or your parent teased you; you and your parent had a difference of opinion; one of you got mad at the other for some reason; you and your parent had a quarrel or an argument; or one of you hit the other." The three days of data for each of the 64 adolescents resulted in 192 days of tracking. During this period adolescents reported a total of 68 arguments with both their parents. This is a rate of .35 arguments with parents per day or about one argument every three days. Further, the average length of each of these arguments was about 11 minutes and, according to the adolescents, the disagreements were moderately upsetting. In addition, most conflicts were with mothers rather than fathers and usually occurred between mothers and their daughters.

The results of these studies indicate that reports of the frequency of parent-adolescent disagreements are directly related to the method used to gather this information. When general levels of conflict are assessed parents and adolescents report that they rarely quarrel. When more specific measures of conflict are obtained, it appears that moderately upsetting arguments may occur as often as twice a week and that a large majority of adolescents may be disciplined by their parents weekly.

Relationship between Parent-Adolescent Conflict and Adolescent Behavior

In this section the question of whether conflict is in some way good for the adolescent or for the parent-adolescent relationship is examined. The idea that conflict facilitates growth is echoed by some developmental theorists such as Erikson (1968) and Kohlberg (1969), and by most life-span theorists who argue that psychological growth takes place in the give-and-take interplay of interpersonal interaction (Baltes & Schaie, 1973). Conflict in general is viewed by some as a normal and essential factor in adolescent development and, within limits, beneficial (Count, 1967; Peskin, 1967). Are these claims true for parent-adolescent conflict?

Very little is known about the possible association between parent-adolescent conflict and adolescent development or the quality of the parent-adolescent relationship. Montemayor (1982) investigated the widely held hypothesis that frequent conflict with parents would be associated with greater peer involvement. The hypothesis was not supported. In this sample of normal adolescents who were all living in intact families, conflict with mothers was associated with spending more time with fathers not peers. This finding is remarkable considering the fact that the adolescents only reported about two arguments per week with their parents. Apparently an aversive event does not have to be frequent for it to have an important impact on a relationship, as Patterson (1980) also has shown.

In a study of the relationship between parent-adolescent conflict and adolescent personality development, Grotevant and his colleagues reported that adolescent identity exploration was positively related to frequency of expressions of disagreement with parents during a family discussion task (Cooper, Grotevant, Moore, & Condon, Note 2).

Taken together the results of these two studies suggest that within some normal range, conflict with parents may be healthy for the personal development of adolescents, but that even infrequent conflict may be associated with less involvement with the disagreeable parent and more involvement with other family members.

At some point normal healthy conflict becomes serious distress. It is not known when this point is reached in a relationship, or what percentage of families with an adolescent could be classified as distressed. According to Offer and Offer (1975) 21 percent of their sample of "modally adjusted" adolescents experienced "tumultuous growth," which included serious conflict with parents. On the basis of this figure and the data reviewed in this presentation, a conservative estimate of the percentage of adolescents who have serious conflict with their parents is between 15 percent and 20 percent. According to the 1980 U.S. Census there are about 25 million individuals between the ages of 12 and 17 years. Fifteen to 20 percent of that group would be between four and five million families in which parent-adolescent conflict would be serious enough for the individuals to feel stressed and, perhaps, to desire help.

A high degree of conflict between parents and their adolescents is not related to psychological growth but is predictive of a variety of adolescent problems. The physical abuse of adolescents by their parents is oftentimes the culmination of a history of intense arguments between parents and adolescents (Garbarino, 1980; Libbey & Bybee, 1979). Similarly, incidents of the physical abuse of parents by adolescents are more frequent in homes that are characterized by turmoil and conflict (Straus, Gelles, & Steinmetz, Note 3). High levels of parent-adolescent conflict are related to adolescents moving away from their parents (Gottlieb & Chafetz, 1977), running away from home (Blood & D'Angelo, 1974; Shellow, Schamp, Liebow, & Unger, 1967), and joining a religious cult (Ullman, 1982). Teenage girls who report that their relations with their parents are very stressful are more likely to marry early (Moss & Gingles,

1959) or become pregnant (McKenry, Walters, & Johnson, 1979) than their schoolmates who report calm relations with their parents. Adolescents who drop out of school in comparison to adolescents who graduate from high school report more conflict and less communication with parents (Bachman, Green, & Wirtanen, 1971; Cervantes, 1965). In addition to school related problems, more male juvenile delinquents than non-delinquents indicate that their parents do not understand them (Duncan, 1978), often nag and scold them (Nye, 1958), and use harsh and restrictive disciplinary techniques (Bandura & Walters, 1959).

Other adolescent problems related to high levels of parent-adolescent conflict are psychiatric disorders (Rutter, Graham, Chadwick, & Yule, 1976), low self-esteem (Bachman, 1970), and suicide (Jacobs, 1971). Negative and conflictual parent-adolescent relations are associated with adolescents' use of heroin (Eldred, Brown, & Mahabir, 1974), depressants and stimulants (Streit, Halsted, & Pascale, 1974), hallucinogens (Sanborn, Daniels, Jones, Salkin, & Shonick, 1971), marijuana (McGlothlin, 1975; Tec, 1970), and illicit drugs in general (Kandel, Kessler, & Margulies, 1978).

Since all of the above studies are correlational, it is impossible to know if parent-adolescent conflict causes problems for adolescents or if the relations between parents and adolescents are strained and unpleasant as a result of the problems that adolescents may already have. But whichever the direction of causality, severe parent-adolescent conflict must be viewed as symptomatic of a variety of serious adolescent problems. In general, high levels of parent-adolescent conflict are associated with a wide range of non-specific acting-out behaviors during adolescence. The particular form of the problem behavior is probably a function of a variety of personal, family, and peer influences.

CONCLUSIONS

The results of this review do not indicate that the old "sturm and drang" view of parent-adolescent relations was right after all. It wasn't. But, perhaps in our attempt to be modern and repudiate this view we have lost sight of the fact that conflict is a part of any relationship, and that the ability to satisfactorily resolve differences is a key element to the continuation of a relationship. Understanding the causes and consequences of conflict with parents may be particularly important during the adolescent period for two reasons. First, some conflict with parents appears to be a normal part of family relations during this time. This conflict may be an essential component of the transformation of relations with parents that occurs during puberty. Understanding this type of conflict is important for our overall understanding of normal adolescent development. A second type of conflict, however, may or may not be associated with transitional stress, and may have its origins in earlier parent-child relations. This conflict, when it is severe, is associated with serious adolescent problem behavior. From clinical perspective, we cannot ignore this type of conflict and need to develop prevention and treatment programs to help families cope with it.

REFERENCE NOTES

1. Rosenthal, D. A. *The influence of ethnicity on parent-adolescent conflict.* Paper presented at the Second National Child Development Conference, Melbourne, August, 1982.
2. Cooper, C. R., Grotevant, H. D., Moore, M. S., & Condon, S. M. *Family support and conflict: Both foster adolescent identity and role taking.* Paper presented at the annual meeting of the American Psychological Association, Washington, D.C., August, 1982.
3. Straus, M. A., Gelles, R. J., & Steinmetz, S. K. *Physical violence in a nationally representative sample of American families.* Paper presented at the Ninth World Congress of Sociology, Uppsala, Sweden, August, 1978.

REFERENCES

Alexander, J. F., & Barton, C. Behavioral systems therapy for families. In D. H. L. Olson (Ed.), *Treating relationships.* Lake Mills, IA: Graphic, 1976.

Ausubel, D. P., Montemayor, R., & Svajian, P. *Theory and problems of adolescent development* (2nd ed.). New York: Grune & Stratton, 1977.

Bachman, J. G. *Youth in transition: The impact of family background and intelligence on tenth-grade boys.* Ann Arbor: Survey Research Center, Institute for Social Research, 1970.

Bachman, J. G., Green, S., & Wirtanen, I. D. *Youth in transition: Dropping out—problem or symptom?* Ann Arbor: Survey Research Center, Institute for Social Research, 1971.

Ballenski, C. B., & Cook, A. S. Mothers' perceptions of their competence in managing selected parenting tasks. *Family Relations,* 1982, *31,* 489–494.

Baltes, P. B., & Schaie, K. W. (Eds.). *Life-span developmental psychology.* New York: Academic Press, 1973.

Bandura, A. The stormy decade: Fact or fiction? *Psychology in the Schools.* 1964, *1,* 224–231.

Bandura, A., & Walters, R. H. *Adolescent aggression.* New York: Ronald Press, 1959.

Bath, J. A., & Lewis, E. C. Attitudes of young female adults toward some areas of parent-adolescent conflict. *Journal of Genetic Psychology* 1962, *100,* 241–253.

Bengtson, V. L., & Starr, J. M. Contrast and consensus: A generational analysis of youth in the 1970s. In R. J. Havighurst & P. H. Dreyer (Eds.), *Youth,* The Seventy-Fourth Yearbook of the National Society for the Study of Education. Chicago: University of Chicago Press, 1975.

Bengtson, V. L., & Troll, L. Youth and their parents: Feedback and intergenerational influence in socialization. In R. M. Lerner & G. B. Spanier (Eds.), *Child influences on marital and family interaction.* New York: Academic Press, 1978.

Block, V. L. Conflicts of adolescents with their mothers. *Journal of Abnormal and Social Psychology,* 1937, *32,* 193–206.

Blood, L., & D'Angelo, R. A progress research report on value issues in conflict between runaways and their parents. *Journal of Marriage and the Family,* 1974, *36,* 486–491.

Blos, P. *On adolescence.* New York: Free Press, 1962.

Boszormenyi-Nagy, I. *Invisible loyalties: Reciprocity in intergenerational family therapy.* New York: Harper & Row, 1973.

Braungart, R. G. Youth and social movements. In S. E. Dragastin & G. H. Elder, Jr. (Eds.), *Adolescence in the life cycle.* New York: Wiley, 1975.

Burr, W. R. Satisfaction with various aspects of marriage over the life cycle: A random middle class sample. *Journal of Marriage and the Family,* 1970, *32,* 29–37.

Burr, W. R., Leigh, G. K., Day, R. D., & Constantine, J. Symbolic interaction and the family. In W. R. Burr, R. Hill, F. I. Nye, & I. L. Reiss (Eds.), *Contemporary theories about the family* (Vol. 2). New York: Free Press, 1979.

Caplow, T., Bahr, H. M., Chadwick, B. A., Hill, R., & Williamson, M. H. *Middletown families.* Minneapolis: University of Minnesota Press, 1982.

Cervantes, L. F. Family background, primary relationships, and the high school dropout. *Journal of Marriage and the Family,* 1965, *27,* 218–223.

Coleman, J. C. Current contradictions in adolescent theory. *Journal of Youth and Adolescence,* 1978, *7,* 1–11.

Connor, R., Johannis, T. B., & Walters, J. Parent-adolescent relationships. *Journal of Home Economics,* 1954, *46,* 183–186.

Count, J. The conflict factor in adolescent growth. *Adolescence,* 1967, *2,* 167–181.

Cromer, G. A comparison of intergenerational relations in the Jewish and non-Jewish family. *Adolescence,* 1978, *13,* 297–309.

Dinkel, R. M. Parent-child conflict in Minnesota families. *American Sociological Review,* 1943, *8,* 412–419.

Douvan, E., & Adelson, J. *The adolescent experience.* New York: Wiley, 1966.

Duncan, D. F. Attitudes towards parents and delinquency in suburban adolescent males. *Adolescence,* 1978, *13,* 365–369.

Edwards, J. N., & Brauburger, M. B. Exchange and parent-youth conflict. *Journal of Marriage and the Family,* 1973, *35,* 101–106.

Eldred, C. A., Brown, B. S., & Mahabir, C. Heroin addict clients' description of their families of origin. *International Journal of the Addictions,* 1974, *9,* 315–320.

Elkin, F., & Westley, W. A. The myth of adolescent culture. *American Sociological Review,* 1955, *20,* 680–684.

Erikson, E. H. *Identity: Youth and crisis.* New York: Norton, 1968.

Fawl, C. L. Disturbances experienced by children in their natural habitat. In R. Barker (Ed.), *The stream of behavior.* New York: Appleton-Century-Crofts, 1963.

Fine, M. J. *Handbook on parent education.* New York: Academic Press, 1980.

Freud, S. Three essays on sexuality. In *Standard edition* (Vol. VII). London: Hogarth Press, 1953. (Originally published, 1905.)

Gant, B. L., Barnard, J. D., Kuehn, H. H., Jones, E. R., & Christophersen, E. R. A behaviorally based approach for improving intrafamilial communication patterns. *Journal of Clinical Child Psychology,* 1981, *10,* 102–106.

Garbarino, J. Meeting the needs of mistreated youths. *Social Work,* 1980, *25,* 122–126.

Ginott, H. G. *Between parent & teenager.* New York: Avon, 1969.

Gnagey, T. D. *How to put up with parents: A guide for teenagers.* Ottawa, IL: Facilitation House, 1975.

Goethals, G. W. Adolescence: Variations on a theme. In R. J. Havighurst & P. H. Dreyer (Eds.), *Youth. The Seventy-Fourth Yearbook of the National Society for the Study of Education.* Chicago: University of Chicago Press, 1975.

Gottlieb, D., & Chafetz, J. S. Dynamics of familial, generational conflict and reconciliation. *Youth and Society,* 1977, *9,* 213–224.

Gottman, J. *Marital interaction: Experimental investigations.* New York: Academic Press, 1979.

Hall, G. S. *Adolescence.* New York: Appleton & Co., 1904.

Hicks, J. A., & Hayes, M. Study of the characteristics of 250 junior high school children. *Child Development,* 1938, *9,* 219–242.

Hill, J. P. The family. In M. Johnson (Ed.), *Toward adolescence: The middle school years. The Seventy-Ninth Yearbook of the National Society for the Study of Education.* Chicago: University of Chicago Press, 1980.

Hoffman, L. W., & Manis, J. D. Influences of children on marital interaction and parental satisfactions and dissatisfactions. In R. M. Lerner & G. B. Spanier (Eds.), *Child influences on marital and family interaction.* New York: Academic Press, 1978.

Hopkins, J. R. Sexual behavior in adolescence. *Journal of Social Issues,* 1977, *33*(2), 67–85.

Jacob, T. Patterns of family conflict and dominance as a function of child age and social class. *Developmental Psychology,* 1974, *10,* 1–12.

Jacobs, J. *Adolescent suicide.* New York: Wiley, 1971.

Johnstone, J. W. C. Social change and parent-youth conflict: The problem of generations in English and French Canada. *Youth and Society,* 1975, *7,* 3–26.

Kandel, D. B., Kessler, R. C., & Margulies, R. Z. Antecedents of adolescent initiation into stages of drug use: A development analysis. In D. B. Kandel (Ed.), *Longitudinal research on drug use.* New York: Wiley, 1978.

Kinloch, G. C. Parent-youth conflict at home: An investigation among university freshmen. *American Journal of Orthopsychiatry,* 1970, *40,* 658–664.

Kohlberg, L. Stage and sequence: The cognitive-developmental approach to socialization. In D. A. Goslin (Ed.), *Handbook of socialization theory and research.* Chicago: Rand McNally, 1969.

Landis, P. H. The ordering and forbidding techniques and teenage adjustment. *School and Society,* 1954, *80,* 105–106.

Libbey, P., & Bybee, R. The physical abuse of adolescents. *Journal of Social Issues,* 1979, *35*(2), 101–126.

Liccione, J. V. The changing family relationships of adolescent girls. *Journal of Abnormal and Social Psychology,* 1955, *51,* 421–426.

Lynd, R. S., & Lynd, H. M. *Middletown.* New York: Harcourt, Brace & Co., 1929.

McGlothin, W. H. Drug use and abuse. *Annual Review of Psychology,* 1975, *26,* 45–64.

McKenry, P. C., Walters, L. H., & Johnson, C. Adolescent pregnancy: A review of the literature. *Family Coordinator,* 1979, *28,* 17–28.

Meissner, W. W. Parental interaction of the adolescent boy. *Journal of Genetic Psychology,* 1965, *107,* 225–233.

Montemayor, R. The relationship between parent-adolescent conflict and the amount of time adolescents spend alone and with parents and peers. *Child Development,* 1982, *53,* 1512–1519.

Moore, B. M., & Holtzman, W. H. *Tomorrow's parents.* Austin: University of Texas Press, 1965.

Morton, T. L., Alexander, J. F., & Altman, I. Communication and relationship definition. In G. R. Miller (Ed.), *Annual review of communication research: Interpersonal communication.* Beverly Hills: Sage Publications, 1976.

Moss, J. J., & Gingles, R. The relationship of personality to the incidence of early marriage. *Marriage and Family Living,* 1959, *21,* 372–377.

National Center for Health Statistics. *Parent ratings of behavioral patterns of youths 12–17 years.* Department of Health, Education, and Welfare. Publication No. (HRA) 74–1619. Series 11, No. 137, 1974.

Nye, F. I. *Family relationships and delinquent behavior.* New York: Wiley, 1958.

Offer, D. *The psychological world of the teenager.* New York: Basic Books, 1969.

Offer, D., & Offer, J. B. *From teenage to young manhood: A psychological study.* New York: Basic Books, 1975.

Patterson, G. R. Mothers: The unacknowledged victims. *Monographs of the Society for Research for Child Development,* 1980, *45,* 1–55.

Peskin, H. Pubertal onset and ego functioning: A psychoanalytic approach. *Journal of Abnormal Psychology,* 1967, *72,* 1–15.

Powell, M. Age and sex differences in degree of conflict with certain areas of psychological adjustment. *Psychological Monographs,* 1955, *69,* 1–14.

Prinz, R. J., Foster, S., Kent, R. N., & O'Leary, K. D. Multivariate assessment of conflict in distressed and non-distressed mother-adolescent dyads. *Journal of Applied Behavior Analysis,* 1979, *12,* 691–700.

Propper, A. M. The relationship of maternal employment to adolescent roles, activities, and parental relationships. *Journal of Marriage and the Family,* 1972, *34,* 417–421.

Prosen, H., Toews, J., & Martin, R. The life cycle of the family: Parental midlife crisis and adolescent rebellion. In S. C. Feinstein, J. G. Looney, A. Z. Schwartzberg, & A. D. Sorosky (Eds.), *Adolescent psychiatry* (Vol. IX). Chicago: University of Chicago Press, 1981.

Punke, H. H. High school youth and family quarrels. *School and Society,* 1943, *58,* 507–511.

Remmers, H. H. *The American teenager.* Indianapolis: Bobbs-Merrill, 1957.

Reuter, E. B. The sociology of adolescence. *American Journal of Sociology,* 1937, *43,* 414–427.

Robin, A. L. A controlled evaluation of problem-solving communication training with parent-adolescent conflict. *Behavior Therapy,* 1981, *12,* 593–609.

Rubin, L. B. The empty nest: Beginning or ending? In L. A. Bond & J. C. Rosen (Eds.), *Competence and coping during adulthood.* Hanover, NH: University Press of New England, 1980.

Rutter, M., Graham, P., Chadwick, O. F. D., & Yule, W. Adolescent turmoil: Fact or fiction? *Journal of Child Psychology and Psychiatry,* 1976, *17,* 35–56.

Sanborn, B., Daniels, J., Jones, S. G., Salkin, B., & Shonick, H. LSD reactions: A family-research approach. *International Journal of the Addictions,* 1971, *6,* 497–507.

Santrock, J. W. *Adolescence: An introduction.* Dubuque: William C. Brown, 1981.

Schowalter, J. E., & Anyan, W. R. *The family handbook of adolescence.* New York: Knopf, 1981.

Schvaneveldt, J. D. Mormon adolescents' likes and dislikes towards parents and home. *Adolescence,* 1973, *8,* 171–178.

Shellow, R. J., Schamp, J. R., Liebow, E., & Unger, E. Suburban runaways of the 1960s. *Monographs of the Society for Research for Child Development,* 1967, *32,* 1–51.

Steinberg, L. D. Transformations in family relations at puberty. *Developmental Psychology,* 1981, *17,* 833–840.

Steinberg, L. D., & Hill, J. P. Patterns of family interaction as a function of age, the onset of puberty, and formal thinking. *Developmental Psychology,* 1978, *14,* 683–684.

Stott, L. H. Home punishment of adolescents. *Journal of Genetic Psychology,* 1940, *57,* 415–428.

Streit, F., Halsted, D. L., & Pascale, P. J. Differences among youthful users and nonusers of drugs based on their perceptions of parental behavior. *International Journal of the Addictions,* 1974, *9,* 749–755.

Stuart, R. B. Behavioral contracting within the families of delinquents. *Journal of Behavior Therapy and Experimental Psychiatry,* 1971, *2,* 1–11.

Sullivan, K., & Sullivan, A. Adolescent-parent separation. *Developmental Psychology,* 1980, *16,* 93–99.

Tec, N. Family and differential involvement with marihuana: A study of suburban teenagers. *Journal of Marriage and the Family,* 1970, *32,* 656–664.

Thornburg, H. D. The amount of sex information learning obtained during early adolescence. *Journal of Early Adolescence,* 1981, *1,* 171–183.

Tolor, A. The generation gap: Fact or fiction? *Genetic Psychology Monographs,* 1976, *94,* 35–130.

Turiel, E. The development of social concepts. In D. DePalma & J. Foley (Eds.), *Moral development.* Hillsdale, N.J.: Erlbaum, 1975.

Turiel, E. The development of concepts of social structure. In J. Glick & A. Clarke-Stewart (Eds.), *Personality and social development* (Vol. 1). New York: Gardner Press, 1977.

Turner, R. H. *Family interaction.* New York: Wiley, 1970.

Ullman, C. Cognitive and emotional antecedents of religious conversion. *Journal of Personality and Social Psychology,* 1982, *43,* 183–192.

Westley, W. A., & Elkin, F. The protective environment and adolescent socialization. *Social Forces,* 1957, *35,* 243–249.

Wish, M., Deutsch, M., & Kaplan, S. J. Perceived dimensions of interpersonal relations. *Journal of Personality and Social Psychology,* 1976, *33,* 409–420.

URBAN POVERTY AND THE FAMILY CONTEXT OF DELINQUENCY

ROBERT J. SAMPSON
University of Chicago
JOHN H. LAUB
Northeastern University and Henry A. Murray Research Center

In 1950, Sheldon and Eleanor Glueck published their now classic study, *Unraveling Juvenile Delinquency*. In one of the most frequently cited works in the history of delinquency research, the Gluecks sought to answer a basic and enduring question—what factors differentiate boys reared in poor neighborhoods who become serious and persistent delinquents from boys raised in the same neighborhoods who do not become delinquent or antisocial? To answer this question, the Gluecks studied in meticulous detail the lives of 500 delinquents and 500 nondelinquents who were raised in the same slum environments of central Boston during the Great Depression era.

The research design of the Gluecks' study provides a unique opportunity to address anew poverty and its sequelae in adolescence. Namely, what is the *process* by which family poverty leads to delinquency within structurally disadvantaged urban environments? It is our contention that sociological explanations of delinquency have too often focused on structural background (e.g., poverty) without an understanding of mediating family processes, especially informal social control. Competing explanations based on behavioral predispositions (e.g., early conduct disorder) have also been ne-

glected in structural accounts of delinquency. On the other hand, developmental models in psychology tend to emphasize family process and early antisocial behavior to the neglect of structural context and social disadvantage.

Based on our reconstruction and reanalysis of the Gluecks' original data, this article rejects a bifurcated strategy by uniting structure and process in an integrated theoretical framework. Our major thesis is that poverty and structural disadvantage influence delinquency in large part by reducing the capacity of families to achieve effective informal social controls. In this sense, we argue that scholars of child and adolescent development must come to grips with structural contexts of disadvantage and not just focus on families "under the roof."

The historical context of the Gluecks' data also serves as a baseline for assessing current research on children and poverty. The boys in the Glueck sample were born in the Depression era and grew to young adulthood in the context of a rapidly changing economy after World War II (1945–1965). This context raises interesting questions relevant to an understanding of how poverty influences developmental patterns of delinquency. For example, are the risk factors associated with crime similar across different structural contexts? Were characteristics of today's "underclass" (e.g., chronic joblessness, poverty) found among these earlier Boston fami-

From *Child Development*, 1994, 65, 523–540. © 1994 by the Society for Research in Child Development, Inc. All rights reserved.

lies? Current debates, especially in public policy circles, seem to imply that criminal behavior is inevitably linked to race and drugs. Yet the delinquency problem in the historical context we are analyzing was generated not by blacks, but by white ethnic groups in structurally disadvantaged positions. And though drugs were not pervasive, delinquency and antisocial behavior were. Indeed, the boys in the Gluecks' delinquent sample were persistent and serious offenders, many of whom can be labeled "career criminals" using contemporary language. By analyzing a white sample that is largely "underclass" by today's economic definition (see Jencks, 1992; Wilson, 1987), we provide an alternative perspective to current thinking about race, crime, and poverty.

FAMILY PROCESS AND INFORMAL SOCIAL CONTROL

The hypotheses guiding our analysis are derived from a general theory of age-graded informal social control over the life course (see Sampson & Laub, 1993). Our general organizing principle is that the probability of deviance increases when an individual's bond to society is weak or broken (Hirschi, 1969). In other words, when ties that bind an individual to key societal institutions (e.g., attachment to family, school, work) are loosened, the risk of crime and delinquency is heightened. Unlike formal sanctions, which originate in purposeful efforts to control crime, informal social controls "emerge as by-products of role relationships established for other purposes and are components of role reciprocities" (Kornhauser, 1978, p. 24).

Our theoretical conceptualization on the family is drawn in part from "coercion theory" as formulated by Patterson (1980, 1982). Unlike most sociological theories, coercion theory places a prominent etiological role on direct parental controls in explaining delinquency. In particular, the coercion model assumes that less skilled parents inadvertently reinforce their children's antisocial behavior and fail to provide effective punishments for transgressions (Patter-

son, 1982; see also Gottfredson & Hirschi, 1990, p. 99). Based on research designed to assess this perspective, Patterson argues that "parents who cannot or will not employ family management skills are the prime determining variables. . . . Parents of stealers do not track; they do not punish; and they do not care" (1980, pp. 88–89).

The emphasis on parent-child interaction in coercion theory shares much in common with Hirschi's (1969) social control theory. The model of Patterson differs mainly in the mediating mechanisms it emphasizes—that is, direct parental controls as found in discipline and monitoring practices. By contrast, Hirschi's (1969) original formulation of control theory emphasized indirect controls in the form of the child's attachment to parents. On balance, however, Patterson's model is consistent with social control theory because direct parental controls are likely to be positively related to relational, indirect controls (Larzelere & Patterson, 1990, p. 305). Moreover, Gottfredson and Hirschi (1990) include direct parental controls in a recent statement of control theory that relies heavily on Patterson's coercion model. Their reformulated theory of effective parenting includes monitoring the behavior of children, recognizing their misdeeds, and punishing (correcting) those misdeeds accordingly in a consistent and loving manner (Gottfredson & Hirschi, 1990, p. 97). In addition, Hirschi (1983) argues that parental affection and a willingness to invest in children are essential underlying conditions of good parenting, and hence, the prevention of misbehavior.

This view of families also corresponds to Braithwaite's (1989) notion of "reintegrative shaming," whereby parents punish in a consistent manner and within the context of love, respect, and acceptance of the child. The opposite of reintegrative shaming is stigmatization, where parents are cold, authoritarian, and enact a harsh, punitive, and often rejecting regime of punishment (1989, p. 56). When the bonds of respect are broken by parents in the process of punishment, successful child rearing is difficult to achieve.

Given their theoretical compatibility, we draw on the central ideas of social control and coercion theory along with the notion of reintegrative shaming to develop a model of informal family social control that focuses on three dimensions—*discipline, supervision,* and *attachment.* In our view, the key to all three dimensions of informal social control lies in the extent to which they facilitate linking the child to family, and ultimately society, through emotional bonds of attachment and direct yet socially integrative forms of control, monitoring, and punishment. These dimensions of informal family control have rarely been examined simultaneously in previous research. Hence our theoretical model permits assessment of the relative and cumulative contributions of family process to the explanation of delinquency.

Poverty and Family Process

The second part of our theory posits that structural background factors influence delinquency largely through the mediating dimensions of family process (see also Laub & Sampson, 1988). Our specific interest in this article is the indirect effect of family poverty on delinquency among those children living in disadvantaged communities. Although examined in the developmental psychology literature (for a recent review see McLoyd, 1990), it is ironic that sociological research on delinquency often fails to account for how structural disadvantage influences parenting behavior and other aspects of family life. As Rutter and Giller (1983, p. 185) have stated, "serious socio-economic disadvantage has an adverse effect on the parents, such that parental disorders and difficulties are more likely to develop and good parenting is impeded" (see also McLoyd, 1990, p. 312). Furthermore, Larzelere and Patterson (1990, p. 307) have argued that many lower-class families are marginally skilled as parents, in part because they experience more stress and fewer resources than do middle-class parents. McLoyd (1990, p. 312) has also expressed the view that "poverty and economic loss diminish the capacity for supportive, consistent, and involved parenting." In reviewing the extant literature, she found that economically disadvantaged parents and those parents who experience economic stress are more likely to use punitive, coercive parenting styles, that is, use of physical punishment, as opposed to reasoning and negotiation. Low-income parents also face heightened risks of spousal violence, drug and alcohol abuse, and criminal involvement (McLoyd, 1990), behaviors that undermine socially integrative parent-child relationships and interactions.

Equally important and relevant here is the large body of literature establishing the effects of stressors such as economic crises and divorce on parenting behavior. For example, Patterson (1988) has shown that stressful experiences increase the likelihood of psychological distress, which in turn leads to changes in parent-child management practices. Specifically, Patterson (1988) found that distressed mothers are more likely to use coercive discipline, thereby contributing to the development of antisocial behavior in children (see also Patterson, DeBaryshe, & Ramsey, 1989, p. 332). Elder and Caspi (1988) examined the effects of stressful economic circumstances on parents and their children. They found that in times of economic difficulty, aversive interactions between parents and children increase while the ability of parents to manage their children diminishes. Using more recent data, Conger et al. (1992) confirmed that economic hardship was indirectly linked to adolescent development largely through its effect on parenting behavior.

It seems clear that poverty and the accompanying stresses resulting from economic deprivation influence parent-child relationships and interactions within the family. Integrating this viewpoint with our general theory of informal social control, we thus hypothesize that the effect of poverty and disadvantaged family status on delinquency is mediated in large part through parental discipline and monitoring practices.

ANTISOCIAL CHILDREN: RECONSIDERING FAMILY EFFECTS

Two research findings raise questions regarding unidirectional models that attribute the development of delinquency as flowing solely from parental influence. The first is empirical research establishing the early onset of many forms of childhood misbehavior (Robins, 1966; West & Farrington, 1973; White, Moffitt, Earls, Robins, & Silva, 1990). In one of the best studies to date, White et al. (1990) examined the predictive power of behavior measured as early as age 3 on antisocial outcomes at ages 11 and 13. They found that teacher and/or parent-reported behavioral measures of hyperactivity and restlessness as a young child (age 3), difficulty in management of the child at age 3, and early onset of problem behaviors at age 5 predicted later antisocial outcomes. White et al.'s (1990) research shows the extent to which later delinquency is foreshadowed by early misbehavior and general difficulty among children.

Second, there is evidence that styles of parenting are in part a reaction to these troublesome behaviors on the part of children. Lytton (1990) has written an excellent overview of this complex body of research, which he subsumes under the theoretical umbrella of "control systems theory." This theory argues that parent and child display reciprocal adaptation to each other's behavior level (see also Anderson, Lytton, & Romney, 1986), leading to what Lytton calls "child effects" on parents. One reason for these child effects is that reinforcement does not work in the usual way for conduct-disordered children. As Lytton (1990, p. 688) notes, conduct-disordered children "may be underresponsive to social reinforcement and punishment." Hence, normal routines of parental child rearing become subject to disruption based on early antisocial behavior— that is, children themselves differentially engender parenting styles likely to further exacerbate antisocial behavior.

The behavior that prompts parental frustration is not merely aggressiveness or delinquency, however. Lytton (1990, p. 690) reviews evidence showing a connection between a child being rated "difficult" in preschool (e.g., whining, restlessness, inadaptability to change, strong-willed resistance) and the child's delinquency as an adolescent—a relation that holds independent of the quality of parents' child-rearing practices. For example, Olweus (1980) showed by a longitudinal path analysis that mothers of boys who displayed a strong-willed and hot temper in infancy later became more permissive of aggression, which in turn led to greater aggressiveness in middle childhood. Moreover, there is intriguing experimental evidence that when children's inattentive and noncompliant behavior is improved by administering stimulant drugs (e.g., Ritalin), their mothers become less controlling and mother-child interaction patterns are nearly normalized (Lytton, 1990, p. 688). All of this suggests that parenting, at least in part, is a reaction to the temperament of children, especially difficult ones.

Further evidence in favor of "child effects" from the criminological literature is found in West and Farrington's (1973) well-known longitudinal study. They showed that boys "troublesomeness" assessed at ages 8 and 10 by teachers and peers was a significant predictor of later delinquency, independent of parental supervision, parental criminality, and family size. However, the reverse was not true—parental effects on delinquency disappeared once early troublesomeness was taken into account. As Lytton observes, this finding "suggests the primacy of child effects" (1990, p. 690).

In short, there is a sound theoretical and empirical basis for expanding our model by introducing early childhood effects. Lytton's review suggests a strategy to ascertain the relative importance of parent and child influences. Namely, one can test the effects of early childhood factors on later delinquency, with parent factors held constant, against the prediction of parents' effects on delinquency, with early childhood factors held constant. The relative strength of each set of variables would be an index of the importance of the main independent variables—child or parent (1990, p. 694). Put more simply, the key question is whether our family process model holds up after we consider early childhood difficulty and antisocial predispositions. If parenting or family effects on delinquency are spurious, then our model should collapse once childhood behaviors are controlled. On the other hand, if control systems theory is correct, we are liable to see both child *and* parent effects on the outcome of adolescent delinquency. We assess our theoretical model of structure and family process by employing this strategy.

METHOD

The present article is based on data from the first wave of the Gluecks' original study of juvenile delinquency and adult crime among 1,000 Boston males born between 1924 and 1935 (Glueck & Glueck, 1950, 1968). As part of a larger, long-term project we have reconstructed and computerized these data, a process that included the validation of key measures found in the original files. For a full description of these efforts and other procedures taken to address prior criticisms of the Gluecks' study, see Sampson and Laub (1993).

The Gluecks' delinquent sample comprised 500 10–17-year-old white males from Boston who, because of their persistent delinquency, had been recently committed to one of two correctional schools in Massachusetts (Glueck & Glueck, 1950, p. 27). The nondelinquent or "control-group" sample was made up to 500 white males age 10–17 chosen from the Boston public schools. Nondelinquent status was determined on the basis of official record checks and interviews with parents, teachers, local police, social workers, recreational leaders, and the boys themselves. The Gluecks' sampling procedure was designed to maximize differences in delinquency, an objective that by all accounts succeeded (Glueck & Glueck, 1950, pp. 27–29).

A unique aspect of the *Unraveling* study was the matching design. The 500 officially defined delinquents and 500 nondelinquents were matched case-by-case on age, race/ethnicity (birthplace of both parents), measured intelligence, and neighborhood deprivation. The delinquents averaged 14 years, 8 months, and the nondelinquents 14 years, 6 months when the study began. As to ethnicity, 25% of both groups were of English background, another fourth Italian, a fifth Irish, less than a tenth old American, Slavic, or French, and the remaining were Near Eastern, Spanish, Scandinavian, German, or Jewish. As measured by the Wechsler-Bellevue Test, the delinquents had an average IQ of 92 and nondelinquents 94. The matching on neighborhood ensured that both delinquents and nondelinquents grew up in disadvantaged neighborhoods of central Boston. These areas were regions of poverty, economic dependency, and physical deterioration, and were usually adjacent to areas of industry and commerce (Glueck & Glueck, 1950, p. 29).

A wealth of information on social, psychological, and biological characteristics, family life, school performance, work experiences, and other life events was collected on the delinquents and controls in the period 1939–1948. These data were collected through an elaborate investigation process that involved interviews with the subjects themselves and their families as well as interviews with key informants such as social workers, settlement house workers, clergymen, schoolteachers, neighbors, and criminal justice and social welfare officials. The home-interview setting also provided an opportunity to observe home and family life (Glueck & Glueck, 1950, pp. 41–53).

Interview data and home investigations were supplemented by field investigations that meticulously culled information from the records of both public and private agencies that had any involvement with a subject or his family. These materials verified and amplified the materials of a particular case investigation. For example, a principal source of data was the Social Service Index, a clearinghouse that contained information on all dates of contact between a family and the various social agencies (e.g., child welfare) in Boston. Similar indexes from other cities and states were utilized where necessary. For *Unraveling,* the Gluecks employed two case collators to sift through the several thousand entries over the 7¹/₂-year project.

The Gluecks also searched the files of the Massachusetts Board of Probation, which maintained a central file of all court records from Boston courts since 1916 and from Massachusetts as a whole from 1924. These records were compared and supplemented with records from the Boys' Parole Division in Massachusetts. Out-of-state arrests, court appearances, and correctional experiences were gathered through correspondence from equivalent state depositories. Of equal importance was the Gluecks' collection of self-reported, parental-reported, and teacher-reported delinquency of the boy.

Measures

Descriptive statistics and intercorrelations for the full set of measures are displayed in Table 1. To tap the central concept of *family poverty,* we created a scale from information on the average weekly income of the family and the family's reliance on outside aid. The latter measures whether the family was living in comfortable circumstances (having enough savings to cover 4 months of financial stress), marginal circumstances (little or no savings but only occasional dependence on outside aid), or financially dependent (continuous receipt of outside aid for support). The resulting standardized scale of poverty was scored so that a high value represents the combination of low income and reliance on public assistance. Although the Gluecks' matching design controls for neighborhood deprivation, there is still considerable variation among families in poverty (see Table 1).

Five additional features of the structural background of families are introduced as control variables. *Residential mobility* is an interval-based measure of the number of times the boy's family moved during his childhood and ranges from none or once to 16 or more times. *Family size* is the number of children in the boy's family and ranges from one to eight or more. *Family disruption* is coded one when the boy was reared in a home where one or both parents were absent because of divorce, separation, desertion, or death. *Maternal employment* is a dichotomous variable where housewives were coded 0 and working mothers (full time or part time) were coded 1. *Foreign-born* indexes whether one or both parents were born outside the United States.

It is possible, of course, that the poverty status and other structural characteristics of families resulted from prior differences among parents that are correlated with dysfunctional family management (Patterson & Capaldi, 1991). To address this possible confounding, we control for the criminality and drinking habits of mothers and fathers as determined from official statistics and interview data. Criminality refers to official records of arrest or conviction, excluding minor auto violations and violation of license laws. Alcoholism/drunkenness refers to intoxication and includes frequent, regular, or chronic addiction to alcohol, and not to very occasional episodes of overdrinking in an atmosphere of celebration. Not surprisingly, there were strong relations between crime and heavy drinking and between mother's and father's crime/drinking. Hence we formed a summary scale ranging from 0 to 4 that measures the extent of what we term *parental deviance* (see Table 1). For example, a subject whose mother and father both had a criminal record and a history of excessive drinking received a score of 4.

The Gluecks also collected data on each parent's mental condition and temperament from official diagnoses and medical reports from hospitals and clinics, and on occasion from unofficial observations made by social workers (Glueck & Glueck, 1950, p. 102). The ordinal variable labeled *parental instability* reflects whether none (0), one (1), or both (2) of the boy's parents were diagnosed with "severe mental disease or distortion" including "marked emotional instability," "pronounced temperamental deviation," or "extreme impulsiveness."

TABLE 1
Descriptive Statistics and Correlations

Variable	Mean	SD	Minimum	Maximum	Valid N
Structural context:					
Family poverty[a]	.00	1.64	-3.64	3.45	998
Residential mobility	6.75	4.72	1	16	999
Family size	5.08	2.21	1	8	999
Family disruption	.47	.50	0	1	1,000
Maternal employment	.40	.49	0	1	993
Foreign born	.60	.49	0	1	987
Parent/child disposition:					
Parental deviance	1.45	1.27	0	4	1,000
Parental instability	.62	.72	0	2	972
Child difficult/antisocial	.72	.80	0	3	884
Family process:					
Erratic/harsh discipline[a]	-.02	1.73	-3.24	3.14	856
Maternal supervision	1.97	.86	1	3	989
Parental-child attachment	3.72	1.21	1	5	960
Adolescent delinquency:					
Official status	.50	.50	0	1	1,000
Self-parent-teacher reported	8.44	6.67	1	26	1,000

Pairwise Pearson Correlation Coefficients

	2	3	4	5	6	7	8	9	10	11	12	13	14
1. Family poverty	.40	.26	.21	-.04	-.07	.38	.25	.20	.35	-.32	-.34	.34	.33
2. Residential mobility		.05	.40	.18	-.18	.50	.35	.27	.28	-.44	-.43	.41	.41
3. Family size			-.09	-.20	.13	.08	.02	.01	.23	-.11	-.02	.16	.17
4. Family disruption				.19	-.13	.38	.24	.15	.13	-.27	-.46	.26	.28
5. Mother's employment					-.02	.17	.16	.08	.10	-.28	-.16	.14	.16
6. Foreign born						-.21	-.10	-.03	.07	.05	.04	-.04	-.07
7. Parental deviance							.35	.22	.36	-.48	-.44	.41	.41
8. Parental instability								.25	.30	-.39	-.31	.36	.34
9. Child difficult/antisocial									.35	-.30	-.30	.45	.45
10. Erratic/harsh discipline										-.51	-.40	.52	.50
11. Maternal supervision											.49	-.63	-.62
12. Parent-child attachment												-.50	-.49
13. Official status													.86
14. Self-parent-teacher reported													

[a]Standardized scale based on z scores.

Taken together, the parental deviance and instability measures capture key dispositional characteristics that have been argued to underlie family poverty and other disadvantaged outcomes.

Family Process.—The three intervening dimensions of family process are style of discipline, supervision, and parent-child attachment. Parenting style was measured by summing three variables describing the discipline and punishment practices of mothers and fathers. The first constituent variable concerns the use of physical punishment and refers to rough handling, strappings, and beatings eliciting fear and resentment in the boy—not to casual or occasional slapping that was unaccompanied by rage or hostility. The second constituent variable measures threatening or scolding behavior by mothers or fathers that elicited fear in the boy. The third component taps erratic and negligent discipline, for example, if the parent vacillated between harshness and laxity and was not consistent in control, or if the parent was negligent or indifferent about disciplining the boy.

The summation of these constituent variables resulted in two ordinal measures tapping the extent to which parents need inconsistent disciplinary measures in conjunction with harsh physical punishment and/or threatening or scolding behavior. In Braithwaite's (1989) scheme, these measures tap the sort of punitive shaming and negative stigmatization by families that engender delinquency. The validity of measures is supported by the high concordance between mother's and father's use of erratic/harsh discipline (gamma = .60). For example, of fathers who employed harsh physical punishment, threatening behavior, and erratic discipline (code = 3), 44% of the mothers were also coded 3. By contrast, less than 1% of boys' fathers coded 0 on the erratic/harsh scale had mothers coded high (3) in erratic/harsh discipline. For reasons of both theoretical parsimony and increased reliability, we created standardized scales that combined mother and father's *erratic/harsh discipline.*

Maternal supervision is an ordinal variable coded 3 if the mother provided supervision over the boy's activities at home or in the neighborhood. If unable to supervise the boys themselves, mothers who made arrangements for other adults to watch the boy's activities were also assigned a 3. A code of 2 was assigned to those mothers providing partial or fair supervision. Supervision was considered unsuitable (code = 1) if the mother left the boy on his own, without guidance, or in the care of an irresponsible person.

As the Gluecks originally observed, attachment is a "two-way street"—parent to child and child to parent (Glueck & Glueck, 1950, p. 125). Accordingly, the Gluecks gathered interview-based information from both the parents and boys themselves on emotional attachment and rejection. For example, the Gluecks developed a three-point ordinal indicator of the extent to which the boy had a warm emotional bond to the father and/or mother as displayed in a close association with the parent and in expressions of admiration. Similarly, the Gluecks measured whether the parents were loving and accepting of the child or were rejecting in emotional attention—that is, whether parents were openly hostile or did not give the child much emotional attention. Because the parent-child and child-parent indicators of attachment were strongly related (gamma = .58), we combined them into a single ordinal scale labeled *parent-child attachment* that ranges from 1 (low) to 5 (high).

Child Effects.—Although the *Unraveling* study was not longitudinal, there are retrospective data on three key dimensions of troublesome childhood behavior. From the parent's interview there is an indicator distinguishing those children who were overly restless and irritable from those who were not. A second measure reflects the extent to which a child engaged in violent temper tantrums and was predisposed to aggressiveness and fighting. The Gluecks' collected data only on habitual tantrums—when tantrums were "the predominant mode of response" by the child to difficult situations growing up (1950, p. 152). This measure corresponds closely to one validated by

Caspi (1987). The third variable is the boy's self-reported age of onset of misbehavior. We created a dichotomous variable where a 1 indexes an age of onset earlier than age 8. Those who had a later age of onset *and* those who reported no delinquency (and hence no age of onset) were assigned a zero.

As expected, all three measures are significantly correlated. For example, of those children rated difficult in childhood, 34% exhibited tantrums, compared to 13% of those with no history of difficultness. Similarly, for those with an early onset of misbehavior, 47% were identified as having tantrums, compared to 20% of those with no early onset (all p's < .05). To achieve theoretical and empirical parsimony, we summed the three indicators to form an ordinal scale that measures *child difficult/antisocial behavior.* The scale ranges from 0, indicating no signs of early conduct disorder or difficulty in child rearing, to a score of 3, indicating that a child was difficult and irritable, threw violent temper tantrums, and engaged in antisocial behavior prior to age 8.

There is evidence of the predictive validity of our child-effects measure derived from self, parent, and teacher reports. Fully 100% of those scoring high on child antisocial behavior were arrested in adolescence, compared to 25% of those scoring low (gamma = .69). More importantly, the child-effects measure predicts criminal behavior well into adulthood. Using data on adult crime collected by the Gluecks as part of a follow-up study (Glueck & Glueck, 1968), 60% of those scoring high on childhood antisocial behavior were arrested at ages 25–32, compared to less than 25% with no signs of early disorder. Perhaps most striking, there is a rather strong monotonic relation between childhood antisocial disposition and arrests even at ages 32–45 (gamma = .37). Hence, although early antisocial behavior was determined by retrospective reports, the techniques used by the Gluecks appear valid (see also Sampson & Laub, 1993, pp. 47–63).

Delinquency.—The outcome of adolescent delinquency is measured using both the official criterion of the Gluecks' research design (1 = delinquent, 0 = control group) and "unofficial" delinquency derived by summing self, parent, and teacher reports. In preliminary analysis we also examined measures for particular offenses (e.g., truancy as reported by parents, teachers, and self) and the total amount of delinquency for all crime types reported by a particular source (e.g., self-report total, parent-report total). Because the results were very similar, the present analysis is based on the sum of all delinquent behaviors that were measured consistently across reporters. That is, we eliminated incorrigibility (e.g., vile language, lying) and other behaviors that were only asked of one source (e.g., teacher reports of school vandalism). The unofficial measure thus reflects adolescent delinquency measured by parents, teachers, and the boys themselves.

Reliability and Validity

Because of their strategy of data collection, the Gluecks' measures pertain to multiple sources of information that were independently derived from several points of view and at separate times. The level of detail and the range of information collected by the Gluecks will likely never be repeated given contemporary research standards on the protection of human subjects. As Robins et al. (1985, p. 30) also point out in their analysis of social-science data from an earlier era analogous to the Gluecks: "In conformity with the precomputer era of data analysis, the coding was less atomized than it would have been today. Consequently, we have only the coders' overall assessment based on a variety of individual items."

This method of data collection limits the extent to which reliability can be determined by traditional criteria (e.g., intercoder reliability). As described above, however, our basic measurement strategy uses multiple indicators of key concepts and composite scales whenever possible and theoretically appropriate. Note also that the Glueck data are different in kind from survey research where measurement error, especially on attitudes, is large. That is, the Glueck data represent the comparison, reconciliation, and integration of multiple sources of information even for individual items (see Glueck & Glueck, 1950, pp. 70–72; 1968, pp. 205–255). Moreover, our measures refer to behavior (e.g., discipline, supervision) and objective structural conditions (e.g., poverty, broken homes)—not attitudes.

To verify the coding of the family-process variables, we also conducted a validation test for the purposes of this article. Selecting a 10% random sample of the delinquent subjects ($N = 50$), we coded from the original interview narratives the three key elements of family process—supervision, parenting style, and parental attachment—blind to the actual codes of the Gluecks. We then compared our scores with those of the Gluecks and in general found excellent correspondence. For example, the correlation (gamma) between our coding and the Gluecks for parental supervision, father's rejection, and mother's rejection was .87, .92, and .98, respectively. We found significant levels of agreement for other key indicators of family process as well, using both gamma and kappa statistics on percent agreement corrected for chance.

Finally, the correlations in Table 1 reveal that our key measures are related in a manner consistent with theory and past research. In particular, erratic/harsh discipline is negatively related to supervision and parent-child attachment (–.51 and –.40, respectively, $p < .05$), whereas maternal supervision is positively related to parent-child attachment (.49, $p < .05$). These and other significant correlations in the predicted and expected direction (see Table 1) support standard criteria for construct validation.

RESULTS

Our analysis begins in Table 2 with an overview of the bivariate association between family process and delinquency as measured by official records and total unofficial delinquency. The magnitude and direction of relationships support the informal social-control model. All relationships are in the expected direction, quite large, and maintain whether one considers official or unofficial delinquency. For example, both official and unofficial delinquency increase monotonically as erratic/harsh discipline increases (gammas = .70 and .59., respectively). Delinquency also declines monotonically with increasing levels of supervision and attachment. In fact, 83% of those in the low supervision category were delinquent, compared to only 10% of those in the high category (gamma = –.84). The unofficial criterion shows an even greater differential. Parental attachment is similarly related to both official and unofficial delinquency.

We next consider the extent to which the three dimensions of informal social control potentially

TABLE 2
Bivariate Association between Family Process and Delinquency

	Discipline Erratic/Harsh			Maternal Supervision			Parent-Child Attachment		
	Low (288)	Medium (224)	High (334)	Low (382)	Medium (252)	High (355)	Low (414)	Medium (194)	High (352)
Officially delinquent (%)	18	51	74	83	58	10	77	47	21
Gamma		.70*			–.84*			–.73*	
Unofficially delinquent[a] (%)	10	39	53	60	39	5	57	32	13
Gamma		.59*			–.72*			–.62*	

[a]Percent unofficially delinquent refers to the trichotomized "high" category.
*$p < .05$.

TABLE 3

OLS Linear Regression Models of Family Process on Structural Context and Parent/Child Disposition

A. Structural Context and Parental Disposition (N = 800)	Family Process					
	Erratic/Harsh Discipline		Maternal Supervision		Parent-Child Attachment	
	β	t ratio	β	t ratio	β	t ratio
Family poverty	.17	4.66*	−.09	−2.84*	−.15	−4.28*
Residential mobility	.07	1.81	−.21	−5.85*	−.17	−4.59*
Family size	.16	4.90*	−.13	−4.30*	−.01	−.29
Family disruption	−.05	−1.35	−.04	−1.16	−.22	−6.75*
Maternal employment	.05	1.54	−.20	−7.04*	−.03	−1.04
Foreign born	.13	4.30*	−.07	−2.60*	−.11	−3.81*
Parental deviance	.23	6.01*	−.24	−7.12*	−.18	−4.86*
Parental instability	.17	4.96*	−.19	−6.26*	−.10	−3.21*
Adjusted R^2	.26		.41		.32	

B. Adding Child Effects (N = 716)	Family Process					
	Erratic/Harsh Discipline		Maternal Supervision		Parent-Child Attachment	
	β	t ratio	β	t ratio	β	t ratio
Family poverty	.16	4.38*	−.06	−1.64	−.17	−4.58*
Residential mobility	.03	.73	−.18	−5.06*	−.15	−3.94*
Family size	.18	5.41*	−.16	−5.26*	−.02	−.58
Family disruption	−.06	−1.56	−.01	−.42	−.19	−5.55*
Maternal employment	.07	2.12*	−.22	−7.29*	−.02	−.70
Foreign born	.13	4.09*	−.08	−2.70*	−.12	−3.77*
Parental deviance	.20	4.90*	−.24	−6.80*	−.19	−4.83*
Parental instability	.13	3.79*	−.16	−5.01*	−.05	−1.44
Child diff./antisocial	.22	6.67*	−.15	−4.94*	−.13	−3.96*
Adjusted R^2	.30		.43		.34	

*$p < .05$.

mediate the effect of more distal, structural factors. To accomplish this goal, Panel A of Table 3 displays the results of ordinary-least-squares (OLS) models of family process variables regressed on structural background factors and parental disposition. The results support the theoretical prediction that structural poverty has significant effects on informal social control. For example, the data in columns 1 and 2 show that poverty, in addition to large families, parental deviance, parental instability, and foreign-born status, contributes significantly to erratic use of harsh/punitive discipline ($\beta = .17$, t ratio = 4.66).

The results for maternal supervision are also consistent with our general social control framework—poverty significantly reduces effective monitoring (t ratio = −2.84). In addition to parental disposition, other features of structural context are salient too, especially residential mobility, family size, and employment by mothers. There has been much debate about the effect of mother's employment outside of the home on delinquency, but relatively little on how supervision might mediate this structural factor (see Hoffman, 1974; Laub & Sampson, 1988; Maccoby, 1958). In the Glueck data and time era (circa 1940), employment by mothers outside of the home appears to have a significant negative effect on mother's supervision. This is exactly the pattern supportive of a social control framework and confirmed by other empirical research (see Maccoby, 1958; Wilson, 1980). It remains to be seen whether employment outside of the home by mothers has any direct effect on delinquency. It is also worth noting that mother's employment has no discernible effect on erratic/harsh discipline and parent-child attachment.

In columns 5 and 6 we turn to the relational dimension of family social control—emotional attachment and bonding between parent and child. Substantively, the results suggest that in families experiencing marital disruption, frequent residential moves, disadvantaged financial/ethnic position, and a pattern of deviant or unstable parental conduct, parents, and children are more likely to exhibit indifference or hostility toward each other. Interestingly, these effects are rather substantial and much larger than those associated with family size and maternal employment.

Panel B displays the replication models that add "child effects" to the explanation of family process. The results suggest that difficult and antisocial childhood behavior disrupts effective parenting. Specifically, children who were rated difficult, habitually engaged in violent tantrums, and exhibited early misbehavior tended to generate lower levels of supervision by their mothers during adolescence. Consistent with a control-systems perspective, troublesome childhood behavior also significantly predicts the erratic/harsh use of discipline by parents and weakened attachment between parent and child. These results support Lytton's (1990) arguments regarding the endogeneity of parental styles of discipline and control of children, especially direct controls. Simply put, parents appear responsive to early behavioral difficulties—angry temperamental children who misbehave provoke in their parents a disrupted style of parenting and control.

Considering the central role of childhood behavior, the finding that the effects of structural context remain largely intact becomes all the more impressive. Indeed, the rationale for introducing child effects was not to establish conclusively the validity of "control systems" theory, but rather to test the validity of our theoretical conceptions about the indirect effects of poverty on adolescent delinquency. In this regard, note that family poverty, independent of child disposition, continues to exert significant and relatively large effects on erratic/harsh discipline and parent-child attachment. Moreover, it is possible that the reduced effect of poverty on supervision in Panel B (t ratio = -1.64, $p < .10$) reflects in part an indirect effect whereby poverty increases early antisocial behavior, which further disrupts parenting. In any case, the data support a structure-process model—poverty and structural context explain informal social control by families, regardless of parental disposition and childhood antisocial behavior.

Explaining Delinquency

Panel A of Table 4 displays the effects of structural context, parental disposition, and family process on adolescent delinquency. The first two columns of data list the ML logistic results for the official delinquency criterion. Columns 3 and 4 list the OLS results for the summary measure of unofficially reported delinquency. In general the results are invariant across method and measurement of delinquency. The majority of structural context and parental disposition factors have insignificant direct effects on delinquency, operating instead through the family process variables. The main exception is family size, which has a direct positive effect on both official and self-parent-teacher-reported delinquency. Residential mobility and family disruption also have small direct effects on unofficial delinquency.

On the other hand, the three family-process variables exhibit significant effects on delinquency in the predicted theoretical direction. Several of these effects are quite large, especially the negative effect of maternal supervision

TABLE 4

OLS Linear and ML Logistic Regression of Delinquency on Structural Context, Family Process, and Parent/Child Disposition

	Delinquency			
	Official Status		Self-Parent-Teacher Reported	
A. Structural Context and Parental Disposition (N = 800)	ML Logistic[a]		OLS Linear	
	b	t ratio	β	t ratio
Family poverty	.10	1.36	.04	1.46
Residential mobility	.03	1.20	.07	2.21*
Family size	.14	2.63*	.08	2.82*
Family disruption	.32	1.36	.06	2.10*
Maternal employment	−.14	−.62	−.02	−.64
Foreign born	.04	.18	−.03	−1.32
Parental deviance	−.00	−.04	.01	.23
Parental instability	.21	1.36	.05	1.60
Erratic/harsh discipline	.38	5.26*	.17	5.25*
Maternal supervision	−1.27	−8.15*	−.36	−9.89*
Parent-child attachment	−.47	−4.51*	−.15	−4.70*
	ML Model χ^2 = 485, 11 df		OLS R^2 = .48	

	Delinquency			
	Official Status		Self-Parent-Teacher Reported	
B. Adding Child Effects (N = 716)	ML Logistic[a]		OLS Linear	
	b	t ratio	β	t ratio
Family poverty	.09	1.18	.02	.64
Residential mobility	.01	.33	.07	1.97*
Family size	.18	3.04*	.10	3.59*
Family disruption	.33	1.24	.07	2.23*
Maternal employment	−.00	−.00	.01	.26
Foreign born	.01	.04	−.03	−1.25
Erratic/harsh discipline	.35	4.22*	.13	3.87*
Maternal supervision	−1.21	−7.06*	−.33	−8.77*
Parent-child attachment	−.50	−4.24*	−.15	−4.54*
Parental deviance	.03	.25	.01	.28
Parental instability	.10	.61	.02	.76
Child difficult/antisocial	1.09	6.35*	.19	6.72*
	ML Model χ^2 = 475, 12 df		OLS R^2 = .52	

*Entries for ML Logistic "b" are the raw maximum-likelihood coefficients; "t ratios" are coefficients divided by SE.
*$p < .05$.

on delinquency (OLS $\beta = -.36$, ML t ratio = -8.15). At the same time, erratic/punitive discipline and parent-child attachment have independent effects on delinquency of similar magnitudes ($\beta = .17$ and $-.15$, respectively). Net of background variables and parental disposition, then, both direct family controls (discipline and monitoring) and indirect social control (affective bonding between child and parent) distinguish nondelinquents from serious, persistent delinquents.

The initial results support the predictions of our theoretical strategy—when an intervening variable mediates the effect of an exogenous variable, the direct effects of the latter should disappear. For the most part that is what Table 4 yields. Moreover, when OLS and ML logistic regression models are estimated without the hypothesized mediating variables, virtually all structural context factors have large, significant effects on delinquency in the expected manner. In particular, the reduced-form t ratio for the effect of poverty on unofficial delinquency is 4.96 (further underscoring the between-family variations in poverty). But, as seen in Table 4, the significant effect of poverty on delinquency is eliminated when discipline, supervision, and attachment are controlled. The calculation of indirect effect estimates reveals that of the total effect of all structural context and parental disposition factors on delinquency, approximately 67% is mediated by family process. The results thus demonstrate the importance of considering indirect effects of poverty and other dimensions of structural background.

Panel B of Table 4 displays two replication models of structural background, parental disposition, family process, and child effects on delinquency. The results suggest three substantive conclusions. First, much like earlier models, family poverty and most other structural background factors influence delinquency largely through the mediating dimensions of family process. Second, the child-effects measure has a significant direct effect on delinquency that is unaccounted for by family process and structural context. Third, and most

important from our perspective, are the robust results regarding family process. Despite controlling for childhood and parental disposition, the dimensions of parental discipline, attachment, and supervision all continue to influence delinquent conduct in the manner predicted by our informal social-control model. Mother's supervision has by far the largest effect on self-parent-teacher-reported delinquency, with a standardized coefficient almost double the child effect ($\beta = -.33$).

On balance, then, our theoretical model remains intact, surviving a test that controls for early childhood antisocial behavior. Hence one way of interpreting Table 4 is that variations in adolescent delinquency unexplained by early propensity to deviance are directly explained by informal processes of family social control in adolescence. The magnitude of the family-process effects is especially noteworthy—for example, independent of all other factors including childhood antisocial behavior, a one-unit increase in mother's supervision (on a three-point scale) is associated with over a 50% decrease in official delinquency. The magnitudes of the standardized effects on unofficial delinquency tell the same story.

Structural Equation Models

To this point in the analysis it is clear that structural context, parental disposition, and child antisocial behavior have similar effects on supervision, attachment, and erratic/harsh discipline. This pattern suggests that the three family-process measures are tapping the same latent construct. Further evidence for this specification was seen earlier in Table 1—all three indicators are highly intercorrelated—in fact, the smallest correlation is $-.40$ between attachment and erratic/harsh discipline. Thus, even though supervision, attachment, and erratic/harsh discipline exhibited independent effects in the OLS regression models, there are both theoretical and empirical reasons to consider an alternative strategy that specifies all three measures as underlying a latent construct of informal social control.

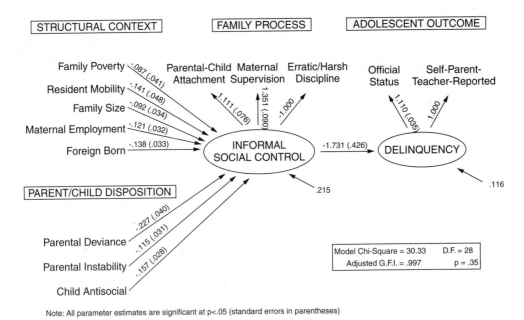

Note: All parameter estimates are significant at p<.05 (standard errors in parentheses)

FIGURE 1   ML Weighted-Least-Squares Covariance-Structure Model of Structural Context, Parent\Child Disposition, Informal Social Control, and Delinquency (*N* =716).

To estimate this alternative conception, we take advantage of recent advances in Jöreskog and Sörbom's (1989) LISREL 7.20 and PRELIS 1.20 programs for maximum-likelihood (ML) estimation of linear covariance-structure models with data that are non-normally distributed. The basic specification of our covariance structure model is shown in Figure 1 (for a similar specification see Larzelere & Patterson, 1990). Both delinquency and informal social control are specified as latent constructs. The former is measured with official delinquency and self-parent-teacher reports, whereas the latent construct of informal social control is hypothesized to generate the correlations among erratic/harsh discipline, parent-child attachment, and maternal supervision. The direction and magnitude of factor loadings support the validity of specified variables as indicators of the latent constructs. As before, structural context and child/parent disposition are treated as exogenous observed variables. However, family disruption was insignifi-

cant in the initial LISREL estimation, and was thus dropped to improve the model fit.

Figure 1 presents the ML weighted-least-squares LISREL estimates of all significant path coefficients. The model fits the data very well, yielding a chi-square of 30 with 28 degrees of freedom (*p* = .35). Indeed, as seen in the adjusted goodness-of-fit index (.99), there is an excellent match between the observed covariances and our theoretical specification of family process. Informal social control also has a large and significant negative effect on the latent construct of delinquency (*t* ratio = − 4.06). Perhaps most striking, the latent family construct new mediates all prior effects of structural context and parent/child disposition. Calculating indirect effect estimates, we find that 68% of the total effect of exogenous factors on delinquency is mediated by informal social control. Note, for example, that poverty has a significant negative effect on informal social control (*t* ratio = −2.12) net of other context variables and parent/child disposition. This finding substantiates earlier OLS analyses. Similarly, both parental deviance and instability independently reduce informal social control, in turn increasing delinquency.

Interestingly, however, note that the child-disposition measure has a large negative effect (t ratio = –5.61) on informal social control but no direct effect on delinquency. This is the only major finding that does not comport with earlier regression analyses—once a family-process measurement model is specified, the influence of childhood antisocial behavior on delinquency works solely through attenuated informal social control. Although this finding needs to be replicated in future analysis, it does support the control-systems hypothesis (Lytton, 1990) that child effects are important primarily for their influence on family management. Similarly, the lack of a direct effect on delinquency suggests that the correlation between childhood and adolescent delinquency is less an indication of a latent antisocial trait than a *developmental process* whereby delinquent children systematically undermine effective strategies of family social control, in turn increasing the odds of later delinquency. In any case, the more general message in Figure 1 is that the latent construct of informal social control is the primary factor in explaining adolescent delinquency.

DISCUSSION

Our major finding is that family process mediated approximately two-thirds of the effect of poverty and other structural background factors on delinquency. Whether analyzed with standard regression techniques or covariance structure models, the data paint a consistent picture. Namely, poverty appears to inhibit the capacity of families to achieve informal social control, which in turn increases the likelihood of adolescent delinquency.

The data thus support the general theory of informal social control explicated at the outset. We believe that this theory has significance for future research by positing how it is that poverty

and structural disadvantage influence delinquency in childhood and adolescence. A concern with only direct effects conceals mediating relations and may thus lead to misleading conclusions regarding the theoretical importance and policy relevance of more distal structural factors such as poverty (see also Conger et al., 1992; Larzelere & Patterson, 1990; McLoyd, 1990). More generally, families do not exist in isolation (or just "under the roof") but instead are systematically embedded in social-structural contexts—even taking into account parental predispositions toward deviance and impulsive temperament.

The data further point to the complex role of social selection and social causation in the genesis of delinquency. Although difficult children who display early antisocial tendencies do appear to self select or sort themselves into later states of delinquency, family processes of informal social control still explain a significant share of variance in adolescent delinquency. Moreover, the covariance structure analyses further suggest that the effect of childhood antisocial/difficult behavior is mediated by family process. Although "child effects" are clearly present, a full understanding of delinquency thus requires that we also come to grips with the socializing influence of the family as reflected in disciplinary practices, supervision and direct parental controls, and bonds of attachment.

Not only do our results point to the indirect effects of poverty on adolescent delinquency, they simultaneously suggest that strong family social controls may serve as an important buffer against structural disadvantage in the larger community. Recall that all boys were reared in economically deprived neighborhoods of central Boston in the Great Depression era, conditions similar to disadvantaged "underclass" communities in many inner-city areas today (see Wilson, 1987). Yet there were marked variations in both family poverty and delinquency risk within these structurally deprived areas of Boston in the 1930s and 1940s, just as there are in the worst inner cities of today. Cohesive families characterized by consistent, loving, and reintegrative punishment, effective supervision, and close emotional ties appear to have overcome these disadvantaged conditions in producing a low risk of adolescent delinquency. In this sense it is mistaken to assume that residents of concentrated poverty areas (e.g., the "underclass") face homogeneous odds—whether it be for negative *or* positive outcomes.

Despite the consistency of results, we recognize that limitations of the data preclude definitive conclusions. Because the Gluecks used a sample of institutionalized delinquents and neighborhood socioeconomic status as one of the matching variables, our conclusions are limited to the relative effects of family poverty on serious and persistent delinquency within a disadvantaged sample (for a critique of this aspect of the Gluecks' research design, see Reiss, 1951). Whether our results hold for adolescents (including noninstitutionalized delinquents) drawn from a wider range of socioeconomic positions is an important issue for future research. Many of the measures we used in the present analysis were also retrospective in nature and may have been confounded by the original coders' global impressions. Issues of temporal order and discriminant validity thus cannot be resolved with certainty (see Bank, Dishion, Skinner, & Patterson, 1990). In particular, a richer set of prospective child-effects and parental-disposition measures is needed to assess more rigorously the role of individual differences. Whether child effects are fully mediated by family processes of informal social control (see Fig. 1) would seem to be an especially salient question for future work.

Nevertheless, it bears emphasis that our findings on family process are consistent with much previous research—including key observations of the Gluecks some 40 years ago. Note also the recent meta-analysis by Loeber and Stouthamer-Loeber (1986, p. 37) where they found that aspects of family functioning involving direct parent-child contacts are the most powerful predictors of delinquency and other juvenile conduct problems. Apparently, the fundamental causes of delinquency are consistent across time and rooted not in race (e.g., black inner-city culture) but generic family processes—such as *supervision, attachment,* and *discipline*—that are systematically influenced by family poverty and structural disadvantage. We hope that future research will address further the connections we have emphasized between poverty and mediating family processes, especially as they bear on both risk and avoidance of adolescent delinquency in disadvantaged communities.

REFERENCES

Anderson, K., Lytton, H., & Romney, D. (1986). Mothers' interactions with normal and conduct-disordered boys: Who affects whom? *Developmental Psychology, 22,* 604–609.

Bank, L., Dishion, T., Skinner, M., & Patterson, G. (1990). Method variance in structural equation modeling: Living with "glop." In G. Patterson (Ed.), *Depression and aggression in family interaction* (pp. 248–279). Hillsdale, NJ: Erlbaum.

Braithwaite, J. (1989). *Crime, shame, and reintegration.* Cambridge: Cambridge University Press.

Caspi, A. (1987). Personality in the life course. *Journal of Personality and Social Psychology, 53,* 1203–1213.

Conger, R., Conger, K., Elder, G. H., Jr., Lorenz, F., Simons, R., & Whitbeck, L. B. (1992). A family process model of economic hardship and adjustment of early adolescent boys. *Developmental Psychology, 63,* 526–541.

Elder, G. H., & Caspi, A. (1988). Economic stress in lives: Developmental perspectives. *Journal of Social Issues, 44,* 25–45.

Glueck, S., & Glueck, E. (1950). *Unraveling juvenile delinquency.* New York: Commonwealth Fund.

Glueck, S., & Glueck, E. (1968). *Delinquents and nondelinquents in perspective.* Cambridge, MA: Harvard University Press.

Gottfredson, M., & Hirschi, T. (1990). *A general theory of crime.* Stanford, CA: Stanford University Press.

Hirschi, T. (1969). *Causes of delinquency.* Berkeley: University of California Press.

Hirschi, T. (1983). Crime and the family. In J. Wilson (Ed.), *Crime and public policy* (pp. 53–68). San Francisco: Institute for Contemporary Studies.

Hoffman, L. W. (1974). Effects of maternal employment on the child: A review of the research. *Developmental Psychology,* **10,** 204–228.

Jencks, C. (1992). *Rethinking social policy: Race, poverty, and the underclass.* Cambridge, MA: Harvard University Press.

Jöreskog, K., & Sörbom, D. (1989). *LISREL VI: A guide to the program and applications.* Chicago, IL: Scientific Software.

Kornhauser, R. (1978). *Social sources of delinquency.* Chicago: University of Chicago Press.

Larzelere, R., & Patterson, G. (1990). Parental management: Mediator of the effect of socioeconomic status on early delinquency. *Criminology,* **28,** 301–323.

Laub, J. H., & Sampson, R. J. (1988). Unraveling families and delinquency: A reanalysis of the Gluecks' data. *Criminology,* **26,** 355–380.

Loeber, R., & Stouthamer-Loeber, M. (1986). Family factors as correlates and predictors of juvenile conduct problems and delinquency. In M. Tonry & N. Morris (Eds.), *Crime and justice* (Vol. **7,** pp. 29–150). Chicago: University of Chicago Press.

Lytton, H. (1990). Child and parent effects in boys' conduct disorder: A reinterpretation. *Developmental Psychology,* **26,** 683–697.

Maccoby, E. (1958). Children and working mothers. *Children,* **5,** 83–89.

McLoyd, V. C. (1990). The impact of economic hardship on black families and children: Psychological distress, parenting, and socioemotional development. *Child Development,* **61,** 311–346.

Olweus, D. (1980). Familial and temperamental determinants of aggressive behavior in adolescent boys: A causal analysis. *Developmental Psychology,* **16,** 644–660.

Patterson, G. (1980). Children who steal. In T. Hirschi & M. Gottfredson (Eds.), *Understanding crime: Current theory and research* (pp. 73–90). Beverly Hills, CA: Sage.

Patterson, G. (1982). *Coercive family process.* Eugene, OR: Castalia.

Patterson, G. (1988). Stress: A change agent for family process. In N. Garmezy & M. Rutter (Eds.), *Stress, coping, and development in children* (pp. 235–264). Baltimore: Johns Hopkins University Press.

Patterson, G., & Capaldi, D. (1991). Antisocial parents: Unskilled and vulnerable. In P. Cowan & M. Hetherington (Eds.), *Family transitions* (pp. 195–218). Hillsdale, NJ: Erlbaum.

Patterson, G., DeBaryshe, B., & Ramsey, E. (1989). A developmental perspective on antisocial behavior. *American Psychologist,* **44,** 329–335.

Reiss, A. J., Jr. (1951). Unraveling juvenile delinquency: II. An appraisal of the research methods. *American Journal of Sociology,* **57,** 115–120.

Robins, L. N. (1966). *Deviant children grown up.* Baltimore: Williams & Wilkins.

Robins, L. N., Schoenberg, S., Holmes, S., Ratcliff, K., Benham, A., & Works, J. (1985). Early home environment and retrospective recall: A test for concordance between siblings with and without psychiatric disorders. *American Journal of Orthopsychiatry,* **55,** 27–41.

Rutter, M., & Giller, H. (1983). *Juvenile delinquency: Trends and perspectives.* New York: Guilford.

Sampson, R. J., & Laub, J. H. (1993). *Crime in the making: Pathways and turning points through life.* Cambridge, MA: Harvard University Press.

West, D., & Farrington, D. P. (1973). *Who becomes delinquent?* London: Heinemann.

White, J., Moffitt, T., Earls, F., Robins, L., & Silva, P. (1990). How early can we tell? Predictors of childhood conduct disorder and adolescent delinquency. *Criminology,* **28,** 507–533.

Wilson, H. (1980). Parental supervision: A neglected aspect of delinquency. *British Journal of Criminology,* **20,** 203–235.

Wilson, W. J. (1987). *The truly disadvantaged: The inner city, the underclass, and public policy.* Chicago: University of Chicago Press.

ADOLESCENTS' INTIMACY WITH PARENTS AND FRIENDS

Tiffany Field, Claudia Lang, Regina Yando, and Debra Bendell

Separate literatures support the importance of intimate relationships of adolescents with parents and peers. In studies on adolescents' relationships with parents, the majority of adolescents have been noted to feel close to and get along with their parents (Richardson, Galambos, Schulenberg, & Petersen, 1984). The parent relationship literature, however, contains very little data on the association between adolescents' intimacy with their parents and other psychological variables such as self-esteem and depression or problem behaviors characteristic of adolescence including drug use and risk-taking.

In contrast, in the literature on adolescents' relationships with peers, those adolescents with supportive friendships are noted to have greater self-esteem, less depression, and better adjustment to school (Berndt & Savin-Williams, 1993). Because the parent and peer relationship literatures do not overlap, little is known about the relative relationships between intimacy with parents and friends and these other important psychological and problem-behavior variables.

The purpose of the present study was to determine how intimacy with mother, father, and close friend varied as a function of demographic variables (sex, ethnicity, and SES), social and school variables (family responsibility-taking, sex of friends, presence of boyfriend/girlfriend, interest in school, and academic expectations), psychological variables (self-esteem and depression), and problem behaviors (drug use and risk-taking). Several of these variables were categorical, and others were submitted to median splits with intimacy scale scores as dependent measures.

METHOD

Subjects

A questionnaire comprised of several scales was administered to 455 adolescents ranging in age from 14 to 19 years ($M = 16.6$). Half the adolescents were female (54%), and their ethnicity consisted of 33% white non-Hispanic, 48% Hispanic, 12% black, and 5% Asian, with the remaining 2% from a variety of ethnic backgrounds. Distribution of their socioeconomic status was 17% low to low middle, 50% middle, and 33% upper middle to upper class.

Procedure

The questionnaire was administered anonymously to the students in their classrooms near the end of the school year. Students were informed that the purpose of the study was to learn more about their interpersonal relationships and how they felt

From *Adolescence*, 30, 117, 133–140 (1995). Copyright © 1995 by Libra Publishers, Inc. Reprinted with permission.

about different areas affecting their lives. The scales required 45 minutes to complete, and answers were checked on computer scan sheets.

Measures

The questionnaire tapped the following areas of interest:

Background and Lifestyle   (Field & Yando, 1991). This section includes questions on demographics (gender, ethnicity, and self-perceived socioeconomic status), relationships (number of close friends, gender of friends, and presence of boyfriend/girlfriend), school (interest in school and academic expectations), problem behaviors (suicidal thoughts and drug/alcohol use), and self-contentment.

Intimacy   (Blyth & Foster-Clark, 1987). This scale (Cronbach's alpha = .85; test-retest reliability = .81) assesses level of intimacy with mother, father, and best friend. Examples of the 24 questions, which are divided into 3 subscales (one for mother, one for father, and one for best friend) are: How important is your mother/father/best friend) to you? The five-choice answers vary from "Not at All" to "Very Much." High scores signify greater intimacy.

Family Responsibility   (Field & Yando, 1991). This 10-item scale (Cronbach's alpha = .65; test-retest reliability = .81) was developed to tap students' feelings of responsibility within the family. Examples of the questions include inquiries about doing housework, making mother/father (to whomever the student feels closest) feel better when she/he is "down," and having more responsibilities than peers. Likert-type answers with four choices from "Rarely" to "Very Often."

Self-Esteem   (Field & Yando, 1991). On this scale students are asked to compare themselves to their peers on the following 20 descriptors: confident, anxious, happy, fearful, competitive, ambitious, hard-working, good-looking, good in

sports, creative, independent, angry, honest, generous, caring, expressive, outgoing, sentimental, good at school work, and moody (Cronbach's alpha = .66; test-retest reliability = .83). The questions were asked as follows: Compared to my peers I would say I am generally (e.g., confident: a) Less; b) The Same; c) More).

Depressed Mood   (Center for Epidemiological Studies Depression Scale, CES–D; Radloff, 1991). This 20-item scale was included to assess depressive symptoms. The subject is asked to report on his/her feelings during the preceding week. The scale has been standardized for high school populations (Radloff, 1991), and has adequate test-retest reliability (.80 – .90) internal consistency, and concurrent validity (Wells, Klerman, & Deykin, 1987). Test-retest reliability over a one-month period for the current sample was .79.

Risk-Taking   (Field & Yando, 1991). The risk-taking scale was designed to tap sports-related and danger-related risk-taking behavior, and was accordingly divided into these two subscales (Cronbach's alpha = .69; test-retest reliability = .84). Thirteen items comprise the "sports-related" risk-taking subscale, and nine items comprise the "danger-related" risk-taking subscale.

Drug Use   Four items, taken from the background information, were used to assess drug abuse. These included questions on smoking and the use of alcohol, marijuana, and cocaine. The answers to these four-choice Likert-type questions range from "Regularly" to "Never," with higher scores signifying more drug use. The questions are asked in the past tense so that students even though the scale was anonymous, would not feel incriminated by their answers.

RESULTS

For these analyses categorical variables and median splits were used to define high and low groups. MANOVAs on the three different clusters (demographic variables, family and school variables, and psychological variables) yielded significant effects. These were followed by univariate ANOVAs on the individual variables within clusters. These analyses were performed with intimacy scale scores as dependent measures.

Demographic Variables

As can be seen in Table 1, intimacy varied as a function of demographic factors as follows: (1) females vs. males reported greater intimacy with their mothers and friends; (2) white and Hispanic vs. black students reported greater intimacy with their fathers and friends; and (3) middle- and upper-class vs. lower-class students reported greater intimacy with their mothers and fathers.

Family, Friends, and School Variables

As can be seen in Table 2, the following effects emerged: (1) *family responsibility-taking:* students with high scores on this scale reported greater intimacy with their mothers, fathers, and best friends; (2) *same-sex friends:* students with

same-sex friends were more intimate with their mothers than were students with opposite-sex friends, and students who had friends from both sexes reported being more intimate with their friends than did students with friends exclusively from the same or opposite sex; (3) *boyfriend/ girlfriend:* students who had a boy/girlfriend reported being less intimate with their friends; (4) *interest in school:* students who were interested in school some or most of the time vs. hardly ever were more intimate with their mothers; and (5) *higher education:* students who reported that they would expect to finish high school, college or a graduate degree indicated greater intimacy with their mothers and fathers than did students who said they would quit school as soon as possible.

TABLE 1
Demographic Variables and Intimacy Scores

Demographic Factors	Intimacy Scores		
	Mother	Father	Friends
Sex			
Male	39.7_a^1	35.8_a	28.7_a^2
Female	42.0_b	33.7_a	32.9_b
Ethnicity			
White	40.6_a	37.0_a	32.3_a
Black	38.6_a	28.0_b^2	28.8_b^2
Hispanic	42.0_a	35.1_a	31.2_a
SES			
Lower	36.5_a^1	28.5_a^2	30.2_a
Middle	41.7_b	34.3_b	30.5_a
Upper	41.8_b	38.0_b	31.0_a

Different subscripts (to be read vertically) indicate group differences
Superscript $^1(p < .05)$ and $^2(p < .01)$ appear by statistically different values.

TABLE 2
Family and School Variables and Intimacy Scores

Family, Friends and School Variables	Intimacy Scores		
	Mother	Father	Friends
Family Responsibility			
Low (< 21)	23.6_a^2	20.5_a^2	30.5_a^1
High (> 22)	28.5_b	24.4_b	31.7_b
Sex of Friends			
Same Sex	41.9_a	34.4_a	30.0_a
Opposite Sex	37.1_b^1	31.5_a	30.2_a
Both Sexes	41.1_{ab}	35.2_a	31.8_b^1
Boy/Girlfriend			
Has	41.4_a	35.1_a	30.3_a^2
Does Not Have	40.1_a	34.1_a	32.0_b
Interest in School			
Hardly Ever	36.3_a^2	30.2_a	30.0_a
Some of the Time	40.0_b	34.1_a	30.6_a
Most of the Time	43.0_b	36.0_a	31.6_a
Academic Expectations			
Quit ASAP	32.8_a^1	20.4_a^1	30.4_a
Finish High School	37.0_b	31.0_b	29.4_a
Finish College	40.5_b	34.4_b	30.9_a
Graduate Degree	41.7_b	35.7_b	31.3_a

Different subscripts (to be read vertically) indicate group differences
Superscript $^1(p < .05)$ and $^2(p < .01)$ appear by statistically different values.

Psychological Variables

As can be seen in Table 3, all of the psychological variables related to intimacy with mothers (except drug use) and fathers (except drug use and risk-taking) as follows: (1) *self-esteem:* students with high self-esteem had more intimate relationships with their mothers and fathers; (2) *depression:* students with higher depression scores had less intimacy with their mothers and fathers; (3) *suicidal thoughts:* students who regularly had suicidal thoughts had less intimacy with their mothers and fathers vs. those who never had suicidal thoughts; (4) *drug use:* no drug use effects were noted; and (5) *danger risk-taking:* students who scored low on danger risk-taking reported more intimacy with their mothers than did students who scored high on danger risk-taking. None of the psychological variables differentiated students with high and low intimacy with friends.

To further explore the relationship between psychological variables and intimacy with mothers, fathers, and friends, correlation analyses were performed. As can be seen in Table 4, the greatest number of significant correlations involved the "intimacy with mother" variable. This was correlated with all variables: measures of well-being including positive relationships with self-esteem and happiness with self and negative relationships with depression, danger risk-taking, and drugs. Intimacy with fathers was correlated with the same measures of well-being excluding danger risk-taking and drug consumption. While intimacy with friends was correlated with intimacy with mothers and with happiness,

TABLE 3

Psychological Variables and Intimacy Scores

Psychological Variables	Intimacy Scores		
	Mother	Father	Friends
Self-Esteem			
Low (< 44)	$25.0_a{}^2$	$21.0_a{}^2$	30.8_a
High (> 45)	27.0_b	23.5_b	31.3_a
Depression			
Low (< 15)	27.0_a	24.1_a	30.9_a
High (> 23)	$23.4_b{}^2$	$19.1_b{}^2$	31.0_a
Suicidal Thoughts			
Regularly	$35.3_a{}^2$	$28.4_a{}^2$	31.2_a
Occasionally	37.3_{ab}	31.4_{ab}	31.3_a
Rarely	38.2_{ab}	31.0_{ab}	31.0_a
Never	43.2_b	37.4_b	31.0_a
Drug Use			
Low (< 7)	24.3_a	21.7_a	30.0_a
High (> 8)	26.0_a	22.4_a	31.7_a
Danger Risk-Taking			
Low (< 17)	27.0_a	22.2_a	31.4_a
High (> 18)	$24.3_b{}^2$	22.5_a	30.4_a

Different subscripts (to be read vertically) indicate group differences
Superscript [1]$(p < .05)$ and [2]$(p < .01)$ appear by statistically different values.

TABLE 4

Correlations Between Psychological and Intimacy Variables

Variables	Intimacy with Mother r	Intimacy with Father	Intimacy with Friends r
Intimacy w/Mom	1.00		
Intimacy w/Dad	.41*	1.00	
Intimacy w/Friends	.15*	.05	1.00
Family Responsibility	.39*	.30*	.06
Self-Esteem	.24*	.22*	.08
Happiness w/Self	.42*	.37*	.16*
Depression	−.23*	−.31*	−.02
Risk (Danger)	−.14*	.07	−.16*
Drugs	−.12*	.04	.03

*(p < .01)

and negatively correlated with danger risk-taking, intimacy with friends was not correlated with the other measures.

DISCUSSION

Not surprisingly, adolescents' perceived intimacy varied as a function of demographic variables including gender and socioeconomic status. Greater perceived intimacy on the part of females with mothers and friends is consistent with the literature on adults who report greater intimacy among females, perhaps related to their greater tendency to self-disclose and greater interest in relationships. Greater intimacy with parents among middle- and upper-class students may relate to the greater accessibility of parents in smaller families, with lower-class families being notably larger and with father frequently absent.

The association between parental intimacy and family responsibility-taking as well as greater interest in school and higher education are probably related to social desirability factors and concerns about pleasing parents. Having friends exclusively from the same or opposite sex (boyfriend/girlfriend) as in an "exclusive relationship," limited intimacy with both parents and friends.

The relationships between parental intimacy and psychological variables were not surprising given similar findings in the literature (Leung & Leung, 1992; Richardson et al., 1984). However, the apparent lack of relationship between peer intimacy and psychological variables was surprising, not only because others have noted positive effects of peer intimacy (Berndt & Savin-Williams, in press), but because adolescence is typically considered a time when students are becoming increasingly autonomous from parents while moving closer to their peers. Students in this sample who had higher self-esteem, less depression, and no suicidal thoughts felt more intimate with their parents (and those low on danger risk-taking were more intimate with their mothers). None of these variables differentiated high and low peer intimacy, and no effects were noted for drug use. However, in a correlation analysis, greater risk-taking was marginally but negatively related to mother and peer intimacy, and drug taking was marginally negatively related to intimacy with mother.

The greatest number of relationships for family, school, and psychological well-being variables were noted for intimacy with mother. Students who felt greater intimacy perceived themselves as having more socially desirable behaviors/aspirations and reported greater well-being. If the maternal relationship can be thought of as the most stable (in terms of duration and/or exposure) in a person's life, that relationship could in turn be contributing to greater perceived stability in the adolescent.

REFERENCES

Berndt, T. J., & Savin-Williams, R. C. (1993). Variations in friendships and peer-group relationships in adolescence. In P. Tolan, & B. Cohler (Eds.), *Handbook of clinical research and practice with adolescents.* New York: Wiley.

Blyth, D. A., & Foster-Clark, F. S. (1987). Gender differences in perceived intimacy with different members of adolescents' social networks. *Sex Roles, 17,* 689–719.

Field, T. M., & Yando, R. (1991). Adolescents' Self-Perceptions scales. *Unpublished Scales.*

Leung, J., & Leung, K. (1992). Life satisfaction, self-concept, and relationship with parents in adolescence. *Journal of Youth & Adolescence, 21*(6), 653–665.

Radloff, L. S. (1991). The use of the Center for Epidemiological Studies Depression Scale in adolescents and young adults. Special Issue: The emergence of depressive symptoms during adolescence. *Journal of Youth and Adolescence, 20*(2), 149–166.

Richardson, R. A., Galambos, N. L., Schulenberg, J. E., & Petersen, A. C. (1984). Young adolescents perceptions of the family environment. *Journal of Early Adolescence, 4,* 131–153.

Wells, V. E., Klerman, G. L., & Deykin, E. Y. (1987). The prevalence of depressive symptoms in college students. *Social Psychiatry, 22,* 20–28.

PART FIVE

PEERS

The most powerful and the most lasting friendships are usually
those of the early season of our lives, when we are most susceptible
to warm and affectionate impressions.
—WILLIAM MELMOTH (1710–1799)

Most adolescents live in three worlds: at home, in school, and among peers. Because the rules in each of these domains can be different, behaviors, languages etc. often must be modified to meet the requirements of each world. For example, some teenagers change significant parts of their attire between school and home. Nevertheless, most adolescents navigate through the three worlds successfully. Evidence suggests that as the childhood attachment to the family diminishes, the peer group becomes more influential.

The peer group proffers powerful rewards, providing popularity, status, prestige, security, and an opportunity to establish close and even intimate friendships. Adolescents seek validation by finding others who share their needs, beliefs, and feelings. Peers provide feedback that most adolescents value, especially when consequences such as compliments or criticism are immediate, as in regard to dress and hairstyles. Reflections from friends on current problems and shared interests help to clarify and confirm perceptions, thus making an important contribution to identity formation.

Hartup (14) provides insights into the dynamics and importance of peer relationships. He distinguishes between "having friends, the identity of one's friends, and friendship quality" in order to assess the impact that peers have on one another. Being liked by one's peers seems to support healthy development. When parents and teachers are perceived as uninterested or insensitive to a young person's problem, many adolescents turn to a friend for comfort and approval. Relying on friends is a healthy coping strategy that plays out differently according to gender. Young women tend to be more relational and talk about their problems with each other for support, whereas young men seek each others' company and enjoy doing things together. Conversely, being disliked by peers puts a teenager at considerable risk. Isolation can lead to feelings of deprivation and contribute to psychological disturbances. Nevertheless, having friends is no guarantee of emotional well-being. Hartup explores the developmental significance of friendships, which include such attributes as equality between friends, choices for conflict resolution, closeness, and mutual support.

Stone and Brown (15) expand the broad and inclusive term *peer group* by focusing on specific subgroups, or "crowds." Adolescent crowds are composed of individuals having distinctive characteristics, similar values, and preferences for common activities. The names of the crowds may differ from one community to another and across time; for instance, jocks are sometimes referred to as athletes or sports. The crowds most commonly recognized are the brains, socies, druggies, populars, loners, normals, rebels, etc. These labels reflect lifestyle, reputation, social status in school, attitude toward school, and perhaps different backgrounds. Adolescents can differentiate clearly between these crowds. Each crowd can be identified by unique patterns of dress, grooming, social activities, academic attitudes and performances, extracurricular activities, school hangouts, and weekend activities. Based on Stone and Brown's research findings, crowds can be placed on a two-dimensional map in which the horizontal identifies *academic engagement* (brains are the highest) and the vertical *peer status* (jocks are the highest). Some crowds are clustered closely together, such as jocks and populars, but others are far apart, such as rebels and brains. Members of any one crowd ascribe positive attributes to their own group as well as to crowds that are close by, but they hold unflattering stereotypes for those that are further away on the two-dimensional map. For example, rebels don't have much good to say about brains. In a delightful way the movie *The Breakfast Club* (1985) depicts the differences in values, clothes, attitudes toward school, and types of social activities teenagers select by depicting the princess, the brain, the delinquent, the jock, and the loner, who grudgingly interact when they are forced to come to school on a Saturday morning as punishment.

Berndt (16) emphasizes that the influence of friends on the attitudes, behaviors, and development of an individual adolescent has been conceptualized by two different models. The first interprets these influences as positive, viewing friends as contributing to adjustment and psychological well-being and enhancing the development of social skills. On certain issues, the peer group may serve as a more effective teacher than parents. The second model emphasizes that friends can be a negative influence, asserting pressure that invites problem behavior. When parents worry that if friends drink at parties, their nondrinking son/daughter will also drink in order to gain acceptance, they espouse this theory. Research by Flannery et al. (39) supports this idea. They found that friends who drink alcohol and an individual's susceptibility to peer pressure are the most significant predictors of an adolescent's substance use. Obviously some individuals are more susceptible and more easily persuaded than others. A college student reflecting on her adolescence wrote, "When I think of my junior-high experience and remember the necessity of obtaining peer acceptance . . . I would have preferred death to any action not totally acceptable to my peers." Her honest acknowledgment of her yielding to peer group standards—no matter what—illustrates these dynamics. Friendship influences work both ways: adolescents usually select friends on the basis of similarities to begin with, and once friendship bonds have been established, individuals may compromise their own or their family's standards to accommodate those of their friends. Berndt acknowledges that both theories have validity in certain situations, but depending too much on either gives an incomplete view of the nature of peer influences.

Adolescents need companions and social support. The type of people chosen to be friends often reflects the individual's needs, aspirations, self-esteem, personality, socioeconomic status, values, and interests.

THE COMPANY THEY KEEP: FRIENDSHIPS AND THEIR DEVELOPMENTAL SIGNIFICANCE

WILLARD W. HARTUP
University of Minnesota

On February 16, 1995, in the small Minnesota town of Delano, a 14-year-old boy and his best friend ambushed and killed his mother as she returned home. The circumstances surrounding this event were described in the next edition of the *Minneapolis Star Tribune* (February 18, 1995): The boy had "several learning disabilities—including attention deficit disorder." He had been "difficult" for a long time and, within the last year, had gotten in trouble with a stepbrother by wrecking a car and carrying a gun to a movie theater. The mother was described as having a wonderful relationship with her daughter but having "difficulties" with her son. The family dwelling contained guns.

Against these child, family, and ecological conditions is a significant social history: The boy was ". . . a lonely and unliked kid who was the frequent victim of schoolmates' taunts, jeers, and assaults. He had trouble with school work and trouble with other kids. . . . He was often teased on the bus and at school because of his appearance and abilities. . . . He got teased bad. Every day, he got teased. He'd get pushed around. But he couldn't really help himself. He was kind of skinny. . . . He didn't really have that many friends."

The boy actually had two good friends: One appears to have had things relatively well together. But with this friend, the subject ". . . passed [a] gun safety course for hunting; they took the class together." The second friend (with whom the murder was committed) was a troublesome child. These two boys described themselves as the "best of friends," and spent much time together. The boys have admitted to planning the ambush (one saying they had planned it for weeks, the other for a few hours). They were armed and waiting when the mother arrived home from work. One conclusion seems relatively certain: this murder was an unlikely event until these two antisocial friends reached consensus about doing it.

An important message emerges from this incident: Child characteristics, intersecting with family relationships and social setting, cycle through peer relations in two ways to affect developmental outcome: (*a*) through acceptance and rejection by other children in the aggregate, and (*b*) through dyadic relationships, especially with friends. Considerable evidence now tells us that "being liked" by other children (an aggregate condition) supports good developmental outcome; conversely, "being disliked" (another aggregate condition) is a risk factor (Parker & Asher, 1987). But the evidence concerning friendships and their developmental significance is weak—mainly because these relationships

From *Child Development,* 1996, 67, 1–13. © 1996 by the Society for Research in Child Development, Inc. All rights reserved.

have not been studied extensively enough or with sufficient differentiation.

On the too-rare occasions in which friendships are taken into account developmentally—either in diagnosis or research—children are differentiated merely according to whether or not they have friends. This emphasis on having friends is based on two assumptions: First, making and keeping friends requires good reality-testing and social skills; "having friends" is thus a proxy for "being socially skilled." Second, friendships are believed to be developmental wellsprings in the sense that children must suspend egoism, embrace egalitarian attitudes, and deal with conflict effectively in order to maintain them (Sullivan, 1953). On two counts, then, having friends is thought to bode well for the future.

Striking differences exist, however, among these relationships—both from child to child and companion to companion. First, enormous variation occurs in who the child's friends are: Some companions are outgoing and rarely get into trouble; others are antisocial; still others are good children but socially clumsy. These choices would seem rather obviously to contribute to socialization—not only by affecting reputations (as the adage admonishes) but through what transpires between the children. Knowing that a teenager has friends tells us one thing, but the identity of his or her friends tells us something else.

Second, friendships differ from one another qualitatively, that is, in their *content* or normative foundations (e.g., whether or not the two children engage in antisocial behavior), their *constructiveness* (e.g., whether conflict resolution commonly involves negotiation or whether it involves power assertion), their *closeness* (e.g., whether or not the children spend much time together and engage in many different activities), their *symmetry* (e.g., whether social power is vested more or less equally or more or less unequally in the two children), and their *affective substrates* (e.g., whether the relationship is supportive and secure or whether it is nonsupportive and conflict ridden). Qualitative differ-

ences in these relationships may have developmental implications in the same way that qualitative variations in adult-child relationships do (Ainsworth, Blehar, Waters, & Wall, 1978).

This essay begins, then, with the argument that one cannot describe friendships and their developmental significance without distinguishing between *having friends, the identity of the child's friends* (e.g., personality characteristics of the child's friends), and *friendship quality.* In the sections that follow, these relationship dimensions are examined separately and in turn. Three conclusions emerge: First, having friends is a normatively significant condition during childhood and adolescence. Second, friendships carry both developmental advantages and disadvantages so that a romanticized view of these relationships distorts them and what they may contribute to developmental outcome. Third, the identity of the child's friends and friendship quality may be more closely tied to individual differences than merely whether or not the child has friends.

HAVING FRIENDS

Measurement Issues

Children's friends can be identified in four main ways: (*a*) by asking the children, their mothers, or their teachers to name the child's friends and determining whether these choices are reciprocated; (*b*) by asking children to assess their liking for one another; (*c*) by observing the extent to which children seek and maintain proximity with one another; and (*d*) by measuring reciprocities and coordinations in their social interaction. Concordances among various indicators turn out to be substantial, but method variance is also considerable; the "insiders" (the children themselves) do not always agree with the "outsiders" (teachers) or the observational record (Hartup, 1992; Howes, 1989).

Some variation among measures derives from the fact that social attraction is difficult for outsiders to know about. Method variance also derives from special difficulties connected with self-reports: First, children without friends almost always can name "friends" when asked to do so (Furman, 1996). Second, friendship frequently seems to investigators to be a dichotomous condition (friend vs. nonfriend), whereas variation is more continuous (best friend/good friend/occasional friend/not friend). Third, whether these categories form a Guttman scale has not been determined, although researchers sometimes assume that they do (see Doyle, Markiewicz, & Hardy, 1994). Fourth, the status of so-called unilateral or unreciprocated friendship choice is unclear. Sometimes, when children's choices are not reciprocated, social interaction differs from when friendship choices are mutual; in other respects, the social exchange does not. Unilateral friends, for example, use tactics during disagreements with one another that are different from the ones used by mutual friends but similar to those used by nonfriends (e.g., standing firm). Simultaneously, conflict *outcomes* among unilateral friends (e.g., whether interaction continues) are more similar to those characterizing mutual friends than those characterizing nonfriends (Hartup, Laursen, Stewart, & Eastenson, 1988).

Developmental Significance

The developmental significance of having friends (apart from the identity of the child's friends or the quality of these relationships) has been examined in three main ways: (*a*) comparing the social interaction that occurs between friends and between nonfriends, (*b*) comparing children who have friends with those who don't, and (*c*) examining the extent to which having friends moderates behavioral outcomes across certain normative transitions.

Behavior with Friends and Nonfriends.—Behaviors differentiating friends from nonfriends have been specified in more than 80 studies (Newcomb & Bagwell, 1995); four are cited here. In the first of these (Newcomb & Brady, 1982), school-aged children were asked to explore a "creativity box" with either a friend or a classmate who was not a friend. More extensive exploration was observed among the children with their friends; conversation was more vigorous and mutually oriented; the emotional exchange was more positive. Most important, when tested individually, the children who explored the box with a friend remembered more about it afterward.

Second, Azmitia and Montgomery (1993) examined problem solving among 11-year-olds (mainly their dialogues) working on "isolation of variables" problems either with friends or acquaintances (the children were required to deduce which pizza ingredients caused certain characters in a series of stories to get sick and die). Friends spontaneously justified their suggestions more frequently than acquaintances, elaborated on their partners' proposals, engaged in a greater percentage of conflicts during their conversations, and more often checked results. Most important, the children working with friends did better than children working with nonfriends—on the most difficult versions of the task only. Clearly, "a friend in need is a friend indeed." The children's conversations were related to their problem solving through engagement in transactive conflicts. That is, task performance was facilitated to a greater extent between friends than between nonfriends by free airing of the children's differences in a cooperative, task-oriented context.

Third, we recently examined conversations between friends and nonfriends (10-year-olds) in an inner-city magnet school while the children wrote stories collaboratively on a computer (Hartup, Daiute, Zajac, & Sholl, 1995). Stories dealt with the rain forest—subject matter that the children had studied during a 6-week science project. Baseline story writing was measured with the children writing alone; control subjects *always* wrote alone. Results indicate that friends did not talk more during collaboration than nonfriends but, nevertheless, (*a*) engaged in more mutually oriented and less individualistic utterances; (*b*) agreed with one another more often (but did not disagree more readily); (*c*) repeated their own and the other's assertions more often; (*d*) posed alternatives and provided elaborations more frequently; (*e*) spent twice as much time as nonfriends talking about writing content, the vocabulary being used, and writing mechanics; and (*f*) spent less time engaged in "off-task" talk. Principal component analyses confirm that the structure of friends' talk was strongly focused on the task (i.e., the text) and was assertively collaborative—reminiscent of the dialogs used by experts and novices as discovered in other social problem-solving studies (Rogoff, 1990). Our stories themselves show that, overall, the ones collaboratively written by friends were better than the ones written by nonfriends, a difference that seems to rest on better use of Standard English rather than the narrative elements included in the text. Results suggest, overall, that the affordances of "being friends" differ from the affordances of "being acquaintances" in social problem solving (Hartup, 1996).

Fourth, we examined conflict and competition among school-aged children playing a board game when they had been taught different rules (Hartup, French, Laursen, Johnston, & Ogawa, 1993). Disagreements occurred more frequently between friends than between nonfriends and lasted longer. Conflict resolution, however, differed by friendship and sex: (*a*) boys used assertions *without rationales* more frequently than girls—but only when friends were observed; (*b*) girls, on the other hand, used assertions *with rationales* more frequently than boys but, again, only with friends. Sex differences in conflict talk, widely cited in the literature (see Maccoby, 1990), thus seem to be relationship manifestations rather than manifestations of individual children.

Based on these and the other available data sets, a recent meta-analysis identified significant friend versus nonfriend effects across four broad-band categories (Newcomb & Bagwell, 1995): *positive engagement* (i.e., talk, smiling, and laughter); *conflict management* (i.e., disengagement and negotiation vs. power assertion); *task activity* (i.e., being oriented to the task as opposed to being off task); and *relationship properties* (i.e., equality in the exchange as well as mutuality and affirmation). Behaviorally speaking, friendships clearly are "communal relationships" (Clark & Mills, 1979). Reciprocity constitutes their deep structure.

Existing data suggest that four cognitive and motivational conditions afford these distinctive interactions: (*a*) friends know one another better than nonfriends and are thus able to communicate with one another more efficiently and effectively (Ladd & Emerson, 1984); (*b*) friends and nonfriends have different expectations of one another, especially concerning assistance and support (Bigelow, 1977); (*c*) an affective climate more favorable to exploration and problem solving exists between friends than between nonfriends—namely, a "climate of agreement" (Gottman, 1983); and (*d*) friends more readily than nonfriends seek ways of resolving disagreements that support continued interaction between them (Hartup & Laursen, 1992).

Unfortunately, the developmental significance of these differences is not known. Only fragmentary information tells us about short-term consequences in problem solving and behavioral regulation. Recalled events (Newcomb & Brady, 1982), deductive reasoning (Azmitia & Montgomery, 1993), conflict rates (Hartup et al., 1988), creative writing (Hartup et al., 1995), and social/moral judgments (Nelson & Aboud, 1985) are better supported by transactions with friends than by transactions with nonfriends. But only a small number of investigations exists in each case—sometimes only one. The bottom line: Process-outcome studies are badly needed to tell us whether friends engage in better scaffolding than nonfriends, or whether it only seems like they do. Once process/outcome connections are established, we can then—and only then—conclude that friendships have normative significance (i.e., that children employ their friends adaptively on a daily basis as cognitive and social resources).

Having Friends Versus Not Having Friends.
Does having friends contribute to developmental differentiation (i.e., contribute to individual differences)? For the answer to this question to be affirmative, children who have friends must differ from those who do not.

Cross-sectional comparisons show that, first, children who have friends are more socially competent and less troubled than children who do not; they are more sociable, cooperative, altruistic, self-confident, and less lonely (Hartup, 1993; Newcomb & Bagwell, 1996). Second, troubled children (e.g., clinic-referred children) are more likely to be friendless than nonreferred control cases (Rutter & Garmezy, 1983). Friendlessness is not always assessed in the same manner in these studies, but the results are consistent: Not one data set suggests that children with friends are worse off than children who do not have them.

Although friended/friendless comparisons are consistent across data sets, the results are difficult to interpret. First, having friends in these studies usually means having good supportive friends; thus having friends is confounded with friendship quality. Second, causal direction is impossible to establish: Friendship experience may contribute to self-esteem, for example, but self-confident children may make friends more readily than less confident children.

Longitudinal studies can be more convincing concerning developmental significance. Unfortunately, few exist. Short-term studies suggest that certain benefits accrue across school transitions: First, attitudes toward school are better among kindergartners (5-year-olds) who have friends at the beginning and who maintain them than those who don't. Making new friends also predicts gains in school performance over the kindergarten year (Ladd, 1990). Second, with data collected from 10-year-olds across a 1-year interval, friendship experience enhanced self-esteem (Bukowski, Hoza, & Newcomb, 1991). Third, psychosocial disturbances have been reported less frequently when school changes occur in the company of good friends than when they don't (Berndt & Hawkins, 1991; Simmons,

Burgeson, & Reef, 1988). Having friends thus seems to contribute specifically to affective outcomes across normative school transitions.

One long-term investigation (Bagwell, Newcomb, & Bukowski, 1994) raises questions, however, about "having friends" as a developmental predictor: Eleven-year-old children were identified as either friended or friendless on two separate occasions; subjects were re-evaluated at 23 years of age. Having friends and sociometric status (i.e., social acceptance) *together* predicted school success, aspirations, trouble with the law, and several other outcomes. Unique contributions to adult adjustment, however, were verified only for sociometric status. And even then, when stability in the childhood adjustment measures was taken into account, neither sociometric status nor friendship predicted adult outcomes.

Comment

Overall, the developmental significance of having friends is far from clear. Social interaction between friends differs from social interaction between nonfriends, but this does not tell us much more than that these relationships are unique social entities. Correlational studies are difficult to interpret because the effects of having friends are difficult to disentangle from the effects of friendship quality. Short-term longitudinal studies suggest that having friends supports adaptation during normative transitions, but more substantial evidence is needed concerning these effects. Child differences may interact with friendship experience in relation to developmental outcome rather than being main effects. Having friends, for example, may differentiate mainly among children who are vulnerable in some way prior to the transition. Stress associated with developmental transitions is known to accentuate differences among vulnerable children to a greater extent than among nonvulnerable ones (Caspi & Moffitt, 1991). Similarly, developmental interventions often have greater effects on vulnerable than on nonvulnerable individuals (see Crockenberg, 1981).

THE IDENTITY OF THE CHILD'S FRIENDS

We turn now to the identity of the child's friends. Several questions can be asked: With whom does the child become friends? Can the identity of a child's friends be forecast from what we know about the child? What is the developmental significance of the company a child keeps?

Who Are Children's Friends?

Consider, first, that children make friends on the basis of common interests and common activities. Common ground is a sine qua non in friendship relations throughout childhood and adolescence, suggesting that friends ought to be similar to one another in abilities and outlook. Folklore sometimes suggests that "opposites attract," but this notion has not found general support in the empirical literature. The weight of the evidence suggests that, instead, "Beast knows beast; birds of a feather flock together" (Aristotle, *Rhetoric,* Book 11).

Similarities between friends, however, vary from attribute to attribute, in most cases according to *reputational salience* (i.e., according to the importance of an attribute in determining the child's social reputation). Considerable evidence supports this "reputational salience hypothesis": Behavior ratings obtained more than 60 years ago by Robert Challman (1932) showed that social cooperation (an attribute with considerable reputational salience) was more concordant among friends than nonfriends; intelligence (an attribute without reputational salience among young children) was not. Among boys, physical activity (reputationally salient among males) was more similar among friends than nonfriends. Among girls, attractiveness of personality and social network size (both more reputationally salient among females than among males) were more similar among friends than nonfriends.

More recent data also suggest that behavioral concordances among school-aged chil-

dren and their friends are greater than among children and nonfriends (Haselager, Hartup, Van Lieshout, & Riksen-Walraven, 1995). Peer ratings were obtained in a large number of fifth-grade classrooms centering on three constructs: prosocial behavior, antisocial behavior, and social withdrawal (shyness). First, friends were more similar to one another than nonfriends within each construct cluster (i.e., mean difference scores were significantly smaller). Second, correlations between friends were greater for antisocial behavior (i.e., fighting, disruption, and bullying) than for prosocial behavior (i.e., cooperation, offering help to others) or social withdrawal (i.e., shyness, dependency, and being victimized). These differences may reflect differences among these three attributes in reputational salience: Fighting, for example, is more consistently related to reputation than either cooperation or shyness (Coie, Dodge, & Kupersmidt, 1990). Our results also show important sex differences: (*a*) Friends were more similar to one another among girls than among boys in both prosocial and antisocial behavior (see also Cairns & Cairns, 1994), and (*b*) friends were more similar among boys than among girls in shyness. These gender variations are consistent with the reputational salience hypothesis, too: Being kind to others and being mean to them have greater implications for girls' social reputation than boys', whereas shyness/withdrawal has more to do with boys' reputations than girls' (Stevenson-Hinde & Hinde, 1986).

Concordance data from other studies are consistent with the reputational salience notion: Among adolescents, friends are most similar to one another in two general areas: (*a*) school-related attitudes, aspirations, and achievement (Epstein, 1983; Kandel, 1978b) and (*b*) normative activities such as smoking, drinking, drug use, antisocial behavior, and dating (Dishion, Andrews, & Crosby, 1995; Epstein, 1983; Kandel, 1978b; Tolson & Urberg, 1993). Sexual activity among adolescents is also consistent with the reputational salience hypothesis. Among girls (both African-American and white) in the United States, friends have been found to be similar in sexual behavior and attitudes, even when age and antisocial attitudes are taken into account. Among boys, however, sexual activity (especially engaging in sexual intercourse) was not concordant (Billy, Rodgers, & Udry, 1984). The authors argue that sexual activity is more closely related to social reputation among adolescent girls than it is among boys, thus accounting for the gender differences in the results.

Still other investigators, employing the social network as a unit of analysis, have discovered that members of friendship networks are concordant on such salient dimensions as sports, academic activities, and drug use (Brown, 1989). Antisocial behavior also distinguishes social networks from one another beginning in middle childhood (Cairns, Cairns, Neckerman, Gest, & Garieppy, 1988).

Friendship Concordances: Sources and Developmental Implications

Similarities between friends are one thing, but where do they come from and where do they lead? Developmental implications cannot be specified without understanding that these similarities derive from three sources: (*a*) *sociodemographic conditions* that bring children into proximity with one another; (*b*) *social selection* through which children construct relationships with children who are similar to themselves rather than different; and (*c*) *mutual socialization* through which children become similar to their friends by interacting with them.

Sociodemographic Conditions.—Demographic conditions determine the neighborhoods in which children live, the schools in which they enroll, and the classes they attend. Concordances among children and their friends in socioeconomic status, ethnicity, and chronological age thus derive in considerable measure from social forces that constrain the "peer pool" and the child's access to it. One should not underestimate, however, the extent to which some of these

concordances derive from the children's own choices. Among children attending schools that are mixed-age, mixed-race, and mixed socioeconomically, friends are still more similar to one another in these attributes than nonfriends are (Goldman, 1981; McCandless & Hoyt, 1961).

Selection.—Some similarities among friends derive from the well-known tendency among human beings (not alone among the various species) for choosing close associates who resemble themselves. Recent studies confirm that the similarity-attraction hypothesis applies to children: Among elementary school children who began an experimental session as strangers, differential attraction was evident in some groups (40%). Within them, more social contact occurred between preferred than between nonpreferred partners, and correlations were higher between preferred than nonpreferred partners in sociability and the cognitive maturity of their play (Rubin, Lynch, Coplan, Rose-Krasnor, & Booth, 1994).

But friendship selection is embedded in assortative processes occurring in larger social networks. Dishion and his colleagues (Dishion, Patterson, & Griesler, 1994) believe that these network concordances emerge through a process called "shopping" in which children and adolescents construct relationships that maximize interpersonal payoffs. Children are not believed to choose friends who are similar to themselves on a rational basis so much as on an experiential one. Accordingly, relationships become established when they "feel right." Similar individuals cleave to one another more readily than dissimilar individuals because they are more likely to find common ground in both their activities and their conversations. Antisocial children are thus most likely to make friends with other antisocial children and, in so doing, their common characteristics merge to create a "dyadic antisocial trait." Similarly, soccer players or musicians make friends, merge themselves dyadically, and set the stage for becoming even more similar to one another.

Selection thus acts simultaneously to determine the identity of the child's friends through two interlocking processes: (*a*) similarity and attraction occurring within dyads, and (*b*) assortative network formation occurring within groups. These processes undoubtedly combine differently from child to child in affecting developmental outcome: Cooperative, friendly, nonaggressive children can choose friends resembling themselves from a wide array of choices; antisocial children can also choose their friends on the basis of similarity and attraction—but frequently from a more restricted range of social alternatives.

Mutual Socialization.—What behavioral outcomes stem from mutual socialization? The weight of the evidence suggests, first, that children and their friends who ascribe to conventional norms move further over time in the direction of normative behavior (Ball, 1981; Epstein, 1983; Kandel & Andrews, 1986). But does antisocial behavior increase over time among children in antisocial networks? Does troublesome behavior escalate among children—especially into criminal activity—through membership in these networks? Answers to these questions have been surprisingly difficult to provide, especially since children perceive their friends as exerting more pressure toward desirable than toward undesirable conduct (Brown, Clasen, & Eicher, 1986). Nevertheless, increases in undesirable behavior through antisocial friends among children who are themselves at risk for antisocial behavior is now relatively well documented (Ball, 1981; Berndt & Keefe, 1992; Dishion, 1990; Dishion et al., 1994). Conversely, "desisting" is forecast as strongly by a turning away from antisocial friends as by any other variable (Mulvey & Aber, 1988).

What occurs on a day-to-day basis between aggressive children and their friends? Jocks and their friends? "Brains" and their friends? One guesses that children model normative behaviors *for* their friends and simultaneously receive reinforcement *from* them. Antisocial children, for example, are known to engage in large amounts of talk with their friends—talk that is deviant even when the children are being videotaped in the laboratory (Dishion et al., 1994, 1995). Ordinary children talk a lot with their friends, too, but the content is not generally as deviant (Newcomb & Bagwell, 1995). Antisocial children use coercion with one another (Dishion et al., 1995); ordinary children, on the other hand, are freewheeling with their criticisms and persuasion but are less likely to be coercive (Berndt & Keefe, 1992; Hartup et al., 1993). Finally, one guesses that friends support one another in seeking environments that support their commonly held worldviews, although not much is known about this.

Other results show that selection *combines* with socialization to effect similarity between friends. Kandel (1978a) studied changes over the course of a year in drug use, educational aspirations, and delinquency in early adolescence, discovering that similarity stemmed from both sources in approximately equal amounts. Relative effects, however, vary according to the norms and the children involved (see Hartup, 1993).

Comment

Children and their friends are similar to one another, especially in attributes with reputational salience. One must acknowledge that effect sizes are modest and that friends are not carbon copies of one another. One must also acknowledge that the reputational salience hypothesis has never been subjected to direct test and it needs to be. Nevertheless, the identity of the child's friends is a significant consideration in predicting developmental outcome. Friends may be generally intimate, caring, and supportive, thus fostering good developmental prognosis. At the same time, the activities in which they support one another (the relationship *content*) may be extremely deviant, suggesting an altogether different prognosis.

FRIENDSHIP QUALITY

Conceptual and Measurement Issues

Qualitative assessment of child and adolescent friendships currently involves two main strategies: (*a*) *dimensional analysis* through which one determines whether certain elements are present or absent in the social interaction between friends (e.g., companionship, intimacy, conflict, or power asymmetries), and (*b*) *typological* or *categorical* analysis through which one identifies patterns in social interaction believed to be critical to social development and adaptation (Furman, 1996).

Dimensional Assessment.—Most current dimensional assessments are based on "provisions" or "features" that children mention when talking about these relationships (Berndt & Perry, 1986; Bukowski, Hoza, & Boivin, 1994; Furman & Adler, 1982; Furman & Buhrmester, 1985; Parker & Asher, 1993); most instruments tap five or six domains. Domain scores, however, are correlated with one another (Berndt & Perry, 1986; Parker & Asher, 1993), and most factor analyses yield two-factor solutions. Both Berndt (1996) and Furman (1996) argue that "positive" and "negative" dimensions adequately describe most dimensional assessments, although some data sets suggest that more elaborate solutions are warranted (e.g., Ladd, Kochenderfer, & Coleman, 1996).

Typological Assessment.—Typological assessment is evolving slowly since the functional significance of friendships remains uncertain. Can one, for example, regard friendships as attachments? Probably not. No one has demonstrated that "the secure base phenomenon," so common among children and their caregivers, constitutes the functional core of children's friendships. Friends have been shown to be secure bases in one or two instances (Ipsa, 1981; Schwartz, 1972), but one is not overwhelmed with the evidence that children and their friends are bound to one another as attachment objects. Children describe their relationships with friends differently from their relationships with their caregivers—as *more* companionable, intimate, and egalitarian and, simultaneously, as *less* affectionate and reliable (Furman & Buhrmester, 1985). For these reasons, some writers describe

friendships as affiliative relationships rather than attachments (Weiss, 1986). The challenge, then, is to describe what good-quality affiliative relationships are.

One new classification system has been devised on the basis of family systems theory (Shulman, 1993). Well-functioning friendships are considered to be balanced between closeness and intimacy, on the one hand, and individuality, on the other. The family systems model suggests three friendship types: *interdependent* ones, with cooperation and autonomy balanced; *disengaged* ones, in which friends are disconnected in spite of their efforts to maintain proximity with one another; and *consensus-sensitive* or *enmeshed* relationships, in which agreement and cohesion are maximized. Empirical data are based largely on children's interactions in a cooperative task adapted from family systems research (Reiss, 1981) and document the existence of interdependent and disengaged relationships— a promising beginning. Once again, however, caution should be exercised: Friendship networks may not revolve around the same equilibrative axes as families do.

DEVELOPMENTAL SIGNIFICANCE

Cross-sectional Studies.—Among the various qualitative dimensions, *support* (positivity) and *contention* (negativity) have been examined most extensively in relation to child outcomes. Support is positively correlated with school involvement and achievement (Berndt & Hawkins, 1991; Cauce, 1986) and negatively correlated with school-based problems (Kurdek & Sinclair, 1988); positively correlated with popularity and good social reputations (Cauce, 1986); positively correlated with self-esteem (Mannarino, 1978; McGuire & Weisz, 1982; Perry, 1987) and psychosocial adjustment (Buhrmester, 1990) as well as negatively correlated with identity problems (Papini, Farmer, Clark, Micke, & Barnett, 1990) and depression—especially among girls (Compas, Slavin, Wagner, & Cannatta, 1986). Results are thus consistent but, once again, impossible to interpret. We cannot tell whether supportive relationships contribute to the competence of the individual child or vice versa.

Longitudinal studies.—Longitudinal studies dealing with friendship quality (positive vs. negative) emphasize school attitudes, involvement, and achievement. Studying children across the transition from elementary to junior high school, Berndt (1989) measured the size of the friendship network, friendship stability, and self-reported friendship quality (positivity) as well as popularity, attitudes toward school, and achievement. First, network size was negatively related to friendship support as reported by the children, suggesting that children recognize what researchers have been slow to learn, namely, that friendships are not all alike. Second, several nonsignificant results are illuminating: Neither number of friends nor friendship stability contributed to changes in school adjustment—either across the board transition or across the first year in the new school. School adjustment was relatively stable across the transition and was related to friendship stability cross-sectionally but not with earlier adjustment factored out. Third, the self-rated supportiveness of the child's friends, assessed shortly after entrance to the new school, predicted increasing popularity and increasingly positive attitudes toward classmates over the next year, suggesting that positive qualities in one's friendship relations support a widening social world in new school environments.

Other investigations focus on friendship qualities as predictors of school adaptation within the school year. Among 5-year-olds enrolled in kindergarten (Ladd et al.,1996), for example, those having friendships characterized by "aid" and "validation" improved in school attitudes over the year with initial attitudes toward school factored out. Perceived conflict in friendships, on the other hand, predicted increasing forms of school maladjustment, especially among boys, including school loneliness and avoidance as well as school liking and engagement.

One other investigation (Berndt & Keefe, 1992) focused on both positive and negative friendship qualities and their correlations across time with school adjustment and self-esteem among adolescents (Berndt & Keefe, 1992). Students with supportive, intimate friendships became increasingly involved with school, while those who considered their friendships to be conflict-ridden and rivalrous became increasingly disruptive and troublesome. Friendship quality was not correlated with changes in self-esteem, possibly because self-esteem was relatively stable from the beginning to the end of the year. Additional analyses (Berndt, 1996) suggest that developmental prediction is better for the negative dimensions in these relationships than the positive ones.

Other investigators have examined the interactions between stress and social support as related to behavioral outcome. With elementary school children, increases in peer support over several years predict both increasingly better adaptation and better grade point averages (Dubow, Tisak, Causey, Hryshko, & Reid, 1991). Other results, however, suggest that support from school personnel was associated with decreases in distress across a 2-year period but not support from friends (controlling for initial adjustment). Regression models showed that, actually, school grades predicted changes in friends' support rather than the reverse (DuBois, Felner, Brand, Adan, & Evans, 1992). Among adolescents, however, results are more complex: Windle (1992) reported that, among girls, friend support is positively correlated with alcohol use but negatively correlated with depression (with initial adjustment levels factored out). Among boys, friendship support is associated with outcome depending on stress levels: When stress is high, friend support encourages both alcohol use and depression; when stress is low or moderate, both alcohol use and depression are associated with having *nonsupportive* friends.

The dissonances encountered in these results would be reduced considerably were the identity of the children's friends to be known. Children and adolescents with behavior difficulties frequently have friends who themselves are troublesome (Dishion et al., 1995). These friends may provide one another with emotional support, but the interactions that occur between them may not be the same as those occurring between nontroubled children and their friends. Knowing who the child's friends are might account for the empirical anomalies.

Other difficulties in accounting for these results derive from the fact that the referents used in measuring social support in these studies (except in Berndt's work) consisted of friendship networks (the child's "friends") rather than a "best friend." And still other complications arise from the use of one child's assessments of relationship qualities (the subject's) when the evidence suggests that discrepancies between partners may correlate more strongly with adjustment difficulties than the perceptions of either partner alone (East, 1991). Nevertheless, these studies provide tantalizing tidbits suggesting that friendship quality bears a causal relation to developmental outcome.

Comment

What kinds of research are needed to better understand the developmental implications of friendship quality? One can argue that we are not urgently in need of cross-time studies narrowly focused on friendships and their vicissitudes. Rather, we need comprehensive studies in which interaction effects rather than main effects are emphasized and that encompass a wide range of variables as they cycle through time: (a) measures of the child, including temperament and other relevant early characteristics; (b) measures of early relationships, especially their affective and cognitive qualities; (c) measures of early success in encounters with relevant institutions, especially the schools; (d) status and reputation among other children (sociometric status); and, (e) friendship measures that simultaneously include whether a child has friends, who the child's friends are, and what these relationships are like.

Coming close to this model are recent studies conducted by the Oregon Social Learning Center (e.g., Dishion et al., 1994; Patterson, Reid, & Dishion, 1992). Child characteristics and family relations in early childhood have not been examined extensively by these investigators, but their work establishes linkages between coerciveness and monitoring within parent-child and sibling relationships, on the one hand, and troublesomeness and antisocial behavior among school-aged boys on the other. These studies also establish that poor parental discipline and monitoring predict peer rejection and academic failures, and that these conditions, in turn, predict increasing involvement with antisocial friends. Among children with these early histories, the immediate connection to serious conduct difficulties in adolescence now seems to be friendship with another deviant child. Exactly these conditions existed in the social history of that Minnesota teenager who, together with his best friend, killed his mother early in 1995.

CONCLUSION

Friendships in childhood and adolescence would seem to be developmentally significant—both normatively and differentially. When children have friends, they use them as cognitive and social resources on an everyday basis. Normative transitions and the stress carried with them seem to be better negotiated when children have friends than when they don't, especially when children are at risk. Differential significance, however, seems to derive mainly from the identity of the child's friends and the quality of the relationships between them. Supportive relationships between socially skilled individuals appear to be developmental advantages, whereas coercive and conflict-ridden relationships are developmental disadvantages, especially among antisocial children.

Nevertheless, friendship and its developmental significance may vary from child to child. New studies show that child characteristics interact with early relationships and environmental conditions, cycling in turn through relations with other children to determine behavioral outcome (Hartup & Van Lieshout, 1995). The work cited in this essay strongly suggests that friendship assessments deserve greater attention in studying these developmental pathways than they are currently given. These assessments, however, need to be comprehensive. Along with knowing whether or not children have friends, we must know who their friends are and the quality of their relationships with them.

REFERENCES

Ainsworth, M. D. S., Blehar, M. C., Waters, E., & Wall, S. (1978). *Patterns of attachment: A psychological study of the Strange Situation.* Hillsdale, NJ: Erlbaum.

Azmitia, M., & Montgomery, R. (1993). Friendship, transactive dialogues, and the development of scientific reasoning. *Social Development, 2,* 202–221.

Bagwell, C., Newcomb, A. F., & Bukowski, W. M. (1994). *Early adolescent friendship as a predictor of adult adjustment: A twelve-year follow-up investigation.* Unpublished manuscript, University of Richmond.

Ball, S. J. (1981). *Beachside comprehensive.* Cambridge: Cambridge University Press.

Berndt, T. J. (1989). Obtaining support from friends during childhood and adolescence. In D. Belle (Ed.), *Children's social networks and social supports* (pp. 308–331). New York: Wiley.

Berndt, T. J. (1996). Exploring the effects of friendship quality on social development. In W. M. Bukowski, A. F. Newcomb, & W. W. Hartup (Eds.), *The company they keep: Friendships in childhood and adolescence.* Cambridge: Cambridge University Press.

Berndt, T. J., & Hawkins, J. A. (1991). *Effects of friendship on adolescents' adjustment to junior high school.* Unpublished manuscript, Purdue University.

Berndt, T. J., & Keefe, K. (1992). Friends' influence on adolescents' perceptions of themselves in school. In D. H. Schunk & J. L. Meece (Eds.), *Students' perceptions in the classroom* (pp. 51–73). Hillsdale, NJ: Erlbaum.

Berndt, T. J., & Perry, T. B. (1986). Children's perceptions of friendship as supportive relationships. *Developmental Psychology, 22,* 640–648.

Bigelow, B. J. (1977). Children's friendship expectations: A cognitive developmental study. *Child Development, 48,* 246–253.

Billy, J. O. G., Rodgers, J. L., & Udry, J. R. (1984). Adolescent sexual behavior and friendship choice. *Social Forces, 62,* 653–678.

Brown, B. B. (1989). The role of peer groups in adolescents' adjustment to secondary school. In T. J. Berndt & G. W. Ladd (Eds.), *Peer relationships in child development* (pp. 188–215). New York: Wiley.

Brown, B. B., Clasen, D. R., & Eicher, S. A. (1986). Perceptions of peer pressure, peer conformity dispositions, and self-reported behavior among adolescents. *Developmental Psychology, 22,* 521–530.

Buhrmester, D. (1990). Intimacy of friendship, interpersonal competence, and adjustment during preadolescence and adolescence. *Child Development, 61,* 1101–1111.

Bukowski, W. M., Hoza, B., & Boivin, M. (1994). Measuring friendship quality during pre- and early adolescence: The development and psychometric properties of the Friendship Qualities Scale. *Journal of Personal and Social Relationships, 11,* 471–484.

Bukowski, W. M., Hoza, B., & Newcomb, A. F. (1991). *Friendship, popularity, and the "self" during early adolescence.* Unpublished manuscript, Concordia University (Montreal).

Cairns, R. B., & Cairns, B. D. (1994). *Lifelines and risks.* Cambridge: Cambridge University Press.

Cairns, R. B., Cairns, B. D., Neckerman, H. J., Gest, S., & Garieppy, J. L. (1988). Peer networks and aggressive behavior: Peer support or peer rejection? *Developmental Psychology, 24,* 815–823.

Caspi, A., & Moffitt, T. E. (1991). Individual differences are accentuated during periods of social change: The sample case of girls at puberty. *Journal of Personality and Social Psychology, 61,* 157–168.

Cauce, A. M. (1986). Social networks and social competence: Exploring the effects of early adolescent friendships. *American Journal of Community Psychology, 14,* 607–628.

Challman, R. C. (1932). Factors influencing friendships among preschool children. *Child Development, 3,* 146–158.

Clark, M. S., & Mills, J. (1979). Interpersonal attraction in exchange and communal relationships. *Journal of Personality and Social Psychology, 37,* 12–24.

Coie, J. D., Dodge, K. A., & Kupersmidt, J. B. (1990). Peer group behavior and social status. In S. R. Asher & J. D. Coie (Eds.), *Peer rejection in childhood* (pp. 17–59). Cambridge: Cambridge University Press.

Compas, B. E., Slavin, L. A., Wagner, B. A., & Cannatta, K. (1986). Relationship of life events and social support with psychological dysfunction among adolescents. *Journal of Youth and Adolescence,* **15,** 205–221.

Crockenberg, S. B. (1981). Infant irritability, mother responsiveness, and social support influences on the security of mother-infant attachment. *Child Development,* **52,** 857–865.

Dishion, T. J. (1990). The peer context of troublesome child and adolescent behavior. In P. Leone (Ed.), *Understanding troubled and troublesome youth.* Newbury Park, CA: Sage.

Dishion, T. J., Andrews, D. W., & Crosby, L. (1995). Anti-social boys and their friends in early adolescence: Relationship characteristics, quality, and interactional process. *Child Development,* **66,** 139–151.

Dishion, T. J., Patterson, G. R., & Griesler, P. C. (1994). Peer adaptations in the development of antisocial behavior: A confluence model. In L. R. Huesmann (Ed.), *Current perspectives on aggressive behavior* (pp. 61–95). New York: Plenum.

Doyle, A. B., Markiewicz, D., & Hardy, C. (1994). Mothers' and children's friendships: Intergenerational associations. *Journal of Social and Personal Relationships,* **11,** 363–377.

DuBois, D. L., Felner, R. D., Brand, S., Adan, A. M., & Evans, E. G. (1992). A prospective study of life stress, social support, and adaptation in early adolescence. *Child Development,* **63,** 542–557.

Dubow, E. F., Tisak, J., Causey, D., Hryshko, A., & Reid, G. (1991). A two-year longitudinal study of stressful life events, social support, and social problem-solving skills: Contributions to children's behavioral and academic adjustment. *Child Development,* **62,** 583–599.

East, P. L. (1991). The parent-child relationships of withdrawn, aggressive, and sociable children: Child and parent perspectives. *Merrill-Palmer Quarterly,* **37,** 425–444.

Epstein, J. L. (1983). Examining theories of adolescent friendship. In J. L. Epstein & N. L. Karweit (Eds.), *Friends in school* (pp. 39–61). San Diego: Academic Press.

Furman, W. (1996). The measurement of friendship perceptions: Conceptual and methodological issues. In W. M. Bukowski, A. F. Newcomb, & W. W. Hartup (Eds.), *The company they keep: Friendships in childhood and adolescence.* Cambridge: Cambridge University Press.

Furman, W., & Adler, T. (1982). *The Friendship Questionnaire.* Unpublished manuscript, University of Denver.

Furman, W., & Buhrmester, D. (1985). Children's perceptions of the personal relationships in their social networks. *Developmental Psychology* **21,** 1016–1022.

Goldman, J. A. (1981). The social interaction of preschool children in same-age versus mixed-age groupings. *Child Development,* **52,** 644–650.

Gottman, J. M. (1983). How children become friends. *Monographs of the Society for Research in Child Development* **48**(3, Serial No. 201).

Hartup, W. W. (1992). Friendships and their developmental significance. In H. McGurk (Ed.), *Childhood social development* (pp. 175–205). Gove, UK: Erlbaum.

Hartup, W. W. (1993). Adolescents and their friends. In B. Laursen (Ed.), *Close friendships in adolescence* (pp. 3–22). San Francisco: Jossey-Bass.

Hartup, W. W. (1996). Cooperation, close relationships, and cognitive development. In W. M. Bukowski, A. F. Newcomb, & W. W. Hartup (Eds.), *The company they keep: Friendships in childhood and adolescence.* Cambridge: Cambridge University Press.

Hartup, W. W., Daiute, C., Zajac, R., & Sholl, W. (1995). *Collaboration in creative writing by friends and nonfriends.* Unpublished manuscript, University of Minnesota.

Hartup, W. W., French, D. C., Laursen, B., Johnston, K. M., & Ogawa, J. (1993). Conflict and friendship relations in middle childhood: Behavior in a closed-field situation. *Child Development,* **64,** 445–454.

Hartup, W. W., & Laursen, B. (1992). Conflict and context in peer relations. In C. H. Hart (Ed.), *Children on playgrounds: Research perspectives and applications* (pp. 44–84). Albany: State University of New York Press.

Hartup, W. W., Laursen, B., Stewart, M. I., & Eastenson, A. (1988). Conflict and the friendship relations of young children. *Child Development,* **59,** 1590–1600.

Hartup, W. W., & Van Lieshout, C. F. M. (1995). Personality development in social context. In J. T. Spence (Ed.), *Annual Review of Psychology,* **46,** 655–687.

Haselager, G. J. T., Hartup, W. W., Van Lieshout, C. F. M., & Riksen-Walraven, M. (1995). *Friendship similarity in middle childhood as a function of sex and sociometric status.* Unpublished manuscript, University of Nijmegen.

Howes, C. (1989). Peer interaction of young children. *Monographs of the Society for Research in Child Development, 53*(Serial No. 217).

Ipsa, J. (1981). Peer support among Soviet day care toddlers. *International Journal of Behavioral Development, 4,* 255–269.

Kandel, D. B. (1978a). Homophily, selection, and socialization in adolescent friendships. *American Journal of Sociology, 84,* 427–436.

Kandel, D. B. (1978b). Similarity in real-life adolescent pairs. *Journal of Personality and Social Psychology, 36,* 306–312.

Kandel, D. B., & Andrews, K. (1986). Processes of adolescent socialization by parents and peers. *International Journal of the Addictions, 22,* 319–342.

Kurdek, L. A., & Sinclair, R. J. (1988). Adjustment of young adolescents in two-parent nuclear, stepfather, and mother-custody families. *Journal of Consulting and Clinical Psychology, 56,* 91–96.

Ladd, G. W. (1990). Having friends, keeping friends, making friends, and being liked by peers in the classroom: Predictors of children's early school adjustment? *Child Development, 61,* 1081–1100.

Ladd, G. W., & Emerson, E. S. (1984). Shared knowledge in children's friendships. *Developmental Psychology, 20,* 932–940.

Ladd, G. W., Kochenderfer, B. J., & Coleman, C. C. (1996). Friendship quality as a predictor of young children's early school adjustment. *Child Development., 67,* 1103–1118.

Maccoby, E. E. (1990). Gender and relationships: A developmental account. *American Psychologist, 45,* 513–520.

Mannarino, A. P. (1978). Friendship patterns and self-concept development in preadolescent males. *Journal of Genetic Psychology, 133,* 105–110.

McCandless, B. R., & Hoyt, J. M. (1961). Sex, ethnicity and play preferences of preschool children. *Journal of Abnormal and Social Psychology, 62,* 683–685.

McGuire, K. D., & Weisz, J. R. (1982). Social cognition and behavior correlates of preadolescent chumship. *Child Development, 53,* 1478–1484.

Mulvey, E. P., & Aber, M. S. (1988). Growing out of delinquency: Development and desistance. In R. Jenkins & W. Brown (Eds.), *The abandonment of delinquent behavior: Promoting the turn-around.* New York: Praeger.

Nelson, J., & Aboud, F. E. (1985). The resolution of social conflict between friends. *Child Development, 56,* 1009–1017.

Newcomb, A. F., & Bagwell, C. (1995). Children's friendship relations: A meta-analytic review. *Psychological Bulletin, 117,* 306–347.

Newcomb, A. F., & Bagwell, C. (1996). The developmental significance of children's friendship relations. In W. M. Bukowski, A. F. Newcomb, & W. W. Hartup (Eds.), *The company they keep: Friendship in childhood and adolescence.* Cambridge: Cambridge University Press.

Newcomb, A. F., & Brady, J. E. (1982). Mutuality in boys' friendship relations. *Child Development, 53,* 392–395.

Papini, D. R., Farmer, F. F., Clark, S. M., Micke, J. C., & Barnett, J. K. (1990). Early adolescent age and gender differences in patterns of emotional self-disclosure to parents and friends. *Adolescence, 25,* 959–976.

Parker, J. G., & Asher, S. R. (1987). Peer relations and later personal adjustment: Are low-accepted children at risk? *Psychological Bulletin, 102,* 357–389.

Parker, J. G., & Asher, S. R. (1993). Friendship and friendship quality in middle childhood: Links with peer group acceptance and feelings of loneliness and social dissatisfaction. *Developmental Psychology, 29,* 611–621.

Patterson, G. R., Reid, J. B., & Dishion, T. J. (1992). *Antisocial boys.* Eugene, OR: Castalia.

Perry, T. B. (1987). *The relation of adolescent self-perceptions to their social relationships.* Unpublished doctoral dissertation, University of Oklahoma.

Reiss, D. (1981). *The family's construction of reality.* Cambridge, MA: Harvard University Press.

Rogoff, B. (1990). *Apprenticeship in thinking.* New York: Oxford University Press.

Rubin, K. H., Lynch, D., Coplan, R., Rose-Krasnor, L., & Booth, C. L. (1994). "Birds of a feather . . .": Behavioral concordances and preferential personal attraction in children. *Child Development, 65,* 1778–1785.

Rutter, M., & Garmezy, N. (1983). Developmental psychopathology. In E. M. Hetherington (Ed.), P. H. Mussen (Series Ed.), *Handbook of child psychology: Vol. 4. Socialization, personality, and social development* (pp. 775–911). New York: Wiley.

Schwartz, J. C. (1972). Effects of peer familiarity on the behavior of preschoolers in a novel situation.

Journal of Personality and Social Psychology, **24,** 276–284.

Shulman, S. (1993). Close friendships in early and middle adolescence: Typology and friendship reasoning. In B. Laursen (Ed.), *Close friendships in adolescence* (pp. 55–72). San Francisco: Jossey-Bass.

Simmons, R. G., Burgeson, R., & Reef, M. J. (1988). Cumulative change at entry to adolescence. In M. Gunnar & W. A. Collins (Eds.), *Minnesota symposia on child psychology* (Vol. **21,** pp. 123–150). Hillsdale, NJ: Erlbaum.

Stevenson-Hinde, J., & Hinde, R. A. (1986). Changes in associations between characteristics and interaction. In R. Plomin & J. Dunn (Eds.), *The study of temperament: Changes, continuities and challenges* (pp. 115–129). Hillsdale, NJ: Erlbaum.

Sullivan, H. S. (1953). *The interpersonal theory of psychiatry.* New York: Norton.

Tolson, J. M., & Urberg, K. A. (1993). Similarity between adolescent best friends. *Journal of Adolescent Research,* **8,** 274–288.

Weiss, R. S. (1986). Continuities and transformations in social relationships from childhood to adulthood. In W. W. Hartup & Z. Rubin (Eds.), *Relationships and development* (pp. 95–110). Hillsdale, NJ: Erlbaum.

Windle, M. (1992). A longitudinal study of stress buffering for adolescent problem behaviors. *Developmental Psychology,* **28,** 522–530.

READING 15

IN THE EYE OF THE BEHOLDER: ADOLESCENTS' PERCEPTIONS OF PEER CROWD STEREOTYPES

MARGARET R. STONE AND B. BRADFORD BROWN
University of Wisconsin–Madison

As a young person moves into adolescence, interactions with peers take on an added level of complexity. In addition to dyadic ("friendship") and small-group ("clique") relations, both of which are apparent in childhood, the adolescent's social world seems to be heavily influenced by the divisions of peers into larger collectives, commonly referred to as "crowds" (Brown, 1990). One's crowd affiliation reveals not only who one "hangs around" with, but also one's reputation among peers. Crowd labels—jock, loner, druggie, popular, nerd, and so on—reflect personality, social position, life style, or cultural background.

Some researchers maintain that the adolescent crowd system serves a singular purpose. Dunphy (1963) suggested that, basically, crowds provide a convenient means of integrating opposite-gender cliques so as to socialize teenagers into heterosexual roles. Coleman (1961) argued that in each high school, the "leading crowd" establishes the values and life styles for all other students to follow. In these conceptualizations, one crowd is much like another.

An original paper prepared for this book of readings.

Others, however, have taken the differences implied by this menagerie of crowd labels more seriously. Building on Erikson's (1968) identity theory, Newman and Newman (1976, p. 268) suggested that "the adolescent . . . scans the range of possibilities that exist in his social environment" and "experiences an internal questioning about the group of which he is most naturally a part." Having a number of groups with well-defined, distinctive characteristics and life styles facilitates the selection of a crowd that will provide a meaningful "provisional identity." Furthermore, one can "try on" different identities by transferring affiliations among crowds with different norms and life styles.

For Newman and Newman's (1976) perspective to be accurate, differences among crowds should be more than vague or superficial. Indeed, even in early adolescence one should observe considerable *consensus* among teenagers about the activities and interests characteristic of each crowd and considerable *differentiation* among crowds on these dimensions, so that each crowd offers a unique and recognizable provisional identity.

Ethnographies of the adolescent social system all mention a variety of crowds with distinctive "personalities" (Buff, 1970; Clark, 1962; Eckert, 1989; Larkin, 1979; Lesko, 1988; Varenne, 1982). There is even a hint of common crowd types across a variety of school settings. In nearly all of these investigations there is a group of athletes, an "elite" or high-status crowd, and a crowd with a more delinquent image. Most ethnographies, however, focus on a small portion of the student body—often one or two cliques of seniors—and it is not clear how readily the students share the ethnographers' interpretations of their (the students') social world.

The present studies were designed to move beyond ethnography by having adolescents systematically identify and describe the major crowds they perceived in their schools. To gather teenagers' own perceptions rather than adults' interpretations of the adolescent social world, the typology of crowds and the descriptive domains with which groups were stereotyped were derived

empirically from pilot testing of adolescent samples rather than abstracted from previous studies of high school peer groups. Study 1 was designed to answer three questions. First, do the number and types of crowds named by respondents vary by grade level or gender? Second, do respondents perceive the crowds they mention as distinct from one another in terms of life-style and behavior? Third, how strong is consensus among respondents regarding the images of crowds?

STUDY 1

Sample

Respondents included 310 students attending the junior (grades 7–9) or senior (grades 10–12) high school in a racially homogenous (96% white) residentially stable, working- to middle-class midwestern community. Each school had about 1,000 students. The sample was evenly divided by grade and gender.

Measures

The self-report questionnaire was designed to identify the stereotypic characteristics that students associated with each major crowd in their school. The format of and coding for the questionnaire were derived from a pilot study of 133 adolescents who were asked to name the major crowds in their school, provide a one-sentence description of each group, then describe the distinguishing features of each crowd.

From these open-ended descriptions, we identified six domains commonly used to characterize crowds: dress and grooming styles; sociability (the way members related to students outside their group); academic attitude (how students felt about school achievement and learning); the crowd's hangout at school; typical weekend activities; and participation in five types of school-sponsored extracurricular activities (athletics, clubs, performing groups, leadership groups, and social events). From three to five descriptive alternatives were identified for each domain (see Table 1). For example, in dress and grooming, crowds were typified either as stylish (wearing designer clothes or the latest fad), athletic or casual in dress, neat and clean, looking tough or messy (leather, ripped jeans too much make-up, etc.) or showing poor taste (outdated styles, clashing colors, "high waters," etc.).

The one-sentence description of each peer group was employed to derive a lexicon of crowd types—that is, a listing of specific crowd labels that seemed to describe the same type of group. Jocks, for example, subsumed groups referred to as jocks, athletes, sports, sporties, football players, and so on. Seven major crowd types were identified: brains (intellectually oriented students), druggies (heavy users of illicit drugs and/or alcohol), jocks (athletically oriented), outcasts (socially inept and/or intellectually retarded), populars (high-status students who lead social activities), toughs (who have a gang-like or delinquent image), and normals (average, middle-of-the-road students who constitute the "masses"). Also, there were categories for special-interest crowds (actors, chess crew, farmers, etc.), hybrids (e.g., popular smarties or "wasted" jocks), and unassignable names.

From this information, a modified forced-choice, self-report questionnaire was derived. On the first page, respondents named (in their own words) all the major crowds they perceived in their school. *Crowd* was defined as "a label attached to students who act the same way or do the same things, whether or not they hang around each other." On successive pages, respondents were instructed to choose, for each crowd in each of the eight domains listed previously, the best description that typified crowd members. The same description could be assigned to more than one crowd. If, in any domain, respondents felt that none of the descriptions listed adequately fit a given crowd, they could write their own.

Procedure

Generating the Data.   Questionnaires were administered to students in three or four classrooms per grade. The classrooms were selected within ability groupings so that the sample

would be reasonably representative of the student body. The questionnaire was administered by a member of the research staff and was completed anonymously. Respondents also indicated their grade level and gender. Usable questionnaires were completed by 95% of the sample.

Data Coding and Analyses.   Coders assigned each crowd identified by the respondents to 1 of the 10 crowd-type categories. Interrater agreement, using Flanders' (1967) statistic, was 0.86. Analyses then turned to an assessment of the number and types of crowds named by respondents across grade level and gender. Next, differentiation between major crowd type images was examined through a series of log-linear analyses (Goodman, 1972) comparing each possible pair of major crowd types for each descriptive domain such as dress, academic attitude. Analyses indicated, for each pair of major crowds in each domain, whether the pair's distribution of responses (among the descriptors for that domain) differed significantly. Finally, consensus among respondents regarding the stereotypic traits of each crowd was operationalized as the proportion of domains for which at least 60% of respondents chose the same description for a given crowd.

Results

The number of crowds mentioned ranged from two to eight, but most students named between four and six groups ($M = 4.47$). Females named more crowds ($M = 5.32$) than males ($M = 5.05$), ANOVA $F (1,298) = 17.28$, $p < .001$. The number of crowds named increased steadily across grades—from an average of 3.92 crowds in grade 7 to 5.23 in grade 12—except for a dip between 9th and 10th grades, the point at which these students made the transition from junior to senior high school.

Jocks were the most frequently mentioned crowd type, acknowledged by two-thirds of the sample. Normals were the only type other than jocks mentioned by a majority of the sample. More females (56%) than males (30%) mentioned a popular crowd $G^2 = 7.28$, $p < .01$. Otherwise, gender differences were not significant, and grade differences did not fluctuate in a systematic fashion. Six major crowd types were mentioned by respondents: druggies, jocks, nobodies, normals, populars, and toughs.

Differentiation. Descriptions differentiated among virtually all pairs of major crowd types. In fact, in the log-linear analyses, descriptions of 93% of the pairings examined differed signifi-

cantly in at least four of the six domains of description, and 60% of the pairings differed on all six categories. Druggies and toughs differed only with regard to weekend activities; otherwise, all pairings of crowds were significantly differentiated in four or more domains.

Consensus on Crowds' Characteristics. Table 1 summarizes characterizations by respondents of each crowd type within each sample. A cursory glance at this table indicates that

TABLE 1

Percentage of Respondents Choosing Various Domain Descriptors for Crowds Named in Study 1.

Domain descriptor	Crowd Type					
	Jocks	Populars	Normals	Nobodies	Druggies	Toughs
Dress and grooming						
Neat and clean	16	10	32	8	7	3
Casual, athletic	52	21	51	8	24	18
Stylish	31	59	16	1	6	4
Tough-messy	1	8	1	30	57	66
Poor taste	0	1	1	51	5	5
Sociability						
Disruptive	2	13	1	5	68	75
Cliquish	45	54	7	8	11	10
Not with it	2	6	16	78	4	4
Friendly	50	25	74	6	13	9
Academic attitude						
Enjoy, try hard	49	50	41	14	1	2
Positive	45	31	53	30	10	10
Take it or leave it	4	9	5	38	22	23
Hate school	0	9	1	14	65	62
Extracurricular activities						
High	53	49	33	3	1	1
Moderate	45	34	61	21	10	11
Low	1	16	6	76	89	88
School hangout						
Common areas	72	56	52	10	2	13
Out-of-way	3	16	7	23	90	76
Special interest	21	13	14	1	2	2
Nowhere	4	14	25	66	6	9
Weekend activities						
Drink, use drugs	4	11	1	6	88	54
Cause trouble	2	5	1	9	3	29
Social, party	72	52	49	9	5	10
Alone, with family	21	31	48	75	3	6

Note: Where figures for a given crowd type on a given category do not add up to 100%, the remainder represents the proportion of respondents who chose the "other" descriptor.

respondents did ascribe different characteristics to different crowd types. But just how strong was the consensus on a given crowd's image? We considered there to be consensus when at least 60% of respondents selected the same description for a crowd type. With this criterion, consensus was not overwhelming. Of the 36 distributions assessed (six domains for each of the six crowd types), there was consensus on only one half of the distributions. Nevertheless, for all crowd types other than the populars, there was consensus on at least one stereotyping domain. In fact, for the druggies, toughs, and nobodies, respondents reached consensus for at least four of the six domains.

Discussion

Over the past several decades, many researchers have preferred to portray the adolescent peer system as a monolithic "youth culture" (Coleman, 1961; Eisenstadt, 1956; Parsons, 1942), an age group with a singular focus, sharing a common set of values, interests, and life styles. Our findings in Study 1 fail to endorse this viewpoint. They instead demonstrate that adolescents perceive their social world as comprised of a diverse array of peer groups with distinctive, well-differentiated life styles. Results of this study confirm ethnographers' account (e.g., Buff, 1970; Cusick, 1973; Larkin, 1979) so strongly that one wonders why the notion of a youth culture still persists.

On the other hand, it is puzzling to note that though crowd identities are distinct from one another, there is only modest consensus about the nature or meaning of the various crowd identities comprising adolescents' social world. Several explanations seem possible. First, it is conceivable that lack of consensus may reflect genuine diversity among crowd members. Second, some students may simply be reluctant to characterize their peers as conforming to a set of group norms.

A more theoretically interesting third possibility is that our expectation of consensus was unrealistic. A finding of consensus would depend upon perceptions being unaffected by the alliances, loyalties, and resentments that typically characterize social systems. It would also require that self-esteem needs had little effect on perceptions of crowds. In fact, it is more sensible to assume that members of a particular crowd would actually get a different view of it than nonmembers and that adolescents would feel more benevolent toward their own crowd and toward "ally" crowds than they would toward crowds of radically different social status.

Symbolic-interactionist theories (e.g., Festinger, 1954) and social identity theory (Tajfel, 1978) suggest that self-enhancement and group loyalty may be more important than accuracy and objectivity in perceptions of self and other. Moreover, adolescents may be even more prone than adults toward biased stereotypes due to the particular characteristics of this life-phase. Research has demonstrated that early and middle adolescents tend toward insecurity, self-consciousness, teasing, and a heightened sensitivity to issues of loyalty, slight, and rejection (Eder, 1985; Elkind, 1967; Gavin & Furman, 1989; Savin-Williams & Berndt, 1990; Youniss & Smollar, 1985).

In order to investigate these possibilities, Study 2 was devised with three objectives. First, we would obtain respondents' perceptions of the structure of the social system. Second, we would sample descriptions of crowds by individuals from various social locations within the crowd system by recruiting participants considered by peers to be affiliated with each of the major crowds. Finally, we would assess the effects of respondents' own crowd affiliation on their perceptions of crowds.

We hoped to replicate our findings regarding the differentiation of crowd images in a more diverse sample. If we again found that controversy was more evident than consensus regarding the characteristics of crowds, we expected to find that the particular crowd to which respondents belong would emerge as a significant variable in explaining such controversy.

STUDY 2

Sample

Questionnaire respondents included 256 students attending the middle (grades 6–8) or senior (grades 9–12) high school in a mid-sized midwestern community. The middle school had about 500 students and the high school had about 1,500 students. The sample included 7th, 9th, and 11th graders (*n*'s = 93, 98, and 98) evenly divided by sex. The sample generally reflected the racial and ethnic composition of the schools: 13% African-American, 4% Asian-American, 4% Hispanic-American, 75% European-American, and 4% multiracial students. Students were invited to complete a self-report questionnaire after being identified through nomination procedures (explained in the next section) as members of seven major crowds. The questionnaire focused on perceptions of crowds and relations between crowds. Of the students recruited for the questionnaire phase, 88% filled out usable questionnaires. Of the remainder, 4% refused or were denied parent permission, 5% did not attend scheduled administrations, and 3% failed to fill out the questionnaire completely and credibly.

Identifying Crowds and Crowd Members. In two or three small focus group-interviews per grade, students were introduced to the concept of the "crowd" and asked if their school had crowds. Participants in every focus group recognized crowds as part of their school world and were able to differentiate between "cliques" and "crowds." Students constructed lists of crowds individually; then a "master" list was compiled through group discussion to obtain consensus regarding the major crowd types at each school (see Brown, 1989).

Through these interviews, six crowds were consistently mentioned and seemed to span both schools. The normals, brains, jocks, and populars were mentioned as in Study 1. In addition, interviewees consistently mentioned the Black crowd (mostly African American students) and the wannabe Black crowd (students of varying

ethnicity who adopt African American styles of dress and behavior and who meet with varying degrees of acceptance from the Black crowd). One of the *most* prominent crowds among the high school students—headbangers—was not mentioned by 7th graders; and a prominent crowd in the middle school—troublemakers—was not mentioned at the high school. The headbangers (also called "stoners") were said to openly use drugs, listen to heavy metal rock music, skip school, fight, wear combat boots and concert t-shirts, and play only hard contact sports if any sport at all. Troublemakers were said to skip school, fight, act loud, and get into trouble with teachers. Previous research (Brown, Lohr, & Trujillo, 1990) and current interview material suggest that the "tough" crowd-type may metamorphose across adolescence from "tough" to "druggie." Thus, these two discontinuous crowds were maintained in the master crowd list.

A second group of 63 informants completed a brief rating survey in which they "nominated" 10 male and female members of these crowds. Students whose nominations for a particular crowd were over 60% of their total nominations were assigned to that crowd and recruited for the questionnaire phase of the study. The questionnaire sample included 37 jocks, 33 populars, 47 normals, 40 Black crowd members, 39 brains, 23 wannabe Black crowd members, and 36 rebel crowd members (7th grade troublemakers and high school headbangers).

Measures.   Respondents were asked to characterize each of the 7 major crowds in their school in domains of dress and grooming, behavior toward people not in their own crowd, academic attitude, extracurricular participation, and weekend activities. Focus groups had assessed the domains and item responses from Study 1 for appropriateness in their particular school; some items were modified or dropped for Study 2. Students had the option to choose "really varies" if they thought that crowd members vary so much that they couldn't give a single answer. Respondents were also asked to rate the status of crowds from 1 ("very low") to 5 ("very high") and the similarity or dissimilarity of each pair of crowds from 1 ("extremely similar") to 10 ("extremely different").

Results

Structure of the Crowd System. Figure 1 presents a map of the seven crowds generated by multidimensional scaling analyses (Kruskal & Wish, 1978) of similarity data. Crowds that are close together on the map were described by respondents as similar to each other; crowds at greater distance on the map were described as relatively different from each other. The analyses indicated that a two-dimensional solution accounted for over 90% of the structure in the data, and that a third dimension did not add much to the "fit." Thus, the two-dimensional map has been used to illustrate students' conceptualization of the mapping of crowds in "symbolic social space." The seven crowds are distributed across the map's quadrants in several "neighborhoods," with the normals closer to the center than any other crowd. Jocks, populars, normals, and brains are to the right of center, while rebels, the Black crowd, and the wannabe Black crowd are at the extreme left. The horizontal dimension of the map is anchored at two ends by the rebel crowds (headbangers and troublemakers) and the brains. Because the ordering of crowds along the horizontal dimension coincides perfectly with the rank ordering of scores for perceived teacher relations, we speculate that this dimension may represent peer perceptions of academic engagement.

The vertical dimension seems to represent peer status, since the jock and popular crowds are at the upper extreme (see also Brown et al., 1994). Specifically, the jocks had the highest average status ranking ($M = 3.65$), followed by the populars ($M = 3.43$), normals ($M = 3.22$), the Black crowd ($M = 2.77$), brains ($M = 2.53$), the wannabe Black crowd ($M = 1.99$), and the rebel crowds ($M = 1.92$).

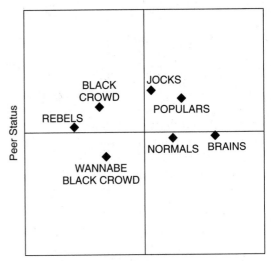

FIGURE 1   Two-Dimensional Social Map Derived from Multidimensional Scaling Analysis of Perceptions of the Similarity of Each Possible Crowd Pair.

Differentiation. Once again, descriptions differentiated among most pairs of crowd types. In loglinear analyses, 89% of the pairings examined differed significantly in at least four of the five domains of description, and 78% differed in all five domains. Jocks and populars differed only with respect to extra-curricular activities and the Black crowd and the wannabe Black crowd were not different in any domain. Differentiation could not be assessed between headbangers and troublemakers because respondents described one or the other of these crowds, depending upon their attendance at junior or senior high school.

Interestingly, patterns of differentiation were sensible in relation to social proximity and distance as seen on the crowd map, with the exception of the rebel crowds. The rebel crowds were differentiated from the Black crowd and the wannabe Black crowd in every domain, but would appear to be similar to them based upon placement on the crowd map. A follow-up examination of crowd maps based on data for each grade separately revealed that the rebel crowd emerged in an isolated position on the 9th and 11th grade maps. On the map derived from 7th grade data, the rebel crowd formed a cluster with the Black and wannabe Black crowds.

Consensus and Controversy on Crowds' Characteristics. Table 2 illustrates that, as in Study 1, consensus was not overwhelming regarding the attitudes and behaviors of crowds. A majority (over 50%) of respondents did agree in describing each crowd with a single descriptor in at least one domain, and there was 60% consensus in at least one descriptive domain for all of the crowds except the Black crowd.

As we had predicted, the crowd to which respondents belonged made a significant difference in their choices of descriptors for crowds. When the sample was divided by respondent crowd, a series of chi squared analyses revealed significant differences in the pattern of responses in a majority of domains regarding descriptions of four of the seven crowds: the jock, popular, Black, and wannabe Black crowds. Disagreement between respondents membership crowds was less intense in descriptions of the normal, brain, and rebel crowds.

As expected, overall patterns of consensus and disagreement in respondents' characterizations of crowds also revealed the effects of crowd similarity and social location. In general, respondents portrayed their own crowd in a significantly more positive light than did their classmates who were not part of the crowd. Additionally, members of similar and/or "neighboring crowds" often endorsed similar views of crowds, while members of very different and/or very socially distant crowds often differed with each other regarding those descriptions.

To illustrate this phenomenon, Table 3 shows descriptions of the jock crowd by members of each crowd. Pair-wise chi-squared tests comparing the pattern of responses revealed no differences between the relatively flattering descriptions of the jock crowd by the jocks and the

populars. In contrast, patterns of responses for the jock crowd and the Black crowd were different in four out of five domains. Moreover, no difference in response patterns emerged in the relatively unflattering descriptions of the jock crowd by members of the Black crowd and the wannabe Black crowd. Thus, the Black crowd disagrees with its distant neighbor regarding the characteristics of the jock crowd, but agrees with its close neighbor. These patterns of agreement fulfilled our expectation that crowds perceived as close on the crowd map and relatively undifferentiated in terms of lifestyle would also have similar perceptions of a given crowd.

General Discussion

The two studies reported here found that in both an overwhelmingly white sample and in an ethnically diverse sample, the adolescent social world was characterized by multiple well-differentiated youth cultures, with values and lifestyles ranging from those promoted by adults to those engendering grave concern. This portrait stands in stark contrast to the traditional view (Coleman, 1961) that adolescents march together in rebellion against adult standards. Perhaps the notion of a singular youth culture has persisted because some researchers have focused too heavily on the most prominent segments of adolescent society. Jocks, for example, the most widely recognized crowd among our respondents, have been the focus (along with jocks' frequent companions— populars) of many studies (Coleman, 1961; Cusick, 1973; Eckert, 1989, Varenne, 1982), whereas few investigators have attended to the nobodies, the normals, or the crowds defined by special-interests and ethnicity that were mentioned by our respondents. Certainly the prominence of jocks in our samples underscores the central role that athletics plays in the adolescent social system, but it is unwise to assume, as some have (Coleman, 1961), that this crowd is capable of shaping the entire adolescent peer culture.

TABLE 2

Percentage of Respondents Choosing Various Domain Descriptors for Crowds Named in Study 2.

Domain descriptor	Crowd Type								
	Jocks	Populars	Normals	Black crowd	Brains	Wannabe black crowd	Rebels	Head-bangers	Trouble-makers
Dress and grooming									
Casual, neat	48	25	60	12	40	8	2	1	5
Expensive/stylish	16	67	4	47	5	47	4	0	12
Tough	12	1	1	19	1	14	21	19	26
Messy, dirty	1	0	1	2	1	2	53	61	37
Out-of-style	4	2	5	3	35	12	4	3	6
Really varies	19	5	29	16	18	17	15	16	14
Sociability									
Hassle people, pick fights	9	4	1	52	1	43	43	22	87
Cliquish, tight-knit	31	51	4	20	12	20	11	13	6
Neutral	26	19	42	15	40	14	17	24	2
Friendly, sociable	19	19	44	2	30	6	6	8	1
Really varies	15	7	9	12	17	17	23	33	4
Academic attitude									
Enjoy, try hard	3	14	4	1	81	1	0	0	0
Positive	26	42	39	4	14	6	1	1	2
Neutral	40	22	45	17	3	15	4	4	5
Slightly negative	20	15	6	24	2	33	16	18	11
Hate school	3	2	2	43	0	32	70	65	80
Really varies	8	5	4	11	0	13	7	12	2
Extracurricular activities									
Most participate	95	63	33	27	20	14	1	1	
Evenly split	3	30	59	38	22	25	7	7	
Most don't participate	2	7	8	35	58	61	93	93	
Weekend activities									
Drink, use drugs	10	8	2	17	0	17	66	80	34
Hassle people, make trouble	6	3	2	35	2	30	20	4	57
Social, party	54	59	32	24	3	21	4	5	1
Small group	15	20	40	6	30	13	1	0	4
Alone, family	2	2	5	2	56	3	0	0	0
Really varies	13	8	19	17	10	17	9	11	4

Note: Troublemakers were a middle school crowd. Since no extra-curricular activities were available at the middle school, this question was omitted on the middle school questionnaire.

TABLE 3

Percentage of Respondents from Each Membership Crowd Who Chose Various Domain Descriptors for Describing the Jock Crowd in Study 2.

Domain	Jocks described by						
	Jocks	Populars	Normals	Black crowd	Brains	Wannabe	Headbangers
Dress and grooming							
Expensive, stylish	8	9	26	11	15	23	19
Casual, neat	51	64	45	32	54	46	50
Out-of-style	0	0	0	16	5	5	3
Tough	14	9	9	21	10	14	6
Messy, dirty	3	0	2	0	0	0	0
Really varies	24	18	19	21	15	14	22
Sociability							
Hassle people, pick fights	3	6	2	26	5	9	14
Cliquish, tight-knit	24	33	23	18	40	22	53
Neutral	16	21	45	26	21	30	17
Friendly, sociable	38	18	15	16	21	22	8
Really varies	19	21	15	13	13	17	8
Academic attitude							
Enjoy, try hard	0	3	2	8	3	0	5
Positive	35	24	28	15	13	39	32
Neutral	49	42	45	31	44	39	32
Slightly negative	8	24	13	23	31	22	24
Hate school	0	0	2	10	0	0	5
Really varies	8	6	11	13	10	0	0
Extracurricular activities							
Most participate	93	96	96	92	93	100	100
Evenly split	7	0	0	8	4	0	0
Most don't participate	0	4	4	0	4	0	0
Weekend activities							
Drink, use drugs	3	12	9	13	8	9	16
Hassle people, make trouble	3	0	4	16	0	17	5
Social, party	60	64	52	37	74	35	51
Small group	14	15	20	16	5	22	16
Alone, family	0	3	0	3	3	9	0
Really varies	20	6	15	16	11	9	11

The set of crowds and characterizations of each crowd were similar in our two samples. Their images did not change systematically across grade levels, except in the case of the rebellious faction of students whose drug-use became prominent in later grades. Because the samples come from two different cohorts of teenagers and include both homogeneous and multi-ethnic secondary schools, it is tempting to conclude—as some researchers have (Buff, 1970; Clark, 1962)—that there is a set of youth subcultures in the United States that seems to transcend time and place. We think this conclusion is unwarranted for several reasons. First, in many ways our samples were homogeneous: midwestern, small to mid-sized communities, comprised primarily of middle-class, European-American teenagers. Extending this work to secondary schools in other regions, in major urban centers, or schools where European-American students comprised a minority could produce a very different picture of the adolescent social system. Second, beyond the similarities of findings in our two studies, there were several notable differences: certain crowd types (brains, nobodies, the Black crowd, and the wannabe Black crowd) were prominent in one study but not the other. In some instances, such as the jocks' purported sociability, the stereotypic image of a crowd was notably different in the two studies.

This brings us to the issue of why, in general, consensus on crowd characteristics was not overwhelming. Certainly, part of the explanation is methodological: our method of assigning the specific crowds that were named in Study 1 to crowd categories was reasonably, but not completely, reliable. Thus, error in assignments could have deflated consensus. On the other hand, Study 2 assured that respondents described the same crowds, and consensus was still rather low. Study 2 demonstrated that a sizable portion of students tend not to perceive peers in categorical, stereotypic terms and also that crowds vary in the extent to which they are seen as comprised of conformists or individuals. The relatively frequent use of the "really varies" response option could however mean that lack of consensus reflect a legitimate diversity in the characteristics of crowd members. It is unwise to assume that all members will march neatly in step with the norms of their crowd.

Most intriguingly, Study 2 supports the notion that social distance structures perceptions of peers in group-wise fashion, so that lack of consensus reflects the differentiation of the adolescent social system just as much as the distinctiveness of crowd images does. It is far more than "statistical noise." Instead, the social construction of crowd images is carried out within crowds and adolescents within a crowd or close to it on the crowd map are likely to have a far more flattering image of the crowd than do teenagers from a different segment of the social system. This finding is similar to Eder's (1985) description of the sharply contrasting image of populars among girls who are inside versus girls who are outside of this group. As in Eder's study, our findings suggest the operation of status competition as well as social distance. The Black crowd is not the most distant crowd from the jocks, though its members' opinions differ most strikingly from theirs. Instead, the Black crowd is next in line in the status ordering of crowds, after the jock/popular/normal cluster. Members of the jock and Black crowds accuse each other of hassling people, causing trouble, and hatred of school, while claiming for themselves a neutral or positive response to outsiders and school.

What emerges, then, from our analyses of adolescents' perceptions of crowd characteristics is an image of an adolescent peer system that is diverse and dynamic. Rather than the monolithic youth culture often perceived by adults, our respondents described a peer-group system well-suited to facilitating the identity exploration that Erikson (1968) mandates for this age group. The range of crowds with well-differentiated norms should help adolescents locate a suitable niche for social support and identity exploration. Simultaneously, social cognitions regarding this range of crowds appears to be structured by the social dynamics and distances that structure everyday social relations. The peer group system seems to accommodate variations in individual dispositions, cognitive capacities, and community characteristics. Approaching adolescent peer groups from the adolescent's own perspective should help us to understand more clearly the role that peer groups play in adolescent development.

REFERENCES

Brown, B. B. (1989). *Social type rating manual.* Madison, WI: National Center on Effective Secondary Schools, University of Wisconsin–Madison.

Brown, B. B. (1990). Peer groups and peer cultures. In S. S. Feldman & G. R. Elliott (Eds.), *At the threshold: The developing adolescent* (pp. 171–196). Cambridge, MA: Harvard University Press.

Brown, B. B., Lohr, M. J., & Trujillo, C. M. (1990). Multiple crowds and multiple lifestyles: Adolescents' perceptions of peer group characteristics. In R. E. Muuss (Ed.), *Adolescent behavior and society: A book of readings* (4th ed., pp. 123–167). New York: Random House.

Brown, B. B., Mory, M. S., & Kinney, D. (1994). Casting adolescent crowds in a relational perspective: Caricature, channel, and context. In R. Montemayer, G. R. Adams, & T. Gulotta (Eds.), *Advances in adolescent development: Volume 5, Personal relationships during adolescence.* Newbury Park, CA: Sage Publications.

Buff, S. A. 1970. Greasers, dupers, and hippies: Three responses to the adult world. In L. Howe (Ed.), *The white majority* (pp. 60–77). New York: Random House.

Clark, B. R. (1962). *Educating the expert society.* San Francisco: Chandler.

Coleman, J. S. (1961). *The adolescent society.* New York: Free Press.

Cusick, P. A. (1973). *Inside high school.* New York: Holt, Rinehart & Winston.

Dunphy, D. C. (1963). The social structure of urban adolescent peer groups. *Sociometry, 26,* 230–246.

Eckert, P. (1989). *Jocks and burnouts: social categories and identity in the high school.* New York: Teachers College Press.

Eder, D. (1985). The cycle of popularity: Interpersonal relations among female adolescence. *Sociology of Education, 58,* 154–165.

Eisenstadt, S. N. (1956). *From generation to generation: Age groups and social structure.* London: Collier-Macmillan.

Elkind, D. (1967). Egocentrism in adolescence. *Child Development, 38,* 1025–1034.

Erikson, E. H. (1968). *Identity, youth and crisis.* New York: Norton.

Festinger, L. (1954). A theory of social comparison processes. *Human Relations, 7,* 117–140.

Flanders, N. A. (1967). Estimating reliability. In E. J. Amidon & J. B. Hough (Eds.), *Interaction analysis: Theory, research, and application.* Reading, MA: Addison-Wesley.

Gavin, L., & Furman, W. (1989). Age differences in adolescents' perceptions of their peer groups. *Developmental Psychology, 25,* 827–834.

Goodman, L. A. (1972). A general model for the analysis of surveys. *American Journal of Sociology, 77,* 1035–1086.

Kruskal, J. B., & Wish, M. (1978). *Multidimensional scaling.* Newbury Park, CA: Sage Publications.

Larkin, R. W. (1979). *Suburban youth in cultural crisis.* New York: Oxford.

Lesko, N. (1988). *Symbolizing society: Stories, rites and structure in a Catholic high school.* New York: Falmer.

Newman, P. R., & Newman, B. M. (1976). Early adolescence and its conflict: Group identity versus alienation. *Adolescence, 11,* 261–274.

Parsons, T. (1942). Age and sex in the social structure of the United States. *American Sociological Review, 7,* 604–616.

Savin-Williams, R., & Berndt, T. (1990). Friendship and peer relations. In S. S. Feldman & G. R. Elliott (Eds.), *At the threshold: The developing adolescent* (pp. 277–307). Cambridge, MA: Harvard University Press.

Tajfel, H. (1978). *Differentiation between social groups: Studies in the social psychology of intergroup relations.* European Monographs in Social Psychology, 14, H. Tajfel, Ed. London: Academic Press.

Varenne, H. (1982). Jocks and freaks: The symbolic structure of the expression of social interaction among American senior high students. In G. Spindler (Ed.), *Doing the ethnography of schooling* (pp. 213–235). New York: Holt, Rinehart & Winston.

Youniss, J., & Smoller, J. (1985). *Adolescent relations with mothers, fathers, and friends.* Chicago: The University of Chicago Press.

FRIENDSHIP AND FRIENDS' INFLUENCE IN ADOLESCENCE

THOMAS J. BERNDT
Purdue University

Friendships have an important influence on adolescents' attitudes, behavior, and development. Theorists do not agree, however, on whether this influence is generally positive or generally negative. One theoretical perspective emphasizes the positive effects of close friendships on the psychological adjustment and social development of adolescents. Theorists who adopt this perspective argue that interactions with friends improve adolescents' social skills and ability to cope with stressful events.[1] A second theoretical perspective emphasizes the negative influence of friends on adolescents' behavior. Theorists who adopt this perspective argue that friends' influence often leads to antisocial or delinquent behavior.[2]

The two perspectives differ not only in their assumptions about the effects of friends' influence, but also in their assumptions about processes or pathways of influence. In the first perspective, the influence of friendships depends on the features of these relationships. For example, friendships that are highly intimate are assumed to enhance adolescents' self-esteem and understanding of other people. In the second perspective, friends' influence depends on the attitudes and behaviors of friends. For example, adolescents whose friends drink beer at parties are assumed to be likely to start drinking beer themselves. Thus, the first pathway of influence focuses on features of friendship and the second focuses on friends' characteristics.

Each perspective contains a kernel of truth, but each provides a one-sided view of the effects of friendships. Theorists who emphasize the positive features of friendship seldom acknowledge that friendships can have negative features, too. Adolescents often have conflicts with friends, and these conflicts can negatively affect adolescents' behavior toward other people. Theorists who emphasize the negative influence of friends' characteristics seldom acknowledge that many adolescents have friends with positive characteristics. These friends are likely to influence behavior positively.

In sum, friends can have positive or negative effects on adolescents via either of the two pathways of influence. In this review, I present evidence for these assertions and argue for more comprehensive and balanced theories of friendship in adolescence.

FRIENDSHIP FEATURES

"How can you tell that someone is your best friend?" Open-ended questions like this one were used by several researchers to assess the age changes in conceptions of friendships. The responses of children and adolescents confirmed that they regard several features of friendship as important. They said that friendships involve mutual liking, prosocial behavior (e.g., "we trade tapes with each other"), companionship (e.g., "we go places together"), and a relative lack of conflicts (e.g., "we don't fight with each other"). Many adolescents, but few elementary school children, also referred to intimacy in friendships. Adolescents said, for example, that they "talk about their problems with best friends" and that "a best friend really understands you." These findings are consistent with hypotheses that intimate friendships emerge in adolescence.[1]

Gradually, researchers shifted from studies of conceptions of friendship to studies of the actual features of friendships. Researchers also devised structured rating scales for assessing the features identified in earlier studies. The new measures made it possible to examine several questions about the nature and effects of friendships.[3]

Recent research has confirmed that intimacy becomes a central feature of friendship in early adolescence. Adolescents usually rate their own friendships as more intimate than do elementary school children. The increase in intimacy may be due partly to adolescents' growing understanding of the thoughts, feelings, and traits of self and others. It may also be due to the fact that adolescents spend more time with their friends than younger children do. Friendships are more significant relationships in adolescence than earlier.

Girls describe their friendships as more intimate than do boys. Some writers have suggested that the sex difference is merely a matter of style: Girls express their intimacy with friends by talking about personal matters, and boys express their intimacy in nonverbal ways. However, scattered evidence suggests that boys' friendships are less intimate because boys trust their friends less than girls do.[4] More boys than girls say that friends might tease them if they talk about something clumsy or foolish that they did. More girls than boys say that they share intimate information with friends because their friends listen and understand them.

This sex difference does not simply reflect a developmental delay for boys. In adulthood, women also tend to have more intimate friendships than men.[5] Still, the difference should not be exaggerated, because significant differences have not been found on all measures in all studies. Yet when differences are found, females' friendships usually appear more intimate than males' friendships.

Intimacy is closely related to other features of friendship. Adolescents' ratings of the intimacy of their friendships are correlated with their ratings of the friends' loyalty, generosity, and helpfulness. In short, friendships that are highly intimate tend to have many other positive features. Such friendships are comparable to the supportive social relationships that help adults cope with stressful life events.[6]

We might ask, then, if intimate and supportive friendships have equally positive effects on adolescents' adjustment and coping. In several studies, adolescents with more supportive friendships had higher self-esteem, less often suffered from depression or other emotional disorders, and were better adjusted to school than subjects with less supportive friendships.[7] These data are consistent with theories about the benefits of friendship, but come from correlational studies and so are open to alternative interpretations. Most important is the possibility that self-esteem and other indicators of adjustment contribute to the formation of supportive friendships rather than vice versa.

Longitudinal studies help to answer questions about causal direction, but longitudinal studies of adolescents' friendships are rare. The available data suggest that supportive friendships have significant but modest effects on some aspects of behavior and adjustment. Supportive friendships are not a panacea: They do not appear to have as powerful or as general an influence on adolescents as some theorists have suggested. Additional research is needed to identify the specific aspects of behavior and development that are most strongly affected by variations in positive features of friendship.

Equally important for future research is greater attention to the negative features of friendship. Adolescents interviewed about their conceptions of friendship commented on conflicts with friends, but many researchers ignored these comments. Many measures of friendship focus exclusively on positive or supportive features. This is a serious omission, because recent studies suggest that conflicts with friends can contribute to negative interactions with other peers and with adults.[8] With friends, adolescents may develop an aggressive interaction style that they then display with other interaction partners. Theories that emphasize the positive effects of supportive friendships need to be expanded to account for the negative effects of troubled friendships. Researchers need to measure both the positive and the negative features of friendships. New research with both types of measures should provide a more complete picture of friendship effects via the first pathway of influence.

FRIENDS' CHARACTERISTICS

You and your friends found a sheet of paper that your teacher must have lost. On the paper are the questions and answers for a test that you are going to have tomorrow. Your friends all plan to study from it, and they want you to go along with them. You don't think you should, but they tell you to do it anyway. What would you really do: study from the paper or not study from it?

Many researchers have used hypothetical dilemmas like this one to measure friends' influence on adolescents. In this dilemma, friends supposedly put pressure on an adolescent to engage in antisocial behavior, cheating on a test. Adolescents' responses to similar dilemmas are assumed to show the degree of adolescents' antisocial conformity to friends. Research with these dilemmas has provided the most direct support for theories of friends' negative influence.[2]

However, research with other methods has shown that the hypothetical dilemmas are based on faulty assumptions about the processes and outcomes of friends' influence in adolescence.[7] Some researchers observed friends' interactions in schools, summer camps, and other settings. Other researchers recorded friends' discussions, in experimental settings, as they tried to reach a consensus on various decisions. Both types of research suggest that the studies of conformity dilemmas—and popular writings about peer pressure—seriously distort reality.

In natural settings, influence among friends is a mutual process. Adolescents influence their friends as well as being influenced by them. Mutual influence is most obvious during interactions between a pair of friends. When two friends talk together, each has chances to influence the other. Even when friends interact in a group, decisions are usually made by consensus after group discussion. Groups rarely divide into a majority that favors one decision and one person who favors another. Therefore, models of group decision making describe friends' influence better than do models of individuals conforming to a majority.

In natural settings, influence seldom results from coercive pressure by friends. Friends' influence often depends on positive reinforcement. For example, friends express their approval of certain opinions and not others. Adolescents who are engaged in a discussion also listen to the reasons that friends give for their opinions. The influence of reasoning, or informational influence, may be as important in adolescents' groups as it is in adults' groups.[9] In addition, friends' influence does not always result from explicit attempts to influence. Adolescents admire and respect their friends, so they may agree with friends simply because they trust the friends' judgment.

Of course, friends sometimes do try to put pressure on adolescents. Adolescents also know that they risk disapproval or ridicule if they advocate opinions different from the opinions of most of their friends. In extremely cohesive groups, like some urban gangs, adolescents may even be threatened with physical harm if they do not go along with important group decisions, such as to attack another gang. But such situations and such groups are uncommon. Few friendship groups are as highly organized as an urban gang. Most adolescents simply choose new friends if they constantly disagree with the decisions of their old friends. The freedom of adolescents to end friendships limits their friends' use of coercive pressure as an influence technique.

Research on adolescents' responses to antisocial dilemmas is also misleading because it implies that friends usually pressure adolescents to engage in antisocial behavior. Experimental studies of friends' discussion suggest a different conclusion. So do longitudinal studies in which friends' influence is judged from changes over time in the attitudes or behavior of adolescents and their friends.[7] These studies show that the direction of friends' influence depends on the friends' characteristics. For example, if an adolescent's friends do not care about doing well in school, the adolescent's motivation to achieve in school may decrease over time. By contrast, if an adolescent's friends have good grades in school, the adolescent's grades may improve.

Viewed from a different perspective, the usual outcome of the mutual influence among friends is an increase over time in the friends' similarity. Often, the increased similarity reflects a true compromise: Friends who differ in their attitudes or behaviors adopt a position intermediate between their initial positions. Some adolescents, however, are more influential than their friends. Other adolescents are more susceptible to influence than their friends. The sources of these individual differences need further exploration.

Finally, longitudinal studies suggest that the power of friends' influence is often overestimated.[10] In one study, friends' influence on adolescents' educational aspirations was nonsignificant. In another study, friends' influence on adolescents' alcohol use was nonsignificant. These findings are unusual, but even the statistically significant effects that are found are often small.

The conclusion that friends have only a small influence on adolescents is so contrary to the conventional wisdom that its validity might be questioned. Many studies seem to support the assertion of popular writers that friends have a strong influence on adolescents, but these stud-ies often have serious flaws.[7] Researchers have frequently used adolescents' reports on their friends' behavior as measures of the friends' actual behavior. Then the researchers have estimated the friends' influence from correlations for the similarity between adolescents' self-reports and their reports on friends. Yet recent studies have shown that adolescents' reports on their friends involve considerable projection: Adolescents assume their friends' behavior is more like their own than it actually is.

Another flaw in many studies is the estimation of friends' influence from correlations for friends' similarity at a single time. However, influence is not the only contributor to friends' similarity. Adolescents also select friends who are already similar to themselves. On some characteristics (e.g., ethnicity), friends' similarity is due entirely to selection rather than to influence. To distinguish between selection and influence as sources of friends' similarity, longitudinal studies are needed. Recent longitudinal studies suggest that friends' influence on adolescents is relatively weak.

However, weak effects should not be interpreted as null effects. Underestimating the influence of friends would be as serious a mistake as overestimating it. At all ages, human beings are influenced by individuals with whom they have formed close relationships. Adolescents have close relationships with friends and, therefore, are influenced by friends. Friends influence adolescents' attitudes toward school and the broader social world. Friends influence adolescents' behavior in school and out of school. This influence is not a social problem unique to adolescence, but one instance of a universal phenomenon. To understand friends' influence better, theorists need to abandon the simplistic hypothesis of peer pressure toward antisocial behavior and consider the multiple processes of friends' influence and the varied effects of these processes.

CONCLUSION

Current thinking about adolescents' friendships is dominated by two theoretical perspectives that are incomplete and one-sided. One perspective emphasizes the benefits of friendships with certain positive features, such as intimacy. Intimacy is a more central feature of friendships in adolescence than in childhood. Intimate friendships have positive effects on adolescents, but these friendships seem to affect only some aspects of psychological adjustment. Moreover, some adolescents have friendships with many negative features, such as a high rate of conflicts. These conflicts often spill over and negatively affect other relationships. Adults concerned about adolescents' friendships should not only try to enhance the positive features of close friendships, but also try to reduce their negative features.

The second theoretical perspective emphasizes the negative influence of friends whose attitudes and behaviors are undesirable. Adolescents are influenced by their friends' attitudes and behaviors, but adolescents also influence their friends. Over time, this mutual influence increases the similarity between adolescents and their friends. Friends' influence does not generally lead to shifts either toward more desirable or toward less desirable attitudes and behaviors. These findings imply that adults concerned about negative influences of friends should try not to reduce friends' influence but to channel that influence in a positive direction.

NOTES

1. T. J. Berndt, Obtaining support from friends in childhood and adolescence, in *Children's Social Networks and Social Supports,* D. Belle, Ed. (Wiley, New York, 1989); R. L. Selman and L. H. Schultz, *Making a Friend in Youth: Developmental Theory and Pair Therapy* (University of Chicago Press, Chicago, 1990); J. Youniss and J. Smollar, *Adolescent Relations With Mothers, Fathers, and Friends* (University of Chicago Press, Chicago, 1985).
2. U. Bronfenbrenner, *Two Worlds of Childhood* (Russell Sage Foundation, New York, 1970); L. Steinberg and S. B. Silverberg, The vicissitudes of autonomy in early adolescence, *Child Development, 57,* 841–851 (1986).
3. T. J. Berndt, Children's comments about their friendships, in *Minnesota Symposium on Child Psychology: Vol. 18. Cognitive Perspectives on Children's Social Behavioral Development,* M. Perlmutter, Ed. (Erlbaum, Hillsdale, NJ, 1986); R. C. Savin-Williams and T. J. Berndt, Friendships and peer relations during adolescence, in *At the Threshold: The Developing Adolescent,* S. S. Feldman and G. Elliott, Eds. (Harvard University Press, Cambridge, MA, 1990).
4. T. J. Berndt, Intimacy and competition in the friendships of adolescent boys and girls, in *Gender Roles Through the Life Span,* M. R. Stevenson, Ed. (University of Wisconsin Press, Madison, in press).
5. W. K. Rawlins, *Friendship Matters: Communication, Dialectics, and the Life Course* (Aldine de Gruyter, Hawthorne, NY, 1992); M. S. Clark and H. T. Reis, Interpersonal processes in close relationships, *Annual Review of Psychology, 39,* 609–672 (1988).
6. S. Cohen and T. A. Wills, Stress, social support, and the buffering hypothesis, *Psychological Bulletin, 98,* 310–357 (1985); H. O. F. Veiel and U. Baumann, *The Meaning and Measurement of Social Support* (Hemisphere, New York, 1992).
7. T. J. Berndt and R. C. Savin-Williams, Variations in friendships and peer-group relationships in adolescence, in *Handbook of Clinical Research and Practice With Adolescents,* P. Tolan and B. Cohler, Eds. (Wiley, New York, 1993).
8. T. J. Berndt and K. Keefe, *How friends influence adolescents' adjustment to school,* paper presented at the biennial meeting of the Society for Research in Child Development, Seattle (April 1991); see also W. W. Hartup, Conflict and friendship relations, in *Conflict in Child and Adolescent Development,* C. U. Shantz and W. W. Hartup, Eds. (Cambridge University Press, Cambridge, England, 1992).
9. T. J. Berndt, A. E. Laychak, and K. Park, Friends' influence on adolescents' academic achievement motivation: An experimental study. *Journal of Educational Psychology, 82,* 664–670 (1990).
10. J. M. Cohen, Sources of peer group homogeneity, *Sociology of Education, 50,* 227–241 (1977); D. B. Kandel and K. Andrews, Processes of adolescent socialization by parents and peers, *International Journal of the Addictions, 22,* 319–342 (1987).

PART SIX

THE SCHOOL

The future of our country which is dependent on the will and wisdom
of its citizens is damaged and irreparably damaged, whenever any of
its children is not educated to the fullest extent of his [her]capacity,
from grade school through graduate school.
—JOHN F. KENNEDY, *"State of the Union Message" (1963)*

Schools are supposed to instill global "American values" and provide every child with the opportunity to attain an academic foundation. Unfortunately, ideal and reality are not always aligned. Many urban students attend schools that are old and overcrowded. Students enter school by walking through metal detectors. Schools have security guards. The children walk to and from school in fear. It is difficult to identify a level playing field and equal opportunities for future success when one compares the educational experiences of affluent children who live in relative safety to the harsh realities of the impoverished. Nevertheless, not all poor children are at risk for failure, and not all who are well off are assured future success. Schools can and do make a difference.

Schools obviously contribute to children's success but under some circumstances can impede and even derail their progress. School organizational patterns can reinforce positive self-esteem, security, and resilience or disconnect children from the protective world of community-based elementary school and place them in the departmentalized, depersonalized, often huge secondary school before they are ready. In the 6–3–3 (six years of elementary, three of junior high, and three years of senior high school) organizational pattern, social and educational transitions occur precisely during the period of most profound personal, physiological, and psychosocial upheaval. Blyth, Simmons, and Carlton-Ford (17) address the issue of adolescent development, especially self-concept, as it relates to different patterns of school transitions. They compare the 6–3–3 to the 8-4 pattern; in the latter system, pupils remain in their elementary schools until they finish the eighth grade. That implies that most enter high school only after they have completed their pubertal changes.

Therefore, they have the advantage of dealing primarily with one major transitional task at a time. Although variations of the 6–3–3 pattern are much more prevalent than the K–8 design, the former was found to have many disadvantages. In particular, girls who attend schools using the 6–3–3 pattern and who experience early physiological changes are at greater risk for diminished self-esteem and decline in academic achievement than girls who attend K–8 schools. Both boys and girls who do not handle transitions well show declines in their participation in extracurricular activities and academic success.

Fordham and Ogbu (18) research the experiences of black American students whose cultural and community values are not appropriately reflected in a school system that espouses "white" values, thus creating a culture clash that can and often does result in diminished school success. In order for some African-American children to succeed in school, they must disconnect themselves from their cultural identity and peer values and adopt the academically oriented standards of the school, a process which the authors refer to as "acting white." The differences between black American and white cultures trace back through slavery, through discrimination, inferior schooling, and exclusion from opportunities available to whites only. The collective experience places those black youth who wish to succeed in school in conflict with their own cultural heritage. Since "acting white" is not sanctioned by the peer group but remains essential for school success, some minority students who aspire to academic success encounter internal and external conflicts. To rectify the dissonance they experience, some young people create ingenious coping strategies to balance their desire for school success and their need to belong.

Steinberg, Dornbusch, and Brown (19) are concerned with the academic success of various ethnic groups as related to parenting styles. Reviewing data of academic performance of African-American, Hispanic-American, Asian-American, and white students, their investigation reveals the complex contexts in youngsters' lives and how these affect behavior, school performance, and development. For example, a firm but supportive authoritative parenting style is known to have a positive effect on a child's academic performance. However, even parenting style is moderated by a teenager's peers' value system. Among black American youth, many families are supportive of academic success, but as Fordham and Ogbu point out, peer groups often do not support the same goal. Lerner's (3) developmental contextualism theory warns that any attribute viewed in isolation can produce a partial or distorted understanding of the complex relationships involved. For instance, Asian-American families are likely to have a nonauthoritative parenting style, which in general can be detrimental to school success. The data indicate that Asian parents are less involved in their children's schooling than any other group. Going to see a teacher on their children's behalf seems inappropriate to many parents, who believe that educators should be in command at school. Therefore, many Asian teens report that it is their peer group which provides very strong support for their academic achievement and help them succeed. Steinberg et al. advocate an ecological analysis to understand the relationships between ethnicity and academic performance.

Schools are designed to open the door to learning, educate the mind, empower the spirit, and make opportunities for future success accessible to all. As President Johnson said, "At the desk where I sit, I have learned one great truth. The answer for all our national problems—the answer for all of the problems of the world—comes to a single word. That word is education." Given that mandate, and considering the complexity of adolescent development, cultural, social, and geographic diversity, and different family styles and values; it is not surprising that schools are overwhelmed and under constant public scrutiny.

THE ADJUSTMENT OF EARLY ADOLESCENTS TO SCHOOL TRANSITIONS

DALE A. BLYTH, *American Medical Association Center for Adolescent Health Analysis*
ROBERTA G. SIMMONS AND STEVEN CARLTON-FORD, *University of Minnesota*

In American society we have historically organized our school systems so that students must make a shift from a relatively protected neighborhood elementary school, which is largely child-centered, to progressively larger, more diverse, and more subject-centered secondary schools. (See Blyth and Karnes, 1981 for literature on this area). While there are a variety of ways in which this basic shift can and does take place, we would like to focus attention on only two primary grade level organizational patterns—the 8-4 and widely used 6-3-3 where students must make two major transitions. The first transition occurs in seventh grade as the students leave a relatively small homogeneous neighborhood elementary school to enter a larger, more departmentalized junior high school containing grades seven through nine. After three years in this junior high environment, these same students must again make a second transition. In tenth grade they must enter an even larger and perhaps more prestigious senior high school. By contrast, the 8-4 pattern requires only one major transition between schools and it delays that transition until ninth grade or about the end of early adolescence. Thus, students are kept in a more child-centered, protective kindergarten-through-eight-grade school until about age 13 or 14. Finally, for ninth grade these students must shift into a vastly larger, considerably more diverse, and fully departmentalized four-year high school.

Since students in our society will eventually have to make the shift from an elementary to a secondary school environment at some point in their lives, we shall examine some of the immediate and longer term psychological, academic, and social adjustments of youth as they make these transitions at various points in their lives (see Blyth, Simmons & Bush, 1978; Simmons, Blyth, Van Cleave, & Bush, 1979). In order to help organize and understand the consequences of these different grade level patterns, we shall focus on four particular questions or hypotheses.

The first question, and perhaps the most obvious, is simply how disruptive are the transitions from one school environment to another? This question can be approached from two theoretical perspectives. First, we can extrapolate on the classical perspective of Benedict (1938) and argue that the more discontinuous or different two school environments are the greater the psychological, academic, and social disruption there will be. As Glen Elder (1968) has noted, transitions between schools and (particularly the entry into junior high school) may be the closest American society comes to a formal right of passage. This perspective suggests that each of the

From *Journal of Early Adolescence*, 1983, *3*. 105–120. Copyright 1983 by Sage Publications. Reprinted by permission of the senior author and Sage Publications. Inc.

transitions a student makes will be disruptive if it represents a marked or discontinuous change from what they are used to.

A second perspective, which similarly predicts disruption as a major consequence of these transitions, is concerned with the relative status of students in the schools before and after the transition. This perspective can be labeled the "top-dog" phenomenon since it refers to the dramatic and potentially disruptive effects of moving from the top position in one school to the bottom or lowest position in the second school. This shift from "top dog" to "bottom dog" may cause a variety of disruptions or difficulties for students. The magnitude of the effect may in part depend on how prestigious the new school is compared to the old. For example, if the new school is seen as a major step toward adulthood, then occupying the lowest position in this school may be more tolerable than if the new school is seen as merely an intermediate and less prestigious step toward adulthood.

In summary, either because of the amount of discontinuity in the two school environments or because of a sharp change in statuses, we would expect the transition into a new school to be at least a short term disruption. Furthermore, previous work by Simmons, Rosenberg, and Rosenberg (1973) as well as that of Douvan and Adelson (1966) suggest that such a major change in social relationships might be more likely to be felt by females than males. This proposed female sensitivity to the school changes is a function of the greater perceived importance of social relations for females in our society.

A second questions which we shall explore is whether or not the timing of the transition in an individual's life course makes a significant difference in how disruptive the change will be. This essentially developmental hypothesis suggest that there may be periods in an individual's life when major social change such as the transition between schools is more likely to be disruptive than if that same change took place a few years earlier or later. In particular, transitions which occur in early adolescence may be more disruptive than changes which occur after the in-

dividual has developed a more mature sense of who he or she is. That is, the physical, social and psychological changes taking place in early adolescence may push children further and faster than they are emotionally mature enough to handle. By ninth and tenth grade, their greater emotional maturity may be sufficient to help them adjust more easily to a major transition. This hypothesis differs from the first one noted above since it suggests that the seventh grade transition will be the most disruptive and that later transitions may be considerably less disruptive and perhaps even constructive.

The third question we will explore focuses on the long term consequences of the transition between school environments. In particular, we are concerned with the extent to which students entering a new school are able to overcome or recover from any disruptive effects that might have occurred. If students are able to cope with the disruption caused by the change in schools within a year or two, then the seriousness of the problem may be minimized.

A fourth and final question focuses on the extent to which any stress experienced by students during school transitions may be viewed as functional in so far as it provides a stronger ability to cope with future disruptive changes. Many theorists (e.g., A. Freud, 1946; Erikson, 1968; and Peskin, 1967) see periods of stress as growth-inducing and distinguish between short-term and long-term mental turmoil. In particular this hypothesis suggests that while the first transition into the junior high school may be stressful in the short run, learning to cope with it will better prepare the youngsters for the subsequent transition into the senior high school. By contrast, the students from the kindergarten-through-eighth-grade school (who have been protected up until this point) will be ill-prepared for the move into very large senior high schools. This hypothesis, unlike the second, would suggest that the transition into the four-year high school will be most disruptive and that the transition of the junior high students into senior high school will be only minimally disruptive.

To review briefly, this paper shall explore four questions. First, to what extent do psychological, academic and social disruptions occur as a consequence of three different transitions occurring in two different organization structures: the entry of students into junior high school in seventh grade and their subsequent entry into a senior high school in tenth grade, or alternatively, the entry of students from a kindergarten-through-eighth-grade school into a four-year high school at ninth grade. Second, what evidence is there that the transition which takes place in early adolescence (namely the entry into the junior high school) is more disruptive than either of the other transitions? Third, how long lasting are the effects of these various transitions? And finally, does the experience provided by one transition facilitate the making of a second transition?

METHODS

Sample

In order to fully explore these issues we shall use data from a five-year longitudinal study of adolescents which followed students as they move from sixth through tenth grade in either the 8–4 or 6–3–3 organizational pattern. The data were collected in the Milwaukee Public Schools between 1974 and 1979. Initially we examined students in six of the seven kindergarten-through-eighth-grade schools and a random sample of twelve kindergarten-through-sixth-grade schools in the same district. Since the kindergarten-through-eighth-grade schools were predominantly white or integrated, only eight of the twelve kindergarten-through-sixth-grade schools shall be used in this analysis. Furthermore, the number of Black students is too small to permit analysis of the issues to be considered in this paper. Therefore, only white students shall be included.

Once the eighteen schools were selected and school permission was obtained, all sixth grade students in each school were asked to participate. Written parental permission was obtained for over 85% of these sixth grade students. A total of 594 white students were available for the initial analyses. It should be noted that the analysis contains only those students who stayed within the Milwaukee Public Schools and who followed the grade organization patterns under study. This approach resulted in substantial sample loss over the five years of the study. We shall present trend analyses which use the maximum number of students that are available for a given year. A separate analysis has been conducted analyzing only the smaller longitudinal sample for which we have a full set of five years worth of data. While there are some differences between the two samples (mostly in terms of the level of significance), none of our interpretations would be drastically altered by considering one sample rather than the other. We have chosen to present the maximum number of cases for a given year since we feel that these fuller samples best represent the process taking place in a given year.

Procedures

Data were collected from each student using a structured personal interview conducted within the schools in sixth, seventh, ninth, and tenth grade. In addition to these interviews, supplemental data were also collected by registered nurses hired by the project. Each nurse was requested to collect information on recent physical growth and to measure each student's height and weight periodically over the five year time period. The data which were collected in eighth grade came from the nurses and a brief questionnaire which was administered to students. Thus, the eighth grade data points are not always available for all variables. In addition to these primary sources of data we also collected data from the principals of each of the schools in sixth, seventh, and tenth grade and obtained official transcripts and achievement test scores from the school district.

Measures

Although a wide range of data was collected on each of the students each year, we shall focus our present attention on only a few key variables within the psychological, academic and social areas. Our primary indicator of psychological adjustment will be global self-esteem as measured by the Simmons and Rosenberg self-esteem scale (see Simmons, et al., 1973, for a copy of the scale and reliability and validity information). In the academic area we shall rely largely on the student's academic grade point average as calculated for core academic courses only. We shall also comment on the results of standardized achievement tests which the schools administered in sixth, seventh, and tenth grade but which are not the same tests from year to year. In the social area, we shall analyze the effects of school transitions on behavior in terms of the amount of participation in extracurricular activities. In addition, we shall note the student's perception of his school environment as anonymous. Anonymity is measured using a four-item scale constructed for this study (see Blyth et al., 1978).

RESULTS

Psychological Adjustment—Self-Esteem

Figure 1 illustrates the mean level of self-esteem for students in each of the two school environments for sixth through tenth grade. It should be recalled that the number of students available for this analysis decreases in the later grade levels because of sample loss. Previous analyses of the self-concept by Simmons, et al. (1973) as well as previous analyses from this data set (e.g. Simmons et al., 1979, Blyth et al., 1978) have indicated that girls are more vulnerable in terms of their self-concept than boys during the early adolescent time period. The generally lower level of self-esteem for girls can be seen by comparing the graph for males with that for females. More importantly for the present concerns, however, are the trends across grade levels for each sex separately.

For males we find a general pattern of increasing self-esteem with advances in grade levels. Even for the boys who are entering the ju-

nior high schools there is no decrease in self-esteem. The only time there is a noticeable interruption of the generally upward trend is when the boys in the junior high school cohort enter the senior high school at tenth grade. There we find a leveling off in self-esteem between ninth and tenth grade. It should be noted that the present trend analysis is not as sensitive to a possible drop in self-esteem between eighth and ninth grade for the K–8 cohort of boys because there is no comparable eighth grade measure of self-esteem. We can only note that in the ninth grade the mean level of self-esteem for the K–8 cohort of boys as they enter a four-year high school is considerably higher than their self-esteem was in seventh grade. It is impossible to tell whether the self-esteem of these boys in eighth grade was somewhere between their seventh and ninth grade means or was actually higher than the ninth grade mean and dropped as a result of the transition.

For females we find a quite different pattern. Only females in the K–8 cohort increase in self-esteem as a function of grade level. As with the boys, it is not possible to accurately determine whether or not there is a drop in self-esteem between eighth and ninth grade as the students enter the four-year high school. In any event, if a drop occurred it was not sufficient to put them at a value less than they were at in the sixth or seventh grade. The really contrasting pattern, however, is for the girls in the junior high cohort. These girls had significantly lower self-esteem than their K–8 counterparts during seventh grade and during the tenth grade. As the trend analyses show, for this group self-esteem is lower in seventh grade than it was in sixth grade. Similarly as the junior high cohort of girls makes the transition into the senior high school in tenth grade, there is another drop in the mean level of self-esteem.

Further analysis of these data which more fully utilize the longitudinal aspect of the data shows the amount of change in self-esteem experienced by each cohort. By controlling the initial sixth grade level of self-esteem we can create adjusted change scores for each group.[1]

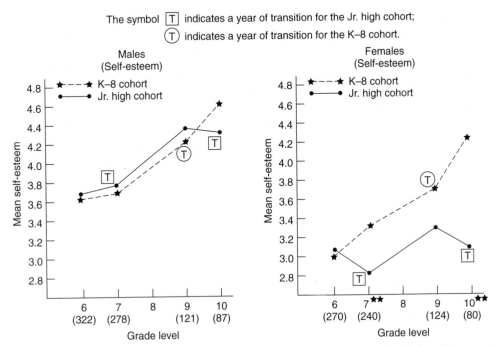

These graphs represent a trend analysis using the maximum number of cases available each year. The decreasing N for each grade level is due to sampling losses as noted in the text.

Levels of significance are based on one-way ANOVA's using school type as the factor and treating each grade level and sex separately. The degree of significance is indicated as follows: *p less than .10 **p less than .05 ***p less than .01.

FIGURE 1   Mean Self-Esteem from Grade 6 to Grade 10 by School Type for Each Sex Separately.

Comparison of these adjusted mean change scores allows us to see which groups are experiencing the relative increments or decrements in self-esteem. The results are shown in Figure 2. As the figure indicates, only those girls who have made the transition into the junior high school experience an adjusted mean loss in self-esteem between sixth and seventh grade. All other groups appear to increase their level of self-esteem. A similar set change analyses looking at changes in self-esteem between sixth grade and ninth grade, and between sixth grade and tenth grade indicate that the junior high girls do not fully recover from this net loss in self-esteem, at least not by ninth or tenth grade.

In summary, the psychological adjustment of students in terms of self-esteem clearly indicates

that girls in the junior high cohort have a more difficult time with school transitions than do boys and that the transition into junior high school is more difficult and has a longer lasting effect than does the transition into a four-year high school in ninth grade. Furthermore, there appears to be an increased vulnerability to the senior high transition when the first transition occurs in the seventh grade. Girls who attend junior high not only show a drop in self-esteem in grade seven, but they are the only group to show a substantial reduction as they move into senior high school (grade ten). For junior high males, however, we find little evidence of a substantial negative or disruptive effect due to transitions. The self-esteem of the K–8 cohort of both girls and boys appears to increase despite their transition

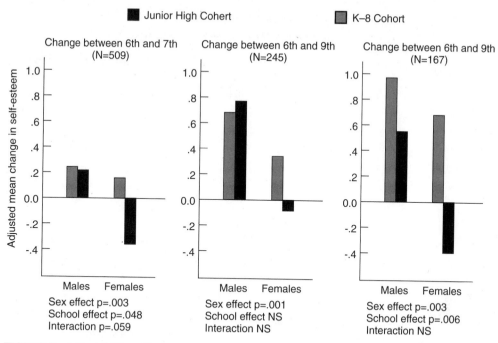

FIGURE 2   Adjusted Mean Change in Self-Esteem by School Type for Each Sex Separately.

into a four-year high school at ninth grade. When this junior high cohort of boys is ready to move on to tenth grade in a senior high school we see a leveling off of self-esteem or perhaps a slight decrease. The apparent lack of a serious self-esteem disturbance in the K–8 cohort suggests that the timing of the transition, particularly for girls, is a major factor affecting the magnitude of any self-esteem disruption. It should be noted that other dimensions of the self-image do not appear to be seriously affected. In particular, there seems to be no significant difference in terms of self-consciousness or stability of the self image as a function of school transitions.

Academic Adjustment—Grade Point Average

Although there are a number of problems associates with grade point averages and how they might change over time, we have elected to use the student's grade point average, calculated on a core set of academic areas, as the best indicator the student has of his performance in school. The mean level of GPA is plotted by grade level for males and females separately in Figure 3. The first observation worth making is the general decrease in grade-point-average as one goes up in grade level. This general pattern is not simply a function of those students who drop out of the study over time.

Looking at the graph for males we see that although there are no initial differences in grade-point-average in sixth grade, there are significant differences between the two groups in seventh grade. In particular, the group of boys who enter the junior high school have a lower GPA than do those who remain in the same kindergarten-through-eighth-grade school. Once again, it is difficult to say whether the K–8 students experience a similar drop in grade point average as they make the transition between eighth and ninth grade because we do not have an eighth grade data point. Nonetheless, the ninth grade GPA for

The symbol $\boxed{T}$ indicates a year of transition for the Jr. high cohort;

$\textcircled{T}$ indicates a year of transition for the K–8 cohort.

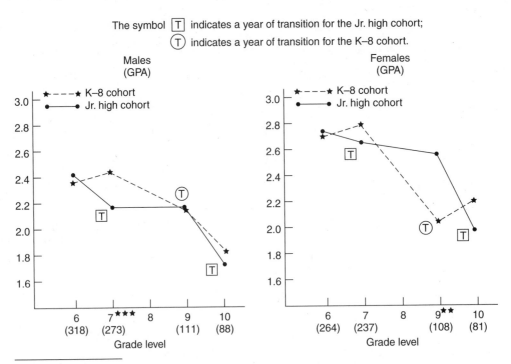

Levels of significance are based on one-way ANOVA's using school type as the factor and treating each grade level and sex separately. The degree of significance is indicated as follows: *p less than .10 **p less than .05 ***p less than .01.

FIGURE 3   Mean GPA from Grade 6 to Grade 10 by School Type for Each Sex Separately.

the K–8 cohort is much lower than it was in seventh grade and is about the same as the mean level of GPA for the ninth graders in the junior high cohort. Both groups of students experience a decrease in mean level of GPA between ninth and tenth grade. There is some indication that the change may be somewhat greater for the boys in the junior high cohort who have now entered the senior high school.

For girls we find a similar pattern for the seventh grade transition; those girls entering a junior high school have a lower mean grade point average than those in the K–8 cohort. Moreover, though it is impossible to assess without an eighth grade data point, there is a considerable decrease in the mean GPA between the seventh and ninth grade for those girls who make the transition into a four-year high school. They par-

tially recovered from this drop by tenth grade. The junior high cohort also experiences a sharp drop in mean grade point average when it moves from the ninth grade in the junior high school to its first year of senior high school.

An examination of change scores between sixth and seventh, ninth and tenth grades indicates that those students entering the seventh grade of the junior high experience a significant drop (p = .000) in adjusted mean grade point average between sixth and seventh grade when compared to students in the K–8 cohort. Similarly the adjusted change scores from sixth to ninth grade indicate that the K–8 females and K–8 males experience a statistically significant (.003) decrease in grade point average. There were no significant adjusted mean changes in GPA between sixth and tenth grade.

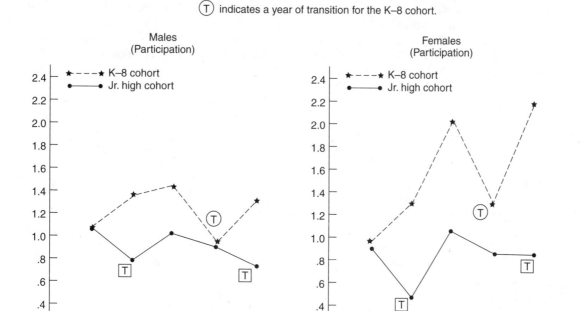

The symbol ⊡ indicates a year of transition for the Jr. high cohort;
Ⓣ indicates a year of transition for the K–8 cohort.

Levels of significance are based on one-way ANOVA's using school type as the factor and treating each grade level and sex separately. The degree of significance is indicated as follows: *p less than .10 **p less than .05 ***p less than .01. ° indicates that there was a significant lack of homogeneity in the variances.

FIGURE 4   Mean Number of Extracurricular Activities from Grade 6 to Grade 10 by School Type for Each Sex Separately.

In summary, we find general support for the hypothesis that a change in school environments is associated with a decrease in grade point average. The effect appears to be somewhat stronger for males during the seventh grade transition and perhaps slightly stronger for girls who make the transition into a four-year high school.

Social Behavior and Attitudes

Participation in Extracurricular Activities
One indication of the extent to which youth in our society are developing positive forms of social behavior is the sheer number of extracurricular activities they participate in at school. Figure 4

contains the mean number of activities that students participated in at school during the course of our study. These graphs, perhaps more than any others, demonstrate the disruption which is associated with entering the junior high. For both males and females we see a dramatic difference between the two cohorts in the mean rate of participation in extracurricular activities during seventh grade. For those students remaining in the K–8 environment, they continue to increase their participation from sixth to seventh and even into eighth grade. On the other hand, for those students entering the junior high school, there is not only a dramatic decrease in participation during seventh grade, but even the gradual recovery from this deficit is insufficient to permit the girls to catch up by ninth or tenth grade.

For males in the K–8 cohort we also see a drop in participation as they enter the ninth grade in the four-year high school. In contrast, the ninth graders in the junior high cohort have reached the "top dog" position in the junior high schools. Even with these differences in environments we find no significant difference in participation between the two cohorts of males in the ninth grade. As already noted, the K–8 cohort of females actually participates more in ninth grade despite the transition they have made. Even more significantly, we found a dramatic recovery to the same or even higher rates of participation for the K–8 cohort of students as they progress to the sophomore year in the four-year high schools. By contrast, the second transition for the junior high cohort once again decreases the mean level of participation for both males and females.

In summary, although both cohorts of students started at about the same level of participation in sixth grade, they end up radically different. While a transition into a new school almost always results in a decreased level of participation regardless of what grade levels are involved, the decrease is persistent and has long term consequences only for the transition which occurs in early adolescence (the junior high cohort). These longer term effects of the transitions into junior high school, like the findings of girls' self-esteem, are perhaps the most telling evidence with regard to the developmental aspect of transitions. Once students are in an environment where actual participation is made difficult or perceived to be difficult, it is hard for them to overcome it. By contrast, greater participation in early adolescence leads to higher levels of participation throughout middle adolescence.

Perceived Anonymity   During each year of the study we asked *different* subsamples of students' questions indicating whether they felt other students and teachers knew their names and who they were.[2] These items were built into a perceived anonymity scale. The best estimate of the mean

level of anonymity for each grade level is plotted in Figure 5 for each sex separately. As the different number of cases each year indicates we did *not* ask all sixth and seventh graders these particular questions. In fact, only a random half of the sixth and seventh grade sample were asked these questions. Since the students measured in sixth and seventh grade were a random subsample of those in the study, the estimated means are quite representative of the total sample. We have included an estimate of the eighth grade level of anonymity based on questionnaire rather than interview data.

As one might expect, the perceived level of anonymity fluctuates in direct proportion to a student's position in the school. When a student enters a new school his or her level of anonymity increases dramatically and gradually decreases over the course of the person's stay at that school. These increases in anonymity are particularly noteworthy at the entry into junior high in seventh grade and again in tenth grade when this cohort enters the senior high school. For males, we also find a significant different in anonymity between those ninth graders in a junior high school and those who have just entered a four-year high school. Those males new to the four-year high school have a higher perceived level of anonymity. For girls, on the other hand, we do not see a significant difference in the ninth grade mean level of perceived anonymity between the two cohorts. While anonymity has clearly gone up for those girls who have entered the four-year high school, it does not increase to a point where it is significantly greater than the perceived anonymity of the ninth grade girls who are the "top dogs" in the junior high school.

In summary, the perceived level of anonymity fluctuates in direct relationship to the entry into a new school. When students enter a new school they perceive a higher level of anonymity than they did in their former school. In addition, other measure of school attitudes such as the extent to which students worry about going into a new grade or think that the new grade level is quite different also indicate the dramatic nature of the transition for many students.

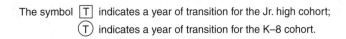

The symbol [T] indicates a year of transition for the Jr. high cohort; (T) indicates a year of transition for the K–8 cohort.

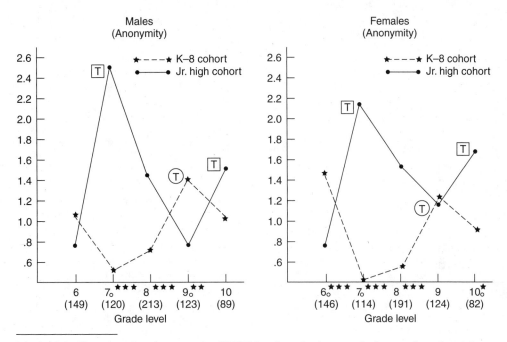

Levels of significance are based on one-way ANOVA's using school type as the factor and treating each grade level and sex separately. The degree of significance is indicated as follows: *p less than .10 **p less than .05 ***p less than .01. ° indicates that there was a significant lack of homogeneity in the variances.

FIGURE 5   Mean Level of Perceived Anonymity from Grade 6 to Grade 10 by School Type for Each Sex Separately.

DISCUSSION

The transition into seventh grade for those students entering a junior high school has some disadvantageous consequences. It places girls at relative risk in terms of their self-esteem and both boys and girls at risk in terms of their grade point average. Furthermore, seventh graders making the transition into junior high school as compared to those staying in the kindergarten-through-eighth-grade schools are in general more likely to view their schools as anonymous places where students are unknown to each other and to teachers. They are also less likely to participate in extracurricular activities. To the extent that the development of a positive self-

picture and a sense of competence are two important tasks of early adolescence, it would appear that the junior high environments studied were not optimal for such development.

The transition into a four-year high school at ninth grade for the K–8 cohort does not appear to have been as disruptive as the seventh grade transition just noted. Caution must be used in making this conclusion, however, since we do not have clear cut eighth grade data points on many of our variables. Nonetheless, with respect to self-esteem we find no significant differences for either boys or girls in the mean level of self-esteem for ninth graders who are the top grade in a junior high as compared to those K–8 students who have just entered a four-year high school.

Whatever drop in self-esteem the K–8 students entering the four-year high school may have experienced, it is not strong enough to place them at a disadvantage with respect to the junior high cohort of girls who is still trying to recover from the serious decrease in self-esteem which occurred in the seventh grade.

Furthermore, an analysis of adjusted group change scores indicated that only the girls in the junior high cohort experienced a net loss in self-esteem in seventh, ninth, and tenth grades. The girls in the K–8 cohort gained in self-esteem over the course of our study. While we do find sizable decreases in the grade point average of those students entering a four-year high school (particularly girls), these differences for girls are short-lived since they are already beginning a recovery by tenth grade. Just as for self-esteem, the junior high cohort of students who made a transition in early adolescence experienced a disruption in their extracurricular participation from which they do not recover. These findings indicate that certain transitions are indeed disruptive and that the degree and nature of disruption appear to depend on the variable studied.

In conclusion, it was only for the perceived degree of anonymity that we found consistent and short term disruptive effects due to transitions regardless of the grade level at which the transition occurred. For the other areas studied the developmental preparedness hypothesis was more appropriate. That is, a transition which is made too early can have relatively long lasting negative effects while transitions made at a later developmental stage may be without serious negative consequences. Thus, the transition into junior high school in early adolescence has negative consequences for youth, particularly in terms of participation and girls' self-esteem. By contrast, the delaying of the transition into secondary schools until ninth grade, as occurred for the K–8 cohort, seems to reduce the magnitude of the disruptions which occur and the time it takes to recover. In spite of some recovery between seventh and ninth grade for the junior high students, they again experience disruption when they make the transition into the senior high school. It is as though the difficulty in coping with the first transition left them vulnerable rather then strengthened for the second transition.

NOTES

1. Adjusted mean change scores are created using the individual's time one scores as a covariate and the new change score as the dependent variable in an analysis of covariance model. We use such adjusted change scores as a way of controlling for differences in where individuals start from. The analysis is identical to a simple analysis of covariance using the time two score, but with a more intuitively clear metric. See Simmons et al., 1979, for more information.
2. The perceived anonymity scale consists of the following questions:
   A kid said: "This school has so many students in it that I feel I don't know lots of kids." Do you ever feel like this about your school?
   A different student said: "Lots of kids don't know me at my school because it is so large." Do you ever feel like this about the *kids* in your school?
   A student said: "At this school the *teachers* don't seem to know who you are or what your name is." Do you ever feel like this about the *teachers* in your school?
   Another student said: "At this school most *students* don't seem to know who you are or what your name is." Do you ever feel like this about the *students* in your school?

REFERENCES

Benedict, R. Continuities and discontinuities in cultural conditioning. *Psychiatry,* 1938, *I* 161–167.
Blyth, D. A., & Karnes, E. L. *Philosophy, Policies, and Programs for Early Adolescent Education: An Annotated Bibliography.* Westport, Conn.: Greenwood, 1981.
Blyth, D. A., Simmons, R. G., & Bush, D. The transitions into early adolescence: A longitudinal comparison of youth in two educational contexts. *Sociology of Education,* 1978, *51,* 149–162.
Douvan, E., & Adelson, J. *The adolescent experience.* New York: John Wiley, 1966.

Elder, G. H., Jr. *Adolescent socialization and personality development.* Chicago: Rand McNally, 1968.

Erikson, E. *Identity: Youth and crisis.* New York: Norton, 1968.

Freud, A. *The Ego and mechanisms of defense.* New York: International University Press, 1946.

Peskin, H. Multiple prediction of adult psychological health from pre-adolescent and adolescent behavior. *Journal of Consulting and Clinical Psychology,* 1972, *38,* 155–160.

Simmons, R. G., Rosenberg, F. and Rosenberg, M. Disturbance in the self-image at adolescence. *American Sociological Review,* 1973, *38,* 553–568.

Simmons, R. G., Blyth, D. A., VanCleave, E. F., & Busch, D. M. Entry into early adolescence: The impact of school structure, puberty, and early dating on self-esteem. *American Sociological Review,* 1974, *44,* 948–967.

READING 18

BLACK STUDENTS' SCHOOL SUCCESS: COPING WITH THE "BURDEN OF 'ACTING WHITE' "

Signithia Fordham and John U. Ogbu
Yale University and University of California, Berkeley

The following vignettes point to the central problem addressed in this paper. The first is from Dorothy Gilliam's column in the *Washington Post* of February 15, 1982, entitled "Success":

> My friend was talking to her son, who is 20, when he blurted out a secret half as old as he. It was the explanation for his ambivalence toward success. It began, he said, in his early school years, when a fifth-grade teacher questioned whether he had really written the outstanding essay he'd turned in about the life of squirrels. It ended when the teacher gave him a grade that clearly showed that she did not believe the boy's outraged denial of plagiarism.

Because the young man is black and the teacher is white, and because such incidents had happened before, he arrived at a youthful solution: "I never tried again," he recently told his mother, who had suffered misery as her son's grades had plummeted and his interest in school had waned. He had sold himself short because he was humiliated.

Today he reads the classics but has only a high school diploma; today he can finally articulate his feelings. Today he feels he was manipulated by society not to achieve, and feels he has been tricked into lowering his performance. He is furious that he blocked his own talents.

As my distraught friend recounted this disturbing episode, we looked at each other and grimaced. Each of us know people of her son's generation, and of our own, who are ambivalent about success (p. B1).

From *Urban Review,* 1986, *18,* 176–206, abridged. Reproduced by permission of the senior author and the publisher.

Gilliam goes on to recount how the existing ecological conditions have led black parents unwittingly to teach their children a double message: "You must be twice as good to go half as far," and "Don't get the big head, don't blow your own horn." Generations of black children have learned this lesson so well that what appears to have emerged in some segments of the black community is a kind of cultural orientation which defines academic learning in school as "acting white," and academic success as the prerogative of white Americans. This orientation embodies both social pressures against striving for academic success and fear of striving for academic success. The following passage from Abdul-Jabbar's autobiography illustrates a part of this *evolved cultural orientation toward schooling:*

> I got there [Holy Providence School in Cornwall Heights, right outside of Philadelphia] and immediately found I could read better than anyone in the school. My father's example and my mother's training had made that come easy; I could pick up a book, read it out loud, pronounce the word with proper inflections and actually know what they meant. When the nuns found this out they paid me a lot of attention, once even asking me, a fourth grader, to read to the seventh grade. When the kids found this out I became a target. . . .
>
> It was my first time away from home, my first experience in an all-black situation, and I found myself being punished for doing everything I'd ever been taught was right. I got all A's and was hated for it; I spoke correctly and was called a punk. I had to learn a new language simply to be able to deal with the threats. I had good manners and was a good little boy and paid for it with my hide (Abdul-Jabbar, 1983, p. 16).

Our main point in this paper is that *one major reason* black students do poorly in school is that they experience inordinate ambivalence and affective dissonance in regard to academic effort and success. This problem arose partly because white Americans traditionally refused to acknowledge that black Americans are capable of intellectual achievement, and partly because black Americans subsequently began to doubt their own intellectual ability, began to define academic success as white people's prerogative, and began to discourage their peers, perhaps unconsciously, from emulating white people in academic striving, i.e., from "acting white." Because of the ambivalence, affective dissonance, and social pressures, many black students who are academically able do not put forth the necessary effort and perseverance in their schoolwork and, consequently, do poorly in school. Even black students who do not fail generally perform well below their potential for the same reasons. We will illustrate this phenomenon with data from a recent ethnographic study of both successful and unsuccessful students in a predominantly black high school in Washington, D.C. . . .

CULTURAL-ECOLOGICAL INFLUENCES ON SCHOOLING

It is well known that some minority groups are academically successful in school, while other minority groups are not (Coleman et al., 1966). The differences in the school performance of the various minority groups exist even when the minority groups face similar language, cultural, and educational barriers in school as well as barriers in the opportunity structure (e.g., job discrimination) in adult life (see Ogbu, 1984, 1987; Ogbu and Matute-Bianchi, 1986). In order to account for this variability, we have suggested that minority groups should be classified into three types: *autonomous minorities,* who are minorities primarily in a numerical sense; *immigrant minorities,* who came to America more or less *voluntarily* with the expectation of improving their economic, political, and social status; and *subordinate* or *castelike minorities,* who were *involuntarily and permanently* incorporated into American society through slavery or conquest. Black Americans are an example par excellence of castelike minorities because they were brought to America as slaves and after emancipation were relegated to menial status through legal and extralegal devices (Berreman, 1960;

Myrdal, 1944). American Indians, Mexican Americans, and Native Hawaiians share, to some extent, features of castelike minorities. American Indians, the original owners of the land, were conquered and sent to live on reservations (Spicer, 1962). Mexican Americans in the Southwest were also conquered and displaced from power; and Mexicans who later immigrated from Mexico were given the status of the conquered group and treated in the same manner (Acuna, 1972; Ogbu, 1978; Schmidt, 1970).

We initially explained the disproportionate and persistent high rates of school failure of subordinate minorities from a cultural-ecological perspective because this perspective allowed us to examine the school performance of the minorities in the context of historical, structural, and cultural forces which affect the schooling of such groups (Ogbu, 1978, 1981). In the case of black Americans we suggested that the disproportionately high rate of low school performance is a kind of adaptation to their limited social and economic opportunities in adult life. That is, the low school performance is an adaptive response to the requirements of cultural imperatives within their ecological structure.

Within their ecological structure black Americans traditionally have been provided with substandard schooling, based on white Americans' perceptions of the educational needs of black Americans; and white Americans have controlled black Americans' education. Another feature of their ecological structure is that black Americans have faced a job ceiling, so that even when they achieved in school in the past, i.e., had good educational credentials, they were not necessarily given access to jobs, wages, and other benefits commensurate with their academic accomplishments. The third component of the ecological structure is that in response to substandard schooling and barriers in the adult opportunity structure, black Americans developed several "survival strategies" and other coping mechanisms.

We suggested how these ecological factors might enter into the schooling of black children

and adversely affect their academic performance. The job ceiling, for example, tends to give rise to disillusionment about the real value of schooling, especially among older children, and thereby discourages them from working hard in school (Hunter, 1980; Ogbu, 1974). Frustrations over the job ceiling and substandard schooling create conflicts and distrust between black Americans and the public schools, making it more difficult for black Americans than for white Americans to believe what the schools say and to behave according to school norms. Survival strategies, such as collective struggle, uncle tomming, and hustling, may encourage black Americans to develop attitudes, perceptions, behaviors, and competencies that are not necessarily congruent with those required to do well in school. The job ceiling and other discriminatory treatment engender among black Americans a feeling of impotence and a lack of self-confidence that they can compete successfully with whites *in matters considered traditionally as white people's domain,* such as good jobs and academic tasks. Finally, the experience of slavery with its attendant "compulsory ignorance" has meant that black Americans have had a limited development of academic tradition.

Under these circumstances, attitudes and behaviors of black students, though different from those of white students, are not deviant of pathological but should be considered as a mode of adaptation necessitated by the ecological structure or effective environment of the black community. That is, the attitudes and behaviors which black children learn in this community as they grow up and which they bring to school are those required by and appropriate for the niche black Americans have traditionally occupied in the American corporate economy and racial stratification system. . . .

A concept which allows one to comprehend more fully the academic attitudes and behaviors of black Americans under this circumstance is that of *status mobility system* (LeVine, 1967; Ogbu, 1978). A status mobility system is the socially or culturally approved strategy for getting ahead within a given population or a given society. It is the people's *folk theory of making it* or getting ahead, however the particular population defines getting ahead. A central premise of the concept is that a given status mobility system generates its own ideal personality types, distinguished by those orientations, qualities, and competencies which one needs to get ahead in the particular population. Furthermore, the way members of a population, including a subordinate population, prepare their children for adulthood, through child rearing as well as formal schooling, is influenced by their ideal images and characteristics of successful members of the population, living or dead; these images are incorporated into the value systems of parents and others responsible for the upbringing of children. As the children get older and begin to understand the status mobility system of their group, they themselves tend to play an active role in learning how to get ahead in the manner prescribed by their culture.

In a given population the orientations, qualities, competencies, and behaviors fostered by the system of status mobility will reflect the social and economic realities of its members. Thus, people's way of bringing up children, through which they inculcate those orientations, qualities, competencies, and behaviors they consider essential for competence in adulthood, is not divorced from their social and economic realities. In the case of subordinate minorities like black Americans, the schooling offered to them by the dominant group usually reflects the dominant group members' perceptions of the place of the minorities in the opportunity structure; equally important, however, are the responses of the minorities, which reflect their perceptions of their social and economic realities, their strategies for getting ahead.

The cultural-ecological explanation has undergone modifications because the original formulation did not explain differences in school success among black students. Why, for example, are some black children academically successful even though as a group black Americans

face a limited adult opportunity structure and are given substandard education? The original formulation has also been criticized for focusing on black school failure while ignoring possible explanations of black school success (Fordham, 1981). But in fairness to the theory, it should be pointed out that it was initially proposed as a response to earlier theories that attributed disproportionately high rates of black school failure to genetic factors (Jensen, 1969) or to cultural deprivation (Bloom, Davis, and Hess, 1965).

COLLECTIVE IDENTITY, CULTURAL FRAME, AND SCHOOLING

Since 1980 (Ogbu, 1980, 1982) the recognition of the above weakness, as well as the need to explain better the academic success of some other minority groups, has led the authors to modify the cultural-ecological explanation. The modification has involved going beyond factors of instrumental exploitation (limitations in opportunity structure, such as "job ceilings") and instrumental responses, to examine the expressive dimension of the relationship between the dominant group and the minorities. Specifically, in studying the expressive dimension of minority-majority group relations, we have isolated two additional factors we believe make the relationship between blacks and whites in America qualitatively different from the relationship between white Americans and other types of minorities, especially the immigrants. These additional factors also shed some light on the intragroup differences or individual differences within the black population. The two factors are an *oppositional collective* or *social identity* and an *oppositional cultural frame of reference* (Fordham, 1981, 1982a; Ogbu, 1980, 1981, 1984).

Our clue to the twin phenomena comes from reviewing cross-cultural studies of minorities. We have found the work of Spicer (1966, 1971), DeVos (1967, 1984). Castile and Kushner (1981), Green (1981), and others particularly helpful in this regard. These scholars have analyzed conflicts and oppositional processes between minority groups and dominant groups in both traditional societies and contemporary urban industrial societies, and they have concluded that the conflicts and opposition often cause the minorities to form oppositional social identities and oppositional cultural frames of reference (Ogbu, 1986a). A close analysis of the relationship between subordinate minorities and the dominant white Americans reveals these same kinds of conflicts and oppositional processes.

Subordinate minorities like black Americans develop a sense of collective identity or sense of peoplehood in opposition to the social identity of white Americans because of the way white Americans treat them in economic, political, social, and psychological domains, including white exclusion of these groups from true assimilation. The oppositional identity of the minority evolves also because they perceive and experience the treatment by whites as collective and enduring oppression. They realize and believe that, regardless of their individual ability and training or education, and regardless of their place of origin (e.g., in Africa) or residence in America, regardless of their individual economic status or physical appearance, they cannot expect to be treated like white Americans, their "fellow citizens"; nor can they easily escape from their more or less birth-ascribed membership in a subordinate and disparaged group by "passing" or by returning to "a homeland" (Green, 1981).

Along with the formation of an oppositional social identity, subordinate minorities also develop an oppositional cultural frame of reference which includes devices for protecting their identity and for maintaining boundaries between them and white Americans. Thus subordinate minorities regard certain forms of behavior and certain activities or events, symbols, and meanings as *not appropriate* for them because those behaviors, events, symbols, and meanings are characteristic of white Americans. At the same time they emphasize other forms of behavior and

other events, symbols, and meanings as more appropriate for them because these are *not* a part of white Americans' way of life. To behave in the manner defined as falling within a white cultural frame of reference is to "act white" and is negatively sanctioned.

The cultural frame of reference of subordinate minorities is emotionally charged because it is closely tied to their sense of collective identity and security. Therefore individuals who try to behave like white Americans or try to cross cultural boundaries or to "act white" in *forbidden domains* face opposition from their peers and probably from other members of the minority community. Their peers often construe such behaviors as trying to join the enemy (DeVos, 1967). Individuals trying to cross cultural boundaries or pass culturally may also experience internal stress, what DeVos (1967) calls "affective dissonance." The reason for the affective dissonance is that such individuals share their minority group's sense of collective oppositional identity, a belief which may cause them to feel that they are, indeed, betraying their group and its cause. The individuals may also experience psychological stress because they are uncertain that white Americans will accept them if they succeed in learning to "act white" (Fordham, 1985; Ogbu, 1986b). Indeed, DeVos (1984) argues that in a situation involving an oppositional process, subordinate-group members may automatically or unconsciously perceive learning some aspects of the culture of their "oppressors" as harmful to their identity. That is, learning itself may arouse a sense of "impending conflict over one's future identity." Of course, not every member of the minority group feels this way. Some did not identify with the oppositional identity and oppositional cultural frame of reference of their group. Some identify only marginally; and some even repudiate their group's social identity and cultural frame of reference (Fordham, 1985).

An oppositional cultural frame of reference is applied by the minorities selectively. The target areas appear to be those traditionally defined as prerogatives of white Americans, both by white people themselves and by the minorities. These are areas in which it was long believed that only whites could perform well and in which few minorities traditionally were given the opportunity to try or were rewarded if they tried and succeeded. They are areas where criteria of performance have been established by whites and competence in performance is judged by whites or their representatives, and where rewards for performance are determined by white people according to white criteria. Academic tasks represent one such area, as was noted in our comment in the vignettes presented earlier.

How do the oppositional identity and oppositional cultural frame of reference enter into the process of subordinate minorities' schooling? The oppositional identity and oppositional cultural frame of reference enter into the process of minority schooling through the minorities' perceptions and interpretations of schooling as learning the white American cultural frame of reference which they have come to assume to have adverse effects on their own cultural and identity integrity. Learning school curriculum and learning to follow the standard academic practices of the school are often equated by the minorities with learning to "act white" or as actually "acting white" while simultaneously giving up acting like a minority person. School learning is therefore consciously or unconsciously perceived *as a subtractive process:* a minority person who learns successfully in school or who follows the standard practices of the school is perceived as becoming acculturated into the white American cultural frame of reference at the expense of the minorities' cultural frame of reference and collective welfare. *It is important to point out that, even though perceptions and behavioral responses are manifested by students, as peer groups and individuals, the perceptions and interpretations are a part of a cultural orientation toward schooling which exists within the minority community and which evolved during many generations when white Americans insisted that minorities were incapable of academic success, denied them the op-portunity to succeed academically, and did not reward them adequately when they succeeded.*

The perception of schooling as a subtractive process causes subordinate minorities to "oppose" or "resist" academic striving, both socially and psychologically. At the social level, peer groups discourage their members from putting forth the time and effort required to do well in school and from adopting the attitudes and standard practices that enhance academic success. They oppose adopting appropriate academic attitudes and behaviors because they are considered "white." Peer group pressures against academic striving take many forms, including labeling (e.g., "brainiac" for students who receive good grades in their courses), exclusion from peer activities or ostracism, and physical assault. Individuals "resist" striving to do well academically partly out of fear of peer responses and partly to avoid affective dissonance. Because they also share their group's sense of collective identity and cultural frame of reference, individuals may not want to behave in a manner they themselves define as "acting white."

FICTIVE KINSHIP AND SCHOOLING

In our study of the twin phenomena of oppositional social identity and oppositional cultural frame of reference among black Americans, we have found the concept of fictive kinship (see Fordham, 1981, 1985) an appropriate one to convey their meanings. In anthropology, fictive kinship refers to a kinshiplike relationship between persons not related by blood or marriage in a society, but who have some reciprocal social or economic relationship. There is usually a native term for it, or a number of native terms expressing or indicating its presence (Brain, 1971; Freed, 1973; Norbeck and Befu, 1958; Pitt-Rivers, 1968). Fictive kinship in the anthropological sense also exists among black Americans. Sometimes black people refer to persons in that kind of relationship as "playkin" (Shimkin, Shimkin, and Frate, 1978).

But there is much wider meaning of fictive kinship among black Americans. In this latter sense the term conveys the idea of "brotherhood" and "sisterhood" of all black Americans. This sense of peoplehood or collective social identity is evident in numerous kinship and pseudokinship terms that black Americans use to refer to one another. The following are examples of the kinship and pseudokinship terms most commonly used by adolescents and adults: "brother," "sister," "soul brother," "soul sister,": "blood," "bleed," "folk," "members," "the people," "my people" (see Folb, 1980; Liebow, 1967; Sargent, 1985; Stack, 1974). In this paper we are using the term fictive kinship in the second, wider sense; that is, fictive kinship is used to denote a cultural symbol of collective identity of black Americans.

More specifically, fictive kinship is used to describe the particular mind set, i.e., the specific world view of those persons who are appropriately labeled "black." Since "blackness" is more than a skin color, fictive kinship is the concept used to denote the moral judgment the group makes on it members (see Brain, 1972). Essentially, the concept suggests that the mere possession of African features and/or being of African descent does not automatically make one a black person, nor does it suggest that one is a member in good standing of the group. One can be black in color, but choose not to seek membership in the fictive kinship system, and/or be denied membership by the group because one's behavior, activities, and lack of manifest loyalty are at variance with those thought to be appropriate and group-specific.

The black American fictive kinship system probably developed from their responses to two types of treatment they received from white Americans. One is the economic and other instrumental exploitation by whites both during and after slavery (Anderson, 1975; Bullock, 1970; Drake and Cayton, 1970; Myrdal, 1944; Spivey, 1978). The other kind of treatment is the tendency of white Americans historically to treat blacks as an undifferentiated mass of people, ascribing to them indiscriminately certain inherent strengths and weaknesses. It appears that blacks

have sometimes responded by inverting the negative stereotypes and assumptions of whites into positive and functional attributes (Fordham, 1982a; Holt, 1972; Ogbu, 1983). Thus, blacks may have transformed white assumptions of black homogeneity into a collective identity system and a coping strategy.

An example of collective treatment by white Americans which may have promoted the formation of black people's sense of collective identity *in opposition* to white identity *and* expressed the oppositional identity in the idiom of fictive kinship occurred following Nat Turner's "insurrection" in Southampton, Virginia, in 1831. After that incident whites restricted the movement of blacks as well as black contact amongst themselves, regardless of their place of residence or personal involvement in the insurrection (Haley, 1976; Styron, 1966). Even black children in Washington, D.C., were forbidden by whites from attending Sunday school with white children after the incident, although local whites knew that black children in Washington, D.C. had no part in the insurrection. What was well understood by blacks in Southampton, Virginia, in Washington, D.C., and elsewhere in the country was that the *onus* for Turner's behavior was extended to all black Americans solely on the basis of their being black. Numerous arbitrary treatments of this kind, coupled with a knowledge that they were denied true assimilation into the mainstream of American life, encouraged blacks to develop what DeVos (1967) calls "ethnic consolidation," a sense of peoplehood (Green, 1981) expressed in fictive kinship feelings and language.

Because fictive kinship symbolizes a black American sense of peoplehood in opposition to white American social identity, we suggest that it is closely tied to their various boundary-maintaining behaviors and attitudes towards whites. An example is the tendency for black Americans to emphasize *group loyalty* in situations involving conflict or competition with whites. Furthermore, black people have a tendency to negatively sanction behaviors and attitudes they consider to be at variance with their group identity symbols and criteria of membership. We also note that, since only black Americans are involved in the evaluation of group members' eligibility for membership in the fictive kinship system, they control the criteria used to judge one's worthiness for membership, and the criteria are totally group-specific. That is, the determination and control of the criteria for membership in the fictive kinship system are in contrast to the determination and control of the criteria for earning grades in school or promotion in the mainstream workplace by white people. Fictive kinship means a lot to black people because they regard it as the ideal by which members of the group are judged; it is also the medium through which blacks distinguish "real" from "spurious" members (M. Williams, 1981).

Black children learn the meaning of fictive kinship from their parents and peers while they are growing up. And it appears that the children learn it early and well enough so that they more or less unconsciously but strongly tend to associate their life chances and "success" potential with those of their peers and members of their community. Group membership is important in black peer relationships; as a result, when it comes to dealing with whites and white institutions, the unexpressed assumption guiding behavior seems to be that "my brother is my brother regardless of what he does or has done" (Haskins, 1976; Sargent, 1985). . . .

"ACTING WHITE" AT CAPITAL HIGH

The setting of the study, Capital High School [a pseudonym] and its surrounding community, has been described in detail elsewhere (Fordham, 1982b, 1984, 1985). Suffice it here to say that Capital High is a predominantly black high school (some 99% black—1,868 out of 1,886 students at the start of the research effort in 1982). It is located in a historically black section of Washington, D.C., in a relatively low-income area.

The influence of fictive kinship is extensive among the students at Capital High. It shows up not only in conflicts between blacks and whites and between black students and black teachers, who are often perceived to be "functionaries" of the dominant society, but also in the students' constant need to reassure one another of black loyalty and identity. They appear to achieve this group loyalty by defining certain attitudes and behaviors as "white" and therefore unacceptable, and then employing numerous devices to discourage one another from engaging in those behaviors and attitudes, i.e., from "acting white."

Among the attitudes and behaviors that black students at Capital High identify as "acting white" and therefore unacceptable are: (1) speaking standard English; (2) listening to white music and white radio stations; (3) going to the opera or ballet; (4) spending a lot of time in the library studying: (5) working hard to get good grades in school; (6) getting good grades in school (those who get good grades are labeled "brainiacs"); (7) going to the Smithsonian; (8) going to a Rolling Stones concert at the Capital Center; (9) doing volunteer work; (10) going camping, hiking, or mountain climbing; (11) having cocktails or a cocktail party; (12) going to a symphony orchestra concert; (13) having a party with no music; (14) listening to classical music; (15) being on time; (16) reading and writing poetry; and (17) putting on "airs," and so forth. This list is not exhaustive, but indicates kinds of attitudes and behaviors likely to be negatively sanctioned and therefore avoided by a large number of students.

As operationally defined in this paper, the idea of "coping with the burden of 'acting white'" suggests the various strategies that black students at Capital High use to resolve, successfully or unsuccessfully, the tension between students desiring to do well academically and meet the expectations of school authorities on the one hand and the demands of peers for conformity to group-sanctioned attitudes and behaviors that validate black identity and cultural frame on the other. Black students at Capital High who choose to pursue academic success are perceived by their peers as "being kind of white" (Weis, 1985, p. 101) and therefore not truly black. This gives rise to the tension between those who want to succeed (i.e., who in the eyes of their peers want to "act white") and others insisting on highlighting group-sanctioned attitudes and behaviors. Under the circumstances, students who want to do well in school must find some strategy to resolve the tension. This tension, along with the extra responsibility it places on students who choose to pursue academic success in spite of it, and its effects on the performance of those who resolve the tension successfully and those who do not, constitute "the burden of 'acting white.' " The few high-achieving students, as we will show, have learned how to cope successfully with the burden of acting white; the many underachieving students have not succeeded in a manner that enhances academic success. It is this tension and its effects on black students' academic efforts and outcomes that are explored in the case study of Capital High students.

Ethnographic data in the study were collected over a period of more than one year. During the study some 33 students in the eleventh grade were studied intensively, and our examples are drawn from this sample. Below we describe 4 cases, 2 underachievers and 2 high achievers.

Underachieving Students

Underachieving black students in the sample appear to have the ability to do well in school, at least better than their present records show. But they have apparently decided, consciously or unconsciously, to avoid "acting white." That is, they choose to avoid adopting attitudes and putting in enough time and effort in their schoolwork because their peers (and they themselves) would interpret their behaviors as "white." Their main strategy for coping with the burden of acting white tends, therefore, to be *avoidance*.

Our . . . example of an underachieving male is *Sidney*. Like most students in the sample, Sidney took the Preliminary Scholastic Aptitude Test (PSAT) and did fairly well, scoring at the

67th percentile on the math section of the test and at the 54th percentile on the verbal section. His scores on the Comprehensive Test of Basic Skills (CTBS) in the ninth grade indicate that he was performing well above grade level: His composite score in reading was 12.2; he scored at the college level on the language component (13.6); on the math component he scored just above the eleventh grade (11.3), making his total battery on these three components 11.8. He scored above college level in the reference skills, science, and social studies sections. On the whole, his performance on standardized tests is far higher than that of many high-achieving males in our sample.

In spite of this relatively good performance on standardized tests, his grade point average is only C. Sidney is surprised and disgusted with his inability to earn grades comparable to those he earned in elementary and junior high school. While he takes most of the courses available to eleventh graders from the Advanced Placement sequence, he is not making the A's and B's at Capital High that he consistently made during his earlier schooling.

Sidney is an outstanding football player who appears to be encapsulated in the very forces which he maintains are largely responsible for the lack of upward mobility in the local black community. He is very much aware of the need to earn good grades in school in order to take advantage of the few opportunities he thinks are available to black Americans. However, he appears unable to control his life and act in opposition to the forces he identifies as detrimental to his academic progress.

His friends are primarily football players and other athletes. He is able to mix and mingle easily with them despite the fact that, unlike most of them, he takes advanced courses; he claims that this is because of his status as an athlete. His friends are aware of his decision to take these advanced courses, and they jokingly refer to him as "Mr. Advanced Placement."

Sidney readily admits that he could do a lot better in school, but says that he, like many of his friends, does not value what he is asked to learn in school. He also reluctantly admits that the fear of being called a "brainiac" prevents him from putting more time and effort into his schoolwork. According to him, the term "brainiac" is used in a disparaging manner at Capital Hill for student who do well in their courses:

Anthropologist: Have you heard the word "brainiac" used here?

Sidney: Yes. [When referring to students who take the Advanced Placement courses here.] That's a term for the smartest person in class. Brainiac-jerk—you know, those terms. If you're smart, you're a jerk, you're a brainiac.

Anthro: Are all those words synonyms?

Sidney: Yes.

Anthro: So it's not a positive [term]?

Sidney: No, it's a negative [term], as far as brilliant academic students are concerned.

Anthro: Why is that?

Sidney: That's just the way the school population is.

Although Sidney takes the Advanced Placement Courses, he is not making much effort to get good grades; instead, he spends his time and effort developing a persona that will nullify any claims that he is a brainiac, as can be seen in the following interview excerpt:

Anthropologist: Has anyone ever called you a [brainiac]?

Sidney: Brainiac? No.

Anthro: Why not?

Sidney: Well, I haven't given them a reason to. And, too, well, I don't excel in all my classes like I *should* be—that's another reason. . . . I couldn't blame it on the environment. I have come to blame it on myself—for partaking *in* the environment. But I *can* tell you that—going back to what we *were* talking about—another reason why they don't call me a "brainiac," because I'm an athlete.

Anthro: So . . . if a kid is smart, for example, one of the ways to limit the negative reaction to him or her, and his or her brilliance, is. . . .

Sidney: Yeah, do something extracurricular in the school . . . [like] being an athlete, cheerleader squad, in the band—like that. . . . Yeah, *something that's important* [emphasis added], that has something to do with—that represents your school.

Sidney admits that the fear of being known as a brainiac has negatively affected his academic effort a great deal. The fear of being discovered as an "imposter" among his friends leads him to choose carefully those persons with whom he will interact within the classroom; all of the males with whom he interacts who also take Advanced Placement courses are, like him, primarily concerned with "mak[ing] it over the hump."

He also attributes his lack of greater effort in school to his lack of will power and time on task. And he thinks that his low performance is due to his greater emphasis on athletic achievement and his emerging manhood, and less emphasis on the core curriculum. He does not study. He spends very little time completing his homework assignments, usually fifteen minutes before breakfast. On the whole, Sidney is not proud of his academic record. But he does not feel that he can change the direction of his school career because he does not want to be know as a brainiac. . . .

Shelvy is our . . . example of the underachieving female students. Her performance on standardized tests supports teachers' evaluation of her academic ability. On her eleventh grade CTBS, her composite score in the three major areas—reading, language, and mathematics—was the highest overall grade equivalent (OGE) possible, 13.6. Because she assumes that she will not be able to go to college (her parents are very poor), she did not see any value in trying to convince her parents to give her the five dollars needed to pay for the PSAT, and so she opted not to take it.

In the elementary school her grades were "mostly VG's, A's, B's and stuff like that." Despite the resistance to academic success by students in the two elementary and two junior high schools (all in the Capital community) she attended prior to coming to Capital High, she continued to obtain good grades. In fact, in the second junior high school she was placed in the only honors section of the ninth grade class. This made it much easier for her because everybody there had been identified as a potentially good student. As she puts it:

> I went to Garden [Junior High School]. That was *fairly* well, but in the seventh grade I had the problem of the same thing—everybody saying, "Well, she thinks she's smart," and all this. I had the same problem in the eighth grade. But in the ninth grade, they placed me in an all-academic section and, you know, everyone in there was smart, so it wasn't recognized—they recognized everybody as being a smart section, instead of an individual.

She made the Honor Role during both her eighth and ninth grade years, and this pattern of academic success continued during her first year at Capital High when she earned two B's, two A's, and two C's.

At the time of this study, however, things had changed for Shelvy. She is no longer enthusiastic about school and is not making any concerted effort to improve the level of her performance. The reason for this development is unclear. However, from her account of students' attitudes and behaviors in the schools she attended and at Capital, we speculate that she finally submitted to peer pressures not to "act white." Therefore she has not resorted to the coping strategies that worked for her in earlier school years.

Speaking of her earlier school experiences, Shelvy says that her first contact with the notion of success as a risky task began in the elementary school, and probably came to full fruition during the sixth grade when, for the first time in her life, she heard the word "brainiac" used to refer to her. She says that ideally everybody wants to be a brainiac, but one is paralyzed with fear that if he or she performs well in school he or she will be discovered, and that would bring some added responsibilities and problems.

Perhaps more than any other underachieving female, Shelvy's academic performance reflects the pain and frustrations associated with trying to camouflage one's ability from peers. Having been a "good student" in elementary school, she knows firsthand how difficult it is to avoid encapsulation in antiacademic peer groups:

> In the sixth grade, it was me and these two girls, we used to hang together all the time. They used to say we was brainiacs, and no one really liked us. . . . It's not something-well, *it's something that you want to be, but you don't want your friends to know* [emphasis added] . . . . Because once they find out you're a brainiac, then the first thing they'll say is, "Well, she thinks she's cute, and she thinks she's smart, she thinks she's better than anyone else." So what most brainiacs do, they sit back and they know an answer, and they won't answer it. . . . 'Cause, see, first thing everybody say, "Well, they're trying to show off." So they really don't—they might answer once in a while, but. . . . Because if you let . . . all your friends know how smart you are, then when you take a test or something, then they're going to know you know the answer and they're going to want the answers. And if you don't give them to them, then they're going to get upset with you.

When asked how their being upset would be manifested, Shelvy replied, "Well, they might start rumors about you, might give you a bad name or something like that."

Shelvy's analysis of the dilemma of the brainiac clearly suggests that the academically successful black student's life is fraught with conflicts and ambivalence. The fear of being differentiated and labeled as a brainiac often leads to social isolation and a social self which is hurt by negative perceptions. Essentially Shelvy claims that a student who is identified as a brainiac is more vulnerable to "social death" than one who is not.

Shelvy is more aware than many of her peers concerning whey she is not performing as well academically as she could and perhaps should. As she explains it, she is keenly aware of her peers' concurrent "embracement and rejection" of school norms and behaviors. In that sense she realizes that seeking school success at Capital High is immersed in boundary-maintaining devices. It is the boundary-maintaining tendencies of her peers, which negatively sanction behaviors associated with the label "brainiac," that are negatively affecting her school performance. Her fear of being labeled a "brainiac" and burdened with all the expectations attendant thereto, as well as her negative perception of the opportunity structure, has led her to resort to lowering her effort in school. Her fear of academic excellence is readily apparent when observed in the classroom context. When she is called upon by teachers, she responds quickly and correctly; however, having learned from negative experiences associated with academic success in the elementary and junior high schools, she "puts brakes" on her academic effort to minimize bringing attention to herself. . . .

High-achieving Students

Students at Capital High who are relatively successful academically also face the problem of coping with the "burden of 'acting white.' " But they have usually adopted strategies that enable them to succeed. These students decide more or less consciously (a) to pursue academic success and (b) to use specific strategies to cope with the burden of acting white.

Martin is our . . . example of a high-achieving male student. His scores on the standardized tests, PSAT and CTBS, are unfortunately not available to help us assess his ability. But he has a relatively good academic record. He graduated tenth in this junior high school class; and in the tenth grade at Capital High, he earned three B's, one A–, and a D. He is a member of the school's chapter of the National Honor Society. Although Martin is still uncertain about his overall academic ability because of absence of reliable scores on standardized tests, he gets good grades in class, attends school regularly, has a positive attitude about school, and receives good evaluations from teachers.

Martin is fully aware of peer pressures to discourage male students at Capital High from striving toward academic success. The most discouraging factor, in his view, is the fear of being labeled a "brainiac" or, worse, a "pervert brainiac." To be known as a pervert brainiac is tantamount to receiving a kiss of death. For a male student to be known as a brainiac, according to Martin, is to question his manhood; to be known as a pervert brainiac leaves little doubt. He claims that there are persistent rumors that some male students taking all or a large number of the Advanced Placement courses are homosexuals; this is far less the case for male students who do not take the advanced courses. Also it is believed at Capital High that males who do *not* make good grades are less likely to be gay.

Martin says that the best strategy for a male student making good grades or wanting to succeed academically and yet escape the label of brainiac is for him to handle his school persona carefully and to cloak it in other activities that minimize hostility against academically successful students. One such "cloaking activity" is "lunching": that is, to avoid being called a brainiac and thereby bringing one's manhood into questions, a male student who desires good grades will often resort to behaviors suggesting that he is a clown, comedian, or does not work very hard to earn the grades he receives.

Martin: Okay. Lunching is like when you are acting crazy, you know, having fun with women, you know. Okay, you still be going to class, but you—like me, okay, they call *me* crazy, 'cause I'll be having fun. . . .

Anthropologist: Do they say you're "lunching"?

Martin: Yeah. Go ask [my girlfriend]. She be saying I'm lunching. 'Cause I be—'cause I be doin' my homework, and I be playin' at the same time, and I get it done. I don't know how I do that.

Anthro: So It's important to be a clown, too—I mean, to be a comedian?

Martin: Yeah. Yeah, a comedian, because you—yeah.

Anthro: A comedian is a male? There's no doubt that a comedian is a male?

Martin: A male, uh-huh! 'Cause if you be all about [concerned only about] your schoolwork, right? And you know a lot of your *friends* not about it, if you don't act like a clown, your friends gonna start calling you a brainiac.

Anthro: And it's not good to be called a brainiac?

Martin: Yeah, it's—I don't want nobody to be calling *me* one, 'cause I know I ain't no brainiac. But if they call you one, you might seem odd to them. 'Cause they'll always be joning on you. See? When I was at Kaplan [Junior High school], that's what they called me—"brainiac," 'cause I made straight A's and B's, that's all in the First Advisory. So that's why. . . .

The interview with Martin left us with the impression that he does not put forth as much effort and time as he might have were he not shackled with the burden of worrying about his peers' perceptions of him as a brainiac. Therefore, although he comes to school every day (he missed only one day during the tenth grade) and completes most of his homework, he does not do more than the officially required academic tasks. . . .

High-achieving females use certain gender-specific strategies to cope with the burden of acting white. But, like the males, they camouflage to avoid being perceived as brainiacs. More than the males, the female high achievers work to maintain low profiles in school. . . .

Katrina's performance on the math component of the PSAT was at the 95th percentile. Only one other student . . . scored higher and another student had a comparable score. Katrina's score on the verbal component was not as high, being at the 75th percentile. But her overall score far surpassed those of most other students. Her performance on the CTBS was equally impressive, with an overall grade equivalent of 13.6, or college level, in every section—math, reading, and language, and in every subsection, as well as in the ancillary sections, namely, reference skills, social studies, and science. She also performed well on the Life Skills examination which measures students' ability to process information in nine different areas. Katrina scored 100% in each of the nine areas.

In the classroom her performance has been equally outstanding. She had A in all subjects except handwriting in the elementary school. Her final grades in ninth grade (i.e., junior high school) were all A's; and in the tenth grade, her first year at Capital High, her final grades were all A's.

Katrina has heard of the term "brainiac" not only at Capital High, but as far back as at the elementary and junior high school levels. And she is very much aware of the nuances associated with the term. She explains:

When they [other students] call someone a "brainiac," they mean he's always in the books. But he probably isn't always in the books. Straight A., maybe—you know, or A's and B's. A Goody-Two-Shoes with the teacher, maybe—you know, the teacher always calling on them, and they're always the leaders in the class or something.

She acknowledges that she is often referred to as a brainiac, but that she always denies it because she does not want her peers to see her that way. To treat her as a brainiac "blows her cover" and exposes her to the very forces she has sought so hard to avoid: alienation, ridicule, physical harm, and the inability to live up to the name.

How does Katrina avoid being called a brainiac and treated with hostility while at the same time managing to keep up her outstanding academic performance? Katrina admits that she has had to "put brakes" on her academic performance in order to minimize the stress she experiences. She says that she is much better at handling subject matter than at handling her peers. To solve the peer problem, she tries not be conspicuous. As she puts it:

Junior high, I didn't have much problem. I mean, I didn't have—there were always a lot of people in the classroom who did the work, so I wasn't like, the only one who did this assignment. So—I mean, I might do better at it, but I wasn't the only one. And so a lot of times, I'd let other kids answer—I mean, not *let* them, but. . . . All right, I *let* them answer questions [laughter], and I'd hold back. So

I never really got into any arguments, you know, about school and my grades or anything.

She is extremely fearful of peer reactions if she were identified as acting white. Since she wants to continue doing well in school, she chooses to "go underground," that is, not to bring attention to herself. Her reluctance to participate in Capital High's "It's Academic" Club, a TV competition program, illustrates her desire to maintain a low profile. "It's Academic" is perhaps the most "intellectual" extracurricular activity at the school. To participate in the three-person team, a student must take a test prepared by the faculty sponsoring it. The three top scorers are eligible to represent the school in the TV competition. Katrina reluctantly took the test at the suggestion of her physics teacher, the club sponsor. However, she had a prior agreement that she would not be selected to participate on the team *even if she had the top score.* She was one of the three top scorers, but because of the prior agreement was made only an alternate member of the team. . . .

To summarize, all the high-achieving students wrestle with the conflict inherent in the unique relationship of black people with the dominant institution: the struggle to achieve success while retaining group support and approval. In school, the immediate issue is how to obtain good grades and meet the expectations of school authorities without being rejected by peers for acting white. Our examples show that successful students at Capital High generally adopt specific strategies to solve this problem.

THE BURDEN OF ACTING WHITE IN COMPARATIVE PERSPECTIVE

The burden of acting white, how black adolescents cope with it, and its effects on their academic careers have not been generally recognized, let alone systematically studied. Nevertheless, there are references here and there suggesting that similar problems are faced by black students in other schools and in other parts of the United States. One example from Philadelphia, that of Abdul-Jabbar, has already been cited. Another is that of E. Sargent, a journalist with the *Washington Post,* who attended public schools in Washington, D.C.

Sargent describes, in a column in the *Washington Post* (Feb. 10, 1985), how he used his emerging sense of black identity to minimize the conflicts associated with academic success among black students. He attributes his ability to deal with the burden of acting white to his broader sense of black American history which he acquired *outside* the public schools. As he puts it:

> While I had always been a good student, I became a better one as a result of my sense of black history. I began to notice that my public-school teachers very rarely mentioned black contributions to the sciences, math, and other areas of study. . . . They never talked about ways blacks could collectively use their education to solve the great economic and social problems facing the race.
>
> My mind was undergoing a metamorphosis that made the world change its texture. Everything became relevant because I knew blacks had made an impact on all facets of life. *I felt a part of things that most blacks thought only white people had a claim to* [our emphasis]. Knowing that there is a serious speculation that Beethoven was black—a mullato [sic]—made me enjoy classical music. "Man, why do you listen to that junk? That's white music," my friends would say. "Wrong, Beethoven was a brother." I was now bicultural, a distinction most Americans could not claim. I could switch from boogie to rock, from funk to jazz and from rhythm-and-blues to Beethoven and Bach. . . . I moved from thinking of myself as disadvantaged to realizing that I was actually "super-advantaged." (pp. D1, D4)

Black students in desegregated and integrated schools also face the burden of acting white. A study by Petroni and Hirsch (1970) shows how the phenomenon operates in a midwestern city. They present several examples of academically successful students at Plains High School and the problems confronting them, as well as the strategies they adopt to cope with the burden of acting white. Take the case of Pat, an academically successful black female whose dilemma they describe. Pat appears to be different from other black students in the school, and she seems to be subjected to different kinds of pressures from black and white students. However, she indicates that the more difficult pressures come from black students:

> I [feel] the greatest pressure from members of my own race. I'm an all A student; I'm always on the Honor Roll: I'm in Madrigals, and so on. Because of these small accomplishments, there's a tendency for the [blacks] to think that I'm better than they are. They think I'm boasting. Take Nancy—Nancy ran for office, and I've heard other [black students] say, "She thinks she's so good." I don't think of it this way. These small accomplishments that I've achieved aren't just for me, but they're to help the black cause. I do things for my race, not just for myself. Most of the time, though, I don't pay too much attention to these kids. It's just a small percentage of [blacks] anyway, who're the troublemakers, and they resent the fact that I'm doing something, and they aren't (Petroni and Hirsch, 1970, p. 20).

The burden of acting white becomes heavier when academically able black students face both pressures from black peers to conform, and doubts from whites about their ability, as the following cases show. The former is described in a series of articles on adolescents' school behavior in a predominantly white suburban school system near Washington, D.C., by Elsa Walsh (1984). Her account highlights the problems of high-achieving black students in integrated schools, especially the paralyzing effects of coping with the burden of acting white.

Our first case is that of "K," whom Walsh identifies as a 13-year-old, academically gifted, female black student. Walsh describes K's feeling of loneliness and isolation in the predominantly white honors courses to which she was assigned. She also points out that black students at the school reject K and often accuse her of being "stuck up" and thinking she is "too good

for them." At the same time, K's white classmates doubt that she actually has the ability to do the work in the honors courses. All of these factors erode K's confidence.

An example of a similar dilemma is Gray's (1985) description of the futility of her efforts to minimize her "blackness" through academic excellence in a predominantly white school and community:

> No matter how refined my speech, or how well educated or assimiliated [sic] I become, I fear I will always be an outsider. I'm almost like a naturalized alien—in this place but not of it. . . . During my pompous period, I dealt with my insecurities by wearing a veil of superiority. Except around my family and neighbors, I played the role—the unblack.
>
> To whites I tried to appear perfect—I earned good grades and spoke impeccable English, was well-mannered and well-groomed. Poor whites, however, made me nervous. They seldom concealed their contempt for blacks, especially "uppity" ones like myself. . . . To blacks, I was all of the above and extremely stuck up. I pretended not to see them on the street, spoke to them only when spoken to and cringed in the presence of blacks being loud in front of whites. The more integrated my Catholic grammar school became, the more uncomfortable I was there. I had heard white parents on TV, grumbling about blacks ruining their schools; I didn't want anyone to think that I, too, might bring down Sacred Heart Academy. So I behaved, hoping that no one would associated [sic] me with "them." (Gray, 1985, pp. E1, E5)

In summary, black students elsewhere, like those at Capital High, in predominantly black schools as well as in integrated schools, appear to face the burden of acting white. Under this circumstance students who are clever enough to use certain deliberate strategies succeed in "making it." In predominantly black schools, they succeed in protecting themselves from the antagonisms of black peers who define their academic striving negatively as acting white. In integrated schools, their problem is further complicated by the negative and often implicit assumptions of whites about the intellectual ability of black people. In such schools, white Americans' doubts may erode the academic confidence of black students who are taking "white courses." . . .

SUMMARY AND IMPLICATIONS

We have suggested in this paper that black students' academic efforts are hampered by both external factors and within-group factors. We have tried to show that black students who are academically successful in the face of these factors have usually adopted specific strategies to avoid them. Although we recognize and have described elsewhere in detail the external, including school, factors which adversely affect black adolescents' school performance (Fordham, 1982a, 1985; Ogbu, 1974, 1978), our focus in this paper is on the within-group factors, especially on how black students respond to other black students who are trying to "make it" academically.

We began by noting that the instrumental factors postulated in our earlier cultural-ecological explanation of minority school performance, namely, inferior schooling, limited opportunity structure, and such peoples' own perceptions of and responses to schooling, are important, but that there are additional factors involved. We identified the additional factors as an oppositional collective or social identity and an oppositional cultural frame of reference, both symbolized, in the case of black Americans, by a fictive kinship system.

Fictive kinship is, then, not only a symbol of social identity for black Americans, it is also a medium of boundary maintenance vis-à-vis white Americans. The school experience of black children is implicated because, under the circumstance, schooling is perceived by blacks, especially by black adolescents, as learning to act white, as acting white, or as trying to cross cultural boundaries. And, importantly, school learning is viewed as a subtractive process. In our view, then, the academic learning and performance problems of black children arise not only from a limited opportunity structure and black people's responses to it, but also from the

way black people attempt to cope with the "burden of 'acting white.' " The sources of their school difficulties—perceptions of and responses to the limited opportunity structure and the burden of acting white—are particularly important during the adolescent period in the children's school careers.

We chose to focus our analysis on the burden of acting white and its effects on the academic effort and performance of black children because it seems to us to be a very important but as yet widely unrecognized dilemma of black students, particularly black adolescents. In other words, while we fully recognize the role of external forces—societal and school forces—in creating academic problems for the students, *we also argue that how black students respond to other black students who are trying to make it is also important in determining the outcome of their education.*

In the case study of Capital High School in Washington, D.C., we showed that coping with the burden of acting white affects the academic performance of both underachieving and high-achieving students. Black students who are encapsulated in the fictive kinship system or oppositional process experience greater difficulty in crossing cultural boundaries; i.e., in accepting standard academic attitudes and practices of the school and in investing sufficient time and effort in pursuing their educational goals. Some of the high-achieving students do not identify with the fictive kinship system; others more or less deliberately adopt sex-specific strategies to camouflage their academic pursuits and achievements.

The strategies of the academically successful students include engaging in activities which mute perceptions of their being preoccupied with academic excellence leading eventually to individual success outside the group, i.e., eventual upward mobility. Among them are athletic activities (which are regarded as "black activities") and other "team"-oriented activities, for male students. Other high-achieving students camouflage their academic effort by clowning. Still others do well in school by acquiring the protection of "bullies" and "hoodlums" in return for assisting the latter in their schoolwork and homework. In general, academically successful black students at Capital High (and probably elsewhere) are careful not to brag about their achievements or otherwise bring too much attention to themselves. We conclude, however, from this study of high-achieving students at Capital High, that they would do much better if they did not have to divert time and effort into strategies designed to camouflage their academic pursuit.

There are several implications of our analysis, and the implications are at different levels. As this analysis clearly demonstrates, the first and critically important change must occur in the existing opportunity structure, through an elimination of the job ceiling and related barriers. Changes in the opportunity structure are a prerequisite to changes in the behaviors and expectations of black adolescents for two salient reasons: (1) to change the students' perceptions of what is available to them as adult workers in the labor force and (2) to minimize the exacerbation of the extant achievement problem of black adolescents who are expected to master the technical skills taught and condoned in the school context but who are, nonetheless, unable to find employment in areas where they demonstrate exemplary expertise. Barring changes in the opportunity structure, the perceptions, behaviors, and academic effort of black adolescents are unlikely to change to the extent necessary to have a significant effect on the existing boundary-maintaining mechanisms in the community. Therefore, until the perceptions of the nature and configuration of the opportunity structure change (see J. Williams, 1985), the response of black students in the school context is likely to continue to be one which suggests that school achievement is a kind of risk which necessitates strategies enabling them to cope with the "burden of acting white." Second, educational barriers, both the gross and subtle mechanisms by which schools differentiate the academic careers of black and white children, should be eliminated.

Third, and particularly important in terms of our analysis, *the unique academic learning and performance problems created by the burden of acting white should be recognized and made a target of educational policies and remediation effort.* Both the schools and the black community have important roles to play in this regard. School personnel should try to understand the influence of the fictive kinship system in the students' perceptions of learning and the standard academic attitudes and practices or behaviors expected. The schools should then develop programs, including appropriate counseling, to help the students learn to divorce academic pursuit from the idea of acting white. The schools should also reinforce black identity in a manner compatible with academic pursuit, as in the case of Sargent (1985).

The black community has an important part to play in changing the situation. The community should develop programs to teach black children that academic pursuit is not synonymous with one-way acculturation into a white cultural frame of reference or acting white. To do this effectively, however, the black community must reexamine its own perceptions and interpretations of school learning. Apparently, black children's general perception that academic pursuit is "acting white" is learned in the black community. The ideology of the community in regard to the cultural meaning of schooling is, therefore, implicated and needs to be reexamined. Another thing the black community can do is to provide visible and concrete evidence for black youths that the community appreciates and encourages academic effort and success. Cultural or public recognition of those who are academically successful should be made a frequent event, as is generally done in the case of those who succeed in the fields of sports and entertainment.

REFERENCES

Abdul-Jabbar, K., and Knobles, P. (1983). *Giant Steps: The Autobiography of Kareem Abdul-Jabbar.* New York: Bantam Books.

Acuna, R. (1972). *Occupied America: The Chicano's Struggle Toward Liberation.* San Francisco: Canfield Press.

Anderson, J. D. (1975). Education and the manipulation of black workers. In W. Feinberg and

H. Rosemont, Jr. (eds.), *Work, Technology, and Education: Dissenting Essays in the Intellectual Foundations of American Education.* Chicago: University of Illinois Press.

Berreman, G. D. (1960). Caste in India and the United States. *The American Journal of Sociology* LXVI: 120–127.

Bloom, B. S., Davis, A., and Hess, R. (1965). *Compensatory Education for Cultural Deprivation.* New York: Holt.

Brain, J. J. (1972). Kinship terms. *Man* 7(1): 137–138.

Bullock, H. A. (1970). *A History of Negro Education in the South: From 1619 to the Present.* New York: Praeger.

Castile, G. P., and Kushner, G., eds. (1981). *Persistent Peoples: Cultural Enclaves in Perspective.* Tucson: University of Arizona Press.

Coleman, J. S., et al. (1966). *Equality of Educational Opportunity.* Washington, D.C.: U.S. Government Printing Office.

DeVos, G. A. (1984). *Ethnic Persistence and Role Degradation: An Illustration from Japan.* Prepared for the American-Soviet Symposium on contemporary Ethnic Processes in the USA and the USSR, New Orleans, April 14–16. Unpublished ms.

DeVos, G. A. (1967). Essential elements of caste: psychological determinants in structural theory. In G. A. DeVos and H. Wagatsuma (eds.), *Japan's Invisible Race: Caste in Culture and Personality,* pp. 332–384. Berkely: University of California Press.

Drake, S. C., and Cayton, H. (1970). *Black Metropolis.* New York: Harcourt, Brace.

Folb, E. A. (1980). *Runnin' Down Some Lines: The Language and Culture of Black Teenagers.* Cambridge, Mass.: Harvard University Press.

Fordham, S. (1985). Black student school success as related to fictive kinship. Final Report. The National Institute of Education, Washington, D.C.

Fordham, S. (1984). Ethnography in a black high school: learning not to be a native. A paper presented at the 83rd Annual Meeting, American Anthropological Association, Denver, Nov: 14–18.

Fordham, S. (1982a). Black student school success as related to fictive kinships: an ethnographic study in the Washington, D.C., public school system. A research proposal submitted to the National Institute of Education.

Fordham, S. (1982b). Cultural inversion and black children's school performance. Paper presented at the 81st Annual Meeting, American Anthropological Association, Washington, D.C., Dec 3–7.

Fordham, S. (1981). Black student school success as related to fictive kinship: a study in the Washington, D.C. public school system. A dissertation proposal submitted to the Department of Anthropology, The American University.

Freed, S. A. (1973). Fictive kinship in a Northern Indian village. *Ethnology* 11(1): 86–103.

Gray, J. (1985). A black American princess: new game, new rules. *The Washington Post,* March 17, pp. E1, E5.

Green, V. (1981). Blacks in the United States: the creation of an enduring people? In G. P. Castile and G. Kushner (eds.), *Persistent Peoples: Cultural Enclaves in Perspective,* pp. 69–77. Tucson: University of Arizona Press.

Haley, A. (1976). *Roots: The Saga of an American Family.* Garden City, N.Y.: Doubleday.

Haskins, K. (1976). You have no right to put a kid out of school. *The Urban Review* 8(4): 273–287.

Holt, G. S. (1972). "Inversion" in black communication. In T. Kochman (ed.), *Rappin' and Stylin' Out: Communication in Urban Black America.* Chicago: University of Illinois Press.

Hunter, D. (1980). Ducks vs. hard rocks. *Newsweek,* Aug. 18, pp. 14–15.

Jensen, A. R. (1969). How much can we boost IQ and scholastic achievement? *Harvard Educational Review* 39: 1–123.

LeVine, R. A. (1967). *Dreams and Deeds: Achievement Motivation in Nigeria.* Chicago: University of Chicago Press.

Liebow, E. (1967). *Tally's Corner.* Boston: Little, Brown.

Myrdal, G. (1944). *An American Dilemma: The Negro Problem and Modern Democracy.* New York: Harper.

Norbeck, E., and Befu, H. (1958). Informal fictive kinship in Japan. *American Anthropologist* 60: 102–117.

Ogbu, J. U. (1987). Variability in minority responses to schooling: non-immigrants vs. immigrants. In G. D. Spindler (ed.), *Education and Cultural Process.* Prospect Heights, Ill.: Waveland Press.

Ogbu, J. U. (1986a). Class stratification, racial stratification and schooling. In L. Weis, (ed.), *Race, Class and Schooling. Special Studies in Comparative Education,* #17, pp. 6–35. Comparative Education Center, State University of New York at Buffalo.

Ogbu, J. U. (1986b). Cross-cultural study of minority education: contributions from Stockton research,

23rd Annual J. William Harris Lecture, School of Education, University of the Pacific, Stockton, Calif.

Ogbu, J. U. (1984). Understanding community forces affecting minority students' academic effort. Paper prepared for the Achievement Council, Oakland, Calif.

Ogbu, J. U. (1983). Minority status and schooling in plural societies. *Comparative Education Review* 27(2): 169–190.

Ogbu, J. U. (1982). Cultural discontinuities and schooling. *Anthropology and Education Quarterly* 13(4): 290–307.

Ogbu, J. U. (1981). Schooling in the ghetto: an ecological perspective on community and home influences. Prepared for NIE Conference on Follow Through, Philadelphia, Feb. 10–11.

Ogbu, J. U. (1980). Cultural differences vs. alternative cultures: A critique of 'cultural discontinuity' hypothesis in classroom ethnographies. A paper presented at the 79th Annual Meeting, American Anthropological Association, Washington, D.C.

Ogbu, J. U. (1978). *Minority Education and Caste: The American System in Cross-Cultural Perspective.* New York: Academic Press.

Ogbu, J. U. (1974). *The Next Generation: An Ethnography of Education in an Urban Neighborhood.* New York: Academic Press.

Ogbu, J. U., and Matute-Bianchi, M. E. (1986). Understanding sociocultural factors in education: Knowledge, identity, and adjustment. In *Beyond Language: Sociocultural Factors in Schooling, Language, and Minority Students.* California State Department of Education. Los Angeles: Education Dissemination and Assessment Center, California State University, Los Angeles, pp. 71–143.

Petroni, F. A., and Hirsch, E. A. (1970). *Two, Four, Six, Eight, When You Gonna Integrate?* New York: Behavioral Publications.

Pitt-Rivers, J. (1968). Pseudo-kinship. In D. L. Sills (ed.), *The International Encyclopedia of Social Science.* New York: Macmillan.

Sargent E. (1985). Freeing myself: discoveries that unshackle the mind. *The Washington Post,* Feb. 10.

Schmidt, F. H. (1970). *Spanish Surname American Employment in the Southwest.* Washington, D.C.: U.S. Government Printing Office.

Shimkin, D. B., Shimkin, E. M., and Frate, D. A. eds. (1978). *The Extended Family in Black Societies.* The Hague: Mouton.

Spicer, E. H. (1971). Persistent cultural systems: a comparative study of identity systems that can adapt to contrasting environments. *Science* 174: 795–800.

Spicer, E. H. (1966). The process of cultural enclavement in Middle America. Proceedings, *36th Congreso Internacional de Americanistas,* Vol. 3, pp. 267–279. Seville.

Spicer, E. H. (1962). *Cycles of Conquest: The Impact of Spain, Mexico and the United States on the Indians of the Southwest, 1533–1960.* Tucson: University of Arizona Press.

Spivey, D. (1978). *Schooling for the New Slavery: Black Industrial Education, 1868–1915.* Westport, Conn.: Greenwood Press.

Stack, C. (1974). *All Our Kin: Strategies for Survival in a Black Community.* New York: Harper & Row.

Styron, W. (1966). *The Confessions of Nat Turner.* New York: Random House.

Walsh, E. (1984). Trouble at thirteen: Being black poses special problems. *The Washington Post,* April 24, pp. A1, A6.

Weis, L. (1985). *Between Two Worlds: Black Students in an Urban Community College.* Boston: Routledge & Kegan Paul.

Williams, J. (1985). The vast gap between black and white visions of reality. *The Washington Post,* March 31, pp. K1, K4.

Williams, M. D. (1981). *On the Street Where I Lived.* New York: Holt, Rinehart & Winston.

ETHNIC DIFFERENCES IN ADOLESCENT ACHIEVEMENT: AN ECOLOGICAL PERSPECTIVE

LAURENCE STEINBERG, SANFORD M. DORNBUSCH, AND B. BRADFORD BROWN
Temple University, Stanford University, and University of Wisconsin–Madison

One of the most consistent and disturbing findings in studies of adolescent achievement concerns ethnic differences in school performance. Many studies indicate that African-American students "generally earn lower grades, drop out more often, and attain less education than do whites" (Mickelson, 1990, p. 44). Although less research has focused on direct comparisons between other ethnic groups, recent reports on adolescent achievement in America suggest that the performance of Hispanic adolescents also lags behind that of their White counterparts, but that the performance of Asian-American students exceeds that of White, African-American, and Hispanic students (see Sue & Okazaki, 1990). Despite the widely held assumption that ethnic differences in achievement are accounted for by group differences on other variables, such as socioeconomic status and family structure, research indicates quite clearly that these patterns of ethnic differences in achievement persist even after important third variables are taken into account.

Although there is considerable agreement that these ethnic differences in school performance are genuine, there is little consensus about the causes of these differences, and a variety of explanations for the pattern have been offered. Among the most familiar are that (a) there are inherited differences between ethnic groups in intellectual abilities, which are reflected in differences in school performance (e.g., Lynn, 1977; Rushton, 1985); (b) that ethnic differences in achievement-related socialization practices in the family lead youngsters from some ethnic groups to develop more positive achievement-related attitudes and behaviors (e.g., Mordkowitz & Ginsburg, 1987); (c) that there are ethnic differences in cultural values, and especially in the value placed on educational success (see Sue & Okazaki, 1990, for a discussion); and (d) that there are ethnic differences in perceived and actual discrimination within educational and occupational institutions (e.g., Mickelson, 1990; Ogbu, 1978).

This article focuses on ethnic differences in school achievement, a phenomenon that, as a recent article in this journal put it, is " in search of an explanation" (Sue & Okazaki, 1990, p. 913). Because the genetic hypothesis has received so little support in studies of school achievement (see Sue & Okazaki, 1990; Thompson, Detterman, & Plomin, 1991), we focus instead on the various environmental accounts of the phenomenon. To do so, we present and integrate several sets of findings from the first wave of data collected as part of a program of research on a large, multiethnic sample of high school students. The research is aimed at understanding

From *American Psychologist*, 1992, 723–729. Copyright © 1992 by the American Psychological Association. Reprinted with permission.

how different contexts in youngsters' lives affect their behavior, schooling, and development.

OVERVIEW OF THE RESEARCH PROGRAM

During the 1987–1988 school year, we administered a 30-page, two-part questionnaire with a series of standardized psychological inventories, attitudinal indices, and demographic questions to approximately 15,000 students at nine different high schools. The schools were selected to provide a window on the contrasting social ecologies of contemporary American adolescents. They included an inner-city school in Milwaukee, Wisconsin, serving a substantially Black population; a San Jose, California, school serving a large number of Hispanic students; a small rural Wisconsin school in a farming community; a semirural California school with youngsters from farm families, migrant workers, and recently arrived Asian refugees; and several suburban schools serving mixtures of working-class and middle-class adolescents from a variety of ethnic backgrounds. All told, our sample was approximately one third non-White, with nearly equal proportions of African-American, Hispanic, and Asian-American youngsters—much like the adolescent population in the United States today (Wetzel, 1987). The sample was quite diverse with respect to socioeconomic status and household composition.

The questionnaires, which were administered schoolwide, contained numerous measures of psychosocial development and functioning, as well as several measures of social relations in and outside of school. The outcome variables fell into four general categories: *psychosocial adjustment* (including measures of self-reliance, work orientation, self-esteem, and personal and social competence); *schooling* (including measures of school performance, school engagement, time spent on school activities, educational expectations and aspirations, and school-related attitudes and beliefs); *behavior problems* (including measures of drug and alcohol use, delinquency, susceptibility to antisocial peer pressure, and school misconduct); and *psychological distress* (including measures of anxiety, depression, and psychosomatic complaints).

This outcome battery is more or less standard fare in the field of adolescent social and personality development. What makes our database different, however, is that it is equally rich in measures of the contexts in which our adolescents live. We have tried to move beyond the simple "social address" models that are pervasive in survey research, in which measures of the environment do not go beyond checklists designed to register the number of persons present in the setting and their relationship to the respondent (see Bronfenbrenner, 1986, for a critique of such models). Accordingly, our measures of family relationships include a number of scales tapping such dimensions as parental warmth, control, communication style, decision making, monitoring, and autonomy granting. Our peer measures include affiliation patterns, peer crowd membership, perceptions of peer group norms, and time spent in various peer activities. Our measure of extracurricular and work settings provide information on the activities the adolescents engage in outside of school. Our measures of the school environment concern the classes the adolescents are taking and the classroom environments they encounter. For each student, we also have information on the family's ethnicity, composition, socioeconomic status, marital history, immigration history, and patterns of language use. For some of these variables, the questionnaire data was supplemented with interviews with both students and parents from a cross section of the schools.

Our large and heterogeneous sample permits us to examine a number of questions about the importance of contextual variations in shaping and structuring youngsters' lives and behavior during the high school years. Because the youngsters in our sample are growing up under markedly different circumstances, we can ask whether and how patterns of development and adjustment differ across these social addresses.

Because we have detailed information on processes of influence within these social addresses, we can look more specifically at mechanisms of influence, both across and within contexts. And because we have information on more than one context in youngsters' lives, we can look at the interactions between contexts and how variations in the way in which contexts are themselves linked affect youngsters' development. Indeed, as we shall argue, ethnic differences in school performance can be explained more persuasively by examining the interplay between the major contexts in which youngsters develop—the family, the peer group, and the school—than by examining any one of these contexts alone.

SOCIALIZATION OF ACHIEVEMENT IN THE FAMILY

According to familial socialization explanations of ethnic group differences of achievement discussed above, we should be able to account for achievement differences among ethnic groups by taking into account the extent to which they use different sorts of parenting practices. Although psychologists have only recently begun examining ethnic differences in adolescent development (Spencer & Dornbusch, 1990), interest among developmentalists in the relation between parenting practices and youngsters' school performance has quite a lengthy history (see Maccoby & Martin, 1983). This literature indicates that adolescent competence, virtually however indexed, is higher among youngsters raised in *authoritative* homes—home in which parents are responsive and demanding (see Baumrind, 1989)—than in other familial environments (Steinberg, 1990). Presumably, better performance in school is just one of many possible manifestations of psychosocial competence. Researchers writing in this tradition have hypothesized that parental authoritativeness contributes to the child's psychosocial development, which in turn facilitates his or her school success (e.g., Steinberg, Elmen, & Mounts, 1989).

Recently, it has been suggested that three specific components of authoritativeness contribute to healthy psychological development and school success during adolescence: parental acceptance or warmth, behavioral supervision and strictness, and psychological autonomy granting or democracy (Steinberg, 1990; Steinberg et al., 1989; Steinberg, Mounts, Lamborn, & Dornbusch, 1991).This trinity—warmth, control, and democracy—parallel the three central dimensions of parenting identified by Schaefer (1965) in his pioneering work on the assessment of parenting practices through children's reports. These components are also conceptually similar to dimensions of parental control proposed by Baumrind (1991a, 1991b) in her recent reports: supportive control (similar to warmth), assertive control (similar to behavioral supervision and strictness), and directive/conventional control (similar to the antithesis of psychological autonomy granting).

The parenting inventory embedded in our questionnaire contained scales designed to assess parental warmth, behavioral control, and psychological autonomy granting. In our model, authoritative parents were defined as those who scored high in acceptance, behavioral control, and psychological autonomy granting. Not surprisingly, these parenting dimensions are moderately intercorrelated with each other and with other aspects of the parent-child relationship. For example, authoritative parents not only are warmer, firmer, and more democrative than other parents, but they are also more involved in their children's schooling, are more likely to engage in joint decision making, and are more likely to maintain an organized household with predictable routines. In view of this, we have used a categorical approach to the study of parenting, in which we used scores on each of our three dimensions to assign families to one of several categories. Using this general model of authoritative parenting, we have documented in several different studies that adolescents who are raised in authoritative homes do indeed perform better in school than do their peers (Dornbusch, Ritter,

Leiderman, Roberts, & Fraleigh, 1987; Lamborn, Mounts, Steinberg, & Dornbusch, 1991; Steinberg et al., 1989; Steinberg et al., 1991).

Can ethnic differences in school performance be explained by ethnic differences in the use of authoritative parenting? According to Dornbusch's earlier work (Dornbusch et al., 1987; Ritter & Dornbusch, 1989), the answer is no. For example, although Asian-American students have the highest school performance, their parents are among the least authoritative. Although African-American and Hispanic parents are considerably more authoritative than Asian-American parents, their children perform far worse in school on average. Given the strong support for the power of authoritative parenting in the socialization literature, these findings present somewhat of a paradox.

One explanation for this paradox is that the effects of authoritative parenting may differ as a function of the ecology in which the adolescent lives. Some writers have speculated that parental authoritarianism may be more beneficial than authoritativeness for poor minority youth (e.g., Baldwin & Baldwin, 1989; Baumrind, 1972). To examine this possibility, we used three demographic variables to partition our sample into 16 ecological niches, defined by ethnicity (four categories: African-American, Asian-American, Hispanic, and White), socioeconomic status (two categories: working class and below versus middle class and above), and family structure (two categories: biological two-parent and nonintact; for details, see Steinberg et al., 1991).

After ensuring that the reliability of each of our three parenting scales was adequate in every ecological niche, we categorized families as authoritative or nonauthoritative. Families who scored above the entire sample median on warmth, behavioral control, and psychological autonomy granting were categorized as authoritative. Families who had scored below the entire sample median on any of the three dimensions were categorized as nonauthoritative. Consistent with previous research (e.g., Dornbusch et al., 1987), we found that authoritativeness is more prevalent among White households than minority households. Also consistent with previous work, we found that Asian-American youngsters are least likely to come from authoritative homes. Again, in light of the superior performance of Asian-American students, this finding runs counter to the family socialization hypothesis.

We contrasted the adolescents from authoritative and nonauthoritative homes within each niche on several outcome variables, including our indices of school performance. Across the outcome variables that are not related to school (psychosocial development, psychological distress, and behavior problems), we found that youngsters from authoritative homes fared better than their counterparts from nonauthoritative homes, in all ethnic groups. When we looked at youngsters' school performance, however, we found that White and Hispanic youngsters were more likely to benefit from authoritative parenting than were African-American or Asian-American youngsters. Within the African-American and Asian-American groups, youngsters whose parents were authoritative did not perform better than youngsters whose parents were nonauthoritative. Virtually regardless of their parents' practices, the Asian-American students in our sample were receiving higher grades in school than other students, and the African-American students were receiving relatively lower grades than other students. Indeed, we found that African-American students' school performance was even unrelated to their parents' level of education (Dornbusch, Ritter, & Steinberg, 1991)—a finding that is quite surprising, given the strong association between parental social class and scholastic success reported in the sociological literature on status attainment (e.g., Featherman, 1980).

GLASS CEILING EFFECT

Why would authoritativeness benefit Asian-American and African-American youngsters when it comes to psychological development and mental health, but not academic performance? One possibility we explored derives from the work of urban anthropologist John Ogbu and his colleagues (e.g., Fordham & Ogbu, 1986; Ogbu, 1978). Ogbu has argued that African-American and Hispanic youngsters perceive the opportunity structure differently than White and Asian-American youngsters do. Because adolescents from what he has called "caste-like" minorities believe that they will face a job ceiling that prohibits them from "receiving occupational rewards commensurate with their educational credentials" (Mickelson, 1990, p. 45), they put less effort into their schoolwork. According to this view, the lower school performance of African-American and Hispanic youngsters is a rational response to their belief that, for them, educational effort does not pay off.

Although Ogbu's (1978) thesis has received a great deal of popular attention, it has been subjected to very little empirical scrutiny. The main tests of his hypothesis have come from ethnographic studies focusing on single peer groups of Black adolescents. Although important in their own right, these studies have not permitted the crucial cross-ethnic comparisons that are at the heart of Ogbu's thesis, because it is impossible to determine from these studies whether the beliefs expressed by the students in these samples are unique to minority adolescents. As several commentators (e.g., Steinberg, 1987) have pointed out, the notion that it is admirable to work hard in school is not widespread among contemporary American adolescents, whatever their color.

On one of our questionnaires, students responded to two questions designed to tap their beliefs about the likelihood of school success: (a) "Suppose you *do* get a good education in high school. How likely is it that you will end up with the kind of job you hope to get?"; and (b), "Suppose you *don't* get a good education in high school. How likely is it that you will still end up with the kind of job you hope to get?" Interestingly, responses to these two questions were only modestly correlated.

When we examined the correlations between our two measures of beliefs about the value of school success and our indices of school performance and school engagement, we found results that are generally consistent with one of the central assumptions of Ogbu's (1978) theory—namely, that the more students believe that doing well in school pays off, the more effort they exert in school and the better they perform there. Of particular interest, however, is the finding that the extent to which students believe that there are *negative* consequences of school failure is a better predictor of their school performance and engagement than the extent to which they believe that there are positive consequences of school success. That is, across ethnic groups, the more youngsters believe that not getting a good education hurts their chances, the better they do in school.

We then looked at ethnic differences in the extent to which youngsters endorse these beliefs. The results were quite surprising. We found no ethnic differences in the extent to which youngsters believe that getting a good education pays off. From the point of view of educators, the new is good: Virtually all students in our sample, regardless of their ethnicity, endorsed the view that getting a good education would enhance their labor market success. However, on the second of these questions—concerning students' beliefs about the consequences of not getting a good education—we found significant variability and significant ethnic differences. Much more than other groups, Asian-American adolescents believe that it is unlikely that a good job can follow a bad education. Hispanic and African-American students are the most optimistic. In other words, what distinguishes Asian-American students from others is not so much their stronger belief that educational success pays off, but their stronger fear that educational failure will have negative consequences. Conversely, unwarranted optimism, rather than excessive pessimism, may be limiting African-American and Hispanic students' school performance.

We noted earlier that academic success and school engagement are more strongly correlated with the belief that doing poorly in school will have negative repercussions than with the belief that doing well will have positive ones. The pattern of ethnic differences on our measures of school performance and engagement is generally consistent with this general principle. In general, Asian-American students, who in our sample were the most successful in school and were most likely to believe that doing poorly in school has negative repercussions, devote relatively more time to their studies, are more likely to attribute their success to hard work, and are more likely to report that their parents have high standards for school performance. Asian-American students spend twice as much time each week on homework as to other students and report that their parents would be angry if they came home with less than an A–. In contrast, African-American and Hispanic students, who do less well in school, are more cavalier about the consequences of poor school performance, devote less time to their studies, are less likely than others to attribute their success to hard work, and report that their parents have relatively lower standards.

In sum, we found that students' beliefs about the relation between education and life success influence their performance and engagement in school. However, it may be students' beliefs about the negative consequences of doing poorly in school, rather than their beliefs about the positive consequences of doing well, that matter. Youngsters who believe that they can succeed without doing well in school devote less energy to academic pursuits, whereas those who believe that academic failure will have negative repercussions are more engaged in their schooling. Although African-American and Hispanic youth earn lower grades in school than their Asian-American and White counterparts, they are just as likely as their peers to believe that doing well in school will benefit them occupationally.

In essence, our findings point to an important discrepancy between African-American and Hispanic students' values and their behavior. In contrast to the differential cultural values hypothesis outlined earlier—which suggests that ethnic differences in achievement can be explained in terms of ethnic differences in the value placed on education—we found that African-American and Hispanic students are just as likely as other parents to value education as well. Yet, on average, African-American and Hispanic youth devote less time to homework, perceive their parents as having lower performance standards, and are less likely to believe academic success comes from working hard.

These ethnic differences in student behaviors have important implications for how students are perceived by their teachers and may help illuminate the relation between ethnicity and student performance. A recent paper by George Farkas and his colleagues (Farkas, Grobe, & Shuan, 1990) helps to make this link more understandable. In a large-scale study of Dallas students, they found that teachers assigned grades to students in part on the basis of such noncognitive factors as their work habits. The lower relative performance of African-American and Hispanic students and the higher relative performance of Asian-American students may be in large measure due to differences in these groups' work habits, which affect performance both directly, through their influence on mastery, and indirectly, through their effects on teachers' judgments.

We noted earlier that our analysis of the influence of authoritative parenting on psychosocial development, including youngsters' work orientation, indicated similar effects across all ethnic groups. Because earlier work had indicated that work orientation is a very strong predictor of school performance, and authoritative parenting a strong predictor of work orientation (Patterson, 1986; Steinberg et al., 1991), we were left with somewhat of a mystery. Why should youngsters who say they value school success, who believe in the occupational payoff of school success, and whose parents rear them in ways known to facilitate a positive work orientation, perform less well in school than we would expect? For African-American students in particular, where was the slippage in the processes linking authoritative parenting, work orientation, and school success? To understand this puzzle, we turned to yet another context—the peer group—and examined how it interacts with that of the family.

PEERS AND PARENTS
AS INFLUENCES ON ACHIEVEMENT

Many of the items on our questionnaire asked students directly about the extent to which their friends and parents encouraged them to perform well in school. We used a number of these items to calculate the degree to which a student felt he or she received support for academic accomplishment from parents and, independently, from peers. We then used these indices of support to predict various aspects of students' attitudes and behaviors toward school.

We found, as have others (e.g., Brittain, 1963), that although parents are the most salient influence on youngsters' long-term educational plans, peers are the most potent influence on their day-to-day behaviors in school (e.g., how much time they spend on homework, whether they enjoy coming to school each day, and how they behave in the classroom). There are interesting ethnic differences in the relative influence of parents and peers on student achievement, however. These differences help to shed light on some of the inconsistencies and paradoxes in the school performance of minority youngsters.

For reasons that we do not yet understand, at least in the domain of schooling parents are relatively more potent sources of influence on White and Hispanic youngsters than they are on Asian-American or African-American youngsters (Brown, Steinberg, Mounts, & Philipp, 1990). This is not to say that the mean levels of parental encouragement are necessarily lower in minority homes than in majority homes. Rather, the relative magnitude of the correlations between parental encouragement and academic success and between peer encouragement and academic success is different for minority than for majority youth. In comparison with White youngsters, minority youngsters are more influenced by their peers, and less by their parents, in matters of academic achievement.

Understanding the nature of peer group norms and peer influence processes among minority youth holds the key to unlocking the puzzle about the lack of relation between authoritative parenting and academic achievement among Asian-American and African-American youth. To fully understand the nature of peer crowds and peer influence for minority youth, it is essential to recognize the tremendous level of ethnic segregation that characterizes the social structure of most ethnically mixed high schools. We discovered this quite serendipitously. To map the social structure of each school, we interviewed students from each ethnic group in each grade level about the crowds characteristic of their school and their classmates' positions in the crowd structure (Schwendinger & Schwendinger, 1985).

For the most part, students from one ethnic group did not know their classmates from other ethnic groups. When presented with the name of a White classmate, for instance, a White student could usually assign that classmate to one of several differentiated peer crowds—"jocks," "populars," "brains," "nerds," and so forth. When presented with the name of an African-American classmate, however, a White student would typically not know the group that this student associated with, or might simply say that the student was a part of the "Black" crowd. The same was true for Hispanic and Asian-American students. In other words, within ethnic groups, youngsters have a very differentiated view of their classmates; across ethnic groups, however, they see their classmates as members of an ethnic group first, and members of a more differentiated crowd second, if at all.

The location of an adolescent within the school's social structure is very important, because peer crowds membership exerts an effect on school achievement above and beyond that of the family (Steinberg & Brown, 1989). Across all ethnic groups, youngsters whose friends and parents both support achievement perform better than those who receive support only from one source but not the other, who in turn perform better than those who receive no support from either. Thus, an important predictor of academic success for an adolescent is having support for academics from both parents and peers. This congruence of parent and peer support is greater for White and Asian-American youngsters than for African-American and Hispanic adolescents.

For White students, especially those in the middle class, the forces of parents and peers tend to converge around an ethic that supports success in school. Working with our data set, Durbin, Steinberg, Darling, and Brown (1993) found that, among White youth, youngsters from authoritative homes are more likely to belong to peer crowds that encourage academic achievement and school engagement—the "jocks" and the "populars." For these youngsters, authoritative parenting is related to academic achievement not only because of the direct effect it has on the individual adolescent's work habits, but because of the effect it has on the adolescent's crowds affiliation. Among White youngsters, authoritatively raised adolescents are more likely to associate with other youngsters who value school and behave in ways that earn them good grades.

The situation is more complicated for youngsters from minority backgrounds, because the ethnic segregation characteristic of most high schools limits their choices for peer crowd membership. We recently replicated Durbin et al.'s (1991) analyses on the relation between parenting practices and peer crowd affiliation separately within each ethnic group. Surprisingly, among African-American and Asian-American students, we found no relation between parenting practices and peer crowd membership. In other words, authoritatively raised minority youngsters do not necessarily belong to peer groups that encourage academic success. Those whose peers and parents do push them in the same direction perform quite well in school, but among authoritatively reared minority youth who are not part of a peer crowd that emphasized achievement, the influence of peers offsets the influence of their parents.

In ethnically mixed high schools, Asian-American, African-American, and, to a lesser extent, Hispanic students find their choices of peer groups more restricted than do White stu-

dents. But the nature, and consequently, the outcome of the restriction vary across ethnic groups. More often than not, Asian-American students belong to a peer group that encourages and rewards academic excellence. We have found, through student interviews, that social supports for help with academics-studying together, explaining difficult assignments, and so on-are quite pervasive among Asian-American students. Consistent with this, on our surveys, Asian-American youngsters reported the highest level of peer support for academic achievement. Interestingly, and in contrast to popular belief, our survey data indicate that Asian-American parents are less involved in their children's schooling than any other group of parents.

African-American students face quite a different situation. Although their parents are supportive of academic success, these youngsters, we learned from our interviews, find it much more difficult to joint a peer group that encourages the same goal. Our interviews with high-achieving African-American students indicated that peer support for academic success is so limited that many successful African-American students eschew contact with other African-American students and affiliate primarily with students from other ethnic groups (Liederman, Landsman, & Clark, 1990). As Fordham and Ogbu (1986) reported in their ethnographic studies of African-American teenagers, African-American students are more likely than others to be caught in a bind between performing well in school and being popular among their peers.

Understanding African-American and Asian-American students' experiences in their peer groups helps to account for the finding that authoritative parenting practices, although predictive of psychological adjustment, appear almost unrelated to school performance among these youngsters. For Asian-American students, the costs to schooling of nonauthoritative parenting practices are offset by the homogeneity of influence in favor of academic success that these youngsters encounter in their peer groups. For African-American youngsters, the benefits to schooling of authoritative parenting are offset by the lack of support for academic excellence that they enjoy among their peers. Faced with this conflict between academic achievement and peer popularity, and the cognitive dissonance it must surely produce, African-American youngsters diminish the implications of doing poorly in school and maintain the belief that their occupational futures will not be harmed by school failure. This, we believe, is one explanation for the apparent paradox between African-American students' espoused values and their actual school behavior.

The situation of Hispanic students is different still. Among these youngsters, as among White youngsters, the family exerts a very strong influence on school performance and the relative influence of the peer group is weaker. Yet Hispanic students report grades and school behaviors comparable with those of African-American students. This illustrates why the influence of the family must be evaluated in terms of the other contexts in which youngsters are expected to perform. Although Hispanic youngsters may be influenced strongly by what goes on at home (at least as much as White youngsters), what goes on in many Hispanic households may not be conducive to success in school, at least as schools are presently structured. As is the case in Asian-American homes, in Hispanic homes, the prevalence of authoritative parenting is relatively lower, and the prevalence of authoritarian parenting relatively higher. In a school system that emphasizes autonomy and self-direction, authoritarian parenting, with its emphasis on obedience and conformity and its adverse effects on self-reliance and self-confidence, may place youngsters at a disadvantage. Without the same degree of support for academics enjoyed by Asian-American students in their peer group, the level of parental authoritarianism experienced by Hispanic students may diminish their performance in school.

CONCLUSION

These findings illustrate the complex mechanisms through which the contexts in which adolescents live influence their lives and their achievement. We began by looking at one process occurring in one context: the relation between authoritative parenting and adolescent adjustment. We found, in general, that adolescents whose parents are warm, firm, and democratic achieve more in school than their peers. At the same time, however, our findings suggest that the effects of authoritative parenting must be examined without the broader context in which the family lives and in which youngsters develop. Our findings suggest that the effect of parenting practices on youngsters' academic performance and behavior is moderated to large extent by the social milieu the encounter among their peers at school.

The nature of this moderating effect depends on the nature of the peers' values and norms: Strong peer support for academics offsets what might otherwise be the ill effects of growing up in a nonauthoritative home, whereas the absence of peer support for academics may offset some of the benefits of authoritativeness. Whether such offsetting and compensatory effects operate in other outcome domains is a question we hope to investigate in further analyses of these data.

We do not believe that we have explained the phenomenon of ethnic differences in achievement in any final sense. We do believe that the ecological approach, with its focus on the multiple contexts in which youngsters live, offers promise as a foundation for future research on this important social issue. Any explanation of the phenomenon of ethnic differences in adolescent achievement must take into account multiple, interactive processes of influence that operate across multiple interrelated contexts.

REFERENCES

Baldwin, C., & Baldwin, A. (1989, April). *The role of family interaction in the prediction of adolescent competence.* Symposium presented at the meeting of the Society for Research in Child Development, Kansas City, MO.

Baumrind, D. (1972). An exploratory study of socialization effects on Black children: Some Black-White comparisons. *Child Development, 43,* 261–267.

Baumrind, D. (1989). Rearing competent children. In W. Damon (ed.), *Child development today and tomorrow* (p. 349–378). San Francisco: Jossey-Bass.

Baumrind, D. (1991a). Parenting styles and adolescent development. In J. Brooks-Gunn, R. Lerner, and A. C. Petersen (eds.), *The encyclopedia of adolescence (pp. 746–758). New York: Garland.*

Baumrind, D. (1991b). Effective parenting during the early adolescent transition. In P. A. Cowan & E. M. Hetherington (eds.), Advances in family research (Vol. 2, pp. 111–163). Hillsdale, NJ: Erlbaum.

Brittain, C. V. (1963). Adolescent choices and parent–peer cross-pressures. *American Sociological Review,* 28, 385–391.

Bronfenbrenner, U. (1986). Ecology of the family as a context for human development: Research perspectives. *Developmental Psychology, 22,* 723–742.

Brown, B., Steinberg, L., Mounts, N., & Phillip, M. (1990, March). The comparative influence of peers and parents on high school achievement: Ethnic differences. In S. Lamborn (Chair), *Ethnic variations in adolescent experience.* Symposium conducted at the biennial meetings of the Society for Research on Adolescence, Atlanta.

Dornbusch, S. M., Ritter, P. L., Liederman, P., Roberts, D., & Fraleigh, M. (1987). The relation of parenting style to adolescent school performance. *Child Development, 58,* 1244–1257.

Dornbusch, S. M., Ritter, P., & Steinberg, L. (1991). Community influences on the relation of family statuses to adolescent school performance: Differences between African Americans and non-Hispanic Whites. *American Journal of Education,* 99, 543–569.

Durbin, D., Steinberg, L., Darling, N., & Brown, B. (1993). *Parenting style and peer group membership among European-American adolescence.* Journal of Research on Adolescence, 3, 87–100.

Farkas, G., Grobe, R., & Shuan, Y. (1990). Cultural differences and school success: Gender, ethnicity, and poverty groups within an urban school district. *American Sociological Review,* 55, 127–142.

Featherman, D. L. (1980). Schooling and occupational careers: Constancy and change in worldly success. In O. Brim, Jr., & J. Kagan (eds.), *Constancy and change in human development* (pp. 675–738). Cambridge, MA: Harvard University Press.

Fordham, S., & Ogbu, J. U. (1986). Black students' school success: Coping with the "burden of 'acting White.' " *Urban Review, 18,* 176–206.

Lamborn, S. D., Mounts, N. S., Steinberg, L., & Dornbusch, S. M. (1991). Patterns of competence and adjustment among adolescents from authoritative, authoritarian, indulgent, and neglectful families. *Child Development, 62,* 1049–1065.

Liederman, P. H., Landsman, M., & Clark, C. (1990, March). *Making it or blowing it: Coping strategies and academic performance in a multiethnic high school population.* Paper presented at the biennial meetings of the Society for Research on Adolescence, Atlanta.

Lynn, R. (1977). The intelligence of the Japanese. *Bulletin of the British Psychological Society, 40,* 464–468.

Maccoby, E., & Martin, J. (1983). Socialization in the context of the family: Parent–child interaction. In E. M. Hetherington (ed.), *Handbook of child psychology: Vol. 4. Socialization, personality, and social development.* (pp. 1–101). New York: Wiley.

Mickelson, R. (1990). The attitude–achievement paradox among Black adolescents. *Sociology of Education, 63,* 44–61.

Mordkowitz, E., & Ginsberg, H. (1987). Early academic socialization of successful Asian-American college students. *Quarterly Newsletter of the Laboratory of Comparative Human Cognition, 9,* 85–91.

Ogbu, J. (1978). *Minority education and caste.* San Diego, CA: Academic Press.

Patterson, G. (1986). Performance models for antisocial boys. *American Psychologist, 41,* 432–444.

Ritter, P., & Dornbusch, S. (1989, March). *Ethnic variation in family influences on academic achievement.* Paper presented at the American Education Research Association Meeting, San Francisco.

Rushton, J. (1985). Differential K theory: The sociobiology of individual and group differences. *Personality and Individual Differences, 6,* 441–452.

Schaefer, E. (1965). Children's reports of parental behavior: An inventory. *Child Development, 36,* 413–424.

Schwendinger, H., & Schwendinger, J. (1985). *Adolescent subcultures and delinquency.* New York: Prager.

Spencer, M., & Dornbusch, S. (1990). Challenges in studying minority youth. In S. Feldman & G. Elliot (eds.), *At the threshold: The developing adolescent* (pp. 123–146). Cambridge, MA: Harvard University Press.

Steinberg, L. (1987, April 25). Why Japan's students outdo ours. *The New York Times,* p. 15.

Steinberg, L. (1990). Autonomy, conflict, and harmony in the family relationship. In S. Feldman & G. Elliot (eds.), *At the threshold: The developing adolescent.* (pp. 255–276). Cambridge, MA: Harvard University Press.

Steinberg, L., & Brown, B. (1989, March). *Beyond the classroom: Family and peer influences on high school achievement.* Paper presented to the Families as Educators special interest group at the annual meetings of the American Education Research Association, San Francisco.

Steinberg, L., Elmen, J., & Mounts, N. (1989). Authoritative parenting, psychosocial maturity, and academic success among adolescents. *Child Development, 60,* 1424–1436.

Steinberg, L., Mounts, N., Lamborn, S., & Dornbusch, S. (1991). Authoritative parenting and adolescent adjustment across various ecological niches. *Journal of Research on Adolescence, 1,* 19–36.

Sue, S., & Okazaki, S. (1990). Asian-American educational achievements: A Phenomenon in search of an explanation. *American Psychologist, 45,* 913–920.

Thompson, L., Detterman, D., & Plomin, R. (1991). Association between cognitive abilities and scholastic achievement: Genetic overlap but environmental differences. *Psychological Science, 2,* 158–165.

Wetzel, J (1987). *American youth: A statistical snapshot.* New York: William T. Grant Foundation Commission on Work, Family, and Citizenship.

PART SEVEN

MORAL JUDGMENT— EGO DEVELOPMENT

*Act only according to the maxim by which you can—at the same
time—will, that it should become a universal law.*
—KANT'S CATEGORICAL IMPERATIVE

Compelling tasks facing adolescents include taking more responsibility for
their actions and personal and moral choices. During this period, moral dilemmas are more common, have more serious consequences, and thus become
more difficult than during childhood. Many choices have only short-lived consequences, some have long-term implications, and some may affect the lives
of other people. Often young people make moral choices based on their definition of rules, rights, and responsibilities. Others frame their decisions more in
the context of interpersonal relationships; some use both. For some adolescents, survival is the only determinant for moral choices.

As a result of the emergence of cognitive growth and social awareness, new
challenges in the form of moral and ego development constitute a major endeavor for youth. Kohlberg's (20) lifetime concern with moral judgment reflects Kant's categorical imperative and is based on the work of Dewey and
Piaget. For these men, moral development is determined by developmental
changes that follow a sequential pattern. The attainment of a moral stage is a
reflection of the individual's current cognitive structure and ability to appreciate the rational nature of rules. According to Kohlberg, moral judgment is a
significant determinant of moral behavior. His stages form a hierarchical sequence; each moral progression depends on the acquisition of new cognitive
skills and attainment of the previous stage. The *preconventional level* reflects
a basic egocentric orientation. Typically found among preschool children, the
orientation is based on a selfish desire for immediate gratification but also a
fear of punishment. At the *conventional level,* individuals are concerned
with pleasing others, maintaining the social order, conforming to rules, and

establishing standards of justice. This level peaks during adolescence and remains a permanent mode of moral reasoning for many. The *postconventional, autonomous,* or *principled level* of moral judgment reflects the philosophy of the Constitution. People work toward changing "bad laws" through building consensus and the democratic process. Eventually they attempt to apply universal ethical principles to moral decisions. To expose injustice, some principled individuals are willing to break laws they consider unfair and accept the social or legal consequences. Progress through these stages is primarily dependent on cognitive development, not on memorizing moral rules. To facilitate the ability to make moral choices, educators need to expose students to arguments and reasoning characteristic of a level above their own, especially if the arguments take the form of open and nonjudgmental debate.

Kohlberg and Gilligan initially collaborated on their research. During the war in Viet Nam, they examined young men's moral choices regarding the draft. Following the Supreme Court's ruling on abortion, Gilligan began to investigate how women made decisions related to their pregnancies. The outgrowth of her influential work, *In a Different Voice,* changed the nature of psychological research. Erikson, Kohlberg, Piaget, and Freud primarily studied and generalized about males and at times made the erroneous assumption that their findings applied equally well to females. Gilligan rejects these theorists' claims of validity because they assumed a male's perspective. She demands that research looks to women's lives to create categories to describe them, rather than accept preexisting definitions based on males. In *Two Moral Orientations,* Gilligan and Attanucci (22) found that men tend to make moral decisions related to justice and care on the basis of law and principles, but women believe that moral choices must be made in the context of the caring relationships of the people involved.

Loevinger's theory of ego development (21) is compatible with Kohlberg's. Her theory grew out of research with females only; it covers the entire human life cycle and encompasses the way a developing person assimilates experiences, feelings, and behaviors. She refuses to establish a simple correspondence between age and stage, which is so characteristic of most theories. However, she does identify a developmental continuum. The *presocial* stage begins with infancy and persists into early childhood. The next level, the *impulsive* stage, is evidenced by the person's desire to get his/her way and the lack of reliable internal controls. During the *self-protective* stage, the concern is still with the self and with immediate gratification, but internal controls are now beginning to emerge that can restrain selfishness. Loevinger believes that adolescents may operate anywhere from *self-protective* to *individualistic* stages. The prevalence of wanting to act like and look like others is characteristic of early adolescents in the *conformist* stage and finds expression in a desire to impress others to gain social approval and acceptance. At the *self-awareness* level, concern for individual values, rather than group standards, starts to develop. At the *individualistic* stage, found only among some of the more mature late adolescents, an increase in respect for individual differences and an awareness that various people fulfill diverse roles become evident. As their egos mature, many adolescents learn to make independent decisions, see themselves as initiators of actions, and begin to take responsibility for their behavior.

The connection between identity and moral development is intriguing. As adolescents develop a sense of who they are, they also begin to develop a more personal commitment to the way they plan to conduct their lives. If they come through their identity crisis with a healthy sense of self and a personal identity, they are more likely to care for others and to take responsibility for their actions. However, if they have little faith in themselves, are unwilling to trust people, place blame on others, and do not attribute success or failure to their own conduct; they are less likely to accept responsibility for what they do.

THE COGNITIVE-DEVELOPMENTAL APPROACH TO MORAL EDUCATION

LAWRENCE KOHLBERG

I. MORAL STAGES

The cognitive-developmental approach was fully stated for the first time by John Dewey. The approach is called *cognitive* because it recognizes that moral education, like intellectual education, has its basis in stimulating the *active thinking* of the child about moral issues and decisions. It is called developmental because it sees the aims of moral education as movement through moral stages. According to Dewey:

> The aim of education is growth or *development,* both intellectual and moral. Ethical and psychological principles can aid the school in the *greatest of all constructions—the building of a free and powerful character*. Only knowledge of the *order and connection of the stages in psychological development can insure this*. Education is the work of *supplying the conditions* which will enable the psychological functions to mature in the freest and fullest manner.[1]

Dewey postulated three levels of moral development: 1) the *pre-moral* or *pre-conventional* level "of behavior motivated by biological and social impulses with results for moral," 2) the *conventional* level of behavior "in which the individual accepts with little critical reflection the standards of his group," and 3) the *autonomous* level of behavior in which "conduct is guided by the individual thinking and judging for himself whether a purpose is good, and does not accept the standard of his group without reflection."

Dewey's thinking about moral stages was theoretical. Building upon his prior studies of cognitive stages, Jean Piaget made the first effort to define stages of moral reasoning in children through actual interviews and through observations of children (in games with rules).[2] Using this interview material, Piaget defined the pre-moral, the conventional, and the autonomous levels as follows: 1) the *pre-moral stage*, where there was no sense of obligation to rules; 2) the *heteronomous stage,* where the right was literal obedience to rules and an equation of obligation with submission to power and punishment (roughly ages 4–8); and 3) the *autonomous stage,* where the purpose and consequences of following rules are considered and obligation is based on reciprocity and exchange (roughly ages 8–12).

In 1955 I started to redefine and validate (through longitudinal and cross-cultural study) the Dewey-Piaget levels and stages. The resulting stages are presented in Table 1.

We claim to have validated the stages defined in Table 1. The notion that stages can be *validated* by longitudinal study implies that stages have definite empirical characteristics.[3] The

From *Phi Delta Kappan,* June 1975, *56,* 670–677, abridged. Reprinted by permission of the author and the publisher. Table 1 from *The Journal of Philosophy,* October 25, 1973, and reprinted by permission of the author and the publisher.

TABLE 1
Definition of Moral Stages

I. PRECONVENTIONAL LEVEL

At this level, the child is responsive to cultural rules and labels of good and bad, right or wrong, but interprets these labels either in terms of the physical or the hedonistic consequences of action (punishment, reward, exchange of favors) or in terms of the physical power of those who enunciate the rules and labels. The level is divided into the following two stages:

Stage I: *The punishment-and-obedience orientation.* The physical consequences of action determine its goodness or badness, regardless of the human meaning or value of these consequences. Avoidance of punishment and unquestioning deference to power are valued in their own right, not in terms of respect for an underlying moral order supported by punishment and authority (the latter being Stage 4).

Stage 2: *The instrumental-relativist orientation.* Right action consists of that which instrumentally satisfies one's own needs and occasionally the needs of others. Human relations are viewed in terms like those of the marketplace. Elements of fairness, of reciprocity, and of equal sharing are present, but they are always interpreted in a physical, pragmatic way. Reciprocity is a matter of "you scratch my back and I'll scratch yours," not of loyalty, gratitude, or justice.

II. CONVENTIONAL LEVEL

At this level, maintaining the expectations of the individual's family, group, or nation is perceived as valuable in its own right, regardless of immediate and obvious consequences. The attitude is not only one of *conformity* to personal expectations and social order, but of loyalty to it, of actively *maintaining,* supporting, and justifying the order, and of identifying with the persons or group involved in it. At this level, there are the following two stages:

Stage 3: *The interpersonal concordance or "good boy—nice girl" orientation.* Good behavior is that which pleases or helps others and is approved by them. There is much conformity to stereotypical images of what is majority or "natural" behavior. Behavior is frequently judged by intention—"he means well" becomes important for the first time. One earns approval by being "nice."

Stage 4: *The "law and order" orientation.* There is orientation toward authority, fixed rules, and the maintenance of the social order. Right behavior consists of doing one's duty, showing respect for authority, and maintaining the given social order for its own sake.

III. POSTCONVENTIONAL, AUTONOMOUS, OR PRINCIPLED LEVEL

At this level, there is a clear effort to define moral values and principles that have validity and application apart from the authority of the groups or persons holding these principles and apart from the individual's own identification with these groups. This level also has two stages:

Stage 5: *The social-contract, legalistic orientation,* generally with utilitarian overtones. Right action tends to be defined in terms of general individual rights and standards which have been critically examined and agreed upon by the whole society. There is a clear awareness of the relativism of personal values and opinions and a corresponding emphasis upon procedural rules for reaching consensus. Aside from what is constitutionally and democratically agreed upon, the right is a matter of personal "values" and "opinion." The result is an emphasis upon the "legal point of view," but with an emphasis upon the possibility of changing law in terms of rational considerations of social utility (rather than freezing it in terms of Stage 4 "law and order"). Outside the legal realm, free agreement and contract is the binding element of obligation. This is the "official" morality of the American government and constitution.

Stage 6: *The universal-ethical-principle orientation.* Right is defined by the decision of conscience in accord with self-chosen *ethical principles* appealing to logical comprehensiveness, universality, and consistency. These principles are abstract and ethical (the Golden Rule, the categorical imperative); they are not concrete moral rules like the Ten Commandments. At heart, these are universal principles of *justice,* of the *reciprocity* and *equality* of human *rights:* and of respect for the dignity of human beings as *individual persons.* . . .

concept of stages (as used by Piaget and myself) implies the following characteristics:

1. Stages are "structured wholes," or organized systems of thought. Individuals are *consistent* in level of moral judgment.
2. Stages form an *invariant sequence.* Under all conditions except extreme trauma, movement is always forward, never backward. Individuals never skip stages; movement is always to the next stage up.
3. Stages are "hierarchical integrations." Thinking at a higher stage includes or comprehends within it lower-stage thinking. There is a tendency to function at or prefer the highest stage available.

Each of these characteristics has been demonstrated for moral stages. Stages are defined by responses to a set of verbal moral dilemmas classified according to an elaborate scoring scheme. Validating studies include:

1. A 20-year study of 50 Chicago-area boys, middle- and working-class. Initially interviewed at ages 10–16, they have been reinterviewed at three-year intervals thereafter.
2. A small, six-year longitudinal study of Turkish village and city boys of the same age.
3. A variety of other cross-sectional studies in Canada, Britain, Israel, Taiwan, Yucatan, Honduras, and India.

With regard to the structured whole or consistency criterion, we have found that more than 50% of an individual's thinking is always at one stage, with the remainder at the next adjacent stage (which he is leaving or which he is moving into).

With regard to invariant sequence, our longitudinal results have been presented in the *American Journal of Orthopsychiatry* (see footnote 8) and indicate that on every retest individuals were either at the same stage as three years earlier or had moved up. This was true in Turkey as well as in the United States.

With regard to the hierarchical integration criterion, it has been demonstrated that adolescents exposed to written statements at each of the six stages comprehend or correctly put in their own words all statements at or below their own stage but fail to comprehend any statements more than one stage above their own.[4] Some individuals comprehend the next stage above their own; some do not. Adolescents prefer (or rank as best) the highest stage they can comprehend.

To understand moral stages, it is important to clarify their relations to stage of logic or intelligence, on the one hand, and to moral behavior on the other. Maturity of moral judgment is not highly correlated with IQ or verbal intelligence (correlations are only in the 30s, accounting for 10% of the variance). Cognitive development, in the stage sense, however, is more important for moral development than such correlations suggest. Piaget has found that after the child learns to speak there are three major stages of reasoning: the intuitive, the concrete operational, and the formal operational. At around age 7, the child enters the stage of concrete logical thought: He can make logical inferences, classify, and handle quantitative relations about concrete things. In adolescence individuals usually enter the stage of formal operations. At this stage they can reason abstractly, i.e., consider all possibilities, form hypotheses, deduce implications from hypotheses, and test them against reality.

Since moral reasoning clearly is reasoning, advanced moral reasoning depends upon advanced logical reasoning; a person's logical stage puts a certain ceiling on the moral stage he can attain. A person whose logical stage is only concrete operational is limited to the preconventional moral stages (Stages 1 and 2). A person whose logical stage is only partially formal operational is limited to the conventional moral stages (Stages 3 and 4). While logical development is necessary for moral development and sets limits to it, most individuals are higher in logical stage than they are in moral stage. As an example, over 50% of late adolescents and adults are capable of full formal reasoning, but only 10% of these adults (all formal operational) display principled (Stages 5 and 6) moral reasoning.

The moral stages are *structures of moral judgment* or *moral reasoning. Structures* of moral judgment must be distinguished from the *content* of moral judgment. As an example, we cite responses to a dilemma used in our various studies to identify moral stage. The dilemma raises the issue of stealing a drug to save a dying woman. The inventor of the drug is selling it for 10 times what it costs him to make it. The woman's husband cannot raise the money, and the seller refuses to lower the price or wait for payment. What should the husband do?

The choice endorsed by a subject (steal, don't steal) is called the *content* of his moral judgment in the situation. His reasoning about the choice defines the structure of his moral judgment. This reasoning centers on the following 10 universal moral values or issues of concern to persons in these moral dilemmas:

1. Punishment
2. Property
3. Roles and concerns of affection
4. Roles and concerns of authority
5. Law
6. Life
7. Liberty
8. Distributive justice
9. Truth
10. Sex

A moral choice involves choosing between two (or more) of these values as they *conflict* in concrete situations of choice.

The stage or structure of a person's moral judgment defines: 1) *what* he finds valuable in each of these moral issues (life, law), i.e., how he defines the value, and 2) *why* he finds it valuable, i.e., the reasons he gives for valuing it. As an example, at Stage 1 life is valued in terms of the power or possessions of the person involved; at Stage 2, for its usefulness in satisfying the needs of the individual in question or others; at Stage 3, in terms of the individual's relations with others and their valuation of him; at Stage 4, in terms of social or religious law. Only at Stages 5 and 6 is each life seen as inherently worthwhile, aside from other considerations.

Moral Judgment vs. Moral Action

Having clarified the nature of stages of moral *judgment,* we must consider the relation of moral judgment to moral *action.* If logical reasoning is a necessary but not sufficient condition for mature moral judgment, mature moral judgment is a necessary but not sufficient condition for mature moral action. One cannot follow moral principles if one does not understand (or believe in) moral principles. However, one can reason in terms of principles and not live up to these principles. As an example, Richard Krebs and I found that only 15% of the students showing some principled thinking cheated as compared to 55% of conventional subjects and 70% of preconventional subjects.[5] Nevertheless, 15% of the principled subjects did cheat, suggesting that factors additional to moral judgment are necessary for principled moral reasoning to be translated into "moral action." Partly, these factors include the situation and its pressures. Partly, what happens depends upon the individual's motives and emotions. Partly, what the individual does depends upon a general sense of will, purpose, or "ego strength." As an example of the role of will or ego strength in moral behavior, we may cite the study by Krebs: Slightly more than half of his conventional subjects cheated. These subjects were also divided by a measure of attention\will. Only 26% of the "strong-willed" conventional subjects cheated; however, 74% of the "weak-willed" subjects cheated.

If maturity of moral reasoning is only one factor in moral behavior, why does the cognitive-developmental approach to moral education focus so heavily upon moral reasoning? For the following reasons:

1. Moral judgment, while only one factor in moral behavior, is the single most important or influential factor yet discovered in moral behavior.
2. While other factors influence moral behavior, moral judgment is the only distinctively *moral* factor in moral behavior. To illustrate, we noted that the Kerbs study indicated that

"strong-willed" conventional stage subjects resisted cheating more than "weak-willed" subjects. For those at a preconventional level of moral reasoning, however, "will" had an opposite effect. "Strong-willed" Stages 1 and 2 subjects cheated more, not less, than "weak-willed" subjects, i.e., they had the "courage of their (amoral) convictions" that it was worthwhile to cheat. "Will," then, is an important factor in moral behavior, but it is not distinctively moral; it becomes moral only when informed by mature moral judgment.

3. Moral judgment change is long-range or irreversible; a higher stage is never lost. Moral behavior as such is largely situational and reversible or "loseable" in new situations.

II. AIMS OF MORAL AND CIVIC EDUCATION

Moral psychology describes what moral development is, as studied empirically. Moral education must also consider moral philosophy, which strives to tell us what moral development ideally *ought to be.* Psychology finds an invariant sequence of moral stages; moral philosophy must be invoked to answer whether a later stage is a better stage. The "stage" of senescence and death follows the "stage" of adulthood, but that does not mean that senescence and death are better. Our claim that the latest or principled stages of moral reasoning are morally better stages, then, must rest on considerations of moral philosophy.

The tradition of moral philosophy to which we appeal is the liberal or rational tradition, in particular the "formalistic" or "deontological" tradition running from Immanuel Kant to John Rawls.[6] Central to this tradition is the claim that an adequate morality is *principled,* i.e., that it makes judgments in terms of *universal* principles applicable to all mankind. *Principles* are to be distinguished from *rules.* Conventional morality is grounded on rules, primarily "thou shalt nots" such as are represented by the Ten Commandments, prescriptions of kinds of actions. Principles are, rather, universal guides to making a moral decision. An example is Kant's "categorical imperative," formulated in two ways. The first is the maxim of respect for human personality, "Act always toward the other as an end, not as a means." The second is the maxim of universalization, "Choose only as you would be willing to have everyone choose in your situation." Principles like that of Kant's state the formal conditions of a moral choice or action. In the dilemma in which a woman is dying because a druggist refuses to release his drug for less than the stated price, the druggist is not acting morally, though he is not violating the ordinary moral rules (he is not actually stealing or murdering). But he is violating principles: He is treating the woman simply as a means to his ends of profit, and he is not choosing as he would wish anyone to choose (if the druggist were in the dying woman's place, he would not want a druggist to choose as he is choosing). Under most circumstances, choice in terms of conventional moral rules and choice in terms of principles coincide. Ordinarily, principles dictate not stealing (avoiding stealing is implied by acting in terms of a regard for others as ends and in terms of what one would want everyone to do). In a situation where stealing is the only means to save a life, however, principles contradict the ordinary rules and would dictate stealing. Unlike rules which are supported by social authority, principles are freely chosen by the individual because of their intrinsic moral validity.

The conception that a moral choice is a choice made in terms of moral principles is related to the claim of liberal moral philosophy that moral principles are ultimately principles of justice. In essence, moral conflicts are conflicts between the claims of persons, and principles for resolving these claims are principles of justice, "for giving each his due." Central to justice are the demands of *liberty, equality,* and *reciprocity.* At every moral stage, there is a concern for justice. The most damning statement a school child can make about a teacher is that "he's not fair." At each higher stage, however, the conception of justice is reorganized. At Stage 1, justice is punishing the bad in terms of "an eye for an eye and a tooth for a tooth." At Stage 2, it is exchanging favors and goods in an equal manner. At Stages 3 and 4, it is treating people as they desire in terms of the conventional rules. At Stage 5, it is recognized that all rules and laws flow from justice, from a social contract between the governors and the governed designed to protect the equal rights of all. At Stage 6, personally chosen moral principles are also principles of justice, the principles any member of a society would choose for that society if he did not know what his position was to be in the society and in which he might be the least advantaged.[7] Principles chosen from this point of view are, first, the maximum liberty compatible with the like liberty of others and, second, no inequalities of goods and respect which are not to the benefit of all, including the least advantaged.

As an example of stage progression in the orientation to justice, we may take judgments about capital punishment.[8] Capital punishment is only firmly rejected at the two principled stages, when the notion of justice as vengeance or retribution is abandoned. At the sixth stage, capital punishment is not condoned even if it may have some useful deterrent effect in promoting law and order. This is because it is not a punishment we would choose for a society if we assumed we had as much chance of being born into the position of a criminal or murderer as being born into the position of a law abider.

Why are decisions based on universal principles of justice better decisions? Because they are decisions on which all moral men could agree. When decisions are based on conventional moral rules, men will disagree, since they adhere to conflicting systems of rules dependent on culture and social position. Throughout history men have killed one another in the name of conflicting moral rules and values, most recently in Vietnam and the Middle East. Truly moral or just resolutions of conflicts require principles which are, or can be, universalizable.

Alternative Approaches

We have given a philosophic rationale for stage advance as the aim of moral education. Given this rationale, the developmental approach to moral education can avoid the problems inherent in the other two major approaches to moral education. The first alternative approach is that of indoctrinative moral education, the preaching and imposition of the rules and values of the teacher and his culture on the child. In America, when this indoctrinative approach has been developed in a systematic manner, it has usually been termed "character education."

Moral values, in the character education approach, are preached or taught in terms of what may be called the "bag of virtues." In the classic studies of character by Hugh Hartshorne and Mark May, the virtues chosen were honesty, service, and self-control.[9] It is easy to get superficial consensus on such a bag of virtues—until one examines in detail the list of virtues involved and the details of their definition. Is the Hartshorne and May bag more adequate than the Boy Scout bag (a Scout should be honest, loyal, reverent, clean, brave, etc.)? When one turns to the details of defining each virtue, one finds equal uncertainty or difficulty in reaching consensus. Does honesty mean one should not steal to save a life? Does it mean that a student should not help another student with his homework?

Character education and other forms of indoctrinative moral education have aimed at teaching universal values (it is assumed that honesty or service are desirable traits for all men in all societies), but the detailed definitions used are relative; they are defined by the opinions of the teacher and the conventional culture and rest on the authority of the teacher for their justification. In this sense character education is close to the unreflective valuings by teachers which constitute the hidden curriculum of the school. Because of the current unpopularity of indoctrinative approaches to moral education, a family of approaches called "values clarification" has become appealing to teachers. Values clarification takes the first step implied by a rational approach to moral education: the eliciting of the child's own judgment or opinion about issues or situations in which values conflict, rather than imposing the teacher's opinion on him. Values clarification, however, does not attempt to go further than eliciting awareness of values; it is assumed that becoming more self-aware about one's values is an end in itself. Fundamentally, the definition of the end of values education as self-awareness derives from a belief in ethical relativity held by many value-clarifiers. As stated by Peter Engel, "One must contrast value clarification and value inculcation. Value clarification implies the principle that in the consideration of values there is no single correct answer." Within these premises of "no correct answer," children are to discuss moral dilemmas in such a way as to reveal different values and discuss their value differences with each other. The teacher is to stress that "our values are different," not that one value is more adequate than others. If this program is systematically followed, students will themselves become relativists, believing there is no "right" moral answer. For instance, a student caught cheating might argue that he did nothing wrong, since his own hierarchy of values, which may be different from that of the teacher, made it right for him to cheat.

Like values clarification, the cognitive-developmental approach to moral education stresses open or Socratic peer discussion of value dilemmas. Such discussion, however, has an aim: stimulation of movement to the next stage of moral reasoning. Like values clarification, the developmental approach opposes indoctrination. Stimulation of movement to the next stage of reasoning is not indoctrinative, for the following reasons:

1. Change is in the way of reasoning rather than in the particular beliefs involved.
2. Students in a class are at different stages; the aim is to aid movement of each to the next stage, not convergence on a common pattern.
3. The teacher's own opinion is neither stressed nor invoked as authoritative. It enters in only as one of many opinions, hopefully one of those at a next higher stage.
4. The notion that some judgments are more adequate than others is communicated. Fundamentally, however, this means that the student is encouraged to articulate a position which seems most adequate to him and to judge the adequacy of the reasoning of others.

In addition to having more definite aims than values clarification, the moral development approach restricts value education to that which is moral or, more specifically, to justice. This is for two reasons. First, it is not clear that the whole realm of personal, political, and religious values is a realm which is nonrelative, i.e., in which there are universals and a direction of development. Second, it is not clear that the public school has a right or mandate to develop values in general. In our view, value education in the public schools should be restricted to that which the school has the right and mandate to develop: an awareness of justice, or of the rights of others in our Constitutional system. While the Bill of Rights prohibits the teaching of religious beliefs, or of specific value systems, it does not prohibit the teaching of the awareness of rights and principles of justice fundamental to the Constitution itself.

When moral education is recognized as centered in justice and differentiated from value education or affective education, it becomes apparent that moral and civic education are much the same thing. This equation, taken for granted by the classic philosophers of education from Plato and Aristotle to Dewey, is basic to our claim that a concern for moral education is central to the educational objectives of social studies.

The term *civic education* is used to refer to social studies as more than the study of the facts and concepts of social science, history, and civics. It is education for the analytic understanding, value principles, and motivation necessary for a citizen in a democracy if democracy is to be an effective process. It is political education. Civic or political education means the stimulation of development of more advanced patterns of reasoning about political and social decisions and their implementation in action. These patterns are patterns of moral reasoning. Our studies show that reasoning and decision making about political decisions are directly derivative of broader patterns of moral reasoning and decision making. We have interviewed high school and college students about concrete political situations involving laws to govern open housing, civil disobedience for peace in Vietnam, free press rights to publish what might disturb national order, and distribution of income through taxation. We find that reasoning on these political decisions can be classified according to moral stage and that an individual's stage on political dilemmas is at the same level as on nonpolitical moral dilemmas (euthanasia, violating authority to maintain trust in a family, stealing a drug to save one's dying wife). Turning from reasoning to action, similar findings are obtained. In 1963 a study was made of those who sat in at the University of California, Berkeley, administration building and those who did not in the Free Speech Movement crisis. Of those at Stage 6, 80% sat in, believing that principles of free speech were being compromised, and that all efforts to compromise and negotiate with the administration had failed. In contrast, only 15% of the conventional (Stage 3 or Stage 4) subjects sat in. (Stage 5 subjects were in between.)

From a psychological side, then, political development is part of moral development. The same is true from the philosophic side. In the *Republic,* Plato sees political education as part of a broader education for moral justice and finds a rationale for such education in terms of universal philosophic principles rather than the demands of a particular society. More recently, Dewey claims the same.

In historical perspective, America was the first nation whose government was publicly founded on post-conventional principles of justice, rather than upon the authority central to conventional

moral reasoning. At the time of our founding, postconventional or principled moral and political reasoning was the possession of the minority, as it still is. Today, as in the time of our founding, the majority of our adults are at the conventional level, particularly the "law and order" (fourth) moral stage. (Every few years the Gallup Poll circulates the Bill of Rights unidentified, and every year it is turned down.) The Founding Fathers intuitively understood this without benefit of our elaborate social science research; they constructed a document designing a government which would maintain principles of justice and the rights of man even though principled men were not the men in power. The machinery included checks and balances, the independent judiciary, and freedom of the press. Most recently, this machinery found its use at Watergate. The tragedy of Richard Nixon, as Harry Truman said long ago, was that he never understood the Constitution (a Stage 5 document), but the Constitution understood Richard Nixon.

Watergate, then, is not some sign of moral decay of the nation, but rather of the fact that understanding and action in support of justice principles are still the possession of a minority of our society. Insofar as there is moral decay, it represents the weakening of conventional morality in the face of social and value conflict today. This can lead the less fortunate adolescent to fixation at the preconventional level, the more fortunate to movement to principles. We find a larger proportion of youths at the principled level today than was the case in their fathers' day, but also a larger proportion at the preconventional level.

Given this state, moral and civic education in the schools becomes a more urgent task. In the high school today, one often hears both preconventional adolescents and those beginning to move beyond convention sounding the same note of disaffection for the school. While our political institutions are in principle Stage 5 (i.e., vehicles for maintaining universal rights through the democratic process), our schools have traditionally been Stage 4 institutions of convention and authority. Today more than ever, democratic schools systematically engaged in civic education are required.

Our approach to moral and civic education relates the study of law and government to the actual creation of a democratic school in which moral dilemmas are discussed and resolved in a manner which will stimulate moral development.

Planned Moral Education

For many years, moral development was held by psychologists to be primarily a result of family upbringing and family conditions. In particular, conditions of affection and authority in the home were believed to be critical, some balance of warmth and firmness being optimal for moral development. This view arises if morality is conceived as an internalization of the arbitrary rules of parents and culture, since such acceptance must be based on affection and respect for parents as authorities rather than on the rational nature of the rules involved.

Studies of family correlates of moral stage development do not support this internalization view of the conditions for moral development. Instead, they suggest that the conditions for moral development in homes and schools are similar and that the conditions are consistent with cognitive-developmental theory. In the cognitive-developmental view, morality is a natural product of a universal human tendency toward empathy or role taking, toward putting oneself in the shoes of other conscious beings. It is also a product of a universal human concern for justice, for reciprocity or equality in the relation of one person to another. As an example, when my son was 4, he became a morally principled vegetarian and refused to eat meat, resisting all parental persuasion to increase his protein intake. His reason was, "It's bad to kill animals." His moral commitment to vegetarianism was not taught or acquired from parental authority; it was the result of the universal tendency of the young self to project its consciousness and values into other living things, other selves. My son's vegetarianism also involved a sense of jus-

tice, revealed when I read him a book about Eskimos in which a real hunting expedition was described. His response was to say, "Daddy, there is one kind of meat I would eat—Eskimo meat. It's all right to eat Eskimos because they eat animals." This natural sense of justice or reciprocity was Stage 1—an eye for an eye, a tooth for a tooth. My son's sense of the value of life was also Stage 1 and involved no differentiation between human personality and physical life. His morality, though Stage 1, was, however, natural and internal. Moral development past Stage 1, then, is not an internalization but the reconstruction of role taking and conceptions of justice toward greater adequacy. These reconstructions occur in order to achieve a better match between the child's own moral structures and the structures of the social and moral situations he confronts. We divide these conditions of match into two kinds: those dealing with moral discussions and communication and those dealing with the total moral environment or atmosphere in which the child lives.

In terms of moral discussion, the important conditions appear to be:

1. Exposure to the next higher stage of reasoning
2. Exposure to situations posing problems and contradictions for the child's current moral structure, leading to dissatisfaction with his current level
3. An atmosphere of interchange and dialogue combining the first two conditions, in which conflicting moral views are compared in an open manner

Studies of families in India and America suggest that morally advanced children have parents at higher stages. Parents expose children to the next higher stage, raising moral issues and engaging in open dialogue or interchange about such issues.[10]

Drawing on this notion of the discussion conditions stimulating advance, Moshe Blatt conducted classroom discussion of conflict-laden hypothetical moral dilemmas with four classes of junior high and high school students for a semester.[11] In each of these classes, students were to be found at three stages. Since the children were not all responding at the same stage, the arguments they used with each other were at different levels. In the course of these discussions among the students, the teacher first supported and clarified those arguments that were one stage above the lowest stage among the children; for example, the teacher supported Stage 3 rather than Stage 2. When it seemed that these arguments were understood by the students, the teacher then challenged that stage, using new situations, and clarified the arguments one stage above the previous one: Stage 4 rather than Stage 3. At the end of the semester, all the students were retested; they showed significant upward change when compared to the controls, and they maintained the change one year later. In the experimental classrooms, from one-fourth to one-half of the students moved up a stage, while there was essentially no change during the course of the experiment in the control group.

Given the Blatt studies showing that moral discussion could raise moral stage, we undertook the next step: to see if teachers could conduct moral discussion in the course of teaching high school social studies with the same results. This step we took in cooperation with Edwin Fenton, who introduced moral dilemmas in his ninth- and eleventh-grade social studies texts. Twenty-four teachers in the Boston and Pittsburgh areas were given some instruction in conducting moral discussion around the dilemmas in the text. About half of the teachers stimulated significant developmental change in their classrooms—upward stage movement of one-quarter to one-half a stage. In control classes using the text but no moral dilemma discussions, the same teachers failed to stimulate any moral change in the students. Moral discussion, then, can be a usable and effective part of the curriculum at any grade level. Working with filmstrip dilemmas produced in cooperation with Guidance Associates, second-grade teachers conducted moral discussions yielding a similar amount of moral stage movement.

Moral discussion and curriculum, however, constitute only one portion of the conditions stimulating moral growth. When we turn to ana-lyzing the broader life environment, we turn to a consideration of the *moral atmosphere* of the home, the school, and the broader society. The first basic dimension of social atmosphere is the role-taking opportunities it provides, the extent to which it encourages the child to take the point of view of others. Role taking is related to the amount of social interaction and social communication in which the child engages, as well as to his sense of efficacy in influencing attitudes of others. The second dimension of social atmosphere, more strictly moral, is the level of justice of the environment or institution. The justice structure of an institution refers to the perceived rules or principles for distributing rewards, punishments, responsibilities, and privileges among institutional members. This structure may exist or be perceived at any of our moral stages. As an example, a study of a traditional prison revealed that inmates perceived it as Stage 1, regardless of their own level.[12] Obedience to arbitrary command by power figures and punishment for disobedience were seen as the governing justice norms of the prison. A behavior-modification prison using point rewards for conformity was perceived as a Stage 2 system of instrumental exchange. Inmates at Stage 3 or 4 perceived this institution as more fair than the traditional prison, but not as fair in their own terms.

These and other studies suggest that a higher level of institutional justice is a condition for individual development of a higher sense of justice. Working on these premises, Joseph Hickey, Peter Scharf, and I worked with guards and inmates in a women's prison to create a more just community.[13] A social contract was set up in which guards and inmates each had a vote of one and in which rules were made and conflicts resolved through discussions of fairness and a democratic vote in a community meeting. The program has been operating four years and has stimulated moral stage advance in inmates, though it is still too early to draw conclusions as to its overall long-range effectiveness for rehabilitation.

One year ago, Fenton, Ralph Mosher, and I received a grant from the Danforth Foundation (with additional support from the Kennedy Foundation) to make moral education a living matter in two high schools in the Boston area (Cambridge and Brookline) and two in Pittsburgh. The plan had two components. The first was training counselors and social studies and English teachers in conducting moral discussions and making moral discussion an integral part of the curriculum. The second was establishing a just community school within a public high school.

We have stated the theory of the just community high school, postulating that discussing real-life moral situations and actions as issue of fairness and as matters for democratic decision would stimulate advance in both moral reasoning and moral action. A participatory democracy provides more extensive opportunities for role taking and a higher level of perceived institutional justice than does any other social arrangement. Most alternative schools strive to establish a democratic governance, but none we have observed has achieved a vital or viable participatory democracy. Our theory suggested reasons why we might succeed where others failed. First, we felt that democracy had to be a central commitment of a school, rather than a humanitarian frill. Democracy as moral education provides that commitment. Second, democracy in alternative schools often fails because it bores the students. Students prefer to let teachers make decisions about staff, courses, and schedules, rather than to attend lengthy, complicated meetings. Our theory said that the issues a democracy should focus on are issues of morality and fairness. Real issues concerning drugs, stealing, disruptions, and grading are never boring if handled as issues of fairness. Third, our theory told us that if large democratic community meetings were preceded by small-group moral discussion, higher-stage thinking by students would win out in later decisions, avoiding the disasters of mob rule.

Currently, we can report that the school based on our theory makes democracy work or function where other schools have failed. It is too

early to make any claims for its effectiveness in causing moral development, however.

Our Cambridge just community school within the public high school was started after a small summer planning session of volunteer teachers, students, and parents. At the time the school opened in the fall, only a commitment to democracy and a skeleton program of English and social studies had been decided on. The school started with six teachers from the regular school and 60 students, 20 from academic professional homes and 20 from working-class homes. The other 20 were dropouts and troublemakers or petty delinquents in terms of previous record. The usual mistakes and usual chaos of a beginning alternative school ensued. Within a few weeks, however, a successful democratic community process had been established. Rules were made around pressing issues: disturbances, drugs, hooking. A student discipline committee or jury was formed. The resulting rules and enforcement have been relatively effective and reasonable. We do not see reasonable rules as ends in themselves, however, but as vehicles for moral discussion and an emerging sense of community. This sense of community and a resulting morale are perhaps the most immediate signs of success. This sense of community seems to lead to behavior change of a positive sort. An example is a 15-year-old student who started as one of the greatest combinations of humor, aggression, light-fingeredness, and hyperactivity I have ever known. From being the principal disturber of all community meetings, he has become an excellent community meeting participant and occasional chairman. He is still more ready to enforce rules for others than to observe them himself, yet his commitment to the school has led to a steady decrease in exotic behavior. In addition, he has become more involved in classes and projects and has begun to listen and ask questions in order to pursue a line of interest.

We attribute such behavior change not only to peer pressure and moral discussion but to the sense of community which has emerged from the democratic process in which angry conflicts are resolved through fairness and community decision. This sense of community is reflected in statements of the students to us that there are no cliques—that the blacks and the whites, the professors' sons and the project students, are friends. These statements are supported by observation. Such a sense of community is needed where students in a given classroom range in reading level from fifth-grade to college.

Fenton, Mosher, the Cambridge and Brookline teachers, and I are now planning a four-year curriculum in English and social studies centering on moral discussion, on role taking and communication, and on relating the government, laws, and justice system of the school to that of the American society and other world societies. This will integrate an intellectual curriculum for a higher level of understanding of society with the experiential components of school democracy and moral decision.

There is very little new in this—or in anything else we are doing. Dewey wanted democratic experimental schools for moral and intellectual development 70 years ago. Perhaps Dewey's time has come.

REFERENCES

1. John Dewey, "What Psychology Can Do for the Teacher," in Reginald Archambault, ed., *John Dewey on Education: Selected Writings* (New York: Random House, 1964).
2. Jean Piaget, *The Moral Judgment of the Child,* 2nd ed. (Glencoe, Ill.: Free Press, 1948).
3. Lawrence Kohlberg, "Moral Stages and Moralization: The Cognitive-Developmental Approach," in Thomas Lickona, ed., *Moral Development and Behavior: Theory, Research and Social Issues* (New York: Holt, Rinehart, and Winston, 1976).
4. James Rest, Elliott Turiel, and Lawrence Kohlberg, "Relations Between Level of Moral Judgment and Preference and Comprehension of the Moral Judgment of Others," *Journal of Personality,* vol. 37, 1969, pp. 225–52, and James Rest, "Comprehension, Preference, and Spontaneous Usage in Moral Judgement," in Lawrence Kohlberg, ed., *Recent Research in Moral Development* (New York: Holt, Rinehart, and Winston, 1973.)
5. Richard Krebs and Lawrence Kohlberg, "Moral Judgment and Ego Controls as Determinants of Resistance to Cheating," in Lawrence Kohlberg, ed., *Recent Research.*
6. John Rawls, *A Theory of Justice* (Cambridge, Mass.: Harvard University Press, 1971).
7. John Rawls, ibid.
8. Lawrence Kohlberg and Donald Elfenbein, "Development of Moral Reasoning and Attitudes Toward Capital Punishment," *American Journal of Orthopsychiatry,* Summer, 1975.
9. High Hartshorne and Mark May, *Studies in the Nature of Character: Studies in Deceit,* vol. 1; *Studies in Service and Self-Control,* vol. 2; *Studies in Organization of Character,* vol. 3 (New York: Macmillan, 1928–30).
10. Bindu Parilch. "A Cross-Cultural Study of Parent-Child Moral Judgment," unpublished doctoral dissertation, Harvard University, 1975.
11. Moshe Blatt and Lawrence Kohlberg, "Effects of Classroom Discussions upon Children's Level of Moral Judgment," in Lawrence Kohlberg, ed., *Recent Research.*
12. Lawrence Kohlberg, Peter Scharf, and Joseph Hickey, "The Justice Structure of the Prison: A Theory and an Intervention," *The Prison Journal,* Autumn–Winter, 1972.
13. Lawrence Kohlberg, Kelsey Kauffman, Peter Scharf, and Joseph Hickey, *The Just Community Approach to Corrections: A Manual, Part I* (Cambridge, Mass.: Education Research Foundation, 1973).

EGO DEVELOPMENT
IN ADOLESCENCE

JANE LOEVINGER
Washington University

The growth of character was considered an appropriate topic for psychologists to study in the early years of this century. But as psychology turned to behavioristic and psychometric methods and principles, the topic was neglected—in fact, it became virtually taboo. In recent years, however, there has been a revival of interest in character development under a variety of names and aspects. Ausubel (1952) has written of ego development; Piaget (1932) and Kohlberg (1964) of the moralization of judgment; Isaacs (1956) and C. Sullivan, Grant, and Grant (1957) of maturation of interpersonal relations; Harvey, Hunt, and Schroeder (1961) of cognitive complexity; Peck and Havighurst (1960) of character structure; Perry (1970) of intellectual-ethical development; and Gedo and Goldberg (1973) of the development of the self. These authors do not all describe the same thing; but each, in describing fully the stages of development of his or her own continuum, impinges on the territory of the others. Many have another thing in common: they are concerned with a kind of development that is characteristic of adolescence and that reaches fruition after physical growth has been largely achieved.

In the early years of psychology, studies of character development were wise essays, whereas current studies mainly emphasize empirical research, each school of thought typically having an anchoring instrument used in most of its research. The best known of these instruments are Kohlberg's test of maturity of moral judgment (Colby & Kohlberg, 1987), derived originally from Piaget's clinical method, and our Sentence Completion Test (SCT) of ego development (Loevinger & Wessler, 1970; Loevinger, Wessler, & Redmore, 1970). The SCT is one of the easiest test to give, unlike Kohlberg's Moral Judgment Instrument. Both tests require extensive training before they can be scored. Much recent research has been done with these two instruments.

Terms such as *ego* and *moral development* have been used with different meanings in other contexts. Psychoanalysts often use the term *ego development* to cover the earliest period of personality development—the first two or three years of life. The objection to that usage is that it leaves no term to describe the dramatic character development that takes place during adolescence. *Moral development* to many people refers to obedience to the norms of adult behavior, a definition that Kohlberg explicitly eschews, as Piaget (1932) did, because it reduces moral judgment to conformity to adult standards. These usages are not likely to give way, however, even among psychologists.

What is meant here by ego development is a continuum that is both a developmental se-

An original paper prepared for this book of readings.

quence and a dimension of individual differences at every age (Loevinger, 1976). The full range of stages is likely to be found only in adult life. Even there, the earliest stages are probably so rare as not to be found in most settings. No single setting yields all stages; indeed, most settings yield only a narrow range of stages. When *ego development* is defined this way, the defining characteristics of the stages cannot be age-specific. This statement is often misunderstood to mean that there is no link of stages to age, but that would be absurd for a developmental continuum. What it means is, rather, that to study age differences one needs a yardstick that does not itself stretch with age.

THE STAGES OF EGO DEVELOPMENT

The earliest stages, ones that are unlikely to be found among adults outside institutional settings, will be omitted here except to note that the next stage is not appropriately called the "first stage." Gedo and Goldberg (1973) point out, however, that in traumatic situations, even normal adults may function at the most primitive level.

The lowest measurable stage—and it is rare in late adolescence and adult life—is the Impulsive Stage. This stage is normal in early childhood and not conspicuously abnormal even in junior high school. The person at this stage is grossly self-indulgent, governed by whim, and preoccupied with satisfying physical appetites. Rules are seen as an arbitrary exercise of power. The interpersonal world is interpreted in oversimplified terms: people are divided into those good (to me) and those mean (to me). Moral goodness may be confused with cleanliness. Persons at this level are unlikely to be found in college. They may become transients or itinerant workers or get by in protected situations where passive obedience will suffice. Money, good looks, ample servants, exceptional talent, or chutzpa may help persons at this level survive in society. Most people outgrow this stage, at latest during the high-school years.

The next level is called the Self-Protective Stage. People at this stage not only have some conception of how to contain and postpone their needs and wishes, but they have the capacity to do so. However, they are still primarily concerned with self, with immediate gratification, and with staying out of trouble. Rules are perceived and understood, but they are used mainly for personal advantage. In children, this pattern is expected, but normally it declines before the end of high school. The small child's love of ritual is part of the normal passage through the Impulsive and Self-Protective Stages. Adults and older adolescents who have remained at this stage may be hostile, manipulative, exploitative, concerned with deceiving and being deceived or ensnared. Hostile humor is a frequent characteristic. Whether it is the bitterness that leads to arrest at the Self-Protective level or living in a world with which they are out of step that has made these persons bitter is not clear. H. S. Sullivan's (1953) conception of the "malevolent transformation" suggests the former possibility. According to Sullivan, when children are made fun of or are made anxious when they are appealing for tenderness, they may more or less permanently adopt the attitude that they are living among enemies. That attitude prevents them from having or appreciating further experiences that would have a favorable influence on their development. Persons of this type can be found in many places in adult life, including colleges and even positions of great power and authority. W. C. Fields is an example of a person who turned himself into a caricature of a Self-Protective person and turned his hostile humor into an outstanding career.

The Conformist Stage is frequent in high school. People at this stage obey the rules because the group approves of the rules and because Conformists identify themselves with the group and identify their welfare with group welfare. Conformist adolescents may be primarily adult-oriented or primarily peer-oriented; in adult life, the difference tends to disappear. Conformists tend to think in clichés and stereotypes:

"One size fits all"—at least within some broad category—all women should stay home with their children, or all women should work; all men enjoy football games; every college student should join a sorority or fraternity; and so forth. Interpersonal interaction is conceived in behavioral terms, often simply as talking. Conformists are concerned with appearances, social acceptance, and belonging. Although the conformist Stage (or type) is widely recognized and described by many authors, by the end of high school and beginning of college the average person has taken a step beyond this stage, at least among people in cities of the United States.

The next milestone, although it is called a transitional level between the Conformist and Conscientious Stages, may in future be recognized as a full stage. It is currently called the Conscientious-conformist transitional level in part because it seems to require no new vocabulary for its description, as all full stages do, and because it is still basically a conformist position. The person at this transitional level sees more than one possible solution to a problem and sees exceptions to rules, contingencies that alter situations, and so on. Whereas the Conformist identifies the individual with the norm of the group to which the person belongs, the Conscientious-Conformist sees a distinction between the person and the norm. In particular, he or she is aware of not always living up to the norms set by society or the family or the school. That recognition may lead to a sense of loneliness or self-consciousness. At one time, this was called the Self-Conscious level, and some persons interpreted that to signify poor adjustment. But no such implication is warranted.

At the next or Conscientious Stage, the person develops a more complex view of the interpersonal world. Rather than just allowing vague exceptions to rules, the person believes that circumstances of individual cases must be accommodated. Whereas the Conscientious-Conformist allows for broad contingencies such as differences due to marital status or age, the Conscientious Stage person recognizes personal needs and wishes and special abilities as legitimate contingencies. People are seen in terms of many individual traits rather than in terms of broad categories or norms. Interpersonal interactions are viewed in the context of the feelings involved, not just the behaviors. The person is aware, in self and others, of richly differentiated feelings rather than the restricted and banal list available to persons of earlier levels. Work is seen as an opportunity for achievement rather than as a chore, and the person achieves according to his or her own standards rather than according to the standards of a group. Most characteristic is attainment of the elements of a mature conscience: long-term goals and ideals, capacity for self-criticism, judging transgressions in terms of intentions as well as in terms of consequences, and putting other people's welfare on a par with one's own.

A problem that may occur at the Conscientious Stage is an excessive sense of responsibility and a need to shape other people in ways deemed for their own good. These are the traits that tend to give way in progress beyond that stage. The next transitional level is called Individualistic. Here the person goes beyond perceiving individual differences to valuing them in self and others. Beginning at this level—often in global terms—are traits that appear in full-fledged form at the Autonomous Stage. These traits include a conception of people as fulfilling different roles, a striving more for self-fulfillment than for achievement per se, toleration for different persons sometimes tempered by a paradoxical intolerance for prejudiced people (often recognized as a paradox by persons at this level), thinking in terms of psychological development and psychological causation. The person at this level understands that independence is not simply a matter of outgrowing the small child's physical dependence or the adolescent's financial dependence; there still remain emotional dependence and interdependence. The sense of responsibility tends to broaden beyond the limits of family and friends to the larger society. Although we like to think that these are typical preoccupations of late adolescence, only the most mature adolescents spontaneously think in those terms.

An added characteristic of the next or Autonomous Stage is the capacity to acknowledge or cope with inner conflict. This capacity is presaged at the Individualistic level by an appreciation of conflict between one's own needs and the impositions of society or of social stereotypes. Since striving for personal autonomy probably characterizes every stage beyond the Impulsive one, that cannot be what is distinctive here. What is characteristic is the recognition that other people have an equal need for autonomy, that they have a right to make their own mistakes—even one's own children and students—and that autonomy must be sought and respected in the context of the inevitable mutual interdependence of social life. Other characteristics of this stage are toleration for ambiguity and existential humor, often in the most intimate sexual and love relations. The latter contrasts with the sarcastic, hostile humor of the Self-Protective Stage. One of the most characteristic aspects of this stage is an added degree of conceptual complexity. At the pre-Conformist stages, people contrast the good with the bad, the right with the wrong. By the Conscientious Stage, such comparisons are rare; they are supplanted by more differentiated comparisons, such as love versus lust or mental versus physical. At the highest stages, comparisons are often multifaceted, including three or four aspects of a situation or a thought, such as comparing one's role as wife, mother, housekeeper, and professional, or comparing one's needs, duties, and desires.

At the highest or Integrated Stage, the person has an integrated sense of personal identity and has integrated his or her own needs and reactions with a view of the larger society in a seamless frame of reference. This stage is rarely observed in random samples and is, therefore, hard to characterize adequately. Perhaps the truest picture of the stage sequence is given simply by stopping at the Autonomous Stage, with the understanding that the sequence is open-ended.

THE NATURAL HISTORY OF EGO DEVELOPMENT

Among high-school seniors and college undergraduate students and their age mates one finds few persons at the Impulsive Stage; of those few, many would probably be in some kind of trouble. In prisons and mental hospitals, we have found relatively more, but they by no means predominate even there. At the other extreme, one could draw a random sample of several hundred persons age 19 or 20 without ever finding a person at the Integrated Stage or even many at the Autonomous Stage. All stages between the Impulsive and the Autonomous Stages would probably be represented.

Holt (1980) has reported results of a survey by Yankelovich, using a national probability sample of almost 1,000 young people between the ages of 16 and 26. The most frequent score was at the Conscientious-Conformist level. For the noncollege sample, most of the remaining cases were below that level; for the college sample, most of the remaining cases were above that level. These results are not as definitive as one might wish because the survey used only 12 items of the SCT rather than the standard form of 36 items, and the test was given orally rather than administered in the usual written form. Unfortunately, there are no better data available to give a picture of the distribution of ego level in the general population. Our own impressions, based on studying a variety of samples form many levels of society, accord with those results; however, our experience would indicate that the Holt study overestimated the frequency of the Autonomous Stage, probably a result of the difficulty of assigning extreme scores with so brief a test. (For carefully revised short forms, see Loevinger, 1985.)

At the end of high school and beginning of college, most samples show young women to be slightly more advanced than matched samples of men of the same age. That was true of both the college and noncollege national samples (Holt, 1980). A meta-analysis of a number of published and unpublished studies (Cohn, 1988) further confirmed this finding. However, a carefully controlled study of 107 couples, selected because they were married—half of the couples in marriage counseling, half not—showed that men and women in adult life are, on average, equal in ego level (Nettles & Loevinger, 1983). It follows that there must be some time in late adolescence or early adult life when young men catch up with young women, and college appears to be that time (Loevinger, Cohn, Redmore, Bonneville, Streich, & Sargent, 1985; Redmore, 1983).

In order to answer the question of when ego development stops, controlled longitudinal studies are required; pretest and posttest should be scored at the same time, with raters blind as to whether they are scoring pre- or posttest. Two of our published studies, covering four different types of schools, meet those criteria.

Loevinger et al. (1985) studied entering freshmen and graduating seniors at a selective midwestern liberal-arts college and at a selective northeastern engineering school. We found that students entering the liberal-arts college tended to cluster about the Conscientious Stage, whereas those entering the technical institute clustered around the Conscientious-Conformist level. By the time of graduation, the difference was less, because the technical students had advanced slightly but the liberal-arts students, on average, had not changed. On college entry, women in the liberal-arts college were on a slightly higher level than the men, but by graduation they were, for the most part, indistinguishable from the men; the women had declined, though only slightly.

Next to age, probably the chief determinants of measured ego level are intelligence and socioeconomic status, whose effects are, in practice, hard to disentangle. Redmore (1983) did a longitudinal study of pharmacy-school students and of some junior-college students, both schools drawing from a lower socioeconomic level than the previous schools. In these colleges, the students were on a slightly lower ego level, clustering around the Conscientious-conformist

level, as is typical of most other college studies. Redmore's study also found the men catching up with the women during college; overall, there was a small but significant gain during the four-year interval.

Several studies have been done of ego level in prisons and mental hospitals. Although these studies are not methodologically rigorous and most have not been published, a general impression can be gleaned from them. The range of ego levels is not noticeably different from that which would be found in an ordinary sample of persons of the same socioeconomic status outside institutions. For about three-fourths of the sample, the distribution resembles that of an ordinary sample—for example, a detachment of the National Guard. However, about one-fourth of the sample is added to those below the Conformist Stage, in addition to those what would be found there normally.

APPLICATIONS

When college professors and administrators formulate goals for undergraduate education, these goals resemble descriptions of higher ego levels, aiming for some spot in the Individualistic-Autonomous range. The objective of helping the students achieve a higher level of personal maturity is often implemented in courses in freshman or sophomore English, anthropology, or the like. Perry (1970) incorporated such goals in a freshman course in how to study. Theories of ego development and related variables have a contribution to make to the process of achieving a liberal education.

According to theory—and such data as exist bear this out—persons do not easily understand materials or arguments or points of view much above their own current level (Blasi, 1976; Rest, 1979; Rest, Turiel, &Kohlberg, 1969). A statement several levels above their own is likely to be misperceived and reworded by these persons so as to represent a statement at their own or at a lower level. Or they may simply be baffled and declare that the whole discussion makes no sense or is irrelevant or trivial (Perry, 1970). Rest made use of this aspect of the continuum in devising his test of moral reasoning. It is part of the cognitive coloring of character development. It is also part of the reason that the highest stages of ego development are hard to describe. Among the many related variables of moral, ego, and interpersonal development, there is substantial agreement as to the characteristics of the lowest stages and least agreement on the highest stages. That is because one cannot adequately understand stages higher than one's own, and each theorist projects onto the theoretical highest stages some of his or her own personal aspirations or ideology. Those working on the SCT more than those in other groups have tried to let data rather than theory be the guide; consequently, we are often criticized for lack of theoretical rigor, and we have to admit to imperfect understanding of the highest stage.

In order to help a student advance, one needs to know where the student is starting from and how to gauge the smallest possible step forward. Thus, to present an Autonomous point of view in a class composed of freshmen, most of whom may be at the Conscientious-Conformist level, would be to risk misunderstanding, total lack of comprehension, or, on occasion, rebellion. However, to present a viewpoint that is lower than the students' own—say, to present a Conformist position to a class already at the Conscientious Stage—is also to risk rejection or condescension from the students.

The theory of the ego as a self-sustaining, self-monitoring frame of reference warns us about how difficult it is to bring about change in ego level. Nonetheless, a number of people have studied the process of change. Many such studies have taken place in schools and colleges (Perry, 1970), in prisons (Hickey & Scharf, 1980; Warren, 1977), and in the workplace (Lasker, 1978). Much of Kohlberg's work, both in prisons and in high schools, focused on the "just community," a system of self-government under a constitution worked out by participants. One element of his theory is that in the course of self-government, moral dilemmas will naturally arise, and their discussion will facilitate growth, much as happens in programs deliberately planned to encourage growth. Warren and her associates have been working with the conception that the treatment and the treator (such as probation officer) should be selected to match the ego level and perhaps some other characteristics of the delinquent client. The core of Lasker's technique is to make explicit the implicit assumptions about interpersonal relations and the self-concept of persons of the stage he is working with; the technique is most effective in helping workers reach the Conformist Stage. Swensen (1980) has elaborated on the use of ego-development theory to choose and to apply therapeutic techniques appropriate to the client's ego level.

CONCLUSION

The field of ego (or moral or character or interpersonal) development still lies outside of the mainstream of psychology. Yet it encompasses some of the most striking phenomena of adolescence, beyond the obvious facts of physical growth and development. Adolescence is a preeminent time not only for observing character development, but also for influencing it. Maturation of character is correlated with age and probably with intelligence and socioeconomic status. But no amount of study of such demographic variables would yield the rich picture of character development that has emerged from such studies of thought samples as the SCT or moral-dilemma interviews. Thus, this field deserves continued study as a permanent part of the science of psychology.

REFERENCES

Ausubel, D. P. (1952). *Ego development and the personality disorders.* New York: Grune & Stratton.

Blasi, A. (1976). Personal responsibility and ego development. In R. deCharms, (Ed.) *Enhancing motivation: Change in the classroom* (pp. 177–199). New York: Irvington.

Cohn, L. D. (1988). *Gender differences in ego development: A meta-analysis.* Unpublished manuscript, Washington University.

Colby, A., & Kohlberg, L. (1987). *The measurement of moral judgment.* Cambridge: Cambridge University Press.

Gedo, J. E., & Goldberg, A. (1973). *Models of the mind: A psychoanalytic theory.* Chicago: University of Chicago Press.

Harvey, O. J., Hunt, D. E., & Schroder, H. M. (1961). *Conceptual systems and personality organization.* New York: Wiley.

Hickey, J., & Scharf, P. (1980). *Toward a just correctional system.* San Francisco: Jossey-Bass.

Holt, R. R. (1980). Loevinger's measure of ego development: Reliability and national norms for male and female short forms. *Journal of Personality and Social Psychology, 39,* 909–920.

Isaacs, K. S. (1956). *Relatability, a proposed construct and an approach to its validation.* Unpublished doctoral dissertation, University of Chicago.

Kohlberg, L. (1964). Development of moral character and moral ideology. In M. L. Hoffman & L. W. Hoffman (Eds.), *Review of child development research* (Vol. 1, pp. 383–431). New York: Russell Sage Foundation.

Lasker, H. M. (1978). Ego development and motivation: A cognitive-developmental analysis of *n* achievement in Curaçao. Unpublished doctoral dissertation, University of Chicago.

Loevinger, J. (1976). *Ego development: Conceptions and theories.* San Francisco: Jossey-Bass.

Loevinger, J. (1985). Revision of the sentence completion test for ego development. *Journal of Personality and Social Psychology, 48,* 420–427.

Loevinger, J., Cohn, L. D., Redmore, C. D., Bonneville, L., Streich, D., & Sargent, M. (1985). Ego development in college. *Journal of Personality and Social Psychology, 48,* 947–962.

Loevinger, J., & Wessler, R. (1970). *Measuring ego development I: Construction and use of a sentence completion test.* San Francisco: Jossey-Bass.

Loevinger, J., Wessler, R., & Redmore, C. (1970). *Measuring ego development II: Scoring manual for women and girls.* San Francisco: Jossey-Bass.

Nettles, E. J., & Loevinger, J. (1983). Sex role expectations and ego level in relation to problem marriages. *Journal of Personality and Social Psychology, 45,* 676–687.

Peck, R. F., & Havighurst, R. J. (1960). *The psychology of character development.* New York: Wiley.

Perry, W. G., Jr. (1970). *Forms of intellectual and ethical development in the college years.* New York: Holt, Rinehart & Winston.

Piaget, J. (1932). *The moral judgment of the child.* New York: Free Press.

Redmore, C. D. (1983). Ego development in the college years: Two longitudinal studies. *Journal of Youth and Adolescence, 8,* 301–306.

Rest, J. R. (1979). *Development in judging moral issues.* Minneapolis: University of Minnesota Press.

Rest, J., Turiel, E., & Kohlberg, L. (1969). Level of moral development as a determinant of preference and comprehension of moral judgments made by others. *Journal of Personality, 37,* 225–252.

Sullivan, C., Grant, M. Q., & Grant, J. D. (1957). The development of interpersonal maturity: Applications to delinquency. *Psychiatry, 20,* 373–385.

Sullivan, H. S. (1953). *The interpersonal theory of psychiatry.* New York: Norton.

Swensen, C. H. (1980). Ego development and a general model for counseling and psychotherapy. *Personnel and Guidance Journal, 58,* 373–381.

Warren, M. Q. (1977). Correctional treatment and coercion: The differential effectiveness perspective. *Criminal Justice and Behavior, 4,* 355–376.

TWO MORAL ORIENTATIONS

CAROL GILLIGAN AND JANE ATTANUCCI

Recent discussions of sex differences in moral development have confused moral stage within Kohlberg's justice framework with moral orientation, the distinction between justice and care perspectives. Studies by Kohlberg (1984), Walker (1984), Baumrind (1986), and Haan (1985) address the question of whether women and men score differently in Kohlberg's scale of justice reasoning and report contradictory findings. In the present study, we address the question of moral orientation and examine evidence of two moral perspectives in people's discussions of actual moral conflicts. In addition, we ask whether there is an association between moral orientation and gender.

The distinction made here between a justice and a care orientation pertains to the ways in which moral problems are conceived and reflects different dimensions of human relationships that give rise to moral concern. A justice perspective draws attention to problems of inequality and oppression and holds up an ideal of reciprocity and equal respect. A care perspective draws attention to problems of detachment or abandonment and holds up an ideal of attention and response to need. Two moral injunctions—not to treat others unfairly and not to turn away from someone in need—capture these different concerns. From a developmental standpoint, inequality and attachment are universal human experiences; all children are born into a situation of inequality and no child survives in the absence of some kind of adult attachment. The two dimensions of equality and attachment characterize all forms of human relationship, and all relationships can be described in both sets of terms—as unequal or equal and as attached or detached. Since everyone has been vulnerable both to oppression and to abandonment, two moral visions—one of justice and one of care—recur in human experience.

This article reports the results of three studies undertaken to investigate the two moral orientations and to determine to what extent men and women differentially raise concerns about justice and care in discussing moral conflicts in their lives. Lyons (1983) operationalized the distinction between justice and care in terms of the perspective toward others which they imply, contrasting a perspective of reciprocity with a perspective of response. Evidence of these perspectives appeared in the kinds of considerations people raised in discussing real-life moral dilemmas. Lyons created a reliable procedure for identifying moral considerations and assigning them to categories. She defines a morality of justice as: fairness resting on "an understanding of relationships as reciprocity between separate individuals, grounded in the duty and obligations of their roles." Reciprocity is defined in terms of maintaining standards of justice and fairness, understood differently at different developmental levels (Kohlberg, 1981, 1984). A morality of care "rests on an understanding of relationships as response to another in their terms" (Lyons, 1983, p. 136). A care perspective involves the question of how to act responsively and protect vulnerability in a particular situation.

The examples presented in Table 1, drawn from discussions of real-life dilemmas, illustrate the concept of moral orientation. Each pair of dilemmas reveals how a problem is seen from a justice and from a care perspective. In each pair of examples, the justice construction is the more familiar one, capturing the way such problems are usually defined from a moral standpoint. In 1J a peer pressure dilemma is presented in terms of how to uphold one's moral standards and withstand pressure from one's friends to deviate from what one knows to be right. In 1C a similar

decision (not to smoke) is cast in terms of how to respond both to one's friends and to oneself; the rightness of the decision not to smoke is established in terms of the fact that it did not break relationships—"my real friends accepted my decision." Attention to one's friends, to what they say and how it will affect the friendship is presented as a moral concern.

In the second pair of examples, a dilemma— whether to report someone who has violated the medical school's alcohol policy—is posed differently from the justice and care perspectives; the decision not to tell is reasoned in different ways. A clear example of justice tempered by mercy is presented in 2J. The student clearly believes that the violator should be turned in ("I was supposed to turn her in") and justifies not doing so on the grounds that she deserved mercy because "she had all the proper level of contriteness" appropriate for the situation. In 2C a student decides not to turn a proctor in because it would "destroy any relationship you have" and therefore, would "hurt any chance of doing any-

TABLE 1
Examples of Justice and Care Perspectives in Real-Life Moral Dilemmas

Justice	Care
1J [If people were taking drugs and I was the only one who wasn't, I would feel it was stupid. I know for me what is right is right and what's wrong is wrong . . . It's like a set of standards I have.] (High School Student)	1C [If there was one person, it would be a lot easier to say no. I could talk to her, because there wouldn't be seven others to think about. I do think about them, you know, and wonder what they say about me and what it will mean . . . I made the right decision not to, because my real friends accepted by decision.] (High School Student)
2J [The conflict was that by all rights she should have been turned into the honor board for violation of the alcohol policy.] [I liked her very much.] [She is extremely embarrassed and upset. She was contrite. She wished she had never done it. She had all the proper levels of contriteness and guilt . . .] [I was supposed to turn her in and didn't.] (Medical Student)	2C [It might just be his business if he wants to get drunk every week or it might be something that is really a problem and that should be dealt with professionally; and to be concerned about someone without antagonizing them or making their life more difficult than it had to be. Maybe there was just no problem there.] [I guess in something like a personal relationship with a proctor you don't want to just go right out there and antagonize people, because that person will go away and if you destroy any relationship you have, I think you have lost any chance of doing anything for a person.] (Medical Student)

thing for that person." In this construction, turning the person in is seen as impeding efforts to help. The concern about maintaining relationship in order to be able to help is not mentioned in 2J; similarly the concern about maintaining the honor board policy is not mentioned in 2C. A further illustration of how justice and care perspectives restructure moral understanding can be seen by observing that in 2J the student justifies not turning in the violator because of questions about the rightness or justification of the alcohol policy itself, while in 2C the student considers whether what was deemed a problem was really a problem for the other person. The case of 2C illustrates what is meant by striving to see the other in the other's terms; it also exemplifies the contrast between this endeavor and the effort to establish, independently of persons, the legitimacy of existing rules and standards. It is important to emphasize that these examples were selected to highlight the contrast between the justice and the care perspectives and that most people who participated in this research used considerations of both justice and care in discussing a moral conflict they faced.

Validity for Lyons' distinction between justice and care considerations was provided by Langdale (1983), who adapted Lyons' procedure in order to code hypothetical dilemmas. Langdale found that Kohlberg's justice-oriented Heinz dilemma elicits significantly more justice considerations than either a hypothetical care-oriented abortion dilemma or subject-generated real-life moral dilemmas. Langdale demonstrated further that the hypothetical Heinz and abortion dilemmas as well as recurrent types of real-life dilemmas are construed by some people predominantly in terms of justice and by others predominantly in terms of care. This negates the suggestion that concerns about justice and care arise from different kinds of moral problems. Instead, Langdale's analysis of moral orientation indicates how the same problem can be seen in different ways. At the same time her study reveals that hypothetical moral dilemmas can "pull" for the justice or the care orientation.

In the present study, we ask the following three questions: (1) Is there evidence of both justice and care concerns in people's discussion of real-life moral conflict? (2) Do people represent both sets of concerns equally or do they tend to focus on one and minimally represent the other? (3) Is there a relationship between moral orientation and gender?

METHOD

Subjects

Subjects were drawn from three research studies conducted over the past six years. As part of each study, the subjects were asked to describe a real-life moral dilemma. All three samples consisted of men and women matched for levels of education; the adults were matched for professional occupations. The decision was made to sample from an advantaged population, since sex differences in adult moral reasoning have been attributed to women's typically lower occupational and educational status (Kohlberg & Kramer, 1969).

Study 1 The design of this study matched participants for high levels of education and professional occupation to examine the variables of age, gender, and type of dilemma. The adolescents and adults included eleven women and ten men. The racial composition (nineteen white and two minority) was not statistically random as race was not a focal variable of the study.

Study 2 In this study first-year students were randomly selected from two prestigious northeastern medical schools to be interviewed as part of a longitudinal study of stress and adaptation in physicians. The twenty-six men and thirteen women students represented the proportions of each gender in the class at large. The nineteen white and twenty minority students (Black, Hispanic, and Asian Americans) were selected to balance the sample's racial composition (the only sample in the present study with such a design). The students ranged from twenty-one to twenty-seven years of age.

Study 3   The ten female and ten male participants were randomly selected from a coeducational private school in a midwestern city. The nineteen white and one minority student ranged in age from fourteen to eighteen years.

See Table 2 for the distribution of subjects by sample in age and gender categories.

Research Interview

All participants were asked the following series of questions about their personal experience of moral conflict and choice.

1. Have you ever been in a situation of moral conflict where you have had to make a decision but weren't sure what was the right thing to do?
2. Could you describe the situation?
3. What were the conflicts for you in that situation?
4. What did you do?
5. Do you think it was the right thing to do?
6. How do you know?

The interviewer asked questions to encourage the participants to clarify and elaborate their responses. For example, participants were asked what they meant by words like responsibility, obligation, moral, fair, selfish, and caring. The interviewers followed the participants' logic in presenting the moral problem, most commonly querying, "Anything else?"

The interviews were conducted individually, tape recorded, and later transcribed. The moral conflict questions were one segment of an interview which included questions about morality and identity (Gilligan *et al.*, 1982). The interviews lasted about two hours.

Data Analysis

The real-life moral dilemmas were analyzed using Lyons' coding procedure. The three coders

TABLE 2

Gender and Age of Subjects by Study
(Moral Orientation Studies)

	15–22 years	23–34 years	35–77 years
Study 1			
Women (N = 11)	4	2	5
Men (N = 10)	4	1	5
Study 2			
Women (N = 13)	9	4	0
Men (N = 26)	12	14	0
Study 3			
Women (N = 10)	10	0	0
Men (N = 10)	10	0	0

trained by Lyons were blind to the gender, age, and race of the participants and achieved high levels of intercoder reliability (a range of 67–95 percent and a mean of 80 percent agreement across samples on randomly selected cases).

The Lyons procedure is a content analysis which identifies moral considerations. The unit of analysis is the consideration, defined as each idea the participant presents in discussing a moral problem. The units are designated in Table 1 with brackets. To reach an acceptable level of reliability in identifying considerations required extensive training; the coders in these studies were all trained by Lyons and achieved reliability at acceptable levels (Lyons, 1983). Typically, a real-life moral dilemma consists of seven considerations with a range of 4 to 17. The coder classifies these considerations as either justice or care. The Lyons score indicates the predominant, most frequent mode of moral reasoning (justice or care). For the present analysis predominance has been redefined, such that a real-life moral dilemma consisting of only care or justice considerations is labeled Care Only or Justice Only (Table 3). A dilemma consisting of 75 percent or more care or justice considerations is labeled Care focus or Justice Focus, respectively. A dilemma in which both orientations are present but neither orientation accounts for 75 percent of the codable considerations is placed

TABLE 3
Moral Orientation of Participants by Category

	Care Only	Care Focus	Care-Justice	Justice Focus	Justice Only
Observed	5	8	27	20	20
Expected*	0.64	4	70	4	0.64

Note: for the typical case, the ratio of care to justice considerations is Care Only, 7:0; Care Focus, 6:1; Care-Justice, 5:2, 4:3, 3:4, 2:5; Justice Focus, 0:7; and Justice Only, 0:7. Since the range of consideration is 4–17, percentages are used to define comparable categories across cases.
*Expected values are based on binomial distribution for N = 7, p = 0.5.

in the Care-Justice category. Thus, dilemmas are described as focused only when more than 75 percent of the considerations fall into one mode.

RESULTS

This article summarizes the real-life dilemma data from three studies with comparable designs, that is, samples with male and female subjects matched for high socioeconomic status. Frequencies and statistical tests are presented across samples.

Looking at Table 3, two observations can be made. First, the majority of people represent both moral orientations: 69 percent (55 out of 80) compared to the 31 percent (25 out of 80) who use Care or Justice Only. Second, two-thirds of the dilemmas are in the Focus categories (Care Only, Care Focus, Justice Only, Justice Focus), while only one-third are in the Care-Justice category. The question addressed by Table 3 is do people tend to focus their discussion of a moral problem in one or the other orientation? Using a binomial model, if one assumes an equal probability of care and justice orientations in an account of a real-life moral dilemma (p = 0.5), then a random sampling of moral considerations (typically N = 7) over eighty trials (eighty participants' single dilemmas) would result in an expected binomial distribution. To test whether the distribution of scores fits the expected distribution, the χ^2 goodness-of-fit test is applied. The observed distribution differs significantly from the expected, χ^2 (4, N = 8) = 133.8, p < 0.001, and provides sup-

TABLE 4
Moral Orientation by Gender of Participants

	Care Focus	Care-Justice	Justice Focus
Women	12	12	10
Men	1	15	30

porting evidence for our contention that an individual's moral considerations are not random but tend to be focused in either the care or justice orientation.

In Table 4, the relationship between moral orientation and gender can be examined. The test of statistical significance, χ^2 (2, N = 80) = 18.33, p < 0.001, demonstrates a relationship between moral orientation and gender such that both men and women present dilemmas in the Care-Justice category, but Care Focus is much more likely to occur in the moral dilemma of a woman, and Justice Focus more likely in the dilemma of a man. In fact, if one were to exclude women from a study of moral reasoning, Care Focus could easily be overlooked.

We did not test the relationship between moral orientation and age, because the majority of participants were adolescents and young adults, providing little age range. Furthermore, in the present analysis, age is confounded with sample (i.e., the young adults are the medical students), making interpretation difficult.

The medical student data (Study 2) raised further questions of interpretation which bear on the issues addressed in this analysis. First, the dilemmas from the medical students when tested separately do not show the same relationship between gender and moral orientation, χ^2 (2, N = 39) = 4.36, n.s. However, consistent with the overall findings, the two Care Focus dilemmas were presented by women.

Examining the pattern of difference in the dilemmas, the Care Focus dilemmas were presented by one white and one minority woman. The relationship between moral orientation and race for both men and women is that the dilemmas presented by white students are more likely to fall in the Care-Justice category and dilemmas of minority students in the Justice Focus category (Fisher's Exact p = 0.045 for women and p = 0.0082 for men).

DISCUSSION

The present exploration of moral orientation has demonstrated that (1) concerns about justice and care are *both* represented in people's thinking about real-life moral dilemmas, but people tend to focus on one set of concerns and minimally represent the other; and (2) there is an association between moral orientation and gender such that both men and women use both orientations, but Care Focus dilemmas are more likely to be presented by women and Justice Focus dilemmas by men.

Our findings indicate that the selection of an all-male sample for theory and test construction in moral judgment research is inherently problematic. If women were eliminated from the present study, Care Focus would virtually disappear. Furthermore, most of the dilemmas described by women could be scored and analyzed for justice considerations without reference to the considerations of care. Thus, the interpretive question hinges on the understanding of the care perspective.

Our analysis of care and justice as distinct moral orientations that address different moral concerns leads us to consider both perspectives as constitutive of mature moral thinking. The tension between these perspective is suggested

by the fact that detachment, which is the mark of mature moral judgment in the justice perspective, becomes *the* moral problem in the care perspective—the failure to attend to need. Conversely, attention to the particular needs and circumstances of individuals, the mark of mature moral judgment in the care perspective, becomes *the* moral problem in the justice perspective—failure to treat others fairly, as equals. Care Focus and Justice Focus reasoning suggest a tendency to lose sight of one perspective in reaching moral decision. The fact that the focus phenomenon was demonstrated by two-thirds of both men and women in our study suggests that this liability is shared by both sexes. The virtual absence of Care Focus dilemmas among men in these samples of advantaged North Americans is the surprising finding of this research.

This finding provides an empirical explanation for the equation of morality with justice in theories of moral development derived from all-male research samples (Piaget, 1932/1965; Kohlberg, 1969, 1984). In addition, the Care Focus dilemmas presented by women offer an explanation for the fact that within a justice conception of morality, moral judgments of girls and women have appeared anomalous and difficult to interpret; Piaget cites this as the reason for studying boys. Furthermore, finding Care Focus mainly among women indicates why the analysis of women's moral thinking elucidated the care perspective as a distinct moral orientation (Gilligan, 1977) and why the considerations of care noted in dilemmas presented by men did not seem fully elaborated (Gilligan & Murphy, 1979). The evidence of orientation focus as an observable characteristic of moral judgment does not justify the conclusion that focus is a desirable attribute of moral decision. However, careful attention to women's articulation of care concerns suggests a different conception of the moral domain and a different way of analyzing the moral judgments of both men and women.

The category Care-Justice in our findings raises important questions that merit investigation in future research. Dilemmas in this "bifocal" category were equally likely among men and women in our study, but it is possible that interviews involving more dilemmas and further questioning might reveal the focus phenomenon to be more common and eliminate the bi-focal category. But it is also possible that such studies might find and elucidate further an ability to sustain two moral perspectives—an ability which according to the present data seems equally characteristic of women and men.

If people know both moral perspectives, as our theory and data suggest, researchers can cue perceptions in one or the other direction by the dilemmas they present, by the questions they raise, or by their failure to ask questions. The context of the research study as well as the interview itself must be considered for its influence on the likelihood of eliciting care or justice reasoning. In the case of the medical student data (Study 2), the findings raise just such contextual questions. In this large-scale study of stress and adaptation which included extensive standard, evaluative inventories as well as the clinical interview, is it possible that the first-year medical students might have been reluctant to admit uncertainty? A large number could not or would not describe a situation in which they were not sure what the right thing to do was. Also, is it possible that the focus on justice represents efforts by the students to align themselves with the perceived values of the institution they are entering? The focus on justice by minority students is of particular interest since it counters the suggestion that a care orientation is the perspective of subordinates or people of lower social power and status.

Evidence that moral orientation organizes moral judgment as well as the discovery of the focus phenomenon has led us to make the following changes in our research procedures which we offer as suggestions for other researchers:

1. That interviewers proceed on the assumption that people can adopt both a justice and a care

perspective and that they encourage participants to generate different perspectives on a moral problem ("Is there another way to think about this problem?") and to examine the relationship between them.

2. That interviewers seek to determine the conception of justice and the conception of care that organizes the moral thinking in the discussion of a particular dilemma. Kohlberg's stages describe the development of justice reasoning. We have described different ways women think about care and traced changes over time in care reasoning. Our work offers guides to thinking about development and the nature of transitions in two perspectives.

Evidence of two moral perspectives suggests that the choice of moral standpoint, whether implicit or explicit, may indicate a preferred way of seeing. If so, the implications of such a preference need to be explored. Orientation preference may be a dimension of identity or self-definition, especially when moral decision becomes more reflective or "post-conventional" and the choice of moral principle becomes correspondingly more self-conscious. Interviewers should attend to where the self stands with respect to the two moral orientations. In our present research we have included the question, "What is at stake for you in the conflict?" to encourage subjects to reveal where they see themselves in the dilemmas they describe and how they align themselves with different perspectives on the problem.

The promise of our approach to moral development in terms of moral orientation lies in its potential to transform debate over cultural and sex differences in moral reasoning into serious questions about moral perspectives that are open to empirical study. If moral maturity consists of the ability to sustain concerns about justice and care, and if the focus phenomenon indicates a tendency to lose sight of one set of concerns, then the encounter with orientation difference can tend to offset errors in moral perception.

REFERENCES

Baumrind, D. "Sex Differences in Moral Reasoning: Response to Walker's (1984) Conclusions that there are None." *Child Development,* 57 (1986) 511–521.

Gilligan, C. "In a Different Voice: Women's conceptions of the Self and Morality." *Harvard Educational Review,* 47 (1977) 481–517.

Gilligan, C., Langdale, S., Lyons, N., & Murphy, J. *The Contribution of Women's Thought to Developmental Theory: The Elimination of Sex Bias in Moral Development Research and Education.* Final Report to the National Institute of Education. Cambridge, Mass.: Harvard University Press (1982).

Gilligan, C. & Murphy, J. "Development from Adolescence to Adulthood: The Philosopher and the Dilemma of the Fact." In D. Kuhn, ed., *New Directions in Child Development: Intellectual Development Beyond Childhood, 5.* San Francisco: Jossey-Bass (1979) 85–99.

Haan, N. "Gender Differences in Moral Development." Paper presented at the American Psychological Association meetings, Los Angeles (1985).

Kohlberg, L. "Stage and Sequence: The Cognitive Developmental Approach to Socialization." In D. Goslin, ed., *The Handbook of Socialization Theory and Research.* Chicago: Rand McNally (1969) 347–480.

Kohlberg, L. *The Philosophy of Moral Development: Moral Stages and the Idea of Justice: Essays on Moral Development, 1.* San Francisco: Harper and Row (1981).

Kohlberg, L. *The Psychology of Moral Development: Essays on Moral Development, 2.* San Francisco: Harper and Row (1984).

Kohlberg, L. & Kramer, R. "Continuities and Discontinuities in Childhood and Adult Moral Development." *Human Development,* 12 (1969) 93–120.

Langdale, S. "Moral Orientations and Moral Development: The Analysis of Care and Justice Reasoning across Different Dilemmas in Females and Males from Childhood through Adulthood." Doctoral dissertation, Harvard Graduate School of Education (1983).

Lyons, N. "Two Perspectives: On Self, Relationships and Morality." *Harvard Educational Review,* 53(2) (1983) 125–145.

Piaget, J. *The Moral Judgment of the Child (1932).* New York: Free Press (1965).

Walker, L. "Sex Differences in the Development of Moral Reasoning: A Critical Review." *Child Development,* 55 (1984) 677–691.

PART EIGHT

IDENTITY DEVELOPMENT

*And of all these facts and feelings the strongest of all was the need to
be known for her true self and recognized.*
—Carson McCullers, *The Member of the Wedding*

Adolescence is the period in the human life cycle during which the definition
and redefinition of a person's identity becomes a primary developmental task.
Although identity formation may remain a lifelong endeavor, for many the
search for a "true self" becomes dominant during adolescence. The current
emphasis on identity has been stimulated by Erikson (23) whose description of
this stage has inspired a diverse and rich body of research. Notable among
those who have expanded Erikson's theory is Marcia, who refined "identity
versus role diffusion" into four distinct statuses, and Phinney (25), who focused on the application of identity theory to minority youth.

Social changes have impacted on education, gender roles, and family problems. In addition, postmodernistic approaches to morals and values have made
establishing a personal identity more of a challenge. Eventually, the adolescent
must define his or her own roles, values, beliefs, and goals, a process Erikson
defines as "identity formation." By trying various options, the individual actively engages in a process of self-exploration, thus providing the potential for
growth and psychosocial maturity, but the risk of derailment and identity diffusion is also present.

Erikson (23) identified eight developmental crises that range from "trust vs.
mistrust" during infancy to the final stage, "integrity vs. despair." Erikson postulated that during the second decade of life, an individual is confronted with
personal and social issues regarding future directions and goals which must be
resolved. "Each youth must forge for himself [herself] some central perspective
and direction, some working unity, out of the effective remnants of childhood
and the hopes of the anticipated adulthood." Failure to get involved in that

process may contribute to *identity diffusion,* characterized by a lack of direction and goals and a feeling of confusion.

Erikson was concerned with the competitive, success-oriented qualities of Western societies; these pressures have intensified since he made his observations. He maintained that adolescents need a period of time for uncommitted experimenting with a variety of personal, vocational, and social roles, a process referred to as *psychological moratorium,* or in the vernacular, "playing the field."

Erikson's theory identifies the main issue of adolescence as "identity vs. role diffusion." However, Marcia, as presented in summary review by Muuss (24), has expanded this model and describes four statuses defined as (1) "identity diffusion," (2) "foreclosure," (3) "moratorium," and (4) "identity achievement." Each is defined by two variables: the degree to which an individual has experienced an identity crisis and the degree to which an individual has made a commitment to a system of values.

The hallmark of a person who is identity diffused is the lack of goal orientation, direction, and commitment. The individual may mention some vague interest in a future career but demonstrates no real understanding of the advantages and disadvantages of a particular occupation. Personal goals are subject to frequent change. Lewis Carroll's *Alice in Wonderland* provides a most fitting illustration of identity diffusion: " 'Who are you?' said the caterpillar. Alice replied rather shyly, '—I—I hardly know, sir, just at present—at least I knew who I was when I got up this morning, but I must have changed several times since then.' " Even though foreclosure individuals have not actively explored identity issues, they show evidence of a commitment to a system of values; these goals are accepted ready made without questioning from others (most commonly from parents). The moratorium adolescent is actively involved in a process of exploration and experimentation with value systems, beliefs, and vocational and sex roles. Unable to make a permanent commitment, they are probers and critics who tend to challenge authority and question the system. Adolescents emerge as identity-achieved after they have successfully resolved the moratorium issues and made a commitment to political, religious, vocational, and sexual values and goals. The result is increasing ego strength and self-acceptance; thus, they are ready to enter Erikson's next stage, "intimacy vs. isolation."

Phinney (25) applied Marcia's paradigm to explore the relationship between ethnicity and self-concept and found that identity formation is an essential process in understanding both self-esteem and adjustment among minority youth. Earlier models of ethnic identity projected an internalized negative view of own-group perceptions among minority children. Phinney's work refutes that and indicates that African-Americans in the diffusion/foreclosure stage do not necessarily hold negative attitudes about their ethnicity or others in their ethnic group. Apparently, living in a predominantly white society creates the additional need for minority youth to deal with their identity as a member of an ethnic group. White people have been referred to by sociologists as the "unmarked marker." Majority whites are under less pressure to deal with their ethnicity because it rarely creates a personal conflict; in that sense, they are "unmarked" by their culture. However, as members of the majority culture, they create many of the accepted standards; therefore, in that sense, they are the "markers." Phinney found that "an achieved ethnic identity was significantly related to positive self-esteem" in minority children who had actively explored ethnicity issues and as a result reached identity achievement. Emerging through the active exploration of self-identity, especially ethnicity issues, minority youth know who they are, know their own past, and accept and take pride in their own culture.

Developing an identity is a personal, complex, and demanding obligation. In their search to find themselves, individuals may range from those who have formed an identity and those who are still exploring to those who have not yet begun the search for the "true self."

YOUTH AND THE LIFE CYCLE

ERIK H. ERIKSON
Harvard University

Question: Are there any points about your concepts of psychosocial development which you would now like to stress in the light of what you have heard about how they have been interpreted during the past decade in the training of professional persons and through them of parents and future parents?

Yes, I am grateful for the opportunity of making a few observations on the reception of these concepts. You emphasize their influence on teaching in various fields; let me pick out a few misunderstandings.

I should confess to you here how it all started. It was on a drive in the countryside with Mrs. Erikson that I became a bit expansive, telling her about a kind of ground plan in the human life cycle, which I seemed to discern in life histories. After a while she began to write, urging me just to go on; she had found my "plan" immediately convincing. Afterwards, a number of audiences of different professional backgrounds had that same sense of conviction—so much so that I (and others) became somewhat uneasy: after all, these psychosocial signposts are hardly *concepts* yet, even if the whole plan represents a valid *conception,* one which suggests a great deal of work.

From *Children* (now *Children Today*), March–April 1960, *7,* 43–49. Reprinted by permission of the author and The Children's Bureau, U.S. Department of Health, Education, and Welfare.

What Mrs. Erikson and I subsequently offered to the White House conference of 1950 was a kind of worksheet, which has, indeed, been used by others as well as myself in scientific investigation, and well integrated in a few textbooks.[3] But its "convincingness" has also led to oversimplification. Let me tell you about a few.

There has been a tendency here and there to turn the eight stages into a sort of rosary of achievement, a device for counting the fruits of each stage—trust, autonomy, initiative, and so forth—as though each were achieved as a permanent trait. People of this bent are apt to leave out the negative counterparts of each stage, as if the healthy personality had permanently conquered these hazards. The fact is that the healthy personality must reconquer them continuously in the same way that the body's metabolism resists decay. All that we learn are certain fundamental means and mechanisms for retaining and regaining mastery. Life is a sequence not only of developmental but also of accidental crises. It is hardest to take when both types of crisis coincide.

In each crisis, under favorable conditions, the positive is likely to outbalance the negative, and each reintegration builds strength for the next crisis. But the negative is always with us to some degree in the form of a measure of infantile anxiety, fear of abandonment—a residue of immaturity carried throughout life, which is perhaps the price man has to pay for a childhood long enough to permit him to be the learning and the teaching animal, and thus to achieve his particular mastery of reality.

You may be interested to know that further clinical research has indicated that our dream life often depicts a recovery of mastery along the lines of these stages. Moreover, nurses have observed that any adult who undergoes serious surgery has to repeat the battle with these nemeses in the process of recovery. A person moves up and down the scale of maturity, but if his ego has gained a positive balance during his developmental crises the downward movements will be less devastating than if the balance, at one stage or another, was in the negative.

Of all the positive aspects mentioned, trust seems to have been the most convincing—so convincing, in fact, that some discussions never reach a consideration of the other stages. I don't mean to detract from the obvious importance of trust as the foundation of the development of a healthy personality. A basic sense of trust in living as such, developed in infancy through the reciprocal relationship of child and mother, is essential to winning the positive fruits of all the succeeding crises in the life cycle: maybe this is what Christmas, with its Madonna images, conveys to us. Yet, it is the nature of human life that each succeeding crisis takes place within a widened social radius where an ever-larger number of significant persons have a bearing on the outcome. There is in childhood, first, the maternal person, then the parental combination, then the basic family and other instructing adults. Youth demands "confirmation" from strangers who hold to a design of life; and later, the adult needs challenges from mates and partners, and even from his growing children and expanding works, in order to continue to grow himself. And all of these relationships must be imbedded in an "ethos," a cultural order, to guide the individual's course.

In our one-family culture (supported by pediatricians and psychiatrists who exclusively emphasize the mother-child relationship) we tend to lose sight of the fact that other people besides parents are important to youth. Too often we ask only where a given youth came from and what he once was, and not also where he was going, and who was ready to receive him and his intentions and his specific gifts. Thus we have movements to punish parents for the transgressions of their children, ignoring all the other persons and environmental factors that entered into the production of a young person's unacceptable behavior and failed to offer support to his positive search.

Another way in which the life cycle theory has been oversimplified is in the omission of stages which do not fit into the preconceived ideas of the person who is adopting or adapting the theory. Thus a large organization devoted to parenthood distributed a list of the stages but omitted *integrity vs. despair*—the problem of senescence. This is too easy a way to dispose of grandparents; it robs life of an inescapable final step; and, of course, it defeats this whole conception of an intrinsic order in the life cycle.

This kind of omission ignores the "cogwheeling" of infantile and adult stages—the fact that each further stage of growth in a given individual is not only dependent upon the relatively successful completion of his own previous stages, but also on the completion of the subsequent stages in those other individuals with whom he interacts and whom he accepts as models.

Finally, I should point to the fact that what my psychoanalytic colleagues warned me of most energetically has, on occasion, come to pass: even sincere workers have chosen to ignore my emphasis on the intrinsic relation of the psychosocial to the psychosexual stages which form the basis of much of Freud's work.

All of these misuses, however, may be to a large extent the fault of my choice of words. The use of simple, familiar words like "trust" and "mistrust" apparently leads people to assume that they know "by feel" what the theory is all about. Perhaps this semantic problem would have been avoided if I had used Latin terms, which call for definitions.

I may point out, however, that I originally suggested my terms as a basis for discussion—discussions led by people who have an idea of the interrelatedness of all aspects of human development. For the eight stages of psychosocial development are, in fact, inextricably entwined in and derived from the various stages of psychosexual development that were described by Freud, as well as from the child's stages of physical, motor, and cognitive development. Each type of development affects the other and is affected by it. Thus, I feel that discussants would do well to study each key word in its origins, in its usage in various periods and regions, and in other languages. Simple words that touch upon universal human values have their counterpart in every living language, and can become vehicles of understanding at international conferences.

Incidentally, I made up one new word because I thought it was needed. To me, "generativity" described the chief characteristic of the mature adult. It was turned into a comfortable, if inaccurate, homespun word before it ever left the Fact-Finding Committee of 1950. I had deliberately chosen "generativity" rather than "parenthood," or "creativity," because these narrowed the matter down to a biological and an artistic issue instead of describing the deep absorption in guiding the young or in helping to create a new world for the young, which is a mark of maturity in parents and nonparents, working people and "creative" people alike.

Enough of this fault-finding! But it *is* interesting to see what can happen to new ideas; and you *did* ask me.

• • •

THE EIGHT STAGES IN THE LIFE CYCLE OF MAN

"Personality," Erikson has written, "can be said to develop according to steps predetermined in the human organism's readiness to be driven toward, to be aware of, and to interact with a widening social radius, beginning with a dim image of a mother and ending with an image of

mankind. . . ." Following are the steps he has identified in man's psychosocial development, and the special crises they bring. In presenting them, he has emphasized that while the struggle between the negatives and positives in each crisis must be fought through successfully if the next developmental stage is to be reached, no victory is completely or forever won.

I. Infancy: Trust vs. Mistrust

The first "task" of the infant is to develop "the cornerstone of a healthy personality," a basic sense of trust—in himself and in his environment. This comes from a feeling of inner goodness derived from "the mutual regulation of his receptive capacities with the maternal techniques of provision"[2]—a quality of care that transmits a sense of trustworthiness and meaning. The danger, most acute in the second half of the first year, is that discontinuities in care may increase a natural sense of loss, as the child gradually recognizes his separateness from his mother, to a basic sense of mistrust that may last through life.

II. Early Childhood: Autonomy vs. Shame and Doubt

With muscular maturation the child experiments with holding on and letting go and begins to attach enormous value to his autonomous will. The danger here is the development of a deep sense of shame and doubt if he is deprived of the opportunity to learn to develop his will as he learns his "duty," and therefore learns to expect defeat in any battle of wills with those who are bigger and stronger.

III. Play Age: Initiative vs. Guilt

In this stage the child's imagination is greatly expanded because of his increased ability to move around freely and to communicate. It is an age of intrusive activity, avid curiosity, and consuming fantasies which lead to feelings of guilt and anxiety. It is also the stage of the establishment of conscience. If this tendency to feel guilty is "overburdened by all-too-eager adults" the child may develop a deep-seated conviction that he is essentially bad, with a resultant stifling of initiative or a conversion of his moralism to vindictiveness.

IV. School Age: Industry vs. Inferiority

The long period of sexual latency before puberty is the age when the child wants to learn how to do and make things with others. In learning to accept instruction and to win recognition by producing "things" he opens the way for the capacity of work enjoyment. The danger in this period is the development of a sense of inadequacy and inferiority in a child who does not receive recognition for his efforts.

V. Adolescence: Identity vs. Identity Diffusion

The physiological revolution that comes with puberty—rapid body growth and sexual maturity—forces the young person to question "all sameness and continuities relied on earlier" and to "refight many of the earlier battles." The developmental task is to integrate childhood identifications "with the basic biological drives, native endowment, and the opportunities offered in social roles." The danger is that identity diffusion, temporarily unavoidable in this period of physical and psychological upheaval, may result in a permanent inability to "take hold" or, because of youth's tendency to total commitment, in the fixation in the young person of a negative identity, a devoted attempt to become what parents, class, or community do not want him to be.

VI. Young Adulthood: Intimacy vs. Isolation

Only as a young person begins to feel more secure in his identity is he able to establish intimacy with himself (with his inner life) and with others, both in friendships and eventually in a love-based mutually satisfying sexual relationship with a member of the opposite sex. A person who cannot enter wholly into an intimate relationship because of the fear of losing his identity may develop a deep sense of isolation.

VII. Adulthood: Generativity vs. Self-Absorption

Out of the intimacies of adulthood grows generativity—the mature person's interest in establishing and guiding the next generation. The lack of this results in self-absorption and frequently in a "pervading sense of stagnation and interpersonal impoverishment."

VIII. Senescence: Integrity vs. Disgust

The person who has achieved a satisfying intimacy with other human beings and who has adapted to the triumphs and disappointments of his generative activities as parent and coworker reaches the end of life with a certain ego integrity—an acceptance of his own responsibility for what his life is and was and of its place in the flow of history. Without this "accrued ego integration" there is despair, usually marked by a display of displeasure and disgust.

• • •

Question: During the past 10 years you have been treating and studying mentally ill young people at a public clinic in a low-income area in Pittsburgh and at a private, comparatively expensive, mental hospital in the Berkshires. Have you found any common denominator in the disturbances of these patients—from such opposite walks of life—that would seem to point to any special difficulty harassing the young people of our land today?

Since 1950, I have concentrated on the life histories of sick young people in late adolescence and early adulthood primarily in order to study one of the crises magnified, as it were, with the clinical microscope. I think that our initial formulations of the identity crisis have been clinically validated and much refined.[4]

Many of these sick young people in their late teens and early twenties had failed during their adolescence to win out in the struggle against identity confusion. They were suffering so seriously from a feeling of being (or, indeed, wanting to be) "nobody" that they were withdrawing from reality, and in some cases even attempting to withdraw from life itself: in other words, they were regressing to a position where trust had to be reinstated. Their malaise proved to be related to the same sense of diffuseness which drives other young adults to incessant and sometimes delinquent activity—an effort to show the world, including themselves, that they are "somebody" even if deep down they do not believe it.

In the meantime, of course, the identity issue has been taken up by many writers and by some magazines, almost in the form of a slogan. We are prone to think that we have cornered an issue when we have found a name for it, and to have resolved it when we have found something to blame. So now we blame "the changing world."

Actually, there is no reason why youth should not participate with enthusiasm in radical change; young people are freer for change than we are. The bewildering thing for them must be that we now complain about change, having eagerly caused it ourselves with inventions and discoveries; that we seem to have played at change rather than to have planned it. If we had the courage of our inventions, if we would grow into the world we have helped to create, and would give youth co-responsibility in it, I think that all the potential power of the identity crisis would serve a better world than we can now envisage.

Let me say a word about identity, or rather about what it is not. The young person seeking an identity does not go around saying, even to himself, "Who am I?" as an editorial in a national magazine suggested last year's college graduates were doing on their way home. Nor does the person with a secure sense of identity usually stop to think or to brag about the fact that he has this priceless possession, and of what it consists. He simply feels and acts predominantly in tune with himself, his capacities, and

his opportunities; and he has the inner means and finds the outer ways to recover from experiences which impair this feeling. He knows where he fits (or knowingly prefers not to fit) into present conditions and developments.

This sense of a coincidence between inner resources, traditional values, and opportunities of action is derived from a fusion of slowly grown, unconscious personality processes—and contemporary social forces. It has its earliest beginning in the infant's first feelings of affirmation by maternal recognition and is nurtured on the quality and consistency of the parental style of upbringing. Thus identity is in a sense an outgrowth of all the earlier stages; but the crucial period for its development to maturity comes with the adolescent crisis.

Every adolescent is apt to go through some serious struggle at one time or another. The crises of earlier stages may return in some form as he seeks to free himself from the alignments of childhood because of both his own eagerness for adulthood and the pressures of society. For a while he may distrust what he once trusted implicitly; may be ashamed of his body, and doubtful of his future. He experiments, looking for affirmation and recognition from his friends and from the adults who mean most to him. Unconsciously, he revamps his repertory of childhood identifications, reviving some and repudiating others. He goes in for extremes—total commitments and total repudiations. His struggle is to make sense out of what has gone before in relation to what he now perceives the world to be, in an effort to find a persistent sameness in himself and a persistent sharing of some kind of essential character with others.

Far from considering this process to be a kind of maturational malaise, a morbid egocentricity of which adolescents must be "cured," we must recognize in it the search for new values, the willingness to serve loyalties which prove to be "true" (in any number of spiritual, scientific, technical, political, philosophical, and personal meanings of "truth") and thus a prime force in cultural rejuvenation.

The strengths a young person finds in adults at this time—their willingness to let him experiment, their eagerness to confirm him at his best, their consistency in correcting his excesses, and the guidance they give him—will codetermine whether or not he eventually makes order out of necessary inner confusion and applies himself to the correction of disordered conditions. He needs freedom to choose, but not so much freedom that he cannot, in fact, make a choice.

In some adolescents, in some cultures, in some historical epochs this crisis is minimal; in others it holds real perils for both the individual and society. Some individuals, particularly those with a weak preparation in their preceding developmental crises, succumb to it with the formation of neuroses and psychoses. Others try to resolve it through adherence—often temporary—to radical kinds of religious, political, artistic, or criminal ideologies.

A few fight the battle alone and, after a prolonged period of agony characterized by erratic mood swings and unpredictable and apparently dangerous behavior, become the spokesmen of new directions. Their sense of impending danger forces them to mobilize their capacities to new ways of thinking and doing which have meaning, at the same time, for themselves and their times. In my book "Young Man Luther"[5] I have tried to show how identity is related to ideology and how the identity struggle of one intense young genius produced a new person, a new faith, a new kind of man, and a new era.

I think I chose to write about Luther and his time because there are many analogies between our time and his, although today the problems which beset all historical crises are global and, as it were, semifinal in character. Today, throughout the world, the increasing pace of technological change has encroached upon traditional group solidarities and on their ability to transmit a sense of cosmic wholeness and technological planfulness to the young.

To me one of the most disturbing aspects of our technological culture is the imbalance between passive stimulation and active outlet in the pleasures that are sanctioned for young people. With the passing of the western frontier and the accelerated appearance of automatic gadgets, young people have become increasingly occupied with passive pursuits which require little participation of mind or body—being conveyed rapidly through space by machines and watching violent fantasies at the movies or on television—without the possibility of matching the passive experience with active pursuits. When an adolescent substitutes passivity for the adventure and activity which his muscular development and sexual drives require, there is always the danger of explosion—and I think that this accounts for much of the explosive, unexpected, and delinquent acts on the part of even our "nice" young people.

This is probably why "Westerns," always on the borderline of the criminal and the lawful, capture the passive imagination of a youth which has traditionally substituted identification with the rugged individualist—the pioneer who ventures into the unknown—for commitment to a political ideology; and which now finds itself confronted with increasing demands for standardization, uniformity, and conformity to the rituals of a status-convention. While the national prototype has historically been based on readiness for change, the range of possibilities of what one might choose to be and of opportunities to make a change have narrowed. To this has been added most recently the rude shaking of the once "eternal" image of our Nation's superiority in productivity and technical ingenuity through the appearance of Sputnik and its successors.

Thus one might say the complexity of the adolescent state and the confusion of the times meet head on.

However, I believe that the "confusion" derives from a hypocritical denial of our true position, both in regard to obvious dangers and true resources. When youth is permitted to see its place in a crisis, it will, out of its very inner dangers, gain the strength to meet the demands of the time.

Clinical experience with young people has, it is true, verified that combination of inner and outer dangers which explains aggravated identity crises. On the other hand, it has convinced me and my colleagues, even in hospital work, of the surprising resources which young people can muster if their social responsibilities are called upon in a total environment of psychological understanding.

Question: Does this kind of confusion have anything to do with juvenile delinquency?

I would not want to add here to the many claims concerning distinct and isolated causes of juvenile delinquency. But I would like to stress one contributing factor: the confused attitudes of adults—both laymen and professionals—towards the young people whom we, with a mixture of condescension and fear, call teenagers.

Except perhaps in some rare instances of congenital defects resulting in a low capacity to comprehend values, juvenile delinquents are made, not born; and we adults make them. Here, I am not referring to their parents exclusively. True, many parents, because of their own personalities and backgrounds, are not able to give their children a chance for a favorable resolution of the identity crisis. Nor am I referring to the failure of society at large to correct those blights on the social scene—such as overcrowded slums and inequality of opportunities for minority groups—which make it impossible for tens of thousands of young people to envisage an identity in line with the prevailing success-and-status ideology.

Rather I am referring to the attitudes of adults—in the press, in court, and in some professional and social institutions—which push the delinquent young person into a "negative identity," a prideful and stubborn acceptance of himself as a juvenile delinquent—and this at a time when his experimentation with available roles will make him exquisitely vulnerable (although he may not admit or even know it) to the opinions of the representatives of society. When a young person is adjudicated as a potential criminal because he has taken a girl for a ride in somebody else's car (which he intended to aban-

don, not to appropriate), he may well decide, half consciously, of course, but none the less with finality, that to have any real identity at all he must be what he obviously *can* be—a delinquent. The scolding of young people in public for the indiscretions they have committed, with the expectation that they show remorse, often ignores all the factors in their histories that force them into a delinquent kind of experimentation. It is certainly no help toward a positive identity formation.

In his insistence on holding on to an active identity, even if it is temporarily a "negative" one from the point of view of society, the delinquent is sometimes potentially healthier than the young person who withdraws into a neurotic or a psychotic state. Some delinquents, perhaps, in their determination to be themselves at all costs and under terrible conditions have more strength and a greater potential for contributing to the richness of the national life than do many excessively conforming or neurotically defeatist members of their generation, who have given up youth's prerogatives to dream and to dare. We must study this problem until we can overcome the kind of outraged bewilderment which makes the adult world seem untrustworthy to youth and hence may seem to justify the choice of a delinquent identity.

Actually, transitory delinquency, as well as other forms of antisocial or asocial behavior, often may be what I have called a *psychosocial moratorium*[4]—a period of delay in the assumption of adult commitment. Some youths need a period of relaxed expectations, of guidance to the various possibilities for positive identification through opportunities to participate in adult work, or even of introspection and experimentation—none of which can be replaced by either moralistic punishment or condescending forgiveness.

Question: The theme of the 1960 White House Conference on Children and Youth charges the Conference with studying and understanding "the values and ideals of our society" in its efforts "to promote opportunities for children and youth to realize their full potential for a creative life in freedom and dignity." . . . Could you add a word about how these values, once identified, can be transmitted in a way that will insure their incorporation into the value systems of the young?

Like every aspect of maturity the virtues which we expect in a civilized human being grow in stages as the child develops from an infant to an adult. What is expected of a child at any time must be related to his total maturation and level of ego-strength, which are related to his motor, cognitive, psychosexual, and psychosocial stages. You can't expect total obedience from a 2-year-old who must test a growing sense of autonomy, nor total truth from a 4-year-old involved in the creative but often guilt-ridden fantasies of the oedipal stage.

It would be in line with the course of other historical crises if in our Nation today a certain sense of moral weakness were producing a kind of frantic wish to enforce moral strength in our youth with punitive or purely exhortative measures.

Today, a sense of crisis has been aggravated by the long cold war and the sudden revelation of the technical strength of a supposedly "backward" rival. We are wondering whether we have made our children strong enough for living in such an unpredictably dangerous world. Some people, who suddenly realize that they have not been responsible guardians of all the Nation's young, now wonder whether they should have beaten moral strength into them or preached certain absolute values more adamantly.

No period, however, can afford to go back on its advances in values and in knowledge, and I trust that the . . . White House Conference will find a way to integrate our knowledge of personality development with our national values, necessities, and resources. What we need is not a plan whereby relatively irresponsible adults can enforce morality in their children, but rather national insistence on a more *responsible* morality on the part of adults, paired with an *informed* attitude toward the *development* of moral values in children. Values can only be fostered gradually by adults who have a clear conception of what to expect and what not to expect of the child as, at each stage, he comes to understand new segments of reality and of himself, and who are firm about what they are sure they *may* expect.

It must be admitted that psychiatry has added relatively little to the understanding of morality, except perhaps by delineating the great dangers of moralistic attitudes and measurers which convince the child only of the adult's greater executive power, not of his actual moral power or true superiority. To this whole question, I can, on the basis of my own work, only indicate that the psychosocial stages . . . seem to open up the possibility of studying the way in which in each stage of growth the healthy child's developmental drives dispose him toward a certain set of qualities which are the necessary fundaments of a responsible character: in *infancy,* hope and drive; in *early childhood,* will and control; in the *play age,* purpose and direction; in the *school age,* skill and method; and in *adolescence,* devotion and fidelity. The development of these basic qualities in children, however, depends on the corresponding development in adults of qualities related to: in *young adulthood,* love, work, and affiliation; in *adulthood,* care, parenthood, and production; and in *old age,* "wisdom" and responsible renunciation.

Now I have given you another set of nice words, throwing to the winds my own warning regarding the way they can be misunderstood and misused. Let me point out, therefore, that I consider these basic virtues in line with our advancing psychoanalytic ego-psychology, on the one hand, and with our advancing knowledge of psychosocial evolution, on the other, and that the conception behind this list can only be studied in the context of advancing science. I will discuss this further in a forthcoming publication,[6] but I mention it now because I thought I owed you a reference to the way in which my contribution of 1950 has gradually led me in the direction of the great problem of the anchoring of virtue in human nature as it has evolved in our universe.

We ought to regard the breaking of a child's spirit—by cruel punishment, by senseless spoiling, by persistent hypocrisy—as a sin against humanity. Yet today we have back-to-the-woodshed movements. Last year in the legislature of one of our greatest States a bill was introduced to allow corporal punishment in the public schools and was lauded by part of the press. This gave the Soviets a chance to declare publicly against corporal punishment, implying that they are not sufficiently scared by their own youth to go back on certain considered principles in the rearing of the young. Actually, I think that we stand with the rest of the civilized world on the principle that if adult man reconsiders his moral position in the light of historical fact, and in the light of his most advanced knowledge of human nature, he can afford, in relation to his children, to rely on a forbearance which step by step will bring the best *out* of them. . . .

REFERENCES

1. Erikson, E. H. *Childhood and society.* New York: W. W. Norton, 1950.
2. ____ . Growth and crises of the "healthy personality." In M. J. E. Senn (Ed.), *Symposium on the healthy personality supplement II; Problems of infancy and childhood.* Josiah Macy, Jr., Foundation, New York, 1950.
3. Stone, L. J., & Church, J. *Childhood and adolescence: A psychology of the growing person.* New York: Random House, 1957.
4. Erikson, E. H. The problem of ego identity. *Journal of American Psychoanalytic Association,* April 1956, **4,** 56–121.
5. ____ . *Young man Luther.* New York: W. W. Norton, 1958.
6. ____ . The roots of virtue. In Sir Julian Huxley (Ed.), *The humanist frame.* New York: Harper & Bros., 1962.

R E A D I N G   2 4

MARCIA'S EXPANSION OF ERIKSON'S THEORY OF IDENTITY FORMATION

ROLF E. MUUSS
Goucher College

Erikson's theory remains in many important ways the starting point for most of contemporary identity research since it provides the foundation for understanding the processes underlying ado-

lescent identity formation, and thus sets the standards against which scholars compare their findings. Much research has emerged that has validated Erikson's psychosocial stages by testing his theoretical assumptions empirically; in addition, this process has generated new ideas and refined old ones. However, it is important to bear in mind that Erikson never endorsed the empirical research intended to explain and validate his theory. By moving into more and more specific and refined substages of Erikson's "Eight Stages of Man," these efforts have tended to trivialize Erikson's theory and tended to fragment "identity formation" into increasingly more specific domains. Current identity formation researchers are becoming increasingly aware of what might have been Erikson's critique: "We have been stretching this construct in a myriad of directions in terms of its definitions, contexts, behavioral expressions, relationship with other components of living" (Archer, 1994: 10).

The early efforts to operationalize Erikson's theory and to develop a structured *Identity Status Interview* to determine identity formation comes from James Marcia. His dissertation "Determination and construct Validity of Ego Identity Status" and the numerous subsequent research studies by him and his followers (Marcia; 1966; 1967; 1968; 1976a; 1976b; Marcia & Friedman, 1970; Marcia, et al., 1993; Schenkel & Marcia, 1972; Toder & Marcia, 1973) constitute such an expansion and elaboration of Erikson's theory and focuses especially on his theoretical construct of the adolescence stage of *identity versus identity confusion.* Marcia identifies various patterns and common issues operating in youths who are exploring the adolescent identity issues. In addition, Marcia's conceptualizations have stimulated others to pursue identity-status research. In part, these scholars have relied on Marcia's interview assessment technique (which, as the most commonly used assessment technique, will become the primary focus in this chapter) and, in part, they have developed alternative ways to measure identity as well as new theoretical constructs for identity-status research.

Marcia's pioneering methodological and empirical contributions to the theory of identity formation are widely recognized. Marcia's conceptualization of identity statuses are assumed to have a "high degree of construct validity and predictive utility" (Archer & Waterman, 1990: 107).

Marcia (et al., 1993) calls for an awareness that theory builders such as Erikson and Blos did not intend developmental issues to be conceptualized as either-or propositions. For example, Marcia has dropped the "versus" from Erikson's original stage labels of his "Eight Stages of Man" in favor of the connecting word "and": Trust and Mistrust, etc. Erikson (1982: 55) actually meant "versus" to express the idea of "complementarity." Marcia argues that Erikson saw the psychosocial stages as a connected series of progression in "forms of relatedness" as well as separation, as an option for males as well as for females. He calls for dialectical language that lets one see the "both . . . and" rather than the "either . . . or" nature of each of the outcomes of the psychosocial stage.

According to Marcia, the criteria for attainment of a mature identity are based on two essential variables that Erikson had already identified: crisis/exploration and commitment.* Crisis/exploration refers to the time during adolescence when the individual actively examines developmental opportunities, identity issues, and questions parentally defined goals and values, and begins to search for personally appropriate alternatives in respect to occupation, goals, values, and beliefs. Commitment pertains to the extent that the individual is personally involved in, and expresses allegiance to, self-chosen aspirations, goals, values, beliefs, and occupation (Berzonsky, 1989; Bilsker & Marcia, 1991; Marcia, 1967). In applying these criteria of the absence or the presence of crisis/exploration as well as that of commitment to Erikson's adolescent stage *identity versus role diffusion,* four identity statuses emerge (Figure 1). They provide the conceptual structure for Marcia's taxonomy of adolescence and represent four distinct modes for conceptualizing the identity issue of adolescence. (Marcia, 1980).

---

*In order to avoid the negative connotations of the term *crisis*, the synonym *opportunity* should be considered; the recent literature also substitutes the term *exploration.*

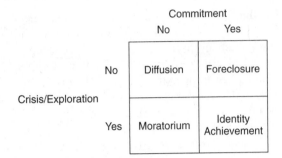

FIGURE 1   Marcia's Four Identity Statuses.

1. The *identity-diffused* or *identity-confused subject* has not yet experienced an identity crisis or exploration nor made any personal commitment to a vocation or a set of beliefs. Identity issues have not yet been a significant issue, or if they ever did become an issue, they were never resolved.

2. The *foreclosure subject* has not yet experienced an identity crisis/exploration but has made definite commitments to goals, values, and beliefs. These commitments emerge from both an identification with parents or significant others and from socialization efforts, pressures, and indoctrination of parents and others. The motivation leading to a foreclosed commitment usually is a reciprocal one. However, the commitments that emerge—in contrast to the commitments of identity achievement—are not the result of any truly personal searching and exploring. In other words, foreclosed commitments are accepted without working (and suffering) through the fundamental existential questions and choices.

3. The *moratorium subject* is in an acute state of crisis/exploration and is actively searching for values to eventually call his or her own. In other words, the moratorium subject is actively struggling to define personal identity by experimenting with alternative roles and beliefs but has not yet made a commitment, or has developed only very temporary tentative kinds of commitments.

4. The *identity-achieved subject* has gone through the process of exploration/crisis but has resolved the identity issues on his or her own terms. As a result of the resolution of these explorations, the individual has made a well-defined personal commitment to an occupation, a religious belief, a personal value system, and has resolved his or her attitude and values toward sexuality.

The specific content areas or decision-making issues that the adolescent is exploring or has made a commitment to are referred to as *domains*. The traditional domains—already identified by Erikson as areas in which adolescents have to make choices—provided the focus for much of the earlier identity research: occupation, ideological views in regard to religious beliefs, and political values. In addition, sex roles and sexuality are significant identity issues for adolescents because reproductively mature sex drive emerges during puberty and makes sexuality an identity issue.

Erikson studied psychosocial development in terms of changes in structure as reflected in the resolution (or lack of resolution) of the developmental tasks posed in each of the stages. The formation of an identity from a structural perspective involves development of overall ego strength; all functions increase as identity develops. In other words, the four identity statuses define the internal structure of the adolescent's ego; however, neither Marcia nor anyone else ever intended them to be used as a rigid typology. Rather than a static entity, each identity status is always an ongoing process. By definition, the *process* by which an individual established a sense of identity is developmental progression through these four stages. The ease or difficulty with which an individual moves (or does not move) through the identity statuses may well be a function, at least in part, of the effectiveness with which the child resolved (or did not resolve) Erikson's four preceding psychosocial stages. To the extent that mistrust, shame and doubt, guilt or inferiority issues linger on into the time of adolescence, a smooth and easy resolution of identity issues is impaired, and some of the adolescent's psychosocial problems (school problems, substance abuse, delinquency, suicide and suicide ideation, sexual promiscuity, etc.) can be understood as the result of developmental deficits from these earlier stages.

Identity statuses may be perceived as a developmental sequence, but no one status is necessarily and inevitably a stepping stone for another, as is the case in Erikson's "Eight Stages of Man." Only the moratorium appears to be an essential and inevitable prerequisite for the achievement of an identity, because an authentic personal identity cannot emerge without the kind of searching and exploring that is the defining characteristic of this stage. Regressive changes from higher to lower statuses in follow-up studies, e.g., from foreclosure or moratorium to identity diffusion, and also from identity achievement to either identity diffusion or moratorium, have been reported in the literature (Adams & Fitch, 1982; Waterman, 1982; Waterman, Geary, & Waterman, 1974) and as one's roles in life change, identity issues may change or reemerge. Apparently, no one has a permanent identity. Marcia introduced the term *status regression* to characterize the return from higher to lower statuses, which is contrary to theoretical exceptions. However, since research has shown that the process of developing an identity actually involves movement back and forth between the stages, this recursive pattern appears to be part of forming and later reestablishing an identity for at least some individuals.

Any one of these identity statuses could become terminal, but the foreclosure subject is in greater danger of closing his or her development than the moratorium subject. However, a basic assumption is that, initially, as children enter into adolescence, they have not yet considered identity issues, hence they are diffuse. Their life goals are still vague, unclear, and undefined. Erikson's postulation of this developmental process from identity diffusion to identity achievement during adolescence is well documented. Identity achievement is, of course, not a terminal status, but always functions as a com-

ponent of the overall progression of Erikson's eight stages. Within that frame of reference, bringing to successful completion the struggle for an authentic identity greatly enhances one's ability to establish a genuine intimate relationship in Erikson's next stage, *intimacy versus isolation,* as Orlofsky (1975) has demonstrated. However, the progression toward the intimacy stage takes place according to the epigenic plan, even though an individual may not have successfully achieved an identity.

Individuals in the process of moving to higher statuses may exhibit some of the characteristics of two or perhaps even three statuses at the same time. For example, a young person may already have developed a goal and a clear commitment to a vocation based on personal choices, while at the same time he or she may still actively search for a personal value system and remain committed to a puritanical attitude toward sex that reflects indoctrination by parents. Marcia found that, as students moved through the four years of college, the proportion of identity-diffused subjects declined significantly while the proportion of identity-achieved subjects increased steadily. This movement toward more mature identity statuses was not a function of college selectivity but of increased psychosocial maturity. This developmental progression from identity diffusion to identity achievement as a function of age and maturity during adolescence is a widely reported research finding. Constantinople (1969: 367) reports "consistent increases in successful resolution of identity, both from the freshman year to senior year across subjects and from one year to the next within subjects." Meilman's (1979) investigations of the age changes in identity status confirmed Erikson's and Marcia's theoretical assumptions. Meilman found that 12-year-olds were identity-diffused (68 percent) or foreclosed (32 percent), but by age 24, the majority (56 percent) had achieved an identity. Even then however, the other statuses were still represented: moratorium, 12 percent; foreclosure, 8 percent; and identity-diffused, surprisingly, 24 percent. Consistent with Meilman's earlier finding, research has repeatedly reported that high school students tend to be predominantly in the foreclosure of the identity statuses (Archer, 1989b). Marcia maintains that the late adolescent years (18 to 21) are the crucial time for identity formation.

Marcia created a semistructured *Identity Status Interview* that he developed as a research tool to assess identity thinking and decision making in the various domains. As such, the interview methodology has contributed in large measure to the understanding of identity formation and has generated much empirical knowledge (Marcia, 1966; 1967; 1968; 1976a; 1976b). The interview is administered individually and designed to sample the subject's commitment to a personal value system and religious and political beliefs, the extent to which the subject has experienced a personal crisis or identity exploration and how he or she has made decisions in regard to any of these. More recent revisions of the interview include more detailed questions to be used as a follow-up for responses that need further exploration. These follow-up questions are designed to unearth and clarify identity issues. Marcia's interview initially covered three core domains: (1) vocational choices, (2) religious beliefs, and (3) political philosophy. When he worked with females, Marcia added two domains: (4) family and career conflict (Marcia & Friedman, 1970), and (5) beliefs about sexual expression (Schenkel & Marcia 1972). Supplemental domains that appear with increasing frequency in the literature and—depending on the purpose of the research—are administered in conjunction with the core domains are: (6) gender role attitudes (Matteson, 1974), (7) avocational interest (Meilman, 1979), (8) relationships with friends and dates (Grotevant & Cooper, 1985), (9) role of spouse (Archer, 1981), (10) role of parent (Archer, 1981), (11) priorities assigned to family and career goals (Marcia & Friedman, 1970), and (12) ethnic identity (Rotheram-Borus, 1989).

IDENTITY DIFFUSION

The identity-diffused individual has no apparent personal commitment to occupation, religion, or politics and has not yet developed a consistent set of personal standards for sexual behavior and, by implication, for any of the goals, values, and choices of the other domains. The diffused subject has not explored identity issues actively nor gone through a genuine struggle in terms of reevaluating, searching, considering, and deciding personal alternatives. Consequently, identity diffusion can encompass a variety of different behavior patterns, from an aimless drifting, to a manipulative selfishness, to a morbid self-preoccupation. Archer and Waterman (1990: 96) actually subdivide the identity-diffused status into "precrisis, apathic, alienated, pathological, marginally involved and commitment-avoiding types." This appears to be one reason why some of the research findings concerned with identity-diffused subjects are not always consistent.

For the child entering adolescence who has not yet been confronted with identity decisions, diffusion appears to emerge due to a precrisis lack of commitment, which, therefore, may be a common experience, perhaps developmentally necessary. Apparently, it is a kind of psychological instability typically experienced by early adolescents, as the data by Meilman (1979) and Archer (1989a, 1989b) convincingly demonstrate. There is also the narcissistic type of identity diffusion. These youths are primarily involved in their own lives, their motto is "to live and let live," and in their selfish approach "use" others for their own advantage and try to get for themselves whatever they can get away with. Apparently suffering from an unresolved ego crisis of Erikson's first stage, *trust versus mistrust,* unable to trust people, they use them. In addition, some identity-diffused subjects avoid anxiety, exploration, and confrontation by means of alcohol or drugs or by otherwise avoiding and/or denying that these issues need to be worked through. Others are alienated from their social, educational, and political world without actively challenging or questioning these institutions. Still other diffused subjects are in a state of psychological fluidity. Uncommitted to a personal system of values, they are open to all kinds of influences. When opportunities arise, they may take advantage of them, often without design or purpose, certainly without any personal commitment. Such individuals may take a "smorgasbord" approach to ideological systems and be most influenced by and overly receptive toward whichever politician or minister they last heard. Diffused college students can become quite vehement in their demand that the professor tell them which of the various theories is best, which is right, or which they should believe. Erikson (1968) maintained that identity diffusion is not the diagnosis of a psychological problem but the description of normal developmental process. Only if it persists over an extended period of time into late adolescence and adulthood could diffusion be considered a pathological condition; the most common diagnostic categories would be: delinquency, schizophrenia, and suicidality.

The classical example of identity diffusion in literature is Shakespeare's Prince Hamlet. He appears confused about his sex role: "Man delights me not, no, nor woman either." He is also estranged from love and procreation: "I say we shall have no more marriage." Finally, Hamlet feels alienated from the ways of his country: ". . . though I am native here, and to the manner born . . ." (Erikson, 1965: 6). In Arthur Miller's *Death of a Salesman,* Biff admits his identity diffusion quite succinctly: "I just can't take hold, Mom, I can't take hold of some kind of life."

FORECLOSURE

Foreclosure status is the most frequently observed identity status during adolescence, and while it declines with increasing age, it remains prevalent even in adulthood. Foreclosure subjects are committed to goals and values, an occupation, and a personal ideology. Consequently, in everyday life they superficially may appear very

much like identity-achieved subjects, with whom they actually share some characteristics. However, foreclosure subjects differ from identity-achieved subjects in that they have not gone through the reflective process of intensive searching and personal exploration. They have never seriously considered other values and other alternatives for themselves. The goals they aim for and the values and beliefs they endorse are those adapted from parents or other "models," such as relatives, media personalities, ministers, or peers. Usually, the choices leading to foreclosure are made relatively early in life. "E.g., ever since I was seven I knew I wanted to be a marine biologist" (Waterman, personal communication). When a young man is asked what he wanted to become, he may answer: "I want to be a dentist: and when asked why, he may respond: "Because my father is a dentist." And even further probing would not change the essence of that response. No personal reason is given, no personal searching seems to have taken place. Foreclosure subjects were "socialized" by or "identified" with their parents, to the extent that parental values rather then personally explored convictions defined their commitment. College serves mainly to reconfirm the childhood value system and to provide an opportunity to attain the individual foreclosed goals rather than as a conscious process to explore vocational options.

The danger is that foreclosure subjects become so solidified in their position and in their attitudes that their identity status becomes terminal, and hence, they do not move easily toward reaching the status of identity achievement. Marcia refers to this phenomenon as "structured foreclosure" as distinguished from the more normal and temporary "developmental foreclosure." There appears to be a certain rigidity in foreclosures' personality structure. If the subjects are not sufficiently challenged to question their preprogrammed assumptions and values, foreclosure may become a permanent part of their personality structure. Waterman (1993) has pointed out that parents, teachers, or friends may effectively influence an individual's life work decisions that actually will bring out the highest potential in that person. Thus, parents may often be quite accurate in assessing their child's needs. (However, authoritarian and/or foreclosed parents may also misjudge their children's needs and exert pressures that reveal their own preferences.) Furthermore, Waterman notes that someone who has found satisfying life work without personal exploration should probably not deliberately disrupt it unless that foreclosure status interferes with the life work and no longer brings fulfillment. If that should happen, then the individual should be encouraged to explore more potentially rewarding possibilities.

Responses from Marcia's interview protocol may illustrate the commitment of foreclosure subjects to parental values. One interviewee commented on his political affiliation with a Republican ideology quite similar to that of his parents: "You still pull that way, Republican, if your parents are that way. You feel like it is where you should be." Another foreclosed adolescent who holds the same religious beliefs as his parents states: "Maybe it's just a habit with me, I don't know. I've thought a lot and you meet all kinds of people here, but I really haven't changed any of my beliefs . . . I plan to bring up my children in the church, just the way dad did with me" (Marcia, 1968: 329).

The foreclosure status is most widely viewed as being shaped through the reciprocal influences of identification processes with, as well as the socialization efforts of, parents. However, the dynamics do not inevitably involve the parents; they could be applied to other potent influential forces, such as a church or the individual's peers. For a certain developmental period, peer group conformity is common, and young adolescents may yield to their family values but lose their budding identity to the peer group. In this situation, foreclosure occurs because the individual's identity submerges too readily and without exploring other alternatives into the roles prescribed for them by others. As a result, adolescents define themselves primarily by their group membership; they act, dress, select food and en-

tertainment, and use language and slang expressions in conformity to peer group standards, expectations, and pressures. Explicit or implicit peer group suggestions may lead to intolerance and even cruelty toward those who behave differently, especially in the junior high school years. When, outside the peer group context, the individual is confronted by parents or teachers with such behavior, he or she may feel ashamed and not understand his or her own cruelty.

The youth group movement of totalitarian systems, such as the Hitler Youth or the Pioneers/Komsomol in Communist Russia, provides such group identity with uniforms, flags, songs, rituals, beliefs, and even heroes as models. A similar vicarious identity is provided by belonging to a gang, a "hood" subculture, a sports team, and other less structured youth groups. Many junior high school students conform rather unquestioningly to the dress and behavior standards of their peer group in order to be accepted, to benefit from the feeling of solidarity with others, and to boost their immature identity through identification with the peer group. In the process, they often overidentify with the peer group, with its heroes and idols, to the extent that they may lose for some time their own personal value system and even the capacity to make independent decisions. According to Keniston, if the "conformity to peer group norms merely replaces conformity to parental norms . . . adolescent development is foreclosed before real self-regulation and independence are achieved" (Keniston, 1971: 377).

The youth group of the totalitarian system may serve as an illustration of political foreclosure, since the youth movement provides the adolescent with a ready-made system of beliefs and even a personal identity that the democratic society does not provide. It is no coincidence that totalitarian systems have large and very active youth groups often with idealistic commitment, while such politically committed youth groups rarely exist in democratic societies. Democratic identity is much harder to attain because it is based on freedom of choice. Rather than supplying a ready-made identity, democratic societies insist on self-made identity. Adolescent imagery, which frequently tends to reduce complex realities to black and white, has an affinity to the totalitarian system, which encourages this kind of absolute dichotomy. The democratic system allows for many different shades of ideological beliefs—and tolerates them all—and therefore provides more ambiguity. It even tolerates totalitarian belief systems, such as the Moonies, Hare Krishna, Koresh's Davidians, Bagwadinians, etc., which cater to the needs of some adolescents for a ready-made value structure. The democratic value structure requires that individuals develop their own ego-identity in order to withstand ambiguity as well as the persuasive arguments of totalitarian ideologies; the problem is that it provides little help to the individual in establishing an identity.

MORATORIUM

The word *moratorium* is defined as a period of delay granted to somebody who is not yet ready to meet an obligation or make a commitment (Erikson, 1968: 157). The moratorium of adolescence is defined as a developmental period during which commitments either have not yet been made or are rather exploratory and temporary. However, applied to identity formation, the concept suggests that there are still many unresolved questions and much ongoing personal exploration. The individual is in an active struggle to find answers, to search, to explore, to try on different roles, and to play the field. In the process of actively pursuing identity concerns, the individual is willing to explore new ideas, new behaviors, and to change. This openness to unconventional, even regressive, alternative experiences (e.g., tolerance for unfamiliar ideas and unconventional behavior, fantasy, imagination, artistic creativity, subjectivism, distrust of logic and certainty, etc.) are used in the service of the ego. If such temporary adaptive regression lead to rational evaluation and purposeful selection, these experiences contribute to the achieve-

ment of a constructive synthesis of identity elements. Moratorium subjects, especially moratorium women, have a greater tendency to use "adaptive regressive experiences" in the identity exploration process (Bilsker & Marcia, 1991). Adaptive regression used in the service of ego development involves a temporary withdrawal from reality in order to master a higher-level synthesis.

Erikson and also Margaret Mead (1961) postulate that the adolescent period is a psychological moratorium, or an "as-if period" when individuals can experiment with different roles "as if" they were committed to these roles. However, since it is only an "as-if period," they are not really held fully responsible for errors that they might make in trying out new roles. Moratorium subjects can still change their values and modify their commitments, and they frequently do, in the process gaining new experiences and exploring a variety of new roles. Therefore, the "as-if period" is the delay society grants to youth to try on different roles—like trying on clothes—to see which fits best. It is in this spirit that the moratorium may try out radical political philosophies, nontraditional religious beliefs such as Oriental mysticism or Hare Krishna-belief, or even different vocational activities such as social work or the Peace Corps. The moratorium may try different interpersonal relationships, cohabitation, homosexuality, bisexuality, and heterosexuality. It is in this sense that the moratorium status is considered the adolescent issue *par excellence.*

If, while exploring moratorium issues on an uncommitted basis, adolescents have sufficient opportunities to search, experiment, play the field and try on different roles, experience and absorb the consequences, the chances are very good that they will eventually find themselves. They will develop an identity, and emerge with commitments to politics, religion, a vocational goal, and a more clearly defined sex role and sexual preference. These more permanent commitments, which lead to identity achievement, are frequently much less radical than some of the tentative and exploratory commitments during the moratorium. According to Marcia, moratorium is truly an essential and necessary prerequisite for identity achievement. However, while the adolescent is in the process of trying out different, new, and unconventional attitudes, values, beliefs, and behaviors, the world does not look very stable or predictable and does not appear to be a very desirable place; rather, the youth views the world and the social institutions as badly in need of improvement. Experiencing moratorium issues often creates subjective discomfort. Moratorium subjects are inclined to express their disenchantment by challenging what they see and hear. Their desire is to change government, politics, the church and education, in short, the system. While they are frequently very good diagnosticians and effective critics who can point to limitations, inconsistencies, and imperfections of the "system," moratorium subjects are not equally effective in producing viable, realistic alternatives because to do so requires life-experiences, identity, willingness to compromise, and a more permanent commitment.

Mead, Friedenberg, and Elkind have expressed concern that society's emphasis on rapid success, visible progress toward some goal, and achievement—as symbolized by scout badges, good grades, promotion, honors, recognition, awards, and diplomas—exerts too much pressure on youth. Such pressure deprives them of the opportunity to experience a true moratorium, an "as-if period" without the necessity of accountability.

IDENTITY ACHIEVEMENT

After an individual has experienced a psychological moratorium and has explored identity issues and crises and, as a result, has begun to develop more permanent personal commitments, he or she has achieved an identity. The achievement of a personal identity inevitably contributes to an increment in ego strength. Successful achievement of an identity means that adolescent development comes, at least for the time being, to completion. The progression to young

adulthood, Erikson's *intimacy vs. isolation* stage, will emerge regardless of the successful or unsuccessful resolution of the identity issues, because stage progression is determined both epigenetically and socially. However, the ability to establish genuine intimacy is very much enhanced if an identity was achieved during adolescence (Orlofsky, 1975).

An identity has developed after the individual has seriously and carefully evaluated various alternatives and has considered different options, but has found a personal value structure and made his or her decisions on his or her own terms. In actuality, it is not at all uncommon for such an individual to choose a position that is fairly close to the parents' values; however, unlike the foreclosure subjects, achievers have considered various options, tried more liberal and often even more radical positions, but finally accepted or rejected them on their own terms. This identity formation process contrasts with that of the foreclosure subject, who remains, often by choice, very close to parental values and expectations and willingly accepts the parental ideology without seriously challenging parental beliefs. The achievement of an identity gives the individual an awareness and acceptance of personal continuity with the past and a more stable orientation toward the future. Identity means that the adolescent has found a new synthesis that "will link the past, the present, and the future" (Keniston, 1965: 212). The function of this sense of identity is to create a new outlook toward the self, to provide inner self-sameness and continuity, and to stabilize values and purposes. Once an identity has been achieved, there is an increase in self-acceptance, a stable self-definition, a willingness to make commitments to a vocation, a religion, a political ideology, and also toward intimacy and a personal commitment in an intimate relationship. Orlofsky, Marcia, and Lesser (1973) were able to show that the identity-achieved subjects have by far the greatest capacity for engaging in interpersonal intimacy. Those subjects still at lower levels of identity have a much greater probability of being stereotyped, pseudo-intimate, or even isolated in their intimate relationships. To achieve a mature ego-identity, the individual must overcome both "his irrational rebelliousness as well as his irrational urge to conform" (Keniston 1971: 364).

Stephen, Fraser, and Marcia (1992) maintain, however, that the individual who has achieved an identity will not necessarily—or even likely—remain in that status without changing. Identity achievers can reenter a period of exploration or crisis if the chosen identity element does not work out for some reason or if more appealing alternatives come up that could precipitate a crisis over whether or not to change. This could set off a moratorium-achievement-moratorium-achievement (MAMA) cycle. Even if this does happen, the identity achiever will probably process the new crisis/exploration issues somewhat more constructively than someone just beginning moratorium crisis/exploration, because that person would already have established effective methods of weathering the upheaval. The earlier success at resolving moratorium issues would most likely help the identity achiever to successfully resolve the situation again. If the MAMA cycle becomes too frequent, however, the individual may come to the conclusion that decisions are only temporary. This could lead to rather tenuously formed commitments.

In addition, adult identity achievers sometimes appear to move back even to the identity-diffused status. This happens because the established commitment lost its importance and its vigor over time. A committed love relationship gone sour can create interpersonal and intrapersonal diffusion. Regression to earlier stages may occur if the person experiences "burn out," for example, on the job or for economic or psychological reasons and therefore can no longer remain with the original commitment. The identity diffusion status for persons at mid-life is not a true regression to early adolescence, but may actually be an enactment of Erikson's stage 7 (*generativity versus stagnation*) crisis/exploration. The adult who burns out is not at all like the drifting identity of the early adolescent-diffused subject.

Individuals who have attained an identity feel in harmony with themselves, accept their capacities, and even more important, their limitations. Such an individual realizes "where he fits (or knowingly prefers not to fit)" into social situations in terms of his own personal preferences.

REFERENCES

Adams, G. R., & Fitch, S. A. (1982). Ego state and identity status development: A cross-lag analysis. *Journal of Adolescence, 4,* 163–171.

Archer, S. L. (1981). Ego identity development among early and mid-adolescents. Paper presented at the Eastern Psychological Association, New York.

Archer, S. L. (1989a). Gender differences in identity development: Issues of process, domain and timing. *Journal of Adolescence, 12,* 117–138.

Archer, S. L. (1989b). The status of identity: Reflections on the need for intervention. *Journal of Adolescence, 12,* 345–359.

Archer, S. L. (1994). An overview. In S. L. Archer (Ed.), *Interventions for adolescent identity development.* Thousand Oaks, CA: Sage.

Archer, S. L., & Waterman, A. S. (1990). Varieties of identity diffusions and foreclosures. *Journal of Adolescent Research, 5,* 96–111.

Berzonsky, M. D. (1989). Identity status: Conceptualization and measurement. *Journal of Adolescence, 4,* 268–282.

Bilsker, D., & Marcia, J. (1991). Adaptive regression and ego identity. *Journal of Adolescence, 14,* 75–84.

Constantinople, A. (1969). An Eriksonian measure of personality development in college students. *Developmental Psychology, 1,* 357–372.

Erikson, E. H. (1965). Youth: Fidelity and diversity. In E. H. Erikson, (Ed.), *The challenge of youth.* Garden City, NJ: Doubleday/Anchor.

Erikson, E. H. (1968). *Identity youth and crisis.* New York: Norton.

Erikson, E. H. (1982). *The life cycle completed.* New York: Norton.

Grotevant, H. D. & Cooper, C. R. (1985). Patterns of interaction in family relationships and the development of identity exploration in adolescence. *Child Development, 56,* 415–428.

Keniston, K. (1965). Social change and youth in America. In E. H. Erikson (Ed.), *The challenge of youth.* Garden City, NJ: Doubleday/Anchor.

Keniston, K. (1971). The tasks of adolescence. In *Developmental psychology today.* Del Mar, CA: CRM Books.

Marcia, J. E. (1966). Development and validation of ego-identity status. *Journal of Personality and Social Psychology, 3,* 551–558.

Marcia, J. E. (1967). Ego identity status: Relationship to change in self-esteem, "general maladjustment," and authoritarianism. *Journal of Personality, 35,* 118–133.

Marcia, J. E. (1968). The case history of a construct: Ego identity status. In E. Vinacke (Ed.), *Readings in general psychology.* New York: Van Nostrand Reinhold.

Marcia, J. E. (1976a). Identity six years after: A follow-up study. *Journal of Youth and Adolescence, 5,* 145–160.

Marcia, J. E. (1976b). Studies in ego-identity. Unpublished research monograph, Simon Fraser University.

Marcia, J. E., & Friedman, M. (1970). Ego identity status in college women. *Journal of Personality, 38,* 249–262.

Marcia, J. E., Waterman, A. S., Matteson, D. R., Archer, S. L., & Orlofsky, J. L. (1993). *Ego identity: A handbook for psychosocial research.* New York: Springer.

Matteson, D. R. (1974). Alienation in exploration and commitment: Personality and family correlates of adolescent identity status. Report for the Project of Youth Research. Copenhagen Royal Danish School of Educational Studies, Copenhagen, Denmark.

Mead, M. (1961). The young adult. In E. Ginzberg (Ed.), *Values and ideas of American youth.* New York: Columbia University Press.

Meilman, P. W. (1979). Cross-sectional age changes in ego identity status during adolescence. *Developmental Psychology, 15,* 230–231.

Orlofsky, J. L. (1975). Intimacy status: Relationship to interpersonal perception. *Journal of Youth and Adolescence, 5,* 73–88.

Orlofsky, J. B., Marcia, J. M., & Lesser, I. M. (1973). Ego identity status and the intimate versus isolation crisis of young adulthood. *Journal of Personality and Social Psychology, 27,* 211–219.

Rotheram-Borus, M. J. (1989). Ethnic differences in adolescents' identity status and associated behavior problems. *Journal of Adolescence, 12,* 361–374.

Schenkel, S., & Marcia, J. E. (1972). Attitudes toward premarital intercourse in determining ego identity status in college women. *Journal of Personality, 40,* 472–482.

Stephen, J., Fraser, E., & Marcia, J. E. (1992). Moratorium-achievement (MAMA) cycles in life-span identify development: Value orientations and reasoning system correlates. *Journal of Adolescence, 15,* 283–300.

Toder, N. L., & Marcia, J. E. (1973). Ego identity status and response to conformity pressure in college women. *Journal of Personality and Social Psychology, 26,* 287–294.

Waterman, A. S. (1982). Identity development from adolescence to adulthood: An extension of theory and a review of research. *Developmental Psychology, 18,* 341–358.

Waterman, A. S. (1993). Finding something to do or someone to be: A Eudaimonist perspective on identity formation. In J. Kroger (Ed.), *Discussions on ego identity.* Hillsdale, NJ: Erlbaum.

Waterman, A. S., Geary, P. S., & Waterman, C. K. (1974). A longitudinal study of changes in ego identity status. *Developmental Psychology, 10,* 387–392.

STAGES OF ETHNIC IDENTITY DEVELOPMENT IN MINORITY GROUP ADOLESCENTS

JEAN S. PHINNEY
California State University, Los Angeles

In his seminal book on adolescent identity, Erikson (1968) devoted a chapter to the issue of race and identity. He pointed out the likelihood that members of an "oppressed and exploited minority" (p. 303) may internalize the negative views of the dominant society, thereby developing a negative identity and self-hatred. A related theme has been expressed by social psychologists. Tajfel (1978) has suggested that membership in a disparaged minority group can create psychological conflict; minority group members are faced with a choice of accepting the negative views of society toward their group or rejecting them in a search for their own identity. Many writers, particularly from minority groups, have addressed this complex issue, exploring the impact of ethnic group membership on one's identity (e.g., Arce, 1981; Baldwin, 1979; Gordon, 1976; Gurin & Epps, 1975; Maldonado, 1975; Zinn, 1980). Maldonado (1975) sums up the views of many of these writers in his statement that "ethnic self-identity is . . . central to the development of the personal identity of minority group members" (p. 621).

Although much conceptual writing has concerned ethnic identity in adults, empirical work investigating the role of ethnicity in develop-ment has focused on young children, where the central issue has been the way in which children learn the label for their own group and the attributes of that label (see Aboud, 1987, for a recent review). Beyond childhood, concerns about ethnicity shift from learning one's ethnic label to understanding the significance of one's group membership. Adolescents are faced with a number of changes that affect this understanding, including increased cognitive abilities, more interactions outside their own community, and greater concern with appearance and social life. These factors, contributing to greater awareness of current social issues such as increased immigration, changing demographics, and legal challenges to affirmative action, are likely to make ethnicity salient for minority youth (Gay, 1978), especially at a time when ego identity formation is the central developmental task (Erikson, 1968).

Erikson's (1968) theory of ego identity development, as operationalized by Marcia (1966, 1980), provides a useful starting point for studying ethnic identity in adolescence. Marcia's paradigm describes four identity statuses based on the presence or absence of exploration and commitment. An individual who has neither engaged in exploration nor made a commitment is said to have a diffuse identity; a commitment made without exploration, usually on the basis of parental values, represents a foreclosed status.

Journal of Early Adolescence, May 1989, 9(1–2), 34–49.
© 1989 Sage Publications, Inc. Reprinted by permission of Sage Publications, Inc.

An individual in the process of exploration without having made a commitment is in moratorium; a firm commitment following a period of exploration is indicative of an achieved identity. Although an achieved identity is seen as the most sophisticated identity status, the paradigm does not suggest a necessary developmental progression. Possible pathways for movement from one status to another have been discussed by Waterman (1982).

Several models of ethnic identity (Arce, 1981; Atkinson, Morten, & Sue, 1983; Cross, 1978; Kim, 1981) share with Marcia's (1980) model the idea that an achieved identity is the result of an identity crisis, which involves a period of search or exploration, leading to a clear commitment. However, these ethnic identity models differ from Marcia in suggesting stages that are presumed to show a progression over time. The Cross (1978) model describes progressive changes in the identity of Black college students during the civil rights era. A study based on this model compared past, present and projected future attitudes of Black college students and found that subjects perceived themselves as progressing from lower to more advanced stages of Black identity (Krate, Leventhal, & Silverstein, 1974). In Kim's (1981) study, based on retrospective interviews with adult Japanese-American women, all of the subjects saw themselves as having changed toward more advanced stages. Atkinson, Morten, & Sue (1983) suggested a similar sequence on the basis of clinical experience, and Arce (1981) discussed the process conceptually with regard to Chicanos. There are, however, no developmental studies that provide empirical support for such a progression.

The current study was part of a research program aimed at developing and testing a model of ethnic identity development that is consonant with Marcia's (1980) ego identity statuses, that reflects the stages and issues described in the ethnic identity literature, and that can be applied across several ethnic groups. Because there is little empirical data on ethnic identity development, the first step was to develop from the existing literature descriptive criteria for each stage of ethnic identity development. This description is presented here, as a basis for the study that follows.

Existing models of ethnic identity development suggest that minority group members begin with an acceptance of the values and attitudes of the majority culture, including often internalized negative views of their own group that are held by the majority. In this first stage, "the person's world view is dominated by Euro-American determinants" (Cross, 1978, p. 17). Parham and Helms's (1985) measure of Black identity development, based on Cross's work, included items for this stage, such as "I believe that the White man is superior intellectually" and "Sometimes I wish I belonged to the White race." Similarly, the model suggested by Atkinson, Morten, & Sue (1983) describes a Conformity Stage, in which individuals show an "unequivocal preference for dominant cultural values over those of their own culture" (pp. 35–36). Kim (1981) identified an initial stage in which "subjects . . . internalized the White societal values and standards and saw themselves through the eyes of the White society" (p. 129).

This first stage of minority identity development might be compared to identity foreclosure, as described by Marcia (1980), in that individuals have taken on without question the values and attitudes to which they have been exposed. However, it is not clear that individuals in this stage necessarily have negative views of their own group. Although there is little evidence on this point, it is possible that young adolescents from families that stressed ethnic pride might have adopted positive attitudes toward their own group and therefore would not manifest preference for the majority culture, even though they were foreclosed in the sense of not having examined the issues for themselves.

Alternatively, many young adolescents might simply not have been faced with the issue of ethnicity in their own lives and might therefore have given it little thought. They would be expected to have little to say on the subject and to consider ethnicity of little importance. By analogy with the ego identity model, this would be considered a diffuse ethnic identity; however, this stage has not been identified in the ethnic identity literature.

All of the minority models cited have assumed that a period of exploration into the meaning of one's ethnicity is central to ethnic identity development. It is not clear what initiates this stage. Cross (1978) suggested that it may be precipitated by "a shocking personal or social event that temporarily dislodges the person from his old world-view, making the person receptive to a new interpretation of his identity" (p. 17); this experience he termed "encounter." Others have suggested that the exploration may result from a growing awareness on the part of minorities of the conflict between the values and attitudes of the majority society and a positive view of themselves or their group (Arce, 1981), for example, differing standards of beauty (Kim, 1981) or negative stereotypes (Mendelberg, 1986).

The period of exploration, or moratorium, has been described in the ego identity literature as a time of experimentation and inquiry (Waterman, 1985). For minority youth, the ethnic identity search (the "immersion" stage in Cross, 1978) is characterized by the attempt to clarify the personal implications of their ethnicity (Cross, 1978). For Kim's (1981) subjects, it involved "an effort to better understand themselves and their people" (p. 147). Empirical support for this stage comes from interviews with middle-class Black and White eighth graders in an integrated school (Phinney & Tarver, 1988). About one-third of the Black subjects were engaged in some form of exploration regarding their ethnicity. They expressed interest in learning more about their culture and were actively involved in doing so: They talked with family or friends about ethnic issues, read books on the subject, and had thought about the effects of ethnicity on their life in the present and future. They often expressed awareness of prejudice as a factor that might interfere with their educational or career objectives.

The optimum outcome of the identity process is an achieved identity. Ego identity achievers have resolved questions about their future direction and have made commitments that will guide

future action (Marcia, 1980). In the area of ethnicity, identity achievement corresponds to acceptance and internalization of one's ethnicity. "Following this period of cultural and political consciousness, . . . individuals develop a deeper sense of belonging to the group. . . . When the person finally comes to feel at one with the group, the internalization process has been completed, and ethnic identity established" (Arce, 1981, p. 186). "Tension, emotionality, and defensiveness are replaced by . . . self-confidence about one's Blackness" (Cross, 1978, p. 18). According to Kim (1981), "Self-concept during this stage is positive. Subjects feel good about who they are and feel proud to be Asian American. They also feel comfortable with both parts of themselves (Asian and American)" (p. 150). Across all groups, then, an achieved ethnic identity is characterized by a clear, confident acceptance of oneself as a member of a minority group, replacing the negative self-image discussed by Tajfel (1978).

The stages of ethnic identity development that have been outlined can be summarized as follows:

1. *Diffuse:* Little or no exploration of one's ethnicity and no clear understanding of the issues.
2. *Foreclosed:* Little or no exploration of ethnicity, but apparent clarity about one's own ethnicity. Feelings about one's ethnicity may be either positive or negative, depending on one's socialization experiences.
3. *Moratorium:* Evidence of exploration, accompanied by some confusion about the meaning of one's own ethnicity.
4. *Achieved:* Evidence of exploration, accompanied by a clear, secure understanding and acceptance of one's own ethnicity.

The understanding of ethnic identity is important because it is implicated in the overall adjustment of minority group adolescents. Although research has shown that minority youth do not differ in self-esteem from White youth (e.g., Rosenberg & Simmons, 1971), concern remains that the failure of minority adolescents to deal with their ethnicity could have negative implications, such as poor self-image or a sense of alienation. For example, Ogbu (1987) stated that the dilemma for a Black student is the need to choose between acting Black and acting White. Many Black youth choose an "oppositional identity" (p. 166), seeking to define themselves in contrast to White culture, with implications for engaging in activities not approved by that culture. It seems likely that adolescents who have not examined and resolved issues regarding their ethnicity would be at greater risk for adjustment problems. Phinney and Alipuria (1990) found that an achieved ethnic identity was significantly related to positive self-esteem in college students. Therefore, the relationship of ethnic identity to adjustment was also considered in this study.

In summary, the goals of the current research were, first, to determine whether the stages of ethnic identity development derived from the literature can be reliably applied to adolescents from diverse ethnic backgrounds, that is, whether these stages describe accurately the way such adolescents deal with ethnicity as a component of their identity; second, to determine the relationship of ethnic identity to independent measures of ego identity and adjustment; and third, to examine differences among ethnic groups in the process.

METHOD

Subjects

Participants were 91 American-born tenth graders (ages 15 to 17) from two high schools in the metropolitan Los Angeles area, including 14 Asian Americans (8 males, 6 females), 25 Blacks (10 males, 15 females), 25 Hispanics (14 males, 11 females), and 27 Whites (15 males, 12 females). The Hispanics were of Mexican and Central American origin; the Asian Americans were of Japanese, Chinese, Korean, Vietnamese, and Philippine origin. Only American-born students were included in order to minimize confounding with a foreign identity. Subjects identified themselves as members of one of the four ethnic groups, and reported that both parents were of that same ethnicity. Subjects were from both lower-class ($n = 40$) and middle-class ($n = 51$) backgrounds, as determined by parents' occupation and education. A chi-square analysis revealed no significant association of class with ethnic group.

These subjects were chosen from an original sample of over 500, drawn from two large, ethnically diverse urban high schools in southern California. The ethnic makeup of the student populations was as follows: School A, Asian = 30.7%, Black = 3.4%, Hispanic = 48.6% White = 16.6%, other = 0.6%; School B, Asian = 16.4%, Black = 28.7%, Hispanic = 22.3%, White = 32.1%, other = 0.6%. Participants were all students enrolled in tenth-grade driver education and career planning classes who signed a consent form and obtained a signed parental permission form and who met the criteria of ethnicity and birthplace. The criteria required eliminating large numbers of foreign-born students, students from other groups, those of mixed ethnicity, those who were not tenth graders, and those who failed to complete the survey. At one school an excessively large sample of Hispanics was obtained. About two-thirds of these students were randomly eliminated in order to obtain a more balanced representation of ethnic groups. While in theory it would be helpful in such a study to control for generation of immigration, the numbers of third- and fourth-generation students were so small for some groups as to make the distinction statistically meaningless.

Measures

Interview. The interview was a revised version of the interview used by Phinney and Tarver (1988). It was based on the interviews employed in ego identity research (Archer, 1982; Grotevant & Cooper, 1981; Marcia, 1966) but focused specifically on the topic of ethnicity. The interview consisted of 20 questions assessing the extent of exploration of ethnicity (e.g., "Do you ever talk with your parents or other adults about

your ethnic background or what it means to be
___?"; "Have you ever thought about whether
your ethnic background will make a difference
in your life as an adult?"); the commitment to an
ethnic identity (e.g., "Some people find these
questions about their background pretty confusing and are not sure what they really think about
it, but others are pretty clear about their culture
and what it means to them. Which is true of
you?"); and attitudes about ethnicity ("Are there
things you especially like or enjoy about your
own cultural background, or things you consider
to be strengths of your culture?"). Each item included open-ended follow-up questions to clarify or determine the reasons for the answer.

Questionnaire.   The questionnaire consisted of
four scales from the Bronstein-Cruz Child/Ado-
lescent Self-Concept and Adjustment Scale
(Bronstein et al., 1987): Self-Evaluation, Social
and Peer Relations, Family Relations, and Sense
of Mastery (reported subscale reliabilities, .69 to
.90, $\bar{X} = .84$); and a scale of ego identity adapted
for the present population from an inventory developed by Rosenthal, Gurney, and Moore
(1981). Each item was rated on a four-point
scale from "Not at all true about me" to "Very
true about me." Ratings of items for each scale
are averaged to yield a score between 1 and 4.

Procedures

Participants were interviewed individually by
a research assistant of the same sex and ethnicity
as the student. In a few instances, schedule conflicts and mismarked data sheets necessitated an
interview done by an opposite-sex researcher,
but in all instances ethnicity was the same. Interviews were tape-recorded in full. Following the
interview, the questionnaire was administered to
participants in a group setting.

Coding of Interviews

A coding manual was developed, describing the
expected characteristics of each stage of ethnic

identity development, as derived from the model
discussed previously. Coding of the responses of
White subjects according to the model was found
to be impossible. Except for a few subjects who
emphasized their European origin (e.g., German,
Hungarian), ethnicity was not an identity issue to
which they could relate; that is, they did not think
of themselves has having an ethnicity other than
simply "American." The term tended to be interpreted as referring to minority groups. Therefore,
the White subjects could not be assigned to stages
and are not included in the analyses, except as a
comparison group for the adjustment and ego
identity scores.

For the minority group subjects, three trained
graduate students (one from each of the three
groups) independently coded the tapes, assigning
an ethnic identity stage on the basis of detailed
descriptions of each stage in the manual. Each
tape was coded by two coders. In case of disagreement, a third coder listened to the tape and
assignment to stage was resolved by discussion.
Coders could not reliably distinguish between the
two lowest stages, diffusion and foreclosure, so
these two stages were combined into a single category representing subjects who had not explored
their ethnicity. In four cases (two Black and two
Hispanic subjects), the three coders could not
agree as to stage, and the four subjects were considered unclassifiable. Of the 60 subjects classified, absolute agreement between the initial two
coders was 80.0%. Cohen's kappa, a conservative
measure of agreement between raters that takes
into account chance agreement, was equal to .647.

RESULTS

Stages of Ethnic Identity

Sixty of the 64 minority group subjects were
reliably assigned to one of three stages of ethnic identity: an initial stage in which there has
been no search (diffusion/foreclosure), a moratorium stage, and an achieved ethnic identity.
The percentages of each ethnic group in each
stage are shown in Table 1. Just over one-half of

TABLE 1
Percentage of Subjects in Each Ethnic Identity Stage

	Ethnic Idenity Stage		
	Diff./Fore.	Moratorium	Achieved
Asian American ($n = 14$)	57.1%	21.4%	21.4%
Black ($n = 23$)	56.5	21.7	21.7
Hispanic ($n = 23$)	52.1	26.9	21.7
Total ($N = 60$)	55.7	22.9	21.3

the subjects were at the lowest stage, with a little less than one-quarter at each of the other stages. The proportions were remarkably similar across groups.

Chi-square analyses showed no significant differences in stage assignment by ethnic group, sex, socioeconomic status, or school. A loglinear analysis to assess simultaneously the effects of ethnic group, sex, and socioeconomic status revealed no significant relationships between the ethnic identity stage and these variables.

Because the stages of ethnic identity were developed conceptually (Cross, 1978) or from an unpublished retrospective study (Kim, 1981), there are virtually no descriptive data available on the characteristics of the stages. To convey a sense of these characteristics, Table 2 provides examples of typical statements by subjects in each stage. Although diffusion and foreclosure could not be reliably distinguished, the examples demonstrate the differences between these categories that were suggested by the literature.

Correlates of Ethnic Identity Stage

For each of the adjustment measures and the measure of ego identity, subjects received scores between 1 and 4. Scores for these scales are shown in Table 3 for subjects at each stage, together with the results of analyses of variance of the effect of ethnic identity stage on adjustment and ego identity.

The scores for ego identity showed a consistent increase from the proposed first stage (diffusion/foreclosure) to the third stage, achieved ethnic identity. A one-way analysis of variance by stages revealed a significant difference among these scores, as shown in Table 3. A similar increase across stages was seen in the scores for self-evaluation, sense of mastery, social and peer interactions, and family relations, with significant differences as noted in the table.

There were no significant differences in ego identity or adjustment by ethnic group, sex, or class. A comparison of ego identity and adjustment scores of the three ethnic groups with the scores for the White students revealed no significant differences.

Ethnic Group Differences

The three ethnic groups showed no significant differences as to stage or adjustment. However, some group differences emerged in responses to individual interview items. To assess satisfaction with their own ethnicity, participants were asked whether they would change their group membership if they could. Thirteen subjects (20.3%), not confined to any one stage, said they would change; significantly more Asian Americans (53.3%) said they would prefer to belong to another group (specifically, to be White) than did Blacks (12.0%) or Hispanics (8.7%) ($\chi^2 = 13.7, p < .01$).

Although there were no sex differences in stage, or interactions of sex and stage, there was a trend among the Black subjects. Five females but no males had achieved ethnic identity. Because of the small numbers, this result should be viewed with caution. However, an earlier study with Black eighth graders also found evidence

TABLE 2
Representative Quotations from Each Stage of Ethnic Identity Development

Diffusion

"My past is back there; I have no reason to worry about it. I'm American now." (Mexican-American male)

"Why do I need to learn about who was the first Black woman to do this or that? I'm just not too interested." (Black female)

"My parents tell me . . . about where they lived, but what do I care? I've never lived there." (Mexican-American male)

Foreclosure

"I don't go looking for my culture. I just go by what my parents say and do, and what they tell me to do, the way they are." (Mexican-American male)

Foreclosure (negative)

"If I could have chosen, I would choose to be American White, because it's America and I would then be in my country." (Asian-American male)

"I would choose to be White. They have more job opportunities and are more accepted." (Mexican-American male)

Moratorium

"I want to know what we do and how our culture is different from others. Going to festivals and cultural events helps me to learn more about my own culture and about myself." (Mexican-American female)

"I think people should know what Black people had to go through to get to where we are now." (Black female)

"There are a lot of non-Japanese people around me and it gets pretty confusing to try and decide who I am." (Asian-American male)

Achieved

"People put me down because I'm Mexican, but I don't care anymore. I can accept myself more." (Mexican-American female)

"I have been born Filipino and am born to be Filipino . . . I'm here in America, and people of many different cultures are here too. So I don't consider myself only Filipino, but also American." (Asian-American male)

"I used to want to be White, because I wanted long flowing hair. And I wanted to be real light. I used to think being light was prettier, but now I think there are pretty dark-skinned girls and pretty light-skinned girls. I don't want to be White now. I'm happy being Black." (Black female)

TABLE 3
Identity and Adjustment Scores, by Ethnic Identity Stage

	Diff./Fore. n = 33	Moratorium n = 14	Achieved n = 13	F(2,56)	P
Ego identity	2.7	2.8	3.1	5.49	<.01
Self-evaluation	2.8	3.1	3.2	5.01	<.01
Sense of mastery	2.9	3.0	3.2	3.88	<.05
Social and peer interactions	3.0	3.0	3.3	3.60	<.05
Family relations	2.7	2.9	3.3	6.48	<.01

of more ethnic identity search and commitment among Black females than among Black males (Phinney & Tarver, 1988)

The three groups perceived different issues to be important in the resolution of ethnic identity. For Asian Americans, pressures to achieve academically, together with concerns about quotas that make it more difficult to get into good colleges, were salient issues. They also felt the need to distinguish themselves from recent immigrants. Many Black females discussed struggling with the realization that White standards of beauty (especially hair and skin color) did not apply to them; Black males seemed more concerned with possible job discrimination and the need to distinguish themselves from a negative image of Black adolescents. For Hispanics, prejudice was a recurrent theme; some subjects also commented on conflicting values between their own and the majority culture.

DISCUSSION

The results of this study provide empirical evidence to three stages of ethnic identity development among American-born minority adolescents. Unlike previous research that has focused on a single group, this study examined ethnic identity across three ethnic groups and showed similar numbers of subjects at each stage across groups. It appears that these youth, regardless of the specific group, face a similar need to deal with the fact of their membership in an ethnic minority group in a predominantly White society, as suggested by Tajfel (1978). In contrast, the White students, even in settings where they were in the minority, did not show evidence of these stages and were frequently unaware of their own ethnicity apart from being American. These results imply an ethnocentric view that is out of touch with the increasingly pluralistic nature of society. For example, projections show that by the mid-1990s minority youth will constitute more than 30% of the 15- to 25-year-olds in the country (Wetzel, 1987).

Of the tenth graders from the three ethnic groups, more than one-half were in the initial stage, characterized by lack of exploration of ethnicity as an identity issue. Evidence was found both of ethnic identity diffusion, in which subjects had little concern and few thoughts about the issue, and of foreclosure, in which they expressed views that appeared to be acquired from others. However, there was little evidence of the negative attitudes toward one's own group that has been described in the literature (Cross, 1978). These two stages showed some overlap, and coders could not clearly distinguish between them. These results suggest that for ethnicity there may be only a single stage that precedes the moratorium.

About one-fourth of the subjects showed evidence of involvement in ethnic identity search and could be considered in moratorium in the area of ethnicity. There was no evidence that this stage was initiated by the dramatic type of encounter experience or accompanied by the intensity of feeling described by Cross (1978). Rather, this stage was characterized by an increasing awareness of the importance of the issue and the need to understand it.

Finally, about one-fourth of the subjects revealed the confident sense of self as a minority group member following a search that indicates an achieved ethnic identity. These identity-achieved subjects, together with the moratorium subjects, made up nearly one-half of the sample. This proportion of minority tenth graders who gave evidence of ethnic identity search was somewhat larger than the one-third of Black eighth graders who were engaged in search in an earlier interview study carried out in similar integrated urban schools (Phinney & Tarver, 1988). Although these results cannot be directly compared, as the samples are different, they suggest the possibility that with increased age, high school students will show greater evidence of ethnic identity search. Future research is needed to examine the proportions of students in each stage across a variety of groups and range of ages in order to further define the stages, and determine whether the stages are sequential and if there is a developmental shift toward ethnic identity achievement.

One aspect of the model is of particular relevance to the development of minority children and youth: the suggestion that negative attitudes toward one's own group are typical of the first stage (Cross, 1978; Kim, 1981). In the present study, subjects in the diffusion/foreclosure stage did not necessarily have negative attitudes. Only one-fifth of all the subjects, including some from each stage, had negative own-group attitudes, for example, a desire to change their ethnicity if they could. It is not clear whether this proportion would be higher at younger ages. The literature on young children has indicated that while preference for the dominant culture declines beyond early childhood, some elementary school children still prefer the majority group over their own (Aboud, 1987; Jahoda, Thomson, & Bhatt, 1972). In the present study, the subjects with negative attitudes were mainly Asian-American students. This finding is surprising in view of the generally positive view of Asians in American society. However, interview responses by these students reveal the lack of the sort of social movement stressing ethnic pride that is available to Blacks and Mexican Americans. For example, Asian-American students had trouble naming leading Asian-American personalities who might serve as role models. Generally, their attitudes tended more toward assimilation than toward ethnic pride and pluralism. Further research is needed to clarify the extent of preference for another group beyond childhood and the possible reasons for this preference.

This study also demonstrates parallels between ethnic identity and ego identity. The ethnic identity stages were significantly related to an independent global measure of ego identity achievement not based on ego identity statuses. In addition, the proportions of subjects at each ethnic identity stage were remarkably similar to the proportions of a large sample of tenth graders in the comparable ego identity statuses, in norms presented by Adams, Bennion, and Huh (1987, p. 28), based on a questionnaire measure. These results are suggestive of a link between ethnic identity and ego identity, but further research is needed to clarify the possible connections.

The process of ethnic identity development has clear implications for overall psychological adjustment. Minority group membership per se did not affect adjustment, as scores did not differ among the three minority groups or between their scores and those of their White peers. However, those minority adolescents who had explored and were clear about the meaning of their ethnicity (ethnic identity achieved) showed higher scores on self-evaluation, sense of mastery, social and peer interactions, and family relations, compared to the diffusion and foreclosed adolescents. These results are similar to those obtained by Phinney and Alipuria (1987) with college students. They suggest that the process of ethnic identity development, not minority group membership per se, is a key factor in understanding the self-esteem and adjustment of minority youth.

The sample in the present study was relatively small. This allowed for in-depth interviews to explore the sensitive topic of ethnicity in open-ended question. In order to extend the findings of the present study and to examine the broader applicability of these stages, a questionnaire measure of ethnic identity development is currently being tested. It is hoped that the model and data presented will stimulate further studies of ethnic identity at different ages, with larger samples that include diverse ethnic groups in varied settings.

REFERENCES

Aboud, F. (1987). The development of ethnic self-identification and attitudes. In J. Phinney & M. Rotheram (Eds.), *Children's ethnic socialization: Pluralism and development* (pp. 32–55). Newbury Park, CA: Sage.

Adams, G., Bennion, L., & Huh, K. (1987). *Objective measure of ego identity status: A reference manual.* Logan: Utah State University.

Andrews, M., & Lochner, B. (1989, April). *Ethnic identity issues in White tenth graders.* Paper presented at the annual meeting of the Western Psychological Association, Reno, NV.

Arce, C. (1981). A reconsideration of Chicano culture and identity. *Daedalus, 110*(2), 177–192.

Archer, S. (1982). The lower age boundaries of identity development. *Child Development, 53,* 1551–1556.

Atkinson, D., Morten, G., & Sue, D. (1983). *Counseling American minorities.* Dubuque, IA: Wm. C. Brown.

Baldwin, J. (1979). Theory and research concerning the notion of Black self-hatred. *The Journal of Black Psychology, 5,* 51–77.

Bronstein, P., Cruz, M., Cowels, C., D'Ari, A., Pienadz, J., Franco, O., Duncan, P., & Frankowski, B. (1987, August). *A measure of child and adolescent self-concept and psychological adjustment.* Paper presented at the annual meeting of the American Psychological Association, New York.

Cross, W. (1978). The Thomas and Cross models of psychological nigrescence: A literature review. *Journal of Black Psychology, 4,* 13–31.

Erikson, E. (1968). *Identity: Youth and crisis.* New York: Norton.

Gay, G. (1978). Ethnic identity in early adolescence: Some implications for instructional reform. *Educational Leadership, 35,* 649–655.

Gordon, V. (1976). The methodologies of Black self-concept research: A critique. *Journal of Afro-American Issues, 4,* 373–381.

Grotevant, H., & Cooper, C. (1981). Assessing adolescent identity. Manual for administration and coding of the interviews. *JSAS Catalog of Selected Documents in Psychology,* 11:52 (Ms. No. 2295).

Gurin, P., & Epps, E. (1975). *Black consciousness, identity, and achievement.* New York: Wiley.

Jahoda, G., Thomson, S., & Bhatt, S. (1972). Ethnic identity and preference among Asian immigrant children in Glasgow: A replicated study. *European Journal of Social Psychology, 2,* 19–32.

Kim, J. (1981). *The process of Asian-American identity development: A study of Japanese American women's perceptions of their struggle to achieve positive identities.* Doctoral dissertation, University of Massachusetts.

Krate, R., Leventhal, G., & Silverstein, B. (1974). Self-perceived transformation of Negro-to-Black identity. *Psychological Reports, 35,* 1071–1075.

Maldonado, D., Jr. (1975). Ethnic self-identity and self-understanding. *Social Casework, 56,* 618–622.

Marcia, J. (1966). Development and validation of ego-identity status. *Journal of Personality and Social Psychology, 3,* 551–558.

Marcia, J. (1980). Identity in adolescence. In J. Adelson (Ed.), *Handbook of adolescent psychology* (pp. 159–187). New York: Wiley.

Mendelberg, H. (1986). Identity conflict in Mexican-American adolescents. *Adolescence, 21,* 215–222.

Ogbu, J. (1987). Opportunity structure, cultural boundaries, and literacy. In J. Langer (Ed.), *Language, literacy, and culture: Issues of society and schooling* (pp. 149–177). Norwood, NJ: Ablex.

Parham, T., & Helms, J. (1985). Attitudes of racial identity and self-esteem of black students: An exploratory investigation. *Journal of College Student Personnel, 26,* 143–147.

Phinney, J., & Alipuria, L. (1990). Ethnic identity in college students from four ethnic groups. *Journal of Adolescence, 13,* 171–183.

Phinney, J., & Tarver, S. (1988). Ethnic identity search and commitment in Black and White eighth graders. *Journal of Early Adolescence, 8,* 265–277.

Rosenberg, M., & Simmons, R. (1971). *Black and White self-esteem: The urban school child.* Washington, DC: American Sociological Association.

Rosenthal, D., Gurney, R., & Moore, S. (1981). From trust to intimacy: A new inventory for examining Erikson's stages of psychosocial development. *Journal of Youth and Adolescence, 10,* 525–537.

Tajfel, H. (1978). *The social psychology of minorities.* New York: Minority Rights Group.

Waterman, A. (1982). Identity development from adolescence to adulthood: An extension of theory and a review of research. *Developmental Psychology, 18,* 341–358.

Waterman, A. (1985). Identity in the context of adolescent psychology. In A. Waterman (Ed.), *Identity in adolescence: Process and contents* (pp. 5–24). San Francisco: Jossey-Bass.

Wetzel, J. (1987). *American youth: A statistical snapshot.* Washington, DC: William T. Grant Foundation.

Zinn, M. (1980). Gender and ethnic identity among Chicanos. *Frontiers, 5,* 18–24.

DATING AND SEXUALITY

Romantic love and sexuality can be experiences filled with contrasting emotions—unsettling but exciting, pleasurable but disturbing. As adolescents' bodies change, they must assimilate new feelings. Children are naturally curious about their bodies and the differences between male and female genitalia, but for the most part, these interests are peripheral. During adolescence, biological changes, social expectations, and gender roles and differences compel sexuality, love, and intimacy to center stage. Individuals begin to search for intimacy and are learning to adapt their behavior to attract others. For some adolescents, this can be an awkward process, because they often feel self-conscious and insecure. Most believe that they are the only ones who suffer from the fear of rejection or unrequited love. Nevertheless, through a process of experimentation, these early adolescent uncertainties are commonly replaced with greater self-assuredness, and eventually relationships are developed and ideally sustained. All of this has an undercurrent of discovery and experimentation. How much more intense is the struggle with these issues when the young person is confronted with the question, "Am I bisexual or homosexual?" How much more difficult and painful for a survivor of childhood sexual abuse? Even for "average" adolescents whose lives have not been filled with trauma, approaching a member of the opposite sex, dating, and early sexual experimentation can be an awkward pleasure that can put them on top of the world but also in the deepest depths.

McDonald and McKinney (26) investigate the relationship between self-esteem and going steady among high school students. Their research concentrated on the effect of going steady on females, since they found no correlation between going steady and self-esteem among males. Adolescent females who went steady when they were younger and are still going steady have lower self-esteem than adolescent females who report that they had gone steady in the past but are no longer going steady. The authors based their analysis on Marcia's statuses: identity diffusion, foreclosure, moratorium, and identity achievement. Perhaps going steady during early adolescence, when that level of dating involvement is not yet normative, is indicative of being foreclosed since by the nature of the commitment which going steady implies, one chooses to close oneself off to other possibilities without the opportunity of exploration that noncommitted dating implies. Gilligan's work provides additional insight since by going steady, a young girl often disconnects from her own interests and desires in order to maintain her steady relationship. Among those girls who did but are no longer going steady, the increase in self-esteem can be explained by their regaining the right to explore possibilities; identity theory suggests that they are leaving foreclosure and entering moratorium. In Gilligan's terms, the girls reconnected to their own voices and experience a renewed sense of self.

Nothing can prepare a child for the trauma of sexual abuse and its devastating aftereffects. In their study, "Unwanted and Illegal Sexual Experiences in Childhood and Adolescence" (27), Kellogg and Hoffman examined the results of traumatic sexual experiences. When young people are the victims of unwanted sexual experiences, their wounds are deep and hard to heal. A variety of teenagers responded to questions regarding frequency and type of unwanted sexual experiences, types of abusive acts, frequency of the experience, feelings about the experience, and wanted sexual experiences. Seventy of the 92 respondents from a sexual abuse clinic reported that they had been forced to engage in unwanted sexual activities. Despite their recognition that they had little or no control over the situation, they reported feelings of self-blame and guilt. The age at the time of the offense, the age of the offender, and the adolescent's understanding of "unwanted" were examined in connection to each other. An adolescent who reported her first "wanted" sexual experience was with her grandfather when she was six reveals her confusion between "wanted" and "unwanted" sexual experiences. The complex and interwoven relationship between a person's ability to understand unwanted sexual experiences and misplaced blame and guilt must be understood in order to heal the wounds caused by sexual abuse.

According to Elkind (10), most adolescents experience a feeling of uniqueness during a time when belonging to a group of friends is extremely important. However, few agonize over the question of a personal sexual identity more than homosexual and bisexual youth. Savin-Williams (28) examined the problems encountered by lesbian, gay male, and bisexual youth. These young people must cope with powerful internal and external stressors and feelings of self-doubt and guilt. The issue is not only the stress that coming to terms with one's sexual orientation involves, but even more the anxiety associated with "coming out" and revealing orientation to peers and family members. The social world of adolescents can be intolerant, even cruel. The response to homosexual and/or bisexual behavior by others can be traumatic for the individual. In a society that is still homophobic, these young people often become the victims of severe verbal and even physical abuse. Some experimental and clinical evidence suggests a relationship between the stress of being a homosexual and the problems of substance abuse, running away from home, prostitution, and suicide.

Romantic love is a confusing and exciting experience whether it results in falling or staying in love. The burgeoning awareness of one's ability to attract a partner can be exhilarating. However, for those who have been wounded by trusted friends and adults, the experience can be catastrophic. One of life's great ironies is that love can be the best and worst thing that happens to us.

STEADY DATING AND SELF-ESTEEM IN HIGH SCHOOL STUDENTS

Donna L. McDonald and John Paul McKinney
Michigan State University

Although steady dating is common among American adolescents, surprisingly little research attention has been paid to the practice. Although not all adolescents progress along an unproblematic course of dating and courtship, the majority appear to follow a pattern of heterosexual dating and going steady. Poffenberger (1964) found that among a group of 11th and 12th graders, 70% of the females and 58% of the males had gone steady at some point. Furthermore, those relationships lasted for relatively long periods of time: 37% of the boys and 57% of the girls had gone steady for a year or more. Mitchell (1976) suggested that dating was one way that adolescents can test their new ideas about themselves and gain a sense of intimacy. McCabe (1984) listed the following functions of adolescent dating: recreation, status grading, socialization, sexual experimentation, and intimacy.

A number of studies have examined gender differences in dating expectations (Collins *et al.,* 1976; Coombs and Kenkel, 1966) and functions (Dornbusch *et al.,* 1981; Newcomber *et al.,* 1983) and the relationship between dating and social class (Lowrie, 1961). Fewer studies have dealt explicitly with the role of self-esteem (Kle-

mer, 1971) or insecurity (Larson *et al.,* 1976) in dating and going steady.

From the point of view of identity formation (Erikson, 1968) early adolescent going steady may be used by those with low self-esteem as a confirmation of one's own worth. Going steady may be one expression of foreclosure in the formation of identity. For most adolescents, it would be a temporary foreclosure, since the majority do not end up marrying their early high school steady partners. There is research that suggests a link between foreclosure in identity formation and low self-esteem (Marcia, 1980). Thus, if the foreclosure hypothesis is correct, one would expect that going steady would be more common among adolescents with lower self-esteem.

From an object relations perspective (Blos, 1979), one might think of going steady as a compensation or substitution for the Oedipal loss in early adolescence. To the extent that the introjected objects were a part of the self system, the perceived loss of parental love could involve a loss of self-love as well. If going steady were such a compensation, one would also predict that going steady would be associated with lower self-esteem. That is, those individuals who experienced the loss most severely would have the lowest self-esteem and would be the most likely to go steady.

From *Journal of Adolescence* 1994, *17,* 557–564. © 1994 The Association for Professionals in Services for Adolescents. Reprinted with permission.

The view that going steady as a compensation for parental loss is consistent with Hetherington's (1972) observation that the daughters of divorcees were more likely to be involved in early and heavy dating than their peers. Conversely, however, the daughters of widows were slower in their dating behavior. It would be reasonable to suppose that the daughters of divorced parents feel more parental rejection than the daughters of widows, since in the case of widows, neither parent chose the separation.

Klemer (1971) found that college women who dated frequently were significantly more likely to have higher self-esteem than their classmates who dated less frequently. The experience of going steady, however, was not related to self-esteem in the same way. In fact, respondents who were going steady had lower self-esteem, although this difference was not significant. Klemer concluded that the women with higher self-esteem, who would have greater opportunity to go steady, since they were dating more, were probably actively avoiding going steady.

The foregoing research prompted three hypotheses: We predicted that adolescents who were going steady, or had gone steady at least once in the past, i.e. prior to our testing, would have lower self-esteem than those who had never gone steady. Secondly, adolescents with low self-esteem should view the dating process as being more important than those with higher self-esteem. The argument here is simply that not only do low self-esteem respondents differ from high self-esteem respondents in their dating behavior, they also differ with respect to the value they place on such behavior. We assume that their behavior is prompted by what they value.

Finally, given the greater importance of relationships and intimacy to women (Gilligan, 1982) we expected that the differences stated in hypotheses 1 and 2 would be more pronounced for girls. In a recent major theory of development, Gilligan has proposed that self-development for women is based more on connection and care, while for men it is based primarily on individuation and separation. Given this hypothesis, we assumed that a woman's self-esteem, a fundamental aspect of the self, would be more related to connections, for example, dating and going steady, than would be true for men. Once again, the hypothesis is based on our assumption about the relationship between behavior and values. If the behaviors involved in intimacy and connection (e.g. dating and going steady) are more characteristic of the self-definition of women, as Gilligan suggests, then the value that one places on those activities should be more closely tied to the value one places on the self (self-esteem) for women.

METHOD

Subjects

Participants were 121 sophomores (75 males; 46 females) at a medium-sized (470 students) midwestern high school. The participants were all White and came from a middle class community that was predominately White (99%). Sophomores were chosen because most driver's licenses are obtained during the sophomore year and dating can occur more freely. Also marriage is rarely seriously considered at this age, and therefore, dating has a more exploratory nature.

Procedure

After permission was obtained from the University Committee for Research on Human Subjects, contacts were made at the high school and permission was obtained from the principal and teacher. (The school administrators are authorized by their board to act *in loco parentis* for such research. Thus, individual parental permissions were not required.)

Questionnaires were distributed by the investigator during the last portion of each sophomore history class. Respondents were told that the study concerned dating patterns among high school students and that their participation was voluntary.

They were instructed not to include their names on the questionnaire so that anonymity could be assured. All the respondents cooperated and completed the questionnaires. The total procedure took approximately 15 minutes.

Measures

Participants were asked to report their present dating pattern by checking one of six categories of dating: not dating, going out in male/female groups, dating different people, dating one person without any definite commitment, dating one person exclusively, and engaged. Using the same six items the respondents then described their past dating patterns, that is, their most advanced dating pattern prior to their current practice.

Participants were then given four questions designed to be an estimate of how much they valued dating: "Being involved in a steady dating relationship is very important to me;" "I feel better about myself when I have a boyfriend/girlfriend;" "When I am not dating someone, I feel like something is missing from my life;" and "I feel that having a boyfriend/girlfriend makes me more acceptable to others." These statements were selected as the most salient from a list of 10 items generated in informal discussions (D.McD.) with high school students about the value of dating. Students were asked to rate these on a 4-point scale according to their level of agreement: strongly agree = 4; agree = 3; disagree = 2; or strongly disagree = 1. Their total "value of dating" score was the sum of their ratings for the four items.

The 10-item Rosenberg scale (1965) was used as the measure of self-esteem. The scale was converted to a Likert-type instrument by asking the respondents to rate each item on a four point scale from strongly agree (4) to strongly disagree (1). Responses were then scored from one (i.e. strongly agreeing with negative statements or strongly disagreeing with positive statements about the self) to four (strongly agreeing with positive or disagreeing with negative statements). An individual's self-esteem score was the sum of ratings of the 10 items.

RESULTS

Judging from the number of students involved in the practice, one can assume that dating is important to them. Although 23 (19%) reported that they were currently not dating, only nine of those students reported never having dated. Twenty-seven (22%) students reported that they were currently dating only one person and would not date another. The most popular socializing pattern was going out in male/female groups. In total, 44 (36%) of the respondents reported socializing in this way. The remaining 27 students (22%) were either dating a number of people or were dating one person but not with any commitment.

Hypothesis 1: Self-Esteem and Steady Dating

The reliability of the Rosenberg measure of self-esteem when converted to a Likert-type scale was acceptable; $\alpha = 0.83$. The correlation between self-esteem and level of dating involvement was significant for the females, $r(45) = -0.25$; $p < 0.05$, but not the males, $r(74) = -0.18$; $p > 0.05$. Lower self-esteem is associated with more advanced dating practices. The difference between these correlation coefficients was not significant, $z_{obs} = 0.94$; $p > 0.10$.

When the category of "going steady" was compared to all of the other "not going steady" categories combined, significant results emerged. A $2 \times 2 \times 2$ (Gender $\times$ Steady dating $\times$ Steady dating in the past) independent cell design, analysis of variance revealed, first of all that males ($N = 75$) had significantly higher self-esteem ($M = 31.65$) than females (N = 46; M = 28.35), $F(1,113) = 11.41$; $p < 0.001$.

The first hypothesis, that adolescents who were going steady or who had formerly gone steady, would have lower self-esteem, was not entirely supported. Although respondents who were going steady had significantly lower self-esteem than those who were not going steady ($M = 28.68$ *vs.* 30.89), $F(1,113) = 7.81$; $p < 0.006$, surprisingly, those who had gone steady in the past had higher self-esteem than those who had never gone steady ($M = 31.54$ *vs.* 29.81), $F(1,113) = 4.35$; $p < 0.04$. Having gone steady in the past interacted with going steady currently differently for the two sexes. For males, going steady in the past meant higher self-esteem than not having gone steady in the past, both for those who were currently going steady and for those who were not. For females, however, going steady in the past meant higher self-esteem for those who were no longer going steady, but lower self-esteem for those who were still (or again) going steady. These differences yielded a significant Gender × Going Steady × Past Going Steady interaction, $F(1,113) = 4.98$; $p < 0.004$.

Hypothesis 2: Self-Esteem and Value of Dating

The reliability of the 4-item value questionnaire was acceptable; $\alpha = 0.78$. Pearson product–moment correlations between self-esteem scores and scores on the value of dating were significant for the males, $r(73) = -0.35$, $p < 0.01$, but not for the females, $r(44) = -0.13$, $p > 0.05$. Negative correlations mean that the more importance attributed to dating the lower the scores on self-esteem. The difference between these two correlation coefficients was not significant, $z_{obs} = 1.14$; $p > 0.10$.

Hypothesis 3: Gender Differences

Since the first hypothesis was not entirely supported in its stated form, it was not meaningful to test the hypothesis that the self-esteem differences between those who go steady and those who do not would be more pronounced for girls.

DISCUSSION

This study establishes a link between going steady and low self-esteem in high school sophomore females. As in Klemer's study with older adolescent respondents, the early adolescent females who go steady have lower self-esteem than those who do not go steady.

One way of interpreting these results is in terms of identity formation. Although the relationship between self-esteem and identity is, admittedly complex, it seems reasonable, as Marcia (1993) suggests, that, "Foreclosures, who have not undergone the differentiation process, should have unrealistically high ego ideals and correspondingly low self-esteem" (p. 24). Surely going steady is to some extent a form of foreclosure since it precludes dating other people. To what extent these adolescents took seriously the exclusivity of this commitment is not known. Nor do we know how many really believe they will some day marry their current steady partner. The arrangement of "going steady," however, is used by adolescents to communicate to their partners and their peers their involvement in an exclusive and presumably faithful relationship that mimics in those respects the marriage relationship of adults. Gilligan speaks of this stage of a young woman's development as ". . . a critical time in girls' lives—a time when girls are in danger of losing their voices and thus losing connection with others . . ." (Gilligan, 1990, p. 25). One way they can lose their voice is by too early limitation of choices. Perhaps this is one reason why those who had tried going steady but were no longer doing so, ended up having even higher self-esteem than their peers. They may have found a renewed sense of self, or in Gilligan's terms, they may have rediscovered their own voice in going from foreclosure to a new moratorium. We do not have the data that would tell us which partner initiated the steady relationship or who terminated it, although these would be important data that we will collect in future studies.

Another possible basis for this heightened self-esteem in girls who have retreated from a steady relationship may lie in the nature of the relationship itself. Early adolescent males may enter into a steady relationship to "get on the map" or "make a statement," and thus pay little attention to the sensitivities of their partner. At a time when their own identity is in need of early building, they may be poorly prepared for the exigencies of intimacy and may, in fact, treat their "steadies" badly. In such an arrangement, the female could easily feel neglected and disappointed. Hope for a happy romance dashed, she may be relieved to end the "steady" arrangement.

Some obvious questions arise out of this sort of research. It would be important to know who initiated the steady relationship, the girl or her partner. In the case of prior steady partnerships, it might be important also to know who ended the relationship. One could then ask whether either of these affects self-esteem. For example, perhaps the girl who was asked to go steady, but later decides for herself against the arrangement, is different in terms of self-esteem from the one who initiates a steady relationship and is rejected later. Secondly, only a longitudinal examination of these issues will help answer the question of which came first, lower self-esteem or a particular pattern of dating relationships. We are currently embarking on a cross-lag panel analysis of these two questions spanning the middle school years, which should give us more information about both of these issues.

REFERENCES

Blos, P. (1979). *The Adolescent Passage: Developmental Issues.* New York: International Universities Press.

Collins, J. K., Kennedy, J. R. and Francis, R. D. (1976). Insights into a dating partner's expectations of how behavior should ensue during the courtship process. *Journal of Marriage and the Family,* **38,** 373–378.

Coombs, R. and Kenkel, W. (1966). Sex differences in dating aspirations and satisfaction with computer selected partners. *Journal of Marriage and the Family,* **28,** 62–66.

Dornbusch, S. M., Carlsmith, J. M., Gross, R. T., Martin, J. A., Jennings, D., Rosenberg, A. and Duke, P. (1981). Sexual development, age and dating: a comparison of biological and social influences upon one set of behaviors. *Child Development,* **52,** 179–185.

Erikson, E. H. (1968). *Identity: Youth and Crisis.* New York: Norton.

Gilligan, C. (1982). *In a Different Voice: Psychological Theory and Women's Development.* Cambridge, MA: Harvard University Press.

Gilligan, C. A. (1990). Teaching Shakespeare's sister: notes from the underground of female adolescence. In *Making Connections: The Relational Worlds of Adolescent Girls at Emma Willard School.* Gilligan, C. A. Lyons, N. P. And Hanmer, T. J. (Eds). Cambridge, MA: Harvard University Press, pp. 6–29.

Hetherington, E. M. (1972). Effects of father absence on personality development of adolescent daughters. *Developmental Psychology,* **7,** 313–326.

Klemer, R. H. (1971). Self-esteem and college dating experience as factors in mate selection and marital happiness: a longitudinal study. *Journal of Marriage and the Family,* **33,** 183–187.

Larson, D. L., Spreitzer, E. A. and Snyder, E. E. (1976). Social factors in the frequency of romantic involvement among adolescents. *Adolescence,* **11,** 7–12.

Lowrie, S. (1961). Early and late dating: some conditions associated with them. *Marriage and Family Living,* **23,** 284–291.

Marcia, J. E. (1980). Identity in adolescence. In *Handbook of Adolescent Psychology,* Adelson, J. (Ed.). New York: Wiley, pp. 159–187.

Marcia, J. E. (1993). The status of the statuses: Research Review. In *Ego Identity: A Handbook for Psychosocial Research,* Marcia, J. E., Waterman, A. S., Matteson, D. R., Archer, S. C. And Orlofsky, J. L. (Eds). New York: Springer-Verlag, pp. 22–41.

McCabe, M. P. (1984). Toward a theory of adolescent dating. *Adolescence,* **73,** 159–170.

Mitchell, J. J. (1976). Adolescent intimacy. *Adolescence,* **11,** 275–280.

Newcomber, S. F., Udry, J. R. and Cameron, F. (1983). Adolescent sexual behavior and popularity. *Adolescence,* **18,** 515–552.

Poffenberger, T. (1964). Three papers on going steady. *Family Life Coordinator,* **13,** 7–13.

Rosenberg, M. (1965). *Society and the Adolescent Self-Image.* Princeton, NJ: Princeton University Press.

UNWANTED AND ILLEGAL SEXUAL EXPERIENCES IN CHILDHOOD AND ADOLESCENCE

Nancy D. Kellogg and Thomas J. Hoffman

University of Texas Health Science Center and St. Mary's University, San Antonio, Texas

WHAT IS SEXUAL abuse? Friedman (1990) indicates that "criminal statutes usually define child sexual abuse as nonconsensual physical contact with a minor for purposes of sexual gratification." A child or teenager may describe sexual abuse as an "unwanted sexual experience," a term first used by P.I. Erikson and A.J. Rapkin (1991). While legal definitions frequently coincide with what a child or teenager would describe as "abuse," this is not always the case. For example, some abused children vacillate between hating the abuse and loving the abuser: for them, sexual abuse may be an illegal yet wanted sexual experience. Conversely, some sexual experiences may be unwanted yet not meet the legal criteria for "abuse." Both illegal and unwanted sexual experiences merit professional attention and treatment.

Regardless of whether a child's sexual experience is wanted or unwanted, professionals are responsible for reporting illegal sexual experiences. Once abuse is uncovered, a professional's interaction with the child and their family can significantly impact the child's healing process (Heger & Emans, 1992) and subsequent investigative efforts. The success of this interaction depends upon an understanding of the child's perception of what has happened and how she feels about it, including whether the child describes the experience as unwanted or wanted. The child's realization that a given sexual experience is "abuse" is in part dependent upon the values and beliefs of their family and culture. For example, in a family or culture that emphasizes absolute obedience to adults, children may describe sexual experiences with adults as permissible, not abusive.

Sexual abuse is a pervasive and underreported problem. Numerous studies have documented its prevalence (Finkelhor & Hotaling, 1984; Kercher & McShane, 1984; Leventhal, 1988; Russell, 1983; Siegal, Sorenson, Golding, Burnham, & Stein, 1987). Finkelhor (1994), after surveying studies from throughout the world, concluded: "In every country where researchers have asked about it, they have found that an important percentage of the adult population—measurable in simple survey of adults—acknowledges a history of sexual abuse." Worldwide there is widespread incest and child molestation. Indeed, Olafson, Corwin, and Summit (1993) point out that "The full realization that child sexual victimization is as common and as noxious as current research suggest would necessitate costly efforts to protect children from sexual assault." Despite the high reported numbers, many child victims never disclose the abuse (Finkelhor, 1979; Russell, 1983).

Reprinted from *Child Abuse & Neglect*, 1995, *19*, 1457–1468, abridged. Copyright (1995) with permission from Elsevier Science LTD, The Boulevard, Langford Lane, Kidlington OX5 1GB, UK.

Several factors influence the decision to disclose, including the child's perception that the sexual experience was or was not abusive.

Regardless of disclosure, child sexual abuse has significant and persistent effects. Numerous studies (Briere, Evans, Runtz, & Wall, 1988; Brown, 1990; Lew, 1988; Parks, 1990) have described the negative effects of child sexual abuse on adult survivors. Distrust of others by survivors is reported throughout the literature (Bolton, Morris, & MacEachron, 1989; Hayward & Carlyle, 1991; Jones & Johnston, 1989; Kilpatrick, 1992; Kohn, 1987; Lew, 1988; Osborn, 1990; Peters, 1988). Self-esteem is also undermined in the abused (Finkelhor, 1979; Grubman-Black, 1990; Peters, 1988).

Kilpatrick (1992) recently did a study of the long-range influence on adults of childhood and adolescent sexual experiences. She concludes that the identity of the sexual partner and the evaluations of the sexual experiences influence adult functioning. Partners who are relatives or close to the family, and behaviors that are abusive, forced, pressured, or inflict guilt impact negatively on respondents in her survey. Those sexual experiences influence intrafamilial stress, depression, marital discord, and self-esteem. These pervasive effects are moderated by the child's perception that a sexual experience is abusive or unwanted.

The goals of this study are to address the following questions:

1. What types of sexual experiences in adolescence are "unwanted" or "wanted?" How do these experiences overlap with legal definitions of sexual abuse?
2. What feelings are associated with unwanted sexual experiences (USE)? Do these feelings impact tendency to disclose?
3. Do the types of sexual experiences and feelings about USE vary among ethnic groups?

METHODS

A six-page anonymous survey was developed by one of the authors. This questionnaire was administered to subjects who fit the age criteria within each of three clinic sites: sexual abuse clinic, family planning clinic, and family practice clinic. All three clinics were located at a large ambulatory care center in downtown San Antonio where 80% of the clients are below the federal poverty level income. Parental consent was not required of subjects from the sexual abuse clinic; in the other two clinics, the need for parental consent was eliminated by enrolling only those subjects over the age of 18. Subjects 18–22 years old were selected because their memories and feelings concerning events prior to their 18th birthday would be most complete.

In the sexual abuse clinic, all cases were filed with law enforcement or the district attorney's office. The family planning patients were females who had appointments for birth control or pelvic examinations. Family practice patients presented with a variety of physical complaints, most not related to sexual issues. All subjects were given complete privacy and anonymity. All subjects were informed that the questionnaire was voluntary and would not affect how they were treated or cared for in the clinic. The physicians in the sexual abuse clinic asked the teenagers if they wished to participate in the study and reviewed the cover letter of the questionnaire with them if they indicated interest. The teenagers were asked to participate in the study during the course of the medical evaluation. The young adults from family planning and family practice clinics were randomly selected.

RESULTS

Patient Information

One hundred and two males and females from the sexual abuse clinic agreed to fill out the questionnaire; six patients refused to participate. Of the study participants, 100 were female and two were males. Ninety-two (91%) indicated they had experienced at least one unwanted sexual experience. The mean age was 13.9 and the median age was 14. Ethnicity reflected that of the San Antonio Community: 68% Hispanic, 25% White, and 7% African American.

One hundred and one females from the family planning clinic filled out the questionnaire; four females refused to take part in the study. Of the respondents, 40 (40%) indicated having at least one unwanted sexual experience prior to their 18th birthday. Mean age for this group was 19.9 and the median age was 20. Ethnicity was similar to that in San Antonio and in the other two study groups: 77% Hispanic; 13.5% White, and 9.5% African American.

Of the 142 participants from the family practice clinic, 60% were females and 40% were males; there were two nonresponders. Of the study participants 33 females (39%) and nine males (16%) indicated they had at least one unwanted sexual experience prior to their 18th birthday. Mean age for this group was 19.8 and the median age was 20. Ethnic distribution was 82% Hispanic, 10.5% White, 7.2% African American, and .3% other. There was no statistical difference in ethnic group distribution among the three site samples.

Unwanted and Wanted Sexual Experiences in Adolescence

Table 1 summarizes the responses of the three clinic populations to the question: "Have you ever had an unwanted sexual experience?" Of note is that only 91% of females from the sexual abuse clinic describe their legally abusive experiences as "unwanted."

Perpetrator, type of act, and frequency of acts were analyzed for USE's. The most common perpetrators from all clinic sites were adult family members (36%) and adult acquaintances (24%) followed by strangers (15%), peer acquaintances (15%) and peer family members (6%). Four percent described their experience as gang-related. By second-order odds ratio there was a moderate (2.4) association found of having an unwanted sexual experience with a peer given one such experience with an adult. This association was strong in the older subjects from family planning and practice populations who were reflecting upon 5 or 6 years of adolescent experience, including sexual events. This association was slight in the younger subjects from the sexual abuse clinic, many of who were not yet dating. Forty-two percent (combined populations) described unwanted sexual experiences with more than one perpetrator. In the combined sample, of the female respondents, 98% of the perpetrators were male. Male subjects were as likely to have had an unwanted sexual experience with a male (44.4%) as with a female (44.4%). Two of the female respondents and one of the male respondents had perpetrators of both genders.

Types of unwanted sexual acts were divided into three categories: penetrating genital or anal injuries (rape, attempted rape, or digital penetration), oral-genital contact (including penile-oral

TABLE 1
Unwanted Sexual Experiences in San Antonio Youth[a]

	Clinic site	% Reporting "yes"
Females	Sexual Abuse (N = 100)	91
	Family Planning (N = 101)	40
	Family Practice (N = 85)	39
Males	Sexual Abuse (N = 2)	100
	Family Planning (N = 0)	—
	Family Practice (N = 57)	16

[a]"Unwanted sexual experiences may be any kind of sexual touching which made you feel uncomfortable, bad, uneasy, etc. It may have come from another teen or adult or someone you didn't know well at all. Have you ever had an unwanted sexual experience (prior to your 18th birthday)?"

penetration), and fondling. Of the 244 different acts enumerated by the sexual abuse population, 51% were penetrating injuries, 37% were fondling, and 12% involved oral-genital contact. Family planning subjects described 108 acts by various perpetrators; 44% involved penetration, 44% were acts of fondling, and 12% involved oral-genital contact. In the family practice population 96 acts were reported and 47% involved penetrating injuries, 39% were fondling, and 14% were of the oral-genital type.

With regard to frequency of the unwanted sexual experiences, there was no statistically significant difference between the three clinic populations. About one-third reported having one experience, one-quarter reported having experiences more than 20 times, and the remainder (about 40%) reported the number of experiences as between two and 20.

All subjects were asked if they ever had a wanted sexual experience (WSE) prior to their 18th birthday. They indicated the age difference in years for their first wanted sexual partner. A sexual experience was considered "illegal" if the partners were 4 or more years apart in age, in accordance with Texas Penal Code Article 22.011 (1994). Utilizing this definition, 20% ($N = 70$) of the combined clinic sample had illegal wanted sexual experiences. In 97% of these cases the subject was the younger of the two partners; two males (3%) in the family practice group had their first wanted sexual experience with a partner 4 or more years younger. Overall, 46% of the family planning and family practice subjects had either an USE or an illegal sexual experience.

Feelings about Unwanted Sexual Experiences

Subjects were asked to "characterize your feelings about the unwanted sexual experience." They were provided with 13 statements and asked to indicate which, if any, was important for them. Most subjects selected more than one statement. Table 2 summarizes responses to this question. When adolescents from the sexual abuse clinic were compared with the combined responses of the young adults from family planning and family practice clinics, sexual abuse subjects were statistically less likely to rank reasons reflecting peer pressure as important: "I did it because I was mad at my family/partner" ($p = .01$); "I did it because I thought I might lose my partner" ($p = .008$); and "I did it because everyone else is doing it" ($p = .002$). Sexual abuse patients were also less likely to select ambivalent or naive feelings: "I didn't know it was wrong at the time" ($p = .02$) and "I wasn't sure so I went along with it" ($p = .03$). "It was the other person's fault," a feeling of victimization, was reported more frequently by the sexual abuse subjects than the subjects from the other two populations ($p = .02$).

As might be expected, subjects having unwanted sexual experiences with peer acquaintances had different feelings and responses than those subjects having unwanted sexual experiences with other types of perpetrator(s). Table 3 summarizes the similarities and differences in feelings by perpetrator type. While the three most common feelings (force, fear, and "It was the other person's fault") did not differ by type of perpetrator, feelings of self-blame ("It was my fault" and "I later regretted it") and risk-taking behaviors ("I was drunk\high" and "I didn't use contraception") were significantly more common in the peer perpetrator group.

A factor analysis indicates three underlying variables concerning feelings about unwanted sexual experiences. Feelings within Factor 1 ("self-blame") related to peer pressure and risk-taking behaviors (alcohol/drug use and no contraception). Factor 2 taps naivete and uncertainty. The third set of reactions relates to feelings more commonly associated with rape: being scared, forced, and victimized. Subjects from the sexual abuse clinic were less likely to have feelings of self-blame and naivete compared with subjects from the other two clinic sites; they were more likely to blame the other person. Those who had USE's with peers were more likely to report risky behavior and have feelings of self-blame.

TABLE 2
Feelings About Unwanted Sexual Experiences
(Percentage in each group ranking a given reason as "important")

	Sexual Abuse (N = 92)	Family Planning (N = 40)	Family Practice (N = 42)	Combined Populations (N = 174)	p Value
"I was forced"	70	73	64	69	NS
"I wasn't sure, so I went along with it"	36	56	50	45	NS
"I got drunk/high"	21	41	19	26	NS
"I did it because I thought I might lose my partner"	15	50	17	24	.005
"I did it because everyone else is doing it"	10	41	17	19	.001
"I wasn't prepared with sexual protection/contraception"	28	46	19	30	.05
"I was threatened/scared"	75	70	60	70	NS
"I wasn't planning on it; it just happened and I later regretted it"	28	46	29	33	NS
"I did it because I was mad at my family"	10	39	12	18	.001
"I did it because I was mad at my partner"	10	27	12	17	.05
"I didn't know it was wrong at the time"	21	51	26	30	.001
"It was the other person's fault"	71	54	55	63	.05
"It was my fault"	25	49	21	30	.005

NS = Not significant.

TABLE 3
Feelings About Unwanted Sexual Experiences by Type of Perpetrator
(Percentage in each group ranking a given reason as "important")

	Peer Perpetrator N = 39	All Others N = 133	p Value
"I was forced"	81	66	NS*
"I wasn't sure, so I went along with it"	46	41	NS
"I got drunk/high"	57	14	.001
"I did it because I thought I might lose my partner"	46	16	.001
"I did it because everyone else is doing it"	38	12	.001
"I wasn't prepared with sexual protection/contraception"	54	22	.001
"I was threatened/scared"	78	67	NS
"I wasn't planning on it; it just happened and I later regretted it"	51	23	.001
"I did it because I was mad at my family"	32	11	.002
"I did it because I was mad at my partner"	30	11	.006
"I didn't know it was wrong at the time"	43	21	.006
"It was the other person's fault"	65	61	NS
"It was my fault"	60	19	.001

NS = Not significant.

Impact on Tendency to Disclose

Subject gender, ethnicity, type of perpetrator, type of unwanted sexual experience, and feelings about unwanted sexual experiences were tested for influence on tendency to disclose. Disclosure of USE was not influenced by subject gender, ethnic group, or type of perpetrator. Severity of USE did impact disclosure tendency: those who experienced either rape or attempted rape were more likely to tell someone else (90%) than those who had other types of unwanted sexual experiences (78%; $p < .05$).

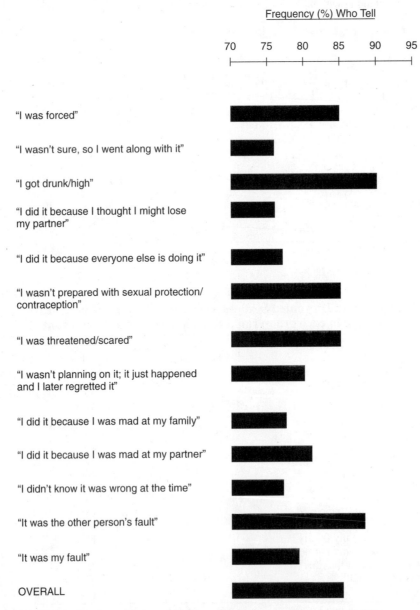

FIGURE 1   Disclosure Rate and Feelings About Unwanted Sexual Experiences.

In Figure 1, all subjects with unwanted sexual experiences who disclosed their experience are compared by the feelings they indicated were important. Overall, 85% disclosed their USE to "someone." Generally, subjects with feelings related to peer-pressure, self-blame, ambivalence and indecisiveness (Factors 1 and 2) were less likely to tell someone about their USE. Eighty-five percent or more of subjects who reported feelings of victimization (Factor 3) disclosed their experience.

Sexual Experiences and Feelings: Differences Between Ethnic Groups

Due to the low number of African Americans and males, comparisons among ethnic groups were made only for Hispanic and White females. It was found that White females (80%) were more likely to have an unwanted sexual experience than Hispanic females (52%; $p < .005$). When considering all types of sexual experiences: unwanted, illegal, and legal, Hispanic females were significantly (66%) less likely than White females (90%) to have an unwanted or illegal sexual experience ($p < .02$; Table 4). However, of the nine females in the sexual abuse clinic who did not characterize their abuse as "unwanted," seven were Hispanic (two were African American).

Feelings of victimization (Factor 3) were most common in all subjects and did not differ by ethnicity. While Hispanic females (18%) were less likely than White females (33%; $p < .05$) to have an USE with a peer, they were more likely to have feelings of self-blame and peer-pressure (Table 5).

DISCUSSION

In this study, the incidence of unwanted sexual experiences in childhood and adolescence was high: 40% of females and 16% of males in a randomly selected population of young adults. An

TABLE 4
Sexual Experiences in Adolescent Females by Ethnicity

Type of Sexual Experience	Hispanic $N = 200$	Non-Hispanic White $N = 46$
None	27 (14%)	1 (2%)
Wanted only[a]	44 (22%)	4 (9%)
Unwanted only	39 (20%)	10 (22%)
Illegal only[b]	24 (12%)	5 (11%)
Both wanted and unwanted	41 (21%)	16 (35%)
Both illegal and unwanted	25 (13%)	10 (22%)

[a]Wanted sexual experience: first wanted sexual experience with a partner within 3 years in age of the subject.
[b]Illegal sexual experience: first wanted sexual experience with a partner who is at least 4 years older than the subject.

TABLE 5
Feelings about Unwanted Sexual Experiences: Differences Between Ethnic Groups (Females only) (Percentage in each group ranking a given reason as "important")

	Hispanic $N = 114$	Non-Hispanic White $N = 40$	p Value
"I wasn't planning on it; it just happened and I later regretted it"	34	13	.01
"It was my fault"	30	13	.03
"I did it because I thought I might lose my partner"	26	10	.04
"I did it because everyone else is doing it"	20	5	.03
"I did it because I was mad at my partner"	18	3	.02

additional 27% of subjects had illegal sexual experiences with partners at least 4 years older or
younger. Presumably these illegal experiences
were not reported because they were described
as "wanted" by the adolescent. In 9% of the respondents from the sexual abuse clinic, abuse
was reported but the experience was not described as "unwanted" by the adolescent. The
complexity of feelings about sexual abuse is exemplified in one 15-year-old female from the
sexual abuse clinic who described unwanted
sexual experiences with two perpetrators but
also indicated that her first "wanted" sexual experience was with her grandfather when she was
6 years old. Clearly legal definitions of abuse do
not always coincide with the adolescent's perception that the experience was "unwanted." In
general, professionals are responsible for reporting illegal sexual experiences. However, in some
regions professionals may be responsible for reporting only those illegal sexual experiences between a child and an adult caretaker. As an example, Texas law formerly required "any
person" to report child abuse "by a person responsible for the child's care, custody or welfare;" in 1989, Texas law changed such that "a
person" is mandated to report child abuse "by
any person" (Texas Family Code Section 34.01).
Regardless of reporting statues, sexual experiences with much older partners merit a careful
clinical assessment, especially for sexually
transmitted diseases and pregnancy.

In this study sample most unwanted sexual
experiences involved adult perpetrators and
more serious acts of penetrating trauma. Over
three-quarters of the USE's involved adults,
strangers, or gang members. Over 40% had
USE's with more than one perpetrator. Penetrating acts of trauma were more common than nonpenetrating trauma and two-thirds of USE's occurred more than one time. Older subjects (mean
age 19.8) with more years of risk as adolescents
were more likely to have USE's with an adult
and a peer than the younger subjects (mean age
13.9) in the sexual abuse clinic. This finding
suggests that an USE with a peer or an adult in

earlier years may predispose one to having another USE with another peer or adult in later
teenage years. Detection and intervention efforts
with first-time victims may be critical in preventing subsequent unwanted or illegal sexual
experiences.

Feelings regarding USE varied by clinic sites,
type of perpetrator, and ethnic groups. The
younger sexual abuse patients who were less
likely to report USE's with peers were also less
likely than the older subjects to have feelings related to peer pressure. The sexual abuse patients
tended to objectify the guilt and blame the perpetrator, in contrast to older females who cited
feelings of ambivalence, indecisiveness, and
self-blame about 50% of the time. The fact that
most of the sexual abuse subjects were involved
in counseling and/or litigation may explain these
findings. The process of litigation may reinforce
feelings of victimization and desire for retribution; counseling may help victims objectify
guilt.

Unwanted sexual experiences with peer perpetrators were significantly associated with self-
blame and failure to protect oneself by engaging
in risky behaviors. Specifically, those subjects
having USE with a peer were more likely to be
drunk or high and less likely to use sexual protection. These responses—self-blame and irresponsible or impulsive behaviors—grouped together
in a factor analysis of all feelings. It is likely that
a risky behavior such as using drugs or becoming
drunk makes one vulnerable to unwanted sexual
experiences for which contraception is not
planned or available. The person who decides to
become drunk or high feels guilty and responsible for the consequences. Recognition and avoidance of high risk situations are crucial decision-
making skills for children and adolescents.

While feelings and severity of USE impacted
tendency to disclose, subject gender, type of
perpetrator, and ethnicity did not influence this
tendency. Ambivalence, self-blame, and peer-
pressure were associated with a lower tendency
to disclose USE. Subjects with feelings of guilt
were less likely to tell someone than those who

were scared or threatened. Victims of penetrating trauma were more likely to disclose their USE than victims of nonpenetrating types of trauma. It is interesting that while USE with peers are associated with feelings of self-blame, disclosure rate is the same with peer as with adult perpetrators of USE. On the other hand, 27% of the subjects had illegal sexual encounters with older peers which were presumably not reported. It appears that the adolescent's perception of the sexual experience as "unwanted" is key to disclosure. Attempts to alleviate feelings of guilt in neutral settings, such as schools, may promote disclosure.

Differences between Hispanic and White females were noted with regard to incidence and types of sexual experiences, type of perpetrator, and feelings about USE. Hispanic females were less likely to have an unwanted or illegal sexual experience and less likely to have a USE with a peer but more likely than White females to have feelings of self-blame and ambivalence about their USE. The lower incidence of USE in Hispanic females differs from that of other studies (Kercher & McShane, 1984). While unwanted and illegal sexual experiences may be less common in Hispanic females, differences in the definition of "unwanted" may account for this finding: Seven of the nine sexual abuse subjects who denied having any unwanted sexual experiences were Hispanic and none were White. Feelings of self-blame and ambivalence may nullify the perception that a sexual experience is "unwanted." Alternately, perpetrators of Hispanic children and adolescents may utilize approaches that tend to inflict more guilt. Kilpatrick (1992) found negative impact in situations where guilt was inflicted. These considerations merit further study and are important in therapeutic management.

SUMMARY AND CONCLUSIONS

A considerable number of adolescents and children in our community have had unwanted or illegal sexual experiences. A number of the sexually abused adolescents did not describe their experience as "unwanted." Over one-quarter of the subject population had illegal sexual experiences with partners at least 4 years older or younger; these experiences were largely unreported. While feelings of victimization were most common in those with an USE, self-blame, ambivalence and naivete were also frequently reported. Self-blame and ambivalence lower the tendency to disclose one's USE. While Hispanic females were less likely than White females to have unwanted or illegal sexual experiences they were more likely to experience guilty and ambivalent feelings about their USE. Professionals who work with children and adolescents should be aware of the complex nature of these perceptions and feelings regarding sexual experiences and how these issues may vary according to ethnicity and the type of experience. This understanding is key to providing appropriate and effective treatment for these children and teenagers.

REFERENCES

Bolton, F. G., Jr., Morris, L. A., & MacEachron, A. E. (1989). *Males at risk.* Newbury Park, CA: Sage Publications, Inc.

Briere, J., Evans, D., Runtz, M., & Wall, T. (1988). Symptomatology in men who were molested as children: A comparison study. *American Journal of Orthopsychiatry, 58,* 457–461.

Brown, M. (1990). From victim to survivor: The treatment of adults who have been sexually abused as children. In S. J. Rossetti (Ed.), *Slayer of the soul* (pp. 83–97). Mystic, CT: Twenty-Third Publications.

Erickson, P., & Rapkin, A. J. (1991). Unwanted sexual experiences among middle and high school youth. *Journal of Adolescent Health, 12,* 319–325.

Finkelhor, D. (1979). *Sexually victimized children.* New York: The Free Press.

Finkelhor, D. (1994) The international epidemiology of child sexual abuse. *Child Abuse & Neglect, 18,* 409–417.

Finkelhor, D., & Hotaling, G. T. (1984). Sexual abuse in the national incidence study of child abuse and neglect: An appraisal. *Child Abuse & Neglect, 8,* 23–33.

Friedman, S. R. (1990). What is child sexual abuse? *Journal of Clinical Psychology, 46,* 372–375.

Grubman-Black, S. D. (1990). *Broken boys/mending men.* Blue Ridge Summit, PA: Tab Books.

Hayward, J., & Carlyle, D. (1991). *Too close for comfort.* Wisbech, Cambs, UK: LDA.

Heger, A., & Emans, S. J. (1992). *Evaluation of the sexually abused child.* New York: Oxford University Press.

Jones, D. R., & Johnston, M. W. (1989). *Child abuse and neglect.* Austin: Joint Study Committee on Treatment of Child Abuse, 71st Legislature.

Kilpatrick, A. (1992). *Long-range effects of child and adolescent sexual experiences.* London: Lawrence Erlbaum Associates.

Kohn, A. (1987, February). Shattered innocence. *Psychology Today, 21*(2), 54–58.

Kercher, G. A., & McShane, M. (1984). The prevalence of child sexual abuse victimization in an adult sample of Texas residents. *Child Abuse & Neglect, 8,* 495–501.

Leventhal, J. M. (1988). Have there been changes in the epidemiology of sexual abuse of children during the 20th century? *Pediatrics, 82,* 766–773.

Lew, M. (1988). *Victims no longer.* New York: Nevraumont Publishing Co.

Olafson, E., Corwin, D. L., & Summit, R. C. (1993). Modern history of child sexual abuse awareness: Cycles of discovery and suppression. *Child Abuse & Neglect, 17,* 7–24.

Osborn, J. (1990). *Psychological effects of child sex abuse in women.* Norwich, England: Social Work Monographs. University of East Anglia.

Parks, P. (1990). *Rescuing the "inner child."* London: Souvenir Press.

Peters, S. D. (1988). Child sexual abuse and later psychological problems. In G. E. Wyatt, & G. J. Powell (Eds.), *Lasting effects of child sexual abuse* (pp. 101–117). Beverly Hills, CA: Sage.

Russell, D. E. H. (1983). The incidence and prevalence of intrafamilial and extrafamilial sexual abuse of female children. *Child Abuse & Neglect, 7,* 133–146.

Siegel, J. M., Sorenson, S. B., Golding, J. M., Burnham, M. A., & Stein, J. A. (1987). The prevalence of childhood sexual assault. *American Journal of Epidemiology. 126,* 1141–1153.

VERBAL AND PHYSICAL ABUSE AS STRESSORS IN THE LIVES OF LESBIAN, GAY MALE, AND BISEXUAL YOUTHS: ASSOCIATIONS WITH SCHOOL PROBLEMS, RUNNING AWAY, SUBSTANCE ABUSE, PROSTITUTION, AND SUICIDE

RITCH C. SAVIN-WILLIAMS
Cornell University

Despite the increasing public visibility of homosexuality and bisexuality in North American culture, the prevailing assumption among clinicians and researchers is that homoerotic attractions and desires are the province solely of adulthood and not of childhood and adolescence. This misunderstanding and the ensuing clinical and empirical silence and neglect are particularly consequential because lesbian, gay male, and bisexual youths are disproportionately at risk for stressors that are injurious to themselves and others. In some cases, the threat for youths is not merely their mental health but their very lives.

A "fact sheet" published by the Center for Population Options (1992) summarized these difficulties.

> Lesbian, gay and bisexual adolescents face tremendous challenges to growing up physically and mentally healthy in a culture that is almost uniformly anti-homosexual. Often, these youth face an increased risk of medical and psychosocial problems,

From *Journal of Consulting and Clinical Psychology,* 1994, 62 (2), 261–269. Copyright © 1994 by the American Psychological Association. Reprinted with permission.

caused not by their sexual orientation, but by society's extremely negative reaction to it. Gay, lesbian and bisexual youth face rejection, isolation, verbal harassment and physical violence at home, in school and in religious institutions. Responding to these pressures, many lesbian, gay and bisexual young people engage in an array of risky behaviors. (p. 1)

In a seminal article, Martin and Hetrick (1988) reviewed the major stressors in the lives of lesbian, gay male, and bisexual youths who sought the services of the Hetrick-Martin Institute (HMI) in New York City. The lesbian, gay male, and bisexual youths, most of whom are also an ethnic minority in North American culture, often felt discredited and isolated from peers, family members, and religious, educational, and social institutions. Many believed that they must remain hidden and invisible; their lives had to be compartmentalized into the public versus the private. One fear of many youths was that family members and peers would discover their "deviant sexuality" and react in such a way that the youths would be expelled from the home or face violence.

Gay male, lesbian, and bisexual youths experience unique stressors in their lives that are directly related to their sexual behavior and identity. This is evident from early empirical studies of lesbian youths. For example, the major problems reported by 60 gay and bisexual male youths ages 16 to 22 years, were their perceived need to keep their homosexuality a secret and their belief that they were rejected by mainstream society because of their sexual behavior and identity (Roesler & Deisher, 1972). According to Rotherham-Borus, Rosario, and Koopman (1991, p. 191), gay and bisexual youths often feel vulnerable because of "issues of disclosing or being discovered by family or friends, reactions by others to their homosexuality, and chronic stress associated with their homosexuality." Their empirical investigation, conducted with HMI African-American and Hispanic gay and bisexual male youths, reported that the most stressful events the youths faced were "coming out" to others, having their sexual orientation discovered by others, and being ridiculed because of their homosexuality. The youths felt that they had little control over the reactions of others: Would they be rejected or neglected? Ridiculed or assaulted? Raped or sexually abused? The stresses caused by coming out to others and being discovered as gay have been extensively covered in other publications (see Review in Savin-Williams & Lenhart, 1990). In the present article, research that addresses verbal and physical abuse and associated outcomes is reviewed, focusing exclusively on investigations conducted with samples of bisexual, lesbian, and gay male youths.

From a traditional scientific perspective, many of these studies are methodologically flawed. They include only a very small number of nonrepresentative lesbian, bisexual, and gay male youths. The vast majority of youths who will eventually identify themselves as lesbian, bisexual, or gay seldom embrace this socially ostracized label during adolescence and thus would never participate in scientific research. Those who do are often in an urban youth-serving agency, come into contact with the legal system, or are members of college campus organizations. At best, the research reported in this article samples a nonrepresentative (e.g., urban, help-seeking, college activists) fraction of an unusual (out to themselves and to others) section of the gay male, bisexual, and lesbian youth population. In addition, measures and procedures in published studies are often not adequately described and the validity and reliability of the instruments are usually unknown. Few studies considered for this review were published in peer-refereed, "rigorous" (i.e., low acceptance rate) journals; most were published as book chapters, conference articles, and invited articles for trade journals. Thus, it is difficult to evaluate their scientific merit. The approach taken in the current review is to include all available data, to note when they converge, and to offer tentative conclusions—fully aware that subsequent research may well present a different perspective on the issues addressed in this review.

Because lesbian, gay male, and bisexual youths who are visible and willing to participate in research studies are often those who are suffering most—physically, psychologically, and socially—clinicians and researchers may unduly present all such youths as weak, vulnerable adolescents who are running away from home, prostituting themselves, abusing drugs, and killing themselves. In actuality, the vast majority of gay male, bisexual, and lesbian youths cope with their daily, chronic stressors to become healthy individuals who make significant contributions to their culture. This article and the research it highlights must be balanced by research that focuses on the strengths, coping skills, and successes of lesbian, bisexual, and gay male youths.

The majority of empirical research conducted to date addresses the problems faced by gay and bisexual male youths and not those faced by lesbian and bisexual female youths. This literature fundamentally reflects the male bias of scientific research. In addition, research indicates that gay and bisexual male teenagers are more likely than lesbian and bisexual female teenagers to externalize their stress, thus increasing their visibility, and that female teenagers face their sexual identity crises later, after adolescence (see Savin-Williams, 1990). The latter finding suggests that it is more difficult to recruit lesbian than gay male adolescents for research purposes because there are fewer female lesbian and bisexual youths who have identified their sexual identity to themselves and to others. One approach to overcome this deficit would be to use adult lesbians and bisexual women's retrospective reports on growing up attracted to other women. There are, however, questionable assumptions regarding the use of retrospective data for highly charged emotional research issues. (Boxer, Cohler, Herdt, & Irvin, 1993). Even if problems of retrospective bias could be overcome, the pace of change in North American culture for lesbian, gay male, and bisexual youths has been so rapid that it is unlikely that the adolescent experiences of adult lesbian and bisexual women are particularly applicable for today's generation of lesbian and bisexual female adolescents. It is for these reasons that this article only reviews data from the lives of lesbian, bisexual, and gay male youths growing up in North America during the past decade (for cross-cultural reports, see Herdt, 1989).

One common theme identified in empirical studies and clinical reports of lesbian, gay male, and bisexual youths is the chronic stress that is often created by peers and family members through their verbal and physical abuse of lesbian, bisexual, and gay male adolescents. In the following sections, the harassment and abuse that threaten gay male, lesbian, or bisexual youth's well-being are reviewed. This response from peers and adults is often associated with several problematic outcomes, such as school-related problems, running away from home, conflict with the law, substance abuse, prostitution, and suicide. The causal link between these stressors and outcomes has not been scientifically established.

VERBAL AND PHYSICAL ABUSE AND HARASSMENT AS STRESSORS

Significant numbers of lesbian, gay male, and bisexual youths report that they have been verbally and physically assaulted, robbed, raped, or sexually abused by family members and peers

(DeStefano, 1988; Martin & Hetrick, 1988; National Gay and Lesbian Task Force, 1982; Remafedi, 1987a, 1987b; Rotheram-Borus et al., 1991). A review of violence inflicted on gay men and lesbians on college campuses revealed that 55% to 72% of those sampled reported verbal or physical abuse (D'Augelli, 1992). The incidence of physical threats of violence reached 25% in several surveys. The most frequent abusers (64%) in D'Augelli's sample of 160 college lesbians and gay men were fellow students and roommates. In 23% of reported incidents, the abusers were faculty, staff, and administrators.

In studies conducted with ethnic-minority youths seeking the services of the HMI, one half reported being ridiculed because of their homosexuality (Rosario, Rotheram-Borus, & Reid, 1992), and 46% had experienced violent physical attacks because of their sexual identity (Hunter & Schaecher, 1990). A survey of the Los Angeles County school system found that the high prevalence of antigay abuse inflicted by classmates was apparently premeditated, rather than a chance occurrence, and that the incidence is escalating dramatically (Peterson, 1989). The most frequent abusers were fellow teenagers. These data correspond with the data collected on antigay violence occurring on college campuses (D'Augelli, 1992).

Peer Harassment

Several studies of lesbian, gay male, and bisexual youths have documented the importance of peers in their lives. For example, among 61 gay and bisexual male college students, 57% reported that the most important person in their life was a gay or lesbian friend (D'Augelli, 1991). By contrast, 15% replied "parents" and 25%, "straight friends." In a study of over 300 lesbian, bisexual, and gay male youths between the ages of 14 and 23 years (Savin-Williams, 1990), youths reported that the most important aspect of their sense of self was having friends of the same sex. For lesbians, relations with parents trailed after female friends, career, academic success, and a love relationship; for gay male youths, relations with parents trailed after all the aforementioned aspects, physical attractiveness, and a social life.

Peer relations can, however, be a source of dissatisfaction and distress. On the basis of intake interviews and records of individual and group counseling of the first 2,000 sexual-minority youths between the ages of 12 and 21 years who either called or visited the HMI, one of the most difficult issues noted by the youths was social isolation (Martin & Hetrick, 1988). Over 95% of the teenagers reported that they frequently felt separated and emotionally isolated from their peers because of their feelings or differentness. Over one half of the gay and bisexual male HMI adolescents had been ridiculed because of their sexuality, usually by peers (Rotheram-Borus et al., 1991). Most abused were youths who failed to incorporate cultural ideals of gender-appropriate behavior and the consequences of nonconformity were known implicitly by most youths.

Other studies support these findings. Thirty percent of Remafedi's (1987b) 29 gay and bisexual male youths were victims of physical assaults, one half of which occurred on school property. Over one half reported regular verbal abuse from classmates, and 40% had lost a friend because of their homosexuality. White male college students in a conservative community feared being verbally and physically harassed; as a result, they were significantly less open about their homosexuality (D'Augelli, 1991). In Sears' (1991) study, 97% of the 36 lesbian, bisexual, and gay male Southern youths recalled negative attitudes by classmates and over one half feared being harassed, especially if they came out in high school. Only two found a peer group that was supportive of lesbian and gay people. Therefore, most passed as heterosexual until graduation.

In D'Augelli's (1992) review, the response to actual harassment or the fear of it among 70% to 80% of the lesbian and gay male college students was to remain hidden. They avoided situations and people that might implicate them as being lesbian or gay. Few (7%) reported the ha-

rassment to authorities, and nearly all (94%) expected to be harassed in the future. In a more detailed study, D'Augelli (1991) reported that the primary fear of the gay male college students (mean age, 21 years) was being rejected by parents. Following closely were the fears of being verbally abused and physically harmed because of their sexual orientation. Those less open had more fears, and those who dreaded physical harassment had lower life satisfaction scores.

Adult Harassment

Violence against lesbian, gay male, and bisexual youths often takes place in the home and neighborhood, perpetuated not only by peers but also by adults, including family members. After coming out to their family or being discovered as gay, many youths are "rejected, mistreated, or become the focus of the family's dysfunction" (Gonsiorek, 1988, p. 116). Youths fear retribution more from fathers than from mothers (D'Augelli, 1991). In a study of over 200 lesbian, gay male, and bisexual youths in Chicago (40% White, 30% Black, 12% Hispanic), relations with the mother were significantly better than with the father (Boxer, Cook, & Herdt, 1991). As a result, youths disclosed their sexual orientation earlier and more often to mothers than to fathers (see also Savin-Williams, 1990); many intensely feared their father's reactions to their sexual identity. Indeed, nearly 10% who disclosed to their fathers were kicked out of their home (Boxer et al., 1991).

The harassment may be more harmful than verbal abuse and may lead to physical assaults, including sexual abuse and rape. Martin and Hetrick (1988) found that problems within the family was the second most common presenting complaint of the HMI youths they interviewed, ranging "from feelings of isolation and alienation that result from fear that the family will discover the adolescent's homosexuality, to actual violence and expulsion from the home" (p. 174). Among the HMI lesbian, gay male, and bisexual youths, nearly one half who had suffered violence because of their sexuality reported that it was perpetuated by a family member (Martin & Hetrick, 1988). Others were abused in institutions such as foster homes, detention centers, and churches. Not infrequently, youths blamed themselves because they felt they must have seduced the adult or did not say "no" convincingly enough. In a later survey of 500 HMI youths—primarily male, Black, or Latino and with a mean age of 16.8 years—Hunter (1990) reported that 40% experienced violent physical attacks from adults or peers. Of the gay-related violence, 61% occurred in the family. Data from studies of male prostitutes, runaways, and homeless youths (discussed later) confirm this home-based violence.

Physical violence in the home may also include sexual abuse. The incidence of sexual abuse was 22% in Martin and Hetrick's study (1988). Similar to the pattern found among female heterosexuals, most cases of sexual abuse of lesbian and bisexual female youths occurred in the home. Among the male youths, sexual abuse was also most likely to occur in the home, usually by an uncle or older brother, but sometimes by a father. Two of Remafedi's (1987a) 29 male subjects were victims of incest, one was abused by an older brother and the other by his stepfather and eight uncles. Heterosexually oriented sexual abuse appears to occur more frequently among lesbians than among gay men (Pratch, Boxer, & Herdt, 1991).

Summary

Although definitive data suggesting that bisexual, lesbian, and gay male youths are more frequently ridiculed and abused by peers and family members than are other subpopulations of adolescents are not available, it is clear that these youths face unique harassment because of their sexual behavior and identity. There is sufficient evidence, however, to suggest that the physical and verbal abuse that lesbian, gay male, and bisexual adolescents receive is a source of great stress to them and is detrimental to their mental health.

There are many potential consequences of peer and family harassment. Although research has not yet addressed the sequential, casual pathway between harassment and negative outcomes, the two are clearly associated. In the following section, I discuss some of the negative outcomes that have been associated by researchers and clinicians with the verbal and physical abuse that lesbian, gay male, and bisexual youths experience.

OUTCOMES ASSOCIATED WITH PEER AND ADULT HARASSMENT

School-Related Problems

Many of the school-related problems experienced by lesbian, gay male, and bisexual youths are in response to the verbal and physical abuse that they receive from peers. Forms of violence range from name calling to "gay bashing" (physical attacks). Because much of this violence occurs in schools, school is too punishing and dangerous for many lesbian, gay male, and bisexual youths to tolerate. Hunter and Schaecher (1990) noted that the consequences of peer harassment include poor school performance, truancy, and dropping out of school. These problems have also been noted by counselors in mainstream schools (Price & Telljohann, 1991; Sears, 1988).

Most of the lesbian, gay male, and bisexual students who attended the gay-sensitive Harvey Milk School in New York City had dropped out of other public schools, largely because of peer harassment (Martin & Hetrick, 1988). Over two thirds of the gay and bisexual male youths in another study (Remafedi, 1987a, 1987b) said they had experienced school-related problems: Nearly 40% were truant, and 28% dropped out of school. These problems were manifested in another study, in which 60% of the gay and bisexual male youths failed a grade (Rotheram-Borus et al., 1991).

Rofes (1989), Peterson (1989), Newton and Risch (1981), and Freiberg (1987) pointed out that schools frequently fail to meet the needs of lesbian, gay male, and bisexual youths or stop the harassment because they fear the repercussions, lack the knowledge or resources, or are simply unaware. Many of the teachers and staff may be bisexual, lesbian, or gay but refuse to offer assistance because they fear that they will be accused of recruiting or converting youth.

In an article addressed to school personnel concerning high school students' attitudes toward homosexuality, Price (1982) concluded, "Adolescents can be very cruel to others who are different, who do not conform to the expectations of the peer group (p. 472)." This assessment echoed Norton's earlier view (1976) that the bisexual, lesbian, or gay male adolescent is "the loneliest person . . . in the typical high school of today (p. 376)." Very little has apparently changed in the last decade.

Runaway and Homeless Youths

There is little empirical verification regarding the percentage of runaways who identify themselves as lesbian, gay, or bisexual or the number of lesbian, gay male, and bisexual youths who run away from home. The National Network of Runaway and Youth Services (1991) reported that 6% of all runaways identified themselves as gay or lesbian. Among 12- to 17-year-old African-American and Hispanic male runaways in New York City, 6% considered themselves gay or bisexual (Rotheram-Borus, Meyer-Bahlburg, et al., 1992). According to the U.S. General Accounting Office (1989), 2% to 3% of homeless and runaway youths who sought services or assistance were reported by shelter staff to be lesbian, gay male, and bisexual youths. Another group, street youths who make money from prostitution, were not counted in this 2%-to-3% range. As I note later, many of these youths are likely to be gay male, lesbian, and bisexual teenagers.

These percentages are probably a gross underestimation because few youths are likely to tell authorities and staff their sexual identity. Indeed,

investigations of runaways in specific locales have revealed that a much larger percentage of runaway and homeless youths are gay, lesbian, or bisexual (Robertson, 1989; Yates, MacKenzie, Pennbridge, & Cohen, 1988). For example, 40% of street youths in Seattle (Orion Center, 1986) and 30% of the runaway youths in Los Angeles (Peterson, 1989, cited in Kruks, 1991) identified themselves as lesbian, bisexual, or gay.

When the directionality of the question is reversed and these youths are asked if they have ever run away from home, the percentages are considerably higher. For example, nearly one half of bisexual and gay male youths in one study (Remafedi, 1987a) had run away at least once; many, repeatedly. Many of the youths seeking the assistance of the Los Angeles Gay and Lesbian Community Services Center are runaways and throwaways (youths thrown out of the home by parents) who have had arguments and fights with their parents (Brownworth, 1992). Nearly one quarter are HIV-positive. These are vulnerable youths who frequently have good reason to run.

> If you leave home because you've been kicked out for being gay or because you can't cope with the homophobia of your surroundings and you go to a totally different city, you are alone, isolated, on the streets, and very, very vulnerable. (Kruks, as cited in Brownworth, 1992, p. 41)

By leaving, they avoid abuse and maintain the family secret (Burnison, 1986), but they also face a world that is prepared to exploit them.

If these youths do not find programs that meet their needs within 1 or 2 weeks of their arrival on the street, drugs, prostitution, pregnancy, criminal activity, and HIV will take them (Coleman, 1989; Peterson, 1989; Rotheram-Borus et al., 1991). For example, the National Coalition for the Homeless (1990) estimated that 12% to 20% of all homeless youths are HIV-positive. Runaway youths are at very high risk because of the "overwhelming concerns about day-to-day survival [that] can overshadow interest in illness prevention" (Remafedi, 1988, p. 141).

Conflict with the Law and Substance Abuse

Research indicates that gay male, lesbian, and bisexual youths are at high risk for conflict with the law and abusing substances. One quarter to one half of gay and bisexual male youths encounter trouble with the law, largely because of substance abuse, prostitution, truancy, and running away (Remafedi, 1987a; Rotheram-Borus et al., 1991). In the latter study, 23% encountered trouble with the police and 14% had been jailed. Rosario, Hunter, and Rotheram-Borus (1992) found that the male youths they interviewed reported an average of three conduct problems out of 13 listed in the *Diagnostic and Statistical Manual of Mental Disorders* (3rd ed., rev.; *DSM-III-R:* American Psychiatric Association, 1987), sufficient for a diagnosis of conduct disorder. Ninety-two percent of their sample had participated in at least one of the 13 behaviors; this prevalence rate was considerably higher than for comparable surveys of other ethnic-minority youth.

Remafedi (1987a) reported that most of the bisexual and gay male youths he questioned had used illegal drugs, especially alcohol and marijuana; tobacco and nitrate inhalants were used by almost one half of the youths. Nearly 60% were currently abusing substances and met psychiatric criteria for substance abuse. Seventeen percent had been in a chemical dependency treatment program.

These data correspond to the number of ethnic-minority lesbian, gay male, and bisexual youths who had a drug or alcohol problem in New York City (Rosario, Hunter, et al., 1992; Rotheram-Borus et al., 1991; Rotheram-Borus, Rosario, et al., 1992). In a sample of 20 lesbians, mean age of 19 years, all had consumed alcohol and three quarters had used drugs, including 28% who reported cocaine or crack use (Rosario, Rotheram-Borus, et al., 1992). In a sample of 136 HMI gay and bisexual male youths, 77% drank alcohol, 42% smoked marijuana, 25% used cocaine or crack, and 15% took hallucinogens during their lifetime (Rotheram-Borus, Rosario, et al., 1992). The authors noted that substance use was considerably higher for their sample than among national surveys (e.g., National Institute on Drug Abuse, 1991): ". . . the lifetime prevalence rates for our youths are 50% higher for alcohol, three times higher for marijuana and eight times higher for cocaine/crack" (p. 17). This increased substance abuse may be indicative of the high stress that lesbian, bisexual, and gay male youths experience because of their sexual orientation. It may also reflect the reality that for many youths, of both sexes, the bar subculture, with its emphasis on alcohol, has been a main entry into adult lesbian and gay male communities.

Although there is little documentation regarding the reasons bisexual, lesbian, and gay male youths use illegal substances and engage in criminal activity, they abuse drugs and commit crimes for many of the same reasons as do heterosexual youths (e.g., peer pressure and hedonism), as well as for reasons specific to their sexual identity. The latter include attempts to fog an increasing awareness that they are not heterosexual, to defend against the painful realization that being lesbian or gay means a difficult life lies ahead, and to take revenge against parents and society for rejecting them (Hammond, 1986).

Prostitution

Coleman's review (1989) of the empirical and clinical literature on prostitution among male adolescents revealed that the vast majority (at least two thirds) of male prostitutes are gay or bisexual. Some boys are situational prostitutes, and others make a living from prostitution. The professional "call" and "kept" boys frequently work gay male urban areas; they are the most gay-identified, usually with a well-integrated sense of their sexual identity. These youths are often from a middle-class background and are sufficiently physically attractive to support their prostitution business. Below them in status are "street hustlers," "bar boys," and "prison punks" who frequently come from lower socioeconomic backgrounds and are conflicted about their sexual identification.

According to Coleman, many of these boys begin prostituting in their early teenage years. They drop out of school, use drugs and alcohol, and run away from home or are thrown out by the family because of their sexual orientation. Many of their parents are heavy alcohol and drug users. Consistent with their family pattern, 20% to 40% of prostitutes also abuse drugs (including heroin) and alcohol. They run away from home to escape a family situation that is frequently chaotic and where they feel misunderstood, unwanted, and rejected. Over one half said they had been physically abused or raped. At some point in their lives most said they had been coerced into having unwanted sex. One half had been treated for at least one sexually transmitted disease and most were at high risk for HIV infection.

Those who become street hustlers face a difficult life. In Minneapolis, 75% of male street hustler youths are gay, with a history of dropping out of school, substance abuse, homelessness, and running away from home (Freiberg, 1985). They view themselves as "sluts and whores," have low self-esteem, and want to quit hustling but see no other option. In desperate need of money, they feel that they have no choice except to mug others or prostitute themselves. Most left home because they were thrown out by their parents, but they did not thereby escape sexual abuse, violence, and drugs. Among HMI gay and bisexual male youths in New York City, 23% had exchanged money or drugs for sex at some point in their lives (Rotheram-Borus, Rosario, et al., 1992).

Many male street hustlers are victims of rape and exploitation (Groth & Birnbaum, 1979). They face the trauma of male–male rape and the difficulties that gay male youths have in being taken seriously in reporting the crime and garnering support from authorities. They often have feelings of being "less of a man" and experience physical, emotional, and psychological problems. Davis and Leitenberg (1987) concluded in their review of adolescent sex offenders that there is little information when the victim of rape is male.

Data on adolescent female–female rape and young lesbian prostitution are difficult to find, although it is clear that, like many heterosexual women, young lesbians have been sexually abused and raped by men (Rothblum, 1990). Rosario, Rotheram-Borus, et al. (1992) reported that 5 of 20 Hispanic and Black New York City lesbian adolescents had exchanged sex for drugs or money. The rate of prostitution among other samples of lesbian adolescents is unknown.

Many youths report that they became prostitutes to survive and to escape physical, sexual, and emotional abuse in their homes and schools. The money helped them become independent from their families; for some, prostitution was a source of excitement and adventure in an otherwise dreary life. On closer examination, it is also clear that many youths turned to prostitution to meet nonsexual needs, such as to be taken care of, to receive affection, and for others to help them cope with their homosexuality. Among their fellow prostitutes, they found camaraderie and kinship that substituted for the neglect or rejection they received from their biological families and peers.

Suicide

Suicide among bisexual, gay male, and lesbian youths has received considerable attention during the last several years. A controversy emerged after the publication of the "Report of the Secretary's Task Force on Youth Suicide" and its quick repudiation by the administration of George Bush in response to conservative and religious opposition. According to the report, suicide is the leading cause of death among lesbian, gay male, and bisexual youths, primarily because of the debilitating effects of growing up in a homophobic society. They are two to three times more likely to kill themselves than are heterosexual youths. In fact, they constitute 30% of all adolescent suicides. The author of the report

(Gibson, 1989, pp. 3–110) suggested that one of the primary culprits "is a society that discriminates against and stigmatizes homosexuals while failing to recognize that a substantial number of its youth has a gay or lesbian orientation."

The empirical documentation is of one accord: The rate of suicide among gay male, bisexual, and lesbian youths is considerably higher than it is for heterosexual youth. Studies of lesbian, gay male, and bisexual youths report suicide attempts in the 20% to 40% range (Remafedi, 1987a; Remafedi, Farrow, & Deisher, 1991; Roesler & Deisher, 1972; Rotheram-Borus, Hunter, & Rosario, 1992; Schneider, Farberow, Kruks, 1989). These rates increase for special populations of gay male, bisexual, and lesbian youths: 41% of the girls and 34% of the boys who report being violently assaulted (Hunter, 1990); 53% among homeless and street youths (Kruks, 1991); 41% of those seeking assistance at service agencies (National Gay and Lesbian Task Force, 1982); and adolescents particularly sensitive to feeling rejected by others (Schneider et al., 1989).

Remafedi et al. (1991) studied 137 gay and bisexual male adolescents, ages 14 to 21 years. Most (82%) are White, volunteered for the research project, and resided in Minnesota or Washington. One third had at least one intentional self-destructive act; one half of these youths had multiple attempts. Remafedi et al. noted that, "the gravity of some attempts is reflected in the rate of subsequent hospitalization (21%), the lethality of methods (54%, moderate to high risk), and the victims' inaccessibility to rescue (62%, moderate to least rescuable) (p. 873)." The suicide attempts were frequently linked with sexual milestones, such as self-identification as gay or coming out to others. The most cited reason for attempting suicide was family problems. Summarizing their psychosocial data predicting suicide attempts, Remafedi et al. concluded that "compared with non-attempters, attempters had more feminine gender roles and adopted a bisexual or homosexual identity at younger ages. Attempters were more likely than peers to report sexual abuse,

drug abuse, and arrests for misconduct (p. 869)." Unlike previous studies, suicide attempts were not related to running away from home, depression, hopelessness, suicidal ideation, violence, discrimination, or loss of friendship. The attempters came from dysfunctional families, used drugs (85% reported illicit drug use), and acted out in other antisocial behaviors (more than one half had been arrested).

A study of 108 gay college men, primarily White (70%) and Latino (15%) and ranging in age from 16 to 24 years, in Los Angeles was undertaken by Schneider et al. (1989). Over one half of the youths reported that they occasionally had suicidal thoughts, considered suicidal action, formed a suicide plan, or made a suicide attempt. This group was characterized as having alcoholism in the family, physical abuse from family members, no religious affiliation, and a perception that those who usually supported them rejected their homosexuality. Twenty percent of the total sample reported that they made at least one suicide attempt; 9% made multiple attempts (2 to 14 times). The youngest attempt was at age 12, and one half of the youths received no treatment after their first attempt. At the time of first attempt, the youths felt hopeless, worthless, alienated, lonely, and helpless. Compared with nonsuicidal gay male youths, attempters were significantly younger when they first became aware of their homoerotic attractions (8 versus 11 years), first labeled their feelings but not themselves as homosexual (12 versus 14 years), and first became involved in a same-sex romantic relationship (16 versus 18 years). Although most attempters were aware of their same-sex attractions before their first suicide attempt, few had reached the point of identifying themselves as gay, felt positive about their sexual orientation, or had told others about their sexual identity. Attempts were most likely to occur when an individual was questioning his heterosexual identity or after same-sex sexual activities. Schneider et al. concluded that "suicidal behavior in gay youths may be the product both of familial factors that predispose youths to suicidal behavior, and of social and intrapersonal stressors involved in coming to terms with an emerging homosexual identity" (p. 381).

A group of younger (aged 14 to 19 years) and more ethnically diverse gay and bisexual male youths (47% Hispanic, 28% Black, 11% White, 14% other) from New York City were studied by Rotheram-Borus, Hunter, et al. (1992). Thirty-nine percent had attempted suicide; of these, 52% made multiple attempts. An additional 37% of the 139 youths thought about suicide every day for at least 1 week, and 49% said they had a family member or friend who had attempted or completed suicide. Nearly 60% reported suicidal ideation during the week before data collection. The attempters did not differ from the nonattempters in stressful life events, but they experienced more gay-related stressors, including coming out to parents (53% versus 30%), being discovered as gay by parents (37% versus 23%) or other family members (41% versus 28%), and being ridiculed for their sexual identity (57% versus 45%).

Psychiatrists who specialize in therapy with adolescent patients have speculated that the most frequent causes of suicide among lesbian, bisexual, and gay male adolescents are feelings of disenfranchisement, social isolation, rejection from family or peers, and self-revulsion (Kourany, 1987). The high risk among lesbian, bisexual, and gay male youths to suicidal ideation, attempts, and completions has been brought to the attention of psychiatrists (Kourany, 1987), social workers (Hunter & Schaecher, 1987), health educators (Remafedi, 1985), and therapists (Coleman & Remafedi, 1989; Rothblum, 1990). Unfortunately and tragically, few have listened.

CONCLUSION

Youths who are known to be lesbian, gay, or bisexual receive considerable verbal and physical abuse from peers and, all too frequently, from parents and other adults. These threats of physical harm and verbal abuse that bisexual, lesbian, and gay male youths are subjected to are sources of great stress to them, are detrimental to their mental health, and often correlate with negative outcomes such as school-related problems, substance abuse, criminal activity, prostitution, running away from home, and suicide.

Social science research does not allow us to generalize these findings to all bisexual, gay male, and lesbian youths, primarily because most of these youths are not "out" to themselves or to others. Thus, the youths studied to date are not a representative subset of the gay male, bisexual, and lesbian youth population—as noted by Rotheram-Borus, Rosario, et al. (1992): "These youths are atypical in that they have publicly disclosed their sexual preferences by seeking services at a social service agency serving homosexual youths . . ." (p. 15). They may also be "unusual" because those most abused are frequently youths who are "cross-gendered"; they do not or cannot abide by cultural definitions of acceptable feminine and masculine behavior and, thus, do not meet cultural ideals of gender-appropriate behaviors and roles. Deviating from acceptable sex roles is particularly problematic during adolescence.

> Males experience intense peer pressure to be "tough" and "macho," and females to be passive and compliant. Although social sex roles are not intrinsically related to sexual orientation, the distinction is poorly understood by most adolescents, as well as by most adults. Adolescents are frequently intolerant of differentness in others and may castigate or ostracize peers, particularly if the perceived differentness is in the arena of sexuality or sex roles. (Gonsiorek, 1988, p. 116)

Peer rejection may not be expressed directly, but it is recognized nevertheless by affected youths.

Although social science research has not addressed the casual pathway between harassment and negative outcomes, the two are clearly associated with each other. Rosario, Hunter, et al. (1992) most explicitly explored the linkages among emotional distress, conduct problems, alcohol and drug use, and sexual risk acts among gay and bisexual ethnic-minority male youths. In their sample, as might be expected, an increase in conduct problems was associated with increased levels of alcohol and drug usage and emotional distress. However, with an increase in conduct problems came a decrease in reported gay-related stress (negative reactions to coming out to others, being discovered as gay, and ridicule from others), suggesting that they may have desensitized themselves to these stresses by their acting-out behavior. Counter to findings with heterosexual youths, the authors' results did not support a single factor underlying multiple problem behavior; thus, it may not be possible to simply generalize research results from heterosexual to sexual-minority youths. Little is known about "normal" developmental pathways among gay male, lesbian, and bisexual youths and how they are similar and divergent from heterosexual youths (Savin-Williams, 1990). What is known is that the issue of sexual identity status is not a minor, insignificant factor in the lives of adolescents. Rosario, Hunter, et al. (1992) noted, ". . . the experience of being gay or bisexual in our society overwhelms any potential differences in social categories involving age, ethnicity, race, social class or geographical region of the country" (p. 19).

The variety of problematic behaviors described in this review may very well end the lives of many bisexual, lesbian, and gay male youths. Running away from home, engaging in high-risk sexual behavior, prostituting oneself, and abusing substances all place youth at high risk for suicide or being the victim of homicide. Those who survive will face throughout their lives the effects of growing up in a homophobic culture. If their social and interpersonal worlds are replete with verbal abuse and the threat of physical harm, youths in North American culture may find it difficult to totally expunge "internalized homophobia," a term Gonsiorek (1988) used to describe lesbian, gay male, and bisexual individuals' incorporation of biases against homosexuality that are prevalent in the social world. "Symptoms" range from covert forms such as self-doubt to overt self-hatred. The latter case "presents in persons who consciously accuse themselves of being evil, second class, or inferior because of their homosexuality. They may abuse substances or engage in other self-destructive or abusive behaviors" (Gonsiorek, 1988, p. 117).

The effects of peer and family harassment may be more severe for bisexual, lesbian, and gay male youth who are early adolescents or ethnic minorities because they may find it more difficult to recognize and accept their homosexuality than do older and White youths. Early adolescents, according to Remafedi (1987a), face several conflicts that hinder their ability to cope with being lesbian, gay, or bisexual: ". . . emotional and physical immaturity, unfulfilled developmental needs for identification with a peer group, lack of experience, and their dependence upon parents who may be unwilling or unable to provide emotional support around the issue of homosexuality" (p. 336).

Ethnic-minority youths who are gay, lesbian, or bisexual may also be at increased risk for the detrimental effects of homosexually oriented verbal and physical abuse. Savin-Williams and Rodriguez (1993) noted three unique tasks that these youths face: ". . . (a) developing and defining both a strong gay identity and a strong ethnic identity; (b) potential conflicts in allegiance, such as reference group identity within one's gay and ethnic community; and (c) experiencing both homophobia and racism" (p. 94). The Black and Hispanic sexual-minority youths at the Harvey Milk School had many signs of emotional isolation, vulnerability, and depression.

> Pervasive loss of pleasure, feelings of sadness, change of appetite, sleep disturbance, slowing of thought, lowered self-esteem with increased self-criticism and self-blame, and strongly expressed feelings of guilt and failure. Again, they repeatedly report they feel they are alone in the world, that no one else is like them, and that they have no one with whom they can confide or talk freely. (Martin & Hetrick, 1988, p. 172)

The dilemma for clinicians and other health care professionals is how best to assist sexual-minority youths. Few youths are willing to seek health care providers because they fear disclosure, humiliation, and discrimination. This may be for good reason: Gonsiorek (1988) noted that, rather than the client's actual problem (e.g., feelings of rejection), his or her sexual orientation may become the focus of treatment for the clinician or agency. Because of their prejudices, staff may allow, or even encourage, discrimination and name calling. Even if they are tolerant, they often lack the knowledge or resources to be of assistance to lesbian, bisexual, and gay male youths.

Guidelines are now available to assist health care providers to overcome these shortcomings (Bergstrom & Cruz, 1983; Kus, 1990; Rofes, 1989; Savin-Williams & Cohen, 1996; Savin-Williams & Lenhart, 1990). Clinicians and researchers should support the well-being of gay male, lesbian, and bisexual youths by conducting research, enacting policies, and encouraging behaviors that will help minimize the internalized homophobia, self-destructive behaviors, and homicide of our youths.

REFERENCES

American Psychiatric Association. (1987). *Diagnostic and statistical manual of mental disorders (3rd ed., rev.).* Washington, DC: Author.

Bergstrom, S., & Cruz. L. (1983). *Counseling lesbian and gay male youth: Their special lives/special needs.* Washington, DC: National Network of Runaway and Youth Services.

Boxer, A. M., Cohler, B. J., Herdt, G., & Irvin, F. (1993). Gay and lesbian youth. In P. H. Tolan & B. J. Cohler (Eds.). *Handbook of clinical research and practice with adolescents* (pp. 249–280). New York: Wiley.

Boxer, A. M., Cook, J. A., & Herdt, G. (1991). Double jeopardy: Identity transitions and parent-child relations among gay and lesbian youth. In K. Pillemer & K. McCartney (Eds.), *Parent-child relations throughout life.* (pp. 59–92). Hillsdale, NJ: Elrbaum.

Brownworth, V. A. (1992, March 24). America's worst-kept secret: AIDS is devastating the nation's teenagers, and gay kids are dying by the thousands. *The Advocate,* pp. 38–46.

Burnison, M. (1986, May). *Runaway youth: Lesbian and gay issues.* Paper presented at the Symposium on Gay and Lesbian Adolescents, Minneapolis, MN.

Center for Population Options. (1992). *Lesbian, gay and bisexual youth: At risk and underserved.* Washington, DC: Author.

Coleman, E. (1989). The development of male prostitution activity among gay and bisexual adolescents. *Journal of Homosexuality, 17,* 131–149.

Coleman, E., & Remafedi, G. (1989). Gay, lesbian, and bisexual adolescents: A critical challenge to counselors. *Journal of Counseling & Development, 68,* 36–40.

D'Augelli, A. R. (1991). Gay men in college: Identity processes and adaptations. *Journal of College Student Development, 32,* 140–146.

D'Augelli, A. R. (1992). Lesbian and gay male undergraduates' experiences of harassment and fear on campus. *Journal of Interpersonal Violence, 7,* 383–395.

Davis, G. E., & Leitenberg, H. (1987). Adolescent sex offenders. *Psychological Bulletin, 101,* 417–427.

DeStefano, A. M. (1988, October 7). New York teens antigay, poll finds. *Newsday* pp. 7, 21.

Freiberg, P. (1985, November 12). Minneapolis: Help for hustlers. *The Advocate,* pp. 12–13.

Freiberg, P. (1987, September 1). Sex education and the gay issue: What are they teaching about us in the schools? *The Advocate,* pp. 42–49.

Gibson, P. (1989). Gay male and lesbian youth suicide. U.S. Department of Health and Human Services, *Report of the secretary's task force on youth suicide, Vol. 3: Prevention and interventions in youth suicide.* Rockville, MD.

Gonsiorek, J. C. (1988). Mental health issues of gay and lesbian adolescents. *Journal of Adolescent Health Care, 9,* 114–122.

Groth, A. N., & Birnbaum, H. J. (1979). *Men who rape: The psychology of the offender.* New York: Plenum.

Hammond, N. (1986, May). *Chemical abuse in lesbian and gay adolescents.* Paper presented at the Symposium on Gay and Lesbian Adolescents, Minneapolis, MN.

Herdt, G. (Ed.) (1989). *Gay and lesbian youth.* New York: Harrington Park Press.

Hunter, J. (1990). Violence against lesbian and gay male youths. *Journal of Interpersonal Violence, 5,* 295–300.

Hunter, J., & Schaecher, R. (1987). Stresses on lesbian and gay adolescents in schools. *Social Work in Education, 9,* 180–189.

Hunter, J., & Schaecher, R. (1990). Lesbian and gay youth. In M. J. Rotheram-Borus, J. Bradley, &

N. Obolensky (Eds.), *Planning to live: Evaluating and treating suicidal teens in community settings* (pp. 297–316). Tulsa: University of Oklahoma Press.

Kourany, R. F. C. (1987). Suicide among homosexual adolescents. *Journal of Homosexuality, 13,* 111–117.

Kruks, G. (1991). Gay and lesbian homeless/street youth: Special issues and concerns. *Journal of Adolescent Health Care, 12,* 515–518.

Kus, R. J. (Ed.) (1990). *Keys to caring: Assisting your gay and lesbian clients.* Boston: Alyson.

Martin, A. D., & Hetrick, E. S. (1988). The stigmatization of the gay and lesbian adolescent. *Journal of Homosexuality, 15,* 163–183.

National Coalition for the Homeless. (1990). *Fighting to live: Homeless people with AIDS.* Washington, DC: Author.

National Gay and Lesbian Task Force (1982). *Gay rights in the United States and Canada.* New York: Author.

National Institute on Drug Abuse. (1991). *National household survey on drug abuse: Population estimates 1990.* Washington, DC: U.S. Government Printing Office.

National Network of Runaway and Youth Services. (1991). *To whom do they belong? Runaway, homeless and other youth in high-risk situations in the 1990s.* Washington, DC: Author.

Newton, D. E., & Risch, S. J. (1981). Homosexuality and education: A review of the issue. *The High School Journal, 64,* 191–202.

Norton, J. L. (1976). The homosexual and counseling. *Personnel and Guidance Journal, 54,* 374–377.

Orion Center. (1986). *Survey of street youth.* Seattle, WA: Author.

Peterson, J. W. (1989, April 11). In harm's way: Gay runaways are in more danger than ever, and gay adults won't help. *The Advocate,* pp. 8–10.

Pratch, L., Boxer, A. M., & Herdt, G. (1991). *First sexual experiences among gay and lesbian youth: Person, age, and context.*

Price, J. H. (1982). High school students' attitudes toward homosexuality. *Journal of School Health, 52,* 469–474.

Price, J. H., & Telljohann, S. K. (1991). School counselors' perceptions of adolescent homosexuals. *Journal of School Health, 61,* 433–438.

Remafedi, G. J. (1985). Adolescent homosexuality: Issues for pediatricians. *Clinical Pediatrics, 24,* 481–485.

Remafedi, G. (1987a). Adolescent homosexuality: Psychosocial and medical implications. *Pediatrics, 79,* 331–337.

Remafedi, G. (1987b). Male homosexuality: The adolescent's perspective. *Pediatrics, 79,* 326–330.

Remafedi, G. J. (1988). Preventing the sexual transmission of AIDS during adolescence. *Journal of Adolescent Health Care, 9,* 139–143.

Remafedi, G., Farrow, J. A., & Deisher, R. W. (1991). Risk factors for attempted suicide in gay and bisexual youth. *Pediatrics, 87,* 869–875.

Robertson, M. J. (1989). *Homeless youth in Hollywood: Patterns of alcohol use.* Berkeley, CA: Alcohol Research Group.

Roesler, T., & Deisher, R. (1972). Youthful male homosexuality: Homosexual experience and the process of developing homosexual identity in males aged 16 to 22 years. *Journal of the American Medical Association, 219,* 1018–1023.

Rofes, E. (1989). Opening up the classroom closet: Responding to the educational needs of gay and lesbian youth. *Harvard Educational Review, 59,* 444–453.

Rosario, M., Hunter, J., & Rotheram-Borus, M. J. (1992). *HIV risk acts of lesbian adolescents.* Unpublished manuscript, Columbia University.

Rosario, M., Rotheram-Borus, M. J., & Reid, H. (1992). *Personal resources, gay-related stress, and multiple problem behaviors among gay and bisexual male adolescents.* Unpublished manuscript, Columbia University.

Rothblum, E. D. (1990). Depression among lesbians: An invisible and unresearched phenomenon. *Journal of Gay & Lesbian Psychotherapy, 1,* 67–87.

Rotheram-Borus, M. J., Hunter, J., & Rosario, M. (1992). *Suicidal behavior and gay-related stress among gay and bisexual male adolescents.* Unpublished manuscript, Columbia University.

Rotheram-Borus, M. J., Meyer-Bahlburg, H. F. L., Rosario, M., Koopman, C., Haignere, C. S., Exner, T. M., Matthieu, M., Henderson, R., & Gruen, R. S. (1992). Lifetime sexual behaviors among predominantly minority male runaways and gay/bisexual adolescents in New York City. *AIDS Education and Prevention, Supplement,* 34–42.

Rotheram-Borus, M. J., Rosario, M., & Koopman, C. (1991). Minority youths at high risk: Gay males and runaways. In M. E. Colten & S. Gore (Eds.), *Adolescent stress: Causes and consequences.* (pp. 181–200). New York: Aldine.

Rotheram-Borus, M. J., Rosario, M., Meyer-Bahlburg, H. F. L., Koopman, C., Dopkins, S. C., & Davies, M. (1992). *Sexual and substance use behaviors among homosexual and bisexual male adolescents in New York City.* Unpublished manuscript, Columbia University.

Savin-Williams, R. C. (1990). *Gay and lesbian youths: Expressions of identity.* Washington, DC: Hemisphere.

Savin-Williams, R. C., & Cohen, K. M. (Eds.). (1996). *The lives of lesbians, gays, and bisexuals: Children to Adults.* Fort Worth: Harcourt Brace.

Savin-Williams, R. C., & Lenhart, R. E. (1990). AIDS prevention among gay and lesbian youth: Psychosocial stress and health care intervention guidelines. In D. G. Ostrow (Ed.), *Behavioral aspects of AIDS and other sexually transmitted diseases* (pp. 75–99). New York: Plenum.

Savin-Williams, R. C., & Rodriguez, R. G. (1993). A developmental, clinical perspective on lesbian, gay male, and bisexual youths. In T. P. Gullotta, G. R. Adams, & R. Montemayor (Eds.), *Adolescent sexuality. Advances in adolescent development, Vol. 5* (pp. 77–101). Newbury Park, CA: Sage.

Schneider, S. G., Farberow, N. L., & Kruks, G. N. (1989). Suicidal behavior in adolescent and young adult gay men. *Suicide and Life-Threatening Behavior, 19,* 381–394.

Sears, J. T. (1988, April). *Attitudes, experiences, and feelings of guidance counselors in working with homosexual students: A report on the quality of school life for Southern gay and lesbian students.* Paper presented at the American Educational Research Association Meeting, New Orleans, LA.

Sears, J. T. (1991). *Growing up gay in the South: Race, gender, and journeys of the spirit.* New York: Harrington Park Press.

U.S. General Accounting Office. (1989). *Homelessness: Homeless and runaway youth receiving services at federally funded shelters.* Washington, DC: Author.

Yates, G., MacKenzie, R., Pennbridge, J., & Cohen, E. (1988). A risk profile comparison of runaway and non-runaway youth. *American Journal of Public Health, 78,* 820–821.

PART TEN

DIVERSITY IN ADOLESCENCE

*Diversity of people and their setting means that one cannot
assume that general rules of development either exist for,
or apply in the same way to, all children and families.*
LERNER AND MILLER

Adolescence as an academic field has become increasingly more concerned
with investigating and understanding diversity. Obviously, adolescents are not
a monolithic group, but can be classified by such well-known variables as ethnicity, gender, and social class. Age is a factor; early and late adolescents differ not only in physical size, but in cognitive ability, behaviors, and psychosocial characteristics. Some researchers contend that gender differences are
paramount in many aspects of the lives of youth; others believe gender differences are the result of the socialization process, and their significance may decline as gender equity becomes a reality. Contemporary concerns with diversity are intended to bring to full awareness the major group differences that do
exist but previously had neither been fully recognized nor understood. However, one must remain aware that differences between groups are almost always much smaller than the wide differences that can be observed within any
one group. Within-group differences are enormous for most measurable
human dimensions, including height, weight, intelligence, dexterity, strength,
and achievement. That fact may explain why within-group differences—that
is, individual differences—have overshadowed our thinking about group differences for almost a century.

Spencer and Dornbusch (29) reviewed the literature concerned with minority
adolescents and found the research to be flawed, biased, and primarily based
on a deficit model. According to the deficit model, only attributes that are
missing or less than the standard are investigated. Past research seems to have
focused on one specific minority group in order to evaluate it against the majority. Despite the abundance of this type of research, it has done surprisingly

little to promote a better understanding of either minority or majority. Another challenge to studies of minority youth comes from the unbelievable and inexcusable paucity of research. To be specific, from 1985 to 1989 only 2% of psychological research articles used African-American subjects.

Political and cultural values and the spirit of the time do affect the distinction between what is considered normal or deviant. For example, homosexuality, which once was classified as abnormal, is no longer considered a psychiatric disorder but the manifestation of a different lifestyle. In addition, the predominance of an ethnic group within a particular social class has frequently blurred and confused significant distinctions between race and class. Although many believe that more blacks live in poverty than whites, in reality more whites than blacks are poor. However, the proportion of blacks who are poor is much larger than the proportion of whites. Trying to control for all of the factors that influence individual behavior and ascertaining what part race versus social class plays in determining behavior can be complex. For example, although not all minority youth are poor, poverty contributes to adversity, and adversity contributes to behavior. Banks (9) adds greatly to this discussion. Spencer and Dornbusch emphasize the importance of making critical distinctions between diverse groups in order to more accurately understand and appreciate the unique characteristics of minority youth.

Lerner's (30) paper, aptly titled "Diversity," further illuminates this topic. According to Lerner, the study of diversity is pivotal to understanding human development because, as the opening quote suggests, not all children experience development sequella the same way at the same time. Lerner (3), associated with the theory of developmental contextualism, focuses on the interaction between individuals who are constantly changing and the context in which these changes take place. Context encompasses not only society, community, and family attributes, but it also includes the physical environment and the interactive relationship between the individual and all of these features. This idea is illustrated effectively in Figure 1 of Reading 3. Lerner urges policy makers, educators, and sociologists to pay more attention to diversity and the numerous contextual factors in an individual's life to appreciate racial, ethnic, gender, national, and cultural variations and similarities and to use that knowledge to plan more effective and sensitive programs and policies.

Sociologists and psychologists in the past have studied monoethnic groups; however, Phinney and Alipuria (31) open up an entirely new field of investigation by examining multiracial and multiethnic individuals. There has been almost no research that identifies children from racially mixed families. Census forms do not even recognize the existence of multiethnics, except for the nondescript category, "Other." Researchers actually have difficulty identifying those who identify themselves as "other" or who leave that question blank. Nevertheless, an awareness of multiethnic identity introduces a hitherto unrecognized diversity variable that could shed light on the relevance of culture and ethnicity to a person's well-being and self-esteem in a multicultural society. Tiger Woods most illustriously brought this point home by referring to himself as "Cablinasian," emphasizing his Caucasian, black American, Indian, and Asian heritage. Phinney's work suggests that a simple distinction between ethnic categories is no longer sufficient as increasingly more children grow up in multiethnic families. Multiethnic individuals literally embody the idea of America as a "melting pot." Strong arguments for and against recognizing multiethnicity as a new demographic category are being brought to bear on the government.

The role that culture, race, ethnicity, gender, and class play in determining how smoothly or painfully anyone will pass through adolescence is yet to be fully acknowledged and appreciated. However, it is only as a result of the more recent focus on diversity that the impact of ethnicity, nationality, gender, social class, cultural differences, and religious affiliation on individual growth and development is better understood.

CHALLENGES IN STUDYING MINORITY YOUTH

MARGARET BEALE SPENCER AND SANFORD M. DORNBUSCH
University of Pennsylvania and Stanford University

SOCIOCULTURAL AND HISTORICAL INFLUENCES

Minority groups are not homogeneous; they differ in their history and in their current sociocultural condition. For example, Cuban, Puerto Rican, and Mexican immigrants are all Hispanics, yet they had different reasons for migrating, came from divergent socioeconomic backgrounds in their native countries, and experience different rates and types of employment in the United States (77, 108). Native Americans are also heterogeneous and widely dispersed: more than two hundred tribal languages are still spoken, and approximately five hundred native entities are recognized by the federal government (53). There is also diversity among African-Americans. For example, adolescents of Jamaican background have had experiences quite unlike those of African-Americans from the rural South (68). Different groups face unique challenges and opportunities within the majority culture. They differ in their adaptive or maladaptive responses, with the effect of either buffering or increasing the impact of inequity. Thus, con-

siderable variation within ethnic groups is the rule rather than the exception.

Demographic variables also influence minority adolescent development. Specifically, the size of the group, its relative distribution in the wider society, and its geographic location, whether urban or rural, are significant factors. Adolescents, for whom personal characteristics and acceptance by peers are central concerns, are particularly sensitive to the absence of fellow members of their minority in the community:

> "I'm the only Black in my Advanced Bio class. I'm the only Black on the soccer team. I'm the only Black in the band." (teenager in a suburban California high school, 88)
> "Sometimes you don't fit in. Like if you're a Puerto Rican on an Italian block." (110, p. 24)

The concentration of an immigrant group in an area increases its visibility and may increase the level of discrimination that it faces. Often a minority group is segregated within a geographic area, forming a cultural island within the larger social unit. This segregation may be involuntary, discrepant findings suggest the need for empirical studies of the role of religion in the lives of minority, particularly African-American, adolescents.

Another significant influence on the life experiences of minority adolescents is the political climate (13, 80). Political developments such as the expansion of school integration or the loss of industrial jobs frequently open or close windows of opportunity within the wider society. Sometimes instrumental changes manifest themselves as shifts in minority-group consciousness, such as the Black Power movement in the 1960s (91), the growing pressure by Hispanics for the election of more Hispanic officials, and the increasing unity among the diverse tribes of Native Americans. American society is changing rapidly, and the changes affect the ways in which minority adolescents perceive their personal situation, the position of their particular minority group, and both their short-term and long-term options.

Now that we have seen some of the demographic, historical, and sociocultural forces that are part of the background of minority adolescent development, let us turn to the subject of identity formation. We shall consider three major influences on adolescent development—family, peers, and schools—and end with a look at the types of future research that can improve our knowledge base and lead to the creation of informed social policy.

ISSUES OF IDENTITY

Adolescence is a crucial period for identity formation. "Identity, a conscious sense of individual uniqueness . . . and a solidarity with a group's ideals" (29, p. 208), is more problematic for minority adolescents, who often find themselves enveloped by the values and standards of the mainstream culture (78). In light of negative evaluations from the majority, the task of developing a positive identity as a member of a minority group may be difficult. When race is linked to membership in a minority group, the message from the wider culture may be, "If you're white you're all right; if you're brown, stick around; if you're black, stay back" (74, p. 98).

The adolescent's awareness of minority status is qualitatively different from that of the child (104). Very young children, for example, often

think of their race and gender as mutable, something that may change as they grow (100, 104, 114). Many parents of minority children have confronted logic similar to that expressed by the adopted three-year-old African-American boy who held his white mother's hand, turned his palm over, studied it, and said, "When I'm big, I'm gonna be white all over, like you." Then he added, "And I'm gonna be a mommy when I get big!" (75)

In contrast to young children, adolescents have the ability to interpret cultural knowledge, to reflect on the past, and to speculate about the future (41, 42, 50). With cognitive maturity, minority adolescents are keenly aware of the evaluations of their group made by the majority culture (17, 32, 78). Thus the young African-American may learn as a child that black is beautiful but conclude as an adolescent that white is powerful (100).

The minority adolescent's awareness of such negative appraisals, of conflicting values, and of restricted occupational opportunities can affect life choices and the strategies selected for negotiating a life course. As one minority adolescent explained: "The future they see is shut off. It's closed. You're afraid to dream for fear of not reaching it, so you don't set up any goals, and that way you don't fail" (74, p. 91).

Minority youths' perceptions of themselves and their group are significant influences on socioemotional development. The "looking-glass self," in which one imagines the reactions of others to one's behavior and personality, affects the adolescent's identity development (19). For minority youth the stigmas of racial stereotypes, often reinforced by poverty, have the potential to distort the image in the mirror.

Yet negative evaluations of one's group need not portend a poor self-concept for minority youth, for minority status is only one of many potential influences on the adolescent's sense of self (20). In other domains—school, home, friends, sports—self-esteem may find positive expression and encouragement (40). The impact of negative appraisals from the wider society may be countered by peers, parents, teachers, and other members of the youth's community (3, 5, 11, 20, 46, 100).

Still, many minority youth are faced with cultural devaluation of the symbols and heroes of their group. Chinese youth, for example, confront American role models who typically personify values antithetical to those of their immigrant parents (107). Adolescents, becoming sensitive to societal inconsistency, are particularly affected by the conflict in values. A Chinese adolescent described her situation: "Chinese people had Chinese opinions. American people had American opinions. And in almost every case, the American version was much better . . . [but] there were too many choices and it was easy to get confused" (109, p. 191).

For other minority youth the problem is not conflicting role models but a lack of successful role models with whom to identify. This situation confronts many African-American youth in the inner cities. Sylvester Monroe, an African-American journalist, reflected on this issue, drawing on his own adolescent experience in an urban housing project: "If you were black, you didn't quite measure up . . . For a black kid there was a certain amount of self-doubt. It came at you indirectly. You didn't see any black people on television, you didn't see any black people doing certain things, and you couldn't rationalize it. I mean, you don't think it out but you say, 'Well, it must mean that white people are better than we are. Smarter, brighter—whatever' " (74, pp. 98–99). In response to such pressures, minority adolescents may strive to conform to white middle-class standards. Not all minority youth, however, have the option of fitting comfortably into the majority culture. For many, racial characteristics and skin color constrain their acceptance by white society, although for others the issue is not acceptance. As minority youth prepare for adult roles, their greatest desire is for just and equitable treatment (99, 102).

This issue of identity development for minority youth is further complicated by the value associated with a group's racial characteristics.

Some youths find it easy—and desirable—to "pass" as whites; others cannot, or choose not to do so. For some minority females the white standard of beauty engenders self-denigration of their appearance (89). These are particularly significant concerns during adolescence, when physical characteristics are very much an object of concern. Adolescents in general are self-conscious and reluctant to stand out in a crowd. The visible minority youth has little choice.

Those minority teenagers who can interact easily or identify with the majority culture may find themselves rejected by their own group (3, 32, 36, 71, 72, 80). Overidentification with the white majority is commonly labeled pejoratively by minority groups. Native Americans who "act white" are "Apples"; Asians are "Bananas"; "Coconuts" describes that group of Hispanics; and African-Americans are "Oreos." The negative metaphors describe individuals who are racially "of color" but behaviorally "white" (71).

In terms of emotional development, adolescence is a time of constant, and often painful, comparison of oneself with others. Because the social network of the teenager is wider than the child's, adolescents are exposed more directly to the ideals and values of the majority culture. Compared to children, they are increasingly literate, have greater access to the media, and are more mobile, with greater physical freedom and financial resources to explore the environment beyond their immediate neighborhood. Even when they have a positive personal identity (40), minority adolescents may develop ambivalent or negative attitudes toward their own group. For example, African-American teenage girls who live in white suburbs are more negative toward their own culture than are younger African-American females (4). Other research suggests that Asian-American high school students are more negative toward their own group than are other minorities (88). Yet a 1985 study of African-American children through early adolescence noted a progressively more positive orientation toward their own group as the children grew older (104).

Minority adolescents clearly have a special task: to negotiate a balance between two value systems: that of their own group and that of the majority (12). Some youths reject the mainstream, forgoing the rewards that are controlled by the majority (32, 63); others denigrate their own culture and completely assimilate the values and behavior of the majority; and still others take the difficult path to biculturality.

Although young children are aware of some racial and cultural differences, minority individuals first consciously confront the issue of biculturality only at adolescence. This event traditionally has been described in terms of conflict, but social scientists now suggest that there is a double consciousness, an ability to perceive social interaction in terms of different standards and values (21).

W. E. B. Du Bois, writing at the beginning of this century, described the African-American of his day as "two warring idols in one dark body" (27). Internal conflict and tension were attributed to individuals who participated in two cultures simultaneously (106). This issue is raised by many individuals:

> "I wanted my children to have the best combination: American circumstances and Chinese character. How could I know these two things do not mix?" (109, p. 254)
>   " 'Got one mind for white folk to see, 'nother for what I know is me." (Negro folk song, cited in I, p. 194)

Stonequist's concept of the "marginal man" views him as "poised in psychological uncertainty between two (or more) social worlds" (106, p. 329). The marginal man was at home nowhere, belonging in neither group, yet wavering between both, uncertain how to act. A study of Mexican-Americans found that many members of this group were caught between two opposing cultures and often sought relief from their problems through alcohol (60).

In forging an identity, minority adolescents may choose among several strategies for dealing with their ethnicity: alienation, separation, as-

similation, and biculturalism (89). Assimilation occurs when the belief systems and life-styles of a minority are replaced by those of the majority culture (92). In contrast, bicultural individuals shuttle successfully between their primary or familial culture and the dominant culture (92). Ramirez proposes a flexibility model, wherein the norms of both groups are available to minority youth and the standard used depends on the situation (92).

Bicultural competence may offer some advantages (97). For example, some bicultural Blackfeet Indians have been able to make situationally based choices of cultural orientations. With models from both their own ethnic group and the majority, individuals have had the advantage of a large repertory of skills and knowledge from which to draw (66).

Discussions of the experiences of Asian-American youth are cast largely in terms of conflict rather than biculturality (107). Work by Phinney indicates that Asian-American attitudes tend toward assimilation rather than ethnic pride (88). Conflict characterizes the feelings of Southeast Asian immigrant youth in particular (80). Adolescent Southeast Asians may not share the orientations of adult refugees, who still look back to their homeland and may feel exiled in America. Biculturality develops as a coping style, as a means of overcoming the feelings of helplessness that often overwhelm these youth. Nidorf characterizes this group as "struggling to select from both cultures those values and beliefs that will facilitate existence" (80, p. 421). There are frequently significant disparities between traditional values and American ideals of behavior. Nidorf notes:

> Effective coping often requires [youth] to embrace American values at the expense of values cherished by the parents. For example, in the United States we believe that the young person must develop autonomy from parents as a means toward achieving the strong sense of personal identity necessary for leading a productive life. However, the Southeast Asian youths are expected by their parents to remain indefinitely in a position of mutual

interdependence with family members, their sense of self-worth and maturation established by subordinating their own needs and by assuming increasing responsibility for meeting the needs of family members . . . The confusing message received by refugee youths from their parents [is] "Become a success in the United States, but find a way to do it without becoming an American." (80, pp. 421–422)

Sung points out that many Chinese youth "perceive of their marginality as a dilemma. They are faced with a situation where courses of action are diametrically opposed or radically different . . . The choices are painful and more often than not immobilizing. Not having the maturity to evaluate or modify their courses of action or to adjust their values, they do nothing; the vacuousness of their . . . inability to decide is extremely uncomfortable" (80, p. 268).

Language is tied to issues of biculturality for many minority youth. Although a large number have made English their dominant language, their parents may still rely on the native tongue. Furthermore, these youths may be rejected by majority peers and teachers despite their efforts toward linguistic and cultural assimilation (37).

The adaptive consequences of biculturality vary from one social context to another and depend on many factors, such as majority attitudes, the strengths of the minority group, color and social visibility, the youth's own resilience or vulnerability, and factors within the family (96, 101, 103).

FAMILY COMPOSITION AND PROCESSES

Minority-group families differ from majority families in their size, structure, and composition, their reliance on kinship networks, and their levels of income and parental education. These variables affect parenting behaviors (69, 90), family interaction processes (24, 26, 52, 61), and children's socioemotional functioning (70). Other research relates these family characteristics to adolescents' school performance (14, 25, 95). Thus, family environment is a mediating factor that strongly shapes the development of minority youth.

Large and extended families are more common among minorities than among non-Hispanic whites (117, 118). In 1980 families with five or more members accounted for 31% of Hispanic households but only 17% of the general population (51, 76). In addition, there are differences in the extent to which minority families interact with their extended-kin networks. African-Americans and Hispanics interact more with grandparents, aunts, uncles, cousins, and other more distant relatives than do non-Hispanic whites, and the support system among African-American extended kin is more active than that of other groups (44, 73, 105, 111).

Single teenage mothers particularly benefit from the availability of other adults to serve as surrogate parents. Research indicates that African-American adolescent mothers in extended families are more likely to remain in school than their peers who lack this support, and are less likely to rely on welfare. These young mothers also report more peer group support and more often say they feel in control of their lives than do African-American adolescent mothers living independently (15, 33). Advantages accruing to other minority adolescents from extended kinship networks have yet to be explored.

Single-parent families are much more common in the African-American and Hispanic groups than in the majority American population. In 1985 the proportion of children and youth living in single-parent households was 18% for non-Hispanic whites, 29% for Hispanics, and 54% for African-Americans (112). The proportion of children and youth who will live in a single-parent household before reaching age 18 is even greater; these statistics merely suggest the magnitude of the population that will experience single parenting during at least part of their childhood.

The presence of a single parent is more likely to continue into adolescence for children of minority families than for those of non-Hispanic white families. Half of all African-American youth are likely to remain with a single parent for their entire childhood, in contrast to only 15% of whites (70). Single motherhood is clearly linked to poverty. Even among whites, about half the children living in single-parent households are below the poverty line. Among minorities, about 70% of African-American and Hispanic children being raised by single mothers are poor (31), and the number of these poor families has more than doubled since 1960 (113).

In comparison with the situation in two-parent households, single parents usually have more limited resources of time, money, and energy. We can speculate that this shortage of resources prompts them to encourage early autonomy among their adolescent children. For African-Americans, Asian-Americans, Hispanics, and non-Hispanics whites, granting adolescents more autonomy in decision making than is typical for their age is associated with negative outcomes such as high rates of deviance and poor grades in school (24). Thus, differences owing to family structure are partially explained by relating early autonomy in decision making to various outcomes. Poor school performance and a high incidence of deviance (truancy, running away from home, smoking, early dating, contacts with police, and arrests) among many minority youth can be explained in part by the association of single parenthood with this parenting practice (24, 25).

Similarly, within both minority and majority groups the extent of joint decision making between adolescents and parents helps explain the higher grades and lower rates of deviance of children whose parents are better educated. Those parents consult with their adolescents more often, and such a decision-making pattern is associated with positive outcomes across all ethnic and social-class groups. Minority parents, who are often less educated than majority whites, tend to employ joint decision making less often; this low frequency is associated, in turn, with lower grades for adolescents and greater deviance (24, 25).

Minority parents, like all parents, are responding to economic, social, and political conditions (5, 11, 14). Minority youth are more likely to come from disadvantaged and female-headed families (18). Although impoverished families often raise competent youth (43), poor parents risk having a diminished capacity for supportive and involved parenting, and thus tend to see an increased incidence of impaired socioemotional functioning among their youth (70). The absence of fathers can be explained in part by economic circumstances. Among African-Americans there has been a reduction since the 1960s in the male-female wage ratio (2, 115). Changes in industrial and occupational opportunities have reduced the capacity of minority men to support their families and, in turn, have affected their marriageability (34, 70, 116, 119).

A carefully documented review has examined how the psychological stress associated with poverty and unemployment adversely affects parenting behaviors. When parents are overburdened, they are less likely to display parenting behaviors that require patience (70). Parents who engage in practices that appear coercive may have valid motives for their behavior. Research is needed that goes beyond the study of behaviors to examine parental strategies and goals.

In spite of the difference in access to resources, there are striking similarities between competent adolescents from African-American blue-collar families and those from white middle-class families. Living in a competent, intact family facilitates highly adaptive levels of functioning among adolescents; family behaviors are more significant than the influences of class and minority status (58). It has been asserted that "middle-class Blacks are ardent defenders of the society's dominant values" (56, p. 131), but they typically do not have the same resources as whites to mobilize toward the shared goals.

Certain aspects of home life can serve to protect minority youth from social patterns of injustice (11, 46, 54). The community and family can filter out racist, destructive messages (5). Parents can provide alternate frames of reference to those presented by the majority (5, 100); they also can provide role models and encouragement.

Among some Asian subgroups parents are concerned that successful adaptation to mainstream society will undermine their cultural traditions and create problems in disciplining and controlling adolescents. A Southeast Asian refugee discussed his teenage daughter's behavior: "She complains about going to the Lao temple on the weekend and instead joined a youth group in a neighborhood Christian church. She refused to wear traditional dress on the Lao New Year. The girl is setting a very bad example for her younger sisters and brothers" (80, pp. 422–423).

Minority parents strive to protect their children from the world, since societal and peer influences often are perceived to be in conflict with the minority group's values. For example, Chinese parents are extremely conservative about dating, for both their daughters and their sons (107). Since the parents themselves have had no dating experience, parental control in this domain is seen as normative—at least by the parents.

> Good girls simply did not go out with boys alone, so the parents are very suspicious and apprehensive about their daughters dating, and watch them very carefully. For the daring girl who tries to go out against her parents' wishes, there will be a price to pay . . . It is no easier for the Chinese boys. The pressure to succeed in school is even greater than for girls, and parental opposition to dating is even more intense . . . Naturally some children do not agree with their parents and have to carry on their high school romances on the sly. These children are bombarded by television, advertisements, stories, magazines and real-life examples of boy-girl attraction. The teenager is undergoing puberty and is experiencing the instinctive urges surging within him or her. In this society, teenagers are titillated, whereas in China they are kept under wraps until they are married. (107, p. 258).

The views and assumptions of minority parents reflect political and social currents. For example, there are different interpretations of the authoritarian parenting style that is frequently characteristic of African-American families (70).

According to some, a socialization geared toward obedience and submission to authority was considered most adaptive for African-American children, given the roles they were expected to fulfill within their majority society (7, 9). McGoldrick pointed out that African-American parents who are strict in disciplining their children are preparing them for adulthood, for they believe that society imposes severe consequences on African-Americans who transgress (67).

Minority parenting is also affected by the activities and resources of adolescent peers. It is of great concern to minority parents that the peer group in inner cities can often offer tangible rewards for delinquent behavior to youths who feel alienated from society (34). Few legitimate routes to success are available for minority youth. Some who participate in the sale of drugs earn more money than their parents. Under such conditions, peer influences can easily outweigh parental control.

PEER INFLUENCES

During adolescence most youths turn increasingly to their peers. Minority teenagers, particularly immigrants, have additional motivation for doing so. Minority adolescents become aware of the differences between their own expectations, those of their parents, and those of the majority culture. And immigrant youth may begin to distrust their parents as they observe that their parents lack power and competence in the new society (80). The effect is compounded if the adolescent loses the ability to speak the minority group's language (30). These factors serve to strengthen the peer group, in place of the parents, as a source of emotional support and guidance. Peers may also play a role in furthering acculturation (22). The desire to be accepted, which is compelling among teenagers, is especially strong among refugee adolescents. For them the greatest threat is not the feeling of belonging to two cultures but the feeling of belonging to none (55, p. 173).

For many immigrant minority youth, peers from their own ethnic group provide a crucial sense of brotherhood or sisterhood within the new culture. Peer groups may form to oppose majority mores and to provide adaptive social supports that reduce feelings of isolation. Refugee youth, who may be living apart from some or all of their family, may form gangs as a substitute. The gangs permit the reenactment of traditional family roles such as protective older sister, older brother, and father (72, 80).

Young refugees, particularly those unaccompanied by family, often must rely on antisocial strategies to negotiate the departure from their homeland and to survive the wait in refugee camps. Gangs permit the continuation of previously adaptive behaviors such as fighting, stealing, and cheating, even though this may cause trouble for the adolescents in their new homeland (72).

For all adolescents, peer acceptance becomes an increasingly important goal. For minority groups, opposition has historically been a survival strategy. To be against anything white (that is, to be against the system at large) is one way for a minority group to define itself in the face of discrimination and racism (63). This can lead to a militant posture, which may be a form of coping (12). Peer dependence among Native Americans has also been described as a method of coping with feelings of isolation (23).

For some minority youth, acceptance by one's own peer group may hinge on rejecting the values and behaviors of the majority culture, particularly the culture of the school (32, 63). Some minority youth defy mainstream values, in particular positive school conduct, in an effort to maintain a separate and self-accepting ethnic identity. As Fordham and Ogbu note, however, placing African-American youths in a school with many high-achieving minority students relieves them of the psychological burden of "acting white" (32). In a context where academic achievement is normative for African-American youths, they can aim for success without being scorned by their peers.

The influence of peers often increases for adolescents who do poorly in school. When African-Americans, particularly males, fail in school, they try to appear successful to their peers in other domains. These youths may act "cool," adopting certain peer-oriented styles of walking, talking, and dressing. They may even identify with drug dealers and pimps as role models. By taking up "oppositional values," these youths define alternative standards of success and new paths for acceptance by their peers (40). Although sometimes adaptive in the short term, such behaviors usually lead to adverse long-term outcomes.

MINORITY ADOLESCENTS IN SCHOOLS

Contrary to the popular stereotype, minority parents are interested in their youngsters' academic performance and strive to encourage them (57, 95). One ethnographic study, among academically successful rural African-American adolescents, reported strong parental support in the form of such comments as "Your education comes first," "I didn't get [an education], so I want you to," and "Go to school or find another house to stay at" (54, p. 133). Such sentiments are shared by other minority groups. A Mexican-American adolescent described her mother's efforts: "My mother keeps telling me: 'Ai, mi hija, tienes que sacar buenas calificaciones en la high school para que no te estes chingando igual que yo.' [Oh, my dear, you must get good grades in high school so you don't get screwed like me.] And you know she has a point. I don't want to be doing that. I've been in the cannery before. Just being there I can tell I wouldn't want to work there. I've got to do well in school so that I don't have to face this in my future" (63, p. 243).

Parenting practices may either support or detract from youths' performance in school. A recent comparative study of minority teenagers found that, after controlling for social class, punitive parenting and permissive parenting were both associated with poor grades. In contrast, authoritative parenting, which is characterized by setting limits in a context of warmth, was associated with better grades. Certain ethnic differences, however, were seen to affect the connection between parenting style and school performance, with the relation weakest among Asian-American adolescents (25).

Reports from Asian-American high school students of both sexes indicate that their families frequently practice authoritarian parenting. Such methods are significantly associated with low grades. Yet Asian-Americans as a whole receive high grades in school (25). The success of Asian youth in American public schools cannot satisfactorily be explained by a model of parenting style developed largely from white middle-class samples; a model that takes cultural contexts into account is needed.

In spite of parental encouragement, minority youth typically achieve lower levels of academic performance than do majority adolescents. Hispanics, for example, are nearly two years behind African-Americans in years of school completed. Their dropout rates are nearly twice those of African-American and non-Hispanic white youth. In addition, Hispanic students are frequently several years below grade level in American public schools (77, 93). In terms of grades and test scores, of all minority groups African-Americans average the fewest As and the most Ds and Fs in high school classes, and consistently have SAT scores that are lower than those of any other group (93). College enrollment rates held steady from 1976 to 1986 for African-American women but declined dramatically for men (34). This trend among African-American men is particularly disturbing since the proportion of African-Americans who finished high school during that same period increased from 68% to 76% (8). The perceptions of James Comer may be typical of the African-American's experience: "The school was, for many of my classmates, 'the white man's world.' I was aware of that very early. I can remember thinking that if Marshall Long can do so well in the Baptist Young People's Union Bible Drill, why could he not do the same in school? . . . I knew many other kids who could think fast, talk fast and act fast in the playground, in church and on the corner, who seemed to be immobilized in the classroom" (16, p. 20).

Ogbu (81, 82, 83, 85, 86) and Fordham (32) set forth a controversial set of ideas that relate the academic performance of minority youth to their perceptions of subordination and exploitation. The lack of equal educational opportunity within American society induces expectations of poor academic performance among African-Americans, according to Ogbu. Furthermore, teachers often underestimate and stereotype minority students, labeling them as educationally handicapped, and have generally low expectations for their academic performance (79). It has also been suggested that school culture and the culture of minority groups differ; school personnel and minority families and their children have difficulty bridging the gap (47, 48, 57).

The most distinctive aspect of Ogbu's thesis is his emphasis on the minority response to the perceived hegemony of white middle-class values in the educational system (12, 84). He portrays African-Americans and Mexican-Americans in the United States as far more likely to reject characteristic American attitudes and behaviors than recent immigrants who seek economic and political opportunities in the United States. Although many members of American minorities lead productive lives by both majority and minority standards, Ogbu has chosen to emphasize that some subgroups define appropriate behavior in opposition to white middle-class standards, particularly in the area of education.

According to Ogbu, minority opposition to the education system stems from a lack of trust in the American social structure (85, 86). It makes little sense to strive to do well academically if one has no occupational opportunities. From the point of view of majority educators, dropping out does not make sense; education is supposed to be the road to upward mobility. Many researchers, however, believe that when minority youth give up high school, this is a rational response to discrimination and perceived socioeconomic barriers (34, 81, 82, 83).

In fact, finishing high school—even completing some college—does not seem to bring the same job opportunities for minorities as for whites. For example, in terms of earnings and employment rates, African-American high school graduates do not do as well as white high school dropouts. In 1976 blacks aged 20–24 who had completed some college had higher unemployment rates than whites who never finished high school (34). Entwisle provides data showing that for youths without college degrees, racial differences in earnings increased between 1973 and 1986 (28). The number of job opportunities available to black and other minority adolescents in urban centers has sharply declined, owing to the shift from manufacturing to service industries, combined with the relocation of industries as well as middle-income residents to the suburbs (8).

Giving up in school because of a perceived lack of reward in terms of job opportunities is not only typical of African-Americans. There is evidence that some Hispanic high school students share a similar sense of futility. Matute-Bianchi's Mexican respondents expressed these views:

> "Mexicans don't have a chance to go on to college and make something of themselves"; "People like us face a lot of prejudice because there are a lot of people who don't like Mexicans"; "There aren't enough good jobs to go around"; "Some people, no matter how hard they try, just have bad luck" . . . to participate in class discussions, to carry books from class to class, to ask the teacher for help in front of others, to expend effort to do well in school—are efforts that are viewed derisively . . . by other Chicanos. Hence to adopt such features presents these students with a forced choice dilemma. They must choose between doing well in school or being a Chicano." (63, pp. 251, 255)

Many aspects of the American educational system have created difficulties for minority adolescents. A form of institutional racism prevails in many American schools, in that well-meaning teachers, acting out of a sense of misguided liberalism, often fail to challenge minority students. That is, knowing the handicaps that these adolescents face, some teachers accept a low level of performance from their minority pupils, substituting warmth and affability for academic challenge and high academic standards. Minority adolescents, like those in the majority, learn best when teachers combine warmth with challenging standards (6, 79). Teachers may expect minority students to fail and communicate these expectations to the students, who fulfill them (64, 65). The result is a form of racism without racists—teaching practices that result in poor minority performance (62, 64, 65, 79).

In contemporary American culture educators and parents tend to believe that innate ability, rather than diligent effort, is responsible for academic achievement. The emphasis on ability as the main predictor of differences in academic performance often traps minority youth in a vicious circle. Minority children who do not immediately perform well in the classroom are likely to be labeled low-ability or educationally handicapped students. Once they are placed in remedial classes, it is rare for them to be reassigned to higher levels later on (94). When minority youth are overrepresented in the lower tracks, the explanation given is their low level of ability and investment of effort; teachers' prejudices and practices are not considered (57).

In American high schools, African-Americans and Hispanics are overrepresented in the lower tracks and underrepresented at higher levels (93). The percentage of African-American students in the category of educable mentally retarded was double that of all other students in this category in 1980 (86, 93). Such labels become self-fulfilling prophecies, since when tracking errors are made—and there are many—only the parents of advantaged students are likely to protest. Minority parents and low-income parents are more likely to accept the track assignments endorsed by school personnel. Mislabeling and tracking serve to perpetuate social inequality.

REFERENCES

1. Ames, R. A. (1950). Protest and irony in Negro folksong. *Science and Society, 14,* 193–213.
2. Aponte, R.; Neckerman, K.; & Wilson, W. (1985). *Race, family structure, and social policy: Race and policy.* Working Paper 7, National Conference on Social Welfare. Washington, D.C.: Project on the Federal Role.

3. Arce, C. H. (1981). A reconsideration of Chicano culture and identity. *Daedalus, 110*(2), 177–192.

4. Banks, J. A. (1984). Black youths in predominantly white suburbs: An exploratory study of their attitudes and self-concepts. *Journal of Negro Education, 53*(I), 3–17.

5. Barnes, E. J. (1980). The black community as the source of positive self-concept for black children: A theoretical perspective. In R. Jones, ed., *Black psychology*. New York: Harper and Row, pp. 106–130.

6. Baron, R.; Tom, D.; & Cooper, H. (1985). Social class, race, and teacher expectations. In J. Dusek & G. Joseph, eds., *Teacher expectancies*. Hillsdale, N.J.: Erlbaum, pp. 251–269.

7. Bartz, K. W., & Levine, E. S. (1978). Childrearing by black parents: A description and comparison to Anglo and Chicano parents. *Journal of Marriage and the Family, 40,* 709–719.

8. Bell-Scott, P., & Taylor, R. L. (1989). Introduction: The multiple ecologies of black development. In P. Bell-Scott & R. L. Taylor, eds., *Journal of Adolescent Research: Special Edition on Black Adolescents* (April), 119–124. Newbury Park, Calif.: Sage Publications.

9. Billingsley, A. (1968). *Black families in white America*. Englewood Cliffs, N.J.: Prentice Hall.

10. Blau, Z. S. (1981). *Black children/white children: Competence, socialization, and social structure*. New York: Free Press.

11. Bowman, P. J., & Howard, C. (1985). Race-related socialization, motivation, and academic achievement: A study of black youths in three-generation families. *Journal of the American Academy of Child Psychiatry, 24*(2), 134–141.

12. Boykin, A. W. (1986). The triple quandary and the schooling of Afro-American children. In U. Neisser, ed., *The school achievement of minority children: New perspectives*. Hillsdale, N.J.: Erlbaum, pp. 57–92.

13. Caplan, N.; Whitmore, J. K.; & Choy, M. H. (1989). *The boat people and achievement in America*. Ann Arbor: University of Michigan Press.

14. Clark, R. (1983). *Family life and school achievement: Why poor black children succeed or fail*. Chicago: University of Chicago Press.

15. Colletta, N. D., & Lee, D. (1983). The impact of support for black adolescent mothers. *Journal of Family Issues, 4,* 127–143.

16. Comer, J. P. (1972). *Beyond black and white*. New York: Quadrangle Books.

17. _____. (1988). Educating poor minority children. *Scientific American, 259* (5), 42–48.

18. Committee for Economic Development (1987). *Children in need: Investment strategies for the educationally disadvantaged*. Washington, D.C.: Committee for Economic Development.

19. Cooley, C. H. (1902). Human nature and the social order. In C. H. Cooley, ed., *Two major works: Social organization and human nature and the social order*. Glencoe, Ill.: Free Press.

20. Cross, W. E., Jr. (1985). Black identity: Rediscovering the distinction between personal identity and reference group orientation. In M. B. Spencer, G. K. Brookins, & W. R. Allen, eds., *Beginnings: The social and affective development of black children*. Hillsdale, N.J.: Erlbaum, pp. 155–171.

21. _____. (1987). A two-factor theory of black identity: Implications for the study of identity development in minority children. In J. S. Phinney & M. J. Rotheram, eds., *Ethnic socialization: Pluralism and development*. Newbury Park, Calif.: Sage Publications, pp. 117–133.

22. DeVos, G. A. (1980). Ethnic adaptations and minority status. *Journal of Cross-Cultural Psychology, II*(I), 101–124.

23. Deyhle, D. (1986). Break dancing and breaking out: Anglos, Utes, and Navajos in a border reservation high school. *Anthropology and Education Quarterly, 17,* 111–127.

24. Dornbusch, S. M.; Carlsmith, J. M.; Bushwall, S. J.; Ritter, P. L.; Leiderman, P. H.; Hastorf, A. H.; & Gross, R. T. (1985). Single parents, extended households, and the control of adolescents. *Child Development, 56,* 326–341.

25. Dornbusch, S. M.; Ritter, P. L.; Leiderman, P. H.; Roberts, D. F.; & Fraleigh, M. J. (1987). The relation of parenting style to adolescent school performance. *Child Development, 58,* 1244–57.

26. Dressler, W. (1985). Extended family relationships, social support, and mental health in a southern black community. *Journal of Health and Social Behavior, 26,* 39–48.

27. Du Bois, W. E. B. (1961). *The souls of black folk*. Greenwich, Conn.: Fawcett Publications. Originally published 1903.

28. Entwisle, D. R. (1990). Schools and adolescence. In S. S. Feldman & G. R. Elliott, eds., *At*

the threshold: The developing adolescent. Cambridge, Mass.: Harvard University Press.

29. Erikson, E. H. (1968). *Identity: Youth and crisis.* New York: W. W. Norton.

30. Fillmore, L. W., & Britsch, S. (1988). Early education for children from linguistic and cultural minority families. Paper presented for the Early Education Task Force of the National Association of State Boards of Education, Alexandria, Va.

31. Ford Foundation. (1984). *Ford Foundation Letter, 15*(5).

32. Fordham, S., & Ogbu, J. U. (1986). Black students' school success: Coping with the "burden of 'acting white.' " *Urban Review, 18*(3), 176–206.

33. Furstenberg, F. F., & Crawford, A. G. (1978). Family support: Helping teenager mothers to cope. *Family Planning Perspectives, 10*(6), 322–333.

34. Gibbs, J. T. (1988). *Young, black, and male in America: An endangered species.* Dover, Mass.: Auburn House.

35. Gibbs, J. T., & Huang, L. N., eds. (1989). *Children of color: Psychological interventions with minority youth.* San Francisco: Jossey-Bass.

36. Gibson, M. A. (1987). The school performance of immigrant minorities: A comparative view. *Anthropology & Education Quarterly, 18*(4), 262–275.

37. Hakuta, K. (1986). *Mirror of language.* New York: Basic Books.

38. Hale-Benson, J. E. (1980). The socialization of black children. *Dimensions, 9,* 43–48.

39. _____. (1982). *Black children: Their roots, culture, and learning styles.* Baltimore: Johns Hopkins University Press.

40. Hare, B. R., & Castenell, L. A., Jr. (1985). No place to run, no place to hide: Comparative status and future prospects of black boys. In M. B. Spencer, G. K. Brookins, & W. R. Allen, eds., *Beginnings: The social and affective development of black children.* Hillsdale, N.J.: Erlbaum, pp. 201–214.

41. Harter, S. (1990). Adolescent self and identity development. In S. S. Feldman & G. R. Elliott, eds., *At the threshold: The developing adolescent.* Cambridge, Mass.: Harvard University Press.

42. Henderson, V. L., & Dweck, C. S. (1990). Motivation and achievement in adolescence: Toward a model of motivational processes. In S. S. Feld-

man & G. R. Elliott, eds., *At the threshold: The developing adolescent.* Cambridge, Mass.: Harvard University Press.

43. Hill, R. (1972). *The strengths of black families.* New York: Emerson-Hall.

44. Hofferth, S. L. (1984). Kin network, race, and family structure. *Journal of Marriage and the Family, 46,* 791–806.

45. Huang, L. N. (1989). Southeast Asian refugee children and adolescents. In J. T. Gibbs & L. N. Huang, eds., *Children of color: Psychological interventions with minority youth.* San Francisco: Jossey-Bass, pp. 278–321.

46. Johnson, D. J. (1988). Racial socialization strategies of parents in three black private schools. In D. T. Slaughter & D. J. Johnson, eds., *Visible now: Blacks in private schools.* New York: Greenwood Press, pp. 251–276.

47. Jordan, C. (1984). Cultural compatibility and the education of ethnic minority children. *Educational Research Quarterly, 8*(4), 59–71.

48. Jordan, C., & Tharp, R. G. (1979). Culture and education. In A. J. Marsella, R. G. Tharp, & T. J. Ciborowski, eds., *Perspectives on cross-cultural psychology.* New York: Academic Press, pp. 265–285.

49. Kasarda, J. (1983). Caught in the web of change. *Society, 21,* 4–7.

50. Keating, D. P. (1990). Adolescent thinking. In S. S. Feldman & G. R. Elliott, eds., *At the threshold: The developing adolescent.* Cambridge, Mass.: Harvard University Press.

51. Keefe, S. E., & Padilla, A. M. (1987). *Chicano ethnicity.* Albuquerque: University of New Mexico Press.

52. Kellam, S.; Ensminger, M. E.; & Turner, R. (1977). Family structure and the mental health of children. *Archives of General Psychiatry, 34,* 1012–22.

53. LaFromboise, T. D. (1988). American Indian mental health policy. *American Psychologist,* 388–397.

54. Lee, C. C. (1985). Successful rural black adolescents: A psychological profile. *Adolescence, 20*(77), 129–142.

55. Lee, E. (1988). Cultural factors in working with Southeast Asian refugee adolescents. *Journal of Adolescence, II,* 167–179.

56. Lewis, J. M., & Looney, J. G., eds. (1983). *The long struggle: Well-functioning working-class black families.* New York: Brunner/Mazel.

57. Lightfoot, S. L. (1978). *Worlds apart: Relationships between families and schools.* New York: Basic Books.

58. Looney, J. G., & Lewis, J. M. (1983). Competent adolescents from different socioeconomic and ethnic contexts. *Adolescent Psychiatry, II,* 64–74.

59. MacLeod, J. (1987). *Ain't no makin' it.* Boulder: Westview Press.

60. Madsen, M. (1964). The alcoholic agringado. *American Anthropologist, 66,* 355–361.

61. Martin, E. P., & Martin, J. M. (1978). *The black extended family.* Chicago: University of Chicago Press.

62. Massey, G. C.; Scott, M. V.; Dornbusch, S. M. (1975). Racism without racists: Institutional racism in urban schools. *The Black Scholar, 7*(3), 10–19.

63. Matute-Bianchi, M. E. (1986). Ethnic identity and patterns of school success and failures among Mexican-descendant and Japanese-American students in a California high school: An ethnographic analysis. *American Journal of Education, 95,* 233–255.

64. McDermott, R. P. (1987a). The explanation of minority school failure, again. *Anthropology & Education Quarterly, 18,* 361–364.

65. _____. (1987b). Achieving school failure: An anthropological approach to illiteracy and social stratification. In G. D. Spindler, ed., *Education and cultural process.* Prospect Heights, Ill.: Waveland Press, pp. 173–209.

66. McFee, M. (1968). The 150% man, a product of Blackfeet acculturation. *American Anthropologist, 70,* 1096–1103.

67. McGoldrick, M. (1982). Normal families: An ethnic perspective. In F. Walsh, ed., *Normal family processes.* New York: Guilford Press, pp. 399–424.

68. McKenry, P. C.; Everett, J. E.; Ramseur, H. P.; & Carter, C. J. (1989). Research on black adolescents. In P. Bell-Scott & R. L. Taylor, eds., *Journal of Adolescent Research: Special Edition on Black Adolescents.* Newbury Park, Calif.: Sage Publications, pp. 254–258.

69. McLanahan, S. (1983). Family structure and stress: A longitudinal comparison of two-parent and female-headed families. *Journal of Marriage and the Family, 45,* 347–357.

70. McLoyd, V. (1990). The impact of economic hardship on Black families and children: Psychological distress, parenting, and socio-

emotional development. *Child Development,* 61, 311–346.

71. Means, R. (1980). Fighting words on the future of the earth. *Mother Jones, 5*(10), 12–38.

72. Messer, M. M., & Rasmussen, N. H. (1986). Southeast Asian children in America: The impact of change. *Pediatrics, 78,* 323–329.

73. Mindel, C. H. (1980). Extended familism among urban Mexican-American Anglos and blacks. *Hispanic Journal of Behavior Science, 2,* 21–34.

74. Monroe, S.; Goldman, P.; & Smith, V. E. (1988). *Brothers: Black and poor—a true story of courage and survival.* New York: Morrow.

75. Mont-Reynaud, R. (1989). Personal communication.

76. Moore, J. W. (1981). Minorities in the American class system. *Daedalus, 110,* 275–298.

77. Moore, J., & Pachon, H. (1985). *Hispanics in the United States.* Englewood Cliffs, N.J.: Prentice Hall.

78. Muga, D. (1984). Academic subcultural theory and the problematic of ethnicity: A tentative critique. *Journal of Ethnic Studies, 12,* 1–51.

79. Natriello, G., & Dornbusch, S. M. (1984). *Teacher evaluative standards and student effort.* New York: Longmans.

80. Nidorf, J. F. (1985). Mental health and refugee youths: A model for diagnostic training. In T. C. Owen, ed., *Southeast Asian mental health: Treatment, prevention, services, training, and research.* Washington, D.C.: National Institute of Mental Health, pp. 391–427.

81. Ogbu, J. U. (1974). *The next generation: An ethnography of education in an urban neighborhood.* New York: Academic Press.

82. _____. (1978). *Minority education and caste.* New York: Academic Press.

83. _____. (1981). Origins of human competence: A cultural-ecological perspective. *Child Development, 52,* 413–429.

84. _____. (1986). The consequences of the American caste system. In U. Neisser, ed., *The school achievement of minority children: New perspectives.* Hillsdale, N.J.: Erlbaum, pp. 19–56.

85. _____. (1987a). Variability in minority school performance: A problem in search of an explanation. *Anthropology & Education Quarterly, 18,* 312–334.

86. _____. (1987b). Social stratification in the United States. In P. Hockings, ed., *Dimensions*

of social life: Essays in honor of David G. Man-delbaum*. New York: Mouton de Gruyter, pp. 585–597.

87. Padilla, A. M. (1980). The role of cultural awareness and ethnic loyalty in acculturation. In A. M. Padilla, ed., *Acculturation*. Boulder: Westview Press, pp. 47–84.

88. Phinney, J. S. (1989). Stages of ethnic identity development in minority-group adolescents. *Journal of Early Adolescence, 9,* 34–49.

89. Phinney, J. S.; Lochner, B. T.; & Murphy, R. (1990). Ethnic identity development and psychological adjustment in adolescence. In A. Stiffman & L. Davis, eds., *Advances in adolescent mental health*. Vol. 5. *Ethnic issues*. Greenwich, Conn.: JAI Press.

90. Portes, P.; Dunham, R.; & Williams, S. (1986). Assessing child-rearing style in ecological settings. Its relation to culture, social class, early-age intervention, and scholastic achievement. *Adolescence, 21,* 723–735.

91. Pugh, R. W. (1972). *Psychology and the black experience*. Monterey, Calif.: Brooks/Cole.

92. Ramirez, M. (1984). Assessing and understanding biculturalism-multiculturalism in Mexican-American adults. In J. L. Mendoza & R. H. Mendoza, eds., *Chicano psychology*. New York: Academic Press, pp. 77–94.

93. Reed, R. (1988). Education and achievement of young black males. In J. T. Gibbs, ed., *Young, black, and male in America: An endangered species*. Dover, Mass.: Auburn House.

94. Rist, R. C. (1970). Student social class and teacher expectations: The self-fulfilling prophecy in ghetto education. *Harvard Education Review, 40* (August), 411–451.

95. Ritter, P. L.; Mont-Reynaud, R.; & Dornbusch, S. M. (forthcoming). In N. F. Chavkin, ed., *Minority parents and the schools*. New York: Teachers College Press.

96. Rosenthal, D. (1987). Ethnic identity development in adolescents. In J. S. Phinney & M. J. Rotheram, eds., *Children's ethnic socialization: Pluralism and development*. Newbury Park, Calif.: Sage Publications, pp. 156–179.

97. Rotheram, M. J., & Phinney, J. S. (1987). Introduction: Definitions and perspectives in the study of children's ethnic socialization. In J. S. Phinney & M. J. Rotheram, eds., *Children's ethnic socialization: Pluralism and development*. Newbury Park, Calif.: Sage Publications, pp. 10–28.

98. Scanzoni, J. H. (1971). *The black family in modern society*. Boston: Allyn & Bacon.

99. Select Committee on Children, Youth, and Families, House of Representatives, 100th Congress (1987). *Race relations and adolescence: Coping with new realities*. Report no. 73–234. Hearing held in Washington, D.C., March 27. Washington, D.C.: U.S. Government Printing Office.

100. Semaj, L. T. (1985). Afrikanity, cognition, and extended self-identity. In M. B. Spencer, G. K. Brookins, & W. R. Allen, eds., *Beginnings: The social and affective development of black children*. Hillsdale, N.J.: Erlbaum, pp. 173–183.

101. Spencer, M. B. (1983). Children's cultural values and parental child-rearing strategies. *Developmental Review, 3,* 351–370.

102. _____. (1987). Black children's ethnic identity formation: Risk and resilience of castelike minorities. In J. S. Phinney & M. J. Rotheram, eds., *Children's ethnic socialization: Pluralism and development*. Newbury Park, Calif.: Sage Publications, pp. 103–116.

103. _____. (1990). Parental values transmission: Implications for black child development. In J. B. Stewart & H. Cheatham, eds., *Interdisciplinary perspectives on black families*. Atlanta: Transaction, pp. 111–131.

104. Spencer, M. B.; Brookins, G. K.; & Allen, W. R., eds. (1985). *Beginnings: The social and affective development of black children*. Hillsdale, N.J.: Erlbaum.

105. Stack, C. B. (1974). *All our kin*. New York: Harper & Row.

106. Stonequist, E. V. (1964). The marginal man: A study in personality and culture conflict. In E. Burgess & D. J. Bogue, eds., *Contributions to urban sociology*. Chicago: University of Chicago Press, pp. 327–345.

107. Sung, B. L. (1985). Bicultural conflicts in Chinese immigrant children. *Journal of Comparative Family Studies, 16*(2), 255–270.

108. Szapocnik, J., & Kurstnes, W. (1980). Acculturation, biculturalism, and adjustment among Cuban-Americans. In A. M. Padilla, ed., *Acculturation*. Boulder: Westview Press.

109. Tan, A. (1989). *The Joy Luck Club*. New York: G. P. Putnam's Sons.

110. Thomas, P. (1967). *Down these mean streets*. New York: Alfred A. Knopf.

111. Tienda, M., & Angel, R. (1982). Headship and household composition among blacks, Hispanics, and other whites. *Social Forces, 61,* 508–531.

112. U.S. Bureau of the Census (1985). *Marital status and living arrangements.* Current Population Reports, ser. P-20, March. Washington, D.C.: U.S. Government Printing Office.

113. U.S. Commission on Civil Rights (1983). *A growing crisis: Disadvantaged women and their children.* Washington, D.C.: U.S. Government Printing Office.

114. Vaughan, G. M. (1987). A social-psychological model of ethnic identity development. In J. S. Phinney & M. J. Rotheram, eds., *Children's ethnic socialization: Pluralism and development.* Newbury Park, Calif.: Sage Publications, pp. 73–91.

115. Walker, H. A. (1988). Black-white differences in marriage and family patterns. In S. M. Dorn-busch & M. H. Strober, eds., *Feminism, children, and the new families.* New York: Guilford Press, pp. 87–112.

116. Wilson, J. W. (1987). *The truly disadvantaged: The inner city, the underclass, and public policy.* Chicago: University of Chicago Press.

117. Wilson, M. N. (1986). The black extended family: An analytical consideration. *Developmental Psychology, 22*(2), 246–258.

118. _____. (1989). Child development in the context of the black extended family. *American Psychologist, 44*(2), 380–383.

119. Wilson, W. J., & Neckerman, K. (1986). Poverty and family structure: The widening gap between evidence and public policy issues. In S. Danziger & D. Weinberg, eds., *Fighting poverty: What works and what doesn't.* Cambridge, Mass.: Harvard University Press, pp. 232–259.

READING 30

DIVERSITY

Richard M. Lerner
Boston College

During the last two decades the study of children and their families has evolved in at least three significant directions: changes in the conceptualization of the nature of the person, the emergence of a life-span perspective about human development, and a stress on the contexts of development. These trends were products and producers of a theoretical perspective once labeled "developmental contextualism." This perspective has promoted a rationale for a synthesis of research and outreach (i.e., for the extension, application, or utilization of research in the "community") that is focused on the diversity of children and on the contexts within which they develop.

From *SRCD Newsletter,* Winter Issue 1992, pp. 2, 12–14. Copyright © 1992 by Richard M. Lerner. Reprinted with permission.

Developmental contextualism stresses that reciprocal relations ("dynamic" interactions) exist among variables from multiple levels of organization (e.g., biology, psychology, social groups, and culture). These dynamic relations structure human behavior. In addition, this system of integrated levels of organization is itself embedded in and interactive with history; this temporality provides a change component to the multiple, integrated levels comprising human life.

Prior to the 1970s, human development theory and research was often predicated on either organismic or mechanistic models of development. Since the 1970s developmental contextual conceptions have been increasingly prominent bases of scholarly activity. The three directions noted above exemplify this role of developmental contextualism.

First, children have come to be understood as active producers of their own development. These contributions primarily occur through the reciprocal relations individuals have with other significant people in their context, for example, children with family members, caregivers, teachers, and peers. Moreover, the content and functional significance of these effects people have on others and, in turn, on themselves, occur as a consequence of people's characteristics and behavioral individuality. Individual differences in people evoke differential reactions in others which provide feedback to people and influence the individual character of their further development. Recognizing individual diversity among people is central to understanding the way in which any given person is an active agent in his or her own development.

The second trend arose in the 1970s and later promoted a concern with variation in developmental pathways across life. This interest in life-span human development led to an understanding that change occurs in more than the childhood or adolescent years. For example, parents develop as distinct individuals across life. Parents develop both as adults in general and, more specifically, in regard to their familial and extra-familial (vocational, career) roles. Thus, a person's unique history of experiences and roles, as well as his or her unique biological (e.g., genetic) characteristics, combine to make him or her unique, and with time, given the accumulation of the influences of distinct roles and experiences, increasingly more unique across the course of life.

The life-span perspective underscores the theme that changing relations between the person and his/her context provide the basis of the individual's unique repertoire of physical, psychological, and behavioral characteristics. This link between person and context was a product and a producer of the third trend emerging in the study of human development since the 1970s. The study of children and their parents became increasingly "contextualized," or placed within the broader "ecology of human development." This focus has involved a concern with the "real life" situations within which children and families exist, and is linked to the study of the bidirectional relations between the family and the other social settings within which children and parents function. These include the work place, day care centers, and the formal and the nonformal educational and recreational settings present in a neighborhood. The contributions of Bronfenbrenner and his colleagues have been a major catalyst in moving the study of human development beyond its status as *"the science of the strange behavior of children in strange situations with strange adults for the briefest possible periods of time."*

With increasing study of the actual contexts within which people live, behavioral and social scientists have shown heightened appreciation of the diversity of patterns of individual and family development that exists. Such diversity—involving racial, ethnic, gender, physical handicaps, national, and cultural variation—has not been a prime concern of empirical analysis. Unfortunately, this is detrimental to the human development knowledge base.

There are several reasons why diversity must become a key concern in the study of development. First, by recognizing diversity, we acknowledge that general rules of development neither exist for nor apply in the same way to all children and families. This acknowledgment does not deny the existence of general features of human development. And the descriptive research that has documented such characteristics has been an important component of past, present, and future scholarship. However, the lawful individuality of human development means that a priori assumptions cannot be made to the effect that characteristics identified in one or several samples exist or function in the same way in another group. Moreover, even when common characteristics are identified in diverse groups, we cannot be certain that the individual or unique attributes of each group—even if they account for only a small proportion of the variance in the respective groups' functioning—are unimportant for understanding the distinctive nature of the groups' development. This point also applies to planning key components of policies or programs that are designed for the groups.

Accordingly, a new research agenda is necessary. This agenda should focus on diversity and context while at the same time attending to general and specific facets of individual development, of family changes, and of the mutual influences between the two. Integrated multidisciplinary and developmental research devoted to the study of diversity and context must be moved to the fore of scholarly concern.

Second, this integrative research can be effectively synthesized with two other foci: with policies and programs; and, second, with collaborations among disciplines and between scholarly and community interests. In regard to the first focus, I have just noted that research in human development that is concerned with one or even a few instances of individual and contextual diversity cannot be assumed to be useful for understanding the life course of all people. Similarly, policies and programs derived from research insensitive to diversity and context cannot be applicable, appropriate, and useful to all settings or for all individuals. Policy development, program (in-

tervention) design, and delivery—outreach—must be integrated with the new research base.

Consider additional advantages to this approach. When attempts are made to explain the diversity of changing person-context relations that characterize the life course, then research-derived outreach potentially becomes a means to test developmental contextual models of change processes. Such explanatory research may derive from descriptive research that documents the similarities in the development of diverse groups. Or, research that reveals differences in developmental pathways may lead to a further search for explanations of distinct histories or person-context relations. In actuality, policies and programs in research-based outreach can be used in a variety of ways to test models of similar or different developmental trajectories.

These points underscore the ideas that (1) policies and programs constitute natural experiments; and (2) the evaluation of such activities provides information about the utility of such outreach endeavors and feedback about the utility of developmental contextual models from which the policies and programs were derived.

To be successful, these kinds of endeavors require collaboration across disciplines with individuals who represent different levels in the profession hierarchy and with the individuals we hope to serve. This is my second point. Colleagues in the research, policy, and intervention communities need to plan and implement their activities in a synthesized manner. All components of this collaboration are equally valuable and essential. The collaborative activities of colleagues in university extension and outreach, in service design and delivery, in elementary, middle (or junior high), and high schools, in policy development and analysis, and in academic research are vital to the success of this new agenda. Moreover, given the contextual embeddedness of research and service activities, collaboration must occur with the people we are trying to both understand and serve. The absence of community perspective, sense of ownership, and values means that research and service activities are not adequately integrated into people's lives.

To many developmentalists, this developmental contextual agenda for research and outreach that is focused on diversity may seem no more than a recapitulation of the philosophy underlying the land grant university system in the United States. In truth, it is just that. Developmental contextualism as a view of human development grew out of the scholarly model found in land grant university colleges of home economics, human ecology, and human development. During these challenging times it may be particularly appropriate to rely again on the land grant model of multidisciplinary scholarship to lead the field of child development, and the American university system, into a new era of needed contributions to society. Today, unprecedented rates of risks affect the children of our nation—poverty; school failure, underachievement, and dropout; unsafe sex, teenage pregnancy, and teenage parenting; drug and alcohol use and abuse; and delinquency, crime, and violence—and demand innovation in addressing societal problems. Given that 50 percent of the youth of our nation are involved in two or more of the above-noted risk categories, the very fabric of American society is challenged. We are all at risk!

Perhaps it is time then to restructure our scholarly agendas, our universities, and our communities around a reinvigorated multidisciplinary vision of the integration of science and outreach focused on diversity and context. Of course, such a view of the structure and role of the American university could be applied to both land grant institutions of higher education and other public and private institutions. It may be, then, that the developmental contextual view of human development can lead universities to become institutions for the communities within which they exist, that is, institutions for the children and families they seek to both understand and to serve. In short, our task is not just to do more or do better. If we are to significantly advance science and service for the children of our nation, we must engage in new ideas and activities. This is the challenge before us as we approach the next century. And this is the path upon which we, as scientists and citizens, must embark.

AT THE INTERFACE OF CULTURES: MULTIETHNIC/MULTIRACIAL HIGH SCHOOL AND COLLEGE STUDENTS

JEAN S. PHINNEY AND LINDA L. ALIPURIA
California State University, Los Angeles, and Claremont Graduate School

THE RACIAL COMPOSITION of the United States is becoming more ethnically diverse. No longer predominantly White, Black, and Native American, the U.S. population now includes greater numbers of Latinos, Asians, and other immigrants. According to the most recent census (Census of Population and Housing, 1990), one in four Americans—and nearly 43% of Californians—were members of minority groups (i.e., non-White or Hispanic). These changing demographics indicate the necessity for (a) a broader research base containing more ethnic minority samples (Graham, 1992) and (b) the consideration of culture in the study of development and behavior (Betancourt & Lopez, 1993; Shweder, 1990).

Central to the study of ethnicity, but scarcely considered by researchers, is the growing proportion of the U.S. population that is ethnically and racially mixed. Currently, almost 5% of all marriages—nearly four times as many as in 1970—are interracial (U.S. Bureau of the Census, 1993). Among some groups of Asian Americans in Hawaii, California, and elsewhere, the proportion of mixed marriages is higher than 50%, according to data from a study of surnames on marriage license applications (Kitano & Daniels, 1988). Studies that elicit parental ethnicity have provided additional evidence for this phenomenon. In a large study of monoethnic high school students conducted in the greater Los Angeles area (Phinney, 1992), 9.8% of the student were ineligible to participate because self-reports indicated that their parents were from two different ethnic groups.

These data are particularly significant to psychologists because research on people of mixed heritage can contribute both theoretically and methodologically to the study of culture and ethnicity (Stephan & Stephan, 1989). Multiethnic individuals combine in one person the issues and conflicts of interacting in two or more cultures, and they therefore provide unique insights into the effects of being bicultural, beyond those of monoethnic minority group members (LaFromboise, Coleman, & Gerton, 1993). One's biculturality is particularly important during middle and late adolescence, when identity issues, including ethnic identity, are highly salient (Phinney, 1990).

There has been little research on people who are multiethnic. Such individuals are rarely given an opportunity to identify themselves on questionnaires, because researchers generally categorize participants as belonging to a single ethnic group—usually on the basis of a self-report item that requires a monoethnic label. Moreover, re-

From *The Journal of Social Psychology*, 1996, *136*(2), 139–158. Reprinted with permission of the Helen Dwight Reid Educational Foundation. Published by Heldref Publications, 1319 Eighteenth St., N.W., Washington, D.C. 20036–1802. Copyright © 1996.

searchers who are interested in studying multiethnic individuals have difficulty locating them (Root, 1992b), and most existing research has been based on small, clinical samples or on samples recruited by word of mouth. Few studies provide data on multiethnic individuals as they are found naturally in the population.

Our purpose in the present study was to provide normative data from the United States for two typical samples of multiethnic youth and a comparison sample of monoethnic youth. We explored psychological well-being, attitudes toward other groups, ethnic identity, and ethnic self-labeling, including the effect of setting, using data from two large surveys. Subsets of multiethnic high school and college students, identified on the basis of parental ethnicity, were examined (a) as a group and (b) in comparison with their monoethnic peers. In addition to providing normative data, the present studies illustrate how multiethnic samples can be identified and described using survey questionnaires that elicit parental ethnicity and how identifying this subgroup can make the study of ethnically diverse samples more precise.

PSYCHOLOGICAL WELL-BEING

One basic question that has been posed concerning individuals who are part of two cultures is whether they are confused outsiders or special individuals who possess a broader understanding. The "marginal man" conceptualization by Park (1928; Wright & Wright, 1972) in the 1920s and by Stonequist (1961) in the 1930s articulated ideas that are still guiding research. Park's (1928) view was that, with migration and the loosening of the bonds to his original culture, the marginal man—a person at the edge of two cultures—becomes "the individual with the keener intelligence, the wider horizon, the more detached and rational viewpoint" (Park, 1950, pp. 375–376). In contrast, Stonequist (1961), a student of Park at the Chicago School, viewed the marginal man as a person caught between two cultures, never fitting in.

Until recently, the dominant U.S. view of the mixed-race person was consistent with that of Stonequist. In popular literature (Berzon, 1978; Nakashima, 1992) and in clinical reports (Gibbs, 1987; Sommers, 1964; Teicher, 1968), multiethnic people have been portrayed as troubled and anxious outsiders who lack a clear identity. However, the results of empirical research with nonclinical U.S. samples have indicated that multiethnic individuals are at no psychological disadvantage in comparison with monoethnic individuals. Researchers using measures of self-esteem have consistently found no significant difference between the self-esteem of multiethnic groups and that of monoethnic comparison groups (Cauce, et al., 1992; Johnson & Nagoshi, 1986; Stephan & Stephan, 1991). In the present study, we compared the self-esteem of multiethnic and monoethnic youths from the same setting. Our expectation was that there would be no difference in self-esteem between these two groups.

ATTITUDES TOWARD
OTHER GROUPS

Park (1928) suggested that being of mixed heritage might be advantageous. Members of minority groups have been reported to have greater cognitive flexibility because they are required to function in two cultures (Ramirez, 1984; Ramirez & Castaneda, 1974). Similarly, multiethnic individuals may exhibit greater bicultural competence (Hall, 1980; Wilson, 1984) and may be less ethnocentric. In a study of college students in Hawaii and New Mexico, Stephan and Stephan (1991) found that multiethnic students were more tolerant than monoethnic students.

The second study in the present article includes a measure of attitudes toward other groups. Our expectation was that either there would be no difference in other-group attitudes between the multiethnic and the monoethnic participants or the multiethnic adolescents would have more positive attitudes toward other groups than the monoethnic participants would.

ETHNIC IDENTITY

Ethnic identity is a component of the more general identity structure described by Erikson (1968). It is generally viewed as a multidimensional construct that includes feelings of ethnic belonging and pride, a secure sense of group membership, and positive attitudes toward one's ethnic group. Ethnic identity may also include a developmental component, that is, the extent to which an individual has achieved a secure sense of his or her ethnicity, based on the process of exploration and commitment (Phinney, 1990, 1992). Ethnic identity is likely to be highly salient for monoethnic minority group members (Phinney & Alipuria, 1990).

Although the ethnic identity issues faced by people of mixed heritage are much the same as those that are faced by monoethnic minority groups, multiethnic individuals may find establishing a secure sense of ethnic identification to be particularly difficult because of the potential conflict between their parents' cultures. For example, identification with one's maternal ethnic group may oblige a person to reject his or her paternal ethnic group. Multiethnic individuals may consciously examine the meaning of their mixed heritage to determine their place in society or they may accept an ascribed position, based on their physical appearance or on the group that will accept them (e.g., Hall, 1992b). Having greater latitude in the choice of one's ethnic identity can be a source of strength, confusion, or both, depending upon the individual (Gibbs & Hines, 1992; Kerwin, Ponterotto, Jackson, & Harris, 1993). It may not be necessary to emphasize one heritage over another; for example, Hall (1992b) found that it was possible for Black/Japanese individuals to feel strongly that they were both Japanese and Black.

Because of the possible pull from more than one culture, multiethnic adolescents may not identify with either of their parents' ethnic groups as strongly as monoethnic adolescents do (Kich, 1992; Stephan & Stephan, 1989). In the only study we have located that addresses this issue, Hiraga, Cauce, Mason, and Ordonez (1993) found that monoracial African-American adolescents identified more strongly with African-American culture than biracial (African-American and White) adolescents did. However, the latter group's identification as White or biracial was not assessed. Because it was unclear whether the ethnic identity of multiethnic adolescents is dual (or multiple) or whether it is a blend of two cultures, we had no basis on which to predict the strength of multiethnic adolescents' ethnic identity in the present research.

ETHNIC SELF-LABEL

A person's ethnic self-label is a part of his or her ethnic identity, but whereas ethnic identity includes a broad range of attitudes, feelings, and self-perceptions, as discussed previously, ethnic self-label refers only to a person's chosen ethnic classification and may vary situationally. Nevertheless, ethnic self-label is viewed as an important indicator of multiethnic youths' ethnic identity (Gibbs & Hines, 1992; Hall, 1992b; Kerwin et al., 1993; Kich, 1992; Salgado de Snyder, Lopez, & Padilla, 1982; Stephan & Stephan, 1989). Theoretically, multiethnic individuals should be able to use their maternal group label, their paternal group label, or a label such as Black Asian or Mixed, indicating a mixed background, but there are many constraints on the choice of an ethnic self-label. People of mixed Black/White parentage in the United States, for example, have not always had a choice regarding ethnic self-label; the existence of a single Black ancestor once qualified as evidence that a person was Black, socially and legally (Williamson, 1980).

At present, the constraints on choice of self-label are less clear. Choice of self-label is no doubt influenced by a person's physical appearance, although we know of no data on this factor. Nevertheless, most mixed individuals do perceive that they have choices with regard to self-label (Stephan & Stephan, 1989; Wilson, 1984). Hall (1992b) found that some of her Black/Japanese participants were comfortable with a Black label or a Japanese label, even when "Other" was an option. Kich (1992) described a developmental process in which the use of a biracial self-label by White/Japanese participants increased as they became more accepting of their biracial identity. Thus, multiethnic youths who describe themselves as Mixed might be expected to have higher self-esteem than multiethnic youths who use a monoethnic label.

Although previous research suggests some variability in the use of labels, the factors that influence choice of self-label have not been systematically investigated. In the present research, we examined the labels used by multiethnic youths in relation to their parents' ethnicity and explored the relationship of these labels to contextual variables, such as the ethnic make-up of the school, and to outcome variables, including self-esteem and ethnic identity.

In summary, the two studies in this article provide normative data on a group that has received little research attention—multiethnic and monoethnic high school and college students in the United States. In addition to documenting the incidence of multiethnic students and exploring factors related to these individuals' use of ethnic self-labels, we compared the multiethnic and the monoethnic students in regard to a number of variables. Study 1 is based on data from a relatively small sample of college students on two campuses; Study 2 is based on data from a larger sample of students from ethnically diverse high schools. The two studies are reported separately, but because they address similar issues, the Discussion sections have been combined.

STUDY 1: COLLEGE STUDENTS

Method

Participants. The participants were 47 multiethnic (ethnically or racially mixed) university students and a comparison group of 345 monoethnic students. All the students were American-born. The students attended two large state universities in southern California that differed in ethnic composition. Twenty-one multiethnic and

195 monoethnic students were from an ethnically diverse campus on which approximately three quarters of the students were ethnic minorities— about one quarter each Asian, Latino, and White; one eighth African-American; and the remainder from the other groups. Twenty-six multiethnic and 150 monoethnic students were from a predominantly White campus with a student body that was 66.4% White, with Latinos being the only sizeable minority group, at 9.5%; the remainder of the student body consisted of small groups of students with African American, Native American, Asian, and Middle Eastern backgrounds.

The participants were selected from a group of more than 500 students at the two universities who had completed questionnaires for a different study (Alipuria, 1990; Lochner & Phinney, 1988; Phinney & Alipuria, 1990). They were chosen on the basis of their parentage, birthplace (United States), and age (17 to 24 years; $Ms =$ 19.9 years and 19.6 years for the ethnically diverse campus and the predominantly White campus, respectively). For the monoethnic students, both parents were from the same ethnic group. The multiethnic students' parents were from two clearly distinguishable ethnic/racial groups, including Latino, Asian-American, African American, Native American, or non-Latino White.

Questionnaire Procedures and Measures. In both university settings, the questionnaires were completed in general education classes, which are required for all undergraduates. The questionnaire contained items about the participants' sex, age, birthplace, and parents' birthplace and included the following measures.

1. Spontaneous ethnic self-label. We obtained the participants' ethnic self-labels, using an open-ended question the respondents answered by filling in a blank with their ethnic group membership. These open-ended responses were subsequently coded with one of the following labels: (a) Asian American, (b) African American or Black, (c) Latino or

Hispanic, (d) White or Caucasian, (e) Native American, or (f) Mixed. Respondents who indicated other groups (e.g., Lebanese) were not included in the sample.

2. Parents' ethnicity. The participants answered a separate question about each parent's ethnicity, using a list of U.S. ethnic groups.

3. Self-esteem. The 10-item Rosenberg (1986) Self-Esteem Scale was used, with a 4-point response scale. The mean of the 10 items for each participant was used in the analyses.

Results

Percentage and Self-Labels of Multiethnic Respondents. The percentage of multiethnic participants in the larger sample of college students was 9.0% (7.3% for the ethnically diverse campus; 11% for the predominantly White campus). On both campuses, the Latino/White combination was the most prevalent (12 out of 21 for the ethnically diverse campus; 13 out of 26 for the predominantly White campus).

A spontaneous self-label indicating a mixed heritage was provided by only about one fifth of the students (19% on the ethnically diverse campus; 23% on the predominantly White campus). Overall, 80% of the students provided a monoethnic label, meaning that on the basis of self-label alone, they were indistinguishable from the monoethnic students. The results of a t test comparing the self-esteem scores of the multiethnic participants who used a monoethnic self-label with the scores of the multiethnic participants who used a multiethnic self-label indicated that there was not a significant difference in self-esteem.

Most of the multiethnic college students had one White parent (17 out of 21 on the ethnically diverse campus; 22 out of 26 on the predominantly White campus). We compared the percentage of these students who described themselves as White with the percentage of those who described themselves as ethnic or Mixed, on the two campuses. Only 1 out of 17 participants (5.9%) used the label White on the ethnically diverse campus, in contrast to 10 out of 22 (45.5%) on the predominantly White campus. The results

of a chi-square test indicated that there was a statistically significant difference between the two campuses in self-label of multiethnic persons with one White parent, $\chi^2(2, n = 9) = 8.3, p < .05$; on the predominantly White campus, these students were significantly more likely to describe themselves as White than were those on the ethnically diverse campus. In addition, 3 out of 7 Latino/White multiethnic students on the predominantly White campus who used a monoethnic non-White label described themselves as Spanish, suggesting European ancestry (Buriel, 1987), but these students' non-White parents were Hispanic or Mexican American, not Spanish. None of the participants on the minority campus described themselves as Spanish.

Self-Esteem of Multiethnic and Monoethnic Students. The multiethnic students' self-esteem scores were compared with those of the monoethnic students, for each campus. The results of one-way analyses of variance (ANOVAs) with follow-up paired comparisons indicated that there were no significant difference in self-esteem between the multiethnic and monoethnic students, for either campus.

STUDY 2: HIGH SCHOOL STUDENTS

Method

Participants. The participants were 194 ethnically or racially mixed high school students and a comparison sample of 696 monoethnic students from the same schools. Both groups were American-born. The multiethnic students had parents from two different ethnic or racial groups. A detailed description of the ethnicity of the multiethnic sample is provided in the Results section. The monoethnic students, whose parents were both members of the same ethnic or racial group, were 232 African Americans, 372 Latinos, 27 Asian Americans, and 65 Whites. Monoethnic students who were members of other groups that were too small to be analyzed were not included in this sample.

The participants were selected from students in predominantly minority (Hispanic and

African American) public and parochial high schools in urban areas of Los Angeles who completed questionnaires as part of a large survey (Phinney, DuPont, Espinosa, Revill, & Sanders, 1994). The multiethnic and monoethnic adolescents were similar in age (ranging from 14 to 19 years for both groups; *Ms* = 16.2 years and 16.1 years for the multiethnic and monoethnic students, respectively). There were more females than males in both groups (70.6% of the multiethnic sample; 54.7% of the monoethnic sample). The percentage of parents who were professionals or had advanced degrees (upper middle class) was 36.1% for the multiethnic group and 23.6% for the monoethnic group. The percentage of parents who had some college education or held white-collar or skilled jobs (middle class) was 51.5% for the multiethnic sample and 45.7% for the monoethnic sample. The percentage of parents who had no college education or held unskilled jobs (lower class) was 9.8% for the multiethnic group and 30.8% for the monoethnic group.

Questionnaire Procedures and Measures. The questionnaire, which was completed in selected, intact, classrooms, contained items about the respondents' sex, age, birthplace, and grade point average and items about the respondents' parents' birthplace, education, and occupation. We used the data on parents' education and occupation to divide the participants into three socioeconomic status (SES) groups: upper middle class (professional, college-educated), middle class (white-collar or skilled work, some college), and lower class (unskilled work, no college), on the basis of the parent with the higher SES. The questionnaire also included the same three measures that had been used with the college sample: spontaneous ethnic self-label, parents' ethnicity, and self-esteem. In addition, the questionnaire contained the following measures.

1. Selected self-label. Toward the end of the questionnaire, the participants answered a second self-label question by selecting a label from a list that included the following choices: (a) Asian, Asian-American, or Oriental; (b) Black or African-American; (c) Hispanic, Latino, or Mexican-American; (d) White, Caucasian, European, not Hispanic; (e) American Indian; (f) Mixed or Parents are from two different groups; (g) Other (write in).

2. Ethnic identity. We assessed ethnic identity, using the 14-item Multi-group Ethnic Identity Measure (MEIM; Phinney, 1992), which has a reliability (Cronbach's alpha) of .81 with monoethnic high school students. Using both positively and negatively worded items, the measure assesses three aspects of ethnic identity: a sense of belonging to and attitudes toward one's ethnic group; ethnic behaviors and customs; and ethnic identity achievement, based on exploration and commitment. The items are rated on a 4-point scale ranging from *strongly disagree* (1) to *strongly agree* (4). We obtained an ethnic identity score by computing the mean of the 14 items.

3. Other-group attitudes. The six-item measure of attitudes toward other ethnic groups, embedded in the MEIM, includes both positively and negatively worded items (e.g., "I like meeting and getting to know people from ethnic groups other than my own" and "I sometimes feel it would be better if different ethnic groups didn't try to mix together"). Possible responses range from *strongly disagree* (1) to *strongly agree* (4). A mean score was used in the analyses. This measure has a reliability of .71 for monoethnic high school students.

Results

Percentage and Ethnicity of Multiethnic Respondents. We were not able to calculate the percentage of multiethnic respondents directly because in restricting the sample of monoethnic students to four ethnic groups (African American, Latino, Asian American, and White), we eliminated a number of potential participants. However, an estimate that included the multiethnic and monoethnic students who had a parent from one of the four selected ethnic groups indicated that 14.5% of the students were multiethnic.

We identified 16 combinations of ethnic groups in the present sample. Various combinations with one African American and/or Latino parent were the most prevalent, as would be expected because these two groups were predominant in the sample. The most prevalent subgroups were Black/Mixed ($n = 44$), Latino/White ($n = 23$), Black/Indian ($n = 21$), Black/Latino ($n = 18$), and Black/White ($n = 14$). A large percentage of the participants (36.1%) had one parent of mixed heritage, and 11.9% of the participants had two parents of mixed heritage.

Self-Labels Used by Multiethnic Respondents. The spontaneous self-labels that were used by the multiethnic students were either (a) the label of one parent or (b) a label that incorporated both parents' ethnicities (e.g., Black/Asian or Mixed). A spontaneous self-label indicating mixed heritage was used by 34% of the students. Sixty-six percent of the respondents used a monoethnic label and hence would be classified as monoethnic on the basis of self-label alone.

The kinds of self-labels the students chose indicated several clear patterns. Students who had one Black parent and one parent from a different minority group used the label Black more often than they used the label of the non-Black parent. For example, of the 18 Black/Latino students, 6 identified themselves as Black; 2 identified themselves as Latino; and 10, as Mixed; of the 21 Black/Indian students, 13 identified themselves as Black; 3 identified themselves as Indian; and 5, as Mixed; and of the 5 Black/Asian students, 1 used the label Black; and 4 identified themselves as Mixed. Students with one Black and one White parent never used the White label; of the 14 Black/White students, 8 used the label Black; and 6 identified themselves as Mixed. Over half the students who reported that both parents were mixed identified themselves as Black.

Adolescents who had one non-Black minority parent and one White parent tended to use the minority label instead of a White label. For example, among the 23 Latino/White students, 15 described themselves as Latino; 4 described themselves as White; and 4, as Mixed; of the 6 Indian/White students, 4 used the label Indian; 1 used White; and 1, Mixed. The only respondents who used the White label as much as a mixed or minority label were the 8 adolescents who had one White and one mixed parent (4 used White, 3 used Mixed, and 1 used Black). In general, the label that was used most frequently was Black, and the label that was used second most frequently was another minority label or Mixed. The label that was used the least frequently was White.

Next we examined the percentage of high school students who used a spontaneous monoethnic self-label, based on the ethnicity of each parent. The number of students who actually had one parent from each group is reported in Column 2 of Table 1, and the number and the percentage of adolescents who used that parent's ethnicity as their spontaneous self-label are reported in Columns 3 and 4 of Table 1. This percentage varied substantially across groups. Over three fourths (76.5%) of the students with one Black parent called themselves Black, but only 18% of the students with one White parent called themselves White.

We examined variation in self-label in relation to the item (type and position on questionnaire) that was completed by the respondents (see Table 1). The number of students who used an ethnic group as a self-label in response to an initial, open-ended question is reported in Column 3, and the number of students who used the same self-label in a second item toward the end of the questionnaire that included a Mixed option is reported in Column 5. With the exception of the Indian self-label, all the monoethnic self-labels were used about half as often in the second question, which included the Mixed option, as they were in the first question. There was a corresponding increase from 66 to 124 in the number of respondents who used the Mixed label, although over a third of the respondents

TABLE 1
Multiethnic High School Students: Parentage, Spontaneous Self-Label, and Selected Self-Label

| | | Self-label | | |
| | | Spontaneous | | Selected |
Ethnic group	No. with one parent from group[a]	n	%[b]	n
Asian American	17	1	5.9	0
Black	102	78	76.5	43
Latino	60	30	50.0	15
American Indian	38	9	23.7	7
White	55	10	18.2	5
Mixed	93	66	71.0	124
		194		194

[a]Most participants are represented twice in this list, once for each parent; however, the 93 mixed participants included 23 with both parents mixed; the latter were counted only one. [b]Percentage using ethnicity of parent from this group as self-label.

still used a monoethnic self-label for both questions. For example, of the 78 students with one Black parent and a spontaneous self-label of Black or African American, 36 identified themselves as Mixed when given that option, and 42 continued to identify themselves as Black or African American.

The results of a *t* test comparing the self-esteem of the multiethnic students who used a multiethnic self-label with that of the multiethnic students who used a monoethnic self-label indicated that there was no significant difference in self-esteem between the two groups.

Comparisons Between Multiethnic and Monoethnic Adolescents: Social Class and Grade Point Average. We compared self-reported social class (lower, middle, and upper middle class) between the monoethnic students and their multiethnic peers who had a parent from the same ethnic group (see Table 2). The results of chi-square analyses conducted for each ethnic category indicated that there was a significant difference in the distribution of social class between the multiethnic and the monoethnic Latinos, $\chi^2(n = 430) = 36.4$, $p < .001$; more of the monoethnic group was lower class, and more of the multiethnic group was middle class and upper middle class. For the White sample, the relationship was significant but reversed, $\chi^2(n =$

116) = 10.5, $p < .01$; compared with the students who had one White parent, almost twice as many of the students with two White parents were upper middle class, and fewer monoethnic students were lower class. There were no significant differences in the distribution of social class in the Black and Asian samples.

We compared the academic performance of the multiethnic and monoethnic students, using an ANOVA that included sex and SES, because of the differences between the multiethnic and monoethnic participants on these variables. The results of a $2 \times 3 \times 2$ (Sex $\times$ SES $\times$ Multi vs. Mono) ANOVA of school grade point average indicated that there were no significant differences in grade point average in relation to sex, SES, or parentage (multi- or monoethnic). The results of 3×2 (SES $\times$ Multi vs. Mono) ANOVAs, conducted separately for each ethnic group, indicated that SES and parentage did not affect grade point average.

Comparisons in Self-Esteem Between Multiethnic and Monoethnic Adolescents. Reliability was calculated separately for the multiethnic and monoethnic participants; Cronbach's alpha = .81 for the multiethnic students and .83 for the monoethnic students. The self-esteem score for the entire group of multiethnic students was compared with that for the entire group of

TABLE 2

**Percentage of Mono- and Multiethnic High School Students Reporting Social Status,
by One Parent (for Multi) or Ethnicity (for Mono)**

| Ethnic group | n | Social class | | | χ^2 | p |
		Lower	Middle	Upper middle		
Asian						
Multi	16	0	38.5	53.9	—	ns
Mono	26	7.7	25.0	38.5		
Black						
Mixed	99	11.1	49.5	39.4	—	ns
Mono	239	12.5	55.7	31.8		
Latino						
Mixed	59	13.6	52.5	33.9	36.3	< .001
Mono	371	48.8	40.7	10.5		
White						
Mixed	54	14.8	51.9	33.3	10.5	< .01
Mono	62	1.6	41.9	56.5		

monoethnic students. The results of a $2 \times 3 \times 2$ (Sex × SES × Multi vs. Mono) ANOVA indicated that there were no differences in self-esteem between the multiethnic and the monoethnic groups. There were, however, differences in self-esteem based on sex, $F(1, 859) = 5.6$, $p < .02$, and on SES, $F(2, 859) = 3.28$, $p < .05$; males and students with a higher SES had higher self-esteem. There were no interactions among any of these variables.

Ethnic Identity.   The reliabilities for the ethnic identity measure were Cronbach's alphas = .85 for the multiethnic students and .83 for the monoethnic students. These figures were slightly higher than what has been reported in previous research (Phinney, 1992).

Relationship of Ethnic Identity to Self-Label and Parents' Ethnicity, for the Multiethnic Sample.   We compared the ethnic identity scores of the multiethnic high school students who spontaneously used a single group label with those of the multiethnic students who used a mixed label. Because sex and SES differed between the two samples, we included these variables in the analyses. The results of a $2 \times 3 \times 2$ (Sex × SES × Label; mixed vs. mono) ANOVA indicated that

there were no differences in ethnic identity on the basis of sex, SES, or spontaneous self-label.

In a second analysis, the multiethnic students who changed their initial spontaneous self-label to Mixed when given that option were compared with the multiethnic students who did not. The participants who changed their ethnic self-label tended to have a lower ethnic identity score ($M = 3.09$) than those who did not ($M = 3.24$), $t(128) = 1.8$, p .07.

Comparisons of Ethnic Diversity Between Multi- and Monoethnic Youth.   We compared the ethnic identity score for the multiethnic and the monoethnic groups, using an ANOVA that included sex and SES. The results of a $2 \times 3 \times 2$ (Sex × SES × Multi vs. Mono) ANOVA indicated that neither sex nor SES affected ethnic identity and that there was no difference between the ethnic identity scores of the multiethnic and the monoethnic groups. Ethnic identity was also analyzed by ethnicity. The monoethnic adolescents from each ethnic group were compared with the multiethnic adolescents who had a parent from the same ethnic group. Because of the sample sizes and because we found no sex differences in the initial analysis, we combined the ethnic identity scores for the males and females in these analyses. The results of a 3×2 (SES $\times$ Multi vs. Mono) ANOVA indicated that the multiethnic Latinos had lower ethnic identity scores ($M = 3.04$) than the monoethnic Latinos did ($M = 3.16$), $F(1,419) = 4.43$, $p < .05$. A similar analysis for the Whites indicated a significant but opposite effect, $F(1, 108) = 4.80$, $p < .05$; the multiethnic Whites had higher ethnic identity scores ($M = 2.91$) than the monoethnic Whites did ($M = 2.70$). There were no ethnic identity differences between the multiethnic and the monoethnic students for the Black and the Asian American groups, and SES did not affect ethnic identity for any ethnic group.

Ethnic Identity and Self-Esteem. The multiethnic and monoethnic groups were considered separately in an analysis of the correlation between ethnic identity scores and self-esteem scores. The correlations for both groups were similar and highly significant: $r = .31$, $p < .001$, for the multiethnic group; and $r = .28$, $p < .001$, for the monoethnic group. For both groups, a higher ethnic identity score was correlated with a higher self-esteem score.

Attitudes Toward Other Groups. The measure of attitudes toward other groups assessed extent of positive feelings toward and willingness to mix with people from other ethnic groups. The reliability scores for the measure (Cronbach's alphas = .77 for the multiethnic students and .76 for the monoethnic students) were slightly higher than what has been reported previously (Phinney, 1992).

Using a $2 \times 3 \times 2$ (Sex $\times$ SES $\times$ Multi vs. Mono) ANOVA, we compared the multiethnic students' scores on attitudes toward other groups with those of the monoethnic students. There were no significant differences based on any of these variables. We then compared the monoethnic students' scores for attitudes toward other groups with those of the multiethnic students who had a parent from the same ethnic group. The results of a $2 \times 3 \times 2$ (Sex $\times$ SES $\times$ Multi vs. Mono) ANOVA indicated that the multiethnic

adolescents with one Black parent had attitudes toward other groups that were significantly more positive ($M = 3.32$) than those of the monoethnic Black adolescents ($M = 3.07$), $F(1, 322) = 4.19$, $p < .05$; there were no effects of sex or SES. For the Latinos, a similar ANOVA indicated no significant main effects, but there was a Sex $\times$ Parentage interaction, $F(1, 416) = 4.01$, $p < .05$; the females did not differ regarding attitudes toward other groups, but the multiethnic Latino males had more positive attitudes toward other groups ($M = 3.47$) than the monoethnic Latino males did ($M = 3.13$). There were no differences in other-group attitudes between the multiethnic adolescents and the monoethnic adolescents for the White or the Asian groups, which were considerably smaller than the other samples, and no effects of sex or SES.

DISCUSSION

By surveying large populations and gathering data on parental ethnicity, we were able to select and examine normal samples of U.S. multiethnic high school and college students and to compare them with their monoethnic peers. The approach we used in the present study differs from those that have been used in most studies on multiethnic/multiracial individuals, in which clinical populations or "snow-ball" techniques have yielded nontypical samples. Our approach also differs from the one used in surveys that determine ethnicity solely on the basis of self-label; such surveys fail to identify many multiethnic individuals.

The present results document the incidence of mixed ethnic youths in ethnically diverse and predominantly White settings in Southern California. Consistent with the data from other studies (e.g., Cauce et al., 1992), the present data indicate that over 10% of the students in both surveys were multiethnic and suggest justification for the study of multiethnic individuals as a group. Although small studies are problematic (Stephan, 1992), mixed individuals can easily be identified and described in large surveys if their parents' ethnicity is elicited. As statistics on intermarriage indicate, the number of people who are multiethnic is increasing. Thus, researchers who study ethnicity should be aware of the presence of this group.

Consistent with the results of several recent studies (e.g., Field, 1993; Grove, 1991; Hiraga et al., 1993), we found that multiethnic young people were not at a psychological disadvantage because of their mixed background. A self-esteem measure did not indicate any difference in terms of psychological well-being between the multiethnic individuals and their monoethnic peers in either study. Furthermore, self-esteem did not vary depending on whether the multiethnic students used a multiethnic or a monoethnic self-label. Thus, contrary to popular views (Berzon, 1978; Nakashima, 1992) and earlier clinical impressions (Gibbs, 1987; Sommers, 1964; Teicher, 1968), multiethnic individuals are not troubled, marginal people. Measures that have been used with monoethnic samples (ethnic identity, self-esteem, and attitudes toward other groups) were found to be just as methodologically reliable when they were used with multiethnic respondents.

However, the multiethnic participants were not identical to their monoethnic peers. At least in some cases, multiethnic youths may have an advantage in intergroup relations; multiethnic male and female high school students with one Black parent and multiethnic males with one Latino parent had more positive attitudes toward other groups than their monoethnic peers did. These results support the findings of Stephan and Stephan (1991) that "there are some positive effects of bicultural socialization in terms of insulation from the ethnocentrism of single-heritage groups" (p. 248). Because multiethnic individuals' dual heritage increases the likelihood that they will have close contact with at least two cultures, these individuals may function as a bridge between groups. Even multiethnic individuals who live in a monoethnic community and consider themselves to be members of one ethnic group will probably be less ethnocentric than monoethnic individuals. Hall (1980) described multiethnic people as ethnically androgynous, that is, able to identify strongly with more than one heritage, and a similar view has been expressed with regard to bicultural individuals (LaFromboise et al., 1993). People who identify with and participate in two cultures may further the appreciation of diversity and the reduction of intergroup conflict.

The present research provides clear evidence of the variability of multiethnic students' ethnic self-labels in differential contexts. First, in the college sample, the use of a White versus a minority self-label by multiethnic respondents with one White parent was related to the ethnic composition of the setting. The White label was used by almost half the respondents with a White parent on the predominantly White college campus but by only 1 student on the minority campus. Thus, for the most part, the spontaneous labels of the multiethnic students conformed to the ethnic composition of the campus. This contextual effect is consistent with the findings of the study with the high school students in that the latter sample was drawn from schools that were predominantly minority and that most mixed adolescents used a minority label. However, it is not clear whether this effect reflects the preselection of setting by a certain type of individual or the influence of setting on the individual. For example, it is conceivable that multiethnic students would decide to attend a predominantly White university or a minority university on the basis of their predominant identification; it is also conceivable that mixed (White and minority) couples with multiethnic adolescents would be more likely to live in minority communities. Further research is needed to disentangle these factors.

Additional factors are also likely to influence the choice of label. The reason multiethnic high school students with one Black parent used the label Black instead of another label may be that the Black community has become more accepting of people of mixed heritage (Hall, 1992b). Physical appearance is another factor in the use of self-label. Although people who have one Black ancestor are no longer obligated to use a Black self-label, those who have identifiable Black features are usually labeled Black, regardless of whether other types of features are also evident. Clearly, then, multiethnic youths' choice of self-label is not without constraints.

Not only does the larger context influence the label; the immediate context—that is, the way the question is asked—is also important. In the high school survey, the students were asked to indicate their ethnicity twice, once at the beginning of the questionnaire, using an open-ended format, and again at the end of the questionnaire, using a list that included the Mixed option. Many more respondents used the Mixed label in the second response than in the first. However, because the way the question was asked was confounded with its position on the questionnaire, we do not know whether this result reflects a preference for the Mixed option or merely an increase in the respondents' ethnic awareness by the end of the survey and the attendant choice of the Mixed label. In either case, the present results are consistent with the variability in self-label that has been documented in previous research (Stephan & Stephan, 1989).

This variability has important implications for research. Many individuals would not be identified as multiethnic with methodology that depends solely on self-label. In the present research, for example, when the format was open-ended, 66% to 80% of the multiethnic participants used self-labels indicating that they belonged to a single ethnic group. Thus, samples in diverse settings may contain three to five times as many multiethnic individuals as might be suggested on the basis of self-report alone.

When unidentified multiethnic individuals are included in monoethnic samples, the potential for error variance increases. Thus, researchers who fail to consider parental ethnicity may obtain results that are distorted or lack statistical significance. This type of difficulty is illustrated by the present findings regarding social class standing. Although the White participants' SES was

higher than that of the minority samples as a whole, the multiethnic White participants' SES was lower than that of their monoethnic White peers. However, among the Latinos, whose SES was generally lower than that of the other groups, the multiethnic adolescents' reported SES was higher than that of their monoethnic peers. Thus, ethnic mixing seems to have had an equalizing effect on social class. These findings are consistent with those of a study conducted in Israel (Yogev & Jamshy, 1983) in which multiethnic Ashkenazi Oriental adolescents' scores for several variables, including SES, fell between those of their monoethnic Ashkenazi and Oriental peers. If researchers are to identify this type of effect, they must specify ethnic background rather than treating multiethnic participants as a group.

Two notable findings in the high school sample were the large number of multiethnic adolescents (about one third of the respondents) who indicated their mixed heritage in an open-ended response format and the large number of parents who were identified as mixed (nearly half the multiethnic adolescents reported that one or both their parents were of mixed heritage). Thus, many of the participants were at least second-generation mixed. These findings may indicate increased recognition and acceptance of the phenomenon of mixed heritage in highly diverse settings and general progress toward the "critical mass" (Hall, 1992a, p. 326) that is necessary for the recognition of multiethnic persons as a legitimate entity. Relatedly, the growing multiethnic segment of the U.S. population is pressuring the government to include a Mixed option on the next census (Thornton, 1992). The formation of local and national social support groups for people of mixed heritage may signal the beginning of a movement for multiethnic pride.

A broader issue involves the changes in the meaning of race and ethnicity that have resulted from the stronger presence of people of mixed heritage. Social psychology in general and social identity theory in particular have regarded groups as discrete entities and conflict between groups as inevitable (Hogg & Abrams, 1988). Multiethnic individuals present a challenge to the view of ethnic groups as distinct and in conflict. Root (1992a) points out that "the presence of racially mixed persons . . . blurs racial and ethnic group boundaries and . . . challenges long-held notions about the biological, moral, and social meaning of race" (p. 3). This idea is developed at a personal level in the recent autobiography of a multiethnic woman (Haizlip, 1994).

Just as psychologists have become more cognizant of the effects of culture and ethnicity (Betancourt & Lopez, 1993), so, too, must they become cognizant of the complex topic of the blending of cultures. There is growing interest in the ways in which minority group members function in the bicultural context of their ethnic and the mainstream cultures (LaFromboise et al., 1993). Multiethnic individuals go beyond this cultural mixing by combining two or more heritages in one person. Through the study of these individuals, researchers may be able to gain valuable insights into the role of group identity in the psychological functioning of people in a multicultural society.

REFERENCES

Alipuria, L. L. (1990). *Self-esteem and self-label in multiethnic students from two southern California state universities.* Unpublished master's thesis, California State University, Los Angeles.

Betancourt, H., & Lopez, S. R. (1993). The study of culture, ethnicity, and race in American psychology. *American Psychologist, 48*(6), 629–637.

Berzon, J. R. (1978). *Neither White nor Black: The Mulatto character in American fiction.* New York: New York University Press.

Buriel, R. (1987). Ethnic labeling and identity among Mexican Americans. In J. Phinney & M. Rotheram (Eds.), *Children's ethnic socialization* (pp. 134–152). Newbury Park, CA: Sage.

Cauce, A. M., Hiraga, Y., Mason, C., Aguilar, T., Ordonez, N., & Gonzales, N. (1992). Between a rock and a hard place: Social adjustment of biracial youth. In M. P. P. Root (Ed.), *Racially mixed people in America* (pp. 207–222). Newbury Park, CA: Sage.

Census of Population and Housing. (1990). Summary tape file 1C [CD-ROM]. (Vital Statistics Summary). Machine readable data files. Washington, DC: The Bureau of the Census.

Erikson, E. (1968). *Identity: Youth and crisis.* New York: Norton.

Field, L. (1993, August). *Reference group orientation and self-concept in biracial adolescents.* Paper presented at the annual convention of the American Psychological Association, Toronto, Canada.

Gibbs, J. T. (1987). Identity and marginality: Issues in the treatment of biracial adolescents. *American Journal of Orthopsychiatry, 57,* 265–278.

Gibbs, J. T., & Hines, A. M. (1992). Negotiating ethnic identity: Issues for Black–White biracial adolescents. In M. P. P. Root (Ed.), *Racially mixed people in America* (pp. 223–238). Newbury Park, CA: Sage.

Graham, S. (1992). Most of the subjects were White and middle class: Trends in the published research on African Americans in selected APA journals, 1970–1989. *American Psychologist, 47,* 629–639.

Grove, K. (1991). Identity development in interracial, Asian/White late adolescents: Must it be so problematic? *Journal of Youth and Adolescence, 20,* 617–628.

Haizlip, S. (1994). *The sweeter the juice: A family memoir in Black and White.* New York: Simon & Shuster.

Hall, C. C. I. (1980). *The ethnic identity of racially mixed people: A study of Black-Japanese.* Unpublished doctoral dissertation, University of California, Los Angeles.

———. (1992a). Coloring outside the lines. In M. P. P. Root (Ed.), *Racially mixed people in America* (pp. 326–329). Newbury Park, CA: Sage.

———. (1992b). Please choose one: Ethnic identity choices for biracial individuals. In M. P. P. Root (Ed.), *Racially mixed people in America* (pp. 250–264). Newbury Park, CA: Sage.

Hiraga, Y., Cauce, A., Mason, C., & Ordonez, N. (1993, March). *Ethnic identity and the social adjustment of biracial youth.* Paper presented at the Society for Research in Child Development, New Orleans.

Hogg, M., & Abrams, D. (1988). *Social identifications: A social psychology of intergroup relations and group processes.* London: Routledge.

Johnson, R. C., & Nagoshi, C. T. (1986). The adjustment of offspring of within group and interracial/intercultural marriages: A comparison of personality factor scores. *Journal of Marriage and the Family, 48,* 279–284.

Kerwin, C., Ponterotto, J. G., Jackson, B. L., & Harris, A. (1993). Racial identity in biracial children: A qualitative investigation. *Journal of Counseling Psychology, 40*(2), 221–231.

Kich, G. K. (1992). The developmental process of asserting a biracial, bicultural identity. In M. P. P. Root (Ed.), *Racially mixed people in America* (pp. 304–320). Newbury Park, CA: Sage.

Kitano, H., & Daniels, B. (1988). *Asian Americans.* Englewood Cliffs, NJ: Prentice Hall.

LaFromboise, T., Coleman, H., & Gerton, J. (1993). Psychological impact of biculturalism: Evidence and theory. *Psychological Bulletin, 114,* 395–412.

Lochner, B., & Phinney, J. (1988, April). *Ethnic identity in Hispanic and White college students.* Paper presented at the Western Psychological Association meeting, Burlingame, California.

Nakashima, C. L. (1992). An invisible monster: The creation and denial of mixed-race people in America. In M. P. P. Root (Ed.), *Racially mixed people in America* (pp. 162–180). Newbury Park, CA: Sage.

Park, R. E. (1928). Human migration and the marginal man. *The American Journal of Sociology, 33,* 881–893.

———. (1950). *Race and culture.* Glencoe, IL: Free Press.

Phinney, J. (1990). Ethnic identity in adolescents and adults: Review of research. *Psychological Bulletin, 108,* 499–514.

———. (1992). The Multigroup Ethnic Identity Measure: A new scale for use with diverse groups. *Journal of Adolescent Research, 7,* 156–176.

Phinney, J., & Alipuria, L. (1990). Ethnic identity in college students. *Journal of Adolescence, 13,* 171–183.

Phinney, J., DuPont, S., Espinosa, C., Revill, J., & Sanders, K. (1994). Ethnic identity and American identification among ethnic minority adolescents. In A. Bouvy, F. van de Vijver, P. Boski, & P. Schmitz (Eds.), *Journeys into cross-cultural psychology* (pp. 167–183). Amsterdam: Swets & Zeitlinger.

Ramirez, M. (1984). Assessing and understanding biculturalism–multiculturalism in Mexican-American adults. In J. Martinez & R. Mendoza (Eds.), *Chicano psychology* (2nd ed., pp. 77–94). Orlando, FL: Academic Press.

Ramirez, M., & Castaneda, A. (1974). *Cultural democracy, bicognitive development and education.* San Diego: Academic Press.

Root, M. P. (1992a). Within, between, and beyond race. In M. P. P. Root (Ed.), *Racially mixed people in America* (pp. 3–11). Newbury Park, CA: Sage.

———. (1992b). Back to the drawing board: Methodological issues in research on multiracial people. In M. P. P. Root (Ed.), *Racially mixed people in America* (pp. 181–189). Newbury Park, CA: Sage.

Rosenberg, M. (1986). *Conceiving the self.* Melbourne, FL: Krieger.

Salgado de Snyder, N., Lopez, C. M., & Padilla, A. M. (1982). Ethnic identity and cultural awareness among the offspring of Mexican interethnic marriages. *Journal of Early Adolescence, 2,* 277–282.

Shweder, R. (1990). Cultural psychology—What is it? In J. Stigler, R. Shweder, & G. Herdt (Eds.), *Cultural psychology: Essays on comparative human development* (pp. 1–43). Cambridge, UK: Cambridge University.

Sommers, V. S. (1964). The impact of dual-cultural membership on identity. *Psychiatry, 27*(4), 332–344.

Stephan, C. W. (1992). Mixed-heritage individuals: Ethnic identity and trait characteristics. In M. P. P. Root (Ed.), *Racially mixed people in America* (pp. 50–63). Newbury Park, CA: Sage.

Stephan, C. W., & Stephan, W. G. (1989). After intermarriage: Ethnic identity among mixed-heritage Japanese-Americans and Hispanics. *Journal of Marriage and the Family, 51,* 507–519.

———. (1991). Intermarriage: Effects on personality, adjustment, and the intergroup relations in two samples of students. *Journal of Marriage and the Family, 53*(1), 241–250.

Stonequist, E. V. (1961). *The marginal man: A study in personality and culture conflict.* New York: Russell & Russell.

Teicher, J. D. (1968). Some observations of identity problems in children in Negro-White marriages. *Journal of Nervous and Mental Disease, 146,* 249–256.

Thornton, M. C. (1992). Is multiracial status unique? The personal and social experience. In M. P. P. Root (Ed.), *Racially mixed people in America* (pp. 321–325). Newbury Park, CA: Sage.

United States Bureau of the Census. (1993). No. 62. Married couples of same or mixed races and origins

1970 to 1992. *Statistical Abstract of the United States: 1993.* (113th ed., p. 54). Washington, DC.

Williamson, J. (1980). *New people: Miscegenation and the Mulattos in the U.S.* New York: Free Press.

Wilson, A. (1984). "Mixed race" children in British society: Some theoretical considerations. *The British Journal of Sociology, 35,* 42–61.

Wright, R. D., & Wright, S. N. (1972). A plea for a further refinement of the marginal man theory. *Phylon, 33,* 361–368.

Yogev, A., & Jamshy, H. (1983). Children of ethnic intermarriage in Israeli schools: Are they marginal? *Journal of Marriage and the Family, 45,* 965–974.

PART ELEVEN

GENDER DIFFERENCES

*The world tells us what we are to be and shapes us by the ends it sets
before us. To men it says, work. To us, it says, seem. The less
a woman has in her head the lighter she is for carrying.*
—OLIVE SCHREINER

Traditional cultural values and societal expectations in the past have—as the above quote clearly illustrates—determined gender roles. As a result of feminists challenges to these stereotypes, a new social awareness of old prejudices is emerging. Consequently adolescents too must learn to establish and maybe revise their concepts of self to include a personal gender identity. Social codes of conduct may define what is expected of males and females, but the process of integrating such standards often means the individual's genuine needs and vulnerabilities become submerged so that a socially prescribed version may surface. For example, if young people are overwhelmed by their emotions but do not feel free to express those feelings, they may use drugs to mask the pain and appear "cool and in control." According to Erikson (23), gender identity is an important aspect of identity formation.

This chapter is concerned with understanding how young males and females see themselves and are socialized to adapt to the roles expected of them. As a result of gender differences, they tend to experience psychopathology differently. Few codes are as rigid as the standards of acceptable behaviors that young males impose on each other. Young adolescents feel pain when they are hit, but they learn to mask their pain to comply with the imperative, "Big boys don't cry." According to Gilligan, young women define themselves in terms of interpersonal relationships, but they are told that in order to grow up, they must become independent and separate. Therefore, to be considered adults, they must disassociate from their relational selves and pretend to desire detachment. Pubertal changes create new levels of personal and social awareness, and psychological adjustments require revised definitions of self. However, it is always within a social context that these psychological and biological transformations take place.

Carol Gilligan's work (32) on gender identity and development has reshaped our conceptualization of gender differences. Her brief overview of the historical paradigm of development indicates that one purpose of adolescence is to become independent. Teenagers renegotiate their power bases to claim their rights to autonomy. It was Gilligan's revolutionary observation that this description primarily fits the developmental paths of males, not females. For girls, feelings of attachment and fears of detachment are especially significant during adolescence. As a result of Gilligan's work, the missing female voice is heard at last.

Suitor and Reavis (33) explored gender roles and the changes in attitudes that have taken place in recent years. Surprisingly, their data demonstrate the persistence of traditional gender roles among high school students during the 1980s. Asked to list how males and females gained prestige in high school, both genders revealed deeply entrenched expectations for males to be aggressive and involved in sports and for girls to gain prestige through physical attractiveness and sociability. The findings suggest only minor changes in perceptions by the end of the decade, and these were reported mainly by males. Male students perceived an increase in prestige for girls who participated in sports and were sexually active; the only decrease in prestige was for young women for cheerleading and owning a car. Revisions in these perceptions were reported by boys, not girls. Although changes are taking place in the roles of women in the workplace, the political system, and the media, gender-based expectations during adolescence appear to change only slowly and are not nearly as free of stereotypes as might have been assumed.

Schonert-Reichl and Beaudoin (34) explored the rarely studied relationships between external and internal patterns of psychopathology among adolescent boys and girls. Externalizers believe that they have little control over their lives. They believe things just seem to happen to them; effort and success are not seen as intrinsically related. In contrast, internalizers believe they have some control over their destiny. Efforts are assumed to lead to success; they see themselves as responsible for what happens to them. Empathy, the social cognition studied, is the ability to see a problem from another person's perspective, and it is comprised of both cognitive and affective dimensions. The authors examined gender differences in regard to empathy and the extent to which psychopathology is externalized or internalized by both genders. The researchers found that females are more likely to be internalizers who demonstrate higher levels of empathy and perspective taking, but they also tend to internalize their distress in quiet, personally debilitating ways, such as depression and eating disorders. Males externalize their problems and demonstrate lower levels of empathy and perspective taking. They express their distress by aggressiveness, acting out behavior, and reveal more conduct disorders.

A clear understanding of the historical changes in gender roles can shed some light on the conflicting messages adolescents receive regarding what is expected of them as their bodies and minds develop. It is clear that gender plays a crucial part in societal, family, peer, school, and later work expectations. Adolescence is a time in life when diverse and even conflicting messages about gender must be reconciled and forged into one's personality structure. Therefore, as Erikson postulated, forming an identity that includes gender roles is a primary developmental imperative.

EXIT-VOICE DILEMMAS
IN ADOLESCENT DEVELOPMENT

CAROL GILLIGAN
Harvard University

In *Exit, Voice and Loyalty: Responses to Decline in Firms, Organizations, and States* (1970), Albert Hirschman contrasts two modes of response to decline in social organizations—the options of exit and voice. Exit, central to the operation of the classical market economy, is exemplified by the customer who, dissatisfied with the product of company A, switches to the product of company B. In comparison to this neat and impersonal mechanism that operates "by courtesy of the Invisible Hand," voice—the attempt to change rather than escape from an objectionable situation—is messy, cumbersome, and direct. "Graduated all the way from faint grumbling to violent protest," voice is political action par excellence, carrying with it the potential for "heartbreak" by substituting the personal and public articulation of critical opinions for the private, secret vote. Introducing exit and voice as the two principal actors in his drama of societal health, Hirschman puts forth a theory of loyalty to explain the conditions for their optimal collaboration. Loyalty, he maintains, the seemingly irrational commitment of "the member who cares," activates voice by holding exit at bay, while sustaining in the im-

plication of disloyalty the possibility of exit as the option of last resort.

To the economist's view of the individual as motivated by the desire for profit and to the political theorist's view of the individual as seeking power in social organizations, Hirschman adds a new dimension—an image of the individual as motivated by loyalty or attachment to stem decline and promote recuperation. Demonstrating the power of attachment to influence action and shift the parameters of choice, Hirschman illustrates across a wide range of situations how the presence of loyalty holds exit and voice in tension and, thus, changes the meaning of both leaving and speaking. The psychological acuity of Hirschman's analysis of exit and voice is matched by the transformation implied by bringing the psychology of attachment to the center of developmental consideration.

In honoring Hirschman's contribution I wish to illuminate the psychological dimensions of his conception by extending it to the seemingly remote domain of adolescent development. Here it is possible to see not only the interplay of exit and voice that Hirschman describes but also the dilemmas posed by loyalty at a time of intense transition in human life. The central themes of Hirschman's work—the importance of values and ideas in the developmental process, the connection between passions and interests, the reflection on historical periods of development—

will be addressed here in the context of the life cycle. But following Hirschman's example of trespass, I will suggest that the analysis of loyalty in family relationships speaks across disciplinary boundaries to the problems of interdependence that face contemporary civilization.

Hirschman's focus on loyalty is in part a correction to the more popular view of the exit option as uniquely powerful in effecting change. In challenging this view, he underscores the problems of attachment which arise in modern societies—problems which have taken on an added intensity and urgency in an age of nuclear threat. This threat which signals the possibility for an irredeemable failure of care also calls attention to the limits of exit as a solution to conflicts in social relationships. Yet "the preference for the neatness of exit over the messiness and heartbreak of voice" (p. 107), which Hirschman finds in classical economics as well as in the American tradition, extends through the study of human development, emerging most clearly in the psychology of adolescence. This paradigm of problem solving, based on an assumption of independence and competition, obscures the reality of interdependence and masks the possibilities for cooperation. Thus, the need to reassess the interpretive schemes on which we rely, the need to correct a "defensive representation of the real world" (p. 2) in which our actions take place, extends across the realm of economics to the psychological domain, calling attention to shared assumptions about the nature of development and the process of change.

This parallel is forcefully evoked by the easy transfer of the characters from Hirschman's drama to the adolescent scene where puberty signals the decline of the childhood world of relations, and exit and voice enter as modes of response and recuperation. The growth to full stature at puberty releases the child from dependence on parents for protection and heightens the possibility of exit as a solution to conflicts in family relationships. At the same time the sexual maturation of puberty—the intensification of sexual feelings and the advent of reproductive

capability—impels departure from the family, given the incest taboo. The heightened availability of and impetus toward exit in adolescence, however, may also stimulate development of voice—a development enhanced by the cognitive changes of puberty, the growth of reflective thinking, and the discovery of the subjective self. Seeing the possibility of leaving, the adolescent may become freer in speaking, more willing to assert perspectives and voice opinions that diverge from accepted family truths. But if the transformations of puberty heighten the potential for both exit and voice, the experience of adolescence also changes the meaning of leaving and speaking by creating dilemmas of loyalty and rendering choice itself more self-conscious and reflective.

Adolescents, striving to integrate a new image of self and new experiences of relationship, struggle to span the discontinuity of puberty and renegotiate a series of social connections. This effort at renegotiation engages the adolescent voice in the process of identity formation and moral growth. But this development of voice depends on the presence of loyalty for its continuation. Hirschman, pointing out that the availability of the exit options tends "to atrophy the development of the art of voice" (1970, p. 43), but also noting that the threat of exit can strengthen the voice's effective use, observes that the decision of whether to exit will often be made in light of the prospects for the efficacy of voice. Development in adolescence, thus, hinges on loyalty between adolescents and adults, and the challenges to society, families, and schools is how to engage that loyalty and how to educate the voice of the future generation.

In the life cycle the adolescent is the truth teller, like the fool in the Renaissance play, exposing hypocrisy and revealing truths about human relationships. These truths pertain to justice and care, the moral coordinates of human connection, heightened for adolescents who stand between the innocence of childhood and the responsibility of adulthood. Looking back on the childhood experiences of inequality and attachment, feeling again the powerlessness and vulnerability which these experiences initially evoked, adolescents identify with the child and construct a world that offers protection. This ideal or utopian vision, laid out along the coordinates of justice and care, depicts a world where self and other will be treated as of equal worth, where, despite differences in power, things will be fair; a world where everyone will be included, where no one will be left alone or hurt. In the ability to construct this ideal moral vision lies the potential for nihilism and despair as well as the possibility for societal renewal which adolescence symbolizes and represents. Given the engagement of the adolescent's passion for morality and truth with the realities of social justice and care, adolescents are the group whose problems of development most closely mirror society's problems with regeneration.

In analyzing these problems I will distinguish two moral voices that define two intersecting lines of development—one arising from the child's experience of inequality, one from the child's experience of attachment. Although the experiences of inequality and attachment initially are concurrent in the relationship of parent and child, they point to different dimensions of relationship—the dimension of inequality/equality and of attachment/detachment. The moral visions of justice and care reflect these different dimensions of relationships and the injunctions to which the experiences of inequality and attachment give rise. But these experiences also inform different ways of experiencing and defining self in relation to others and lend different meanings to separation. These different conceptions of self and morality (Gilligan, 1982, chap. 2) have been obscured by current stage theories of psychological development that present a single linear representation, fusing inequality with attachment and linking development to separation. But the problems in this portrayal are clarified by observing how the axis of development shifts when dependence, which connotes the experiences of connection, is contrasted with isolation rather than opposed to independence.

To trace this shift and consider its implications for the understanding of progress and growth, I will begin with theories of identity and moral development that focus on the dimension of inequality/equality, noting that these theories have been derived primarily or exclusively from research on males. Then I will turn to research on females to focus the dimension of attachment/detachment and delineate a different conception of morality and self. Although these two dimensions of relationship may be differentially salient in the thinking of women and men, both inequality and attachment are embedded in the cycle of life, universal in human experience because inherent in the relation of parent and child. By representing both dimensions of relationships, it becomes possible to see how they combine to create dilemmas of loyalty in adolescence and to discern how different conceptions of loyalty give rise to different modalities of exit and voice.

CURRENT THEORIES OF ADOLESCENT DEVELOPMENT

The theories that currently provide the conceptual underpinning for the description of adolescent development trace a progression toward equality and autonomy in the conception of morality and self. All of these theories follow William James (1902/1961) in distinguishing the once from the twice-born self and tie that distinction to the contrast between conventional and reflective moral thought. This approach differentiates youth who adopt the conventions of their childhood society as their own, defining themselves more by ascription than choice, from youth who reject societal conventions by questioning the norms and values that provide their justification. The distinction between two roads to maturity and the clear implication that the second leads far beyond the first appears in Erikson's division between the "technocrats" or "compact majority" and the "neo-humanists" (1968, pp. 31–39). The same contrast appears in Kohlberg's division of moral development into preconventional, conventional, and principled thought (Kohlberg, 1981).

This dual or tripartite division of identity formation and moral growth generates a description of adolescent development that centers on two major separations—the first from parental authority and the second from the authority of societal conventions. In this context, loyalty, the virtue of fidelity that Erikson (1964) cites as the strength of adolescence, takes on an ideological cast, denoting a shift in the locus of authority from persons to principles—a move toward abstraction that justifies separation and renders "the self" autonomous. Key to this vision of self as separate and constant is the promise of equality built into the cycle of life, the promise of development that in time the child will become the adult.

Tracing development as a move from inequality to equality, adolescence is marked by a series of power confrontations, by the renegotiation of authority relationships. To emerge victorious the adolescent must overcome the constraint of parental authority through a process of "detachment" described by Freud as "one of the most significant, but also one of the most painful, physical accomplishments of the pubertal period . . . a process that alone makes possible the opposition, which is so important for the progress of civilization, between the new generation and the old" (Freud, 1905/1963). This equation of progress with detachment and opposition leads problems in adolescence to be cast as problems of exit or separation. Observing that, as "at every stage in the course of development through which all human beings ought by rights to pass, a certain number are held back; so there are some who have never got over their parents' authority and have withdrawn their affection from them either very incompletely or not at all," Freud concludes that this failure of development in adolescence is one that occurs mostly in girls (p. 227).

Thus, exit, in resolving the childhood drama of inequality, symbolized for Freud by the Oedipal dilemma, becomes emblematic of adolescent growth. Yet the option of exit, as Hirschman observes, leaves a problem of loyalty in its wake, a problem which if not addressed can lead to the decline of care and commitment in social relationships (p. 112). In this light, adolescent girls who demonstrate a reluctance to exit may articulate a different voice—a voice which speaks of loyalty to persons and identifies detachment as morally problematic. To represent this perspective on loyalty changes the depiction of adolescent growth by delineating a mode of development that relies not on detachment but on a change in the form of attachment—a change that must be negotiated by voice.

Yet the preference for the neatness of exit over the messiness and heartbreak of voice, the focus on inequality rather than attachment in human relations, and the reliance on male experience in building the model of human growth have combined to silence the female voice. This silence contributes to the problems observed in adolescent girls, particularly if these problems are seen to reflect a failure of engagement rather than a failure of separation. But this silence and the implicit disparagement of female experience also creates problems in the account of human development—a failure to trace the growth of attachment and the capacity for care and loyalty in relationships.

The omission of female experience from the literature on adolescent development was noted by Bruno Bettelheim in 1965, and the significance of this omission was underlined by Joseph Adelson who edited the *Handbook of Adolescent Psychology,* published in 1980. Adelson had asked a leading scholar to write a chapter for the handbook on female adolescent development, but after surveying the literature she concluded that there was not enough good material to warrant a separate chapter. In their chapter on psychodynamics, Adelson and Doehrman observe that "to read the psychological literature on adolescence has, until very recently, meant reading about the psychodynamics of the male youngster writ large" (1980, p. 114). They end their chapter by noting that "the inattention to girls and to the processes of feminine development in adolescence has meant undue attention to such problems as impulse control, rebelliousness, superego struggles, ideology and achievement, along with a corresponding neglect of such issues as intimacy, nurturance, and affiliation" (p. 114). They found particularly troubling the fact that current biases in the literature reinforce each other, with the result that "the separate, though interacting emphases on pathology, on the more ideologized, least conformist social strata, and on males has produced a psychodynamic theory of adolescence that is both one-sided and distorted" (p. 115).

In girls' accounts of their experiences in the adolescent years, problems of attachment and detachment emerge as a central concern. Because girls—the group left out in the critical theory-building studies of adolescent psychology—have repeatedly been described as having problems in adolescence with separation, the experience of girls may best inform an expanded theory of adolescent development.

THE MISSING LINE
OF ADOLESCENT DEVELOPMENT

In adolescence the renegotiation of attachment centers on the inclusion of sexuality and inclusion of perspective in relationships—each introducing a new level of complication and depth to human connection. Conflicts of attachment that arise at this time are exemplified by the problems that girls describe when they perceive the inclusion of themselves (their views and their wishes) as hurting their parents, whereas including their parents implies excluding themselves. The revival of the Oedipal triangular conflict which psychoanalysts describe demonstrates how such problems tend to be recast by girls as a drama of inclusion and exclusion rather than of dominance and subordination. If the "Oedipal wish" is conceived as a desire to be included in the parents' relationship—to be a "member of the wedding" in Carson McCullers' phrase—then the Oedipal threat in the adolescent years is that of exclusion, experienced as endangering one's connection with others.

But adolescents, gaining the power to form family relationships on their own, confront the implications of excluding their parents as they remember their own experience of having been excluded by them. Construed as an issue of justice, this exclusion seems eminently fair, a matter of simple reciprocity. Construed as an issue of care, it seems, instead, morally problematic, given the association of exclusion with hurt. In resisting detachment and criticizing exclusion, adolescent girls hold to the view that change can be negotiated through voice and that voice is the way to sustain attachment across the leavings of adolescence.

Adolescents, aware of new dimensions of human connection, experiment in a variety of ways as they seek to discover what constitutes attachment and how problems in relationships can be solved. Girls in particular, given their interest in relationships and their attention to the ways in which connection between people can be formed and maintained, observe that relationships in which voice is silenced are not relationships in any meaningful sense. This understanding that voice has to be expressed in relationship to solve rather than escape the dilemmas of adolescence, calls attention not only to the limitations of exit but also to the problems that arise when voice is silenced. In sum, adolescent girls who resist exit may be holding on to the position that solutions to dilemmas of attachment in adolescence must be forged by voice and that exit alone is no solution but an admission of defeat. Thus, their resistance may signify a refusal to leave before they can speak.

Hirschman, describing how the high price of exit and the presence of loyalty in family relationships encourages the option of voice, also indicates that resort to voice will be undertaken in a conflict situation when the outcome is visualized as either possible victory or possible accord. But adolescents in their conflicts with their parents cannot readily visualize victory, nor can they visualize full accord, for given the closeness of the relationships, a meeting of minds may suggest a meeting of bodies which is precluded by the incest taboo. Therefore, exit must be part of the solution, and some accommodation must be found, some mixture of leaving and speaking which typically may occur in different proportions for boys and girls.

The focus on leaving in the psychology of adolescence, manifest by measuring development by signs of separation, may be an accurate rendition of male experience, at least within certain cultures, since the more explosive potential of tensions between adolescent sons and parents highlights the opposition between dependence and independence which renders exit appealing. In contrast, the propensity toward staying, noted as the "problem" in female development, may reflect the different nature of the attachment between daughters and parents and the greater salience for girls of the opposition between dependence and isolation. In this way the two opposites of the word dependence—isolation and independence—catch the shift in the valence of relationships that occurs when connection with others is experienced as an impediment to autonomy and when it is experienced as a protection against isolation. This essential ambivalence of human connection creates an ongoing ethical tension that rises sharply in adolescence and leads to exit-voice problems.

The ways in which adolescents consider decisions about staying and leaving, silence and speaking, illustrate the interplay of exit, voice, and loyalty that Hirschman describes. But the dilemmas of adolescence become more intense when they involve conflicts of loyalty, especially when attachment to persons vies with adherence to principles. Psychological theorists typically have given priority to principles as the anchor of personal integrity and focused their attention on the necessity and the justification for leaving. But in doing so, they have tended to overlook the costs of detachment—its consequences both to personal integrity and to societal functioning. Since adolescent girls tend to resist detachment and highlight its costs to others and themselves, we may learn about ways of solving problems through voice within the context of ongoing rela-

tionships by observing the way that they struggle with conflicts of loyalty and exit-voice decisions.

In a series of studies (conducted by the Center for the Study of Gender, Education, and Human Development), concerns about detachment have emerged saliently in girls' and women's moral thinking, pointing to an ethic of care that enjoins responsibility and responsiveness in relationships. In a study of high school girls, these concerns were so insistent and focused so specifically on problems of speaking and listening that it seemed important to inquire directly about situations in which voice failed: we sought to explore empirically the conceptual distinction between problems of inequality and problems of detachment. Thus, two questions were added to the interview schedule in the second year of the study—one pertaining to incidents of unfairness and one to incidents of not listening. Asked to describe a situation in which someone was not being listened to, girls spoke about a wide variety of problems that ranged across the divide between interpersonal and international relations. "The Nicaraguan people," one girl explained, "are not being listened to by President Reagan." Asked how she knew, she said that Mr. Reagan, in explaining his own position, did not respond to the issues raised by the Nicaraguans and, thus, appeared to discount their view of their situation. The absence of response, as it indicated not listening, was acutely observed by girls in a wide range of settings and interpreted as a sign of not caring. The willingness to test the extent of detachment, to ascertain whether not listening signified a transitory distraction or a more deeply rooted indifference, appeared critical to decisions girls made about silence and speaking.

The same moral outrage and passion that infused girls' descriptions of not listening was also apparent in their accounts of unfairness. Yet, over the high school years, concerns about listening tended increasingly to temper judgments about fairness, reflecting a growing awareness of differences in perspective and problems in communication. The amount of energy devoted to solving these problems, the intensity of the search for ways to make connection and achieve understanding, led girls to express immense frustration in situations where voice failed. When others did not listen and seemed not to care, they spoke of "coming up against a wall." This image of wall had as its counterpart the search for an opening through which one could speak. The nature of this search, together with the intensity of its frustration, are conveyed in the following girl's description of an attempt to reestablish communication with her mother without abandoning her own perspective:

> I called my mother up and said, "Why can't I talk to you anymore?" And I ended up crying and hanging up on her because she wouldn't listen to me . . . She had her own opinion about what was truth and what was reality, and she gave me no opening . . . And, you know, I kept saying, "Well, you hurt me." And she said, "No, I didn't." And I said, "Well, why am I hurt?" you know. And she is just denying my feelings as if they didn't exist and as if I had no right to feel them, even though they were . . . I guess until she calls me up or writes me a letter saying I want to talk instead of saying, well, this and this happened, and I don't understand what is going on with you, and I don't understand why you are denying the truth . . . until she says, I want to talk, I can't, I just can't.

Simone Weil, in a beautifully evocative and paradoxical statement, defines morality as the silence in which one can hear the unheard voices (1977, p. 316). This rendering of morality in terms of attention and perception is central to Iris Murdoch's vision (1970) and appears as well in Hannah Arendt's question as to whether the activity of thinking as such, "the habit of examining whatever happens to come to pass or to attract attention, regardless of results and specific content," can be considered a moral act (1972, p. 5). The visions of these women philosophers illuminate the activities of care that high school girls describe, their equation of care with the willingness "to be there," "to listen," "to talk to," and "to understand." In girls' narratives about conflict and choice, these activities of care taken on a moral dimension, and the willingness and the ability to care become a source of empowerment and a standard of self-evaluation. Detachment, then, signifies not only caring in the sense of choosing to stand apart but also not being able to care, given that in the absence of connection one would not know how to respond. Thus, girls' portrayal of care reveals its cognitive as well as affective dimensions, its foundation in the ability to perceive people in their own terms and to respond to need. As this knowledge generates the power not only to help but also to hurt, the uses of this power become a measure of responsibility in relationships.

In adolescence when both wanting and knowing take on new meanings, given the intensity of sexual feelings and the discovery of subjectivity, conflicts of responsibility assume new dimensions of complexity. The experience of coming into a relationship with oneself and the increasing assumption of responsibility for taking care of oneself are premised in this context not on detachment from others but on a change in the form of connection with others. These changes in the experience of connection, both with others and with oneself, set the parameters of the moral conflicts that girls describe when responsibility to themselves conflicts with responsibility to others. Seeking to perceive and respond to their own as well as to others' feelings and thoughts, girls ask if they can be responsive to themselves without losing connection with others and whether they can respond to others without abandoning themselves.

This search for an inclusive solution to dilemmas of conflicting loyalties vies with the tendency toward exclusion expressed in the moral opposition between "selfish" and "selfless" choice—an opposition where selfishness connotes the exclusion of others and selflessness the exclusion of self. This opposition appears repeatedly in the moral judgments of adolescent girls and women, in part because the conventional norms of feminine virtue, which hold up selflessness as a moral ideal, conflict with an understanding of relationships derived from experiences of connection. Since the exclusion of self as well as of others dissolves the fabric of connection, both exclusions create problems in relationships, diminishing the capacity for care and reducing one's efficacy as a moral agent.

The bias toward voice in girls' moral thinking contains this recognition and directs attention toward the ways that attachments can be transformed and sustained. "There is not a wall between us," one adolescent explains in describing her relationship with her parents, "but there is a sort of strain or a sieve." This metaphor of connection continuing through a barrier to complete attachment conveys a solution that avoids detachment while recognizing the need for distance that arises in adolescence. The following examples further illustrate the mixture of exit and voice in adolescent girls' thinking about relationships, indicating the value they place on loyalty or continuing attachment. In addition, these examples suggest how attachments can be sustained across separation and how relationships can expand without detachment.

> I have been very close to my parents mentally . . . We have a very strong relationship, but yet it is not a physical thing that you can see . . . In my family we are more independent of each other, but yet we have this strong love.
>
> All the boyfriends that I have ever really cared about, they are still with me . . . in mind, not in body, because we are separated by miles. But they will always be with me. Any relationship that I have ever had has been important to me. Otherwise I wouldn't have had it.

Such evocations of the mind-body problem of adolescence convey a view of continuing connection as consonant with autonomy and growth. Within this vision, dependence and independence are not opposed but are seen instead to commingle, as exemplified by the following description of a relationship between close friends:

> I would say we depend on each other in a way that we are both independent, and I would say that we are very independent, but as far as our friendship goes, we are dependent on each other because we know that both of us realize that whenever we need something, the other person will always be there.

In this way, the capacity to care for others and to receive care from them becomes a part of rather than antithetical to self-definition.

Defined in this context of relationships, identity is formed through the gaining of voice or perspective, and self is known through the experience of engagement with different voices or points of view. Over the high school years, girls display an increasing recognition that attachment does not imply agreement and that differences constitute the life of relationships rather than a threat to their continuation. The ability to act on this recognition generates a more empirical approach to conflict resolution, an approach which often leads to the discovery of creative solutions to disputes. Hirschman describes how the willingness to trade off the certainty of exit for the uncertainty of improvement via voice can spur the "creativity-requiring course of action" from which people would otherwise recoil. Thus, he explains how loyalty performs "a function similar to the underestimate of the prospective tasks' difficulties" (p. 80). The observation of girls' persistence in seeking solutions to problems of connection, even in the face of seemingly insurmountable obstacles, extends this point and indicates further how attachment to persons rather than adherence to principles may enhance the possibility for arriving at creative forms of conflict resolution.

Yet the vulnerability of voice to exclusion underscores how easily this process can fail when a wish for victory or domination defeats efforts at reaching accord. "If people are thinking on two different planes," one girl explains, then "you can't understand." Asked whether people on different planes can communicate, she describes how voice depends on relationship while exit can be executed in isolation.

> Well, they can try, maybe they can . . . if they were both trying to communicate. But if one person is trying to block the other out totally, that person is going to win and not hear a thing that the other person is saying. If that is what they are trying to do, then they will accomplish their objective: to totally disregard the other person.

This vulnerability of voice to detachment and indifference becomes a major problem for girls in adolescence, especially when they recognize a difference between their own perspectives and commonly held points of view. Given a relational construction of loyalty, the drama of exit and voice may shift to the tension between silence and speaking, where silence signifies exit and voice implies conflict and change in relationships. Then development hinges on the contrast between loyalty and blind faith, since loyalty implies the willingness to risk disloyalty by including the voice of the self in relationship. This effort to bring the subjectively known self into connection with others signifies an attempt to change the form of connection and relies on a process of communication, not only to discover the truth about others but also to reveal the truth about oneself.

"If I could only let my mother know the list (that I had grown inside me . . . of over two hundred things that I had to tell my mother so that she would know the true things about me and to stop the pain in my throat), she—and the world—would become more like me, and I would never be alone again" (Kingston, 1976, pp. 197–198). So the heroine of Maxine Hong Kingston's autobiographical novel, *The Woman Warrior,* defines the parameters of adolescent development in terms of the contrast between silence and voice. The silence that surrounds the discovery of the secret, subjectively known self protects its integrity in the face of disconfirmation but at the expense of isolation. In contrast, voice—the attempt to change rather than escape from an objectionable situation—contains the potential for transformation by bringing the self into connection with others.

In adolescence, the problem of exclusion hinges on the contrast between selfish and selfless behavior. This is juxtaposed against a wish for inclusion, a wish that depends upon voice. In recent years the exit option has become increasingly popular as a solution to conflicts in human relationships, as the high incidence of divorce attests. The meaning of such leaving, although commonly interpreted as a move toward separation and independence, is, however, more complex. For example, the more unencumbered access to exit from marriage can spur the exercise of voice in marriage, which in turn can lead to the discovery of the truth about attachment. The distinction between true and false connection, between relationships where voice is engaged and relationships where voice is silenced, often becomes critical to exit decisions both for women considering divorce and for adolescent girls. Given the tendency for girls and women to define loyalty as attachment to persons, exit constitutes an alternative to silence in situations where voice has failed. Thus, the recognition of the costs of detachment, not only from others but also from oneself, becomes key to girls' development in adolescence since it encourages voice while sustaining exit as the option of last resort.

The wish to be able to disagree, to be different without losing connection with others, leads outward in girls' experience from family relationships to relationships with the world. The adolescent girl who seeks to affirm the truths about herself by joining these truths with her mother's experiences aspires through this connection to validate her own perceptions, to see herself as part of the world rather than as all alone. But the difficulty for girls in feeling connected both to their mothers and to the world is compounded in a world where "human" often means male.

Consequently, the problem of attachment in adolescent development is inseparable from the problem of interpretation, since the ability to establish connection with others hinges on the ability to render one's story coherent. Given the failure of interpretive schemes to reflect female experience and given the distortion of this experience in common understandings of care and attachment, development for girls in adolescence hinges not only on their willingness to risk disagreement with others but also on the courage to challenge two equations: the equation of human with male and the equation of care with self-sacrifice. Together these equations create a self-perpetuating system that sustains a limited conception of human development and a problematic representation of human relationships.

By attending to female voices and including these voices in the psychological schemes through which we have come to know ourselves, we arrive at a correction of currently defective modes of interpretation. As the understanding of morality expands to include both justice and care, as identity loses its Platonic cast and the experience of attachment to others becomes part of the definition of self, as relationships are imagined not only as hierarchies of inequality but also as webs of protection, the representation of psychological development shifts from a progression toward separation to a chronicle of expanding connection.

ADOLESCENT DEVELOPMENT IN THE CONTEMPORARY CONTEXT

The student protest movements of the late 1960s focused on the consequences of social inequality and held up against existing unfairness the ideals of justice and rights. But these movements contained as a countercultural theme a challenge to the existing state of relationships, articulated by the generation of "flower children" that included a large female representation. With the disillusionment of the 1970s, these movements for change degenerated into privatism and retreat, as concerns with both justice and care focused increasingly on the self. Yet concomitant changes on the world scene, such as the growing awareness of global pollution and the escalation of the nuclear threat, have underlined the illusory nature of the exit solution and drawn attention to the reality of interdependence. The need to develop the art of voice, then, becomes a pressing agenda for education. The popularity of psychotherapy may reveal the extent to which voice has been neglected in a society that has come increasingly to rely on exit solutions and to prefer neat, impersonal, and often secret forms of communication.

As the youth of both sexes currently oscillate between moral nihilism and moral indignation, given the impending potential for an irretrievable failure of care on the part of the older generation, the relativism that has diluted the engagement between adolescents and adults may give way to a recognition of the moral challenges which they commonly face: the challenges of fairness—that coming generations be allowed their chance to reach maturity; the challenge of care—that the cycle of violence be replaced by an ecology of care that sustains the attachments necessary to life.

When Erikson (1965) pointed to adolescence as the time in the life cycle when the intersection of life history and history becomes most acute, he called attention to the relationship between the problems of society and the crises of youth. In this light the current increase of problems among adolescent girls, including the startling rise of eating disorders among the high school and college population (Crisp *et al.*, 1976; Bruch, 1978), may reveal a society that is having problems with survival and regeneration. The anorexic girl, described in literature as not wishing to grow up, may more accurately be seen as dramatizing the life-threatening split between female and adult (Steiner-Adair, 1984). This tragic choice dramatizes the extent to which care and dependence have been doubly disparaged by their association with women and children rather than seen as part of the human condition. To heal the division between adult and female, thus, requires a revisioning of both images, and this revision retrieves the line that has been missing from the description of human development.

The unleashed power of the atom, Einstein warned, has changed everything except the way we think, implying that a change in thinking is necessary for survival in a nuclear age. Our indebtedness to Hirschman is that he charts the direction for a change in thinking that also carries with it the implication of a change of heart. By describing modes of conflict resolution that do not entail detachment or exclusion, he aligns the process of change with the presence of loyalty or strong attachment. Thus, he offers an alternative to the either/or, win/lose framework for conflict resolution, which has become, in this nuclear age, a most dangerous game. In this article I have tried to extend the optimism of Hirschman's conception by demonstrating the potential for care and attachment that inheres in the structure of the human life cycle. By describing development around a central and ongoing ethical tension between problems of inequality and problems of detachment, I have called attention to dilemmas of loyalty as moments when attachment is at stake. The importance at present of expanding attachment across the barriers of what Erikson called "sub-speciation" brings problems of loyalty to the center of our public life. As the contemporary reality of global interdependence impels the search for new maps of development, the exploration of attachment may provide the psychological grounding for new visions of progress and growth.

REFERENCES

Adelson, J. (1980). *The Handbook of Adolescent Psychology.* New York: John Wiley & Sons.

Adelson, J., & Doehrman, M. J. (1980). "The Psychodynamic Approach to Adolescence." In J. Adelson, ed., *The Handbook of Adolescent Psychology.* New York: John Wiley & Sons.

Arendt, H. (1972). *The Life of the Mind: Thinking.* New York: Harcourt Brace Jovanovich.

Bettelheim, B. (1965). "The Problems of Generations." In E. Erikson, ed., *The Challenge of Youth.* New York: Anchor Books/Doubleday.

Bruch, H. (1978). *The Golden Cage: The Enigma of Anorexia Nervosa.* Cambridge, Mass.: Harvard University Press.

Crisp, A. H., Palmer, R. L., & Kalucy, R. S. (1976). "How Common is Anorexia Nervosa? A Prevalence Study." *British Journal of Psychiatry, 128* 549–559.

Erikson, E. (1964). *Insight and Responsibility.* New York: W. W. Norton.

_____. (1965). "Youth: Fidelity and Diversity." In E. Erikson, ed., *The Challenge of Youth.* New York: Anchor Books/Doubleday.

_____. (1968). *Identity: Youth and Crisis.* New York: W. W. Norton.

Freud, S. (1961). "Three Essays on the Theory of Sexuality," VII (1905). In J. Strachey, ed., and trans., *The Standard Edition of the Complete Psychological Works of Sigmund Freud.* London: Hogarth Press.

Gilligan, C. (1982). *In a Different Voice: Psychological Theory and Women's Development.* Cambridge, Mass.: Harvard University Press.

Hirschman, A. O. (1970). *Exit, Voice, and Loyalty: Responses to Decline in Firms, Organizations and States.* Cambridge, Mass.: Harvard University Press.

James, W. (1961). *The Varieties of Religious Experience (1902).* New York: Collier.

Kingston, M. H. (1976). *The Woman Warrior: Memoirs of a Girlhood among Ghosts.* New York: Alfred A. Knopf.

Kohlberg, L. (1981). *The Philosophy of Moral Development: Moral Stages and the Idea of Justice: Essays on Moral Development, 1.* San Francisco: Harper and Row.

Murdoch, I. (1970). *The Sovereignty of Good.* Boston: Routledge & Kegan Paul.

Steiner-Adair, C. (1984). "The Body Politic: Normal Female Adolescent Development and the Development of Eating Disorders." Unpublished doctoral dissertation. Harvard Graduate School of Education.

Weil, S. (1977). "Human Personality." In G. Panichas, ed., *The Simone Weil Reader.* New York: David McKay.

FOOTBALL, FAST CARS, AND CHEERLEADING: ADOLESCENT GENDER NORMS, 1978–1989

J. JILL SUITOR AND REBEL REAVIS
Louisiana State University

During the past decade, there has been substantial interest in examining and explaining changes in gender-role attitudes and behaviors in the United States. This line of research has shown that gender-role attitudes have become markedly less traditional over the past two decades (cf. Mason & Lu, 1988; McBroom, 1987; Thornton, Alwin, & Camburn, 1983). This work has also revealed a decrease in traditionalism regarding the division of household labor across the 1970s and early 1980s (cf. Robinson, 1988; Shelton & Coverman, 1988), although the changes on these behavioral dimensions of gender roles are far less dramatic than are the changes in stated attitudes.

While this literature has shed a great deal of light on changes in *adults'* gender-role attitudes and behaviors, much less attention has been directed toward changes in gender roles among adolescents. This segment of the population should be of particular interest to scholars since adolescents are the harbingers of American gender roles in the coming decades.

Data from several sources suggest that adolescents entered the 1980s with surprisingly traditional gender-role attitudes. For example, Thornton and her colleagues' 1980 findings (1983) revealed that although adolescents held more liberal gender-role attitudes than did their mothers, a substantial proportion maintained relatively traditional attitudes. In fact, almost half of the adolescents agreed with the statement that "It is much better for everyone if the man earns the living and the woman takes care of the home and family." Similarly, Corder and Stephan (1984) found that while 70% of the school-age girls they surveyed in 1978 wanted to combine parenting, marriage, and employment, only 40% of the boys wanted their future wives to combine these roles. Consistent with this pattern, Hansen and Darling (1985) found that the majority of the adolescents they studied in 1981 held relatively traditional attitudes toward the division of household labor.

Studies of adolescents' views toward girls' participation in sports in the late 1970s and early 1980s also demonstrated the persistence of traditional gender-role attitudes, and the characteristics of the people they would most like to date or be friends with. Feltz (1978) reported that participation in sports accrued less status for girls than did other behaviors or attributes, while Williams and White (1983) found that the lowest ratings were assigned to girls who participated in sports. Kane (1988), using data collected in 1982, found that girls were least likely to choose athletics as the way they would like to be remembered in high school. She also found that the "gender-appropriateness" of the sport in which the girls participated greatly affected both girls' and boys' choices of friends and dating partners. Girls who were associated with sports that were seen as gender-appropriate (e.g., tennis) were substantially more likely to be viewed as desirable friends and partners than were girls who were associated with less gender-appropriate sports (e.g., basketball).

Studies of other dimensions of adolescents' behaviors also suggest the persistence of traditional gender roles a decade ago. For example, Canaan's (1990) findings revealed that boys used different mechanisms from girls to create and maintain their position in the social hierarchy in their high schools in the late 1970s and early 1980s. While boys used joke-telling to demonstrate their masculinity by defining their superiority to other males and females, girls used note-passing to develop friendships and to subordinate other females. Further, Eckert (1989) found that physical appearance and dress were of greater importance to girls' than boys' social status among adolescents in the early 1980s. Last, while cheerleading was an important means by which girls could accrue prestige (Eckert, 1989; Eicher, Baizerman, & Michelman, 1991; Foley, 1990), this activity was never mentioned as an avenue by which boys could do so.

Taken together, these findings suggest that American adolescents entered the 1980s with relatively traditional gender roles, as exemplified by both their stated attitudes and differences in the ways in which boys and girls accrued prestige. However, if changes in adolescents' attitudes and behaviors paralleled those of adults during the 1980s, we would expect to find substantially less gender-role traditionalism among teenagers who were graduating from high school at the end of the 1980s. On this basis, it was anticipated that there would be fewer differences in the ways boys and girls acquired prestige in high schools by the end of the decade.

The data used in the present paper were collected between 1978 and 1982, and between 1989 and 1990 from students enrolled in a large public university in the northeastern United States. A total of 565 students completed ques-

tionnaires; 69 students were omitted from the analysis because their date of graduation from high school was either before 1978, or between 1983 and 1988. The final sample included 271 students who graduated between 1978 and 1982, and 225 students who graduated between 1988 and 1989. Fifty-nine percent of the students were women; 41% were men.

All of the students were enrolled in introductory-level sociology courses: 85% of the students were enrolled in Introduction to Sociology; 15% were enrolled in a lower division course in family sociology. There were no statistically differences between the responses of students enrolled in the two courses; therefore, the data were combined for the analysis.

The data were collected during the first few weeks of the semester, prior to any discussion of issues involving gender roles. Data were collected from students enrolled in a total of nine classes taught by four professors; the findings did not differ significantly by instructor or class (within cohort).

MEASUREMENT

The students were asked to respond to the following requests: (1) "List five ways in which males could gain prestige in the high school you attended"; and (2) "List five ways in which females could gain prestige in the high school you attended." The logic behind this approach is that individuals generally acquire prestige by adhering to group norms. Therefore, the means of acquiring prestige should provide an indicator of the norms that exist in a particular group.

The respondents mentioned a total of 61 ways in which students in their high schools acquired prestige. Since several categories were similar, they were combined for the analysis. For example, "being friendly," "being outgoing," and "having a good personality" were combined into the category labeled "sociability"; "pretty," "handsome," and "having a good body" were combined into the category labeled "physical attractiveness." The 13 categories that were listed

TABLE 1

College Students' Reports of Mechanisms by Which Girls and Boys Acquired Prestige in Their High Schools in 1978–82 and 1988–89 (percent of students mentioning each mechanism)

Mechanisms for Gaining Prestige	1978–82 (n=271)		1988–89 (n=225)		Cohort Difference (sig. of diff. between cohorts)	
	Reports on		Reports on			
	Girls	Boys	Girls	Boys	Girls	Boys
Participation in Sports	33.6**a	90.0	43.6**	84.0	*	*
Grades/Intelligence	56.1	55.0	60.1	56.0	ns	ns
Physical Attractiveness	59.0**	39.1	58.2**	41.8	ns	ns
Popularity with Opposite Sex	43.2	40.6	41.8*	35.1	ns	ns
General Sociability	56.8**	42.1	54.7**	44.4	ns	ns
Clothes	40.6**	15.9	36.9**	22.2	ns	ns
Ownership/Use of Car	5.9**	45.0	5.3**	25.3	ns	**
Participation in School Clubs/Government	35.4*	29.9	29.3*	23.1	ns	ns
Cheerleading	32.9**	0.0	23.6**	0.0	*	ns
Drugs/Drinking	2.6**	11.4	2.7**	6.7	ns	ns
"Class Clown"	3.0**	11.1	1.8**	9.8	ns	ns
"Toughness"/Physical Aggressiveness	1.9**	17.7	3.6**	13.8	ns	ns
Sexual Activity	1.9*	4.8	8.4	7.6	**	ns

aLevel of significance shown is difference between girls and boys within each cohort.
*$p < .05$
** $p < .01$

most frequently are included individually in the analysis; the remainder were combined in an "other" category which was taken into consideration in the analysis, but is not shown in Table 1.

The students were also asked to specify their gender, the year in which they graduated from high school, and the city/town in which they attended high school.

RESULTS

Table 1 shows the distribution of students' reports of ways in which boys and girls acquired prestige in the high schools from which they had recently graduated. For example, 33.6% of the students who graduated between 1978 and 1982 reported that participation in sports was one of the ways in which girls gained prestige, while 90% of the students reported participation in sports as a way boys gained prestige.

The findings presented in the left-hand column of Table 1 show substantial differences in most of the avenues by which boys and girls acquired prestige in high school in the early 1980s. Boys gained prestige primarily through (1) sports, (2) grades and intelligence, (3) access to cars, (4) sociability, (5) popularity with the opposite sex, (6) physical appearance, and (7) participation in school activities (e.g., school government, clubs). In contrast, girls gained prestige primarily through (1) physical attractiveness, (2) sociability, (3) grades and intelligence, (4) popularity with the opposite sex, (5) clothes, (6) participation in school activities, and (7) cheerleading.

The reports of students who graduated in the late 1980s are shown in the middle column of Table 1. Boys in the late 1980s continued to acquire prestige primarily through sports and grades and intelligence, while girls continued to accrue prestige primarily through grades and intelligence, and physical attractiveness. Thus, while grades and intelligence were important for both boys and girls throughout the 1980s, sports continued to play a much larger role in the prestige structure for boys than girls, while physical attractiveness continued to play a much larger role for girls than boys.

Some other behaviors and attributes by which students gained prestige also remained highly segregated by gender throughout the 1980s. For example, while a notable minority of students in both cohorts stated that boys in their high school had gained prestige through "toughness" or rowdiness, or by being a "class clown," almost no students in either cohort reported that these were avenues by which girls gained prestige. Conversely, although cheerleading was mentioned with some frequency by members of both cohorts as a way in which girls gained prestige, not one student in either cohort mentioned cheerleading as a way in which boys gained prestige.

The most important change between the earlier and later cohorts was in the area of prestige acquired through participation in sports—particularly for girls; 34% of the students who graduated in 1978–82 mentioned sports participation as a way in which girls gained prestige, compared to 44% of those who graduated in 1988–89. In contrast, sports became a slightly less important avenue for boys; 90% of the 1978–82 graduates mentioned sports for boys, compared to 84% of the 1988–89 graduates. While these changes suggest a move toward parity in the role of sports

for boys' and girls' prestige, it is important to recognize that among the 1988–89 graduates, sports participation is still almost two times more likely to be named as a source of prestige for boys than girls.

Another difference worth noting is the decrease in the role of cheerleading. While almost 33% of the students who graduated in 1978–82 reported that cheerleading was a means of gaining prestige for girls, only 24% mentioned it in 1988–89. However, the fact that almost one-quarter of the members of the later cohort listed cheerleading for girls, while none listed it for boys, suggests that this activity remains gender segregated, and continued to be an important means of acquiring prestige for girls.

It is interesting to note that boys' acquisition of prestige through access to cars declined substantially across the decade, going from third to sixth place. The reasons for this remain unclear, and cannot be accounted for by any of the variables included in the study. For example, although a slightly larger proportion of students from the 1988–89 cohort attended high school in a city, this factor does not account for the finding; the importance of access to cars declined to the same degree among the subsample of students who attended high school in the suburbs.

Separate analyses by gender of the respondent revealed that men and women had generally similar perceptions of the ways in which boys and girls had acquired prestige in high school (tables not shown). The few differences of interest involved girls' participation in sports and girls' sexual activity.

When the responses are divided by gender, it becomes clear that the overall change in the prestige girls acquired through participation in sports was due to changes in the *boys'* perceptions. Between 1978–82 and 1988–89, the percentage of women who mentioned sports as a way in which girls gained prestige increased only slightly (from 39% to 44%); however, the percentage of men who listed girls' sports as a means of gaining prestige almost doubled (from 26% to 46%).

The other interesting difference between women's and men's reports involved sexual activity as a means through which girls gained prestige. As shown in Table 1, sexual activity for girls was mentioned substantially more frequently among 1988–89 than among 1978–82 graduates. However, this change was due almost entirely to reports by men. In the early 1980s, women and men were approximately equally likely to report that girls gained prestige through being sexually active. In contrast, among members of the later cohort, 16% of the men reported that girls in their high school gained prestige through sexual activity, compared to only 4% of the women.

SUMMARY AND CONCLUSIONS

The findings presented here suggest there was relatively little change in gender norms among high school students between the early and late 1980s. A comparison between the reports of students who graduated in 1978–82 and those who graduated in 1988–89 shows that boys continued to acquire prestige in high school primarily through sports, grades, and intelligence, while girls continued to acquire prestige primarily through a combination of physical appearance, sociability, grades, and intelligence. The only noteworthy differences between the reports in the early and late 1980s were an increase in girls' acquisition of prestige through participation in sports and sexual activity, a decrease in the role of cheerleading, and a reduction in the importance of car ownership as a means by which boys accrued prestige.

The findings also indicated that most of the change that occurred in the ways girls accrued prestige could be accounted for by changes in *boys,'* rather than girls' perceptions. Further, the particular mechanisms that boys viewed as increasingly important were those that have traditionally been avenues by which men, rather than women, have gained prestige—participation in sports and engaging in sexual activities. Thus, much of the change that occurred in-

volved a greater acceptance of girls in traditionally "male" activities rather than the reverse, a pattern consistent with changes that have occurred in the occupational structure across the same period (U.S. Bureau of the Census, 1992).

One limitation of the present study is that the data were collected from only one university. It is possible that this university differs from many others in ways that could affect the findings. However, data collected at another university, but not presented in the present paper, suggest that the findings presented here may be replicated elsewhere. Between 1985 and 1989 one of the authors collected data from students enrolled in a medium-sized state university in New England. Analysis of those data revealed the same pattern of findings presented here, although the student bodies of the two universities differ substantially on demographic dimensions that might have affected gender norms (percentage of minorities; socioeconomic status; religion; percentage who attended high school in urban areas). The similarity between the reports of students in the two universities provides further support for the contention that there has been relatively little change in high school gender roles across the 1980s.

Thus, it appears that gender-role traditionalism continues to play an important role in the prestige structure of American adolescents.

REFERENCES

Canaan, J. E. (1990). Passing notes and telling jokes: Gendered strategies among American middle school teenagers. In F. Ginsburg, & A. L. Tsing (Eds.), *Uncertain terms: Negotiating in American culture.* Boston: Beacon Press.

Corder, J., & Stephan, C. W. (1984). Females' combination of work and family roles: Adolescents' aspirations. *Journal of Marriage and the Family, 46,* 391–402.

Eckert, P. (1989). *Jocks and burnouts: Social categories and identity in the high school.* New York: Teachers College.

Eicher, J. B., Baizerman, S., & Michelman, J. (1991). Adolescent dress, Part II: A qualitative study of suburban high school students. *Adolescence, 26,* 679–686.

Feltz, D. (1978). Athletics in the social status system of female adolescents. *Review of Sport and Leisure, 3,* 98–108.

Foley, D. E. (1990). The great American football ritual: Reproducing race, class, and gender inequality. *Sociology of Sport Journal, 7,* 111–135.

Hansen, S. L., & Darling, C. A. (1985). Attitudes of adolescents toward division of labor in the home. *Adolescence, 20,* 60–72.

Kane, M. J. (1988). The female athletic role as a status determinant within the social systems of high school adolescents. *Adolescence, 23,* 253–264.

Mason, K. O., & Lu, Y. H. (1988). Attitudes toward women's familial roles: Changes in the United States, 1977–1985. *Gender and Society, 2,* 39–57.

McBroom, W. H. (1987). Longitudinal change in sex-role orientations: Differences between men and women. *Sex Roles, 16,* 439–452.

Robinson, J. P. (1988). Who's doing the housework? *American Demographics, 10,* 24–29.

Shelton, B. A., & Coverman, S. (1988). *Are men's roles converging with women's?: Estimating change in husbands' domestic labor time, 1975–1981.* Paper presented at the Annual Meetings of the American Sociological Association, Atlanta, Georgia.

Thornton, A., Alwin, D. F., & Camburn, D. (1983). Causes and consequences of sex-role attitudes and attitude change. *American Sociological Review, 48,* 211–227.

Williams, J. M., & White, K. A. (1983). Adolescent status systems for males and females at three age levels. *Adolescence, 70,* 381–389.

U.S. Bureau of the Census. (1992). *Statistical Abstract of the United States, 1992.* Washington, DC.

READING 34

SOCIAL COGNITIVE DEVELOPMENT AND PSYCHOPATHOLOGY DURING ADOLESCENCE

KIMBERLY A. SCHONERT-REICHL
KATHLEEN BEAUDOIN
University of British Columbia

ABSTRACT

Despite recent advances in the study of developmental psychopathology, we know relatively little about the manner in which social cognitive development interrelates with psychopathology during the adolescent years. This study examined the relationship of social cognition to level of internalizing and externalizing patterns of symptom expression in a sample of 220 adolescent boys and girls (ages 12–19). Girls reported more depressive symptoms and higher levels of perspective taking, empathy, and personal dis-

Paper presented at the 24th Annual Symposium of the Jean Piaget Society, June 2–4, 1994, Chicago, IL.

tress. Boys reported more conduct disorders. Among girls, internalizing symptoms were negatively correlated with perspective taking and positively associated with personal distress. In the sample of boys, internalizing symptoms were positively associated with personal distress and externalizing symptoms were negatively associated with perspective taking and empathy. Results support the need to further examine the interrelations among social cognitive and socioemotional factors with psychopathology in order to elucidate the role of these mechanisms on adaptive functioning during adolescence.

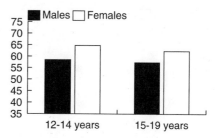

FIGURE 1 Depressive Symptoms in Younger and Older Adolescents

BACKGROUND

Piaget (1965) argued that, "Difficult children, whom parents and teachers send or ought to send up for psycho-therapeutic treatment, supply the richest material for analysis" (p. 112). Nevertheless, the manner in which psychopathology interrelates to cognitive and social cognitive development during adolescence is not well understood, partly because scarce research has been conducted examining adolescent psychopathology from a cognitive developmental perspective. Two aspects of social cognitive ability that appear to be particularly relevant to the study of psychopathology are perspective taking and empathy. The ability to take the perspective of others is a fundamental social skill (Mead, 1934; Piaget, 1965). The relationship of empathy to psychopathology is somewhat less clear. For example, whereas some studies have found empathy to be negatively related to antisocial, externalizing behaviors (e.g., Miller & Eisenberg, 1988), other studies have found empathy to be positively associated with emotional vulnerability (e.g., Davis, 1983).

PURPOSE AND RATIONALE

The purpose of the present investigation was to examine the social cognitive correlates of externalizing and internalizing patterns of symptoms

among adolescent boys and girls. Increased knowledge of the social cognitive variables that are related to psychopathology during adolescence may provide important information necessary for the design and implementation of successful treatment and intervention programs. Furthermore, a better appreciation of the manner in which internalizing and externalizing symptomatology interacts with social cognition among adolescent boys and girls will contribute to our understanding of developmental psychopathology. Given the findings from recent research suggesting that social cognition may modify risk for psychopathology (e.g., Beardslee, Schultz, & Selman, 1987; Downey & Walker, 1989; Garmezy, 1987) it seems important to turn our attention to the relation between social cognitive abilities and psychopathology among adolescents.

METHOD

Subjects

The sample consisted of 220 (110 males, 110 females) adolescents, enrolled in a public secondary school (grades 8 to 12) located near a large Western Canadian city. Students were selected from all grades and ranged in age from 12 through 19 years, with a mean age of 14.93 years (SD = 1.49). The students were predominantly from either middle- or upper-middle class families. In the sample, 20% of the students were Asian, 2% were Hispanic, and 67% were White (the remainder belong to other ethnic groups). Data were collected with respect to demographic

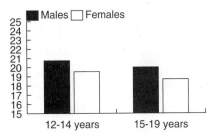

FIGURE 2   Conduct Disorders in Younger and Older Adolescents

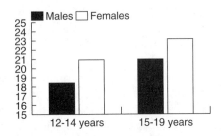

FIGURE 3   Perspective Talking in Younger and Older Adolescents

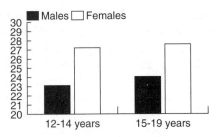

FIGURE 4   Empathy in Younger and Older Adolescents

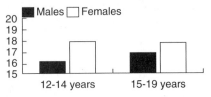

FIGURE 5   Personal Distress in Younger and Older Adolescents

information (e.g., sex, race/ethnicity, age, parental educational level), empathy, and internalizing and externalizing dimensions of psychopathology.

Procedure

Questionnaires were administered to students in their classrooms during a 50-minute classroom period. The order of questionnaires was counterbalanced to control for order effects. Informed consent was obtained by students and their parents.

Measures

Empathy and Perspective Taking. For the present investigation, dimensions of social cognitive development were assessed during the Interpersonal Reactivity Index (IRI; Davis, 1983), a multi-dimensional measure of empathy. The IRI is a 28-item self-report questionnaire that assesses both cognitive and affective dimensions of empathy and is comprised of four 7-item subscales. Three of these subscales (i.e., perspective

taking, empathic concern, personal distress) are of special interest for the present investigation.

Internalizing Symptomatology. Internalizing symptomatology was assessed using the Reynold's Adolescent Depression Survey (RADS, Reynolds, 1987). This 30-item self-report measure was designed for use with 13- to 18-year-olds and taps the severity of depressive symptomatology in adolescents.

Externalizing Symptomatology. Externalizing symptomatology of psychopathology was assessed using a self-report, 16-item conduct disorder subscale of the Adolescent Psychopathology Scale (APS; Reynolds, 1993).

RESULTS

Sex Differences in Externalizing-Internalizing Symptomatology, Empathy, Perspective Taking, and Personal Distress

Adolescents were grouped into younger adolescents (12–14 years) and older adolescents (15–19 years). A series of 2×2 (Sex $\times$ Age

TABLE 1
Social Cognitive Correlates of Internalizing and Externalizing Symptoms by Sex

Male Subjects (N = 110)

Variable	1	2	3	4	5
1. Depressive Symptoms—		.16	−.08	−.08	.48***
2. Conduct Disorder		—	.34***	.34***	.20*
3. Perspective Taking			—	.63***	.10
4. Empathy				—	.09
5. Personal Distress					—

*** p ≤ .001, ** p < .01, *p < .05

TABLE 2
Social Cognitive Correlates of Internalizing and Externalizing Symptoms by Sex

Female Subjects (N = 110)

Variable	1	2	3	4	5
1. Depressive Symptoms—		.47***	−.22*	−.01	.25*
2. Conduct Disorder		—	−.32***	−.11	−.14
3. Perspective Taking			—	.28**	−.12
4. Empathy				—	.10
5. Personal Distress					—

***p ≤ .001, ** p < .01, *p < .05

Group) ANOVAs were computed in order to analyze gender and age differences for depression, conduct disorder, perspective taking, empathy, and personal distress. Girls scored significantly higher than boys on depression, $F(1, 185) = 6.85$, $p < .01$, perspective taking, $F(1, 206) = 9.55$, $p < .005$, empathy, $F(1, 185) = 31.91$, $p < .001$, and personal distress, $F(1, 199) = 3.78$, $p < .05$. Boys scored higher than girls on conduct disorders, $F(1, 204) = 6.57$, $p < .01$. With respect to age differences, older adolescents scored significantly higher than younger adolescents on perspective taking, $F(1, 206) = 9.23$, $p < .005$. No other main effects for age or two-way interactions reached significance (see Figures 1 to 5).

Interrelations of Psychopathology and Social Cognitive Abilities

Pearson product-moment correlations were calculated separately by sex to determine the relationships among depression, conduct disorders, perspective taking, empathy, and personal distress (see Tables 1 and 2). For boys, depressive symptomatology was positively associated with personal distress whereas conduct disorders were negatively associated with perspective taking, empathy, and personal distress. Perspective taking and empathy were significantly and positively related. For girls, depressive symptomatology was positively associated with conduct disorders and personal distress, and negatively associated with perspective taking. Conduct disorders were negatively associated with perspective taking. As with boys, perspective taking and empathy were significantly and positively related.

For empathy, the 2-way interaction of conduct disorders and sex, $F(3, 199) = 2.83$ $p = .09$ approached significance (see Figure 6). A significant 3-way interaction of sex by age by depression was found with respect to empathy as well $F(1, 199) = 8.40$ $p < .01$ (see Figure 7).

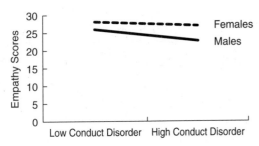

FIGURE 6   Interaction between Sex by Level of Conduct Disorder for the Empathy Subscale of the Interpersonal Reactivity Index

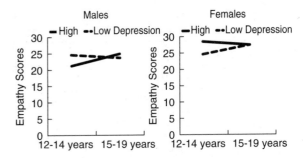

FIGURE 7   Interaction among Sex, Age and Level of Depression for the Empathy Subscale of the Interpersonal Reactivity Index

CONCLUSIONS AND SIGNIFICANCE

Our results suggest that gender differences exist in both the manner in which psychopathology is manifested as well as in the social cognitive concomitants. Girls express their disturbance in terms of more internalized, depressive symptoms whereas boys express their disturbance in an externalizing pattern of symptom expression. With respect to social cognitive abilities, depressive symptomatology is associated with lower levels of perspective taking for girls whereas conduct disorders are associated with lower levels of empathy for boys. Higher levels of depressive symptoms are associated with higher levels of personal distress (i.e., a self-oriented aversive response to another's emotional state) for both boys and girls. Clearly, the relationship between adolescent psychopathology and social cognitive development is a complex one. Further research should continue to explore the role of these dimensions of social cognitive development in relation to adolescent disturbance.

REFERENCES

Beardslee, W. R., Schultz, L. H., & Selman, R. L. (1987). Level of social cognitive development, adaptive functioning, and DSM-III diagnoses in adolescent offspring of parents with affective disorders: Implications of the development of the capacity for mutuality. *Developmental Psychology, 23*, 807–815.

Davis, M. H. (1983). Measuring individual differences in empathy: Evidence for a multidimensional approach. *Journal of Personality and Social Psychology, 44*, 113–126.

Downey, G., & Walker, E. (1989). Social cognition and adjustment in children at risk for psychopathology. *Developmental Psychology, 25*, 835–845.

Garmezy, N. (1987). Stress, competence, and development: Continuities in the study of schizophrenic adults, children vulnerable to schizophrenia, and the study of stress-resilient children. *American Journal of Orthopsychiatry, 57*, 159–174.

Mead, G. H. (1934). *Mind, self and society.* Chicago: University of Chicago Press.

Miller, P. A., & Eisenberg, N. (1988). The relation of empathy to aggressive and externalizing/antisocial behavior. *Psychological Bulletin, 103*, 324–344.

Piaget, J. (1965). *The moral judgment of the child.* New York: Free Press. (Original work published in 1932).

Reynolds, W. M. (1993). *The Adolescent Psychopathology Scale.* Unpublished manuscript.

_____. (1987). *Reynolds Adolescent Depression Scale: Professional Manual.* Odessa, FL: Psychological Assessment Resources.

PART TWELVE

HEALTH ISSUES OF ADOLESCENTS

The main cause of youth mortality is their own behavior.
—FRANK FARLEY

Adolescent health issues can be viewed via two different routes:

1. Adolescents suffer from the same medical diseases that afflict children and adults. Some disorders are more pronounced at the time of puberty, such as acne and hormonal imbalance, but most naturally occurring conditions are less common during the second decade than at any other period in the life cycle. In regard to physical health, adolescence is the healthiest period of life as assessed by such criteria as: number of doctor visits, number of prescriptions used, and frequency and duration of hospital stays. Only 27 percent of adolescent deaths are due to natural causes. Late adolescents are also at the peak of their physical strength.

2. However, many injuries and health-compromising situations are not the result of natural causes but reflect the health-endangering behaviors that have become common during adolescence. Farley's quote applies not only to mortality, but to injuries as well. Youth are prone to take chances. For careless, reckless, chance-taking behaviors there frequently exists underlying psychological problems; however, the manifestations of injuries, STD, and drug overdoses require medical treatment. Seventy-three percent of adolescent deaths are due to dangerous behaviors or violence rather than natural causes.

The impact of these behaviors is the concern of this section. An awareness of these health problems is essential to place adolescent health issues in their rightful context. Many of these behaviors are referred to briefly in other selections (see bracketed references). Some of the prevalent health-endangering conditions are: automobile accidents (1); other accidents (sports, drowning, fire, firearms, etc.) (1, 38); suicide, suicide attempts and ideation (1, 13, 28, 35, 36, 38); homicide and injuries as a result of violence (1, 38); smoking and alcohol abuse (1, 13, 35, 38); marijuana and other illicit drug abuse (1, 13, 28, 35, 37, 38, 39); psychiatric disorders, depression, anorexia, and bulimia (1, 34, 36); unprotected sex, inviting STD and pregnancy (1, 35, 37, 38).

An important survey of 12,118 students in 7th through 12th grades, interviewed by Resnick et al. (35), sheds insights on the social contexts that appear to shape health-related behavior. Various adolescent health practices, the dependent variables, are of greatest social concern: emotional behavior, suicidal thoughts or actions, violence, substance abuse, and sexual behavior. The question being considered is, how do the independent variables—that is, connectedness to home, affinity for school, and individual characteristics—influence what adolescents do in respect to these dependent variables? Positive parent-adolescent relationships and comfortable feelings about school, teachers, and learning provide significant protection against these health-risking behaviors, except for pregnancy. Among individual characteristics, positive self-esteem plays an important role in contributing to healthy behaviors. A close family bond emerges by far as the most influential factor in reducing smoking, alcohol abuse, drug use, violence, sex, and suicide during the high school years. These results hold up across diverse social and economic conditions. An unequivocal message emerges from these findings: parents do make a real difference, more than had been assumed. They can serve as powerful insulators against undesirable peer pressure. Hence, if young people are to stay alive and healthy, they need close emotional ties to their families.

The adolescent eating disorders (Muuss, 36) of anorexia nervosa and bulimia have become major medical and psychological health-compromising behaviors. They are not new phenomena; however, they are observed with increasing frequency, especially among white, affluent, young females in Western societies. The etiology is still poorly understood, and different explanations have been advanced, such as psychosexual, family system, and social theories. Social exaggerations of what constitutes physical attractiveness play a major role, because social messages create ambivalent feelings about food and unrealistic body ideals. Therefore females often develop a disturbed body image, perceiving themselves as overweight even if by medical standards they are normal. The anorexic and bulimic often hold distorted body ideals and develop neurotic eating patterns to achieve the desired "ideal" weight. Apparently females experience more concern with appearance and demonstrate more intense desire to lose weight than do males. As eating and related behaviors take on a compulsive quality, the individual loses control (bulimia) or appears overcontrolled (anorexia). The behaviors such as starving, binge-purge cycles, exercises, and diuretics often occur in secret, and the individual denies having a problem and refuses help. Treatment for those who are unwilling to admit they have a problem is difficult to implement.

Runaways and homeless youth constitute a limited, but often forgotten, subgroup of adolescents who live on the outer fringe of conventional society. The report by Kipke et al. (37), based on 409 interviews of youth from the streets (70%) and shelters (30%), invites serious reflection concerning the fate of approximately 1 million youth who run away from home each year. These street youth, mostly out of school and unemployed, struggle to survive and inevitably face more health risks than any other youth group. Characterized by lives filled with violence, sex, drugs, hopelessness, and the belief that dying young is natural, these young people are involved in a disturbing array of life-threatening behaviors. Participation in survival sex (providing sex in exchange for goods needed to survive), involvement in alcohol and substance abuse, and incidence of sexually transmitted disease are rampant. HIV risk-related behaviors are at epidemic proportion among this population who attempt to survive on the streets.

PROTECTING ADOLESCENTS FROM HARM

Findings from the National Longitudinal Study on Adolescent Health

Michael D. Resnick, PhD; Peter S. Bearman, PhD; Robert Wm. Blum, MD, PhD; Karl E. Bauman, PhD; Kathleen M. Harris, PhD; Jo Jones, PhD; Joyce Tabor; Trish Beuhring, PhD; Renee E. Sieving, PhD; Marcia Shew, MD, MPH; Marjorie Ireland, PhD; Linda H. Bearinger, PhD, MS; J. Richard Udry, PhD

Context.—The main threats to adolescents' health are the risk behaviors they choose. How their social context shapes their behaviors is poorly understood.

Objective.—To identify risk and protective factors at the family, school, and individual levels as they relate to 4 domains of adolescent health and morbidity: emotional health, violence, substance use, and sexuality.

Design.—Cross-sectional analysis of interview data from the National Longitudinal Study of Adolescent Health.

Participants.—A total of 12,118 adolescents in grades 7 through 12 drawn from an initial national school survey of 90,118 adolescents from 80 high schools plus their feeder middle schools.

Setting.—The interview was completed in the subject's home.

Main Outcome Measures.—Eight areas were assessed: emotional distress; suicidal thoughts and behaviors; violence; use of 3 substances (cigarettes, alcohol, marijuana); and 2 types of sexual behaviors (age of sexual debut and pregnancy history). Independent variables included measures of family context, school context, and individual characteristics.

Results.—Parent-family connectedness and perceived school connectedness were protective against every health risk behavior measure except history of pregnancy. Conversely, ease of access to guns at home was associated with suicidality (grades 9–12; $P < .001$) and violence (grades 7–8; $P < .001$; grades 9–12; $P < .001$). Access to substances in the home was associated with use of cigarettes ($P < .001$), alcohol ($P < .001$), and marijuana ($P < .001$) among all students. Working 20 or more hours a week was associated with emotional distress of high school students ($P < .01$), cigarette use ($P < .001$), alcohol use ($P < .001$), and marijuana use ($P < .001$). Appearing "older than most" in class was associated with emotional distress and suicidal thoughts and behaviors among high school students ($P < .001$); it was also associated with substance use and an earlier age of sexual debut among both junior and senior high students. Repeating a grade in school

From the *Journal of the American Medical Association,* September 10, 1997, Volume 278. Copyright © 1997, American Medical Association. Reprinted with permission.

From the Adolescent Health Program, University of Minnesota, Minneapolis (Drs. Resnick, Blum, Beuhring, Sieving, Shew, Ireland, and Bearinger), and the Carolina Population Center, University of North Carolina at Chapel Hill (Drs. Bearman, Bauman, Harris, Jones, and Udry and Ms. Tabor).

was associated with emotional distress among students in junior high ($P < .001$) and high school ($P < .01$) and with tobacco use among junior high students ($P < .001$). On the other hand, parental expectations regarding school achievement were associated with lower levels of health risk behaviors; parental disapproval of early sexual debut was associated with a later age of onset of intercourse ($P < .001$).

Conclusions.—Family and school contexts as well as individual characteristics are associated with health and risky behaviors in adolescents. The results should assist health and social service providers, educators, and others in taking the first steps to diminish risk factors and enhance protective factors for our young people.
JAMA. 1997;278:823–832

Numerous reports have documented the health status of youth in the United States, concluding that the main threats to adolescents' health are predominantly the health-risk behaviors and choices they make.[1-18] Data indicate that more than 3 of every 4 deaths in the second decade of life are caused by social morbidities: unintentional injuries, homicides, and suicides. Juvenile homicide rates have continued to escalate until recently,[17] and suicide rates among adolescents aged 14 years or younger have increased by 75% over the past decade.[3] Cigarette smoking among teenagers has increased by as much as 2% per year since 1992, when 19% of high school seniors reported smoking. Marijuana use has increased in each of the last 3 years among 8th-, 10th-, and 12th-grade students.[19]

Some children who are at high risk for health-comprising behaviors successfully negotiate adolescence, avoiding the behaviors that predispose them to negative health outcomes; while others, relatively advantaged socially and economically, sustain significant morbidity as a consequence of their behaviors. These issues of vulnerability and resilience have stimulated an interest in the identification of protective factors in the lives of young people—

factors that, if present, diminish the likelihood of negative health and social outcomes.[20-26] Of the constellation of forces that influence adolescent health-risk behavior, the most fundamental are the social contexts in which adolescents are embedded[20]; the family and school contexts are among the most critical. Yet, how adolescents' connections to these contexts shape their health-risk behaviors is poorly understood.

In the present analysis we seek to identify particular risk and protective factors at the school, family, and individual levels as they relate to 4 broad domains critical to adolescent health and morbidity (emotional health, violence, substance use, and sexuality), using data collected as part of the National Longitudinal Study of Adolescent Health (Add Health).

METHODS

The Add Health Design

Add Health is a longitudinal study of adolescents in grades 7 through 12 and the multiple social contexts in which they live. The primary sampling frame included all high schools in the United States that had an 11th grade and at least 30 enrollees in the school (N=26,666). From this a systematic random sample of 80 high schools was selected proportional to enrollment size, stratified by region, urbanicity, school type, and percentage white. For each high school, the largest feeder school (typically a middle school) was also recruited when available. Overall, 79% of the schools contacted agreed to participate, for a final sample of 134 schools. Schools varied in size from fewer than 100 to more than 3000 students.

The schools provided a roster of all enrolled students and 96% (n=129) hosted a confidential in-school survey from September 1994 to April 1995. The survey was completed by 90,118 of 119,233 eligible students in grades 7 through 12. The in-school survey was administered only once, in year 1. Survey data will be the subject of future reports.

School administrators also completed a half-hour self-administered questionnaire yielding information on the provision of health services, school policies, school environments, and characteristics. Two phases of school administrator data were collected 1 year apart, beginning in year 1. A total of 130 administrator questionnaires were completed in year 1 and are included in this analysis.

The Main In-Home Sample

From students on the school rosters as well as students who were not on an enrolled roster but who completed an in-school questionnaire, a random sample of 15,243 adolescents stratified by grade and sex was selected for in-home interviews; 12,118 (79.5%) completed the 90-minute interviews. Of these, 75% had completed an in-school questionnaire.

The first phase of in-home interviews was conducted between April and December 1995 and is the focus of this report. A second phase was collected a year later. Data collected during the in-home phase of Add Health provide information on sensitive health-risk behaviors such as drug and alcohol use, sexual behavior, and criminal activities in addition to detailed information on health status, health service utilization, family dynamics, peer networks, romantic relationships, decision making, aspirations, and attitudes. During the more sensitive portions of the interview, adolescents listened to questions through earphones and directly entered their responses into a laptop computer, thereby greatly reducing any potential for interviewer or parental influences on their responses.

For 85.6% of the participating adolescents, a parent (in most instances a mother) also completed a half-hour interview in year 1. Parent interview data are not included in this article.

Through a set of linked identifiers—the in-school and in-home data sets and the school administrator and parent surveys—school administrator and parent surveys were merged. Extensive precautions were taken to maintain confidentiality and to guard against deductive disclosure of participants' identities. All protocols received institutional review board approval. More detailed methodologic information is available in a separate article.[27]

Analysis and Reporting

A series of checks for invalid and inconsistent responses resulted in deletion of 546 (4.5%) of the core sample of 12,118 adolescents. Each case in the core sample was assigned a weight based on the sampling design so that the sample is nationally representative of US adolescents in grades 7 through 12. These sample weights were used in every statistical procedure with the exception of Cox regression (which does not permit weighting in SAS).

The final sample of 11,572 adolescents was randomly partitioned into exploratory and validation samples of approximately equal size. Investigators identified theoretically relevant and empirically significant independent variables with the exploratory sample; confirmatory analyses were completed and results are reported for the validation sample. Separate analyses were performed for grades 7 and 8 and 9 through 12 except for pregnancy history, for which questions were restricted to females aged 15 years and older regardless of grade and age of first intercourse, which latter category included both sexes and all grades regardless of sexual experience. An analysis modeling age of first intercourse excluded sexually experienced youth who reported having intercourse before age 11 years (2.0% of the sexually experienced subsample) on the assumption they represented a distinct subgroup of youth who had been sexually abused or had participated in nonconsensual sex.[28]

Items used in the measurement of the dependent and independent variables were identified from a variety of standardized, validated instruments used in national and state surveys of adolescents. Dependent variables were selected to capture the major indexes of adolescent health and risk behaviors (Table 1).[29] Independent variables were derived from a resiliency framework, which posits that young people's vulnerability to health-compromising outcomes is affected by both the nature and number of stressors as well as the presence of protective factors that buffer the impact of those stressors (Tables 2 and 3). Adverse or successful outcomes are described as emanating from the interplay of environmental factors, familial factors, and individual characteristics.[30-38] Individual characteristics reflect both genetic predispositions (e.g., the timing and tempo of puberty) and social and cognitive developmental variables (e.g., self-image, future perspective). Longitudinal studies by both Werner and Smith[25] and Quinton and Rutter[39] have identified the role of environmental and familial contexts as well as individual characteristics in promoting heightened or diminished well-being among children who have experienced multiple life stressors.

In the present analysis, school characteristics (i.e., school type, dropout rate, attendance rate, classroom size, teacher training, characteristics of student body), including "school connectedness"—a concept that emerges from the interactions of the individual with the school environment[40,41]—are used to represent a key environmental force in the lives of in-school youth. Familial factors incorporate 4 components: parent-family relationships (connectedness, shared activities, parental presence); norms and expectations for adolescent behavior (school achievement, sexual behaviors); parental model-

TABLE 1
Dependent Variables

Variables	Select Descriptors of Variables	No. of Items Constituting Variable (Reliability Coefficient)
Emotional distress	In the past week or past year: felt depressed, lonely, sad, or fearful, moody, cried, or had a poor appetite	17 (α =.87)*
Suicidality	In the past year: seriously thought about committing suicide or attempted 1, 2, or more times	2
Violence	In the past year: had a physical fight, injured someone, was in a group fight, threatened someone with a weapon, used a weapon in a fight, or shot or stabbed someone	8 (α =.82)*
Substance use		
Cigarette use	A 7-category composite variable from never smoked to smoked > 1 pack/d	4
Alcohol use	Frequency: an 8-category variable from never/almost never to daily/almost daily used alcohol	2
Marijuana use	A 7-category composite variable from never used to used marijuana $\geq$ 6 times in past month	3
Sexual behaviors		
Age of sexual debut	Age at first intercourse: a continuous variable, with nonsexually active youth handled as event not having occurred	1
Pregnancy history	Among sexually experienced females $\geq$ 15 y, those who ever reported a history of pregnancy; dichotomous yes/no variable	1

*For most measures including 3 or more items, Cronbach[29] α coefficient was used to assess internal consistency.

TABLE 2
Generic Independent Variables

Variables	Select Descriptors of Variables	No. of Items Constituting Variable (Reliability Coefficient)
Family context		
Parent-family connectedness	Closeness to mother and/or father, perceived caring by mother and/or father, satisfaction with relationship to mother and/or father, feeling loved and wanted by family members	13 (α =.83)*
Parent-adolescent activities	No. of different activities engaged in with mother and/or father in past 4 wk (summed)	10 for mother, 10 for father
Parental presence	A parent present: before school, after school, at bedtime, or dinner (summed)	
Parental school expectations	Mother's and/or father's expectations for you to complete high school and college	2 (r=0.45)†
Family suicide attempts and/or completions	Suicidal attempts and/or completions by family members in the past 12 mo	2
School context		
School connectedness	Feel that teachers treat students fairly; close to people at school; feel part of your school	6 (α =.75)*
Student prejudice	On a 5-point scale, agreement that students in school are prejudiced	1
Attendance‡	Quasi-continuous variable (average daily attendance)	1
Dropout rate‡§	Estimated dropout rate by grade in school	6
School type‡§	Five categories: comprehensive public, magnet public, parochial, technical, other	9
Classroom size‡	Average size of class from $\leq$ 20 to $\geq$ 35	1
Master's degree‡	% of teachers with master's degree from $\leq$ 10% to $\geq$ 90%	1
College‡	Proportion of students who are college bound	1
Parent-teacher organization‡	% of parents involved with a parent-teacher organization, ranging from does not exist to $\geq$ 90%	1
Individual characteristics		
Self-esteem	On a 5-point scale (agree to disagree): good personal qualities, a lot to be proud of, like yourself, feel loved and wanted, as good as other people	10 (α =.86)*
Religious identity	Pray frequently, view self as religious, affiliate with a religion	3
Same-sex attraction or behavior§	Ever had same-sex romantic attraction or same-sex intercourse	3
Perceived risk of untimely death	Perceive self at risk for untimely death	1
Paid work $\geq$ 20 h/wk§	No. of hours per week worked for pay during school year	1
Self-report of physical appearance§	Appear older or younger than most age mates	1 each
Repeated a grade§	Repeated 1 or more grades	1
Grade point average	Available grades in English, math, history/social studies, and science in most recent reporting period	4

*For most measures including 3 or more items, Cronbach[29] α coefficient was used to assess internal consistency.
†Pearson correlation coefficient was used to assess reliability of 2-item measures where appropriate.
‡Derived from school administrator questionnaire.
§Item coded dichotomously, e.g., yes/no, any/none.

ing (family suicide involvement); and household features (access to weapons, substances).[30,31,37] Individual characteristics include such factors as employment, academic performance, and sexual orientation as well as self-belief components including religious identity and self-esteem.[25,39]

Independent variables within each context were divided into 2 sets: generic (those that were expected to be associated with every dependent variable, such as parent-family connectedness, school connectedness, and self-esteem) and domain-specific variables (those that applied to specific dependent variables such as household access to alcohol, school policies on fighting, and knowledge of condom use). In the present analysis, the selection of risk and protective factors was guided by an emphasis on variables that can be used for assessment or are amenable to prevention and intervention efforts.

All dependent and independent variables were standardized separately for each grade category to a mean of 0 and an SD of 1 before conducting the multivariate analyses, except for dichotomous variables and age at first intercourse. In the case of multi-item scales, individual items were standardized before summing items to form scales; summed-scale scores were re-standardized to a mean of 0 and SD of 1. Consequently, parameter estimates can be interpreted as standardized β (with the exception of dichotomous variables); within any particular analysis, odds ratios and relative risks can be compared with each other for effect size.

Multivariate Analysis

Our analytic strategy was to highlight relevant variables, their measurement, and the interrelationships of variables within domains. This broad approach provides a foundation for future, more focused analyses. The impact of each of the 3 contexts (family, school, and individual characteristics) on each of the adolescent health and risk behaviors was assessed using multiple linear regression for the continuous and quasi-continuous outcome variables, logistic regression for preg-

nancy history, and Cox regression for age of sexual debut. Each of these analyses controlled for the effects of key demographic variables: sex, race, ethnicity, family structure, and poverty status. In these analyses, race was categorized as black vs non-Hispanic white as the reference group; ethnicity as "other" ethnic group, which included subcategories of Hispanic (98% white, 2% black), Asian/Pacific Islander, American Indian, and "other" (1% designated 2 or more ethnic identities) vs non-Hispanic white as the reference group; family structure as 2 parents in the home vs 2 parents not in the home; and poverty status as 1 or more parents on welfare vs neither parent on welfare. While a simpler indicator of poverty status, this designation has been shown to work with adolescent respondents.[42,43]

Because of the complex patterns of intercorrelation between variables from each of the 3 contexts, the total variance in each dependent variable explained by a combination of family, school, and individual context measures is typically less than the sum of the variances explained by each context analyzed independently.

To ensure adequate control for demographic effects, in the first step of analyses demographic variables were forced into regression equations and retained regardless of their statistical significance. In the second step of analyses, the set of generic independent variables was introduced; significant generic measures along with demographic variables were retained in subsequent regression models. In the third step of analyses, a set of domain-specific independent variables was introduced into regression models, and significant domain-specific measures were retained. In a fourth and final step, the models developed on the exploratory sample were cross-validated by recomputing parameter estimates on the validation sample, with all retained variables from the estimation analysis forced into the validation analysis. Thus, independent variables found in final models included the full set of demographic variables as well as generic and domain-specific measures that remained significant on cross-validation. For linear regression analysis, potential

TABLE 3
Domain-Specific Independent Variables

Variables	Select Descriptors of Variables	No. of Items Constituting Variable
Sexual behavior domain		
Perceived parental disapproval of adolescent sex	On a 5-point scale, perceived mother's and/or father's disapproval of their adolescent having sex at this time with anyone or a special person	2 (r=0.82)*
Perceived parental disapproval of adolescent contraception	On a 5-point scale, perceived mother's and/or father's disapproval of their adolescent using contraception at this time	2
Length of time since sexual debut	Interval, in months, between first intercourse and the current date	6
Effective contraceptive use with first/last sex	Use of oral contraceptive pills, Norplant, Depo-Provera, intrauterine device, condoms, or condoms plus female barrier method with first/last sex (response categories: neither, 1, or both occasions)	6
Substance use in connection with sex	Level of alcohol and other drug use involved with first/last sex	6 (α =.65)†
Sex in exchange for drugs or money‡	Ever given sex in exchange for drugs or money	1
Virginity pledge‡	Made public or written pledge to remain a virgin until marriage	1
Perceived benefits of sexual activity	On a 5-point scale (strongly agree to strongly disagree), having sex would relax you, give you physical pleasure, make you more attractive, make you less lonely	5 (α =.70)†
Perceived obstacles to contraceptive use	On a 5-point scale (strongly agree to strongly disagree), birth control is a hassle to use, too expensive, interferes with pleasure, requires too much planning ahead, conveys that you are looking for sex	7 (α =.82)†
Perceived susceptibility to pregnancy	On a 5-point scale (strongly agree to strongly disagree), perceived chance of getting pregnant after having unprotected sex on a single occasion in the near future	1
Perceived consequences of pregnancy	Pregnancy: one of the worst things that could happen at this time, would be embarrassing, would force growing up too fast	8 (α =.70)†
Condom use knowledge	Knowledge regarding correct use of condoms (summed)	No. correct of 5
Contraceptive use self-efficacy	Confidence in ability to use contraception or to refuse sex in various situations	3 (α =.65)†

design effects resulting from the use of a cluster sampling design were adjusted with the use of a mixed-models linear regression procedure (SAS PROC MIXED)[44] with specified use of a block diagonal covariance structure.

RESULTS

Prevalence of Behaviors by Demographic Variables

The distribution of key risk behaviors in the national sample of adolescents is presented in Table 4. Prevalence data are presented by grade group, place of residence, region, self-reported poverty status, and sex.

Emotional Distress and Suicidality.—Two indicators of risk to adolescents' emotional well-being are assessed: emotional distress (a recent history of physical and emotional symptoms of distress) and suicidality (a history of suicidal ideation and attempts in the past year). Overall, 87.4% (10,010/11,453) of adolescents indicated that they had neither suicidal thoughts nor attempts over the past year. A total of 10.2% of girls (599/5745) and 7.5% of boys (428/5708) reported

TABLE 3
Domain-Specific Independent Variables (*continued*)

Variables	Select Descriptors of Variables	No. of Items Constituting Variable
School-based reproductive health services on premises†§	Family planning counseling services, sexually transmitted disease treatment, or prenatal or postnatal services	4
Violence, emotional distress, and suicidality domains		
Household access to guns‡	Reported easy availability of a gun in the home	1
History of victimization and/or witnessing violence	Within the past 12 mo, witnessed or been a victim of a shooting or stabbing	5 (α =.66)†
Weapon carrying	Weapon carrying at school, in connection with substance use	4 (α =.74)†
Sale of illicit drugs	Any sale of illicit drugs within the past 12 mo	1
Involvement with deviant/ antisocial behaviors	Destruction of property, theft, skipping school in past year; ever suspended or expelled from school	10 (α =.78)†
Body image	Perceived weight, from very underweight to very overweight	1
School policies on fighting§	Warning/minor action, suspension, or expulsion for fighting with or injuring a student or teacher or carrying a weapon at school	4
Mental health services at school‡§	Emotional counseling, rape counseling, or programs for dealing with effects of violence provided on school premises	3
Substance abuse domains		
Household access to cigarettes‡	Reported easy availability of cigarettes in the home	1
Household access to alcohol‡	Reported easy availability of alcohol in the home	1
Household access to illicit substances‡	Reported easy availability of illicit drugs in the home	1
School policies on smoking§	Warning/minor action, suspension, or expulsion for smoking at school	1
School policies on alcohol§	Warning/minor action, suspension, expulsion for possessing or drinking alcohol at school	2
School policies on illicit drugs§	Warning/minor action, suspension, expulsion for possessing or using drugs at school	2
Substance use programs at school‡§	Drug education, drug abuse, or alcohol abuse program	3

*Pearson correlation coefficient was used to assess reliability of 2-item measures where appropriate
†For most variables including 3 or more items, Cronbach[29] α coefficient was used to assess internal consistency.
‡A dichotomously categorized variable, e.g., yes/no, any/none.
§Derived from a school administrator questionnaire.

having considered suicide without having attempted it over the past year, while 3.6% of all adolescents (415/11,453) (5.1% of girls [295/5745] and 2.1% [120/5708] of boys) reported suicide attempts. Of adolescents, 3.6% (412/11,438) reported a parental suicide attempt during the previous year, while 0.9% of the young people surveyed (103/11,438) reported suicide completions among their parents.

Family Context.—Family context variables explained 14% to 15% of the variability in emotional distress (9th–12th graders and 7th–8th graders, respectively) and 5% to 7% of the variability in suicidality for all adolescents (Table 5). The key aspect of family context that accounted for these relationships, after controlling for the influence of demographic factors, was parent-family connectedness (Table 6). The presence of parents at key times during the day (at waking, after school, at dinner, and at bedtime), shared activities with parents, and high parental expectations for their child's school achievement were also moderately protective against emotional distress for both younger and older adolescents. A recent family history

TABLE 4
Distribution (Percentage) of Risk Behaviors by Demographic Variables

Demographic Variables	Risk Behavior							
	Emotional Distress*	Suicide Attempt (≥1)	Violence Perpetration*	Smoke ≥6 Cigarettes/d	Alcohol (Beer or Wine) Use ≥ 2 d/mo	Marijuana Use at Least Once in Past Month	Had Sex	Pregnancy History
Grade								
7th–8th	17.7	3.7	9.2	3.2	7.3	6.9	17.0	11.8
9th–12th	18.4	3.6	7.8	12.8	23.1	15.7	49.3	19.4
Sex								
Male	15.7	2.1	11.0	10.0	20.1	13.5	39.9	
Female	20.1	5.1	5.7	9.2	15.6	11.9	37.3	18.6
Geography								
Urban	18.6	3.5	9.0	6.9	14.9	11.1	37.7	22.4
Suburban	17.5	3.7	8.2	10.2	19.2	13.8	38.2	17.6
Rural	19.9	3.6	8.4	11.9	17.7	10.5	41.9	15.7
Region								
West	20.7	4.3	8.5	5.4	15.3	14.9	31.7	18.9
Midwest	20.4	4.2	8.4	12.8	18.4	15.0	38.0	18.9
Northeast	18.2	3.6	8.8	11.3	19.5	15.0	35.6	13.9
South	17.4	3.0	8.1	8.2	17.7	9.0	42.8	19.7
Poverty								
Parents receive welfare	23.2	4.7	13.0	10.2	16.1	15.3	44.9	24.0
Parents do not receive welfare	17.2	3.6	7.6	9.5	18.1	12.4	37.9	17.7

*Continuous variable reported as a mean score; higher score indicative of higher risk.
†Percentage of those who are sexually active.

TABLE 5

Percent Variance in Dependent Variables Explained by Each Context Independently, After Controlling for Demographic Factors*

Dependent Variables	Demographic Factors†		Family Context		School Context		Individual Characteristics		3 Models and Demographics Combined‡	
	Grades 7–8	Grades 9–12	Grades 7–8	Grades 9–12	Grades 7–8	Grades 9–12	Grades 7–8	Grades 9–12	Grades 7–8	Grades 9–12
Emotional distress	4.2	5.9	14.6	13.5	17.6	13.1	21.8	21.0	30.0	27.1
Suicidality	1.0	1.2	4.8	7.0	3.1	3.0	2.5	5.9	7.1	9.9
Violence	6.6	8.0	6.5	4.6	7.1	5.8	43.9	49.6	44.4	50.6
Substance use										
Cigarette use	2.2	6.2	6.4	7.8	3.7	5.7	11.4	10.0	14.5	14.4
Alcohol use	1.0	2.9	8.5	6.1	5.6	4.3	7.1	7.3	13.7	12.5
Marijuana use	1.6	2.0	5.6	8.6	4.8	5.6	4.8	7.4	10.2	13.7

*For history of pregnancy and age of sexual debut, no R^2 available using logistic regression or Cox regression.
†The factors include poverty status, family structure, race, ethnicity, and sex.
‡Explanatory variables significant in the 3 context-specific analyses were retained in the combined analysis regardless of changes in significance due to intercorrelations among them.

of suicidality was associated with higher distress as well as adolescent suicidality.

Except for parent-family connectedness, no family context variables significantly protected against adolescent suicidality. However, having a gun easily available at home was slightly associated with suicidality for older adolescents. Overall, 24.2% of respondents (2771/11,468) reported that guns were easily accessible at home.

School Context.—School context had a limited but consistent influence on adolescent emotional health, accounting for 13% to 18% of the variability in emotional distress among older and younger adolescents, respectively, and 3% of the variability in suicidality (Table 5). School connectedness was associated with lower levels of emotional distress and suicidal involvement among both younger and older adolescents (Table 6). Perceived student prejudice was associated with emotional distress among both groups of students. No other aspect of the school environment was associated with either emotional distress or suicidality.

Individual Characteristics.—Individual characteristics accounted for 21% to 22% of the variability in emotional distress among students and

for 3% to 6% of the variability in suicidality among 7th and 8th graders and 9th through 12th graders, respectively (Table 5).

Self-esteem was inversely related to emotional distress, regardless of grade (Table 6). Other factors associated with emotional distress, regardless of grade level, included: being held back 1 or more grades in school, a low grade point average, and perceived risk of untimely death. Among 9th through 12th graders, emotional distress tended to be higher among those with same-sex attraction or behavior, those working 20 or more hours per week, and those who reported looking older than their peers. More emotional distress was reported by 7th and 8th graders who indicated looking "younger than most."

A smaller set of individual characteristics played a role in suicidality. Suicidality across grade cohorts was associated with a perceived risk of an untimely death. Low self-esteem and appearing older than one's peers was associated with suicidality among 9th through 12th graders, while a low grade point average showed significant association with suicidality among 7th and 8th graders.

Involvement Violence.—Although most young people reported never having been the victim of

TABLE 6
Explaining Emotional Distress, Suicidality, and Violence
(Parameter Estimates and P Values)*

Variables	Emotional Distress		Suicidality		Violence	
	Grades 7–8 (P Value)	Grades 9–12 (P Value)	Grades 7–8 (P Value)	Grades 9–12 (P Value)	Grades 7–8 (P Value)	Grades 9–12 (P Value)
Family	n=1785	n=3760	n=1790	n=3789	n=1787	n=3758
Parent-family connectedness	-.37 (<.001)	-.33 (<.001)	-.17 (<.001)	-.24 (<.001)	-.21 (<.001)	-.13 (<.001)
Parent-adolescent activities	.06 (<.01)	.04 (<.05)	. . .	. . .	. . .	. . .
Parental presence	-.07 (<.01)	-.06 (<.001)	. . .	. . .	. . .	. . .
Parental school expectations	-.07 (<.01)	-.08 (<.001)	. . .	. . .	. . .	-.07 (<.001)
Recent family suicide attempts/completions	.09 (<.01)	.07 (<.001)	.12 (<.001)	.06 (<.001)	.13 (<.001)	.07 (<.001)
Household access to guns†	. . .	. . .	. . .	.13 (<.001)	.14 (<.01)	.27 (<.001)
School	n=1800	n=3812	n=1788	n=3799	n=1792	n=3803
School connectedness	-.43 (<.001)	-.36 (<.001)	-.17 (<.001)	-.18 (<.001)	-.27 (<.001)	-.26 (<.001)
Perceived student prejudice	.06 (<.01)	.06 (<.001)	. . .	. . .	. . .	. . .
Individual	n=1754	n=3628	n=1768	n=3865	n=1769	n=3892
Self-esteem	-.38 (<.001)	-.38 (<.001)	. . .	-.21 (<.001)	. . .	. . .
Same-sex attraction or behavior	. . .	.23 (<.001)	. . .	. . .	. . .	. . .
Perceived risk of untimely death	.10 (<.001)	.14 (<.001)	.08 (<.001)	.06 (<.001)	.05 (<.01)	. . .
Paid work ≥ 20 hr/wk†	. . .	.16 (<.001)	. . .	. . .	. . .	. . .
Appears older than most†	. . .	.17 (<.001)	. . .	.27 (<.001)	. . .	. . .
Appears younger than most†	.20 (<.01)	. . .	. . .	. . .	. . .	. . .
Repeated a grade†	.22 (<.001)	.12 (<.01)	. . .	. . .	. . .	. . .
Grade point average	-.14 (<.001)	-.07 (<.001)	-.12 (<.001)	. . .	-.07 (<.001)	. . .
History of victimization/ witnessing violence	. . .	. . .	. . .	. . .	.30 (<.001)	.44 (<.001)
Weapon carrying	. . .	. . .	. . .	. . .	.18 (<.001)	.22 (<.001)
Deviant behavior	. . .	. . .	. . .	. . .	.26 (<.001)	.22 (<.001)
Drug selling	. . .	. . .	. . .	. . .	.39 (<.001)	.11 (<.001)

*Ellipses indicates that the variables were excluded from the final model.
†Item coded dichotomously; e.g., yes/no, any/none. Risk estimate compares reporting affirmatively to item with all others.

violent behavior, 24.1% (2767/11,486) indicated they had been a victim. Additionally, 12.4% of students (1425/11,490) indicated that they had carried a weapon over the previous 30 days.

Family Context.—Controlling for demographic factors, family variables explained relatively little of the variability in violence perpetration, 7% and 5% among younger and older students, respectively (Table 5). Items associated with higher levels of violence for all students included household access to guns and a recent history of family suicide attempts or completions (Table 6). Factors associated with somewhat lower levels of interpersonal violence included parental and family connectedness. In addition, higher parental expectations for school achievement were weakly associated with lower levels of violence among older adolescents.

School Context.—School context accounted for 6% to 7% of the variability in violence among students (Table 5). Specifically, higher levels of connectedness to school were associated with somewhat lower levels of violence, applicable to both student cohorts (Table 6).

Individual Characteristics.—Individual characteristics accounted for 44% of the variability in violent behavior among 7th and 8th graders and 50% of variability among 9th through 12th graders (Table 5). Among both younger and older adolescents, involvement in violence was associated with having been a victim or a witness to violence, frequency of carrying a weapon, involvement in deviant or antisocial behaviors, and involvement in selling marijuana or other drugs within the past year (Table 6). Among younger students, interpersonal violence was associated with lower grade point average and higher perceived risk of untimely death.

Substance Use

Cigarette Use.—Overall, 25.7% of adolescents (2907/11,293) reported being current smokers, with 9.2% of females (524/5681) and 10.0% of

males (563/5612) smoking 6 or more cigarettes per day.

Family Context.—Family context measures explained 6% to 8% of the variability in frequency of cigarette use among younger and older groups (Table 5). Variables associated with some increased frequency of cigarette use among both groups included easy household access to cigarettes and family history of recent suicidal behavior (Table 7). Nearly 1 in 3 respondents (31.4% [3602/11,468]) reported that cigarettes are easily available at home with little sex variability. High levels of connectedness to parents and family members were associated with somewhat less frequent cigarette use among both groups. Among 9th through 12th graders, less frequent cigarette use also had small but significant associations with more frequent parental presence in the home, greater number of shared activities between adolescents and their parents, and higher perceived levels of parental expectations related to adolescent school completion.

School Context.—School variables accounted for only 4% of the variability in cigarette use frequency among 7th and 8th grade students and 6% of the variability among 9th through 12th grade students (Table 5). Among both younger and older students, high self-reported levels of school connectedness were associated with less frequent cigarette use. No other school context variables were significantly associated with cigarette use (Table 7).

Individual Characteristics.—Individual characteristics explained 11% of the variability in cigarette use among 7th and 8th grade students and 10% of variability in this behavior among 9th through 12th graders (Table 5). Correlates of increased frequency of cigarette use among both student cohorts included appearing older than peers and low grade point average (Table 7). Correlates of use among younger students included high perceived risk of early death and having repeated a grade in school. Among older students, working 20 or more hours per week

TABLE 7
Explaining Substance Use (Parameter Estimates and P Values)*

Variables	Cigarette Use		Alcohol Use		Marijuana Use	
	Grades 7–8 (P Value)	Grades 9–12 (P Value)	Grades 7–8 (P Value)	Grades 9–12 (P Value)	Grades 7–8 (P Value)	Grades 9–12 (P Value)
Family	n=1760	n=3687	n=1785	n=3783	n=1776	n=3656
Parent-family connectedness	-.19 (<.001)	-.13 (<.001)	-.24 (<.001)	-.14 (<.001)	-.18 (<.001)	-.19 (<.001)
Parent-adolescent activities	. . .	-.04 (<.001)	. . .	. . .	. . .	. . .
Parental presence	. . .	-.06 (<.001)	. . .	-.13 (<.001)	-.07 (<.01)	-.08 (<.001)
Parental school expectations	. . .	-.05 (<.01)	. . .	. . .	. . .	. . .
Recent family suicide attempts/completions	.09 (<.01)	.04 (<.01)	. . .	. . .	. . .	. . .
Household access to substances†	.25 (<.001)	.38 (<.001)	.32 (<.001)	.22 (<.001)	.75 (<.001)	1.00 (<.001)
School	n=1768	n=3737	n=1785	n=3796	n=1773	n=3669
School connectedness	-.19 (<.001)	-.25 (<.001)	-.23 (<.001)	-.21 (<.001)	-.22 (<.001)	-.24 (<.001)
Individual	n=1705	n=3542	n=1721	n=3584	n=1735	n=3463
Self-esteem	. . .	-.11 (<.001)	-.08 (<.001)	-.05 (<.01)	. . .	-.09 (<.001)
Religious identity	-.07 (<.01)	-.08 (<.001)	-.06 (<.01)	-.11 (<.001)	. . .	-.10 (<.001)
Same-sex attraction or behavior†	. . .	. . .	. . .	-.19 (<.01)	. . .	.17 (<.05)
Perceived risk of untimely death	.11 (<.001)	. . .	.06 (<.01)	. . .	.10 (<.001)	.06 (<.001)
Paid work ≥ 20 h/wk†	. . .	.37 (<.001)	. . .	.33 (<.001)	.20 (<.01)	.20 (<.001)
Appears older than most†	.33 (<.001)	.21 (<.001)	.38 (<.001)	.34 (<.001)	. . .	.22 (<.001)
Repeated a grade in school†	.18 (<.01)	. . .	. . .	. . .	. . .	. . .
Grade point average	-.24 (<.001)	-.21 (<.001)	-.15 (<.001)	-.13 (<.001)	-.18 (<.001)	-.16 (<.001)

*Ellipses indicate that the variables were excluded from the final model.
†Dichotomously categorized variable, e.g., yes/no, any/none. Risk estimate compares reporting affirmatively to item with all others.

was associated with increased cigarette use. Items slightly associated with decreased frequency of cigarette use included high levels of personal importance placed on religion and prayer among all students and among older students, high levels of self-esteem.

Alcohol Use

Overall 17.9% of students (2042/11,436) reported drinking alcohol more than monthly, with 9.9% (1129/11,436) drinking at least 1 day a week.

Family Context.—Family context variables accounted for 9% of the variability in frequency of alcohol use among 7th and 8th grade students and 6% of the variability among 9th through 12th grade students (Table 5). For both groups, easy household access to alcohol was associated with more frequent alcohol use (Table 7). As with cigarettes, alcohol was readily available in over a quarter (28.5% [3268/11,474]) of respondents' homes. High levels of connectedness to parents and family members were associated with less frequent alcohol use among both groups of students. Among older students, more frequent parental presence in the home was associated with less frequent use.

School Context.—School variables accounted for 4% to 6% of variability in frequency of alcohol use among students (Table 5). High levels of school connectedness were associated with less frequent alcohol use among both groups (Table 7).

Individual Characteristics.—Individual characteristics explained 7% of the variability in frequency of alcohol use among both groups of students (Table 5). Items associated with increased frequency of use for both younger and older students included self-report of appearing older than peers, low grade point average, and low self-esteem (Table 7). Among 9th through 12th grade students, increased alcohol use was also associated with working 20 or more hours per week and same-sex attraction or behavior. For 7th and 8th grade students, perceived risk of un-

timely death was associated with more frequent use. High levels of importance placed on religion and prayer appeared to be a significant protective factor among both groups.

Marijuana Use

One quarter of all young people (25.2% [8315/11,116]) reported ever having smoked marijuana, with 12.7% (1406/11,116) reporting that they had smoked at least once during the previous month. About 6% (670/11,116) of females and males were heavy users (using 4 or more times during the previous 30 days).

Family Context.—Family context measures explained 6% to 9% of the variability in marijuana use among both groups of students (Table 5). More frequent marijuana use was associated with easy household access to illicit substances in both age groups (Table 7). High levels of parent-family connectedness were associated with less frequent marijuana use, as was a greater frequency of parental presence in the home.

School Context.—School variables explained 5% to 6% of the variability in marijuana use among students (Table 5). For both groups, high levels of school connectedness were associated with less frequent use. No other school factor was related to marijuana use (Table 7).

Individual Characteristics.—Individual characteristics accounted for 5% of variability in frequency of marijuana use among 7th and 8th graders and 7% among 9th through 12th graders (Table 5). Among both groups of students, appearing older than age mates, low grade point average, and perceived risk of untimely death were associated with more frequent marijuana use (Table 7). Among 9th through 12th grade students, working 20 or more hours per week and same-sex attraction or behavior were associated with greater use. Protective factors, evident among high school students only, included personal importance placed on religion and prayer and high levels of self-esteem.

Sexual Behaviors

Approximately 17% (646/3788) of 7th and 8th graders and nearly half (49.3% [3754/7614]) of 9th through 12th graders indicated that they had ever had sexual intercourse.

Family Context.—Significant family factors associated with delaying sexual debut included high levels of parent-family connectedness, parental disapproval of their adolescent being sexually active, and parental disapproval of their adolescent's

using contraception. Recent family suicide attempt or completion was associated with a slightly increased risk of early sexual debut (Table 8).

School Context.—Three factors were associated with some delay in sexual debut: higher levels of connectedness to school; attending a parochial school; and attending a school with high overall average daily attendance (Table 8).

Individual Characteristics.—Adolescents who reported having taken a pledge to remain a vir-

T A B L E 8

Predicting Sexual Behaviors (Parameter Estimate, *P* Value, 95% Confidence Interval [CI], and Relative Risk [RR] or Odds Ratio [OR])

	Age of Sexual Debut	Pregnancy History
	Grades 7–12 RR* (95% CI)	Sexually Experienced Females ≥ 15 y OR* (95% CI)
Family	n=5017	n=909
Parent-family connectedness	0.85 (0.81–0.88)	. . . †
Recent family suicide attempts/completions	1.07 (1.03–1.12)	. . .
Perceived parent disapproval of adolescent sex	0.79 (0.75–0.83)	. . .
Perceived parent disapproval of adolescent contraception	0.75 (0.71–0.79)	0.65 (0.53–0.81)‡
Parental-adolescent activities	. . .	0.69 (0.56–0.85)
School	n=5177	n=1007
School connectedness	0.77 (0.74–0.81)	
Average daily attendance	0.95 (0.91–0.99)¶	
Parochial School‖	0.78 (0.63–0.97)¶	
Individual	n=4982	n=863
Religious identity	0.93 (0.89–0.97)§	. . .
Same-sex attraction or behavior	1.39 (1.17–1.65)‡	. . .
Perceived risk of untimely death	1.11 (1.06–1.16)‡	. . .
Paid work ≥ 20 h/wk‖	1.36 (1.21–1.53)†	. . .
Appears older than most‖	1.56 (1.38–1.78)‡	. . .
Pledge of virginity‖	0.25 (0.19–0.33)‡	. . .
Grade point average	0.80 (0.76–0.84)‡	. . .
Appears younger than most‖	0.83 (0.69–0.99)¶	. . .
Effective contraceptive use first/last sex	. . .	0.73 (0.60–0.88)§
Time since sexual debut	. . .	1.76 (1.41–2.19)‡
Perceived consequences of pregnancy	. . .	0.61 (0.51–0.73)‡

*Value < 1 associated with decreased risk (increased age of sexual debut).
†Ellipses indicate that the variables were excluded from the final model.
‡*P* < .001.
§*P* < .01.
‖Dichotomously categorized variable, eg, yes/no, any/none. Risk estimate compares reporting affirmatively for item with all others.
¶*P* < .05.

gin were at significantly lower risk of early age of sexual debut (Table 8). Nearly 16% of females (911/5715) and 10% of males (539/5692) reported making such pledges. A higher level of importance ascribed to religion and prayer was also associated with a somewhat later age of sexual debut, as was self-report of appearing younger than peers and a higher grade point average. Self-report of looking older than peers, working 20 or more hours per week, same-sex attraction or behavior, and perceived risk of untimely death were all associated with earlier sexual debut.

History of Pregnancy

Among sexually experienced females aged 15 years and older, 19.8% (369/1860) reported having ever been pregnant.

Family Context.—A greater number of shared activities with parents and perceived parental disapproval of adolescent contraceptive use were protective factors against a history of pregnancy.

School Context.—No school factors were associated with students' pregnancy histories.

Individual Characteristics.—A history of pregnancy was associated with length of time since age of sexual debut. Protective factors included perceived (negative) consequences of becoming pregnant and use of effective contraception at first and/or most recent intercourse.

COMMENT

The goal of this study has been to identify school, family, and individual protective factors and risk factors for major areas of adolescent morbidity. It is clear that when demographic characteristics are controlled, social contexts count. Specifically, we find consistent evidence that perceived caring and connectedness to others is important in understanding the health of young people today. While these findings are confirmatory of other studies, they are also unique because they represent the first time certain protective factors have been shown to apply across the major risk domains.

Family

With notable consistency across the domains of risk, the role of parents and family in shaping the health of adolescents is evident. While not surprising, the protective role that perceived parental expectations play regarding adolescents' school attainment emerges as an important recurring correlate of health and healthy behavior. Likewise, while physical presence of a parent in the home at key times reduces risk (and especially substance use), it is consistently less significant than parental connectedness (e.g., feelings of warmth, love, and caring from parents). The home environment also plays a role in shaping negative health outcomes. If homes provide a venue in which adolescents have easy access to guns, alcohol, tobacco, and illicit substances, adolescents are more likely to have an increased risk of suicidality, involvement in interpersonal violence, and substance use. In this context we note that restricting access to tobacco both within and outside the home is a focus of the recent surgeon general's report on smoking and health.[45] The present data support the importance of those recommendations. It supports the notion of restricting access to alcohol; those who grow up where alcohol is easily accessible may be more likely to drink as teens. And it supports the American Medical Association's recommendation[46] to remove guns from the home, as those with easy access to guns in the home were more likely to be violent and more likely to attempt suicide.

Hewlett[47] and Fuchs and Reklis[48] have identified the time deficit that surrounds many of the children of the United States: the increasing scarcity of time that parents have for their children, driven largely by workforce pressures. Compared with 1960, children in the United States have lost, on average, 10 to 12 hours per week of parental time.[48] The present study confirms the importance of time availability of parents for their children. While the monitoring function is important, time availability becomes critical in those variables that constitute family connectedness and parental activities. As economic and social policies press both parents into the workforce, consideration should be given to the sequelae for children when flexible time options are not made available.

School

Connectedness with school is another protective factor in the lives of young people. Indeed, other population-based studies have suggested that school connectedness, along with an adolescent's sense of connectedness to parents, family, and other adults, serves as a protective factor against a variety of risk behaviors.[23] Steinberg[49] has described how school engagement is a critical protective factor against a variety of risky behaviors, influenced in good measure by perceived caring from teachers and high expectations for student performance. While much emphasis is placed on school policies governing adolescent behaviors, such policies appear in the present analysis to have limited associations with the student behaviors under study.

Individual

A number of individual characteristics emerged as salient correlates of risky behaviors across a variety of domains in this analysis. In the sample, 17.9% (1366/7638) of 9th through 12th grade students reported working during the school year at least 20 hours per week. Greenberger and Steinberg[50] cautioned against adolescents' working long hours, focusing on the adverse consequences of fatigue as well as excessive leisure income. The present study affirms that 20 or more hours per week of work during the teenage years is associated with higher levels of emotional distress, substance use, and earlier age of sexual debut;

although, as emphasized by Bachman and Schulenberg,[51] this association must be examined longitudinally.

Low grade point average and being retained in school were related by varying degree to higher levels of emotional distress, substance use, involvement in violence, and earlier onset of sexual intercourse. Byrd and colleagues[52] have reported that after adjusting for multiple potential confounding variables, old-for-grade high school students were significantly more likely to be involved in a multiplicity of risk behaviors. The prevalence of adolescents who are retained at least 1 year (21.3% [2462/11,561]) and the associated health-risk behavior problems suggest that targeted strategies for all young people who have school-related learning and behavior problems warrant closer examination. Consistently, it appears that those who are academically at risk are at high risk in other ways as well. The "full-service school" as a community-based vehicle for organization and delivery of educational, social, and health services provides an excellent framework for community planning and action to address the health and educational needs of young people who are highly distressed and engaged in serious health-compromising behaviors.[53]

To be "out of sync" for grade level is clearly a risk factor but so too is perceiving oneself as physically older than age mates independent of one's chronological age. These findings are consistent with those of Brooks-Gunn and Peterson[54] and Peterson and Crockett.[55] The present analyses indicate that not only did those who perceived themselves as looking older than peers initiate intercourse at a younger age, but they were also more likely to use cigarettes, alcohol, and marijuana. They were also significantly more likely to have participated in violence and to have expressed emotional distress and suicidality than adolescents who saw themselves as looking age-appropriate. Except for emotional distress, the same behavioral vulnerabilities were not seen in general for those who reported appearing younger than their age. To be out of sync from peers, thus, appears to put a young person at risk. While perceived difference from age mates can be explored with adolescents during preventive health assessments and physical examinations, such perception does not lend itself to direct preventive or intervention efforts.

Among the nearly 88% (9945/11,326) of the population who reported having a religion, the perceived importance of religion and prayer was protective. Those who ascribed importance to religion and prayer tended to have a later age of sexual debut and were also less likely to use all substances. This is consistent with other studies of risk and protective factors that link religiosity, spirituality, and religious identity with "conventional" behaviors.[23,56] While the work of Werner and Smith[25] suggests that religiosity would also be protective against emotional distress, there is nothing in the present study to support that finding.

It is tempting to compare our prevalence data for major adolescent risk behaviors with other national school-based data sets such as the Youth Risk Behavior Survey.[45] However, such direct comparisons should be undertaken with care. Each data set uses particular approaches to measurement (i.e., single-item vs multi-item indicators), and, more importantly, there are branching patterns in the questionnaires that lead to different results. For example, 1 instrument asks all respondents questions about suicide attempts, while another survey asks this question of students who acknowledged previous suicidal ideation. Such comparisons will be undertaken in more detail in the future.

CONCLUSION

This is the first report from the Add Health study, the first nationally representative data set including longitudinal data on the health status, risk behaviors, and social contexts of adolescents. These analyses are limited insofar as they do not incorporate the longitudinal in-home or parent data sets.

There is a generation of research yet to be done using the Add Health data set. These analyses should add to our understanding of adolescent health, risk behaviors, resilience, and protective factors—especially adolescent development over time. This study, although cross-sectional, should assist health and social service providers, educators, and others in taking the first steps of establishing priorities and committing to practices and programs that enhance protective factors as well as reduce risk.

REFERENCES

1. *Kids Count Data Book: State Profiles of Child Well-Being.* Baltimore, Md: Annie E Casey Foundation; 1997.
2. Children's Defense Fund. *The State of America's Children: Yearbook, 1996.* Washington, DC: Children's Defense Fund; 1997.
3. Centers for Disease Control and Prevention. *Mortality Trends: Causes of Death and Related Risk Behaviors Among US Adolescents.* Atlanta, Ga: Centers for Disease Control and Prevention; 1993.
4. Centers for Disease Control and Prevention. *Adolescent Health State of the Nation.* Atlanta, Ga: Centers for Disease Control and Prevention; 1995. Publication 099–4112. Monograph series 1.
5. Centers for Disease Control. Health risk behaviors among persons aged 12–21 years—United States. *MMWR Morb Mortal Wkly Rep. 1992;43:* 213–235.
6. Perry, C., ed. *Preventing Tobacco Use Among Young People: A Report of the Surgeon General.* Washington, DC: US Dept of Health and Human Services, Public Health Service; 1994:5–10.
7. Centers for Disease Control and Prevention. Premarital sexual experience among adolescent women—United States, 1970–1988. *MMWR Morb Mortal Wkly Rep.* 1991;39:929–932.
8. _____. Measuring the health behavior of adolescents: the Youth Risk Behavior Surveillance System and recent report on high-risk adolescents. *Public Health Rep.* 1993;108:1–96.
9. _____. Sexual behavior among high school students—United States, 1990. *MMWR Morb Mortal Wkly Rep.* 1992;40:885–888.
10. Alan Guttmacher Institute. *Sex in America's Teenagers.* New York: Alan Guttmacher Institute; 1994.
11. National Research Council, Commission on Behavioral and Social Science and Education, Panel

on High Risk Youth. *Losing Generations: Adolescents in High Risk Settings.* Washington, DC: National Academy Press; 1993:64–68.

12. Millstein S, Petersen A, Nightingale E. *Promoting the Health of Adolescents: New Directions for the 21st Century.* New York, NY: Oxford University Press; 1993.

13. American Medical Association. *Guidelines for Adolescent Preventive Services.* Chicago, Ill: American Medical Association; 1994.

14. Hechinger F. *Fateful Choices: Healthy Youth for the 21st Century.* New York, NY: Carnegie Council on Adolescent Development, Carnegie Corporation of New York; 1992.

15. McAnarney E, Beach RK, Casamassimo P, et al. Adolescence. In: Green M, ed. *Bright Futures: Guidelines for Supervision of Infants. Children and Adolescents.* Arlington, Va: National Center for Education and Maternal and Child Health; 1994:196–259.

16. Irwin C, Brindis C, Holt K, Langlykke K, eds. *Health Care Reform: Opportunities for Improving Adolescent Health.* Arlington, Va: National Center for Education and Maternal and Child Health; 1994.

17. Sells CW, Blum R. Morbidity and mortality among US adolescents: an overview of data and trends. *Am J Public Health,* 1996;86:513–519.

18. Blum R, Beuhring T, Wunderlich MJ, Resnick M. Don't ask, they won't tell: health screening of youth. *Am J Public Health.* 1996;86: 1767–1772.

19. Johnston L, O'Malley P, Bachman J. *National Survey Results on Drug Use from the Monitoring the Future Study, 1975–1994.* Rockville, Md: National Institute on Drug Abuse; 1996:1.

20. Rutter M. Resilience: some conceptual considerations. *J Adolesc Health.* 1993;14:626–639.

21. Luthar S, Ziegler E. Vulnerability and competence: a review of research on resilience in children. *Am J Orthopsychiatry.* 1991;61:6–22.

22. Hawkins J, Catalano R, eds. *Communities That Care: Action for Drug Abuse Prevention.* San Francisco, Calif.: Jossey-Bass Publishers Inc; 1992:8–24.

23. Resnick MD, Harris LJ, Blum RW. The impact of caring and connectedness on adolescent health and well-being. *J Paediatr Child Health.* 1993;29 (suppl 1):S3–S9.

24. Garmezy N. Resiliency and vulnerability to adverse developmental outcomes assisted with poverty. *Am Behav Scientist.* 1991;34:416–430.

25. Werner E, Smith R. *Overcoming the Odds: High Risk Children from Birth to Adolescence.* Ithaca, NY: Cornell University Press, 1992.

26. Perry C, Kelder S, Komro K. The social world of adolescents: families, peers, schools in the community. In: Millstein S, Petersen A, Nightingale E, eds. *Promoting the Health of Adolescents.* New York, NY: Oxford University Press; 1993:73–96.

27. Bearman P, Jones J, Udry JR. *The National Longitudinal Study on Adolescent Health:* Research Design. Chapel Hill, NC: Carolina Population Center; 1997. [Available at: http://www.cpc.unc.edu//projects/addhealth/design.html].

28. Resnick MD, Blum RW. The association of consensual sexual intercourse during childhood with adolescent health risk and behaviors. *Pediatrics.* 1994;94:907–913.

29. Cronbach L. Coefficient alpha and the internal structure of tests. *Psychometrika.* 1951;16:297–334.

30. Werner E. High-risk children in young adulthood: a longitudinal study from birth to 32 years. *Am J Orthopsychiatry.* 1989;59(1):72–81.

31. Radke-Yarrow M, Zahn-Waxler C. Research on children with affectively ill parents: some considerations for theory and research on normal development. *Dev Psychopathol.* 1990;2:349–366.

32. Sameroff JA, Seifer R. Early contributions to developmental risk. In: Rolf J, Masten AS, Cicchetti D, Nuechterlein KH, Weintraub S, eds. *Risk and Protective Factors in the Development of Psychopathology.* Cambridge, England: Cambridge University Press; 1989:52–66.

33. Rutter M. Psychosocial resilience and protective mechanisms. *Am J Orthopsychiatry.* 1987;57: 316–331.

34. Richmond JB, Beardslee WR. Resiliency: research and practical implications for pediatrics. *J Dev Behav Pediatr.* 1988;9:157–163.

35. McLoyd VC. The impact of economic hardships on black families and children: psychological distress, parenting, and socioemotional development. *Child Dev.* 1990;61:311–346.

36. Allen JP, Aber JL, Leadbeater BJ. Adolescent problem behaviors: the influence of attachment and autonomy. *Psychiatr Clin North Am.* 1990;13:455–467.

37. Garmezy N, Masten AS, Tellegen A. The study of stress and competence in children: a building block for developmental psychopathology. *Child Dev.* 1984;55:97–111.

38. Hauser ST, Jacobson AM, Wertlieb D, Brink S, Wentworth S. The contribution of family envi-

ronment to perceived competence and illness adjustment in diabetic and acutely ill adolescents. *Fam Relations.* 1985;34:99–108.

39. Quinton D, Rutter M. *Parental Breakdown: The Making and Breaking of Intergenerational Links.* Aldershot, England: Avebury; 1988.

40. Hawkins JD, Catalano RF, Miller JY. Risk and protective factors for alcohol and other drug problems in adolescence and early adulthood: implications for substance abuse prevention. *Psychol Bull.* 1992;112:64–105.

41. McBride CM, Curry SJ, Cheadle A, et al. School-level application of a social bonding model to adolescent risk-taking behavior. *J Sch Health.* 1995;65:63–68.

42. Looker D. Accuracy of proxy reports of parental status characteristics. *Sociol Educ.* 1989;62:249–260.

43. Kayser B, Summers G. The adequacy of student reports of parental SES characteristics. *Sociol Methods Res.* 1973;1:298–305.

44. Littell RC, Milliken GA, Stroup WW, Wolfinger RD. *SAS System for Mixed Models.* Cary, NC: SAS Institute Inc; 1996.

45. Kann L, Warren CW, Harris WA, et al. Youth risk behavior surveillance—United States, 1995. *MMWR Morb Mortal Wkly Rep.* 1996;45(SS-4):1–84.

46. Koop CE, Lundberg GD. Violence in America: a public health emergency. *JAMA.* 1992; 267:3075–3076. Corrections: *JAMA.* 1992; 268:3074 and 1994; 271:1404.

47. Hewlett S. *When the Bough Breaks: The Cost of Neglecting Our Children.* New York, NY: Harper-Collins Publications Inc; 1991:90–93.

48. Fuchs V, Reklis D. The status of American children. *Science.* 1992;255:41–46.

49. Steinberg L. *Beyond the Classroom: Why School Reform Has Failed and What Parents Need to Do.* New York, NY: Simon & Schuster; 1996;62–77.

50. Greenberger E, Steinberg L. *When Teenagers Work: The Psychological and Social Costs of Adolescent Employment.* New York, NY: Basic Books Inc Publishers; 1986.

51. Bachman JG, Schulenberg, J. How part time work intensity relates to drug use, problem behavior, time use and satisfaction among high school seniors: are these consequences or merely correlates? *Dev Psychol.* 1993;29:220–235.

52. Byrd RS, Weitzman M, Doniger A. Increased drug use among old for grade adolescents. *Arch Pediatr Adolesc Med.* 1996;150:470–476.

53. Dryfoos JG. *Full-Service Schools: A Revolution in health and Social Services for Children, Youth and Families.* San Francisco, Calif: Jossey-Bass Publishers Inc; 1994:1–17.

54. Brooks-Gunn J, Peterson AC, eds. *Girls at Puberty: Biological and Psychological Perspectives.* New York, NY: Plenum Publishing Corp; 1983.

55. Peterson AC, Crockett L. Pubertal timing and grade effects on adjustments. *J Youth Adolesc.* 1985;3:47–62.

56. Jessor R, Jessor S. *Problem Behavior and Psychological Development: A Longitudinal Study of Youth.* New York, NY: Academic Press; 1977.

This research is based on data from the Add Health project, a program project designed by J. Richard Udry, PhD, and Peter S. Bearman, PhD, and funded by grant PO1 HD31921 from the National Institute of Child Health and Human Development given to the Carolina Protection Center, University of North Carolina at Chapel Hill, with cooperative funding participation by the National Cancer Institute; the National Institute of Alcohol Abuse and Alcoholism; the National Institute on Deafness and Other Communication Disorders; the National Institute on Drug Abuse; The National Institute of General Medical Sciences; the National Institute of Mental Health; the National Institute of Nursing Research; the Office of AIDS Research; the National Institutes of Health (NIH); the Office of the Director, NIH; the Office of Research on Women's Health, NIH; the Office of Population Affairs, Department of Health and Human Services (DHHS); the National Center for Health Statistics, Centers for Disease Control and Prevention, DHHS: the Office of Minority Health, Centers for Disease Control and Prevention, DHHS; the Office of Minority Health, Office of the Assistant Secretary for Health DHHS; the Office of the Assistant Secretary for Planning and Evaluation, DHHS; and the National Science Foundation

The authors wish to thank Elizabeth McAnarney, MD, and Robert DuRant, PhD, for their careful review of early manuscript drafts; Blake Downes and Michelle Burlew for their statistical consultation and assistance; and Linda Boche for her patience and perseverance in numerous manuscript and table revisions.

Persons interested in obtaining data files from the National Longitudinal Study on Adolescent Health should contact Jo Jones, PhD, Carolina Population Center, 123 W Franklin St., Chapel Hill, NC 27516–3997 (e-mail: jo_jones@unc.edu).

EATING DISORDERS:
ANOREXIA NERVOSA AND BULIMIA

ROLF E. MUUSS

ANOREXIA NERVOSA

Anorexia nervosa, which implies a strong desire for a thinner body, is defined, somewhat incorrectly, by a medical dictionary as a "lack of appetite due to nerves." Actually, the concern with body weight and the desire for a thinner body are more important than the issue of appetite and eating. The disorder has fittingly been referred to as "weight phobia," a morbid fear of becoming fat (Palmer, 1980). The diagnosis requires that the loss of weight and accompanying behavior patterns cannot be accounted for by starvation due to poverty, depression, delusion, and other disorders. Although these conditions may produce similar symptoms, weight phobia is absent. Diagnosis can be difficult because the anorexic denies she is undernourished, rationalizes her behavior, and does not perceive the severity of her condition. Some anorexics feel that they live in an overwhelming, chaotic, and uncontrollable world and have a need to feel in control over their own bodies. The anorexic limits her food intake, and self-starvation may be her means of establishing personal control. Anorexics in general have a strong need to control their emotional behavior and their environment.

This paper is based on several previous publications. Copyright © 1989 by Rolf E. Muuss.

Gender, Age, and Occupational Aspirations

Of those afflicted by anorexia nervosa, 90% to 95% are adolescent girls and young women. Anorexia is relatively rare in males; however, currently the rate for males is increasing more rapidly than for females. The frequency listed in the *Diagnostic and Statistical Manual of Mental Disorders* (DSM-IV, 1994) is 0.5% to 1.0% among females age 12 to 18, and that rate is on the increase. If one were to include milder, subclinical tendencies, the figure would be higher, especially in the college population. The mean age for the onset of anorexia is 17, but age of onset has a bimodal distribution. The early peak is at 14 at the time of pubertal maturation and the concomitant increase in body fat (Graber, et al., 1994). The second peak occurs at 18, when young women leave their parents for college. Occupational groups for whom lean physique and physical agility are of utmost importance—ballet dancers, actresses, fashion models, and competitive athletes—are more inclined to show anorexic eating patterns than others.

Characteristics of Anorexia Nervosa

Much of the anorexic's thoughts and behaviors focuses on appearance, body image, control, and thoughts about food. Even though anorexics are by no means a homogeneous group and research findings are not always conclusive, they can be distinguished from control groups by self-doubt, neurotic anxieties, control of emotions, inhibited interpersonal relationships, lack of assertiveness, and unwillingness to take risks. The literature identifies common anorexic personality characteristics as moralistic, idealistic, perfectionistic, ascetic, and asexual (Banks, 1996). Self-denial, internalized hostility, and suicidal tendencies are also common. An unrealistic fear of becoming fat continues unabated even after the person is undernourished and appears emaciated.

Concern about weight and appearance is, of course, quite normal in adolescent girls. Many adolescents go on diets, mostly temporary and usually unsuccessful. Anorexia often begins as such a dieting attempt, but it develops unnoticeably into a more serious obsession with weight as essential nutritional foods are eliminated. The young woman is actually able to sustain her diet and continue to lose weight past her initial goal and past medically suggested norms. She diets as though she cannot stop. The desire to become thinner and thinner prevails and becomes stronger as she continues to lose weight. As she experiences success she enjoys feeling more and more in control of her body. Her exaggerated fear of the consequences of regaining weight may be so strong that she eventually starves herself to death. Thousands of young women die each year as a result of anorexia and bulimia, or the medical complications associated with these disorders.

The anorexic may exhibit the following behaviors and characteristics:

Very Limited Food Intake.—The disease is characterized primarily by self-starvation. Mainly low-calorie foods comprise the diet, and some anorexics become vegetarians. They especially avoid carbohydrates and fatty foods and show obsessive concern with calories. They may use calorie counters and request a medical weight scale for their birthday and weigh themselves repeatedly. Patients refuse to maintain minimum weight for their age and height. They experience intense fear of gaining weight, losing control, and becoming fat.

Preoccupation with Thoughts about Food. Although most anorexics deny feeling hungry, many of their life events are related to food and food preparation. They may do the food shopping and prepare elaborate meals for others which they will not eat. They may avoid coming to the dinner table, offering the excuse that they prefer to eat on their own when in fact they skip the meal. They tend to develop bizarre rituals, such as cutting food into tiny pieces or moving it around on the plate pretending to eat without doing so. Some will collect recipes, while others hoard, even shoplift, crumble, or throw away food.

Weight Reduction.—In addition to reducing food intake, anorexics prefer low-calorie foods such as lettuce, carrots, and diet soft drinks. They are more successful in staying with their diet than most teenagers, and in the process they overshoot their initial weight goal, obtaining satisfaction and feelings of enormous success from suppressing hunger and seeing pounds melt away. Some anorexics become preoccupied with fitness, which symbolizes thinness. They may engage in compulsive exercise, such as bicycling, walking, swimming, or aerobics to the point of exhaustion. The initial, reasonable attempt to lose weight becomes inappropriately prolonged and more pathological as it is compounded by one or several of these reducing techniques.

With overall food consumption too low for normal bowel functions, anorexics often resort to the use of laxatives and diuretics medication, which relieve constipation and also deprive the body of nutrients. Anorexics may develop a dependency on laxatives and use increasingly larger quantities. Laxative abuse can cause abdominal distress and anal soreness, and chronic use leads to complications in the form of metabolic disorders and overall physical deterioration (Palmer, 1980). Potassium deficiency from the abuse of laxatives may throw the regulating mechanism of the digestive juices out of balance.

A serious deficiency may cause the kidneys to malfunction. Constipation often becomes an excuse for not eating: "I would eat more if I were not constipated." Through the use of diuretics, dramatic weight loss, which is gratifying, can result. To maintain the weight loss, diuretics must be used repeatedly. Weight-reducing drugs such as amphetamines may be taken without medical prescriptions or supervision. In the process, the patient exposes herself to the danger of drug dependency.

Self-induced vomiting is another technique of weight reduction. Anorexics who resort to frequent vomiting often exhibit teeth marks on their knuckles and deterioration of tooth enamel. Some anorexics can even vomit "at will." Frequent vomiting, like heavy dependence on laxatives, can have serious metabolic consequences. One criteria for anorexia, according to DSM-IV (1994), is 15% loss of body weight for age and height, but many lose 25% and more. If untreated, anorexics continue to lower their "ideal" body weight. A weight loss of more than 35% can be life threatening (Palmer, 1980). The outcome of all these weight-reducing efforts is emaciation and eventually death.

Preoccupation with Body Size and Body Image.—The psychopathology also is obvious in body image distortion. The anorexic perceives herself as overweight and may claim, "I feel fat," or she may point to imagined layers of fat under her skin. This fear of appearing fat persists even though she looks thin, is undernourished, and suffers from malnutrition. Preoccupation with body image manifests itself in a variety of behaviors, such as gazing in the mirror, obsessive and frequent weighing, and a great concern with scaling down the size of clothing. Moving from size 12 to size 6 is experienced as exhilarating success. Anorexics consistently and considerably overestimate the size of their body or body parts. In the final stage of the disease, they look like scarecrows and their eyes appear relatively large.

Medical Conditions Frequently Associated with Anorexia Nervosa

As the psychopathological conditions become more severe, they turn into physiopathological disorder and may manifest themselves in such symptoms as (DSM-IV, 1994):

> hypothermia—body temperature as low as 35°C (95°F)
>
> bradycardia—slowness of heart beat
>
> hypotension—loss of normal blood pressure
>
> cardiac arrest—one of the causes of death among anorexics
>
> dehydration—loss of body fluids
>
> skin abnormalities—dryness of skin and yellowish color due to high level of carotene
>
> amenorrhea—discontinuation or irregular menses
>
> fluid and electrolyte abnormalities

Other conditions include metabolic changes such as hyperactivity or, more commonly, lethargy. Starvation reduces the metabolic rate, and the anorexic feels cold. Even in warm weather, she needs to wear several layers of clothes, which both provides warmth and hides the thin body. In order to conserve body heat, fine silky hair, called lanugo, grows. In short, the anorexic seems to be caught between a strong weight phobia and the experiences of physical discomfort and pain, symptoms which she is willing to endure but which place her in conflict with her family.

Early Characteristics

Some anorexics were "model children"—obedient, "perfect" little girls—often referred to as "people pleasers." Parents will comment: "She never gave us any trouble before." As children, they were well-behaved, conscientious, cooperative overachievers in school. They were quiet but manifested an underlying fear of not being respected and admired by others. Often they remember being chubby as children and being teased about it.

They may smile and give the appearance of happiness even though they are actually quite miserable. Controlling parents have told them how they should feel; hence they have difficulties in recognizing and expressing their emotions. Some anorexics show perfectionistic tendencies combined with an inability to make choices, while others fear making wrong choices.

A stressful personal experience or crisis often seems to trigger the onset of the disorder. Such crises may include parental divorce, a death in the family, family quarrels, breaking up with a boyfriend, weight loss after an illness, leaving home to go to college, and failing in important endeavors. Already as children, anorexics were fearful of change and may have experienced an aversion to unfamiliar events.

Family Patterns

There is a high probability that the sisters or mother of an anorexic also suffered from problems related to eating, food, or body preoccupation. In addition, family histories may reveal such conditions as depression, obesity, diabetes, or alcoholism. Frequently, the family is preoccupied with food and eating. However, no single identifiable family pattern is always—or even usually—associated with anorexia. Though many anorexics come from what appears to be intact families, these emphasize physical appearance and stress academics. Anorexic families tend to be overprotective and rigid; even though they experience conflict, they are unable to resolve conflicts. They also may exhibit *enmeshment,* or overlapping identities and overinvolvement of family members with each other (Banks, 1996). Rigidity and enmeshment are illustrated in the situation where all family members must always eat the same thing. If one person has a particular serving, or some special dish, everyone else must follow suit.

Theories about Causation of Anorexia Nervosa

No consensus exists about the nature and causes of anorexia nervosa, nor is there agreement about its treatment. Nevertheless, several theories have been advanced and have implications for treatment.

Psychosexual Theory.—Psychosexual theory asserts that the patient has psychosexual problems; specifically, she is unwilling to accept her role as a woman, and she fears sexual intimacy. Psychosexual theory views anorexia as a defense against the process of sexual maturation since it is associated with amenorrhea, the loss or irregularity of menstrual functions, and loss of libido. Breast development returns to an earlier, even prepubertal stage. The extremely anorexic female is infertile. Interest in the opposite sex and sexual intimacy are reduced. An emaciated and childlike appearance may also serve as a deterrent against sexual advances by men.

Social Theory.—Culture's hyper-valuation of physical appearance creates unrealistic expectations and body dissatisfaction for young women. Positive personality attributes are commonly associated with being dainty, thin, glamorous, and attractive, and society accords a wide range of preferential treatments to the model-like beauty (Muuss, 1983). Vulnerable females aspire to these exaggerated ideals of attractiveness. Early on, preschool children prefer to play with the thinner over the more opulent doll. Women's fashion magazines and the mass media relentlessly bombard consumers with highly glamorized, idealized, sexualized, hardly attainable models of feminine beauty. Physical attractiveness, as depicted by media models, is presented as the easy route to health, popularity, admiration, acceptability, love, and success. As adolescents identify with these unrealistic ideals of attractiveness, dissatisfaction with their body commonly evolves (Turner, et al., 1997). Eventually, at least for some, body image self-consciousness develops and creates a fear of becoming fat along with anxieties in regard to food and eating. Consequently three out of four adolescent girls believe that they are overweight even though they are actually quite normal. Anorexics have a compulsive desire to stay on a diet, to become thinner, and to aspire toward hardly attainable beauty ideals. Some hold on to this belief even when they have become medically underweight. Slenderness becomes a highly desirable goal that is perceived as crucial for the attainment of social, personal, sexual, and professional success (Muuss, 1983). The pervasive attitude among young women appears to be that "slenderness is next to godliness."

In addition, Americans are preoccupied with food. There is hardly a social event without an overabundance of tasty, high-caloric delicacies that the hostess continuously offers her guests. To decline her repeated, sincere offers is almost indecent or offensive. Within some families, appreciation and consumption of foods are synonymous with being obedient, accepted, and loved. Young women receive ambiguous messages about food and their bodies; women's magazines offer scrumptious recipes alongside advice on dieting or new diet plans. In the advertisements, women much more relentlessly than men are bombarded with remainders of inadequacy of their bodies, weight, nutrition, and appearance. Adolescent females, prone to succumb to such social pressures, are particularly vulnerable to these messages.

Family Systems Theory.—Minuchin, et al. (1978) believe that the conflicts exist within the family rather than the individual. Superficially, families of anorexics make a good first impression, but actually they are rigid and overprotective. They do not discuss their problems and thus are unable to define and resolve them. A major characteristic of these families is conflict avoidance. While family members may appear to be close, they actually are too concerned and too involved with each other; individual boundaries are not respected and independence in thought and action is discouraged. This phenomenon, referred to as *enmeshment,* interferes with identity formation, a critical developmental task of adolescence. Thus, the pathology within the family system is displaced on the

adolescent, who then presents the problem. Family therapy views the anorexic only as a symptom of the disturbed family system and directs the therapeutic efforts toward the whole family. In support of family systems theory, some evidence indicates that if through some other treatment method the adolescent alone recovers, the level of neuroticism in the rest of the family increases (Crisp, et al. 1974).

In addition to these common explanations, other theories have been advanced, such as the biological theory postulating a disturbance of the hypothalamus and the biological regressions hypothesis (Palmer, 1980).

Course of the Disorder

The anorexic rarely initiates seeking help on her own. To the contrary, she stubbornly refuses to acknowledge that she has a problem and needs help. Denial is common, and she may be quite inventive in explaining her appearance and behavior by developing a plausible rationale for her unusual eating patterns. She is resistant to therapy and uncooperative when made to go. She may sabotage her treatment plan at night or in secret. The earlier the diagnosis is made and the treatment begun, the better the prognosis and the less likely the need for hospitalization. The longer the symptoms persist, the more difficult the treatment becomes.

Long-range follow-up studies indicate higher mortality rates, more frequent rehospitalization, greater chances for psychological impairment (phobias and depression), and greater risks for marital and social maladjustment for anorexics than for those not afflicted. Of all known psychiatric disorders, anorexia has one of the highest mortality rates. Some deaths are the direct outcome of starvation; others result from complications of the disorder, such as cardiac arrest, while still others result from suicide. Of those who survive, one-third will remain anorexic, checking in and out of hospitals over an extended period of time, and another third will continue to walk a tightrope between recovery and relapse. Only one-third experience complete recovery (Neuman & Halvorson, 1983).

BULIMIA

Bulimia is a Greek word meaning "ox" and "hunger." The disorder was so named because the sufferer eats like a hungry ox; that is, the bulimic indulges in unrestrained eating sprees. Some experts claim that bulimia is on the increase and has reached epidemic proportions, especially on college campuses. Bulimia has only recently been recognized as a serious, separate medical and psychological problem.

Characteristics of Bulimia

A characteristic of bulimia, which distinguishes it from anorexia, is binge eating. A binge is a period of eating large quantities of food rapidly. It is a gorging process—usually carried out in secret—that can go on for hours. The bulimic consumes 1,000 to 10,000 calories at a time. Usually the binge is a response to an intense emotional experience, not the result of a strong appetite.

The fear of having to keep such mass of unwanted calories in the body leads to fear of weight gain and the desire of undoing the effect of the binge. Thus, episodes of purging follow the binge. The purge may be accomplished by a combination of several methods such as vomiting (80% to 90%), laxatives (30% to 50%), diuretics, enemas, compulsive exercising, weight reducing drugs (e.g., amphetamines), and intermittent periods of strict dieting. Eventually, a pattern of alternating periods of fasting and periods of bingeing-purging takes on a compulsive quality.

Neuman & Halvorson (1983) and DSM-IV (1994) list characteristics that are important in identifying the victim of bulimia:

1. Excessive concern with weight gain and body image
2. Periods of strict dieting followed by eating binges
3. Frequent overeating, especially when distressed
4. Planning binges or opportunities to binge
5. Bingeing on high-caloric, easily ingested, often sweet foods
6. Feeling out of control in regard to eating patterns
7. Guilt or shame following bingeing-purging episodes
8. Secretiveness about binges and purges
9. Awareness that the eating problem is abnormal
10. Disappearing after a meal for the purpose of purging
11. Self-deprecating thoughts and feelings of hopelessness and depression
12. Resistance to seeking professional help and sabotaging treatment

Age, Frequency, and Demographics

In contrast to anorexia, bulimia usually begins in late adolescence. Like anorexia, bulimia is predominantly a middle- or upper-class disorder; however, its incidence is increasing in other ethnic groups and lower-class adolescents (Graber et al., 1994) and in diverse cultures around the world (Pate, et al., 1992).

Different figures regarding the frequency of bulimia among females have been reported. DSM-IV (1994) places the prevalent figures for late adolescent and young adult females at 1% to 3%. However, the National Association of Anorexia Nervosa estimates that 15% to 20% of college women exhibit subclinical bulimic eating patterns such as gorging and vomiting. Great variations exist in the degree of the severity of the disorder. Some persons binge and purge occasionally, while for others this becomes a highly repetitive obsession, similar to addictive behavior. Regardless of severity, without treatment the condition tends to become progressively more severe.

Bulimia also occurs in men, but with much lower frequency. Only 5% to 10% of all bulimics are males; athletes for whom weight is a qualifying condition are especially vulnerable.

In particular, wrestlers are prone to indulge in purging episodes to meet weight requirements before a match.

Factors Triggering Bulimic Episodes

Bingeing may follow intense, negative emotional experiences and can emerge as a way of coping with loneliness, anger, stress, depression, or rage. It commonly is triggered by some unhappy experiences, such as academic or vocational failure, real or imagined rejection by a lover, or interpersonal problems. During exam time on college campuses, the frequency of bingeing and purging increases greatly. Bingeing becomes a symbolic but ineffective escape from the pressures of life.

Bulimia commonly starts as a more or less normal dieting behavior. After too many calories have been consumed, the urge to eliminate them quickly becomes overpowering. Eventually these calorie elimination methods become compulsive, uncontrollable, and pathological. An awareness of the uncontrollability of the behavior and the associated depression causes some bingers to seek psychiatric or medical help. The compulsive nature of the behavior shows itself in that the gorging may continue for hours unabated, long after hunger feelings have been satisfied, and may stop only when all food has been consumed or there is great discomfort. Sixty percent report that they would like to stop during the binge but cannot. Toward the end of the episode, the bulimic feels bloated, nauseated, exhausted, even physically and emotionally sick.

Vomiting after the binge brings a sense of temporary relief and even euphoria. Bulimics sometimes describe the vomiting episode in sexual terms, ascribing to it an orgasmic quality: "After vomiting I feel a pleasant release, a warm calmness, a sense of total relaxation and tiredness." However, such initial euphoria is quickly replaced by disgust, guilt, shame, and self-condemnation. "My God, I have done it again, even though I resolved to never do it again. I am worthless," or

"I hate myself. I have no control. I'm desperate." The binge episode-purge is followed by deep feelings of hopelessness, eventually depression, and even by suicidal ideation.

Associated Medical and Personality Features

Prolonged bulimic eating patterns can produce a variety of health problems, depending in part on the purging method. Frequent and repeated vomiting can lead to erosion of tooth enamel, inflamed esophagus, including tears in the esophagus and hiatal hernia, cardiac arrhythmia, EEG abnormalities, gastric ruptures, and sore throats. A relatively uncommon, but potentially dangerous, method of purging from unwanted calories is ingested syrup of ipecac, a quick way to trigger the vomit reflex. Bulimics may use it in spite of the unpleasant, sickening smell. Laxative and diuretic abuse contributes to impairment of the natural evacuation process and to colon damage, urinary infection, impairment of kidney functions, and chronic indigestion. Other medical problems include bloodshot eyes, facial puffiness, swollen glands, and overexpanded and possibly ruptured stomach. Regular bingers frequently feel tired and lethargic. Dramatic changes in blood sugar level can result from bingeing on sugary foods.

The behavior and personality patterns of bulimics include perfectionism; they may be high achievers and are often academically or vocationally successful. Their predominant fear is not only of getting fat, but of being unable to stop eating voluntarily. In other words, their greatest fear is losing control, which leads to lowered self-esteem and sometimes self-loathing. The feeling that they cannot stop eating when they should has a devastating impact on their self-esteem, and the outcome of the binge-purge episode is shame, guilt, depression, low self-esteem, and even self-hate.

As a result of the binge-purge cycle, bulimic females look surprisingly normal—neither too thin nor too heavy. They rarely look as thin and emaciated as the anorexic patient and cannot easily be identified by their general physical appearance. Their weight may fluctuate drastically over a short period of time—by as much as 10 to 20 pounds—because of the binge-purge cycle. Often, bulimics are quite attractive; however, they do not perceive themselves as such but show an exaggerated preoccupation with appearance and body image. They have negative feelings about their body and incorrectly evaluate themselves as unattractive and fat. They are extremely concerned with sexual attractiveness and may show an underlying fear of rejection.

The binge itself is surrounded by a great deal of secretiveness. Bulimics are "closet eaters," and often parents and husbands of bulimics are not aware of their loved one's condition. The bulimic's secretiveness leads to dishonesty, even in primary interpersonal relationships, a situation which precludes referral to mental health professionals. Nourishment becomes a substitute for tenderness, affection, love, sex, happiness, and fulfillment—that is, those things which the bulimic feels life owes her but which are not forthcoming. Often bulimics have no real friends; their preoccupation with food, their need for secrecy, and/or their anxiety in social situations may become a way of preventing genuine intimacy. Nevertheless, bulimics tend to be more extroverted than anorexics. The underlying fear is: "If other people get to know me, they won't like me."

Of those suffering from bulimia, 25% to 40% use alcohol, marijuana, amphetamines, and barbiturates, substances which contribute to lower self-control and reduced willpower to stay on a diet. The use of these substances may provide temporary relief from the feelings of guilt and depression that follow the binge-purge, yet ironically they lower resistance to temptation and may trigger another episode.

Bulimic Eating Patterns

The foods consumed during the binge are usually high in calories and easily consumable: ice cream, candy, cookies, bread, and cheese. Ice cream is preferred because it still tastes good when vomited. When on a binge, bulimics will eat almost anything that is available, including cake mixes and unprepared foods. The occasion is not a culinary feast, but a rapid gulping down of enormous quantities of food, often without chewing properly. The consumption of these masses of food is not a pleasurable pastime, but a dreaded compulsion; after the first couple bites, there is very little appreciation for the taste. Bingeing usually takes place in secret, alone, and hurriedly.

In extreme cases, bulimics spend as much as $70 to $100 on food in anticipation of just one binge. This may cause financial difficulties and debt. Some bulimics will even steal to support their binges. Some plan their binges in terms of both foods purchased and times when nobody is around. Because of the compulsive nature of the disorder, any interruption while bingeing may be upsetting and arouse anger. The preparation for the binge and the actual gorging may take priority over everything else, leaving little time and energy for other activities. Bulimic students may have insufficient time for studying, forcing them eventually to drop out of school.

A case study of a student's binge-purge behavior shows the compulsive nature of the disorder, the quantities of foods consumed, and the preoccupation with food:

> The first vomiting period perpetuated itself into a five-year-long habit in which I had daily planned and unplanned binges and self-induced vomiting sessions up to four times daily. I frequently vomited each of the day's three meals as well as my afternoon "snack" of three or four hamburgers, four to five enormous bowls of ice cream, dozens of cookies, bags of various potato chips, packs of Swiss cheese, two large helpings of French fries, at least two milk-shakes, and to top it off, an apple or banana followed by two or more pints of cold milk to help me vomit more easily.
>
> During the night, I sneaked back into the kitchen in the dark so I would not risk awakening any family member by turning on a light . . . Every night I wished that I could, like everyone else, eat one apple as a midnight snack and then

stop. However, every night I failed, but continuously succeeded in consuming countless bowls of various cereals, ice cream sundaes, peanut butter and jelly sandwiches, bananas. potato chips, Triscuits, peanuts, Oreos, orange juice and chocolate chip cookies. Then I tiptoed to the bathroom to empty myself. Sometimes the food did not come up as quickly as I wanted; so, in panic I rammed my fingers wildly down my throat, occasionally making it bleed from cutting it with my fingernails. Sometimes I would spend two hours in the bathroom trying to vomit; yet there were other nights when the food come up in less than three minutes. I always felt immensely relieved and temporarily peaceful after I had thrown up. There was a symbolic sense of emptying out the anxiety, loneliness and depression inside of me, as well as a sense of rebellion to hurt my body, to throw up on the people who hurt me, so to speak. (R. E. Muuss, personal communication)

Cognitive Deficiencies and Thinking Distortions of the Bulimic

Most bulimics experience cognitive distortions, some of which are related to food, weight loss expectations, eating, dieting, and body image. Some of these cognitive distortions are also applicable to anorexics. Correcting these irrational beliefs is an essential step toward changing bulimic behavior.

1. *Inaccurate nutritional information* (Loro, 1982). In general, bulimics are not adequately informed as to the requirements for a nutritional, well-balanced diet. They do not understand its importance and often totally eliminate from their diet some foods which they believe to be fattening, e.g., bread, chocolate, potatoes, and meats. They follow one-sided or bizarre dietary guidelines and jump from one fad to another. They may possess a small library of diet books.

2. *Unreasonable expectations about food and weight reduction* (Brownell & Foreyt, 1986; Loro, 1982). Bulimics hold distorted or incorrect beliefs about foods and eating. They do not realize that a calorie is a calorie regardless of whether it comes from protein, carbohydrates, or fat. Instead, they have unrealistic expectations about the "miraculous" benefits of eating large amounts of proteins and avoiding carbohydrates.

3. *Unrealistic goal setting and adherence to rigidly defined standards* (Loro, 1982). Many bulimics use a very restrictive approach to eating by keeping lists of "forbidden" items, such as ice cream, cookies, chocolate, steak, pizza—often their favorite foods. They begin by stoically denying themselves these delicacies. As they refrain from eating these items, increasingly stronger cravings emerge, which lead to feelings of deprivation. As resentment increases, forbidden foods appear more and more enticing. Eventually, usually under the influence of alcohol, marijuana, or other drugs or because of depression, stress, or frustration, bulimics break down and consume these foods, not in moderation but now in excessive quantities. The binge leads to another purging episode, which is experienced as lack of self-control, triggering, guilt feelings, self-condemnation, and often additional binge-purge cycles.

4. *Perfectionistic thinking* (Brownell & Foreyt, 1986; Burns, 1980; Loro, 1982). Bulimics establish rigidly high standards for themselves in terms of dieting or their weight loss goal, which they plan to achieve in an unreasonably short period. However, their goals are often beyond reach, making failure inevitable. They are unable to accept their appearance and continuously strive for a thinner body. Furthermore, they perceive even a slight deviation from the weight-loss regimen as devastating failure; for example, "if I deviated by as much as just one slice of bread from my diet, I would have to eat a bag of cookies, two boxes of doughnuts, several candy bars, two bags of English muffins with jam, you name it. Afterwards I vomit." The bulimic is unable to accept

minor transgressions for what they are, instead perceiving them as catastrophic. By having perfectionistic expectations that are impossible to attain, bulimics continuously set themselves up for failure, disappointment, and self-castigation.

5. *All-or-none reasoning (dichotomous thinking)* (Brownell & Foreyt, 1986; Burns, 1980; Loro, 1982). Binge eaters tend to categorize along all-or-none, black/white, yes/no lines. Thought and actions tend toward the extreme, as in the case of the person quoted earlier for whom eating one slice of bread too many led to another binge. Patients need to learn that ambivalence is normal and that there are shades of gray. Typical all-or-none reasoning prompts such statements as "If I gain any weight, I will be fat"or "If I weigh over 100 pounds, nobody will like me" or "If I can't stick with my diet, I am a total failure." This kind of dichotomous thinking increases the fear of failure and the tendency to overreach when it does occur. Dichotomous thinking also manifests in categorizing food as having moral qualities: some are "good," such as vegetables and cottage cheese, while others are "bad," such as ice cream, cookies, and steak. Even in their approach to physical exercises, bulimics either push themselves to the point of exhaustion or do not make any effort at all. They rarely find a workable position in which minor transgressions are tolerable. They need to learn that moderation is acceptable.

6. *Egocentric view of the world (personalization)* (Brownell & Foreyt, 1986; Garner, et al., 1982). A prevalent belief among adolescents, but especially pronounced among bulimics, is the feeling that everybody is watching them and knows their thoughts. Believing they are being observed, they become preoccupied with what they believe others think of them; they experience pervasive anxiety that their bingeing and purging will be discovered. For example: "Two people laughed and whispered something to each other when I walked by. They were probably saying that I looked unattractive. I have gained three pounds" (Garner, et al., 1982, p. 16). For the bulimic, self-worth is dependent on the achievement of weight loss goals and on the opinion of others. The bulimic must learn to decenter her thinking and apply the same standards to herself that she applies to others. Her feelings toward others do not depend on their gaining or losing a couple of pounds, and she must learn that the same is true for herself. If asked "Does your love for others depend on their gaining or losing a couple of pounds?" the typical reply is "no, of course not." The bulimic must learn to apply her compassionate approach for others to herself.

7. *Unfounded beliefs and superstitions* (Brownell & Foreyt, 1986; Garner, et al., 1982). The superstitious person is convinced that if the first event occurs, the second event will inevitably follow. Many such unfolded associations can be found in the cognitive distortions of the bulimic. For example, "If I eat the forbidden foods, I will gain pounds." In fact, even though only a limited amount of food was consumed, the bulimic believes she will be grossly fat.

8. *Overgeneralization* (Burns, 1980; Neuman & Halvorson, 1983). The bulimic who deviates from her diet tends to overgeneralize: "I can't stay on my diet. I'll never get better. My eating will never improve." As a result of such overgeneralized thinking, the bulimic incorrectly assumes that she has only a narrow margin for success and fears that she will never improve. A further step in that kind of reasoning leads to the overgeneralization that because everything is hopeless anyway, even trying is useless.

9. *Disturbed affect.* Bulimics have problems understanding their emotions and expressing them appropriately. This may be due to social isolation and superficial interpersonal interactions. Parents may have told them as children what they should feel, thus

inhibiting and distorting their true feelings. Out of touch with their feelings, they may suffer from an inability to express appropriately their anger and aggression or may have difficulties asserting themselves. The binge may be a substitute for the expression of anger; in fact, frustrating or anger-arousing situations often precede the binge episode. Bulimics, however, are not aware of this relationship. For them, bingeing seems to numb all feelings.

10. *The negative filter.* According to Beck (1976), the *negative filter* is a cognitive distortion through which the patient screens out positive experiences and successes. Actual accomplishments and achievements are evaluated as unimportant and not utilized for the development of a positive self-concept. Instead, the attention is directed toward failures which are evaluated as important. Since the bulimic has thus preprogrammed herself for failure, the negative filter exaggerates these experiences, while consistently discounting her successes.

THE TREATMENT OF ANOREXIA NERVOSA AND BULIMIA

The problem of therapy—just as with alcoholics—is that little can be done unless the patient admits she needs help and cooperates in her treatment. Without the patient's cooperation, almost nothing can be accomplished. However, even if she realizes that she may need help, her need for secrecy and her pathological fear of becoming fat tend to outweigh the distress and discomfort of her eating problem. Helping her to understand that fact might be the first step in treatment. To create treatment motivation may be very difficult since the patient does not fully understand the tragic absurdity of her own eating pattern, has developed distorted cognitive rationalizations, and is quite secretive about it all and less than frank in expressing what she does know. Both anorexic and bulimic patients actively resist treatment. Pressure from family members, friends, and relatives to seek help or to change

eating patterns is stubbornly resisted and often leads to animosity and increased secretiveness. Such well-meaning "intruders" initially are perceived as tormenters and persecutors. Only later, after treatment succeeds, will she appreciate that they were trying to help her.

Therapists do not agree on an ideal treatment for anorexia nervosa and bulimia, and limited research information exists on the effectiveness of various treatment modalities. Anorexia and bulimia are unique in that they are simultaneously psychological and medical disorders. Hence, disagreement even exists as to which professional group should treat the disorders. While some experts favor psychological intervention, others place emphasis on medical intervention, which may be more desirable if the patient cannot tolerate the idea that she suffers from a psychological problem. However, the major treatment modalities used for bulimia are similar to those used with anorexic patients.

Hospitalization, Including Intravenous Feeding.—In severe cases of anorexia nervosa, when intravenous feeding and constant supervision are required, hospitalization is the first step in the treatment process. It may include concurrent psychotherapy or family therapy. In extreme cases where physical danger exists, the anorexic is force-fed through a stomach tube. According to Neuman and Halvorson (1983), the following conditions indicate a need for hospitalization: extreme weight loss and emaciation, prolonged depression, suicidal ideation, alcohol and drug abuse, a general inability to cope with life stress, and physical side effects, such as dehydration or electrolyte imbalance. In many programs, some limitation of physical activities is part of the treatment. Restoration of normal body weight and the consumption of a balanced diet at regular mealtimes without supervision is the goal. The hospital can provide the necessary restrictions, structure, and supervision to reteach healthy nutrition and eating habits.

Hospitalization is less common for bulimics because they exhibit fewer dramatic and life-threatening symptoms, such as emaciation or extremely low body weight. However, hospitalization may be indicated if the patient vomits 10 or more times per day or continues to sabotage her treatment plan in secret. In the hospital, the patient is denied the opportunity to binge and to vomit secretly or use laxatives, and her behavior can be regulated and the treatment plan monitored. Psychiatric and medical treatment can be coordinated so that they supplement each other.

Psychotherapy, Especially Cognitive Therapy. Cognitive therapy, in which the therapist identifies and disputes the cognitive distortions, is an especially promising treatment. Such an approach concentrates on eliminating the adolescent's incorrect, irrational, and self-defeating cognitions and beliefs about foods, health, body image, and self. Especially significant for therapy are the irrational demands in the form of "should" and "must" which the patient makes on herself and others. Changing such neurotic beliefs is an important step in modifying behavior. A major therapeutic task is challenging the "anorexic rhetoric," which consists of irrational and unproven assumptions (Piazza, et al., 1983). Simultaneously, cognitive therapy—through self-assertiveness and social skills training—can foster the development of positive social attitudes and a positive self-concept.

Family Therapy.—Family therapy is especially indicated with the younger—frequently anorexic-patient who still lives with her parents. Often, the parents themselves have unmet dependency and security needs. The adolescent's behavior is a response to family needs that interfere with her own movement toward independence, individuation, and autonomy (Goldstein, 1981). Family therapy may start with a brief hospital stay for the anorexic patient. The aim of family therapy is not just to restore the weight and modify the eating behavior of the adolescent, but to change the structure of the family by establishing clearer intergenerational boundaries and helping the adolescent in developing a personal identity, independence, and autonomy—and helping other family members to accept and encourage these new attributes.

Group Therapy.—Group therapy may be especially appropriate for patients when family therapy cannot be provided. Seeing that others have similar eating problems and being able to openly share the "secret" with the group can be a source of great relief. Discussing experiences with a role model of a former bulimic who has overcome her difficulties can have a tremendous therapeutic value. In addition, since the bulimic is highly vulnerable and may not be able to cope alone with the temptation to binge, group members through personal or telephone contact can provide a vital support system.

Behavior Therapy.—Behavior theory assumes that eating patterns have been learned and therefore can be unlearned. Behavior modification has been very successful in initially helping to regulate and normalize the patient's eating habits. Therapy focuses on the extinction of undesirable eating patterns and the reinforcement of desirable eating patterns. It involves the establishment of behavioral contingencies, that is, the agreement, often contractually defined, between certain desirable behaviors on the adolescent's part (e.g., maintaining a certain body weight, eating three meals a day without purging, daily consumption of the basic food groups, limiting exercises, and abstaining from the use of laxatives) and specific reinforcements (e.g., money, privileges, or other rewards). These contingencies are in the form of "if, then" statements. Ideally, but depending on the motivational factors and age, these contingency statements can be defined by the adolescent within reasonable limits.

If no reinforcement can be identified for an obstinate adolescent, it may become necessary to introduce aversive contingencies (e.g., "if your body weight drops below 85 pounds, then hospitalization will follow" or "intravenous feeding will be resumed.")

Obviously numerous other methods of treatment, such as psychoanalysis and psychotropic drugs, have been applied to the intricacies of this psychological/medical problem.

REFERENCES

Banks, C. G. (1996). "There is no fat in heaven": Religious asceticism and the meaning of anorexia nervosa. *Ethos, 24,* 107–135.

Beck, A. (1976). *Cognitive therapy and the emotional disorders.* New York: International University Press.

Brownell, K. D., & Foreyt, J. P. (Eds.). (1986). *Handbook of eating disorders.* New York: Basic Books.

Burns, D. (1980, November). The perfectionist's script for self-defeat. *Psychology Today,* 34–52.

Crisp, A. H., Harding, B., & McGuinness, B. (1974). Anorexia nervosa: Psychoneurotic characteristics of parents: Relationship to prognosis. *Journal of Psychosomatic Research, 18,* 167–173.

Diagnostic and Statistical Manual of Mental Disorders (4th ed.). (1994). Washington, DC: American Psychiatric Association.

Garner, D. M., Garfinkel, P. E., & Bemis, K. M. (1982). A multidimensional psychotherapy for anorexia nervosa. *International Journal of Eating Disorders, 1,* (Winter), 3–46.

Goldstein, M. J. (1981). Family factors associated with schizophrenia and anorexia nervosa. *Journal of Youth and Adolescence, 10,* 455–471.

Graber, J., Brooks-Gunn, J., Paikoff, R., & Warren, M. (1994). Prediction of eating disorders: An 8-year study of adolescent girls. *Developmental Psychology, 30,* 823–834.

Loro, A. D. (1982, August). Cognitive problems with social implications in a bulimarexic woman. Paper presented at the 90th Annual Convention of the American Psychological Association, Washington, DC.

Minuchin, S., Rosman, B. L., & Baker, L. (1978). *Psychosomatic families: Anorexia nervosa in context.* Cambridge, MA: Harvard University Press.

Muuss, R. E. (1983, August 24). Das körperliche Erscheinungsbild: Vorteil oder Behinderung. Vortrag beim international Herbst-Seminar-Kongress für Sozialpädiatrie, Brixen, Italy.

Neuman, P. A., & Halvorson, P. A. (1983). *Anorexia nervosa and bulimia.* New York: Van Nostrand Reinhold.

Palmer, R. L. (1980). Anorexia nervosa: A guide for sufferers and their families. New York: Penguin Books.

Pate, J. E., Pumariega, A. J., Hester, C., & Garner, D. M. (1992). Cross-cultural patterns in eating disorders: A review. *Journal American Academy of Child and Adolescent Psychiatry, 31,* 802–809.

Piazza, E., Rollins, N., & Lewis, F. S. (1983). Measuring severity and change in anorexia nervosa. *Adolescence, 18,* 293–305.

Turner, S., Hamilton, H., Jacobs, M., Angood, L., & Dwyer, D. (1997). The influence of fashion magazines on the body image satisfaction of college women. *Adolescence, 32,* 603–614.

STREET YOUTH IN LOS ANGELES: PROFILE OF A GROUP AT HIGH RISK FOR HUMAN IMMUNODEFICIENCY VIRUS INFECTION

MICHELE D. KIPKE, PhD; SUSAN O'CONNOR, MPH; RAY PALMER, MA; RICHARD G. MACKENZIE, MD
Adolescence Medicine, Children's Hospital Los Angeles

Inner-city, street youth are increasingly being recognized as a population at high risk for a wide range of physical and mental health problems.[1-4] This population is largely composed of out-of-school and unemployed youths, many of whom are involved in the juvenile justice system, runaway or homeless, gang involved, and/or involved in the drug dealing and street prostitution subcultures. Previously cited findings suggest that these adolescents are more likely to be sexually active and to have had sexual intercourse at an earlier age,[5-7] to have had a greater number of sexual partners,[5,7-9] to have elevated rates of unintended pregnancies,[10] sexually transmitted diseases (STDs),[1,11,12] and alcohol and other drug abuse,[2,13-15] and to be involved in injecting drug use (IDU).[15,16] Contraceptive use, including the use of condoms during sexual intercourse, is the exception rather than the norm in this population.[5,17]

Current trends suggest that youths who live in urban settings,[18] particularly out-of-school and runaway, homeless youth, are at increased risk for infection with the human immunodeficiency virus (HIV).[19] Early in the epidemic, youths in New York City (NY) were disproportionately affected.[20] While New Yorkers aged 13 to 21 years

accounted for only 3% of all adolescents nationwide, they represented 20% of the nation's adolescents with acquired immunodeficiency syndrome by 1989.[21] Since that time, HIV-seropositive adolescents have been identified throughout the country.[22,23] However, rates are still reportedly high among street youths found in urban settings. Of the 750,000 to 1.5 million youths who runaway from their homes each year,[24] an estimated 4% to 6% are currently HIV infected.[25] These youths are known to congregate in urban settings, such as Los Angeles, Calif, San Francisco, Calif, San Diego, Calif, Boston, Mass, and New York City. Seroprevalence studies conducted in New York City[25] and San Francisco[26] report seroprevalence rates of 5.3% and 8.2%, respectively. Among HIV-infected youth, aged 12 to 23 years, who received care at a medical center in Los Angeles, 51% reported having been homeless, 52% had engaged in "survival sex" (i.e., the exchange of sexual favor for money, food, a place to stay, clothes, and/or drugs), 53% had an alcohol or other drug abuse problem, 19% had injected drugs, and 49% had been sexually abused.[27] Among HIV-infected youths receiving care at a medical center in Bronx, NY, 18% reported having been homeless, 30% reported having engaged in survival sex, and 36% reported having been incarcerated.[28]

To date, few studies have been conducted to evaluate urban street youths' involvement in

From *Archives of Pediatric and Adolescent Medicine,* 1995, *149,* 513–519. Copyright © 1995 by the American Medical Association. Reprinted with permission.

sexual and drug use behaviors. Existing studies have relied on convenience sampling techniques, which may underestimate the degree to which these youths are engaging in the kinds of behaviors that put them at risk for HIV infection. Numerous studies have surveyed high school and college students,[29–31] although these students, by virtue of the fact that they are attending school, may be at relatively lower risk than their out-of-school peers. Thus, in the end, we know little about the out-of-school youth population who may be at even greater risk through their contact with the street subculture. Studies conducted with incarcerated youths can report findings only for those youths who committed offenses for which they were caught, therefore providing limited information about the larger group of youths who are involved in illegal activities. Furthermore, findings from survey studies with runaway and homeless youths may underestimate their degree of risk given that they tend to recruit youths from shelters and drop-in centers.[17,32,33] The findings from these studies can be generalized only to those youths who are willing to use such services, not the estimated 65% of runaway, homeless youths who are living on the streets and not using shelter services.[34]

The purpose of this study was to conduct epidemiologic research to characterize an urban street youth population, their use of drugs, and their involvement in HIV risk-related sexual and drug use behaviors. Rather than rely on convenience sampling techniques, we used a probability sampling strategy to recruit youths from both shelter and drop-in settings and street and natural hangout locations. This study was conducted in the Hollywood area of Los Angeles, an area with a large street youth subculture where runaway, homeless youths are known to congregate.

RESULTS

Sample Characteristics

Youths recruited into the study ranged in age from 13 to 23 years, with nearly 80% falling between the ages of 16 to 21 years (Table 1). The majority of these youths were male (74%), with the males being significantly older than the females (P <.001). More than half (52%) were white, and 48% were from ethnic minority groups: black (22%), Latino (15%), Native American (6%), Asian/Pacific Islanders (2%), or another ethnic minority group (3%). Of the 409 youths recruited, 295 (72%) reported living in a shelter, squat, or abandoned building at the time of the interview, and 82% of those reported having been homeless for 2 or more months. Of the 114 youths who reported having a place to stay at the time of the interview (i.e., with parents, other family, a boyfriend or girlfriend), 82% reported having lived on the streets, in a shelter, squat, or abandoned building at some time during the previous 12 months. Thus, this sample can be described as largely homeless and/or precariously housed. Fourteen percent of the sample reported being affiliated with a gang, 15% were currently employed, 20% reported being actively involved in drug dealing, and 9% reported having been in jail within the previous 12 months. Forty-two percent of the males reported being either bisexual or homosexual, compared with 27% of the females (P <.001).

Sexual Behaviors

Of the total sample, 283 (70%) reported being sexually active at the time of the interview (sexual intercourse within the previous 30 days). Of these youths, 68% reported having engaged in oral intercourse 63% in vaginal intercourse, and 26% in anal intercourse. The majority of the sexually active youths (68%) had engaged in more than one type of sexual intercourse—e.g., only 12% had engaged exclusively in oral intercourse, 20% had engaged only in vaginal intercourse, and one person had engaged exclusively in anal intercourse. Forty-three percent of the sample (46% of males and 32% of females; P=.01) reported having ever engaged in survival sex. Of the youths who reported having engaged in survival sex, 48% reported exchanging sex for food or a place to stay, 22% for drugs, and 82% for money. When these youths were asked when they had last engaged in

TABLE 1
Demographic Profile of the Study Sample (N=409)

| | No. (%) | | | |
	Total	Males	Females	*P**
Age, y				
13–15	**36** (9)	21 (7)	15(14)	.02
16–18	**147**(36)	95(31)	52(49)	.001
19–21	**178**(44)	143(47)	35(33)	.01
22–23	**48**(12)	44(15)	4 (4)	.003
Gender				
F	**106**(26)			
M	**303**(74)			
Race				
Black	**89**(22)	65(22)	24(23)	.80
Latino	**60**(15)	46(15)	14(13)	.62
White	**213**(52)	155(51)	58(55)	.53
Asian	**9** (2)	7 (2)	2 (2)	.80
Native American	**25** (6)	20 (7)	5 (5)	.48
Other	**13** (3)	10 (3)	3 (2)	.94
Residence status				
Homeless	**295**(72)	213(70)	82(77)	. . .
Not homeless	**114**(28)	90(30)	24(23)	.16
Length of time homeless				
<2 mo	**55**(19)	35(16)	20(24)	.14
2 mo-1 y	**100**(34)	76(36)	24(28)	.24
<1 y	**140**(48)	100(48)	40(48)	.97
Sexual orientation				
Heterosexual	**243**(62)	167(57)	76(73)	.005
Bisexual	**67**(17)	45(16)	22(21)	.18
Homosexual	**85**(22)	79(27)	6 (6)	.001
Survival sex				
No	**232**(57)	161(54)	71(68)	. . .
Yes	**173**(43)	139(46)	34(32)	.01
Tested for human immunodeficiency virus†				
No	**88**(22)	64(22)	24(23)	. . .
Yes	**308**(78)	227(78)	81(77)	.85

*Reflects *P* value of χ^2 test comparing males and females.
†The total does not equal 409 because of missing values.

survival sex, 16% indicated that it had been within the past 7 days, 22% within the past 30 days, and 32% within the past 6 months. Homosexual and bisexual males were significantly more likely to have ever engaged in survival sex (*P* <.001).

Among these sexually active youths, the average (±SD) number of sexual partners within the past 30 days was 11.7 ± 30.2, with 52% reporting one partner, 24% reporting two to five partners, and 24% reporting more than five sexual partners. Nearly 8% of the sexually active youths had had more than 50 sexual partners during the previous 30 days. Forty-one percent of the sexually active youths reported sexual relations with a primary sexual partner only, 16% with a primary and other partners, and 41% with other partners only. Youths with both primary and other sexual partners or with other partners only

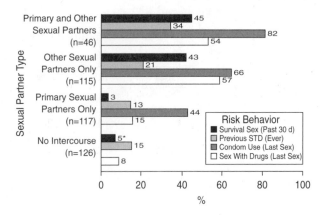

FIGURE 1   Sexual Behaviors and Partner Type Within the Past 30 Days.
STD indicates sexually transmitted disease; asterisk, inaccurate reporting of no sexual activity and recent involvement in survival sex.

were significantly more likely to be engaging in survival sex (P <.001), to have been previously infected with an STD (P <.01), and to have been high on drugs or alcohol the last time they had sexual intercourse (P <.001) (Figure 1). Youths with other sexual partners were significantly more likely to report having used a condom during oral, vaginal, and anal intercourse (P <.001).

Across the three different types of sexual intercourse (oral, vaginal, and anal), youths were less likely to use a condom during their last sexual encounter with a primary sexual partner than with other sexual partners. Subjects were significantly less likely to report condom use during oral and vaginal intercourse with a primary partner than with other partners (21% vs 43% for oral intercourse and 52% vs 73% for vaginal intercourse, respectively) (Figure 2). These same trends were observed across gender, ethnicity, and homeless status. Youths were significantly more likely to report using a condom if they had a condom at the time of the survey (P <.001). Furthermore, youths who reported that they usually carry a condom with them were significantly more likely to report condom use during oral (P <.003), vaginal (P <.001), and anal (P <.03) intercourse.

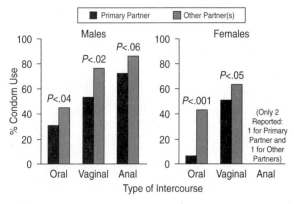

FIGURE 2   Rates of Condom Use by Sexual Partner at the Last Sexual Encounter.

Drug Use Behaviors

Alcohol and other drug use was highly prevalent (Table 2). Nearly all of the youths (79%) reported having used alcohol at some time in their lives, and 50% of those who had ever used alcohol reported use within the past week. Among users, marijuana (55%), methamphetamine or speed (62%), and crack cocaine (38%) were clearly the drugs of choice within the previous 30 days. Other commonly used drugs included cocaine, LSD, and heroin. With the use of the

TABLE 2
Rates of Lifetime and Recent Substance Abuse and Injecting Drug Use (N=395)

	No. (%)	
	Lifetime Use	Recent Use (Past 30 d)*
High risk, high dependency	**310**(79)	**201**(65)
Coke	212(54)	61(29)
Crack	169(43)	64(38)
Speed	269(68)	167(62)
Speedball	93(24)	15(16)
Heroin	94(24)	23(25)
Opium	77(19)	5 (7)
Phencyclidine	15 (4)	5(33)
Alcohol	310(79)	156(50)†
High risk, low dependency	**152**(39)	**24**(16)
Mescaline	65(16)	5(8)
Ecstasy	131(33)	21(16)
Low risk, low dependency	**359**(91)	**198**(55)
Lysergic acid diethylamide	265(67)	81(31)
Mushrooms	190(48)	29(15)
Peyote	82(21)	12(15)
Marijuana	305(77)	167(55)†
Injecting drug use	118(30)	68(58)
Needle use		
Sharing	70(59)‡	32(47)§
Cleaning	39(33)‡	6(18)‖

*Percentages are calculated with the number of recent users (past 30 days) as the numerator and lifetime users as the denominator.
†Denotes use within the past week.
‡Of those who reported lifetime injecting use.
§Of those who reported injecting drug use within the past 30 days.
‖Of those who reported sharing needles within the past 30 days.

risk-dependency spectrum described above, nearly 65% of drug-using youths reported recent use of drugs that fell within the HRHD (high risk, high dependency) category, 16% reported use of drugs that fell within the HRLD (high risk, low dependency) category, and 55% reported use of drugs that fell within the LRLD (low risk, low dependency) category. Injecting drug use and needle sharing were also found to be prevalent among the study sample. Thirty percent of the total sample reported having ever injected drugs; 58% of these youths reported IDU within the previous 30 days. Among the youths who had ever injected drugs, 59% reported having ever shared needles. Among the injectors, 47% reported having shared needles within the previous 30 days, yet only 18% reported having cleaned their needles before use.

High-risk sexual and drug user behaviors were found to be significantly intercorrelated. Youths who used HRHD and HRLD drugs were found to be 2.9 times more likely to report having multiple sexual partners (50% and 24%, respectively; $P < .001$) than youths who used LRLD drugs or no drugs at all (Table 3). Similarly, youths who used HRHD and HRLD drugs were nearly 3.6 times more likely to have been high on alcohol or drugs the last time they had sex and 2.2 times more likely to have engaged in survival sex than youths who used LRLD drugs or no drugs.

TABLE 3

Condom Use and Other Risk Behaviors by Involvement in Lifetime Drug Use Patterns*

Risk Behavior	% of Subjects		Univariate†			Multivariate‡		
	HRHD/ HRLD (n=145 [37%])	LRLD/ No Drugs (n=81 [21%])	OR	CI	P	OR	CI	P
Condom use (at last sex)	36	46	0.7	0.5–1.0	.29	0.9	0.52–1.4	.76
Anal	71	86	0.4	0.2–1.0	.28	0.8	0.47–1.3	.74
Oral	24	31	0.8	0.5–1.3	.61	0.9	0.45–1.8	.83
Vaginal	58	70	0.6	0.4–1.0	.32	0.8	0.43–1.6	.73
Sex while high (at last sex)	44	15	3.6	2.5–6.1§	<.001	3.8	2.5–5.7‖	.01
Primary partner	28	13	2.6	1.4–4.8¶	.02	3.3	1.3–8.5¶	.02
Other partner	60	19	4.9	2.9–8.6§	<.001	4.4	2.2–8.8§	<.001
Survival sex (ever)	54	34	2.2	1.7–3.0§	<.001	3.8	2.3–6.2§	<.001
Multiple partners#	50	24	2.9	2.2–3.9§	<.001	1.5	1.1–2.3¶	.05
Previous STD	26	11	2.5	1.6–3.8‖	.005	1.5	1.0–2.5¶	.05
Tested for HIV	86	69	2.5	1.8–3.6‖	.01	2.6	1.6–4.4¶	.03

*HRHD indicates high risk, high dependency; HRLD, high risk, low dependency; LRLD, low risk, low dependency; OR, odds ratio; CI, confidence interval; STD, sexually transmitted disease; and HIV, human immunodeficiency virus.
†Unadjusted analysis logistic regression where the dependent variable is drug use (HRHD/HRLD=1 and LRLD/no drugs=0).
‡Multiple logistic regression adjusted for age, gender, race, sexual orientation, and length of time homeless.
§P <.001.
‖P <.01.
¶P <.05.
#Sexually active with primary and/or other partners (coded 1) vs sexually active with a primary partner or not sexually active (coded 0). For dichotomous independent variables, if risk behavior was present, the variable was coded with a 1; otherwise the value was 0.

Youths who used high-risk drugs were also 2.5 times more likely to have had a previous STD. Interestingly, these youths were 1.2 times more likely to have been tested for HIV.

COMMENT

Despite efforts to overcome sampling limitations of previously reported studies, there are some limitations to this study. First, the findings from this study rely on subjects' self-report, which cannot be independently verified. The levels of reported involvement in risk-related sexual (e.g., survival sex, unprotected intercourse) and drug use behaviors (e.g., IDU, needle sharing) may actually underestimate the actual prevalence given that these data were collected by a previ-

ously unknown interviewer. A second limitation is that the data are cross-sectional and therefore do not lend themselves to interpretation about the temporal relationship between subjects' lifestyle (e.g., homelessness) and other risk variables explored by this study. Finally, given the limited use of probability sampling techniques used to conduct research with this population, it is unclear how generalizable these findings are to street youth populations from other cities (e.g., Boston, New York, or San Francisco). This sample, however, is likely to be representative of the street youth population within the target geographic area. Future research should employ street-based probability sampling techniques to evaluate similarities and differences among street youth populations from different geographic areas.

Despite these limitations, the study provides evidence that HIV risk-related sexual and drug use behaviors are particularly prevalent within the street youth population. Our findings also suggest that previous research conducted with street youths has underestimated their involvement in HIV risk-related behaviors and therefore their risk for HIV infection. While it had previously been reported that from 26% to 30% of runaway, homeless youths are engaged in survival sex,[1,32,37] in this study, 43% of the sample reported involvement in this high-risk activity. Furthermore, while previous studies report elevated rates of alcohol and other drug abuse among runaway, homeless youths,[15] the rates reported herein far exceed those reported. Interestingly, the findings suggest that high-risk sexual behaviors (survival sex, multiple sexual partners, lack of condom use) and drug use behaviors (IDU, needle sharing, sex while high) cluster with one another to form an HIV high-risk profile. This would suggest that these youths are at particularly high risk for HIV and could become infected from risky sexual or drug use behaviors. Another important finding is the difference in condom use reported with primary and other sexual partners. While these youths perceive there to be a greater need for use of condoms with their sexual partners with whom they have less trusting, intimate relationships, they mistakenly believe there to be less need to use condoms with their primary partners. Thus, these youths would appear to have a false sense of security or believe that they are at lower risk for becoming HIV infected from sexual partners with whom they have intimate, trusting relationships. Condom use during anal intercourse was consistently high with primary and other sexual partners, suggesting that street outreach as well as other types of interventions (e.g., the media) have been effective in alerting these youths to the risk associated with involvement in unprotected anal intercourse.

Substance abuse and multiple sexual partners were significantly associated with a previous diagnosis of an STD. Thus, an STD, when seen in a clinical setting, may be a marker for other high-risk sexual and drug use behaviors. Finally, given that these risk-related behaviors were found to cluster, the presence of any one could suggest the need for HIV testing and efforts toward risk reduction of risk-related sexual and drug use behaviors.

The fact that rates of risk-related sexual and drug use behaviors were so much higher than those reported in other studies suggests the need for additional research with urban, out-of-school, street youths. The use of probability sampling techniques is clearly needed to gain a better estimate of risk within the target population. These findings also suggest the need for public health policies and a national agenda to respond to the special needs of this population. Their elevated levels of risk suggests the need for specialty services that are accessible, affordable, and culturally relevant. To curtail the spread of HIV among this generation, new and innovative educational promotions and preventive interventions will need to be developed and targeted to this growing yet largely hidden population.

REFERENCES

1. Yates GL, MacKenzie, R, Pennbridge, J, Cohen E. A risk profile comparison of runaway and non-runaway youth. *Am J Public Health.* 1988;81:208–210.

2. Robertson MJ. *Homeless Youth: Patterns of Alcohol Use.* Berkeley, Calif: Alcohol Research Group, School of Public Health, University of California at Berkeley; 1989.

3. Institute of Medicine. *Research on Children and Adolescents With Mental, Behavioral, and Developmental Disorders: Mobilizing a National Initiative.* Washington, DC: National Academy Press; 1989.

4. Council on Scientific Affairs. Health status of detained and incarcerated youth. *JAMA.* 1990;263:987–991.

5. Nadar PR, Wexler DB, Patterson TL, et al. Comparison of beliefs about AIDS among urban, suburban, incarcerated, and gay adolescents. *J Adolesc Health Care.* 1989;10:413–418.

6. Baker C, Morris R, Huscroft S, et al. Survey of sexual behaviors as HIV risk factors in incarcerated minors. In: Program and abstracts of the VII International Conference on AIDS; June 1991; Florence, Italy. Abstract M.D. 4098.

7. Centers for Disease Control and Prevention. Health risk behavior among adolescents who do and do not attend school—United States, 1992. *MMWR Morb Mortal Wkly Rep.* 1994;43:129–132.

8. DiClemente RJ, Lanier MM, Horan PF, Lodico M. Comparison of AIDS knowledge, attitudes, and behaviors among incarcerated adolescents and a public school sample in San Francisco. *Am J Public Health.* 1991;81:628–630.

9. Rotheram-Borus MJ, Koopman C, Ehrhardt AA. Homeless youth and HIV infection. *Am Psychol.* 1991;46:1188–1197.

10. Deisher RW, Farrow JA, Hope K, Litchfield C. The pregnant adolescent prostitute. *AJDC.* 1989;143:1162–1165.

11. Alexander-Rodriquez T, Vermund ST. Gonorrhea and syphilis in incarcerated urban adolescents: prevalence and physical signs. *Pediatrics.* 1987;80:561–564.

12. Fullilove MT, Golden E, Fullilove RE, et al. Crack cocaine use and high-risk behaviors among sexually active black adolescents. *J Adolesc Health.* 1993;14:295–300.

13. Stricof RL, Novick LF, Kennedy J, Weisfuse IB. HIV seroprevalence of adolescents at Covenant House/under 21 in New York City. Read before the American Public Health Association Conference; October 1988; Boston, Mass.

14. Fullilove RE, Fullilove MT, Bowser B, Gross S. Crack users: the new AIDS risk group? *Cancer Detect Prev.* 1990;14:363–368.

15. Kipke MD, Montgomery S, MacKenzie RG. Substance use among youth seen at a community-based health clinic. *J Adolesc Health.* 1993;14:289–294.

16. Hudson RA, Petty BA, Freeman AC, et al. Adolescent runaways' behavioral risk factors, knowledge about AIDS and attitudes about condom usage. Read before the V International Conference on AIDS; June 1989; Montreal, Quebec.

17. Anderson J, Freese T, Pennbridge J. Sexual risk behavior and condom use among street youth in Hollywood. *Fam Plan Perspect.* 1994;26:22–25.

18. Burke DS, Brundage JF, Goldenbaum M. et al. Human immunodeficiency virus infection in teenagers: seroprevalence among applicants for US military services. *JAMA.* 1990;263:2074.

19. Kipke MD, Hein K. Acquired immunodeficiency syndrome (AIDS) in adolescents. In: Schydlower M, Shafer M, eds. *Adolescent Medicine: State of the Art Reviews.* Philadelphia, Pa: Hanley & Belfus Inc; 1990;1:429–449.

20. Hein K: Lessons from New York City on HIV/AIDS in adolescents. *N Y State J Med.* 1990;90:143–146.

21. Vermund SV, Hein K, Gayle H, Cary JM, Thomas PA, Drucker E. Acquired immunodeficiency syndrome among adolescents: case surveillance profiles in New York City and the rest of the United States. *AJDC.* 1989;143:1120–1225.

22. Hein K. Fighting AIDS in adolescents. *Issues Sci Technol.* 1991;7:67–72.

23. Centers for Disease Control. *HIV/AIDS Surveillance Report.* Atlanta, Ga: Centers for Disease Control; July 1992:1–18.

24. National Network of Runaway and Youth Services Inc. *To Whom Do They Belong?* Washington, DC: National Network of Runaway and Youth Services, Inc; 1985.

25. Stricof RL, Kennedy JT, Nattell TC, Weisfuse IS, Novick LF. HIV seroprevalence in a facility for runaway and homeless adolescents. *Am J Public Health.* 1991;81:50–53.

26. Schalwitz J, Goulart M, Dunnigan K, Flannery D. Prevalence of sexually transmitted diseases (STD) and HIV in a homeless youth medical clinic in San Francisco. In: Program and abstracts of the Sixth International Conference on AIDS; June 23, 1990; San Francisco, Calif. Abstract 231.

27. Belzer M, Marcus B. *Medical Course of HIV Infection in Youth.* Los Angeles, Calif: Society for Adolescent Medicine; 1994.

28. Futterman D, Hein K, Reuben N, Dell R, Shaffer N. Human immunodeficiency virus-infected adolescents: the first 50 patients in a New York City program. *Pediatrics.* 1993;91:730–735.

29. Gayle HD, Keeling RP, Garcia-Tunon M, et al. Prevalence of the human immunodeficiency virus among university students. *N Engl J Med.* 1990;323:1538–1541.

30. D'Angelo LJ, Getson PR, Luban NL, Gayle HD. Human immunodeficiency virus infection in

urban adolescents: can we predict who is at risk? *Pediatrics.* 1991;88:982–986.

31. DiClemente RJ. The emergence of adolescents as a risk group for human immunodeficiency virus infection. *Pediatr AIDS HIV Infect.* 1990;1:10–35.

32. Rotheram-Borus MJ, Meyer-Bahlburg HFL, Rosario M, et al. Lifetime sexual behaviors among predominantly minority male runaways and gay/bisexual adolescents in New York City. *AIDS Educ Prev.* Fall 1992;suppl:34–42.

33. Rotheram-Borus MJ, Koopman C. Sexual risk behaviors, AIDS knowledge, and beliefs about AIDS among runaways. *Am J Public Health.* 1991:81:208–210.

34. Kipke MD, O'Connor SL, Palmer R, LaFrance S. Street youth, outreach and HIV risk; facing the challenge in two communities. In: Program and abstracts of the American Public Health Association Meeting; October 24, 1993; San Francisco, Calif. Abstract 3144.

35. Burnam MA, Koegel P. Methodology for obtaining a representative sample of homeless persons, the Los Angeles Skid Row Study. *Eval Rev.* 1988;12:117–152.

36. Robertson MJ, Westerfelt A, Irving P. Research note: the impact of sampling strategy on estimated prevalence of major mental disorders among homeless adults in Alameda County, CA. In: Program and abstracts of the American Public Health Association Meeting; November 12, 1991; Atlanta, Ga. Abstract 2180.

37. Pennbridge JN, Freese TE, MacKenzie RG. High-risk behaviors among male street youth in Hollywood, California. *AIDS Educ Prev.* Fall 1992;suppl:24–33.

38. Gable RS. Toward a comparative overview of dependence potential and acute toxicity of psychoactive substances used nonmedically. *Am J Drug Alcohol Abuse.* 1993;19:263–281.

PART THIRTEEN

PSYCHOSOCIAL PROBLEMS AND RISK TAKING

we get bored with the routine
and crave beauty
and excitement . . .
our attitude toward life
is come easy go easy . . .
—Don Marquis, the lesson of the month

In the poem, a moth and the poet Archy seek to understand each other. Archy is the voice of reason and maturity; the moth speaks for those youth whose philosophy is "come easy go easy" and who live in an environment where life is cheap. Especially worrisome is that juveniles at increasingly younger ages are engaging in careless acts that endanger their health and lives. The younger individuals are when these pleasures- and excitement-seeking behaviors begin, the greater the probability that they will become more permanently involved in a risk-filled lifestyle. Adolescence should be a healthy and exciting time of life; however, there are those who, like the moth, *"wad up our life into one little roll and then we shoot the roll."*

Muuss and Porton (38) review the risk-taking literature, describe well-known individual variations in the level of risk involvement, and summarize some findings regarding the frequency of the more common risk behaviors. Many individuals engage in multiple hazardous acts that seem to interact and reinforce each other. For example, a high school dropout has an increased probability of being involved in juvenile delinquency and becoming an unwed parent and substance abuser. Without implying causality or directionality, many risky acts seem to be associated with one another; e.g., the more frequently teenagers consume alcohol, the greater the probability that they also are sexually active.

Attempts to provide "stand-alone" interventions are usually unsuccessful because serious risk-taking behaviors do not occur in isolation. Effective programs provide a holistic approach that recognizes and addresses the interrelated nature of risk-related problems. The problems of risk-taking adolescents have become a public policy issue and hence are of concern to psychologists, sociologists, legislators, educators, and physicians. At-risk youth are often described in contrast to resilient individuals. Resilient adolescents may live under the same demographic risk conditions but can withstand risk temptations. Some of the well-known protective features that contribute to resilience are family connectedness, self-esteem, and positive peer and/or adult role models. Understanding what helps resilient youth not to succumb to risk temptation may provide insights for prevention and intervention.

Flannery, Vazsonyi, Torquati, and Fridrich (39) explored ethnic and gender differences in early adolescent substance abuse. To predict who was at risk, the researchers compared the potential power of interpersonal and intrapersonal domains among 6th and 7th graders in predicting substance abuse. Susceptibility to peer pressure, peer alcohol abuse, parental monitoring, family connectedness, and adolescent school adjustment were the interpersonal factors examined. Impulsivity and aggression, depression, self-efficacy, and academic achievement were the intrapersonal variables. Gender differences were apparent among both ethnic groups. Males reported that they were more aggressive than females. Although females reported being more depressed than males, depression and impulsivity are not as powerful as aggression for predicting drug use. The interpersonal variable that had the most predictive power appears to be relationships with peers who are involved in substance abuse. However, successful school adjustment correlated to low levels of involvement in substance abuse. Youngsters who are aggressive and disengaged from school and those who associate with substance-abusing peers are more likely to be substance abusers.

The investigation of Pakiz, Reinherz, and Giaconia (40) is remarkable because it follows subjects over many years to identify the early precursors of life-long antisocial behaviors. When children were as young as age 5 for males and 9 for females, their teachers could discern hostile and acting-out behaviors that would continue into later life. Low self-esteem, which is frequently observed among at-risk adolescents, appears as early as age 9 for antisocial females. Adolescents who externalize often fail to take responsibility for their actions and blame circumstances or others for their lack of achievement; they do not recognize the connection between their own lack of effort and their failure. Another well-known and strong predictor of future antisocial acts is poor school performance. Family connectedness or dysfunction is also a powerful indicator of the likelihood of future behaviors.

Evaluating which precursors of antisocial behavior were most influential in sustaining problems is essential to designing effective interventions. The finding that teachers can assess young children's problematic behavior and accurately predict future difficulties suggests the need for early prevention by way of systematic interventions in elementary school, not just in high school. This is not a new insight but was identified in a different context three centuries ago. "Of all the adult male criminals in London, not two in a hundred have entered upon a course of crime who have lived an honest life up to the age of twenty. . . . Almost all who enter a course of crime do so between the ages of eight and sixteen" (A. A. Cooper Schaftesbury, 1671–1713).

Most at-risk adolescents have some awareness of the risks involved in substance abuse, dropping out of school, unprotected sex and other antisocial acts. Their decisions to take chances are not based on what they know, but on risk calculations that overemphasize the value of momentary pleasure and excitement and undervalue long-range negative consequences. Mark Twain, when told that he could add five years to his life if he gave up smoking and drinking, is supposed to have sneered at the suggestion. "Five years without smoking and drinking are not worth living." His response serves as a powerful metaphor for the kind of risk calculations that some adolescents make when they weigh the pleasure of the moment against the payback of the future.

INCREASING RISK BEHAVIOR AMONG ADOLESCENTS

ROLF E. MUUSS AND HARRIET D. PORTON

The concept "risk-taking behavior" appears with increasing frequency in both the professional literature and the popular press. To take a risk means that one consciously chooses a behavior that is potentially dangerous to one's physical or mental health and may result in injury, disability, and even death. Some youth are careless, impulsive, sensation-seeking, and willing to take chances. The resulting behaviors, which may be spontaneous or experimental, usually bring short-term benefits, pleasure, or immediate gratification, even though they potentially pose danger for injuries, arrests, incarceration, sexually transmitted diseases, drug dependency, and other health problems.

Since such risk behavior among adolescents may lead to consequences that can be devastating, the topic has become a major educational, psychological, medical, legal, and public policy issue. Risk taking has implications not only for the individual involved but for society at large, including loss of productivity, unemployment, medical expenses, loss of life, suffering inflicted on innocent victims by drunken drivers, and casualties of inappropriate gun use. The negative outcome of risk-taking behavior impairs not only the current but, even more important, the future status of considerable segments of the

population and encompasses all socioeconomic levels. While the mortality rate of all other age groups has been declining, an increase for 15- to 25-year-olds to 95.8 per 100,000 has been reported (Irwin & Millstein, 1990). This increase in youth mortality is especially problematic since the mortality from natural causes in this age group has declined by 90% between 1933 and 1985. Without any injuries, accidents, or other health-impairing consequences of risk-taking behavior, the teens must be viewed as the healthiest period in the human life cycle. Nevertheless, the high death rate of adolescents is due to accidents and violence. Many of these violent deaths must be attributed to the consequences of self-inflicted risk or destructive behaviors: motor vehicle accidents (38%), suicide (10%), violent death and death as a result of injuries (10%), homicide (9%), drowning (4%), and fire (2%). These figures must be contrasted with the relatively low death rate of 27% for all natural causes (Gans et al., 1990). In addition to and not included in these figures, every year a surprisingly large number of those in the 17- to 24-year-old range are injured through accidents. Males experience about twice the death rate as female adolescents.

Data suggests that an increasingly larger segment of today's youth are becoming involved in risk-taking behavior. However, what is even more serious is the fact that such activity begins at earlier and earlier ages. During the second half of this century, the age at which adolescents—and now even children—begin experimenting with some of these dangerous, health-impairing behaviors has decreased significantly. Pre- and early adolescents are especially at risk since they are ever more impressionable than middle or late adolescents. Risk-enhancing experiences and influences can solidify into risk-seeking personality patterns. Ponton, author of *The Romance of Risk,* claims that the most important factor in risk taking is the teenager's own character.

INDIVIDUAL VARIATION IN RISK-TAKING BEHAVIOR

The danger, frequency, and level of involvement in risk-taking behavior show rather remarkable individual differences. On the one hand are the careful, shy, and fearful individuals who attempt to avoid virtually any behavior that is potentially dangerous. However, most youth will, under certain circumstances, engage in moderately risky acts that sometimes, even though relatively rarely, result in accidents and lead to tragic consequences. At the other extreme are the excitement-seeking, impulse-driven daredevils who by their very behavior surprise and even frighten others and appear to be willing to chance injury and death. Approximately 25% of adolescents live a lifestyle that has the potential of impairing their later adjustment and their future health, identified as "severe or dangerous risk-taking" behavior (Dryfoos, 1990). These daredevils seem to challenge repeatedly the probability of mishaps and, sooner or later, endanger themselves and sometimes even others through their behavior.

A *simulated estimation model* illustrating the magnitude of the problem was advanced by Dryfoos (1990). He classified risk-taking behaviors into four categories:

1. alcohol and drug consumption and abuse
2. unsafe sexual behavior, with the potential of STD and pregnancy
3. school-related problems: underachievement, school failure, and dropping out of school
4. antisocial and delinquent behavior: involvement in crime and violence

Approximately 50% of all adolescents in the United States are at no-risk or relatively low risk. Some may occasionally drink, but they are not involved in serious crime or unsafe sex. A moderate risk group of about 25% is involved in at least one of these risk behaviors. These adolescents are the experimenters who may try drugs or get involved, often temporarily, in minor delinquent acts. A high risk group made up of the next 15% is involved in two or three of the risk behaviors but with lower frequency and severity than the fourth group. The very high risk group (10%) is involved in most if not all high-risk behaviors; young people in this category have unprotected sex, often with multiple partners, commit serious crimes, are heavy drug users, and are unsuccessful in school (Dryfoos, 1990).

Even though youth themselves are responsible for the consequences of their sensation-seeking behavior, we still must ask: What can be done? What is actually being done? What are the social-psychological factors that trigger these risk-taking behaviors? What educational programs are most effective in reducing these behaviors? Which programs are actually effective? Can information reduce the danger of risk-taking behaviors? Why has risk-taking behavior among adolescents increased? Why are early adolescents especially vulnerable? Why are warnings from parents and teachers and labels on cigarette packages and beer bottles so ineffective?

RISK-TAKING BEHAVIOR IS NORMATIVE

An average youth normally is willing to take at least some risks under some circumstances. To understand the developmental nature of the issue, one must consider that an essential aspect of the second decade of life is to learn to make independent decisions, to take the initiative, and to experiment with a wide range of behaviors. In

---

such situations, it is almost inevitable that inexperienced and naive youth will make some inappropriate, undesirable, and even detrimental decisions that produce negative consequences. Actually, it is not possible and may not entirely be desirable to eliminate all risk-taking behavior. Therefore, some risk taking appears not only normative but may even be a desirable growth experience, especially if channeled into constructive activities under supervision. Some of the more exciting and challenging sports, such as ski jumping, hang gliding, and mountain climbing, inevitably include at least some risk, especially for the beginner. It is also important to consider that society provides models and glamorizes daring and death-defying behavior, especially in movies and on TV, which also glorify sexual conquests. Even in real-life, society admires and rewards courageous and risk-defying soldiers on the battlefield, stunt artists, circus performers, car racers, and mountain climbers.

The need for recognitions, lure of sensations, and personal development needs contribute to a willingness to try out unfamiliar and challenging patterns of behavior. Many youth feel challenged and excited when confronted with dangerous endeavors. Some are actually quite anxious to test the limits of their endurance, courage, and strength. They feel they have to prove to themselves and to others, how courageous, tough, skillful, and daring they are in facing danger. Thirty-five percent of 12th grade pupils consider it exciting to engage in an activity that is dangerous, while 45% are quite willing to take some risk to demonstrate their courage and their skillfulness.

THE INTERACTING NATURE OF VARIOUS RISKY BEHAVIORS

In the past, risk-taking behaviors were studied in isolation, and the preventive and educational programs developed to combat these problems almost always focused on one particular health-compromising behavior. For example, schools sponsored pregnancy prevention programs and drug and alcohol awareness education. In contrast to this, contemporary theory and research increasingly focus on the mutual interacting nature of adolescent risk-taking behaviors and strongly support the belief that the phenomena of risk taking must be viewed in its broader, psychosocial context.

An analysis of the risk-taking data show that many daring individuals contribute disproportionally to the risk casualties. For example, 50% of pregnant teenagers drop out of school before graduating, thus starting a cycle of poverty, unemployment, welfare dependency, and other negative consequences, not only for the young mother but also for her children. Of the youth who are imprisoned, 63% used drugs on a regular basis; 32% were under the influence of alcohol when they committed their offense, and 39% were under the influence of drugs. As Figure 1 reveals, the relationship between sexual activity level of youth and frequency of alcohol consumption is impressive.

Among 25% of suicide victims, a blood alcohol level of more than 0.10 was measured, while another 25% had lower, but still measurable blood alcohol content. Smoking cigarettes at an early age places young adolescents, especially young women, at greater risk to use drugs later and is also associated with dropping out of school. In addition, young smokers face the well-known, long-term health risks of smoking: cancer, emphysema, and heart and circulatory problems. Ketterlinus et al. (1992) could demonstrate that sexually active youth, in comparison to sexually inexperienced youth, are also more likely to be involved in many other problems: theft, personal violence, drug abuse, and school problems, to mention only a few. For males the age of first sexual intercourse (especially before their 15th birthday) is associated with other risks.

ANTECEDENT AND PREDISPOSITIONS OF JUVENILE RISK-TAKING BEHAVIOR

The emergence of new developmental tasks during the second decade of life must also be considered. Adolescents have to become independent, function autonomously, and modify

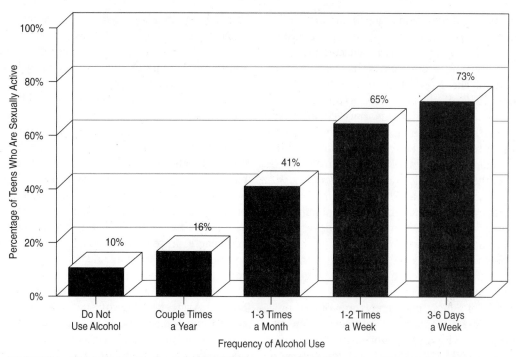

FIGURE 1   The Relationship Between Alcohol Consumption and Sexual Activity in 10th Graders.
(From S. A. Small and T. Luster, "Understanding Adolescent Sexuality and Pregnancy: An Ecological Perspective"
[Paper presented at 1990 Creating Caring Communities Conference, Michigan State University].

attachments to parents and guardians. During this period of life, they must learn to function on their own. These challenges may inspire youngsters to overassert themselves, to challenge conventional authorities, and to try out previously forbidden activities. In addition, there is an increased desire during adolescence to impress peers of both sexes to gain acceptance, recognition, social status, and admiration. These desires may lead to an overidentification with the peer group. While this accelerates the process of gaining independence from parents, it often simultaneously creates a new dependency on peers. Such a peer-group dependency increases the danger to succumb to implicit or explicit peer pressure to take chances (Muuss, 1992a). The smoking behavior of friends is the single most reliable predictor whether an early adolescent will begin to smoke (Center for Disease Control, 1987). The somewhat insecure and peer-status-seeking individuals are especially

vulnerable and may do things they would otherwise not do when pressured or taunted ("Are you chicken?") by those they try to emulate.

Behaviors that are prohibited for children and adolescents but allowed or tolerated for adults seem especially enticing and attractive. Therefore, it is not surprising that youth, even at an early age, attempt to imitate "prohibited" adult behaviors. In addition, adolescents today seem to enjoy more freedom and frequently have more money to spend, but less of a feeling of personal social responsibility, than young people in the past. In contemporary society, social observers and even politicians bemoan the loss of a consensus of values. Families appear to be less inclined to transmit firm binding value structures, which used to serve as guides around which adolescents could orient their behavior. Furthermore, the social pressure of the peer group to participate in smoking cigarettes, drinking alcohol, trying drugs, and engaging in sexual intercourse and other adult behaviors begins earlier today. Partially because family structure has changed, the family is less protective, provides less supervision, and in general has become less influential. The U.S. Census Bureau reports that in 1995, 27% of children and adolescents lived in single-parent households compared to 9.8% in 1960. Furthermore, parents today spent 40% less time in direct personal interaction with their offspring than they did in 1965. Other institutions, such as the school, also seem to experience diminished authority and are confronted with more and more serious discipline problems. At the same time, the influence of the peer group appears to have increased.

Since many youth are still unable to correctly anticipate the full consequences or dangers of their potentially destructive behavior, they take chances that a more mature person would avoid. An often cited reason for adolescents' danger-defying behavior is the egocentric belief that they are invulnerable and that accidents and mishaps happen to other people but not to them. The reasons for this are, especially among early adolescents, their limited life experiences, lack of knowledge, and still undeveloped cognitive, social, and emotional maturity. Youth frequently lack the self-confidence and ego strength to resist temptations to experiment with risky behavior, especially when pressured by peers. In comparison to adults, adolescents are less risk averse and tend to focus on the immediate desirable benefits of such behaviors rather than on their long-term negative consequences (Zimring, 1982). In addition youth have a foreshortened time perspective, so that immediate gratification is valued higher than some potentially dangerous consequences in the distant future.

In spite of all the negative consequences, a certain youthful exuberance, enthusiasm, and passion for enjoyment, excitement, sensation, and delight with risk appear necessary in the process of becoming independent. As long as such explorations remain within limits, they are quite normal. These behaviors are problematic only when they result in tragic outcomes. Even if teens possess the cognitive knowledge to comprehend the potentially disastrous consequences of their behavior, that understanding may not deter them. Educational programs designed to convey knowledge and create an awareness of health risks in the future have not been very successful because the benefits of such risk avoidance are either in the distant future (e.g., smoking) or exist in terms of probability (driving without a seat belt has a low probability risk of injury). Most adolescents have been exposed to sex education classes; however, for a variety of reasons, these have had surprisingly little influence on their sexual activity, as the significant increase in teenage pregnancy and venereal disease indicates.

The question must be asked, why are some individuals so much more inclined to take chances and to endanger their future and their health? A great variety of studies—too numerous to cite—have repeatedly and fairly consistently identified some of the personal, social, and environmental conditions that are found to predispose adolescents to take chances, to get involved in dangerous and health-endangering behaviors, or to defy common sense. While it would be incorrect to label these factors as causes, their association with risk behavior has been widely observed. However, the effects may be two-directional; for example, substance abuse may contribute to school failure, but academic difficulties may also contribute to substance abuse. Some of these widely recognized predisposing variables are: alienation from parents, family, and society; lack of parental support and supervision; family disorganization, especially abusive parents; a negative attitude toward school and education; low expectation for academic success; repeated academic failure; a tolerant attitude toward deviant behavior; excitement-seeking personality traits; low self-esteem; peers who endorse and demonstrate risky, antisocial, or deviant behaviors; lack of religious commitment, moral conviction, and traditional values; depression; availability and affordability of cigarettes, drugs, guns or more general risk opportunities; poverty; high population density, high unemployment, economic hardship, and community disorganinzation; and male gender. It is still true that males are much more likely to be involved in such risk behaviors than females. However, the gender gap is narrowing. Obviously, none of the factors in isolation is an inevitable cause of risk-taking; however, they are predisposing influences that become more potent as several of them operate cumulatively as is often the case.

THE PREVALENCE OF NOTEWORTHY RISK-TAKING BEHAVIORS

Statistical data can never capture the full nature and extent of personal risk, especially since some individuals contribute repeatedly to the following numbers.

1. **Sexually transmitted diseases.** Every year 2.5 million teenagers contract STD. For girls in the age range 15–19 years, gonorrhea has increased in the last 40 years by 400%. (Gans et al., 1990). The rate of contracting gonorrhea is 17% among sexually active youth, and the risk of genital herpes is also high.
2. **Pregnancy among adolescents.** Every year about 1 million adolescents become pregnant; 513,000 teenagers give birth. The birth rate of 57 of every 1,000 teenagers is the highest ratio among industrialized nations. Ten thousand babies are born every year to mothers who are under 15.
3. **Tobacco consumption.** According to the Center for Disease Control and Prevention, 1 million teenagers start smoking annually. Of those who continue, one-third will suffer from tobacco-related health problems later in life. Each year, 100,000 lung cancer deaths can be attributed to smoking behavior, which often becomes a permanent habit in the early teens. Twenty percent of 12th grade students smoke regularly.
4. **Alcohol consumption.** Ninety-three percent of youth have consumed alcohol, 72% within the last month (Irwin & Millstein, 1990). Thirty percent of high school seniors admit binge drinking in the preceding two weeks. The mean age of first alcohol use is 12.6 years. Cigarettes and alcohol are considered the "gateway drugs" that precede more serious substance abuse.
5. **Drug use.** Among 10th graders, illegal drug use has increased from 15% to 34% from 1992 to 1996. While the use of "soft drugs" (alcohol, tobacco, and marijuana) has shown signs of declining among middle and late adolescents, the use of heroin and cocaine is still rising. However, especially worrisome is a recent report that the use of soft drugs has doubled in the age range 9 to 12 years in the last 3 years.
6. **School dropout.** Estimates of the high school dropout rate ranges from 14% to 25%. The consequences of dropping out of school become more serious as workplace demands increasingly require technical skills based on education. The consequences of lack of skill and education are well known: less earning potential, less stable employment, limited opportunity for advancement and unemployment. Dropping out and pregnancy are associated for females. Of those who terminate their education before graduation, 30% end up under the supervision of the criminal justice system.
7. **Delinquency and Crime.** According to Census Bureau data, 53,503 youth are in prisons or security facilities. However, since only 3% to 6% of those who commit punishable offenses are imprisoned (Muuss, 1992b), the actual number of serious offenses committed by youth approximates 1 million. Youth ages 13 to 21 make up 14.3% of the entire population; however, their arrest rate in the 1980s was 35.5%. According to Dryfoos (1990), if the less serious non-index offenses (e.g., truancy, running away, and vandalism) are included, 6 million youth ages 10 to 17 self-reported that they participated in unlawful acts within the previous year.

8. **Homicide.** Adolescents are both victims of and the perpetrators of homicide. In 1995 in the United States, teenagers committed almost 4,000 homicides. The decade from 1985 to 1995 saw a 141% increase in the number of murders committed by teenagers.

9. **Running away from home.** Running away from home can be a temporary solution to interpersonal conflict without dramatic consequences. However, youth, especially those from physically and sexually abusive families, who leave home for extended periods of time or permanently and live in shelters or become homeless, expose themselves to numerous risk factors: alcohol, drugs, promiscuous sex, prostitution, venereal disease, antisocial behavior, and suicidal tendencies. Estimates vary, but between 750,000 and 1.3 million run away each year and a half million young people are homeless.

10. **Suicide and suicide attempts.** Suicide is the third leading cause of death in the United States. An estimated 5,000 to 6,000 youth take their own lives each year, accounting for 13.3% of all death in the 15- to 24-year-old range. Since 1960 the rate of suicide has more than doubled. The magnitude of the problem becomes even more obvious when one considers the estimate, that about 9% to 10% of all American high school students have attempted to kill themselves and 25% thought about it during the preceding year.

Even though data can identify only some of the more common risk-taking behaviors, summing all the incidents in all categories would probably give a highly distorted figure of the prevalence of risk-taking. Some adolescents are known to be especially willing to take risks and hence contribute repeatedly to these statistics by being counted in numerous categories. Those who are heavily involved in the use of alcohol and drugs are most likely to be involved in sexual promiscuity, truancy, and many other risky behaviors. For some, risk taking is so natural that it sooner or later leads to

damaged health, serious injuries, incarceration, and even death. The argument advanced here is that risky behavior should not be viewed each by itself in isolation, but needs to be understood as an overarching personality characteristic that repeatedly breaks through in various realms of life.

RISK-TAKING BEHAVIOR AS A PERSONALITY VARIABLE

A psychodynamic connection among diverse health- and life-threatening behaviors leads to such concepts as "problem behavior syndrome" (Jessor & Jessor, 1977), "covariation of risk behavior" (Irwin, 1990), "overlap in high risk behavior" (Dryfoos, 1990) and "risk-taking behavior as a personality variable." Implied is the idea that these risk behaviors are interrelated; individuals who are heavily involved in one are likely to do several. The interrelationship of some risk behaviors is convincingly illustrated in Figure 1 for sex and alcohol and in Figure 2 for smoking and the use of other harmful drugs. Evidence for positive correlations and associations between a great many risk behaviors are quite pervasive (Irwin, 1990). The fact that risk behaviors are interrelated suggests new approaches to intervention and prevention. Until recently, school, religion, psychology, medicine, and society have focused on the dangers of specific, narrowly defined behaviors and have developed programs to address the dynamics of that particular problem. Categorical intervention programs have been developed for specific problems, such as the prevention of pregnancy, compensatory education, antismoking campaigns, and those aimed at preventing alcohol and substance abuse and suicide. Comprehensive intervention programs focus on the predisposing factors and antecedent conditions rather than on specific behavior manifestations.

Even today such programs still work in isolation from each other, as if such problems developed independently of each other and as if those involved were only at risk through these specifi-

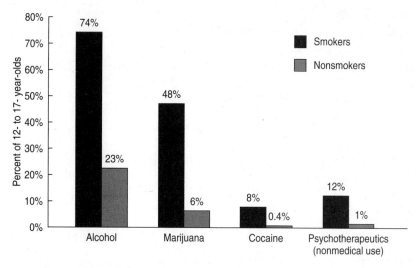

FIGURE 2   Differences Between Adolescent Cigarette Smokers and Non-smokers in the Use of Other Harmful Substances.
(From *National Household Survey* on Drug Abuse: Main findings 1985 [Washington, DC: National Institute on Drug Abuse].

cally identified behaviors. More and more voices demand programs that have as their primary objective to treat risk-taking behavior as a personality variable, no matter what the specific nature of the endangering behavior is. The complex association of diverse but problematic risk-taking, antisocial, and health-endangering behaviors has increasingly become the focus of contemporary research. Data like those demonstrating the association between alcohol and sex (See Figure 1) or sex and other problem-behaviors (Ketterlinus et al., 1992) could be provided for a great many other behaviors. Youth who are seriously involved in risky behaviors are frequently unconventional in many ways; they express and demonstrate a diminished willingness to accept and respect traditional social values in a postmodernistic society with little agreement about what such values ought to be.

Figure 2 impressively demonstrates that 12- to 17-year-olds who smoke are much more at risk to use other health-impairing substances than nonsmokers. More specifically, the danger is 3 times as great that smokers also consume alcohol, 8 times as high that they smoke marijuana, 20 times as great that they use cocaine, and 12 times as great that they abuse prescribed medicine for nonmedical purposes compared to nonsmokers.

AGE AS FACTOR IN RISK-TAKING BEHAVIOR

Adolescents seem to differ from both young children and adults in their perception of risk. They tend to underestimate their own risk as compared to others, and they have a much more tolerant attitude toward risk-taking (Gardner, 1992). Consequently, they are more inclined to engage in dangerous acts. However, the desire to try such risk behaviors occurs today at progressively younger ages, including preadolescence. The earlier some of these behaviors begin, especially the use of addictive substances but also aggression and delinquency, the more likely they are to develop into a permanent personality pattern, rather than stay on the level of youthful experimentation with new, challenging, or forbidden experiences. Individuals who fall into the very high risk group (Dryfoos, 1990) generally began their risk taking early.

Age of initiation thus is an important consideration, since the age when youth begin experimentation with cigarettes, alcohol, and marijuana appears to be decisive for the likelihood that an individual will use and abuse these substances not only in adolescence but into adulthood. After a habit such as smoking has been established, especially early in life, giving it up can be quite difficult. Youth who engage in these health-impairing behaviors at an early age (9 to 14 years) consume greater amounts later and tend to become lifelong addicts. For adolescents who regularly use substances in 12th grade, the use of drugs generally began much earlier. The earlier and the more frequently adolescents use soft drugs, the greater the probability is that they will later turn to hard drugs and become involved in several other risky behaviors. In addition, repeated drug use may have a negative impact on psychosocial development, success in school, ability to learn and concentrate, and development of healthy social relationships with peers and family.

Early onset of antisocial and serious delinquent acts are important predictors of chronic delinquency in adolescence and adulthood. In contrast, those who commit their first delinquent act relatively late (16 or older) are more likely to manifest a transitory pattern of delinquent behavior (Tolan, 1987). Thus, a well-established relationship exists between the age of the beginning of delinquent acts and the permanence, extent, and severity of subsequent antisocial behaviors. An antisocial and delinquent pattern of behavior almost never arises *de novo* in adulthood, but early manifestation of such inclinations generally exists in childhood or early adolescence.

Similarly, those who became sexually active before age 15 are more likely to have numerous partners and less likely to use contraceptives; thus, they are at greater risk for STD and pregnancy. Many individuals who started risk-taking behaviors early in life derail from their optimal developmental course. One can only conjecture what these individuals might have accomplished since for so many the negative consequences of their risk-taking impair or endanger optimal future development.

Youth who do not begin using cigarettes, alcohol, or illegal drugs before their 21st birthday are less inclined to begin after that age. However, even if they do, they are less in danger to become abusers or addicts. The second decade of life must therefore be considered a critical period for the permanent establishment of risk-taking behavior, instigating a danger that continues into later life. The decisive issue is not just that youth get involved in risky behavior—to some extent that has always taken place—but that the risk-taking today begins so much earlier than in the past.

RESILIENT YOUTH

Some youth who are exposed to dangerous personal and ecological risk conditions somehow are capable of resisting these temptations or, after a brief period of experimentation, are willing to evaluate such behaviors and give them up. Naturally, the question arises, what are the protective factors that make it possible for them to resist the pressure of the peer group, the alluring messages of advertisements, and their own sensation and pleasure-seeking impulses? Research has identified several specific factors:

1. A family climate—often defined as authoritative—that is demanding but also supportive and provides love and security but also encourages independence. Resilient individuals come from families that are effective in communicating family rules and an ethical value structure.
2. Enduring contact with at least one supportive and caring individual who provides help and assistance if needed.
3. A social network of support through friends, relatives, and other stable interpersonal relationships, especially people who do not support risk-taking behavior. The choice of friends in this respect is a more important issue than many parents realize (Muuss, 1992a).
4. Personal qualities that strengthen an individual to resist peer pressure and temptation and jeopardize well-being including: a sense of social responsibility, emotional stability, cooperative-

ness, sensitivity to others, independence, the ability to postpone the gratification of personal needs, the ability to control impulses, future-oriented outlook on life, self-confidence, positive self-esteem, the feeling of self-control, and the ability to ask for help and advice.

Even though the latter characteristics can be promoted through systematic educational and therapeutic programs, they seem to play only a subordinate role in the educational goals of our schools. From the point of view of educators, this insight requires a substantial rethinking of curriculum development and cooperation and communication with all agencies involved in the development of prevention and intervention programs for at-risk children of all ages.

REFERENCES

Center for Disease Control. (1987). Psychosocial predictors of smoking in adolescents. *Morbidity and Morality Weekly Reports, 36,* 1s–47s.

Dryfoos, J. (1990). *Adolescents-at-risk: Prevalence and prevention.* New York: Oxford.

Gans, J. E., Blyth, D. A., Elster, A. B., & Gaveras, L. L. (1990). *America's adolescents: How healthy are they?* Vol. 1 of the AMA Profiles of Adolescent Health Series. Chicago: American Medical Association.

Gardner, W. (1992). The life span theory of risk taking. In N. Bell (Ed.), *Adolescent and adult risk taking: The eighth Texas Tech symposium on interfaces in psychology.* Newbury Park: Sage.

Irwin, C. E. (1990). The theoretical concept of at-risk adolescents. In V. C. Strasburger & D. E. Greydanus (Eds.), *The at-risk adolescent.* Philadelphia: Hanley & Belfus, Inc.

Irwin, C. E., & Millstein, S. (1990). Biopsychosocial correlates of risk-taking behavior during adolescence. In R. E. Muuss (Ed.), *Adolescent behavior and society: A book of readings.* New York: McGraw-Hill.

Jessor, R., & Jessor, S. (1977). Problem behavior and psychosocial development. New York: Academic Press.

Ketterlinus, R. D., Lamb, M. E., Nitz, K., & Elster, A. B. (1992). Adolescent nonsexual and sex-related problem behavior. *Journal of Adolescent Research, 7,* 431–456.

Muuss, R. E. (1992a). Störungen in den sozialen Beziehungen während der Pubertät. *Hufeland Journal, 7,* 104–11.

Muuss, R. E. (1992b). Die Delinquenz von Jugendlichen. *Biologische Medizin, 21,* 3–12.

National Institute on Drug Abuse. (1985). *National Household Survey on Drug Abuse: Main Findings 1985.* Washington, DC: U.S. Government Printing Office.

Small, S. A., & Luster, T. (1990, November). Understanding adolescent sexuality and pregnancy: An ecological perspective. Paper presented at the Creating Caring Communities Conference. Michigan State University, East Lansing, MI.

Tolan, P. H. (1987). Implications of age of onset for delinquency risk. *Journal of Abnormal Child's Psychology, 15,* 47–65.

Zimring, F. E. (1982). *The changing legal world of adolescence.* New York: The Free Press.

ETHNIC AND GENDER DIFFERENCES IN RISK FOR EARLY ADOLESCENT SUBSTANCE USE

Daniel J. Flannery, Alexander T. Vazsonyi, Julia Torquati, and Angela Fridrich
Kent State University and University of Arizona

Despite an increasing awareness of its physical and social consequences, drug use continues to occur with epidemic proportion among adolescents. Recently researchers have used an epidemiological approach to examine both the number (Bry *et al.*, 1982) and types of factors (Jessor and Jessor, 1978; Kandel, 1978; Newcomb *et al.*, 1986; Smith and Fogg, 1978) that predict substance use risk in adolescence. An underlying assumption of the epidemiological approach is that individual variables are of little importance; knowing the overall number of variables that predict risk is sufficiently informative.

The purpose of this study was to use a risk factor approach to directly compare the influence of the interpersonal and intrapersonal domains for predicting substance use in early adolescence. Unlike early epidemiological approaches, we were interested in examining the specific influence of individual factors and the general influence of variables by domain. Focusing on the overall *number* of risk variables may be adequate when asking questions about level of use and mean differences between groups. An examination of specific variables is more appropriate, however, when examining similarities and differences in the underlying *pattern* of factors that predict substance use risk.

The question of whether to examine mean differences or pattern reflects one of the biggest ongoing disputes in substance use research, whether (1) a multiple pathway model of drug use is most appropriate, where several different factors may lead to substance use and abuse; or (2) a specific pattern or combination of variables accounts for all types of drug use in all types of users (Brook *et al.*, 1990). Much research points to the importance of a multivariate framework for understanding substance use. Specifically, simultaneous consideration of personality, perceived environment, and behavioral systems has been found to be more heuristic than simplistic, univariate explanations of substance use (Bloch *et al.*, 1991; Huba and Bentler, 1982). Several recent studies have examined risk factors by various domains.

Brook and her colleagues (Brook *et al.*, 1990; Brook *et al.*, 1984) have examined the influence of family and personality factors on adolescent alcohol use. In an early study of Black and Anglo high school students, Brook *et al.* (1984) found that peer, personality, and family factors each independently predicted adolescent risk for initiation of alcohol use. Coombs *et al.* (1991) recently showed that, among Caucasian and Hispanic youth, friend marijuana use was the most realistic predictor of an adolescent's own drug use. These data are consistent with the find-

From *Journal of Youth and Adolescence,* 1994, *23*(2), pp. 195–213. Copyright © 1994 Plenum Publishing Corporation. Reproduced with permission.

ings of Newcomb *et al.* (1986) who, in a sample of 10th–12th graders, showed that peer drug use (vs. parent factors) had the highest average correlation with an individual's self-reported drug use.

In the present study we examine risk for substance use by comparing the specific influence of the *inter*personal and *intra*personal domains. A total of 10 risk variables were included, 5 from each domain. Variables were chosen based on previous research on adolescent samples indicating they predicted substance use (see Brook *et al.,* 1990). Interpersonal risk was assessed via perceived susceptibility to peer pressure and peer alcohol use (Brook *et al.,* 1989; Coombs *et al.,* 1991), parental monitoring (Wells & Rankin, 1988), parent-child involvement (Penning and Barnes, 1982), and adolescent school adjustment (Brook *et al.,* 1990). Intrapersonal risk was assessed by impulsivity and aggression (Block *et al.,* 1986), depression (Brook *et al.,* 1985; Kandel & Davies, 1982), self-efficacy (Simons *et al.,* 1988) and academic achievement (Johnston *et al.,* 1984).

Regarding ethnic differences, previous research has shown that Anglo and Hispanic youth use substances at nearly equivalent levels (Newcomb and Bentler, 1986). Examining mean levels does not, however, convey information about pattern or process. In the present study we expect that mean levels of use between groups will be similar. Further, we expect that the factors predicting risk for substance use (i.e., the pattern underlying levels of use) will be similar for Caucasian and Hispanic youth (Coombs *et al.,* 1991).

There remains some controversy in the literature over factors that may contribute to gender differences in risk for early drug use. Block *et al.* (1986) found that the personality correlates of illegal drug use were similar for boys and girls, a finding confirmed for marijuana use (Donovan *et al.,* 1983). Baumrind (1985) suggests girls are more receptive than boys to interpersonal influences on drug use (cf. Brook *et al.,* 1990). In general, little research has been conducted that specifically examines risk factors for males vs. females. While some consistent mean

level differences have been identified (e.g., boys are more aggressive, girls are more depressed and more concerned about doing well in school), there is little reason to expect gender differences in the *pattern* of variables that may reflect the underlying processes predicting substance use in early adolescence.

The present study extends previous risk factor approaches (e.g., Brook *et al.,* 1990; Bry *et al.,* 1982; Coombs *et al.,* 1991; Newcomb and Bentler, 1986) in several ways. First, we allow individuals to be identified as at risk on any individual variable and examine that variable's unique contribution to predicting substance use. In previous studies one summative risk score was typically computed and treated as a single predictor variable of risk. Second, most studies of risk for substance use have employed older adolescent samples, usually 10th–12th graders. If a risk factor approach is to inform prevention/intervention efforts, we need to examine risk in its earliest stages (i.e., early adolescence). Finally, this study advances previous research by specifically examining gender differences in risk within and between ethnic groups (Brook *et al.,* 1990).

METHOD

Subjects and Procedure

All students in Grades 6 and 7 in three local, urban middle schools were asked to participate. The three schools were all of the middle schools in one large school district in a moderately sized southwestern city. According to information provided by school administrators, families represented all socioeconomic levels; local census tract data indicated mean household income for the district was \$33,880 (range = \$17,067–\$48,621). Information about the survey was sent directly to parents by school administrators. A passive consent procedure was employed: parents were sent a consent form and were asked to indicate whether their child was permitted to take part in the study. If parents indicated consent or no form was returned by the parents, the child was considered eligible for the study. Students were surveyed in their classrooms during two 30-minute periods on consecutive days.

Of the original available sample of 1437 students, 67 (4.7%) did not participate due to parental concerns, 134 students were absent during data collection or chose not to participate (9.3%), and 66 surveys (4.6%) were not usable due to incomplete or missing data (defined as a completion rate below 50% of all items). The final sample consisted of 1170 students in Grades 6 and 7 (mean age = 12.7 years) about equally divided between males (52%) and females (48%). The sample was ethnically diverse, although predominantly Caucasian (64%) and Hispanic (24%). Seventy-four percent of adolescents came from intact families. Lifetime use of alcohol in the sample was 49.4%, tobacco 17%, inhalants 11.7%, marijuana 4.7%, hallucinogens 2.2%, amphetamines 1.9%, and cocaine 1.1%.

Measures

Substance Use Lifetime substance use was assessed for beer/alcohol, tobacco, inhalants, marijuana, hallucinogens, cocaine/crack, and amphetamines. Subjects rated lifetime use for each substance on a 5-point scale: (1) *never*, (2) *1–2 times*, (3) *3–9 times*, (4) *10–39 times*, and (5) = *40 or more times*. Lifetime use was the sum of scores across all seven substances (range = 7–35). This measure is similar to scales used in other large surveys of early adolescent substance use (e.g., Kandel, Newcomb *et al.*, 1986).

Peer Pressure Perceived susceptibility to peer pressure was assessed using 4 items from the misconduct scale of the Peer Pressure Inventory (PPI) developed by Brown *et al.* (1986). Two content valid items were added to assess substance using behaviors. Adolescents rated the six hypothetical situations in which friends urge participation in an antisocial behavior. On a 4-point scale, responses ranged from *definitely would to definitely would not*. Internal consistency in this sample was high (alpha = .87).

Peer Substance Use One item asked early adolescents to indicate "How often do your close friends drink beverage alcohol?" Students responded on a 4-point scale: (1) often, (2) occasionally, (3) rarely, and (4) never. Because of the young age of our sample, we used peer alcohol use rather than peer marijuana use (see Coombs *et al.*, 1991).

Parental Monitoring Four core items from Patterson and Dishion's (1985) measure of parental monitoring were used to assess degree of parental supervision. Two content valid items were added for this sample. Cronbach's alpha for the 6 items was .77.

Parent-Child Involvement Seven items assessed parent-child involvement, focusing on issues of (1) closeness, e.g., "When you have a problem, how often do you go to your mother/father?" and "How often do you share your thoughts and feelings with your mother/father?" and (2) activities, e.g., "How often do your parent(s) help with your homework?" A mean score was calculated across the 7 items (alpha = .74).

School Adjustment Five items assessed an adolescent's school behavior and motivation to succeed. For example, subjects responded to questions like "How important is it to you to get good grades in school?" or "I disobey at school." Items were answered on a 3-point scale, generally ranging from either *none* to *a lot* or *not true* to *very true*. One summary score was computed, with high scores indicating high academic integration (alpha = .64).

Self-Efficacy Eighteen items from Wheeler and Ladd's (1982) self-efficacy scale assessed the adolescent's ability to perform a persuasive task in the presence of peers. Items described social situations followed by an incomplete statement: "Some kids want to play a game. Asking them to play is _____ for you." Adolescents responded on a 4-point scale, ranging from (1) *very hard* to (4) *very easy*. Higher scores indicated a greater sense of self-efficacy with peers. These items have been shown to be appropriate for use with early adolescents; test-retest reliabilities range from .80 for females to .90 for males (alpha for this sample = .89).

Impulsivity   Five items assessed sensation seeking behaviors (Buss and Plomin, 1984). Adolescents rated statements such as "I think planning takes the fun out of things" or "I enjoy new and exciting experiences if they are a little frightening or unusual." Responses ranged from (1) *strongly disagree* to (5) *strongly agree.* One summary score was computed. Coefficient data for these items was .71.

Aggression and Depression   Aggression and depression were assessed using items from Achenbach's (1991) Youth Self-Report (YSR). The YSR is a commonly used clinical instrument designed to elicit self-report information about adolescent's competencies and behavior problems. Adolescents were asked to rate their behavior for the past six months by responding whether statements were *not true, somewhat or sometimes true,* or *very true or often true* for them. The factor structure and internal consistency of the items have been shown to be highly reliable (Achenbach, 1991; depression alpha = .85, aggression alpha = .88 for this sample).

Academic Achievement   Academic achievement was assessed by having adolescents report an overall letter grade that best represented their average level of achievement in school. They were asked "What grades do you *usually* get on your report card?" Eight grade categories were listed as possible responses. The grade checked was transformed to a numeric grade, ranging from A = 4.0 to F = 0.

Plan of Analysis   One-way analyses of variance (ANOVAs) were conducted to examine overall ethnic differences. In addition, because we were interested in examining gender differences in behavior, one-way ANOVAs were also performed by gender with ethnicity. Pearson correlation analyses were employed to illustrate the relationship between variables. To examine patterns of substance use risk, data were analyzed using a series of multiple regressions. First, in a hierarchical regression, lifetime substance use was regressed on all interpersonal and intrapersonal variables together. Interpersonal variables were entered first, based on recent research showing the importance of variables in this domain for predicting adolescent substance use (Brook *et al.,* 1990; Coombs *et al.,* 1991). Significant predictors were retained for a second within-domain stepwise regression. This second step showed which variables contributed the most unique variance to substance use risk and permitted a specific comparison of variance accounted for by the intrapersonal versus interpersonal domain.

To determine risk status, a dichotomous weighing scheme was employed (e.g., Bloch *et al.,* 1991; Newcomb *et al.,* 1986). First, a risk cut-off score was established by determining, within each ethnic group, the score representing the top 20% for each variable. Individuals scoring in the top 20% received a risk score of 1 on that variable. Individuals scoring in the bottom 80% received a risk score of 0 for that variable. Based on 10 risk variables across domains, any individual's risk could range from 0 (no risk) to 10 (high risk on each variable measured). The procedure used to define risk in this sample was somewhat more conservative than in previous studies, where risk was defined as the top third of the sample (Bloch *et al.,* 1991) or the top quartile (Newcomb and Bentler, 1986).

RESULTS

One-way ANOVAs were employed to examine differences in mean levels of behavior. Only two differences emerged when comparing all Caucasian youth to all Hispanic youth: Caucasian adolescents reported having higher school grades, $F(1, 1005) = 39.54$, $p < .01$ and better school adjustment, $F(1, 1019) = 9.51, p < .01$. As expected, overall levels of substance use were not significantly different in the two ethnic groups. Consistent with expectations, an examination of

TABLE I
One-Way ANOVAs by Gender Within Ethnicity[a]

	Caucasians					Hispanics				
	Males (N = 370)		Females (N = 369)			Males (N = 144)		Females (N = 131)		
Variable	Mean	SD	Mean	SD	F	Mean	SD	Mean	SD	F
Drug use	8.5	2.3	8.3	2.4	.8	8.6	2.7	8.7	3.1	.00
Aggression	9.8	6.8	8.7	6.3	5.1[b]	9.0	6.2	10.7	6.9	4.9[h]
Impulsivity	16.5	4.4	15.3	3.9	16.8[d]	16.0	4.5	16.9	4.3	2.9
Depression	6.8	5.6	7.8	6.3	5.3[b]	5.9	4.6	8.7	6.4	17.3[d]
Self-efficacy	59.9	9.9	57.9	10.1	7.3[c]	59.1	9.7	59.0	9.8	.01
Grades	3.1	.7	3.3	.6	14.2[d]	2.8	.8	2.9	.7	2.5
Pressure	10.3	4.4	10.1	4.2	.2	10.3	4.2	11.2	4.5	2.7
Friend drink	1.4	.8	1.4	.8	.5	1.4	.8	1.6	.8	4.7[b]
Monitor	19.2	3.8	20.1	3.4	10.3[d]	19.3	4.2	19.4	3.6	.00
Relations	2.5	.6	2.5	.6	.94	2.5	.6	2.4	.7	1.5
Adjustment	10.6	2.3	11.3	2.0	21.1[d]	10.4	2.2	10.6	2.1	.6

[a]For Caucasian df males = (1, 369); for females df = (1,368). For Hispanic df males = (1, 143); females, df = (1,130).
[b]$p < .05$.
[c]$p < .01$.
[d]$p < .001$.

gender differences within each ethnic group showed that for Caucasian youth males rated themselves to be more aggressive, more impulsive, and more self-efficacious than their female peers (Table I). Conversely, females rated themselves to be better adjusted at school and to have better grades. In addition, Caucasian females reported higher levels of depression and more monitoring by their parents than Caucasian males. Fewer gender differences emerged in the Hispanic group. Hispanic females rated themselves to be more aggressive, more depressed, and were more likely to have friends who drank beverage alcohol compared to their male peers.

Table II contains correlations on Caucasian youth for all variables assessed in this sample. As shown in Table II, lifetime substance use for both males and females was most highly related to perceived susceptibility to peer pressure and whether or not an adolescent had a close friend who used beverage alcohol. In fact, susceptibility to peer pressure was highly related to many areas of individual functioning including school adjustment, being aggressive and impulsive, and whether or not parents monitored behavior. It is interesting to note that for both genders, poor school adjustment was significantly related to increased substance use. Similar patterns were evident for Hispanic youth (see Table III). Specifically, increased drug use was positively related to perceptions of pressure from peers, having close friends who drink alcohol, and to poor school adjustment. Further, perceived susceptibility to pressure from peers was also related to increased aggression, impulsivity, and less monitoring by parents.

Regression Analyses

To examine differences in intrapersonal and interpersonal risk for lifetime substance use, a series of regression analyses were employed. Because we were interested in ethnic and gender differences, the regression analyses were conducted for both males and females within each ethnic group. In the first series of hierarchical regressions, all 10 intrapersonal and interpersonal variables were entered in a single step. Those variables that were significant were then retained in a stepwise model that compared interpersonal

TABLE II
Pearson Correlations for Caucasian Youth[a]

	1	2	3	4	5	6	7	8	9	10	11
1. Drug use		.37	.31	.17		−.23	.55	.52	−.33	−.20	−.41
2. Aggression	.46		.50	.45		−.19	.48	.32	−.36	−.32	−.59
3. Impulsivity	.32	.44		.18	.12	−.24	.44	.24	−.33	−.27	−.45
4. Depression	.30	.65	.24		−.39	−.12		.13	−.14	−.21	−.16
5. Self-efficacy	.19		.15	−.27				.17			
6. Grades	−.29	−.20	−.11	−.16	.11		−.32	−.22	.18		.39
7. Pressure	.56	.49	.47	.19	.20	−.22		.46	−.50	−.25	−.60
8. Friend drink	.50	.37	.29	.29	.17	−.20	.48		−.33	−.19	−.38
9. Monitor	−.38	−.38	−.34	−.22	−.15	.22	−.45	−.28		.41	.49
10. Relations	−.34	−.33	−.26	−.29		.19	−.29	−.25	.40		.36
11. Adjustment	−.51	−.51	−.34	−.19	−.14	.35	−.54	−.38	.39	.34	

[a]Correlations for males are above the diagonal; correlations for females are below the diagonal. For males, $N = 370$; for females, $N = 369$. All values presented in the table are significant at $p < .05$.

TABLE III
Pearson Correlations for Hispanic Youth[a]

	1	2	3	4	5	6	7	8	9	10	11
1. Drug use		.52	.26			−.17	.65	.58	−.27	−.28	−.38
2. Aggression	.29		.30	.57		−.33	.56	.27	−.26	−.27	−.43
3. Impulsivity	.31	.49					.34	.26	−.20	−.18	−.17
4. Depression	.23	.57	.30		−.18						
5. Self-efficacy	−.24			−.21		−.19					
6. Grades	−.18								.20	.17	.39
7. Pressure	.51	.54	.59	.35		−.18		.50	−.28	−.30	−.47
8. Friend drink	.51	.30	.33			−.20	.61			−.27	−.37
9. Monitor	−.36	−.22	−.43				−.37	−.33		.44	.27
10. Relations	−.21	−.32	−.26	−.31		.19	−.30		.36		.35
11. Adjustment	−.45	−.56	−.47	−.35		.34	−.61	−.45	.37	.32	

[a]Correlations for males are above the diagonal; correlations for females are below the diagonal. For males, $N = 144$; for females, $N = 131$. All values presented in the table are significant at $p < .05$.

and intrapersonal variables to determine the variance accounted for by each domain. At this first step as much as 65% of the variance was accounted for in male substance use and 45% of the variance in female substance use.

For both male and female Caucasian early adolescents, perceived pressure from peers to engage in antisocial behavior and having close friends who drink beverage alcohol were the most consistent and powerful predictors of self-reported substance use. While the relative magnitude of the individual beta weights was

slightly different, the same pattern emerged for Hispanic males. Specifically, substance use was best predicted by having a friend who drinks and perceived susceptibility to peer pressure. School adjustment also entered for Hispanic males, a variable uniquely absent from the Caucasian male model.

For both ethnic groups, aggression entered the model for males, but not for females. School adjustment was the most consistent significant predictor of female substance use across ethnicity, and was the only significant predictor for

Hispanic females. Grades added to the predictive model for Caucasian females but not for any other group. Across both gender and ethnicity, interpersonal variables accounted for a greater proportion of the variance in substance use than intrapersonal variables, accounting for as much as 49% of the variance for Hispanic males vs. no variance for Hispanic females.

DISCUSSION

The most striking and consistent finding for this early adolescent sample was the significant contribution of the interpersonal domain to predicting risk of drug use. Specifically, having a friend who drinks beverage alcohol and perceived susceptibility to pressure from peers were the two best and most consistent predictors of drug use. This finding was consistent across both gender and ethnicity. The importance of peer drug and alcohol use and the general influence of peers to predicting adolescent drug use are well documented (Brook *et al.*, 1990; Coombs *et al.*, 1991). Consistent with these studies, we found significant and direct peer influences for early adolescents. Further, we showed that, when comparing the influence of interpersonal to intrapersonal variables directly, the interpersonal domain consistently accounts for more variance in early adolescent substance use risk.

As expected, males in both ethnic groups reported themselves to be more aggressive than females. Aggression was also the most powerful intrapersonal variable for predicting drug use. This is consistent with previous work on drug use in older adolescent samples (Brook *et al.*, 1990). While other researchers have shown that depression and impulsivity predict drug use (Pandina and Schuele, 1983), our data suggest that these are not as important as aggression, at least when they are simultaneously compared in a single model with other intrapersonal factors.

School adjustment was a significant predictor in all but the Caucasian male model of drug use risk. As expected, self-reported grades were also a significant predictor for Caucasian females. These findings are consistent with those of Brook *et al.* (1990), who pointed out the highly robust influence of school achievement and behavior on patterns of adolescent substance use. These data also support assertions that nondrug using adolescents are responsible, achievement-oriented youth (Brook *et al.*, 1990). Positive school adjustment and academic achievement can provide a context in which children and adolescents experience success and gain reinforcement for their efforts. Developing a positive sense of self-worth in school may help buffer against the possibility of turning to a deviant peer group for reinforcement and reward.

Contrary to expectations, several variables did not predict drug use risk in our sample. For example, even though females in both ethnic groups reported greater mean levels of depression vs. males, depression did not enter the predictive model for any group (but see Simons *et al.*, 1988). In light of previous findings, our data may be interpreted in at least two ways: (1) given the impact of peers on behavior in 6th and 7th grades, depression and impulsivity are simply not as influential in predicting drug use at this early age; or (2) when compared directly with other intrapersonal and interpersonal variables in a risk-based model, interpersonal variables generally have more predictive power than depression and impulsivity.

Parental monitoring and involvement also did not emerge as significant predictors of early adolescent substance use. While both were significantly and inversely correlated with substance use, neither was a consistently significant predictor in regression analyses. By comparing parent, peer, and personality variables directly, the present study suggests parental monitoring's impact on substance use may not be direct; rather, any effect of parental monitoring on early adolescent substance use may be mediated by peer or other interpersonal variables (Chassin *et al.*, 1993). Direct vs. indirect effects models of the influence of parental monitoring on early adolescent substance use and its implication for prevention efforts awaits further investigation.

Several limitations regarding this sample require mention. First, the data were collected using early adolescent self-reports. The value of obtaining parent or teacher reports has been well documented (Brook *et al.,* 1990). Any time self-reports are gathered regarding sensitive topics, the question of validity and accuracy of responses is raised. We took several steps to help ensure the confidentiality of responses and the validity of the data, including discarding inconsistent protocols and incomplete surveys. Further, as adolescents are the target of prevention efforts, their perspective regarding factors that lead to further substance use is quite useful and necessary.

Second, the data are cross sectional in nature. In order to examine underlying causal structures and the etiological process that leads to high risk for early substance use, longitudinal data are required. The cross-sectional nature of the data also does not permit conclusions about the direction of peer influence. Is the impact of peers on self-drug use due to assortative pairing wherein individuals select friends who are similar to themselves (Kandel, 1985; e.g., drug users seek out deviant friends), or does associating with deviant peers lead to substance use and other problem behaviors? Only longitudinal data can address the direct causal pathway between peer influence and an individual's drug use in early adolescence.

IMPLICATIONS FOR PREVENTION EFFORTS

Our data have several implications for prevention efforts. First, it is clear that levels of substance use and risk continue to be quite high at very young ages. Starting and concentrating prevention efforts in the early elementary years is the only effective means of prevention; we cannot afford to wait until middle or late adolescence to intervene. Second, our findings point out the highly significant influence of peer behavior and peer pressure on an early adolescent's decision to use substances. In terms of selecting appropriate prevention program goals, focusing on the interpersonal domain is most appropriate for early adolescents. This may include an emphasis on (1) problem solving with peers,

(2) making responsible choices (e.g., choosing friends), and (3) developing strategies to deal effectively with pressure from peers to engage in socially undesirable behavior.

This is not to say that other intrapersonal variables such as aggression and depression should be ignored. For some children and adolescents, these variables may also place them at risk for drug use and other problem behaviors (which may lead to or be associated with drug use). When designing school- and community-based prevention efforts, however, one must decide on a clear focus that will benefit the greatest number of program participants. Our findings, using a large, ethnically diverse, economically representative sample, suggest that the influence of peers deserves early and focused attention.

Finally, what is most compelling about our data is that, despite differences on some specific variables, the significant predictors, across gender, were the same for Caucasian and Hispanic youth. Other researchers comparing different samples have also identified consistencies between ethnic groups (see Brooks *et al.,* 1990). What does this mean for our prevention efforts? If the same factors place adolescents in both ethnic groups at risk for substance use, then both adolescents should be exposed to the same prevention efforts. For example, our data suggest that a Caucasian youth who has friends who drink beverage alcohol is at high risk for using substances. A Hispanic youth in the same situation is also at high risk. Both youth may benefit from prevention efforts with similar goals. While this data speaks to similarity of *pattern* in predicting risk for drug use and the importance of the interpersonal domain, a true examination of *process* awaits specific comparisons of relationships between groups and longitudinal research designs.

REFERENCES

Achenbach, T. M. (1991). *Manual for the Youth Self-Report and Profile.* University of Vermont, Department of Psychiatry, Burlington.

Baumrind, D. (1985). Familial antecedents of adolescent drug use: A developmental perspective. In Jones, C. L., and Battjes, R. J. (eds.), *Etiology of*

Drug Abuse: Implications for Prevention (Research Monograph No. 56, pp. 13–44). National Institute of Drug Abuse, Rockville, MD.

Bloch, L. P., Crockett, L. J., and Vicary, J. R. (1991). Antecedents of rural adolescent alcohol use: A risk factor approach. *J. Drug Educat.* 21: 361–377.

Block, J., Keyes, S., and Block, J. H. (1986). Childhood personality and environmental antecedents of drug use: A prospective longitudinal study. Paper presented at the meeting of the Society for Life History Research in Psychopathology, Palm Springs, CA.

Brook, J. S., Brook, D. W., Gordon, A. S., Whiteman, M., and Cohen, P. (1990). The psychosocial etiology of adolescent drug use: A family interactional approach. *Genet. Social Gen. Psychol. Monogr.* 116: 109–267.

Brook, J. S., Gordon, A. S., Brook, A., and Brook, D. (1989). The consequences of marijuana use on intrapersonal and interpersonal functioning in Black and White adolescents. *Genet. Social Gen. Psychol. Monogr.* 115: 349–369.

Brook, J. S., Whiteman, M., Gordon, A., Nomura, C., and Brook, D. (1984). Onset of adolescent drinking: A longitudinal study of intrapersonal and interpersonal antecedents. *Adv. Alcohol Subst. Abuse* 5: 91–110.

Brook, J. S., Whiteman, M., and Gordon, A. (1985). Stability of personality during adolescence and its relationship to stage of drug use. *Genet. Social Gen. Psychol. Monogr.* 111: 317–330.

Brown, B. B., Clasen, D., and Eicher, S. (1986). Perceptions of peer pressure, peer conformity, disposition, and self-reported behaviors among adolescents. *Develop. Psychol.* 22: 521–531.

Bry, B. H., McKeon, P., and Pandina, R. J. (1982). Extent of drug use as a function of number of risk factors. *J. Abnorm. Psychol.* 91: 273–279.

Buss, A. H., and Plomin, R. (1984). *Temperament: Early Developing Personality Traits.* Erlbaum, Hillsdale, NJ.

Chassin, L., Pillow, D., Curran, P., Molina, B., and Barrera, M. (1993). Relation of parental alcoholism to early adolescent substance use: A test of three mediating mechanisms. *J. Abnorm. Psychol.* 102: 3–19.

Coombs, R. H., Paulson, M. J., and Richardson, M. A. (1991). Peer vs. parental influence in substance use among Hispanic and Anglo children and adolescents. *J. Youth Adolesc.* 20: 73–88.

Donovan, J. E., Jessor, R., and Jessor, L. (1983). Problem drinking in adolescence and young adulthood: A follow-up study. *J. Studies Alcohol* 44: 109–137.

Huba, G. J., and Bentler, P. M. (1982). A developmental theory of drug use: Derivation and assessment of a causal modeling approach. In Baltes, B. P., and Brion, J. (eds.), *Life-Span Development and Behavior* (Vol. 4), Academic Press, New York.

Jessor, R., and Jessor, S. L. (1978). Theory testing in longitudinal research on marijuana use. In Kandel, D. B. (ed.), *Longitudinal Research on Drug Use: Empirical Findings and Methodological Issues.* Hemisphere, Washington, DC.

Johnston, L. D., O'Malley, P. M., and Bachman, J. G. (1984). *Drugs and American High School Students, 1975–1983.* National Institute of Drug Abuse DHHS Publication No. ADM 84–1317. Government Printing Office, Washington, DC.

Kandel, D. B. (1978). Homophily, selection and socialization among youth. *Ann. Rev. Sociol.* 6: 235–385.

Kandel D. B., (1980). Drug and drinking behavior among youth. *Ann. Rev. Sociol.* 6: 235–285.

Kandel, D. B., and Davies, M. (1982). Epidemiology of depressive moods in adolescents. *Arch. Gen. Psychiat.* 39: 1205–1212.

Kandel, D. B. (1985) On processes of peer influences in adolescent drug use: A developmental perspective. Alcohol and substance abuse in adolescents. *Adv. Alcohol Substance Abuse* 4: 139–163.

Newcomb, M. D., and Bentler, P. M. (1986). Substance use and ethnicity: Differential impact of peer and adult models. *J. Psychol.* 120: 83–95.

Newcomb, M. D., Maddahian, E., and Bentler, P. M. (1986). Risk factors for drug use among adolescents: Concurrent and longitudinal analysis. *Am. J. Public Health* 76: 525–531.

Pandina, R. J., and Schuele, J. A. (1983). Psychosocial correlates of adolescent alcohol and drug use. *J. Studies Alcohol* 44: 950–973.

Patterson, G. R., and Dishion, T. J. (1985). Contributions of families and peers to delinquency. *Criminology* 23: 63–79.

Penning, M., and Barnes, G. E. (1982). Adolescent marijuana use: A review. *Int. J. Addict.* 17: 749–791.

Simons, R. L., Conger, R. D., and Whitebeck, L. B. (1988). A multistage social learning model of the influences of family and peers upon adolescent substance abuse. *J. Drug Issues* 18: 293–315.

Smith, J. M., and Fogg, C. P. (1978). Psychological predictors of early use, late use, and nonuse of marijuana among teenage students. In Kandel, D. B. (ed.), *Longitudinal Research on Drug Use: Empirical Findings and Methodological Issues.* Hemisphere Publishing, Washington, DC.

Wells, L. E., and Rankin, J. H. (1988). Direct parental controls and delinquency. *Criminology* 26: 263–285.

Wheeler, V. A., and Ladd, G. W. (1982). Assessment of children's self-efficacy for social interactions with peers. *Develop. Psychol.* 18: 795–805.

EARLY RISK FACTORS FOR SERIOUS ANTISOCIAL BEHAVIOR AT AGE 21

BILGE PAKIZ, ED.D., HELEN Z. REINHERZ, SC.D., AND ROSE M. GIACONIA, PH.D.
San Diego and Simmons College

Serious antisocial behavior appears to reach a peak during young adulthood, the period from ages 18–29 *(Robins & Regier, 1991)*. Although there are a multitude of studies regarding prevalence, antecedents, and early manifestations of antisocial behavior in younger children *(Loeber, 1990a; Offord, Boyle & Racine, 1991)* and adults *(Robins, 1978)*, few have examined the early manifestations of antisocial behavior in the important transitional period of young adulthood *(Rutter & Giller, 1983)*. The present article attempts to bridge this gap by identifying risk factors for antisocial behavior at age 21 that can be recognized from ages five through 18.

A number of risk factors for antisocial behavior in the emotional, behavioral, familial, and educational domains have been cited in prior research. Early behavioral problems have been noted as one of the strongest predictors of later antisocial behavior, including adult offenses *(Farrington, 1990; Loeber, 1990a; Patterson, DeBaryshe, & Ramsey, 1989; White, Earls, Robins, & Silva, 1990)*. Findings have indicated that the course of chronic delinquency follows a succession of anticipated paths *(Patterson et al., 1989)*, including a progression from less serious to more serious acts *(Loeber, 1991)*.

Among the most frequently cited predictors of antisocial behavior is early aggressive behavior *(Huesman, Eron, Lefkowitz, & Walder, 1984; McCord, 1983; Rutter & Giller, 1983)*. A prior study with the current sample *(Pakiz, Reinherz & Frost, 1992)* found that early aggression was strongly associated with delinquent behavior at age 15.

From *American Journal of Orthopsychiatry, 67*(1), January 1997. Copyright © 1997 by the American Orthopsychiatric Association, Inc. Reproduced by permission. Research was supported by NIMH Grant 41569.

Similarly, according to Farrington *(1991)*, early aggression and violent behavior showed significant continuity and predicted chronic offending in young adulthood in a sample of males.

Male predominance in antisocial behavior has been well documented across studies *(Henggeler, 1989; Robins, 1986)*. In addition to higher prevalence rates in males, prior research has identified different pathways *(Offord & Bennett, 1994)* and adult consequences *(Reid, 1993; Robins, 1986)* for males and females.

Family characteristics have been identified as risk factors in various studies. They indicate that families failing to provide supportive and consistent environments may encourage maladaptive coping strategies in their members. Poor parental child-rearing practices have been noted to increase the risk for future antisocial behavior *(Farrington, 1990; Kazdin, 1987; Sampson & Laub, 1993)*. Similarly, serious socioeconomic deprivation, defined by large family size, poor living conditions, or low family income, has been noted to have an impact on antisocial behavior *(Rutter & Giller, 1983; Farrington, 1990)*.

Additional components of the family milieu that have been linked to delinquent outcomes include such extreme forms of family dysfunction as parental criminality *(Henggeler, 1989)* and drug abuse *(Patterson, Reid & Dishion, 1992)*, and a history of abuse or neglect *(Kolko, Kazdin, Thomas & Day, 1993)*. Further, some earlier research identified a modest association between broken homes and antisocial acts *(Henggeler, 1989)*. The literature also suggests that key parental strategies of monitoring, supervision, and discipline may confound the effects of divorce or parental deviance on antisocial behavior *(Henggeler, 1989; Mrazek & Haggerty, 1994; Sampson & Laub, 1993)*.

Prior research has examined the relationship of self-perception to acting out behavior. Henggeler *(1989)* suggested that even though low self-esteem appears to be related to antisocial behavior, the link between the two phenomena is not definitive, since most studies have not established a causal connection, while Patterson et al. *(1992)* underscored the necessity of accounting for the influence of covariates, such as parental discipline or subjects' aggression, on self-esteem of antisocial youth.

Longitudinal studies have helped generate useful information for prediction and prevention of behavior problems. Through the description of early precursors, longitudinal studies have played a critical role in the development of prevention strategies to reduce rates of antisocial behavior, with its high social costs *(Mrazek & Haggerty, 1994; Robins, 1981)*.

Unlike studies based on incarcerated or clinical samples *(Robins, 1978)*, samples of males only *(Farrington, 1990; Loeber & Dishion, 1983; McCord, 1983; Patterson et al., 1992)*, or community samples in which retrospective data were examined *(Robins & Regier, 1991)*, the present article uses prospective data collected over an 18-year period from a single group of youth in the community. It examines risk factors for antisocial behavior in a population of 21-year-olds, evaluating data gathered from the preschool years through early adulthood, and providing information from multiple informants in the emotional, social, and educational domains, as well as on life events and family characteristics. The findings provide needed information on early childhood precursors of antisocial behavior in the period of young adulthood *(Rutter & Giller, 1983)*.

Based on prior research and findings from the longitudinal study of which this paper is a part, it was hypothesized that the following early factors would be associated with an increased risk for antisocial behavior at age 21: male gender; early behavior problems, aggression, or hostility; negative family environment; academic problems; and lack of social support and low self-esteem.

METHOD

Sample

The respondents in the present study were 375 young adults who had enrolled in a public school kindergarten in the northeastern U.S. in

1977 and had been followed in an ongoing 18-year longitudinal panel study. The current analysis was based on data collected at six points in time: 1977 (age five), 1978 (age six), 1981 (age nine), 1987 (age 15), 1990 (age 18), and 1993 (age 21).

Most sample attrition since the inception of the project in 1977 ($N = 777$) has occurred when students have transferred from the public school system to parochial schools. Of those who stayed in public schools through third grade ($N = 519$), approximately 73% ($N = 375$) remained in the study at age 21. Participants and nonparticipants were compared throughout the study on variables thought to be associated with poor outcomes (e.g., gender, socioeconomic status (SES), academic difficulties, and behavior) but no meaningful differences were found at any data collection wave *(Reinherz, Giaconia, Lefkowitz, Pakiz & Frost, 1993)*. This suggests that nonresponse affected findings only minimally.

At the most recent (1993) data collection, the mean age of the study group ($N = 375$) was 21, with an equal number of males and females. Participants' families were predominantly working- or lower-middle-class, and 98% were white. Three percent ($N=11$) of the young adults were married and 6.5% ($N=25$) had children. Nearly 84% ($N=315$) were employed, and 60% ($N=223$) reported living with a parent.

Procedure

Measures that were used to assess performance in specific domains at each data period were chosen for psychometric reliability and validity, as well as for their wide use in community and epidemiological studies. Data from multiple informants (e.g., self-reports and teacher and parent reports) were utilized at the first five time points to overcome the bias inherent in relying exclusively on self-report data.

At age 21, a semistructured interview was administered to the young adults. Each respondent also completed a number of standardized, self-administered questionnaires on emotional, behavioral, and academic adjustment.

Measures

Antisocial Behavior at Age 21 This outcome measure was defined via the symptom counts of self-reported antisocial behavior as identified by the Antisocial Personality Disorder section of the National Institutes of Mental Health Diagnostic Interview Schedule, Version III-Revised (DIS-III-R)*(Robins, Helzer, Cottler, & Goldring, 1989)*. This is a highly structured interview designed to be administered by lay interviewers and developed for use as a comprehensive diagnostic instrument in epidemiological studies of psychiatric disorders.

In the present study, symptom counts of antisocial behavior were utilized as a continuous dependent variable to define antisocial behavior not as a disorder, but as a behavioral cluster reflecting a high level of social dysfunction. Thus, those respondents with serious adult antisocial behavior who would not necessarily meet all criteria for a diagnosis of antisocial personality disorder could be included. Kazdin *(1989)* suggested including a behavioral constellation rather than a single antisocial act in identifying youth who have more serious behavior problems. The DIS-III-R types of behavior included in the current study range from illegal occupations (e.g., handling stolen goods or dealing drugs), to financial irresponsibility (e.g., failure to pay debts or being frequently fired from jobs), to overt aggression (e.g., physical fights with partner or using a weapon).

Early Risk Factors Behavioral and emotional characteristics were measured via six instruments. At age six, the Kindergarten Behavior Questionnaire *(Behar, 1977)*, a self-administered checklist completed by teachers was used to measure individual scores on hyperactivity-hostility. At age nine, teachers completed the Child and Adolescent Adjustment Profile (CAAP) *(Ellsworth, 1977)* to assess hostility.

At ages 15 and 18, externalizing behavior and attention problems were measured using subscales of the Youth Self-Report (YSR) *(Achenbach, 1991)*, a self-administered questionnaire widely used in clinical and epidemiological studies, and included in the current analyses. Alpha reliability coefficients in the current sample for the total scale for both genders were 0.93 and 0.92, respectively.

At the same time points, global self-esteem was evaluated using the Piers-Harris Children's Self-Concept Scale *(Piers, 1986).* At age 15, reliability coefficients for the total scale were 0.91 for boys and 0.92 for girls.

At age 15, items were selected from the Diagnostic Interview Scale for Children *(National Institute of Mental Health, 1983)* to assess respondents' perceptions of behavior problems in school. The alpha reliability coefficient for the scale was 0.74 for the total sample.

Academic and additional behavioral components were assessed via self-reports of grades at 18 and of being expelled or suspended at ages 15 and 18. Lifetime occurrence of marijuana abuse or dependence, diagnosed by age 18, was determined using the DIS-III-R *(Robins et al., 1989).*

Social Support   At ages 15 and 18, an assessment of social support was provided by the Arizona Social Support Inventory *(Barrera, 1980).* This measure yields a rating of both perceived and actual support levels. In the current analysis, availability of and need for assistance (i.e., having people to help with everyday tasks) was assessed. At age 18, the alpha reliability coefficient for overall need for support was 0.68.

Family environment at ages five and six was assessed via a family "disadvantage index," composed from parents' responses to the study questionnaire. This index classified respondents by three groupings: lower SES, single-parent household, and large family (more than three children).

At ages 15 and 18, family milieu items were selected from the structured interview administered to respondents. These items included information on the participants' living conditions, and on parental divorce, incarceration, and drinking and drug problems. Data on the lifetime occurrence of physical, emotional, and sexual abuse were also reported by the respondent.

Analysis

The antisocial behavior component symptom counts identified by the DIS-III-R were included as a continuous dependent variable. The validity of the outcome measure was tested by examining its relationship to maternal reports of delinquency measured by the Young Adult Behavior Check List (YABCL) *(Achenbach, 1993)* and to overall functioning at age 21 according to the Global Assessment of Functioning (GAP) *(American Psychiatric Association, 1994),* as reported by the interviewers.

The independent variables consisted of hypothesized risk factors from the first five time points covering behavioral-emotional, familial, and academic domains. Because the literature identifies differences in developmental patterns for male and female antisocial behavior *(Offord & Bennett, 1994; Zahn-Waxler, 1993),* each gender was analyzed separately to examine the early risk factors for antisocial behavior in young adulthood.

Preliminary correlation analyses were performed for males and females to select key variables from a pool of risk factors identified by the literature. Separate hierarchical regression analyses were employed for each gender to explore the relationship between hypothesized risk factors and antisocial behavior at age 21. Initial regression analyses utilized a backward stepwise method of entry of variables from the earliest developmental periods to maximize their effects *(Cohen & Cohen, 1983).* Final regression models for each gender included those variables identified in the preliminary hierarchical regression analyses, which were entered in chronological order for each final model. An alpha level of .05 was employed to test the effects of all variables.

RESULTS

Findings indicate strong correlations between the outcome measure of self-reported antisocial behavior and maternal and interviewer ratings. Mothers' ratings of delinquency on the YABCL were correlated with the outcome variable at $p < .001$ ($r=0.25$).

Interviewer ratings of young adult functioning on the GAF scale were also strongly correlated to the outcome measure ($p < .001$; $r = -0.39$), with antisocial youth receiving, overall, lower ratings from the interviewers. These findings substantiate the behavioral and emotional adjustment difficulties reported by the antisocial youth in the present study at age 21.

Many hypothesized risk factors from a number of data points were found to be related to serious antisocial behavior at age 21. Variables at ages as early as five, reported by different informants, were identified from psychosocial, behavioral, familial, and academic domains.

As suggested by the literature, and because gender was found to be correlated with the dependent variable ($p < .001$; $r = -0.31$), separate regression analyses were estimated for each gender. Differences in levels of severity of antisocial behavior for males and females were explored through t-tests for independent samples. Findings indicated that males had significantly higher levels of antisocial behavior ($M = 2.09$ (male), $M = 0.80$ (female); $t = 6.26$, $p < .000$).

Male Regression Model

A number of predictors from early data-collection points were included in the initial regression model for males. These variables were as follows. *1)* At age 5, mother- and teacher-rated problem behavior and family disadvantage index scores. *2)* At age 9, measures of hostility and behavior problems, as reported by mothers and teachers, and self-esteem scores. *3)* At age 15, self-reports of depressive symptoms, self-esteem problems, family cohesion problems and parental divorce, acting-out problems, and maternal and self-reports of aggression and attention problems. *4)* At age 18, self-reports of externalizing and attention problems; school expulsions; lifetime diagnosis of depression; marijuana or alcohol disorder; such family characteristics as lack of cohesion and physical abuse; and a need for positive feedback from family members and friends. Of these variables, which were entered into the preliminary regression analysis, eight were included in the final model (see Table 1).

TABLE 1
Regression of Antisocial Behavior at Age 21 on Past Risk Factors for Males ($N=188$)

Variable	R^2 Change	β[a]	Part. Corr.
Ages 5–6			
FDI[b]		0.149*	0.167
Behavior problems[c]	0.07*	0.134*	0.206
Age 15			
Acts out in school[d]	0.13***	0.181**	0.371
Age 18[d]			
Av. school grade[c]		−0.190**	−0.183
Externalizing score[e]		0.215**	0.188
Parent jailed		0.203***	0.195
Family phys. abuse		0.151*	0.148
Lifetime marijuana abuse/dependence[f]	0.34***	0.308***	0.290
Total R^2 for full model	0.54	$F=15.47$***	

[a]Total betas utilized at each step.
[b]Family Disadvantage Index.
[c]Teacher ratings.
[d]Self-reports.
[e]Youth Self-Report *(Achenbach, 1991).*
[f]Diagnostic Interview Schedule-III-R *(Robins et al., 1989).*
*$p < .05$; **$p < .01$; ***$p < .001$.

For antisocial males in the current sample, two variables from ages five and six—teacher-rated behavior problems and a history of socioeconomic deprivation—emerged as significant predictors of later antisocial behavior, explaining 7% of the variance in antisocial behavior in young adulthood ($p < .05$).

One factor at age 15—self-reported acting out in school—was significantly associated with later behavior problems in males, explaining 13% of male antisocial behavior at age 21 ($p < .001$).

Five variables from age 18 were identified as risk factors for antisocial behavior at age 21 in males. From the academic and behavioral domains, self-reports of average grade in school, higher scores of lifetime diagnosis of marijuana abuse or dependence, as measured by the DIS-III-R, and higher levels of externalizing problems, as measured by the YSR, were associated with antisocial behavior at age 21. From the familial domain, self-reports of lifetime occurrence of physical abuse by parents, and of parental incarceration were both related to antisocial behavior at age 21. These five variables from age 18 explained 34% of the variance in antisocial behavior in young adulthood ($p < .001$).

For males, risk factors from ages five, six, 15, and 18 were found to be significantly related to antisocial behavior at age 21. Combined, these eight variables explained 54% of the variance in antisocial behavior in young adulthood ($F = 15.47$; $p < .001$).

Female Regression Model

To predict antisocial behavior in females, a number of variables from earlier ages were entered into the preliminary regression analysis. These included: *1)* At age 9, teacher and mother ratings of hostility and behavior problems, and self-reports of self-esteem. *2)* At age 15, mothers' ratings of hostility and attention problems; and self-reports of depressive symptoms, of self-esteem, attention, and behavior problems, and of parental divorce. *3)* At age 18, self-perceptions of external-

izing and attention problems; a lifetime diagnosis of depression, alcohol, or marijuana dependence; post-traumatic stress disorder; and such family characteristics as cohesion and physical or sexual abuse. Of these variables, eight remained in the final model for females (see Table 2).

For females, two variables from age nine, one of them teacher-rated and one self-rated, were linked with antisocial behavior at age 21. Teachers' ratings of girls' hostile behavior on the CAAP *(Ellsworth, 1977)* and girls' self-reports of low self-esteem *(Piers, 1986)* at age nine explained 16% of female antisocial behavior at age 21 ($p < .001$).

The final model for females identified three associated self-reported variables from age 15; being suspended from school, having attention problems as rated by the YSR, and having experienced parental divorce explained 5% of the variance in antisocial behavior in females at age 21 ($p < .001$).

Three variables from age 18 were also associated: high externalizing scores on the YSR, having a history of family sexual abuse, and expressed need for social support and assistance were identified as explaining 22% of the variance in antisocial behavior in females at age 21 ($p < .001$).

For females, the current model identified eight risk factors from behavioral, educational, and familial domains that, together, explained 43% of the variance in antisocial behavior in young adulthood ($F = 14.04$; $p < .001$).

Comparison of Final Regression Models

A comparison of the final models for males and females in the current sample reveals similarities as well as differences in the patterns and types of risk factors influencing antisocial behavior in young adulthood. For males, hostility and higher scores on the family disadvantage index at ages five and six had predictive value, explaining 7% of the variance in antisocial behavior. For females, hostility and low self-esteem at age nine were the earliest precursors of later deviance, explaining 16% of the variance.

TABLE 2
Regression of Antisocial Behavior at Age 21 on Past Risk Factors for Females (N=187)

Variable	R^2 Change	β[a]	Part. Corr.
Age 9			
Hostile: CAAP[b,c]		0.238***	0.299
Low self-esteem[d,e]	0.16***	–0.156*	–0.248
Age 15[e]			
School suspension		0.136*	0.152
Attention problems[f]		–0.219**	–0.055
Parental divorce	0.05***	0.115	0.156
Age 18[e]			
Externalizing score[f]		0.197**	0.181
Family sexual abuse		0.394***	0.362
Need social support[g]	0.22***	.135*	.129
Total R^2 for full model	0.43	F=14.04***	

[a]Total betas utilized at each step.
[b]Child and Adolescent Adjustment Profile *(Ellsworth, 1977).*
[c]Teacher ratings.
[d]Higher scores=better functioning on Children's Self Concept Scales *(Piers, 1984).*
[e]Self-reports.
[f]Youth Self-Report *(Achenbach, 1991).*
[g]Arizona Social Support Inventory *(Barrera, 1980).*
*p <.05; **p <.01; ***p <.001.

Both male and female final models included a number of risk factors from age 15. Although only one variable—acting out in school—was identified for males, it explained 13% of the variance by itself, compared to only 5% explained by three variables for females at that age. As did males, females at age 15 reported problems—i.e., suspensions—in school. Attention problems and parental divorce at age 15 also had predictive value for females.

Not surprisingly, variables from age 18 were the strongest predictors for both genders. For males, five variables from that time point explained 34% of their variance in antisocial behavior in young adulthood (see Table 1). For females, three variables explained 22% of variance (Table 2).

DISCUSSION

Gender Differences

In the current study, separate analyses for males and females identified gender-specific risk factors for antisocial behavior at age 21. These analyses also showed more serious levels of deviance for the males, and demonstrated the importance that timing of specific life experiences had for both genders. For example, although both males and females exhibited hostility and behavior problems in early childhood, the pivotal period for males was ages five and six, while for females it was age nine. These findings are consistent with those of prior research identifying higher rates of antisocial behavior for males *(Quay, 1986; Regier et al., 1988)* and different patterns in female antisocial behavior *(Loeber, 1990a).*

Precursors

At Ages Five and Nine.   Teachers in this study were the best detectors of the earliest manifestations of behavior problems. They ascertained conduct problems in boys by age six and girls by age nine, and their assessment of hostile and acting-out behavior in the young children pointed to meaningful connections between early and late problem behavior.

Another risk factor from early childhood identified in the current study was low global self-esteem at age nine for antisocial females. The significance of this finding suggests that young girls with low self-esteem may be at risk not only for future depression *(Allgood-Merten & Lewmsohn, 1990; Kaslow, Rehm, & Siegel, 1984)*, but also for externalizing behavior. An earlier study with the same sample population *(Pakiz et al., 1992)* found that boys who were antisocial at age 15 had problems with low self-esteem. While prior studies have established a connection between low self-esteem and deviance, this link needs to be examined for a possible bidirectional relationship *(Henggeler, 1989; Patterson et al., 1992)*.

Ages 15 and 18.   It appeared from findings in the current study that early behavior problems persist into mid- and late-adolescence. As with teacher reports identifying behavior problems from age nine, self-reports of acting out at home and in school at ages 15 and 18 were found to be related to antisocial behavior at age 21 for both genders. These findings have a high level of support from earlier research, which has shown that the strongest predictor of adult problem behavior is similar behavior at earlier ages *(Robins, 1978)*. Current findings lend some support to the assertion that antisocial behavior has strong stability over the life span *(Patterson et al., 1992)*.

Previous studies *(Farrington, 1990)* have identified attention problems in younger children as a precursor of antisocial behavior, but research on such problems in mid-adolescence has been limited. Reports of attention difficulties at age 15 by females in the current study suggest that further research is needed to identify challenges encountered by older youth in areas not readily visible to others.

Academic performance in mid- and late-adolescence emerged as a significant predictor of later antisocial behavior in the current sample, with antisocial males reporting lower grades at age 18 and antisocial females reporting a higher number of school suspensions at age 15. Prior research, too, has established a relatively strong connection between academic failure and antisocial behavior *(Henggeler, 1989; Kazdin, 1987)* and has linked truancy and academic problems to early antisocial behavior *(Robins & Hill, 1966)*.

In the present sample, a set of familial predictors from mid- to late-adolescence was associated with antisocial behavior in young adulthood for both males and females. Factors linked to deviance in young adulthood (e.g., coming from a large or low-income family) in prior research *(Farrington, 1990; Rutter & Giller, 1983)* were also found in the current sample of males at age five. Other familial predictors were parental divorce reported at age 15 and a history of family sexual abuse reported at 18 for females, and parental incarceration and a history of physical abuse at age 18 for males. Such factors are indicative of a nonsupportive family milieu; in Werner's *(1990)* longitudinal study of Hawaiian youth, disrupted or disturbed family relationships were related to antisocial outcomes, while Robbins and Ratcliff *(1979)* identified certain family factors (e.g., an antisocial father) as predictive of children's antisocial behavior in adulthood.

Dysfunction in the families of antisocial young adults in the present sample was also indicated by the lifetime family abuse they reported. Findings from recent studies suggest a strong link between a childhood history of neglect and abuse and antisocial symptoms in adulthood *(Kolko et al., 1993; Lunz & Widom, 1994)*.

At Age 18.   Reports by antisocial males in the study indicated a lifetime diagnosis of marijuana abuse or dependence at age 18. Similar connections between drug use and antisocial behavior have been established in prior studies: Robins and Ratcliff *(1979)* found a link between adult antisocial behavior and early drug and drinking problems; Loeber *(1990b)* found early initiation and continuity of drug use intertwined with progression toward antisocial behavior; and Windle *(1990)* suggested that this interrelationship is stronger for males.

Antisocial females in this study reported a perceived need for social support and assistance at age 18. Although prior studies have identified the availability of a supportive network of family or friends as a protective mental health factor for youth *(Masten, Best, & Garmezy, 1990)*, this issue has not been explored in depth relative to antisocial behavior. Moreover, most research exploring the influences of peer groups on deviance has focused on the negative consequences of peer support systems *(Elliott, Huizinga, & Ageton, 1985; Farrington, 1986)*. The relationship between lack of perceived support, as reported by the females in the current study, and antisocial behavior remains to be tested further.

Implications for Research and Preventive Interventions

Although a multitude of studies point to consequences of early aggression in males, data on young adult outcomes for females is still limited. More research is needed to investigate the patterns and correlates of female deviance over time in changing social and familial structures and expectations for female behavior *(Pakiz et al., 1992; Robins, 1986)*.

The current study has identified persistent patterns of behavior problems for antisocial males and females from early childhood to late adolescence and different ages emerged as significant periods of risk for each gender. These findings have strong implications for educators and practitioners. The current results demonstrate teachers' ability to identify problem behavior of antisocial youth as early as ages five and nine. There is ample evidence from prior research that early onset of problem behavior is indicative of a poor lifetime prognosis *(Offord & Bennett, 1994)*.

The current findings point to other risk factors, in addition to early behavior problems, that may influence later deviance. The information about low self-esteem, academic problems, and other familial and behavioral indicators (e.g., physical or sexual abuse in the family, and drug abuse or dependence) should be useful to practitioners and educators, who may have the opportunity to distinguish the earliest manifestations of deviant conduct. Teachers' skill in noticing early signs of later behavioral maladjustment could be a powerful asset in setting guidelines for timely recognition of these youth.

Although the present study identifies important early precursors of antisocial behavior, it has some limitations for generalization. Findings are based on an almost completely white, working-class community sample from the northeastern U.S. and their applicability to other populations with different social, economic, racial, and ethnic backgrounds remains to be tested.

Serious antisocial behavior is a critical social concern demanding attention. At a time when antisocial behavior in young people seems to be increasing significantly *(Loeber, 1990a)*, it is of utmost importance that interventions be designed to modify such behavior at the earliest possible age. Results of the present study, the data for which were collected prospectively over a period of 18 years from a community population, should assist in understanding the continuity and desistance of problem behavior and the salience of early predictors of later antisocial behavior. In identifying early indicators of future problem behavior, the present findings point to a number of key domains for early intervention that may ameliorate such behavior before it becomes persistent and fixed *(Loeber & Dishion, 1983)*.

REFERENCES

Achenbach, T. M. (1991). *Manual for the Youth Self-Report and 1991 Profile.* Burlington: University of Vermont Department of Psychiatry.

Achenbach, T. M. (1993). *Young Adult Behavior Check-List.* Burlington: University of Vermont Department of Psychiatry.

Allgood-Merten, B., & Lewinsohn, P. M. (1990). Sex differences and adolescent depression. *Journal of Abnormal Psychology, 99,* 55–63.

American Psychiatric Association. (1994). Global Assessment of Functioning Scale. In *Diagnostic and Statistical Manual of Mental Disorders (4th Edition,* p. 32). Washington, DC: Author.

Barrera, M. (1980). A method for the assessment of social support networks in community survey research. *Connections, 3,* 8–13.

Behar, L. B. (1977). The Preschool Behavior Questionnaire. *Journal of Abnormal Child Psychology, 5,* 265–275.

Cohen, J., & Cohen, P. (1983). *Applies multiple regression/correlation analysis for the behavioral sciences.* Mahwah, NJ: Erlbaum.

Elliott, D. S., Huzinga, D., & Ageton, S. S. (1985). *Explaining delinquency and drug use.* Beverly Hills, CA: Sage Publications.

Ellsworth, R. B. (1977). *CAAP Scale: The measurement of child and adolescent adjustment.* Unpublished manuscript. Institute for Program Evaluation, Roanoake, VA.

Farrington, D. P. (1986). The sociocultural context of childhood disorders. In H. C. Quay & J. S. Werry (Eds.), *Psychopathological disorders of childhood* (pp. 391–423). New York: Wiley.

_____. (1990). Implications of criminal career research for the prevention of offending. *Journal of Adolescence, 13,* 93–113.

_____. (1991). Longitudinal research strategies: Advantages, problems and prospects. *Journal of the American Academy of Child and Adolescent Psychiatry, 3,* 369–374.

Henggeler, S. W. (1989). *Delinquency in adolescence.* Newbury Park, CA: Sage Publications.

Huesman, R. L., Eron, L. D., Lefkowitz, M. M., & Walder, L. O. (1984). Stability of aggression over time and generations. *Developmental Psychology, 6,* 1120–1134.

Kaslow, N. J., Rehm, L. P., & Siegel, A. W. (1984). Social-cognitive and cognitive correlates of depression in children. *Journal of Abnormal Child Psychology, 12,* 605–620.

Kazdin, A. E. (1987). *Conduct disorders in childhood and adolescence.* Newbury Park, CA: Sage Publications.

_____. (1989). Conduct disorder. *The Psychiatric Hospital, 8,* 153–158.

Kolko, D. J., Kazdin, A. E., Thomas, A. M., & Day, B. (1993). Heightened child physical abuse potential: Child, parent and family dysfunction. *Journal of Interpersonal Violence, 2,* 169–192.

Loeber, R. (1990a). Development and risk factor of juvenile antisocial behavior and delinquency. *Clinical Psychology Review, 10,* 1–41.

_____. (1990b). Disruptive and antisocial behavior in childhood and adolescence: Development and risk factors. In K. Hurrelman & F. Losel (Eds.), *Health hazards in adolescence* (pp. 233–257). New York: Walter de Gruyter.

_____. (1991). Antisocial behavior: More enduring than changeable? *Journal of the American Academy of Child and Adolescent Psychiatry, 30,* 393–397.

Loeber, R., & Dishion, T. (1983). Early predictors of male delinquency: A review. *Psychological Bulletin, 1,* 68–99.

Lunz, B. K., & Widom, C. S. (1994). Antisocial personality disorder in abused and neglected children grown up. *American Journal of Psychiatry, 151,* 670–674.

Masten, A. S., Best, K. M., & Garmezy, N. (1990). Resilience and development: Contributions from the study of children who overcome adversity. *Development and Psychopathology, 2,* 425–444.

McCord, J. (1983). A longitudinal study of aggression and antisocial behavior. In K. T. Van Duesen & S. A. Madnick (Eds.), *Prospective studies of crime and delinquency* (pp. 269–275). Boston: Kluwer-Nijhoff Publishing.

Mrazek, P. J., & Haggerty, R. J. (Eds.). (1994). *Reducing risks for mental disorder.* Washington, DC: National Academy Press.

National Institute of Mental Health. (1983). *Diagnostic Interview Schedule for Children.* Washington, DC: Author.

Offord, D., & Bennett, K. J. (1994). Conduct disorder: Long-term outcomes and intervention effectiveness. *Journal of the American Academy of Child and Adolescent Psychiatry, 8,* 1069–1078.

Offord, D., Boyle, M. H., & Racine, Y. (1991). Ontario Child Health Study: Correlates of disorder. *Journal of the American Academy of Child and Adolescent Psychiatry, 6,* 856–860.

Pakiz, B., Reinherz, H. Z., Frost, A. K. (1992). Antisocial behavior in adolescence: A community study. *Journal of Early Adolescence, 12,* 300–313.

Patterson, G. R., DeBaryshe, B. D., & Ramsey, E. (1989). A developmental perspective on antisocial behavior. *American Psychologist, 2,* 329–335.

Patterson, G. R., Reid, J. B., & Dishion, T. J. (1992). *Antisocial boys.* Eugene, OR: Castalia Publishing.

Piers, E. V. (1986). *The Piers-Harris Children's Self-Concept Scale, revised manual.* Los Angeles: Western Psychological Services.

Quay, H. C. (1986). Conduct disorders. In H. C. Quay and J. S. Werry (Eds.), *Psychopathological disorders of childhood* (3rd ed., pp. 35–72). New York: Wiley.

Regier, D. A., Boyd, J. H., Burke, J. D., Jr., Rae, D. S., Myers, J. K., Kramer, M., Robins, L. N., George, L. K., Karno, M., & Locke, B. Z. (1988). One-month prevalence of mental disorders in the United States. *Archives of General Psychiatry, 45,* 977–986.

Reid, J. B. (1993). Prevention of conduct disorder before and after school entry: Relating interventions to developmental findings. *Development and Psychopathology, 5,* 243–262.

Reinherz, H. Z., Giaconia, R. M., Lefkowitz, E. S., Pakiz, B., & Frost, A. K. (1993). Prevalence of Psychiatric disorders in a community population of older adolescents. *Journal of the American Academy of Child and Adolescent Psychiatry, 32,* 369–377.

Robins, L. N. (1978). Sturdy childhood predictors of adult antisocial behavior: Replications from longitudinal studies. *Psychological Medicine, 8,* 611–622.

_____. (1981). Epidemiological approaches to natural history research: Antisocial behaviors in children. *Journal of the American Academy of Child Psychiatry, 20,* 566–580.

_____. (1986). The consequences of conduct disorders in girls. In D. Olweus, J. Block, & M. Radke-Yarrow (Eds.), *Development of antisocial and prosocial behavior: Research, theories and issues* (pp. 385–478). NY: Academic Press.

Robins, L. N., Helzer, J., Cottler, L., & Goldring, E. (1989). *NIMH Diagnostic Interview Schedule, Version III-Revised.* Department of Psychiatry, Washington University, St. Louis, MO.

Robins, L. N., & Hill, S. Y. (1966). Assessing the contributions of family structure, class and peer groups to juvenile delinquency. *Journal of Criminal Law, Criminology and Police Science, 57,* 325–334.

Robins, L. N., & Ratcliff, K. S. (1979). Risk factors in the continuation of childhood antisocial behavior into adulthood. *International Journal of Mental Health, 7,* 96–116.

Robins, L. N., & Regier, D. A. (Eds.). (1991). *Psychiatric disorders in America: The Epidemiologic Catchment Area Study.* New York: Free Press.

Rutter, M., & Giller, H. (1983). *Juvenile delinquency: Trends and perspectives.* New York: Penguin Books.

Sampson, R. J., & Laub, J. H. (1993). *Crime in the making: Pathways and turning points through life.* Cambridge, MA: Harvard University Press.

Werner, E. E. (1990). Antecedents and consequences of deviant behavior. In K. Hurrelman & F. Losel (Eds.), *Health hazards in adolescence* (pp. 219–231). New York: Walter De Gruyter.

White, L. J., Earls, F., Robins, L., & Silva, P. (1990). How early can we tell?: Predictors of childhood conduct disorder and adolescent delinquency. *Criminology, 4,* 507–533.

Windle, M. (1990). A longitudinal study of antisocial behaviors in early adolescence as predictors of late adolescent substance use: Gender and ethnic group differences. *Journal of Abnormal Psychology, 1,* 86–91.

Zahn-Waxler, C. (1993). Warriors and worriers: Gender and psychopathology. *Development and Psychopathology, 5,* 79–89.

NAME INDEX

SUBJECT INDEX